Data–Driven Intelligent Business Sustainability

Sonia Singh
Toss Global Management, UAE

S. Suman Rajest
Dhaanish Ahmed College of Engineering, India

Slim Hadoussa
Brest Business School, France

Ahmed J. Obaid
University of Kufa, Iraq

R. Regin
SRM Institute of Science and Technology, India

A volume in the Advances in Business Information
Systems and Analytics (ABISA) Book Series

Published in the United States of America by
  IGI Global
  Business Science Reference (an imprint of IGI Global)
  701 E. Chocolate Avenue
  Hershey PA, USA 17033
  Tel: 717-533-8845
  Fax: 717-533-8661
  E-mail: cust@igi-global.com
  Web site: http://www.igi-global.com

Library of Congress Cataloging-in-Publication Data

Names: Singh, Sonia, 1978- editor. | Rajest, S. Suman, 1988- editor. |
  Hadoussa, Slim, 1980- editor. | Obaid, Ahmed J. (Ahmed Jabbar), editor.
  | Regin, R., 1985- editor.
Title: Data-driven intelligent business sustainability / edited by: Sonia
  Singh, S. Suman Rajest, Slim Hadoussa, Ahmed J. Obaid, and R. Regin.
Description: Hershey : Business Science Reference, [2024] | Includes
  bibliographical references and index. | Summary: "The purpose of this
  book series is to provide a comprehensive analysis of how data-driven
  decision making is influencing the prospects for sustainable commercial
  and economic growth. Novel research with the intent of elucidating fresh
  perspectives through methodically sound and evidence-based analysis is
  required for consideration for inclusion in this proposed book series.
  Data-driven decision making has skyrocketed in popularity in recent
  years, thanks to technological advancements that have allowed us to
  collect and analyse data on an unprecedented scale. Today's
  technological and business environment makes it difficult to sustain a
  thriving corporation that can innovate, grow, and supply the market with
  cutting-edge products and services that stimulate the economy. The
  problem has been posed to the research community"-- Provided by
  publisher.
Identifiers: LCCN 2023020995 | ISBN 9798369300497 (hardcover)
Subjects: LCSH: Decision making. | Production management. | Big data.
Classification: LCC HD30.23 .D37159 2024 | DDC 658.4/03--dc23/eng/20230602
LC record available at https://lccn.loc.gov/2023020995

This book is published in the IGI Global book series Advances in Business Information Systems and Analytics (ABISA)
(ISSN: 2327-3275; eISSN: 2327-3283)

British Cataloguing in Publication Data
A Cataloguing in Publication record for this book is available from the British Library.

For electronic access to this publication, please contact: eresources@igi-global.com.

Advances in Business Information Systems and Analytics (ABISA) Book Series

Madjid Tavana
La Salle University, USA

ISSN:2327-3275
EISSN:2327-3283

MISSION

The successful development and management of information systems and business analytics is crucial to the success of an organization. New technological developments and methods for data analysis have allowed organizations to not only improve their processes and allow for greater productivity, but have also provided businesses with a venue through which to cut costs, plan for the future, and maintain competitive advantage in the information age.

The **Advances in Business Information Systems and Analytics (ABISA) Book Series** aims to present diverse and timely research in the development, deployment, and management of business information systems and business analytics for continued organizational development and improved business value.

COVERAGE

- Business Information Security
- Data Management
- Business Process Management
- Strategic Information Systems
- Performance Metrics
- Business Systems Engineering
- Data Governance
- Business Decision Making
- Algorithms
- Data Analytics

IGI Global is currently accepting manuscripts for publication within this series. To submit a proposal for a volume in this series, please contact our Acquisition Editors at Acquisitions@igi-global.com or visit: http://www.igi-global.com/publish/.

Titles in this Series

IGI Global
PUBLISHER of TIMELY KNOWLEDGE

701 East Chocolate Avenue, Hershey, PA 17033, USA
Tel: 717-533-8845 x100 • Fax: 717-533-8661
E-Mail: cust@igi-global.com • www.igi-global.com

Table of Contents

Detailed Table of Contents

Chapter 1

D. Lavanya, PSNA College of Engineering and Technology, India
Divya Marupaka, Unikon IT Inc., USA
Sandeep Rangineni, Pluto TV, USA
Shashank Agarwal, CVS Health, USA
Latha Thammareddi, DXC Technology, USA
T. Shynu, Agni College of Technology, India

In today's fast-paced and data-driven corporate market, the capacity to fully utilize information is critical. Business intelligence (BI) is the foundation of informed decision-making, allowing firms to turn unprocessed information into actionable insights. It is a process that starts with understanding data integration methodologies and learning extract, transform, load (ETL) procedures, which serve as the foundation for effective BI systems. Businesses, and hence the BI landscape, are continually evolving in our rapid digital world. While an established basis in data integration is still essential, there is a compelling movement toward the future—a future in which predictive analytics, including machine learning, will play critical roles in influencing the way we extract value from data. This chapter will conduct a thorough examination of these key aspects. The authors begin by delving into the complexities of data integration, uncovering the processes and procedures that serve as the foundation for solid business intelligence operations.

Chapter 2

A. Sabarirajan, PSNA College of Engineering and Technology, India
N. Arunfred, SRM Institute of Science and Technology, India
V. Bini Marin, SRM Institute of Science and Technology, India
Shouvik Sanyal, Dhofar University, Oman
Rameshwaran Byloppilly, City University, Ajman, UAE
R. Regin, SRM Institute of Science And Technology, India

Food waste is a pressing issue within the restaurant industry, contributing to environmental concerns and economic losses. This research study investigates food waste reduction strategies in Dindigul restaurants, aiming to provide valuable insights into sustainable practices. A diverse sample of 151 restaurant stakeholders, comprising customers, owners, managers, chefs, and staff, participated in the study. The findings reveal notable demographic patterns among respondents, emphasizing the importance of tailored strategies for distinct segments. The distribution of food waste highlights specific stages and categories as major contributors, underscoring the need for targeted efforts in preparation, spoilage, and plate waste reduction. Perceptions of food waste reduction strategies varied, with composting and surplus food donation receiving favorable feedback. Challenges and barriers, including staff awareness, tools for waste tracking, storage limitations, and customer resistance to portion control, were identified as significant obstacles.

Chapter 3

  P.S. Venkateswaran, PSNA College of Engineering and Technology, India
  M. Lishmah Dominic, PSNA College of Engineering and Technology, India
  Shashank Agarwal, CVS Health, USA
  Himani Oberai, GLA University, India
  Ila Anand, Christ University
  S. Suman Rajest, Dhaanish Ahmed College of Engineering, India

This research aims to investigate how artificial intelligence (AI) can be used to improve marketing and brand loyalty. Artificial intelligence (AI) is one of the most revolutionary technologies because it allows computers to independently execute mental skills often reserved for humans, such as problem solving and reasoning. In order to make judgments (like which marketing actions to take) and reason (about those decisions) in real time, machines represent, learn, store, and refine their knowledge progressively based on past experiences and existing information (e.g., predicting customer satisfaction). AI, with its ability to analyze vast datasets, predict customer behaviors, and deliver personalized experiences, is reshaping the way companies approach and enhance their customer loyalty strategies. This exploration delves into the multifaceted role of AI in revolutionizing the realm of customer loyalty, shedding light on its applications, benefits, and the transformative potential it brings to the forefront of modern marketing.

Chapter 4

  Thangaraja Arumugam, Vellore Institute of Technology, Chennai, India
  R. Arun, St. Joseph's College of Engineering, India
  R. Anitha, Dr. S.N.S. Rajalakshmi College of Arts and Science, India
  P. L. Swerna, Apollo Arts and Science College, India
  R. Aruna, Vellore Institute of Technology, Chennai, India
  Vimala Kadiresan, HELP University, Malaysia

The revolutionary effects of artificial intelligence (AI) and socially responsible marketing on the real estate market are examined in this chapter. Real estate is being redefined by changing consumer values as well as increased social and environmental consciousness. A flexible tool like artificial intelligence (AI) encourages innovation by providing data-driven insights, individualized marketing, and operational efficiencies. The concept simultaneously connects real estate transactions with significant societal and environmental contributions. The investigation starts with the key cause selection process, in which real estate professionals make choices that go beyond transactions and resonate as statements of intent with customers and communities. Forging relationships beyond typical buyer-seller interactions, creating emotionally compelling narratives becomes essential. AI boosts customer experiences, improves relationships, and synchronizes them with client values.

Technological changes have helped the methodology of execution where we can examine the sector in addition to the manner enterprise is carried out. Productive development has facilitated correct manufacturing in large volumes. The advanced technology, together with information in analytics, smart devices, computerization, and artificial intelligence (AI), is converting the system of society and persons to interact on a basic level. The evolution and development of artificial intelligence (AI) have transformed the effectiveness of commercial enterprises globally. However, business adoption of AI-based total packages by businesses remains constrained because of a lack of know-how approximately the generation. The technology can assist the organisation in understanding the clients and permit it to target the customers better and personalize advertising and marketing movements and messages. Advertising takes the benefit of facts to big data: consumer needs research, marketplace analyses, client insights, and competition intelligence.

Welfare signifies the quality of life in the ecological, economic, and social environments. It is crucial as it affects employee behavior and organizational productivity. The provision of welfare amenities by employers can positively impact the workforce. For managers to achieve goals via their teams, offering necessary and desirable workplace facilities is key. Technology and industry-specific tools are instrumental in advancing employee wellness programs. With the rise of remote and hybrid work models, integrating innovative social technologies is vital to enhance employee well-being in the corporate sphere. This process involves understanding well-being, selecting appropriate technologies, protecting data privacy, managing change, evaluating program success, and fostering a culture oriented towards well-being. Goals include improving job satisfaction, encouraging a healthy work-life balance, and addressing stress and mental health issues.

The tea industry faces significant operational and financial challenges in the competitive global market, necessitating focused research to support its growth and sustainability. Access to robust data is critical for convincing management to adopt new strategies, and this study aims to provide valuable data for the industry's advancement. The United Planters Association of Southern India (UPASI), representing tea and other plantation crops in Tamil Nadu, Kerala, and Karnataka since 1893, plays a crucial role. The rich biodiversity of the Nilgiris provides an ideal environment for tea and other crops. Still, traditional farming methods often rely on inefficient information dissemination through various means, resulting in outdated or missing critical data. This gap leads to poor planning, unsustainable farming practices, environmental damage, and reduced farmer income.

Chapter 8
An Empirical Study on Challenges of Working From Home During COVID-19 on Work-Life Domains in the Education Sector in Bengaluru 111

    Riya Singh, Kristu Jayanti College, India
    Nidhi Raj Gupta, Kristu Jayanti College, India
    Ahmad Y. A. Bani Ahmad, Middle East University, Jordan

The chapter looks at the challenges faced by academicians at the time of COVID-19. Additionally, it examines how Bengaluru academicians reconcile work and life, as well as how this pandemic condition has affected teaching performance. Academicians are not only being challenged with teaching methodology due to the pandemic but are forced to create and innovate new ideas of teaching-learning implemented by the New Education Policy. The chapter ends with the findings on the effectiveness of WFH, quality of communication, and return to work. It concludes that although WFH created great difficulty in social interaction, which forced them to return to work, but has increased the productivity of educators in this changing phase and developed a new learning dimension in the higher education industry, even though this domain of working is feasible for several business organizations and the years to come. The COVID-19 pandemic has forced many people to work from home.

Chapter 9
Leveraging MIS Technologies for Preserving India's Cultural Heritage on Digitization, Accessibility, and Sustainability 122

    A. Sabarirajan, PSNA College of Engineering and Technology, India
    Latha Thamma Reddi, DXC Technology, USA
    Sandeep Rangineni, Pluto TV, USA
    R. Regin, SRM Institute of Science And Technology, India
    S. Suman Rajest, Dhaanish Ahmed College of Engineering, India
    P. Paramasivan, Dhaanish Ahmed College of Engineering, India

Written documents, inscriptions, and artefacts have been left behind by India's long and eventful past, providing a wealth of essential information about the country's cultural legacy. India's history spans many millennia, making it one of the world's oldest civilizations. However, given the fragile nature of these old materials and their widespread distribution across the world, preserving and gaining access to them can be a difficult and time-consuming endeavour. This study investigates the application of management information system (MIS) technologies with the goal of enhancing digital archiving and preservation techniques for India's immense cultural heritage in order to overcome the challenges described above. The research endeavours to provide solutions to problems that arise in relation to the maintenance and accessibility of historical documents and artefacts by centering its attention on digitalization, data management, and cloud storage.

Chapter 10

N. Geethanjali, PSNA College of Engineering and Technology, India
Kishore Kandepu, Oberon IT Inc., USA
Seema Bhakuni, Doon Group of Institutions, India
P. Paramasivan, Dhaanish Ahmed College of Engineering, India
C. Satheesh, Dhaanish Ahmed College of Engineering, India
J. Rahila, Dhaanish Ahmed College of Engineering, India

Human resource information system (HRIS) is a human resource management (HRM) tool that allows an employer to design and manipulate a complete human sources method through records generation. The rising hyper-competitive generation over the previous few years has enhanced the need for maintaining records and inventions in human resource control for competitiveness. The revolution in the records era is absolutely and swiftly redefining the way matters are completed in almost every subject of human activity. Human assets and records generation are two factors that many corporations are looking to make use of as strategic weapons to compete. Human resource generation or human aid facts methods shape the interplay between human resource control and data technology. There has been a sizable increase within the wide variety of companies collecting, storing, and reading records regarding their human assets through using human aid data systems.

Chapter 11

M. Sriramkumar, PSNA College of Engineering and Technology, India
Rosario Huerta-Soto, Universidad Cesar Vallejo, Peru
Jenny Elizabeth Vega-García, Universidad Cesar Vallejo, Peru
P. Paramasivan, Dhaanish Ahmed College of Engineering, India
J. Rahila, Dhaanish Ahmed College of Engineering, India
S. Manikandan, Dhaanish Ahmed College of Engineering, India

The management information system deals with processes going through computer data and is integrated with other methods to deliver information faster and more efficient way to support decision-making and other administrative tasks. The function of MIS in organizational decision-making is the primary subject of this chapter. How decisions are made in an organization utilizing MIS, what problems the organization runs into throughout this process, and some suggestions to solve these problems are covered. It offers a concise explanation of how MIS enhances decision-making. The areas of health and customization have been affected by the rapid advancement of information technology and telecommunications. At all levels of management, from the top to the lowest, the highest quality judgments can be achieved with the best alignment of various technologies. The ability of information technology to organize accurate and pertinent data offers significant prospects for quick and effective fraud that improves the standard of decision-making.

Chapter 12

Distributed ledger and blockchain technologies have revolutionized the way businesses imagine and operate across organizational boundaries. Non-repudiation plays a vital role in communications to overcome disputes and establish trust. The incorporation of blockchain-based messaging enables the usage of a decentralized network of nodes, surmounting the conventional methods. Key market players are emphasizing accessing partnerships with technology-based companies, thereby bolstering its regional demand over the forecast period. This chapter focuses on market analysis and forecasting for the forecast period of 2021–2030 in terms of revenue. Further, the chapter briefly focuses on the determinants such as drivers, restraints, and opportunities impacting the market for blockchain messaging apps in different applications and end-user segments.

Chapter 13

The economic value of green spaces and their enormous potential can positively impact both community development and business growth. This chapter explored the value of OSM data especially green space data for business development. Strategic investment in parks and other green spaces has positive effects on the environment as well as the economy. Integration of OSM data with other essential datasets can provide businesses with useful tools for utilizing green spaces. OSM improves client segmentation, market analysis, and distribution channels, promoting sustainable business practices. OSM can also help in developing revenue strategies, discovering competitors, and optimizing logistics. When used in business growth, OSM green space data offers a variety of alternatives, from site selection to eco-friendly campuses, eco-tourism, and conservation projects. Additionally, OSM data encourages civic participation, ecological regrowth, and eco-aware consumer marketing.

Chapter 14

This study's objective is to investigate the various categories of stakeholders and propose strategies for efficiently managing those stakeholders regarding the potential dangers and difficulties that may be encountered by the organization while attempting to manage them throughout COVID-19. In general, the management of stakeholders is a ubiquitous activity, and businesses should adhere to an effective and efficient structure to perform this role. This chapter aimed to investigate whether there are any novel or original approaches to managing stakeholders, as well as to provide some potential solutions to the challenges of doing so during this pandemic. In addition, the authors tried to shed some light on the crucial relationship between stakeholder management and business reputation. According to the results, more research is needed to provide novel insights into stakeholder management. A manager or project manager can utilize the results from this article in several ways.

New technology has transformed how organizations function in recent decades. With recent advancements, companies may work faster and more efficiently. Human resources departments profited since they have several duties that touch internal and external clients. Electronic human resource management (e-HRM) uses the latest web-based and computer-based technologies, including artificial intelligence, machine learning, and deep learning applications, to conduct human resource management activities. These tools make human resource professionals' tasks easier and allow them to focus on strategic work rather than paperwork. Digital human resource management (DHRM) has moved to recruiting, career management, training and development, performance management, and pay. This chapter examines information technology (IT), digital human resource management, planning, and decision-making.

This research observes the connection between the major components such as emotional intelligence (EI), employee job performance (JP), and organisational role stress (ORS). There has been previous research that has been carried out pertaining to EI and JP. However, there have been a very limited number of studies where a third variable has mediated emotional intelligence and job performance variables. There are even fewer studies wherein organisational role stress has been considered as a mediator. Most of the studies pertaining to emotional intelligence have been carried out in the Western context, and very few Indian studies exist. The information technology (IT) sector is considered one of the most rapidly growing sectors in India, and there is very limited research on the EI of Indian employees in the IT sector; hence, the same has been covered in this study. The current study is descriptive, as the variables under investigation are continuous.

Sustainable development is a novel interdisciplinary field of study. The field of sustainable leadership is an innovative approach to effective leadership that was recently created to resolve issues associated with sustainable development. Before incorporating sustainable development into a company's strategy, the company's senior executives must first integrate sustainability into daily operations. Even though leaders play a crucial role in bringing about change, there is still a lack of knowledge about leadership and its relationship to sustainable practices; therefore, additional research is required to demonstrate this. There is a gap in the literature between sustainable practices, sustainability performance, and IT employees' leadership skills. In response, a survey questionnaire was created to collect data, and structural equation modeling (SEM) was used to examine the moderating influence of IT managers' leadership abilities on the relationships between sustainable practices and sustainability performance.

Chapter 18

Jyoti P. Kanjalkar, Vishwakarma Institute of Technology, India
Gaurav N. Patil, Vishwakarma Institute of Technology, India
Gaurav R. Patil, Vishwakarma Institute of Technology, India
Yash Parande, Vishwakarma Institute of Technology, India
Bhavesh Dilip Patil, Vishwakarma Institute of Technology, India
Pramod Kanjalkar, Vishwakarma Institute of Technology, India

This chapter presents a college recommendation system using machine learning with the features of branch, caste, location, and fees. The system aims to provide personalized recommendations to students based on their preferences and past academic performance. The dataset used in the study consists of information about various colleges, including their location, fees, available branches, and the percentage of students belonging to different castes. The system uses a combination of machine learning algorithms, including decision trees and random forests, to provide accurate and efficient recommendations. The Adaboost algorithm is used to find colleges with similar features to the student's preferences, while decision trees and random forests are used to make predictions based on past data. The proposed system is evaluated using metrics such as accuracy, precision, recall, and F1 score. The results show that the system provides highly accurate and personalized recommendations to students.

Chapter 19

Srinivas Kolachina, Koneru Lakshmaiah Education Foundation, India
Swarna Sumanth, Koneru Lakshmaiah Education Foundation, India
Venkat Rama Chowdary Godavarthi, Koneru Lakshmaiah Education Foundation, India
Pavan Kumar Rayapudi, Koneru Lakshmaiah Education Foundation, India
S. Suman Rajest, Dhaanish Ahmed College of Engineering, India
Nasir Abdul Jalil, Universiti Teknologi PETRONAS, Malaysia

Talent management is the constant system that includes attracting and retaining high-quality employees who have developed skills, professional planning, and interest in growth. This management continuously motivates the employees to improve their tasks and performances. The dependent variable measures the bundles of human resource management practices recruitment, performances, staffing, training, and developmental compensation. The independent variables of human resources are talent retention, career management, employee training, and talent attraction, while the dependent variables are employee engagement for growth in management. Talent management defines talent development as the work or efforts that were learned and the employee's improvement to continue the organizational performance. In order to understand the impact more clearly, a survey has been done on 65 employees taken on a random basis. The use of 13 questions was taken into consideration. The responses collected are then put into SPSS software to analyze the results using the proper testing method.

The relevance of data in India's socio-economic development has been defined in several policy documents in the digital economy. Using Indian law to regulate a contract creates major concerns, which can sometimes compromise it as a negotiating chip in cross-border agreements. As previously stated, Indian courts can revoke foreign arbitral verdicts if they determine that the arbitrators misapplied Indian law. As a result, a party to a contract governed by Indian law risked falling victim to the "public policy" fallacy. This will reduce the interest of foreign investors and create more cross-border issues. Many countries have modified the UNCITRAL model law to avoid such situations according to their requirement. Even the Indian government recently introduced MAP effective from May 6; the same model law was modified to give faster resolution in cross-border disputes under sections 64 and 65 of the Insolvency, Restructuring, and Dissolution Act 2018.

The Pink Tax is an additional sum of money that is paid daily by women for comparable or comparable-in-value edible products. Specifically, the Pink Tax is a tax on pink products. There are a lot of people who either don't comprehend the justification for the presence of this tax in society or have a limited awareness of it. It is often referred to by the name "hidden tax." While the Pink Tax is not a legitimate form of taxation, it does still exist. The regulations that prevent price discrimination based on gender are only present in a select number of state and municipal governments, but the federal government does not have any such laws. The objective of this study is to bring attention to a tax that frequently isn't focused on within the day-to-day activities of women, to investigate the price differences between commodities in which women pay a higher amount compared to men for the same product, and to investigate the reason why female products are so expensive.

The emergence of big data (BD) has opened up new opportunities for addressing social and environmental challenges. This chapter examines the potential of BD to drive green social welfare and sustainable environmental management. The chapter highlights how big data can be used to develop new approaches for monitoring and managing natural resources and addressing social issues such as poverty and inequality.

It explores how big data can be used to promote sustainable development, from enhancing resource efficiency to improving disaster management. The chapter also discusses challenges associated with using big data for social welfare and sustainable development, including privacy concerns and improved data quality. Ultimately, the chapter concludes that big data has the potential to transform our approach to sustainable development but that a coordinated effort is required to ensure that it is used effectively and responsibly.

Chapter 23

Rupayan Roy, Department of Fashion Technology, National Institute of Fashion Technology, Kannur Campus, Kannur, India

Swetha Ramakrishnan, Department of Fashion Technology, National Institute of Fashion Technology, Kannur Campus, Kannur, India

This chapter provides an overview of virtual try-on technology and its potential impact on the retail industry. It defines the technology and its various types, including AR, VR, and 3D modeling. The chapter also discusses the benefits of virtual try-on technology, including improved customer engagement, reduced return rates, and increased sales. However, the chapter also explores the limitations of the technology, such as technical constraints and cost barriers. Privacy and ethical considerations are also discussed. The chapter examines the future of virtual try-on technology, particularly the potential impact of emerging technologies such as 5G, AI, and AR/VR. It emphasizes the need for retailers to invest in this technology and prioritize user experience to stay competitive and meet changing consumer needs. Overall, this chapter provides a comprehensive overview of virtual try-on technology and its significance in the digital age of retail.

Chapter 24

Lucio Laureti, Lum University Giuseppe Degennaro, Italy

Alberto Costantiello, Lum University Giuseppe Degennaro, Italy

Alessandro Massaro, Lum University Giuseppe Degennaro, Italy

Angelo Leogrande, Lum University Giuseppe Degennaro, Italy

In this chapter, the authors investigate the role of "renewable energy consumption" in the context of circular economy. They assume that the consumption of renewable energy is a proxy for the development of circular economy. They use data from the environmental, social, and governance (ESG) dataset of the World Bank for 193 countries in the period 2011-2020. They perform several econometric techniques (i.e., panel data with fixed effects, panel data with random effects, pooled ordinary least squares [OLS], weighted least squares [WLS]). The results show that "renewable energy consumption" is positively associated among others to "cooling degree days" and "adjusted savings: net forest depletion" and negatively associated among others to "greenhouse gas (GHG) net emissions/removals by land use change and forestry (LUCF)" and "mean drought index." Furthermore, they perform a cluster analysis with the application of the k-Means algorithm and find the presence of four clusters. Finally, they compare eight different machine-learning algorithms to predict the value of renewable energy consumption.

The potential wide applications of big data analytics have created a high demand for data analysts in various industries, including business, healthcare, bioinformatics, politics, and management. As a result, higher education institutions are capitalizing on this opportunity by offering different data science programs to attract students and cater to industry needs. Over the past decade, there has been a rapid emergence of data science programs both nationally and globally. This chapter will begin by reviewing the impact of big data analytics on different industries. It will then proceed to describe various data science programs, including their curriculum design, course offerings, and target industry sectors for employment. Additionally, the chapter will address the weaknesses of some curricula and propose new teaching areas that are relevant to improve the learning outcomes of students. The aim of the suggestions is to better prepare data science students for the ever-evolving demands of big data analytics in the industry.

In a timeframe marked by intensifying ecological crises, the function of human resource management (HRM) in nurturing an environment-centric innovation ethos is significantly under-researched. This empirical inquiry aims to address this lacuna by investigating the nexus between chosen elements of green human resource management (GHRM) and the culture of green innovation in India's prominent cement manufacturing firms. Adopting a correlational research approach and making use of statistical methodologies like partial least squares (PLS), the study reveals a noteworthy positive linkage between green recruitment and selection (GRS), green training and development (GTD), and green performance appraisal (GPA) with green innovation culture (GIC). These insights add valuable dimensions to both the theoretical understanding and practical applications of HRM and sustainability, more so within the Indian cement industry.

These days people use computers more frequently. Because of rapid growth, many enterprises have started doing online business. The primary data for the study was collected through a questionnaire, which was distributed to the respondents via Google Forms. Secondary data is used to collect all published data through journals, magazines, and articles. The current study aims to identify the variables influencing ladies' beauty products. The study is also intended to identify the issues faced by the users of Nykaa products while purchasing them through online media and to find solutions to solve the issues and thus make online purchases easier and more convenient for the ladies.

Preface

The advent of big data analytics and machine learning has ushered in a new era of data-driven decision-making. Businesses can now harness the power of advanced analytics to gain deeper insights into their operations and the world around them. Predictive analytics, for example, allows organizations to anticipate market trends, consumer preferences, and potential supply chain disruptions. This foresight is invaluable in helping businesses adapt and thrive in a rapidly changing business aspect. This book represents a modern approach to business management and strategic planning, pivoting on the utilization of extensive data analysis and intelligent systems. This concept integrates the principles of sustainable development with advanced data analytics, AI technologies, and business intelligence. It starts with the recognition that today's business aspect is increasingly competitive and deeply intertwined with social, environmental, and economic factors. In this context, businesses must adapt and evolve to thrive and contribute positively to the world. The core of data-driven intelligent business sustainability lies in harnessing the power of big data and analytics. This involves collecting vast amounts of data from various sources, such as market trends, customer behaviours, supply chain operations, and environmental impacts. By applying advanced analytics, machine learning, and AI, businesses can extract meaningful insights from this data, enabling them to make more informed decisions. This enhances efficiency and profitability but also aids in identifying sustainable practices that can reduce environmental footprints and promote social responsibility. Moreover, this approach fosters innovation and resilience. Businesses can anticipate changes and adapt quickly by continuously analyzing market trends and customer preferences. This agility is crucial in a fast-paced world where consumer demands and market conditions constantly evolve. Also, through predictive analytics, companies can foresee potential challenges and opportunities, allowing them to be proactive rather than reactive. Another key aspect is stakeholder engagement. Data-driven sustainability initiatives can provide transparency and accountability, which consumers, investors, and regulators increasingly demand. Companies can build trust and strengthen their brand reputation by openly sharing data about environmental and social impacts. Intelligent data-driven strategies can optimize resource use, reduce waste, and lower carbon emissions in environmental sustainability. For instance, predictive analytics can aid energy management, forecasting peak usage times and suggesting adjustments to reduce consumption. Similarly, supply chain analytics can identify inefficiencies, reduce resource wastage, and promote sustainable sourcing practices. Environmental sustainability, for instance, can benefit immensely from data-driven approaches. Organizations can use data analytics to monitor and reduce their carbon footprint, track resource usage, and optimize energy consumption. Supply chains can be analyzed to identify efficiency improvements and waste reduction opportunities. Sustainability goals can be integrated into business strategies, aligning economic success with environmental stewardship.

Social sustainability is equally important. Businesses can improve their social footprint by analyzing data related to employee satisfaction, community impact, and customer feedback. This includes promoting fair labour practices, engaging in community development, and ensuring that products and services are accessible and beneficial to a broad spectrum of society. Economically, the data-driven approach ensures long-term viability. By aligning business operations with sustainable practices, companies can mitigate risks associated with resource scarcity, regulatory changes, and shifting consumer preferences. This alignment secures the company's future and contributes to global economic stability. The integration of AI and machine learning further elevates this approach. AI-driven systems can automate complex data analysis, uncover patterns and correlations that might be invisible to human analysts, and offer predictive insights that drive strategic decision-making. These technologies also enable real-time monitoring and management of business operations, ensuring that sustainability goals are continuously met.

Ethical considerations are paramount in this approach. The responsible use of data, respecting privacy and data protection laws, and ensuring that AI systems are unbiased and transparent are essential components of a sustainable data-driven strategy. Companies must navigate the fine line between leveraging data for business insights and maintaining ethical standards. Continuous learning and adaptation are fundamental. The business environment, technology, and societal needs are always evolving. As such, businesses must remain agile, constantly updating their strategies, technologies, and practices to stay ahead. This requires a culture of continuous learning, innovation, and flexibility. This book is not just a business strategy; it's a holistic approach that aligns the latest in technology and data analytics with the imperative of sustainable development. It's about creating profitable and efficient businesses that are responsible, resilient, and responsive to the planet's needs and inhabitants. As businesses embark on this journey, they will find that sustainability and success are complementary and complementary, paving the way for a future where business and sustainability go hand in hand.

ORGANIZATION OF THE BOOK

The book is organized into 27 chapters. A brief description of each of the chapters follows:

Chapter 1 involves Information use, which is crucial in today's fast-paced, data-driven corporate environment. Business intelligence (BI) helps organisations turn raw data into actionable insights for informed decision-making. The first step is to understand data integration methodology and ETL procedures, which underpin efficient BI systems. Businesses and BI are always changing in our fast-paced digital era. While data integration is still crucial, predictive analytics, particularly machine learning, will shape how we extract value from data in the future. This chapter will thoroughly examine these crucial points. We start by exploring data integration's intricacies and the processes that underpin business intelligence operations. ETL processes are explained step-by-step for beginners and experts. Our adventure continues. We explore uncharted ground using predictive analytics and machine learning. We will show how these tools alter corporate intelligence and allow decision-makers to anticipate patterns and make data-driven decisions.

Chapter 2 identifies that restaurants squander food, causing environmental and economic problems. This study examines Dindigul restaurant food waste reduction measures to learn about sustainable practices. An eclectic group of 151 restaurant stakeholders—customers, owners, managers, chefs, and staff-participated. The demographic characteristics of responses emphasise the need for a segmented strategy. Specific phases and categories contribute most to food waste, emphasising the need to reduce preparation, spoilage, and plate waste. Composting and surplus food donation were popular food waste reduction measures. Staff awareness, waste tracking tools, storage limits, and customer portion control opposition were major difficulties. The report recommends how restaurants can improve food waste reduction, stressing worker engagement and effective solutions to address this global issue.

Chapter 3 examines how AI may boost marketing and brand loyalty. AI is one of the most innovative technologies because it lets computers solve problems and think like humans. Machines represent, learn, store, and refine their knowledge based on past experiences and available facts to make real-time decisions (like marketing actions) (e.g., predicting customer satisfaction). AI's capacity to analyse massive datasets, forecast consumer behaviour, and provide personalised experiences is changing how firms approach and improve customer loyalty initiatives. This inquiry examines AI's varied role in transforming client loyalty, including its applications, benefits, and potential to revolutionise modern marketing and customer engagement techniques. Businesses are always looking for new methods to engage, understand, and connect with their customers as consumer behaviour and technology change. AI has revolutionised marketing.

Chapter 4 examines the transformative implications of AI and socially responsible marketing on real estate. Consumer values and social and environmental awareness are redefining real estate. Data-driven insights, personalised marketing, and operational efficiency from AI foster innovation. The idea links real estate deals to social and environmental benefits. The study begins with the primary cause selection process when real estate professionals make decisions beyond transactions and communicate with consumers and communities. Creating emotional storylines and building relationships beyond buyer-seller interactions is crucial. AI enhances customer connections and aligns them with client values. Milestones include VR property tours, sustainability integration, and immersive AI-driven chatbots. For accountability and trust, donation matching services elevate transactions to charitable activities and emphasise moral AI and data security. The chapter concludes with an AI-driven measurement and adaptability approach that shows how to improve over time. Real estate professionals ensure their social and environmental contributions are valuable. This chapter invites real estate professionals to embrace a moment when AI and socially responsible efforts reinvent real estate deals. These visualising transactions go beyond economics for a better, more caring future.

Chapter 5 analytics, technology has improved the execution process so we can assess the sector and business. Productive development allows large-scale proper manufacture. Advanced technology, analytics, smart devices, computerization, and AI transform society and people's basic interactions. AI has altered global business effectiveness. A lack of generation knowledge limits businesses' adoption of AI-based whole packages. Technology can help the company better understand customers, target them, and tailor marketing communications. Advertising uses big data for consumer needs research, market analytics, client insights, and competition intelligence. This chapter discusses the theoretical and conceptual underpinnings of AI and ML and how they help marketers revolutionise modern marketing.

Chapter 6 discusses how welfare is quality of life in ecological, economic, and social contexts. It is important because it affects employee behaviour and corporate productivity. Employer welfare amenities can boost work performance. Offering required and desirable workplace facilities helps managers achieve goals through their staff. Employee wellness programmes benefit from technology and industry-specific solutions. As remote and hybrid work models grow, innovative social technologies are needed to improve corporate employee well-being. This process includes understanding well-being, choosing appropriate technologies, safeguarding data privacy, managing change, measuring programme performance, and developing a well-being culture. Job happiness, work-life balance, stress reduction, and mental wellness are priorities. Organizations increasingly see employee well-being as essential to productivity, talent retention, and success. The goal is establishing a supportive workplace that promotes employee satisfaction and productivity, benefiting the workforce and company.

Chapter 7 reviews the competitive worldwide market, and the tea sector has operational and financial issues that require concentrated research to expand and survive. For management to adopt new strategies, robust data is needed, and this study attempts to supply that data for industrial advancement. The United Planters Association of Southern India (UPASI), representing tea and other plantation crops in Tamil Nadu, Kerala, and Karnataka since 1893, is essential. The great biodiversity of the Nilgiris is perfect for tea and other crops. Traditional farming systems sometimes use inadequate information-sharing methods, resulting in obsolete or missing important data. This mismatch causes poor planning, unsustainable farming, environmental damage, and lower farmer revenue. This study recommends using communication technologies to update tea producers' access to critical information and best practices. A system like this will promote sustainable farming, environmental conservation, and revenue. Economic intelligence, industrial relations, liaisons, public relations, scientific research, and publications are UPASI services. The study shows how UPASI could help farmers by fostering informed and sustainable farming.

Chapter 8 introduces COVID-19 and presents academics with challenges. It also analyses how Bengaluru academics balance work and life and how the pandemic has influenced teaching. The epidemic and the New Education Policy drive academics to innovate teaching-learning methods. The article concludes with WFH effectiveness, communication quality, and work return. Even while WFH made social connections impossible, forcing them to return to work, it enhanced educators' productivity in this transition phase. It developed a new learning dimension in higher education, even though this work area is conceivable for various business organisations in the future. Bengaluru, India, Academics work from home due to the COVID-19 pandemic. Working from home has benefits, but it also has drawbacks, especially for educators. This study examines Bengaluru academics' pandemic-related home-based challenges. The study used mixed methodologies. A quantitative survey was given to 100 Bengaluru academics.

Chapter 9 predicts India's long and exciting past has left behind written records, inscriptions, and artefacts that reveal its cultural heritage. One of the earliest civilizations, India has a millennia-old history. Due to their fragility and global distribution, conserving and accessing these historical documents can be challenging and time-consuming. This study examines the use of Management Information System (MIS) technology to improve digital archiving and preservation of India's vast cultural heritage to address the issues above. The research uses digitalization, data management, and cloud storage to solve historical document and artefact preservation and accessibility issues. This study recommended an interdisciplinary strategy and ongoing financing to preserve India's rich history. Provide user-friendly interfaces, evaluate legal and ethical issues, and showcase successful case studies.

Chapter 10 explains Human Resource Information Systems (HRISs) allow employers to build and manage a comprehensive human resources system by creating records. A hypercompetitive generation has evolved in recent years, requiring more innovation and record-keeping in human resource management to stay competitive. The changes recorded during the time rapidly changed practically every aspect of human existence. Many companies are building strategic advantages in human resources and record generation to stay competitive. Human resource generation approaches and aid facts impact the link between HRM and IT. Many businesses use human aid data systems to collect, store, and interpret human asset records. Business numbers have increased due to this tendency. HRIS has become vital for businesses to compete aggressively and successfully. HRIS and corporate competitiveness are the subject of this chapter's specialisation. HRIS's needs, components, features, and capabilities may be covered in this chapter.

Chapter 11 develops how the management information system processes computer data and integrates it with other ways to deliver information faster and more efficiently for decision-making and administrative activities. The role of MIS in organisational decision-making is the focus of this research. How MIS-based organisations make decisions, what issues they face, and how to fix them. It briefly explains how MIS improves decision-making. The rapid expansion of IT and telecommunications has altered health and customization. With optimal technology alignment, to-bottom management can make the best quality decisions. Information technology can arrange accurate and relevant facts, making fraud faster and more effective and improving decision-making. Business leaders, administrators, and senior officials can use decision-support systems to address problems. Management information systems assist business managers in making educated decisions by providing organised, condensed information at the proper time.

Chapter 12 Distributed ledger and blockchain technologies have transformed cross-organizational business thinking. Non-repudiation helps resolve disagreements and build confidence in communications. Web3 is projected to boost user-centric experiences and enable inclusive decentralisation. For instance, blockchain-based messaging allows a decentralised network of nodes, surpassing conventional approaches. Centralized messaging programs often crash and violate privacy, compromising user communication security. Privacy mitigation is growing, driving demand for transparency-driven social media solutions with improved data integrity and security. Key market participants focus on technology partnerships to boost regional demand throughout the forecast period.

Chapter 13 shows Green spaces have great economic potential and can boost community and corporate growth. This chapter examined how OSM data, particularly green space data, may help businesses. Strategic park and green space investment benefits the environment and economy. OSM data integrated with other essential datasets can help businesses use green spaces. OSM enhances client segmentation, market analysis, and distribution channels for sustainable companies. OSM can also help with revenue planning, competitor discovery, and logistics optimization. In corporate growth, OSM green space data can be utilised for site selection, eco-friendly campuses, eco-tourism, and conservation programmes. OSM data also promotes civic engagement, ecological regeneration, and eco-friendly marketing.

Chapter 14 examines several stakeholder groups and proposes ways to efficiently manage them during COVID-19, considering the potential risks and challenges the company may face. Stakeholder management is common, and businesses should use an efficient framework. This article investigated new stakeholder management methods and offered some solutions to the epidemic's difficulties. Also, we tried to illuminate the critical relationship between stakeholder management and business reputation. Results suggest further research is needed to shed light on stakeholder management. A manager or project manager can use this article's findings in various ways. We believe project managers should prioritise individuals affected by their efforts. The stakeholder management plan helps the project manager prioritise stakeholders.

Chapter 15 discusses how new technology has changed companies in recent decades. Recent advances may help companies work faster and more efficiently. HR departments benefited from their many internal and external client interactions. E-HRM combines the newest web-based and computer-based technologies, including AI, ML, and DL, to manage human resources. These solutions simplify HR responsibilities and let professionals focus on strategy rather than paperwork. Digital HRM now includes recruiting, career management, training and development, performance management, and remuneration. IT, Digital HRM, planning, and decision-making are covered in this chapter. It examines cloud-based and computerised HR systems. Big Data, social media, gamifying HRM, online talent, performance, and training management are featured. It teaches HR and the "Internet of Things" concepts. Overreliance on technology is also discussed. Business processes are evolving due to digitization. Digitalization heavily influences HRM due to employee software, IT-enabled HR procedures, social networks, and mobile solutions. Digital HR management is used by companies (HR). Creatively manage human resources to compete in business. Companies are using digitally enabled, employee-focused HR, according to studies. HR must be improved for performance and market competitiveness. Modern HRM employs technology better and replaces traditional HRM. This article discusses how HRM is becoming e-HRM or using IT devices. All HR data, services, tools, apps, and conversations in a company are saved and shared electronically under E-HRM.

Chapter 16 examines the relationship between Emotional Intelligence (EI), Job Performance (JP), and Organizational Role Stress (ORS). Previous research has examined EI and JP. Few studies have mediated emotional intelligence and job performance with a third variable. A few research studies have explored organisational role stress as a moderator. Western studies on emotional intelligence predominate, with few Indian studies. The information technology (IT) sector is one of India's fastest-growing, and there is little research on Indian IT workers' EI. This study addresses that gap. The continuous variables in this study make it descriptive. Data was acquired by survey. The study variables were measured using standardised and accurate questionnaires. A poll of 200 IT software professionals found a significant positive correlation between EI and JP. Organizational role stress partially influenced the EI-JP relationship.

Chapter 17 says that sustainable development is a new interdisciplinary field. Sustainable leadership is a new leadership style that addresses sustainable development challenges. Before adopting sustainable development into a company's strategy, senior leaders must integrate it into daily operations. Leaders are vital to change, but little is known about leadership and sustainable practices; thus, further research is needed. A literature gap exists between sustainable practises performance and IT personnel' leadership skills. In response, a survey questionnaire was designed, and Structural Equation Modeling (SEM) was utilised to evaluate how IT managers' leadership abilities moderated the links between sustainable practises and sustainability performance. The research showed that all leadership techniques sustain performance. Sustainable leadership techniques, including labour relations, employee appreciation, and shared vision, improve business performance.

Chapter 18 shows a machine-learning college recommendation system, including branch, caste, location, and fees. The algorithm makes recommendations based on student interests and academic performance. The study used data on colleges' locations, fees, branches, and caste breakdowns. Machine learning algorithms like Decision Trees and Random Forests make accurate and efficient recommendations. Decision trees and random forests anticipate based on prior data, whereas the Adaboost algorithm finds universities that match student interests. The suggested method is assessed by accuracy, precision, recall, and F1 score. The results reveal that the system gives pupils accurate, individualised recommendations. The paper also compares machine learning techniques and finds that the proposed method outperforms standard recommendation systems. The machine learning-based college recommendation system with branch, caste, location, and pricing elements can assist students in choosing colleges and succeed in school and work.

Chapter 19 discusses how talent management is a continuous process of acquiring and maintaining skilled, professional, and growth-oriented individuals. Management constantly encourages employees to enhance their work. The dependent variable assesses HRM procedures like recruitment, performance, staffing, training, and development compensation. Human resources' independent variables are talent retention, career management, employee training, and talent recruitment, while the dependent variables are employee engagement for management growth. Talent management defines talent development as learning and improving employee performance to maintain organisational performance. A random survey of 65 employees was conducted to better understand the impact. Thirteen questions were considered. SPSS is used to analyse the responses using the correct testing procedure. Most responders (23.08 percent) are between 15 and 35 since they know the market better. 38.46 percent of respondents were between 35 and 50 and 50 to 60. Besides findings and comments, the essay finishes with important Talent Management insights for any firm.

Chapter 20 detects several digital economy policy documents outlining data's role in India's socioeconomic development. Using Indian law to control a contract raises problems and can damage its negotiating power in cross-border deals. As mentioned, Indian courts can overturn foreign arbitral rulings if the arbitrators misapplied Indian law. Thus, the "public policy" fallacy could affect an Indian Law contract party. This will deter foreign investors and increase cross-border concerns. Many countries have updated the UNCITRAL Model Law to avoid similar scenarios. The Indian government introduced MAP on May 6, and sections 64 and 65 of the Insolvency, Restructuring, and Dissolution Act 2018 were updated to speed up cross-border dispute resolution. This article suggests prioritising Article 9 of Model Law—Appointment of Foreign Judges (Masters in relevant field)—and accurate legal enforcement after considering multinational regulatory organisations, practises, and laws to resolve cross-border disputes quickly.

Chapter 21 analyzes how women pay the Pink Tax daily on comparable or comparable-value eating products. The Pink Tax applies to pink goods. Many people don't understand or are unaware of the tax's justification. People call it the "hidden tax." Despite being illegal, the Pink Tax exists. The federal government does not prohibit gender-based price discrimination, but a few state and municipal governments do. This study seeks to raise awareness of a tax that women rarely consider, to examine the price discrepancies across goods in which women pay more than males, and to explain why feminine items are so expensive.

Chapter 22 focuses on how Big Data (BD) has expanded social and environmental solutions. This research investigates how BD might promote green social welfare and environmental sustainability. According to the research, Big Data can be utilised to improve natural resource management and societal challenges like poverty and inequality. It examines how Big Data may improve resource efficiency and disaster management for sustainable development. The chapter also addresses privacy and data quality issues when using Big Data for social welfare and sustainable development. The report finds that Big Data can alter sustainable development, but it needs a unified effort to use it effectively and responsibly.

Chapter 23 discusses virtual try-on technology and its possible impact on retail. It defines AR, VR, and 3D modelling technology. According to the chapter, virtual try-on technology improves client engagement, return rates, and sales. The essay also discusses the technical and cost limits of the system. Also covered are privacy and ethics. According to the chapter, new technologies like 5G, AI, and AR/VR may affect virtual try-on technology. Retailers must invest in this technology and prioritise user experience to be competitive and fulfil evolving consumer expectations. This chapter covers virtual try-on technology and its importance in digital retail.

Chapter 24 examines "Renewable Energy Consumption" in Circular Economy in this chapter. We presume Circular Economy development is proxied by renewable energy usage. We use 2011–2020 World Bank Environmental, Social, and Governance-ESG statistics for 193 countries. We focus on the ESG dataset's Environmental variables to determine country-level Circular Economy implementation paths. We use Panel Data with Fixed Effects, Panel Data with Random Effects, Pooled Ordinary Least Squares-OLS, and Weighted Least Squares-WLS. We found that "Renewable Energy Consumption" is favourably associated with "Cooling Degree Days" and "Adjusted Savings: Net Forest Depletion" and negatively associated with "Greenhouse Gas-GHG Net Emissions/Removals by Land Use Change and Forestry-LUCF" and "Mean Drought Index". A cluster analysis using the Elbow Method-optimized k-Means method yields four clusters. We conclude by comparing eight machine-learning techniques to estimate Renewable Energy Consumption. We found that Polynomial Regression predicts the best and that Renewable Energy Consumption would grow 2.61 percent. We propose using process mining to apply data analytics to force governments to make renewable energy policy decisions.

Chapter 25 explained that Big data analytics has many applications in business, healthcare, biology, politics, and management; therefore, data analysts are in demand. Thus, higher education institutions are offering data science degrees to attract students and meet industry needs. National and worldwide data science programmes have grown rapidly in the past decade. This chapter will examine how big data analytics affects different sectors. Next, it will discuss data science programmes' curricula, course options, and target industry sectors. Additionally, the chapter will explore the flaws of existing curricula and recommend new teaching areas to boost student learning. Our proposals aim to better equip data science students for industry-changing big data analytics demands.

Chapter 26 addresses that HRM's role in fostering an environment-centric innovation mindset is understudied during a period of intensifying ecological challenges. To fill this gap, this empirical study examines the relationship between Green Human Resource Management (GHRM) and Green Innovation in India's leading cement manufacturers. Using correlational research and statistical methods like Partial Least Squares (PLS), the study found a favourable correlation between Green Recruitment and Selection (GRS), Green Training and Development (GTD), Green Performance Appraisal (GPA) and Green Innovation Culture (GIC). These insights enhance HRM and sustainability theory and practise, particularly in the Indian cement sector. This research also prepares for future research in Green HRM, a growing field.

Chapter 27 states that Computers are used increasingly, and electronic and digital sources are becoming essential due to new development technologies and the vast web network to boost sales, which is rapidly expanding in our country. Due to increasing expansion, many businesses are going online. Despite men buying more online than women, studies have emerged. Participants completed a Google Forms questionnaire to provide the study's primary data. Secondary data collects all journal, magazine, and article data. This study investigates what factors affect women's beauty products. The study also aims to discover Nykaa product buyers' online shopping concerns and offer ways to make online shopping easier for women.

Data-Driven Intelligent Business Sustainability aims to provide an in-depth examination of the impact of data-driven decision-making on the ability to achieve long-term commercial and economic success. In order to be considered for inclusion in this proposed book series, research must be novel to provide new insights through methodologically sound and evidence-based analysis. Recent years have seen a meteoric rise in data-driven decision-making, powered by advances in our capacity to collect and interpret information on an unimaginable scale. One of the greatest problems in today's technical and business climate is maintaining a healthy firm that can develop and continue to provide cutting-edge goods and services to the public and boost economic growth. Researchers are asked to solve the topic of how to ensure the long-term success of organisations by using evidence-based decision-making in this book series. When deploying and utilising critical technology, we zero in on how firms do so to maximise their impact. Numerous significant technologies have dramatically altered how businesses are operated. Blockchain, the Internet of Things (IoT), and artificial intelligence (AI) are examples of such technologies. How businesses make decisions, interact with clients, and introduce new offerings is now influenced by cutting-edge tech. The foundation for the connection between organisations and their many stakeholders has shifted thanks to new tools and techniques, including chatbots, virtual assistants, m-commerce, virtual teams, and interactions via the metaverse. The rapid pace of digitization has created new risks for businesses, particularly cybersecurity threats, and artificial intelligence has introduced new ethical questions and puzzles. Therefore, it is essential to create plans for long-term company expansion. This book series seeks contributions to modern machine learning methods, causal inference, and other data-driven approaches that might help businesses make better managerial decisions.

Sonia Singh
Toss Global Management, UAE

S. Suman Rajest
Dhaanish Ahmed College of Engineering, India

Slim Hadoussa
Brest Business School, France

Ahmed J. Obaid
University of Kufa, Iraq

R. Regin
SRM Institute of Science and Technology, India

Chapter 1
Evolving Business Intelligence on Data Integration, ETL Procedures, and the Power of Predictive Analytics

D. Lavanya
PSNA College of Engineering and Technology, India

Shashank Agarwal
iD https://orcid.org/0009-0003-7679-6690
CVS Health, USA

Divya Marupaka
iD https://orcid.org/0009-0005-1893-4842
Unikon IT Inc., USA

Latha Thammareddi
iD https://orcid.org/0009-0005-6338-7972
DXC Technology, USA

Sandeep Rangineni
iD https://orcid.org/0009-0003-9623-4062
Pluto TV, USA

T. Shynu
Agni College of Technology, India

ABSTRACT

In today's fast-paced and data-driven corporate market, the capacity to fully utilize information is critical. Business intelligence (BI) is the foundation of informed decision-making, allowing firms to turn unprocessed information into actionable insights. It is a process that starts with understanding data integration methodologies and learning extract, transform, load (ETL) procedures, which serve as the foundation for effective BI systems. Businesses, and hence the BI landscape, are continually evolving in our rapid digital world. While an established basis in data integration is still essential, there is a compelling movement toward the future—a future in which predictive analytics, including machine learning, will play critical roles in influencing the way we extract value from data. This chapter will conduct a thorough examination of these key aspects. The authors begin by delving into the complexities of data integration, uncovering the processes and procedures that serve as the foundation for solid business intelligence operations.

DOI: 10.4018/979-8-3693-0049-7.ch001

1. INTRODUCTION

Predictive analytics is a datasets-driven process that makes forecasts about future occurrences or outcomes using historical data, statistical methodologies, and modern machine learning algorithms (Abu-Rumman, 2021). It is a proactive strategy for decision-making that enables organizations to find undetected patterns, trends, and linkages in their data and then utilize this information to predict what will happen next (Bloch & Sacks, 2018).

Predictive analytics is a valuable technique in the context of business intelligence (BI) (Marjamäki, 2023) for generating insights into possible scenarios in the future (Chung & Chung, 2013). It helps with risk evaluation, resource allocation, and strategy planning (Abu-Rumman and Qawasmeh, 2021). Predictive analytics, for example, can be used by a retail organization to forecast consumer demand for products based on previous sales data, fluctuations in demand, and other factors (Alayli, 2023). As a result, they can optimize their inventory levels, pricing methods, and marketing efforts (Dayal et al., 2009; Kavya & Arumugam, 2016).

Machine Learning: Machine learning, an element of artificial intelligence, entails the creation of algorithms and models that allow computers to acquire knowledge from data as well as make predictions or judgments without having to be explicitly programmed (Al Shraah et al., 2022). Machine learning algorithms have been developed to improve their performance automatically once they become privy to additional data, enabling them to gradually adapt and make more precise forecasts over time (Massaro et al., 2019). Machine learning is an important component of business intelligence because it provides the level of automation required to conduct predictive activities quickly (Lee & Cheang, 2021; 2022). It can analyze massive amounts of data to unearth useful insights that people would find impossible or impractical to discern (Al Shraah et al., 2013). Machine learning models, for example, can be used to anticipate customer attrition, identify potential fraud, and enhance marketing campaigns by examining past customer data (Lishmah Dominic et al., 2023; Vashishtha & Dhawan, 2023).

Significance: Predictive analytics and machine learning are crucial in business intelligence because they allow firms to:

Anticipate Trends: Businesses may foresee trends in the market, consumer preferences, and demand for products or services by studying past data and recognizing patterns, helping businesses stay far ahead of their competitors (Al-maaitah et al., 2021).

Enhance Decision-Making: Predictive analytics and machine learning deliver data-driven insights that assist companies in making better informed and strategic decisions, whether in marketing, operations, or resource allocation (Anand et al., 2023).

Improve Customer Engagement: These strategies allow for individualized suggestions, promotional efforts, and customer service, which leads to increased client contentment and loyalty (Ramos et al., 2023).

Optimize Operations: Organizations can use predictive analytics to improve supply chain management, control of inventory, maintenance schedules, and labor planning, resulting in cost savings and enhanced efficiency (Kuragayala, 2023).

Retailers utilize predictive analytics to forecast product demand, enhance pricing tactics, and provide personalized product recommendations (Saxena et al., 2023). Amazon's recommendation system, which proposes things to customers based on their online activity and purchasing history, is a popular example (Said & Tripathi, 2023; Venkateswaran & Viktor, 2023).

Predictive analytics is utilized in the financial sector for creditworthiness evaluation, identification of fraud, and portfolio of investments optimization. Machine learning algorithms are used by credit card issuers to detect possibly forged transactions in real-time (Atasever, 2023; Vashishtha & Kapoor, (2023).

Healthcare providers use machine learning to forecast disease outbreaks, diagnose medical disorders, and prescribe individualized treatment approaches. Watson for Oncology from IBM helps oncologists make decisions about treatment according to the medical information provided by a patient and the most recent medical literature (Sabti et al., 2023).

Amazon, which uses machine learning algorithms to forecast consumer preferences and maximize inventory, and Walmart, which uses predictive analytics to improve inventory management and product availability, are two notable retail companies that use predictive analytics for sales forecasting (Srinivas et al., 2023).

1.1. Netflix Case Study: Personalizing Content Recommendations

Background

With such a large library of content, Netflix, the top streaming entertainment service in the world, struggled to keep its members interested. It needed to provide highly customized content recommendations that were tailored to each customer's tastes and preferences in order to keep and gain customers (Khaled Lafi Al-Naif and Ata E. M. Al Shraah, 2018).

Solution

Netflix implemented a predictive analytics and machine learning solution to revolutionize its content recommendation system. Here's how it worked:

Data Gathering: Netflix amassed a vast amount of user behavior data. Users' viewing habits, ratings, search terms, and even the time of day they watched content were all included.

Data Integration: To guarantee accuracy and consistency, the data from diverse sources were combined into a single data repository. ETL procedures were used in this step to clean and prepare the data (Tripathi & Al-Shahri, 2023).

Feature Engineering

Data scientists and engineers at Netflix created features that recorded viewer preferences and viewing patterns (Pandit, 2023). These characteristics included preferences for certain genres, performers, and directors, as well as subtle trends like "viewed with family" or "binge-watched."

Machine Learning Models: Netflix used deep learning models like neural collaborative filtering as well as machine learning methods like matrix factorization and collaborative filtering. These algorithms conducted data analysis to identify user preferences and forecast the type of material they could find appealing (Hochbaum, 2018).

A/B testing: Netflix uses A/B testing to continuously test and improve its recommendation algorithms. In order to be sure that any adjustments produced better suggestions, they could compare the performance of the new models to those of the old ones (Ocoró et al., 2023).

Results: Netflix's use of machine learning and predictive analytics in its recommendation engine had a significant impact:

Improved User Engagement: Tailored suggestions resulted in higher user engagement. Those who subscribed were more inclined to keep utilizing the service while spending more time watching content.

Reduced Churn: Netflix decreased subscriber churn rates by recommending material that matched consumers' preferences. Because there wasn't enough interesting content, users weren't as likely to quit their memberships.

Content Discovery: Customers discovered a wider variety of content, which includes specific genres and foreign films, which they might not have found otherwise. This raised subscribers' overall satisfaction (Lin et al., 2019).

Content Production: Netflix invested in the creation of original content using data-driven insights (Balasudarsun et al., 2022).

Competitive Advantage: Netflix has a distinct advantage over rivals in the streaming market thanks to its personalized recommendation system (María et al., 2023).

The case study of Netflix shows how the integration of predictive analytics and machine learning with data from diverse sources and processing through ETL procedures may completely change a company (Venkateswaran et al., 2023). Netflix grew its user base, kept its members, and cemented its position as the industry leader in streaming entertainment by providing tailored content recommendations. The importance of data-driven decision-making is shown by this case study, which also shows how business intelligence is changing in the digital age.

2. FOUNDATIONS OF PREDICTIVE ANALYTICS

In Fig.1 we can see the 5 phases of existing signal processing that make up the proposed fault detection technique. As indicated in, the procedure begins with capturing the stator current from the machine in various states and then processing it for wavelet-based de-noising (Kompella, 2021). In this step, the signal is divided into four levels in order to filter out the noise that was picked up during the data capture process. The appropriate threshold value is estimated in real-time, and the noise is then eliminated. The second stage, which involves removing approximated frequency components to obtain fault detection using PFFC, begins once the noise has been eliminated. The PFFC uses a Wiener filter to estimate the regular motor stator current components and subtract them from the test signal.

Predictive modeling is an important tool in analytics and data science that enables organizations to generate precise forecasts about future results using historical data. Predictive modeling, at its heart, entails utilizing statistical or predictive machine learning algorithms to detect patterns, connections, and trends in data and subsequently applying those findings to estimate what might happen next. The following are the 8 fundamental steps of predictive modeling and its function in deriving insights from past data (Liang & Liu, 2018); Močarniková & Greguš, 2019).

Figure 1. Foundations of predictive analytics

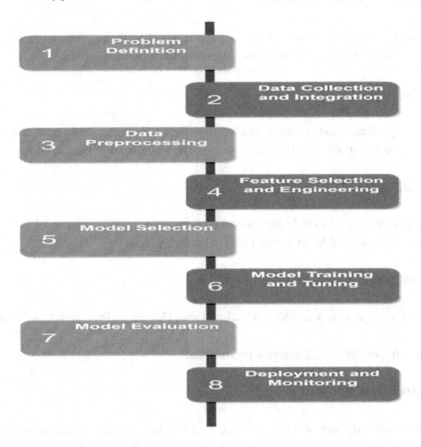

Problem Identification

- Identify the organization's problem you want predictive modeling to solve.
- Determine the variable of interest (what exactly you want to forecast) as well as any relevant traits or circumstances that could influence it.

Data Gathering and Integration

- Collect historical data from a variety of sources while guaranteeing data accuracy and uniformity.
- Combine data from several sources to generate a uniform dataset.

Data Preparation

- By dealing with missing numbers, outliers, and inconsistencies, you can explore and clean the data.
- As needed, normalize numerical characteristics and encode category variables.

Engineering and Feature Selection

- Select the most crucial features for modeling while avoiding those that are unnecessary.
- Create new features that record important information or interactions.

Model Choice

- Based on the problem's nature and data characteristics, select a suitable predictive model.
- Models that are commonly used include linear regression decision trees and neural networks.

Model Development and Tuning

- A training dataset is used to train the chosen model.
- Model parameters should be fine-tuned for optimal performance.

Model Assessment

- Use relevant measures such as Mean Absolute Error (MAE) or Precision to evaluate the model's performance.
- Determine whether the model can predict fresh data.

Monitoring and Deployment

- If the model fulfills the performance criteria, deploy it in a production environment.
- Monitor the model's efficiency on a regular basis and retrain as appropriate.

These eight steps provide a streamlined structure for incorporating predictive modeling into a Business Intelligence system (Lishmah Dominic et al., 2023). The goal is to use past data to produce informed predictions that improve business intelligence and facilitate data-driven decision-making (Lin et al., 2019)

Machine Learning Algorithms

An overview of several common machine learning algorithms, such as regression, decision trees, neural networks, etc., are as follows.

Linear Regression

Linear regression is used to model the connection between a dependent variable (goal) and any number of independent variables (features) by matching a linear equation to the data that has been observed.

It is frequently utilized to anticipate values in numbers and is straightforward yet effective for applications such as price forecasting, forecasting sales, and trend analysis.

Logistic Regression

Logistic regression, as opposed to linear regression, is used for classification tasks with binary or categorical output (e.g., yes/no, spam/not spam). It simulates the likelihood of an example relating to a specific class.

Decision Trees

Decision trees are adaptable and understandable algorithms that can be used for classification as well as regression. They divide the feature space into parts and make decisions using an if-else set of rules. Decision trees are the foundation for more sophisticated algorithms such as random forest construction and gradient boosting.

Forests at Random

Random forests are a collaborative learning strategy that mixes numerous decision trees to increase forecast accuracy while reducing overfitting. They are noted for their resilience and ease of use, and they perform effectively for regression and classification analyses.

Machines for Gradient Boosting

Gradient Boosting is an additional ensemble method that combines the forecasts of weak models (often decision trees) to create a strong predictive model. Gradient boosting algorithms such as XGBoost and Light GBM are widely used.

SVMs (Support Vector Machines)

SVM is a strong method that may be used for classification as well as regression. It determines the optimum hyperplane for separating data points of distinct classes whilst optimizing the space between them.

Artificial Neural Networks

In recent years, neural networks, especially deep learning networks, have been increasing in prominence. They are modeled after the neural network of the human brain and are made up of layers of linked neurons. Deep neural networks have attained state-of-the-art performance in a variety of domains, including visual tasks with Convolutional Neural Networks (CNNs) and sequential data with Recurrent Neural Networks (RNNs) (Mohamad Rodzi et al., 2015).

K-Nearest Neighbors

K-NN is a straightforward instance-based learning method that may be used for regression and classification. It makes projections based on the feature's majority class or the average of the k-nearest data values.

Naive Bayes

The probabilistic algorithm Naive Bayes is based on Bayes' theorem. Among other things, it is often used for the classification of text and spam detection.

Algorithms for Clustering

Clustering techniques such as K-Means, Hierarchical Clustering, and DBSCAN are used in unsupervised training exercises to group data points based on similarity. These are only a few of the numerous machine-learning algorithms that are accessible. The algorithm you use is determined by the characteristics of the data, the query you are attempting to answer, and other criteria such as interpretability and processing resources. Experimenting with numerous algorithms to determine the one that performs best for a specific task is typical.

Data Source and Integration

Data for predictive analytics originates from:

- Historical Data: Records of past events or transactions
- Databases and Warehouses: Structured data repositories
- Streaming and Real-time Data: IoT, social media, sensors
- External Sources: Government datasets, online data
- Surveys and Questionnaires: Specific information collection
- Text, Image, Audio Data: Emails, images, audio, and videos
- Geospatial and Log Data: Geographic info, system logs
- Customer and Market Data: Call logs, market reports

3. DATA INTEGRATION AND ETL PROCESS

Predictive analytics relies heavily on data integration and ETL (Extract, Transform, Load) operations. They prepare and organize data so that it may be utilized to develop predictive algorithms and extract important insights (Fig. 2).

1. Data Gathering and Aggregation

Data integration entails gathering information from a variety of sources of information, which may include databases, auxiliary datasets, web-based services, and others. Access to a diverse set of data sources is critical in predictive analytics for gaining a full picture of the problem and boosting model accuracy (Venkateswaran 2015).

2. Data Cleaning and Transformation

ETL operations, particularly the "Transform" step, are concerned with cleaning and preparing data. These covers dealing with values that are missing, outliers, and anomalies. Developing accurate predictive models requires clean and well-structured data.

3. Feature Development

Feature engineering is an important component of ETL for predictive analytics. It entails either developing new features from current data or picking relevant characteristics to improve model performance. Efficient feature engineering can significantly improve a model's predictive power.

4. Time-Series Data Handling

Many predictive analytics systems work with data that is time-series based, which includes stock prices, weather information, or sales data collected over time. ETL processes frequently involve dealing with timestamps, gathering data over extended periods, and generating lag features for time-dependent forecasts.

5. Data Sampling and Splitting

Data collection and splitting into validation, training, and test sets can also be part of ETL procedures. These kinds of subsets are employed to precisely train models, tune parameters, and measure model performance.

6. Scalability and automation

As data quantities increase, ETL operations must become more automated and scalable to handle the increased volume of data efficiently. Automation guarantees that data streams are always up to date and ready for predictive analyses.

7. Data Protection and Compliance

Organizations frequently work with sensitive or restricted data in predictive analytics. To ensure data integrity, ETL operations should conform to data privacy and compliance standards, such as encryption, controls on access, and audit trails.

8. Monitoring and Maintenance

To discover problems or failures, ETL procedures must be monitored continuously. To react to alterations in sources of data, business requirements, or adjustments in data dissemination, regular maintenance is required.

9. Greater Model Accuracy

The precision and dependability of predictive models are directly affected by the quality of data generated by ETL operations. More exact predictions result from clean, organized data with informative properties.

10. Faster Decision-Making

Because ETL methods speed the data preparation phase, firms may create predictive models more quickly. This enables nimbler, data-driven decision-making.

Figure 2. Source of data predictive analytics

4. MODEL DEPLOYMENT AND OPERATIONALIZATION

Deploying predictive models in real-world corporate environments entails a series of processes to guarantee that the models are functional, accessible, and capable of producing value. Here is a thorough description of the procedure:

4.1. Emerging Trends and Future Outlook

Predictive analytics is a rapidly changing area, with new trends and technology appearing all the time. Here are some of the most notable emerging trends in predictive analytics, as well as prospective future developments:

XAI (Explainable AI): The ability to explain is becoming increasingly important in predictive analytics, particularly in financial, healthcare, and legal applications. Future improvements will center on the development of AI and machine learning models capable of providing visible and interpretable information.

Ethics and Fairness in AI: The ethical implications of predictive analytics are getting attention. Future improvements will stress the construction of models that are equitable, impartial, and follow rigorous ethical norms.

AutoML and Augmented Analytics: AutoML (Automated Machine Learning) simplifies the model-building process and makes it more accessible to a wider audience. Augmented analytics, which mixes AI with analytics, continues to increase, making it easier for users to acquire insights from data.

Time–Series Forecasting: With the increased availability of time-series information (for example, IoT data), advances in predictive analytics will concentrate on more accurate and scalable time-series forecasting approaches, such as deep learning models.

NLP (Natural Language Processing): The combination of NLP with predictive analytics is becoming more common. Text analysis and sentiment analysis will be improved in the future to produce more accurate forecasts using unstructured textual data.

Edge Analytics: Edge computing and analytics will become more prevalent, enabling predictive models to operate on Internet of Things (IoT) devices to make real-time decisions without depending on centralized cloud resources.

RPA (Robotic Process Automation): RPA, paired with predictive analytics, can intelligently automate corporate activities. This trend will only continue to increase as businesses strive for greater efficiency.

Prescriptive Analytics: Prescriptive analytics, which goes beyond predicting outcomes and offers suggestions as well as steps that enhance decision-making in real-time, will become more common (Tambaip et al., 2023).

Privacy-Preserving Techniques: In response to growing data privacy concerns, future innovations will concentrate on approaches such as federated learning and homomorphic encryption to do analytics on encrypted data while maintaining privacy. These trends and developments highlight the changing predictive analytics landscape, stressing transparency, automation, real-time adaption, and ethical considerations. They influence the evolution of data-driven choices across industries collectively.

4.2. Practical Implications of Implementing Predictive Analytics and Machine Learning in BI

It's critical to understand the deep practical ramifications that these technologies bring to businesses of all kinds and across a range of industries as we dig into the transformational area of predictive analytics and machine learning within the domain of Business Intelligence (BI). We will go deeper into these ramifications in this part, highlighting their importance in the data-driven environment of today (fig.3).

Figure 3. Deploying predictive models in business environments

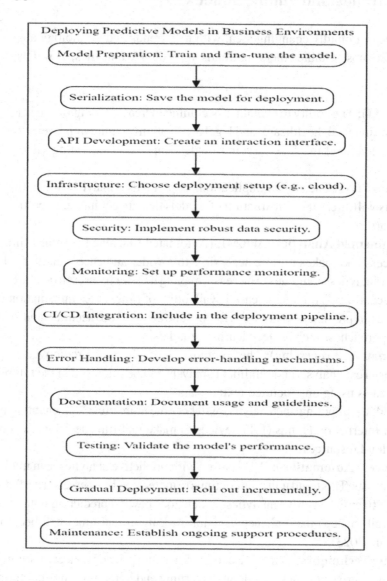

Enhanced Decision-Making: The improvement of decision-making processes is one of the most immediate and useful effects of predictive analytics and machine learning in BI. Organizations can use historical data, statistical methods, and sophisticated algorithms to make more educated, data-driven decisions. Think about a retail company that uses demand prediction to optimize its inventory management. Reduced expenses, fewer stockouts, and higher customer satisfaction result from this. It goes without saying that using these technologies can help businesses expand and build closer relationships with their clients.

Enhanced Client Engagement: Customer involvement is another area with strong practical implications. Businesses may now personalize their interactions with customers thanks to predictive analytics and machine learning. For instance, a streaming service like Netflix makes content suggestions using recommendation algorithms to keep viewers interested and satisfied. This degree of personalization enhances revenue while also increasing client loyalty. The practical implication for firms is clear: utilizing these technologies can promote greater client ties and spur expansion.

Operations Optimization: Machine learning and predictive analytics can simplify many organizational operational processes. Predictive models, for instance, can forecast patient admission rates in the healthcare industry, allowing hospitals to manage resources effectively. Costs are reduced as a result, and patient care is improved. The practical implication is that these technologies make it possible for businesses to improve their operations, which saves money and boosts productivity.

5. CONCLUSION

The convergence of traditional data integration and ETL (Extract, Transform, Load) techniques with the immense potential of predictive analytics and machine learning has emerged as a driving force in the dynamic realm of business intelligence. This chapter provides a comprehensive exploration of these pivotal components, laying the foundation for effective and insightful business intelligence operations, as outlined by Stalin et al. (2021).

Predictive analytics and machine learning have assumed paramount importance in contemporary business environments, equipping organizations with the ability to not only react to changes but also proactively anticipate trends. These technologies empower businesses to enhance their decision-making processes, engage customers more effectively, optimize their operations, and gain strategic advantages in an intensely competitive market, as highlighted by Rajni and Borah in 2015.

At the core of this transformative journey are eight fundamental elements of predictive modeling. These elements, combined with a diverse spectrum of machine learning algorithms, serve as indispensable tools for organizations seeking to extract maximum value from their data resources. The choice of a specific algorithm is often dictated by the nature of the data and the specific objectives at hand. For instance, linear regression may be employed for forecasting price trends, while neural networks can be used for the intricate task of pattern identification.

Furthermore, this chapter underscores the critical importance of data integration and ETL processes in ensuring the quality and accessibility of data for predictive analytics. In the realm of data-driven decision-making, clean and well-structured data acts as the bedrock upon which reliable predictive models are built. The ability to harness such data resources effectively empowers organizations to make informed and data-driven decisions, providing them with a significant competitive edge.

As we look toward the future, the landscape of predictive analytics is set to evolve further. Exciting developments on the horizon, such as Explainable AI (XAI), ethics in AI, automation through AutoML, advanced time-series prediction techniques, natural language processing (NLP), edge analytics, and more, promise to reshape the predictive analytics arena. These emerging trends underscore the growing need for transparency in AI systems, automation to streamline processes, real-time adaptability to changing market conditions, and a keen focus on ethical considerations in the deployment of these technologies.

In summary, the amalgamation of data integration, ETL procedures, predictive analytics, and machine learning holds immense promise for organizations seeking strategic insights and a competitive advantage in the ever-evolving digital landscape. By comprehending and harnessing the potential of these technologies, businesses can adapt their business intelligence strategies to meet the demands of the future. The ability to make data-driven decisions and anticipate market trends is no longer a luxury but a necessity in the competitive world of business and these tools provide the means to achieve just that. Moreover, they underscore the importance of continuous learning and adaptation to remain at the forefront of the business intelligence field.

REFERENCES

Abu-Rumman, A. (2021). Effective Knowledge Sharing: A Guide to the Key Enablers and Inhibitors. In D. Tessier (Ed.), *Handbook of Research on Organizational Culture Strategies for Effective Knowledge Management and Performance* (pp. 133–156). IGI Global. doi:10.4018/978-1-7998-7422-5.ch008

Abu-Rumman, A. & Qawasmeh, R. (2021). Assessing international students' satisfaction of a Jordanian university using the service quality model. *Journal of Applied Research in Higher Education*. doi:10.1108/JARHE-05-2021-0166

Al-maaitah, T. A., Tha'er Majali, M. A., & Almaaitah, D. A. (2021). The Impact of COVID-19 on the Electronic Commerce Users Behavior. *Journal of Contemporary Issues in Business and Government*, 27(1), 772–783.

Al-Naif, K. L., & Al Shraah, A. E. M. (2018). Working capital management and profitability: Evidence from Jordanian mining and extraction industry sector. *IUG Journal of Economics and Business.*, 2(1), 42–60.

Al Shraah, A., Abu-Rumman, A., Alqhaiwi, L. A., & AlSha'ar, H. (2022). The impact of sourcing strategies and logistics capabilities on organizational performance during the COVID-19 pandemic: Evidence from Jordanian pharmaceutical industries. *Uncertain Supply Chain Management*, 10(3), 1077–1090. doi:10.5267/j.uscm.2022.2.004

Al Shraah, A., Irtaimeh, H. J., & Rumman, M. A. (2013). The Strategic Human Resource Management Practices in Implying Total Quality Management (TQM): An Empirical Study on Jordanian Banking Sector. *International Journal of Management*, 4(5), 179–190.

Alayli, S. (2023). Unravelling the Drivers of Online Purchasing Intention: The E-Commerce Scenario in Lebanon. *FMDB Transactions on Sustainable Social Sciences Letters*, 1(1), 56–67.

Anand, P. P., Kanike, U. K., Paramasivan, P., Rajest, S. S., Regin, R., & Priscila, S. S. (2023). Embracing Industry 5.0: Pioneering Next-Generation Technology for a Flourishing Human Experience and Societal Advancement. *FMDB Transactions on Sustainable Social Sciences Letters*, 1(1), 43–55.

Atasever, M. (2023). Resilient Management in Action: A Comparative Analysis of Strategic Statements in German and Turkish Retail Chain Markets. *FMDB Transactions on Sustainable Management Letters*, 1(2), 66–81.

Balasudarsun, D., Sathish, D., Venkateswaran, D., Byloppilly, D. R., Devesh, S., & Naved, D. M. (2022). Predicting consumers' online grocery purchase intention within middle-class families. *Webology*, 19(1), 3620–3642. doi:10.14704/WEB/V19I1/WEB19239

Bloch, T., & Sacks, R. (2018). Comparing machine learning and rule-based inferencing for semantic enrichment of BIM models. *Automation in Construction*, 91, 256–272. doi:10.1016/j.autcon.2018.03.018

Chung, P. T., & Chung, S. H. (2013). On data integration and data mining for developing business intelligence. In *2013, IEEE Long Island Systems, Applications and Technology Conference (LISAT)*. IEEE. 10.1109/LISAT.2013.6578235

Dayal, U., Castellanos, M., Simitsis, A., & Wilkinson, K. (2009). Data integration flows for business intelligence. *Proceedings of the 12th International Conference on Extending Database Technology: Advances in Database Technology*. 10.1145/1516360.1516362

Hochbaum, D. S. (2018). Machine Learning and Data Mining with Combinatorial Optimization Algorithms. In Recent Advances in Optimization and Modeling of Contemporary Problems (pp. 109-129). INFORMS. doi:10.1287/educ.2018.0179

Kavya, V., & Arumugam, S. (2016). A Review on Predictive Analytics in Data Mining. *International Journal of Chaos, Control, Modelling and Simulation, 5*(1/2/3), 1-8.

Kuragayala, P. S. (2023). A Systematic Review on Workforce Development in Healthcare Sector: Implications in the Post-COVID Scenario. *FMDB Transactions on Sustainable Technoprise Letters, 1*(1), 36–46.

Lee, C. S., & Cheang, P. Y. S. (2021). Predictive Analysis in Business Analytics: Application of Decision Tree in Business Decision Making. *Advances in Decision Sciences, 26*(1), 1–29. doi:10.47654/v26y2022i1p1-29

Lee, J., & Cheang, B. (2022). Predictive Analysis in Business Analytics: Application of Decision Tree in Business Decision Making. *Journal of Business Analytics, 8*(2), 123–136.

Liang, T.-P., & Liu, Y.-H. (2018). Bibliometrics study. *Expert Systems with Applications, 111*, 2–10. doi:10.1016/j.eswa.2018.05.018

Lin, Y., Wang, H., Li, J., & Gao, H. (2019). Data source selection for information integration in the big data era. *Information Sciences, 479*, 197–213. doi:10.1016/j.ins.2018.11.029

Lishmah Dominic, M., Sowmiya, S., & Venkateswaran, P. S. (2023). Study on importance of entrepreneurship skill development programme (ESDP) for sustainable growth of MSMEs in India. *Proceedings on Engineering Sciences, 5*(3), 553–564. doi:10.24874/PES05.03.018

María, J. J. L., Polo, O. C. C., & Elhadary, T. (2023). An Analysis of the Morality and Social Responsibility of Non-Profit Organizations. *FMDB Transactions on Sustainable Technoprise Letters, 1*(1), 28–35.

Marjamäki, P. (2023). *Evolution and trends of business intelligence systems: a systematic mapping study*. Academic Press.

Massaro, A., Vitti, V., Galiano, A., & Morelli, A. (2019). Business Intelligence Improved by Data Mining Algorithms and Big Data Systems: An Overview of Different Tools Applied in Industrial Research. *Computer Science and Information Technology (Alhambra, Calif.), 7*(1), 1–21. doi:10.13189/csit.2019.070101

Močarniková, K., & Greguš, M. (2019). Conceptualization of Predictive Analytics by Literature Review. In *Data-Centric Business and Applications* (pp. 205–234). Springer International Publishing.

Mohamad Rodzi, N. A. H., Othman, M. S., & Yusuf, L. M. (2015). Significance of data integration and ETL in the business intelligence framework for higher education. In *2015 International Conference on Science in Information Technology (ICSITech)*. IEEE. 10.1109/ICSITech.2015.7407800

Ocoró, M. P., Polo, O. C. C., & Khandare, S. (2023). Importance of Business Financial Risk Analysis in SMEs According to COVID-19. *FMDB Transactions on Sustainable Management Letters*, *1*(1), 12–21.

Pandit, P. (2023). On the Context of the Principle of Beneficence: The Problem of Over Demandingness within Utilitarian Theory. *FMDB Transactions on Sustainable Social Sciences Letters*, *1*(1), 26–42.

Ramos, J. I., Lacerona, R., & Nunag, J. M. (2023). A Study on Operational Excellence, Work Environment Factors and the Impact to Employee Performance. *FMDB Transactions on Sustainable Social Sciences Letters*, *1*(1), 12–25.

Sabti, Y. M., Alqatrani, R. I. N., Zaid, M. I., Taengkliang, B., & Kareem, J. M. (2023). Impact of Business Environment on the Performance of Employees in the Public-Listed Companies. *FMDB Transactions on Sustainable Management Letters*, *1*(2), 56–65.

Said, F. B., & Tripathi, S. (2023). Epistemology of Digital Journalism Shift in South Global Nations: A Bibliometric Analysis. *FMDB Transactions on Sustainable Technoprise Letters*, *1*(1), 47–60.

Saxena, D., Khandare, S., & Chaudhary, S. (2023). An Overview of ChatGPT: Impact on Academic Learning. *FMDB Transactions on Sustainable Techno Learning*, *1*(1), 11–20.

Srinivas, K., Velmurugan, P. R., & Andiyappillai, N. (2023). Digital Human Resources and Management Support Improve Human Resources Effectiveness. *FMDB Transactions on Sustainable Management Letters*, *1*(1), 32–45.

Stalin, K. G., Meharajan, T., & Venkateswaran, P. S. (2019). Impact of HRM practices on select IT companies' performance in Madurai. *International Journal of Scientific & Technology Research*, *8*(12), 169–172.

Tambaip, B., Hadi, A. F. F., & Tjilen, A. P. (2023). Optimizing Public Service Performance: Unleashing the Potential of Compassion as an Indicator of Public Service Motivation. *FMDB Transactions on Sustainable Management Letters*, *1*(2), 46–55.

Tripathi, S., & Al-Shahri, M. (2023). Problems and Prospects on the Evolution of Advertising and Public Relations Industries in Oman. *FMDB Transactions on Sustainable Management Letters*, *1*(1), 1–11.

Vashishtha, E., & Dhawan, G. (2023). Comparison of Baldrige Criteria of Strategy Planning and Harrison Text. *FMDB Transactions on Sustainable Management Letters*, *1*(1), 22–31.

Vashishtha, E., & Kapoor, H. (2023). Implementation of Blockchain Technology Across International Healthcare Markets. *FMDB Transactions on Sustainable Technoprise Letters*, *1*(1), 1–12.

Venkateswaran, P.S., (2015), Influence of information systems in Engineering Institutions at Madurai District, Tamil Nadu, India. *International Journal of Applied Engineering Research, 9*(21), 10513-10528.

Venkateswaran, P. S., Singh, S., Paramasivan, P., Rajest, S. S., Lourens, M. E., & Regin, R. (2023). A Study on The Influence of Quality of Service on Customer Satisfaction Towards Hotel Industry. *FMDB Transactions on Sustainable Social Sciences Letters*, *1*(1), 1–11.

Venkateswaran, P. S., & Viktor, P. (2023). A Study on Brand Equity of Fast-Moving Consumer Goods with Reference to Madurai, Tamil Nadu. *FMDB Transactions on Sustainable Technoprise Letters*, *1*(1), 13–27.

Chapter 2
A Case Study on Food Waste Reduction Strategies in Dindigul Restaurants Using the Food Supply Chain

A. Sabarirajan
PSNA College of Engineering and Technology, India

N. Arunfred
SRM Institute of Science and Technology, India

V. Bini Marin
SRM Institute of Science and Technology, India

Shouvik Sanyal
Dhofar University, Oman

Rameshwaran Byloppilly
City University, Ajman, UAE

R. Regin
SRM Institute of Science And Technology, India

ABSTRACT

Food waste is a pressing issue within the restaurant industry, contributing to environmental concerns and economic losses. This research study investigates food waste reduction strategies in Dindigul restaurants, aiming to provide valuable insights into sustainable practices. A diverse sample of 151 restaurant stakeholders, comprising customers, owners, managers, chefs, and staff, participated in the study. The findings reveal notable demographic patterns among respondents, emphasizing the importance of tailored strategies for distinct segments. The distribution of food waste highlights specific stages and categories as major contributors, underscoring the need for targeted efforts in preparation, spoilage, and plate waste reduction. Perceptions of food waste reduction strategies varied, with composting and surplus food donation receiving favorable feedback. Challenges and barriers, including staff awareness, tools for waste tracking, storage limitations, and customer resistance to portion control, were identified as significant obstacles.

DOI: 10.4018/979-8-3693-0049-7.ch002

1. INTRODUCTION

Food waste has emerged as a pervasive and pressing global issue, with profound implications for sustainability, economic efficiency, and environmental conservation. The enormity of the problem is evident in its far-reaching consequences, spanning from the depletion of natural resources to the exacerbation of greenhouse gas emissions (Alayli, 2023). Moreover, it extends to a missed opportunity to alleviate food insecurity and promote economic prudence. Within this multifaceted context of food waste reduction, the restaurant industry assumes a significant role, given its substantial contribution to the generation of food waste (Anand et al., 2023). In light of these challenges, this research paper embarks on a comprehensive exploration of food waste reduction strategies within the dynamic landscape of Dindigul's restaurant sector.

The ramifications of food waste are multifaceted and touch upon multiple dimensions of our modern world. Beyond the evident environmental implications, food waste exerts considerable pressure on the sustainable use of natural resources, such as water, land, and energy, which are pivotal to food production (Ramos et al., 2023). Furthermore, it significantly adds to the global burden of greenhouse gas emissions (Atasever, 2023). As food decomposes in landfills, it releases methane, a potent greenhouse gas that contributes to climate change. This highlights the inextricable link between food waste and environmental conservation, emphasizing the urgency of addressing this issue (Pandit, 2023).

Food waste also bears profound economic consequences. From the perspective of individual households to entire nations, the financial toll of discarded food is significant (Ocoró et al., 2023). For households, it translates into wasted money spent on groceries that are ultimately discarded, and for nations, it represents the inefficient allocation of resources that could be directed toward other critical needs. Additionally, within the restaurant industry, food waste amplifies operational costs, affecting profit margins and overall economic efficiency. Therefore, the reduction of food waste is not just an environmental imperative but also an economic one (Tambaip et al., 2023).

Moreover, the issue of food waste is intrinsically linked to social justice and food security. While we grapple with the paradox of food waste, millions of people worldwide face hunger and malnutrition (Said & Tripathi, 2023). The inefficiencies in food production and distribution, coupled with the staggering amount of food waste, underscore the stark inequities within our global food system (Sabti et al., 2023). Addressing food waste is not only a matter of environmental and economic prudence but also a moral obligation to ensure equitable access to food for all (Priscila et al., 2023).

Restaurants, as integral components of the food supply chain, bear a unique and critical responsibility in mitigating food waste and embracing sustainable practices. The food service industry is both a significant contributor to food waste and a potential catalyst for change. Within this sector, food waste arises from various stages of the supply chain, from food production and processing to distribution and consumption. The restaurant industry plays a pivotal role in the consumption phase, making it a locus of intervention for waste reduction efforts.

Understanding the intricacies of food waste within the restaurant industry is paramount to developing effective strategies for its reduction (María et al., 2023). The strategies employed must be context-specific and responsive to the unique dynamics and challenges that restaurants face. By delving into the restaurant sector's complexities, we can tailor strategies that resonate effectively with stakeholders and drive meaningful change (Kuragayala, 2023).

This research paper aims to illuminate the effectiveness of diverse food waste reduction strategies by offering insights into their impact as perceived by a spectrum of restaurant stakeholders (Saxena et al., 2023). To achieve this goal, the study evaluates the perceptions of a diverse group of respondents, encompassing customers, restaurant owners, managers, chefs, and staff. This comprehensive approach ensures a holistic understanding of the challenges and opportunities associated with food waste reduction in Dindigul's vibrant restaurant scene.

The research journey commences with an examination of the demographic profile of respondents, recognizing the rich diversity within the restaurant industry. This diversity encompasses different roles, age groups, and levels of experience (Srinivas et al., 2023). These demographic insights are pivotal in shaping food waste reduction strategies that can effectively resonate with those actively involved in the industry. Subsequently, the study delves into the distribution of food waste within the restaurant setting (Tripathi & Al-Shahri, 2023). It scrutinizes critical stages and categories that substantially contribute to waste generation. This meticulous examination seeks to uncover patterns and insights that are instrumental for restaurants seeking to prioritize and target their waste reduction efforts effectively.

Additionally, the research investigates the perceived effectiveness of various food waste reduction strategies, unraveling the strategies that resonate most positively with restaurant stakeholders. By soliciting and assessing feedback and preferences from both restaurant professionals and customers, this research contributes to the development of strategies that are harmonious with the needs and expectations of the industry. In addition to highlighting successful strategies, the paper also sheds light on the challenges and barriers that restaurants encounter in their pursuit of food waste reduction. These challenges are diverse and range from issues related to staff awareness and tools for waste tracking to storage limitations and customer resistance to portion control. Recognizing and understanding these challenges represents a crucial area for intervention and improvement. By addressing these obstacles, restaurants can advance more effectively toward their goals of reducing food waste (Venkateswaran et al., 2023).

This research endeavor aspires to provide actionable insights and practical recommendations for Dindigul restaurants and similar establishments as they navigate the intricate landscape of food waste reduction. By addressing the multifaceted dimensions of this issue, including demographic diversity, waste distribution, strategy effectiveness, and prevailing challenges, this study endeavors to foster a more sustainable and responsible approach to food management within the restaurant industry. Through these comprehensive efforts, the paper aims to contribute to the creation of a more sustainable and responsible food ecosystem within the restaurant industry, with the ultimate goal of minimizing food waste and its far-reaching consequences.

2. REVIEW OF LITERATURE

Food waste (FW) represents a multifaceted and intricate challenge that encompasses various dimensions, including sustainable production, which is an ongoing and multidimensional process involving numerous parameters (Schanes, 2018). A study conducted in the United States (US) revealed a staggering 70 million tonnes of edible food loss (Dou et al., 2016). The Food and Agriculture Organization (FAO) report by Gustavsson et al. (2011) underscores that one-third of food produced for human consumption is lost globally, amounting to a staggering 1.3 billion tonnes annually. Ludovica (2021) introduced the Restaurant Food Waste Map (RFWM) as a tool to delineate the phases contributing to the food waste phenomenon and to pinpoint mitigation strategies within food waste generation processes. Food waste carries substantial and diverse ethical implications, impacting society, the environment, and the economy (Eriksson et al., 2017; Principato et al., 2021; Vandermeersch et al., 2014; Venkateswaran et al., 2019).

The term "surplus food" refers to excess food production that remains unconsumed even under appropriate storage conditions (Mourad et al., 2016). The broader definition of "food waste" encompasses both "food loss" and "surplus food" (Ostergren et al., 2014). While there is no unanimous consensus on gender influence, some studies suggest that single women in households generate more waste per capita than other household types (Koivupuro et al., 2012). Additionally, Betz et al. (2015) found that women tend to produce more plate waste than men in the food service industry. Downstream in the supply chain, food waste is generated by individuals in homes or food-service establishments for various reasons, including poor planning, oversized portions, and food safety concerns (Buzby et al., 2014).

Hari Krishna et al. (2023) discuss innovative business research. Innovative research methodologies, including those driven by artificial intelligence, could potentially be applied to address food waste challenges in the food supply chain. Bhanushali et al. (2022) emphasize the use of data mining, and it is helpful in identifying points of food waste generation and opportunities for reduction. Venkateswaran et al. (2018) explore the concept of a technology acceptance model. A similar model could be applied to assess the adoption of technology-driven solutions for food waste reduction in the Dindigul restaurant industry.

The ReFed Restaurant Guide (2018) offers insights into critical points for reducing food waste in food service establishments. These include menu design, portion size choices, waste tracking and analytics, inventory management, and production planning, among others (Venkateswaran & Viktor, 2023).

Ramesh et al. (2022) specifically focus on the impact of training and development programs on employee performance in small and medium-sized enterprises (SMEs), highlighting the role of proper training in reducing food waste in restaurants.

3. RESEARCH METHODOLOGY

This study employs a mixed-methods research design, combining both quantitative and qualitative approaches to provide a comprehensive understanding of food waste reduction strategies in Dindigul restaurants. The research design consists of three primary components: a survey questionnaire, data analysis, and qualitative interviews. To ensure the representation of Dindigul restaurants, a stratified random sampling technique is employed. A sampling plan is developed to obtain a sample size of 151 participants. The sampling strata are based on the roles of participants, including customers, restaurant owners, managers, chefs, and staff. This approach allows for a diverse and balanced representation of restaurant stakeholders.

A structured survey questionnaire is administered to collect quantitative data. The questionnaire includes sections on demographic information, food waste generation, perceived effectiveness of food waste reduction strategies, and challenges faced by restaurants in waste reduction. Respondents are selected randomly from each stratum. Quantitative data from the survey questionnaire are analyzed using statistical software. Descriptive statistics, including frequencies, percentages, means, and standard deviations, are computed to summarize demographic profiles, food waste distribution, and perceptions of strategies. The study acknowledges certain limitations, including the potential for response bias in self-reported data and the geographical specificity of Dindigul, which may limit the generalizability of findings to other regions. However, efforts are made to mitigate these limitations through a diverse sample and rigorous data analysis.

4. DATA ANALYSIS

The demographic profile of the respondents reveals insightful patterns within the study sample. Among the roles, customers constitute the largest group, comprising 37.7% of the total respondents, while restaurant owners and managers make up 17.9% and 16.6%, respectively. Chefs and cooks, as well as staff members, each represent 9.9% of the respondents (Vashishtha & Kapoor, 2023). Turning to age groups, the "41 to 50 years" category stands out as the most common, accounting for 45.0% of respondents, followed by "20 to 30 years" at 25.2% and "above 60 years" at 16.6%. Interestingly, the "31 to 40 years" age group is the least represented, with only 0.7% of respondents falling within it. As for experience levels, the "5 to 10 years" range prevails, encompassing 45.0% of respondents, followed by "below 5 years" at 25.8% and "11 to 15 years" at 12.6%. Experience periods of "16 to 20 years" and "above 20 years" are reported by 6.6% and 9.9% of respondents, respectively.

Table 1. Demographic profile of the respondents

Respondent's Role	Frequency	Percent	Cumulative %
Restaurant Owners	27	17.9	17.9
Restaurant Managers	25	16.6	34.4
Chefs and Cooks	15	9.9	44.4
Staff Members	27	17.9	62.3
Customers	57	37.7	100.0
Age Group	**Frequency**	**Percent**	**Cumulative %**
20 to 30 years	38	25.2	25.2
31 to 40 years	1	0.7	25.8
41 to 50 years	68	45.0	70.9
51 to 60 years	19	12.6	83.4
Above 60 years	25	16.6	100.0
Experience	**Frequency**	**Percent**	**Cumulative %**
Below 5 years	39	25.8	25.8
5 to 10 years	68	45.0	70.9
11 to 15 years	19	12.6	83.4
16 to 20 years	10	6.6	90.1
Above 20 years	15	9.9	100.0

These demographic insights offer a comprehensive view of the study's participant composition, which is crucial for interpreting research outcomes within specific respondent segments.

Based on the data presented in Table 1, several significant insights can be drawn regarding the distribution of food waste in restaurants. In terms of average daily food waste, it is apparent that a majority of the respondents fall within the range of 31 to 40 kg, constituting 40.4% of the total distribution. This is followed by the 21 to 30 kg range, accounting for 22.5%.

Table 2. Distribution of food waste in restaurants

Distribution	Frequency	Percent	Cumulative %	Mean	SD	Variance
Average daily food waste Less than 20 Kg 21 to 30 Kg 31 to 40 Kg 41 to 50 Kg	45 34 61 11	29.8 22.5 40.4 7.3	29.8 52.3 92.7 100	2.25	0.967	0.936
Waste % on total food produced / day Less than 5% 6 to 10% 11 to 15% 16 to 20%	34 50 41 26	22.5 33.1 27.2 17.2	22.5 55.6 82.8 100.0	2.39	1.02	1.04
Major Food Waste Category Spoilage Plate waste Preparation Others	35 45 59 12	23.2 29.8 39.1 7.9	23.2 53.0 92.1 100.0	3.32	0.919	0.845

The cumulative percentage indicates that a substantial portion of respondents, around 92.7%, generate up to 40 kg of food waste per day (Table 2). The mean daily waste is 29.8 kg, with a relatively low standard deviation of 7.3, suggesting relatively consistent waste generation across respondents (Figure 1).

Figure 1. Distribution of food waste in restaurants

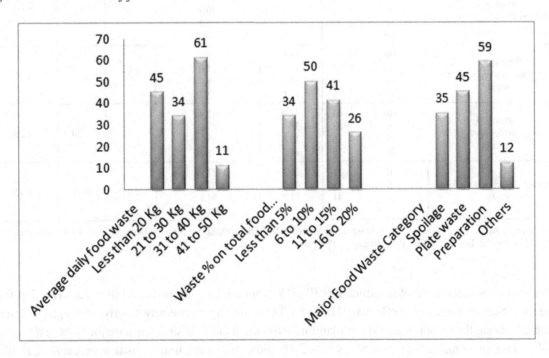

Regarding waste percentages in relation to total food produced daily, it is noteworthy that the largest segment, comprising 33.1% of respondents, generates 6 to 10% of waste. Meanwhile, the percentage distribution of waste categories offers valuable insights into specific areas contributing to food waste. The major food waste categories include preparation errors, accounting for 39.1%, followed by spoilage at 23.2% and plate waste at 29.8% (Vashishtha & Dhawan, 2023). This highlights the significance of effective preparation processes in waste reduction efforts. The mean waste percentage in major food waste categories is 23.2%, with relatively low variability indicated by the standard deviation of 7.9. In conclusion, this data sheds light on the distribution of food waste, emphasizing the importance of addressing specific waste generation stages and categories to implement targeted reduction strategies effectively (Table 3).

Table 3. Effectiveness of food waste reduction strategies

	Response	N	Percent	Cumulative %	Mean	SD	Variance
Overall Impact of Food Waste Strategies	SA	41	27.2	27.2	2.14	0.952	0.907
	A	65	43.0	70.2			
	NA	29	19.2	89.4			
	DA	15	9.9	99.3			
	SDA	1	0.7	100.0			
Strategy 1 Menu planning to minimize leftovers	HE	26	17.2	17.2	2.46	1.06	1.13
	E	70	46.4	63.6			
	N	15	9.9	73.5			
	IE	40	26.5	100.0			
Strategy 2 Portion control measures	HE	1	0.7	0.7	2.97	0.98	0.95
	E	59	39.1	39.7			
	N	47	31.1	70.9			
	IE	32	21.2	92.1			
	HIE	12	7.9	100.0			
Strategy 3 Staff training on reducing food waste	HE	22	14.6	14.6	2.52	1.08	1.18
	E	61	40.4	55.0			
	N	52	34.4	89.4			
	HIE	16	10.6	100.0			
Strategy 4 Donating surplus food to local charities	HE	64	42.4	42.4	1.92	1.00	1.00
	E	53	35.1	77.5			
	N	16	10.6	88.1			
	IE	18	11.9	100.0			
Strategy 5 Composting food waste	HE	41	27.2	27.2	2.11	0.86	0.75
	E	61	40.4	67.5			
	N	41	27.2	94.7			
	IE	8	5.3	100.0			

SA – Strongly Agree, A – Agree, NA - Neither agree nor disagree, DA – Disagree, SDA – Strongly Disagree, HE - Highly effective, E – Effective, N – Neutral, IE – Ineffective, HIE - Highly Ineffective

A significant percentage of respondents (70.2%) either strongly agreed (SA) or agreed (A) that food waste reduction strategies were effective (HE or E). This indicates a generally positive perception of these strategies among the respondents. Menu planning was considered effective by a majority of respondents (63.6%). The mean rating for this strategy was 2.46, indicating a relatively positive perception. Portion control measures received mixed feedback. While 39.7% found them effective (E), a notable percentage

(31.1%) remained neutral (N). The mean rating was 2.97, suggesting a moderately positive perception but with some variability in responses. Staff training was perceived as effective (40.4%) by a significant portion of respondents. The mean rating of 2.52 suggests a relatively positive perception. Donating surplus food received positive feedback, with 42.4% finding it highly effective (HE) (Figure 2).

Figure 2. Effectiveness of food waste reduction strategies

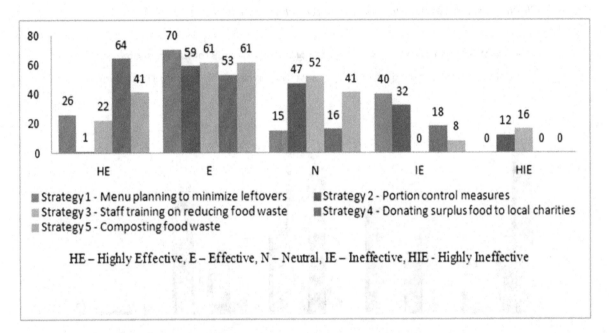

The mean rating was 1.92, indicating a generally positive perception. Composting food waste was perceived positively, with 67.5% of respondents considering it effective (E). The mean rating of 2.11 suggests a relatively positive perception. The findings suggest that the surveyed individuals generally perceive food waste reduction strategies positively, with variations in effectiveness ratings across specific strategies. Strategies such as donating surplus food and composting food waste received more favorable responses, while portion control measures had mixed feedback. These insights can inform decision-makers and organizations in implementing and prioritizing food waste reduction strategies based on their perceived effectiveness.

Table 4. Challenges and barriers to food waste reduction in restaurants

Challenges and Barriers	HI	MI	LI	NI	N	Mean	SD
Lack of staff awareness and commitment	72	38	11	26	4	1.99	1.16
Inadequate tools for tracking food waste	28	27	71	25	0	2.62	0.97
Limited storage and handling capacity	11	36	94	10	0	2.68	0.71
Resistance to portion control by customers	17	47	35	46	6	2.81	1.04

HI - High Impact, MI - Moderate Impact, LI - Low Impact, NI - No Impact

The data from Table 4 outlines the challenges and barriers encountered in the quest to reduce food waste within restaurant establishments. These challenges are categorized into four impact levels: High Impact (HI), Moderate Impact (MI), Low Impact (LI), and No Impact (NI). Notably, inadequate tools for tracking food waste emerge as a highly impactful barrier, with a mean score of 2.62, indicating its substantial hindrance to food waste reduction efforts (Figure 3).

Figure 3. Challenges and barriers to food waste reduction in restaurants

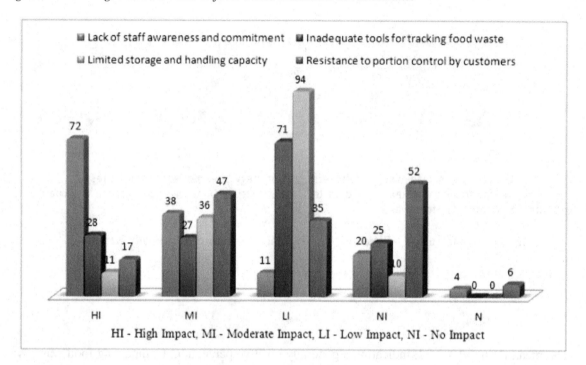

Limited storage and handling capacity also pose a significant challenge, rated as high-impact with a mean score of 2.68. Resistance from customers to portion control is another noteworthy concern, with a high impact rating (mean score of 2.81) and moderate variability in perception among respondents. While the lack of staff awareness and commitment is rated moderately impactful (mean score of 1.99), it still warrants attention. These insights can guide tailored strategies to address these barriers and enhance food waste reduction initiatives in restaurant settings.

5. SUGGESTIONS

In light of the diverse demographics among restaurant stakeholders, it is prudent to adopt a segmented strategy for the implementation of food waste reduction efforts. Tailoring strategies to different segments allows for a more personalized and effective approach. By recognizing that different groups, including customers, restaurant owners, managers, chefs, and staff, may have unique perspectives and needs, restaurants can design strategies that resonate with each segment.

A key priority in food waste reduction should be to focus on specific stages of the food preparation and consumption process where waste is most prevalent. The research identifies that preparation errors, spoilage, and plate waste are the major contributors to food waste in restaurants. Therefore, it is advisable for restaurants to prioritize and concentrate their efforts on these critical stages. This can involve enhancing training programs for kitchen staff to minimize errors, implementing more effective inventory management practices to reduce spoilage, and making menu adjustments to prevent over-preparation.

Additionally, it is evident from the research that certain food waste reduction strategies, such as composting and surplus food donation, are well-received and effective. Restaurants should consider emphasizing and strengthening these successful strategies, allocating resources and efforts to further enhance their impact. Expanding the utilization of these strategies can significantly contribute to waste reduction.

Furthermore, one of the key findings of the research underscores the crucial role of staff awareness and commitment in food waste reduction. To address this, restaurants should invest in ongoing training programs and awareness campaigns. Ensuring that all staff members have a deep understanding of the importance of waste reduction and actively participate in related initiatives is essential for the success of any food waste reduction program. A segmented approach to food waste reduction, with a focus on specific waste-contributing stages, an emphasis on effective strategies, and a commitment to raising staff awareness, is integral to creating a more sustainable and responsible food management system within the restaurant industry.

The comprehensive study conducted on food waste reduction strategies within the context of Dindigul restaurants has yielded invaluable insights into a critical and prevalent issue. This research sheds light on the multifaceted challenges associated with food waste, the distribution of waste within the restaurant setting, and the perceived effectiveness of various strategies. The significance of these findings cannot be overstated, as they have far-reaching implications for the restaurant industry's sustainability and the responsible management of resources.

6. CONCLUSION

Food waste is an issue of paramount concern within the restaurant industry. The analysis reveals that specific stages and categories of food production and consumption significantly contribute to the generation of waste. This knowledge is indispensable for decision-makers in the restaurant sector, as it enables them to pinpoint areas where interventions and strategies are most needed.

One of the most noteworthy takeaways from this research is the recognition of the importance of tailored strategies. The demographic diversity among restaurant stakeholders highlights the need for customized approaches to food waste reduction. Different segments of stakeholders, including customers, restaurant owners, managers, chefs, and staff, may possess distinct perspectives and needs. By developing strategies that cater to the specific characteristics and expectations of these segments, restaurants can enhance the effectiveness of their waste reduction initiatives.

The research also underscores the critical importance of focused waste reduction efforts. It identifies that preparation errors, spoilage, and plate waste are the primary culprits behind food waste in restaurants. As a result, it is imperative for restaurants to concentrate their efforts on these specific stages. Implementing enhanced training programs for kitchen staff to minimize errors, adopting more efficient inventory management practices to reduce spoilage, and making menu adjustments to prevent over-preparation are strategic steps that can significantly contribute to waste reduction.

Moreover, the study highlights the favorable perception of certain food waste reduction strategies, such as composting and surplus food donation. These strategies have proven to be well-received by stakeholders, which suggests that they should be emphasized and expanded. By allocating resources and efforts to strengthen these successful approaches, restaurants can enhance their waste reduction impact and contribute to sustainability goals.

In addressing food waste reduction, it is vital to confront and overcome various challenges. The research findings reveal hurdles related to staff awareness and commitment, inadequate tools for tracking food waste, limited storage capacity, and resistance to portion control. These challenges should not be overlooked but viewed as opportunities for intervention and improvement. Restaurants and decision-makers can use these insights to develop strategies and initiatives that effectively address these challenges.

In conclusion, the findings of this study serve as a valuable guide for restaurants and decision-makers in their pursuit of effective food waste reduction strategies. By understanding the challenges, the distribution of waste, and the effectiveness of various approaches, the restaurant industry can take significant steps toward sustainability and responsible resource management. These findings contribute to broader sustainability efforts within the food supply chain and align with the global imperative to reduce food waste and its associated environmental and economic impacts.

REFERENCES

Alayli, S. (2023). Unravelling the Drivers of Online Purchasing Intention: The E-Commerce Scenario in Lebanon. *F MDB Transactions on Sustainable Social Sciences Letters, 1*(1), 56–67.

Anand, P. P., Kanike, U. K., Paramasivan, P., Rajest, S. S., Regin, R., & Priscila, S. S. (2023). Embracing Industry 5.0: Pioneering Next-Generation Technology for a Flourishing Human Experience and Societal Advancement. *FMDB Transactions on Sustainable Social Sciences Letters, 1*(1), 43–55.

Atasever, M. (2023). Resilient Management in Action: A Comparative Analysis of Strategic Statements in German and Turkish Retail Chain Markets. *FMDB Transactions on Sustainable Management Letters, 1*(2), 66–81.

Betz, A., Buchli, J., Göbel, C., & Müller, C. (2015). Food waste in the Swiss food service industry-Magnitude and potential for reduction. *Waste Management (New York, N.Y.), 35*, 218–226. doi:10.1016/j.wasman.2014.09.015 PMID:25305683

Bhanushali, M. M., Narang, P., Sabarirajan, A., & Turai, A. K., S. K., & U, K. S. (2022). Human Resource Management based Economic analysis using Data Mining. In *Proceedings of the 2022 3rd International Conference on Intelligent Engineering and Management (ICIEM)* (pp. 872-876). 10.1109/ICIEM54221.2022.9853202

Buzby, J. C., Wells, H. F., & Hyman, J. (2014). *The estimated amount, value and calories of postharvest food losses at the retail and consumer levels in the United States.* Economic Information Bulletin Number 121. Economic Research Service/USDA.

Dou, Z., Ferguson, J. D., Galligan, D. T., Kelly, A. M., Finn, S. M., & Gie-gengack, R. (2016). Assessing U.S. food wastage and opportunities for reduction. *Global Food Security, 8*, 19–26. doi:10.1016/j.gfs.2016.02.001

Eriksson, M., Osowski, C. P., Malefors, C., Björkman, J., & Eriksson, E. (2017). Quantification of food waste in public catering services—A case study from a Swedish municipality. *Waste Management (New York, N.Y.)*, *61*, 415–422. doi:10.1016/j.wasman.2017.01.035 PMID:28161338

Gustavsson, J., Cederberg, C., Sonesson, U., van Otterdijk, R., & Meybeck, A. (2011). *Global Food Losses and Food Waste: Extent, Causes and Prevention*. FAO.

Hari Krishna, S., Madala, R., Ramya, P., Sabarirajan, A., Dobhal, D., & Sapate, S. (2023). Ethically Governed Artificial Intelligence Based Innovative Business Research in Finance and Marketing System. In *Proceedings of the 2023 Eighth International Conference on Science Technology Engineering and Mathematics (ICONSTEM)* (pp. 1-7). 10.1109/ICONSTEM56934.2023.10142352

Koivupuro, H.-K., Hartikainen, H., Silvennoinen, K., Katajajuuri, J.-M., Heikintalo, N., Reinikainen, A., & Jalkanen, L. (2012). Influence of socio-demographical, behavioral, and attitudinal factors on the amount of avoidable food waste generated in Finnish households. *International Journal of Consumer Studies*, *36*(2), 183–194. doi:10.1111/j.1470-6431.2011.01080.x

Kuragayala, P. S. (2023). A Systematic Review on Workforce Development in Healthcare Sector: Implications in the Post-COVID Scenario. *FMDB Transactions on Sustainable Technoprise Letters*, *1*(1), 36–46.

María, J. J. L., Polo, O. C. C., & Elhadary, T. (2023). An Analysis of the Morality and Social Responsibility of Non-Profit Organizations. *FMDB Transactions on Sustainable Technoprise Letters*, *1*(1), 28–35.

Mourad, M. (2016). Recycling, recovering, and preventing "food waste": Competing solutions for food systems sustainability in the United States and France. *Journal of Cleaner Production*, *126*, 461–477. doi:10.1016/j.jclepro.2016.03.084

Ocoró, M. P., Polo, O. C. C., & Khandare, S. (2023). Importance of Business Financial Risk Analysis in SMEs According to COVID-19. *FMDB Transactions on Sustainable Management Letters*, *1*(1), 12–21.

Ostergren, K. A., Gustavsson, J., Hansen, O.-J., Møller, H., Anderson, G., Bellettato, C., Gaiani, S., & ... . (2014). *FUSIONS Definitional Framework for Food Waste*. EU FUSIONS.

Pandit, P. (2023). On the Context of the Principle of Beneficence: The Problem of Over Demandingness within Utilitarian Theory. *FMDB Transactions on Sustainable Social Sciences Letters*, *1*(1), 26–42.

Principato, L., Di Leo, A., Mattia, G., & Pratesi, C. A. (2021). The next step in sustainable dining: The restaurant food waste map for the management of food waste. *Ital. J. Mark.*, *2021*(3), 189–207. doi:10.100743039-021-00032-x

Principato, L., Mattia, G., Di Leo, A., & Pratesi, C. A. (2021). The household wasteful behavior framework: A systematic review of consumer food waste. *Industrial Marketing Management*, *93*, 641–649. doi:10.1016/j.indmarman.2020.07.010

Priscila, S. S., Rajest, S. S., Tadiboina, S. N., Regin, R., & András, S. (2023). Analysis of Machine Learning and Deep Learning Methods for Superstore Sales Prediction. *FMDB Transactions on Sustainable Computer Letters*, *1*(1), 1–11.

Ramesh Kumar, V., Selvaraj, M., Venkateswaran, P. S., Sabarirajan, A., & Shatila, K., & Varsha Agarwal. (2022). The impact of training and development programs on employees' performance: The case of Lebanese SMEs. *International Journal of Intellectual Property Management, 12*(3).

Ramos, J. I., Lacerona, R., & Nunag, J. M. (2023). A Study on Operational Excellence, Work Environment Factors and the Impact to Employee Performance. *FMDB Transactions on Sustainable Social Sciences Letters, 1*(1), 12–25.

ReFed. (2018). *Restaurant Food Waste Action Guide*. Rethink Food Waste.

Sabti, Y. M., Alqatrani, R. I. N., Zaid, M. I., Taengkliang, B., & Kareem, J. M. (2023). Impact of Business Environment on the Performance of Employees in the Public-Listed Companies. *FMDB Transactions on Sustainable Management Letters, 1*(2), 56–65.

Said, F. B., & Tripathi, S. (2023). Epistemology of Digital Journalism Shift in South Global Nations: A Bibliometric Analysis. *FMDB Transactions on Sustainable Technoprise Letters, 1*(1), 47–60.

Saxena, D., Khandare, S., & Chaudhary, S. (2023). An Overview of ChatGPT: Impact on Academic Learning. *FMDB Transactions on Sustainable Techno Learning, 1*(1), 11–20.

Schanes, K., Dobernig, K., & Gözet, B. (2018). Food waste matters-A systematic review of household food waste practices and their policy implications. *Journal of Cleaner Production, 182*, 978–991. doi:10.1016/j.jclepro.2018.02.030

Srinivas, K., Velmurugan, P. R., & Andiyappillai, N. (2023). Digital Human Resources and Management Support Improve Human Resources Effectiveness. *FMDB Transactions on Sustainable Management Letters, 1*(1), 32–45.

Tambaip, B., Hadi, A. F. F., & Tjilen, A. P. (2023). Optimizing Public Service Performance: Unleashing the Potential of Compassion as an Indicator of Public Service Motivation. *FMDB Transactions on Sustainable Management Letters, 1*(2), 46–55.

Tripathi, S., & Al-Shahri, M. (2023). Problems and Prospects on the Evolution of Advertising and Public Relations Industries in Oman. *FMDB Transactions on Sustainable Management Letters, 1*(1), 1–11.

Vandermeersch, T., Alvarenga, R. A. F., Ragaert, P., & Dewulf, J. (2014). Environmental sustainability assessment of food waste valorization options. *Resources, Conservation and Recycling, 87*, 57–64. doi:10.1016/j.resconrec.2014.03.008

Vashishtha, E., & Dhawan, G. (2023). Comparison of Baldrige Criteria of Strategy Planning and Harrison Text. *FMDB Transactions on Sustainable Management Letters, 1*(1), 22–31.

Vashishtha, E., & Kapoor, H. (2023). Implementation of Blockchain Technology Across International Healthcare Markets. *FMDB Transactions on Sustainable Technoprise Letters, 1*(1), 1–12.

Venkateswaran, P. S., Sabarirajan, A., Arun, B., Muthupandian, T., & Manimaran, D. S. (2018). Technology Acceptance Model for Making Decision to Purchase Automobile in Coimbatore District. *International Journal of Mechanical Engineering and Technology, 9*(11), 1608–1613.

Venkateswaran, P. S., Sabarirajan, A., Rajest, S. S., & Regin, R. (2019). The theory of the Postmodernism in consumerism, mass culture and globalization. *Journal of Research on the Lepidoptera*, *50*(4), 97–113. doi:10.36872/LEPI/V50I4/201075

Venkateswaran, P. S., Singh, S., Paramasivan, P., Rajest, S. S., Lourens, M. E., & Regin, R. (2023). A Study on The Influence of Quality of Service on Customer Satisfaction Towards Hotel Industry. *FMDB Transactions on Sustainable Social Sciences Letters*, *1*(1), 1–11.

Venkateswaran, P. S., & Viktor, P. (2023). A Study on Brand Equity of Fast-Moving Consumer Goods with Reference to Madurai, Tamil Nadu. *FMDB Transactions on Sustainable Technoprise Letters*, *1*(1), 13–27.

Chapter 3
The Role of Artificial Intelligence (AI) in Enhancing Marketing and Customer Loyalty

P.S. Venkateswaran

iD https://orcid.org/0000-0001-8958-103X

PSNA College of Engineering and Technology, India

M. Lishmah Dominic

PSNA College of Engineering and Technology, India

Shashank Agarwal

iD https://orcid.org/0009-0003-7679-6690

CVS Health, USA

Himani Oberai

GLA University, India

Ila Anand

Christ University

S. Suman Rajest

iD https://orcid.org/0000-0001-8315-3747

Dhaanish Ahmed College of Engineering, India

ABSTRACT

This research aims to investigate how artificial intelligence (AI) can be used to improve marketing and brand loyalty. Artificial intelligence (AI) is one of the most revolutionary technologies because it allows computers to independently execute mental skills often reserved for humans, such as problem solving and reasoning. In order to make judgments (like which marketing actions to take) and reason (about those decisions) in real time, machines represent, learn, store, and refine their knowledge progressively based on past experiences and existing information (e.g., predicting customer satisfaction). AI, with its ability to analyze vast datasets, predict customer behaviors, and deliver personalized experiences, is reshaping the way companies approach and enhance their customer loyalty strategies. This exploration delves into the multifaceted role of AI in revolutionizing the realm of customer loyalty, shedding light on its applications, benefits, and the transformative potential it brings to the forefront of modern marketing.

DOI: 10.4018/979-8-3693-0049-7.ch003

1. INTRODUCTION

In today's rapidly evolving business landscape, cultivating customer loyalty has become an indispensable goal for organizations seeking sustained success (Abu-Rumman, 2021). Customer loyalty not only drives repeat business but also transforms satisfied customers into brand advocates, amplifying a company's reach and influence (Abu-Rumman and Qawasmeh, 2021). To navigate this competitive terrain and effectively nurture brand loyalty, businesses are turning to a potent ally: Artificial Intelligence (AI). AI is not just a buzzword; it's a powerful tool that has fundamentally altered the marketing paradigm, enabling organizations to harness the potential of data-driven insights, automation, personalization, and predictive analytics like never before (Al Shraah et al., 2022).

This explores the pivotal role that AI plays in modern marketing, providing a comprehensive overview of its applications, implications, and the profound impact it has on how businesses interact with customers, make decisions, and stay competitive in a digitally-driven world (Al Shraah et al., 2013).

The last few decades have witnessed a seismic shift in the way businesses operate and market their products and services (Alayli, 2023). The rise of the internet, social media, and digital technologies has not only ushered in an era of unprecedented connectivity but has also inundated consumers with an overwhelming amount of information and choices (Anand et al., 2023). Traditional marketing strategies have struggled to keep pace with the demands of this digital age, where attention spans are shorter and competition is fiercer than ever (Arslan et al., 2021).

In this new landscape, data emerged as the currency of the digital realm, with companies accumulating vast repositories of information on consumer behavior, preferences, and interactions (Atasever, 2023). However, the sheer volume and complexity of this data presented a challenge: how to turn it into actionable insights that could inform marketing strategies and drive business growth? The answer came in the form of AI (Rad et al., 2019).

Artificial Intelligence, in the context of marketing, refers to the application of advanced algorithms and machine learning techniques to analyze, interpret, and leverage data for marketing purposes. AI has the capacity to process and make sense of enormous datasets, providing marketers with valuable insights that were previously unattainable through manual analysis (Tambaip et al., 2023).

2. REVIEW OF LITERATURE

It's no secret that artificial intelligence (AI) has the potential to upend many industries, including marketing (Andrianto et al., 2019). To keep up with customers' ever-shifting wants and demands in today's competitive market, businesses are increasingly turning to artificial intelligence (AI) to create and distribute innovative new offerings (Hossain et al., 2021). Bringing AI to marketing gives companies a chance to boost client loyalty, individualise their offerings, and expand their operations (Wang et al., 2021). The focus of this study is on the potential benefits that can be reaped when fresh services are combined with artificial intelligence in the field of marketing (Kim et al., 2018).

The SOR model has been refined by academics to fit their specific research settings (Kim et al., 2020). Hossain et al. (2021) assumed that consumers' trust, commitment, and CRM performance would be influenced by their interactions, hence they used this model. Since consumer trust is so crucial to the success of the sharing economy, we develop this model further by making it the stimulus (Paudel et al., 2022). Customers have the ability to give and receive feedback (Pandit, 2023). The organism is founded on the judgments and opinions of consumers and reflects the mechanisms at work between an initial stimulus and the consumer's ultimate response (Islam and Rahman, 2017; Venkateswaran, 2015).

According to academic research, trust between strangers is the primary difficulty in the sharing economy (e.g., home sharing, automobile sharing). The sharing economy's transaction model necessitates dealing with strangers, which carries the risk of property loss, bodily harm, and even death (Demeter et al., 2021). The sharing economy is characterised by regulatory uncertainty (Ranchordás, 2014). Sharing one's house with another person involves a two-tiered system of trust (Hawlitschek et al., 2016).

There has been a lot of interest in recent years in how to use AI in marketing (Huang and Rust, 2018). The revolutionary potential of machine learning, NLP, and predictive analytics to transform marketing and propel corporate success is undeniable (Ramos et al., 2023).

Machine learning algorithms can sift through mountains of client data including clickstreams, cart contents, and demographics to produce highly specific recommendations, articles, and ads (Roberts et al., 2021).

Marketers now have access to cutting-edge resources for acquiring and analysing client data thanks to advancements in AI. Organizations can gain a broad understanding of customers' ideas, preferences, and attitudes with the use of sentiment analysis, social media monitoring, and customer sentiment prediction models (Khaled Lafi Al-Naif and Ata E. M. Al Shraah, 2018).

3. MARKETING STRATEGIES USING AI

3.1 Marketing Strategies Using AI

Sentiment analysis, in its essence, is the process of using natural language processing (NLP), machine learning, and computational linguistics to determine the emotional tone, attitude, or sentiment expressed within text, speech, or multimedia content (Balas-Timar & Lile, 2015). By analyzing the words, phrases, and context used in written or spoken communication, sentiment analysis algorithms aim to categorize content as positive, negative, or neutral and sometimes even delve into more nuanced emotions like joy, anger, or sadness (Roman et al., 2020).

The significance of sentiment analysis transcends industries and applications, making it a critical tool in the modern age for several reasons:

In the realm of business, understanding customer sentiment is vital. Sentiment analysis allows companies to gather insights from customer feedback, reviews, and social media mentions to improve products, services, and customer satisfaction (Said & Tripathi, 2023). Businesses can monitor their online reputation by analyzing sentiments expressed in social media conversations, news articles, and blog posts. This enables proactive management of brand perception and crisis response (Ogunmola et al., 2021).

Sentiment analysis provides a deep understanding of market trends, consumer preferences, and competitor performance. Companies can adapt their strategies based on these insights (Rad et al., 2022). Political Analysis: In politics, sentiment analysis can gauge public opinion, track political discourse, and measure voter sentiment. It's a valuable tool for political campaigns, pollsters, and policymakers (Rad & Rad, 2021).

Sentiment analysis is integrated into customer support systems and chatbots to detect and address customer frustration or dissatisfaction in real time, leading to improved service. By analyzing customer sentiment, businesses can identify areas for product improvement and innovation, helping them stay competitive in the market (Figure 1).

Figure 1. Sentiment analysis of the customers
Source: Sentiment Analysis (2022)

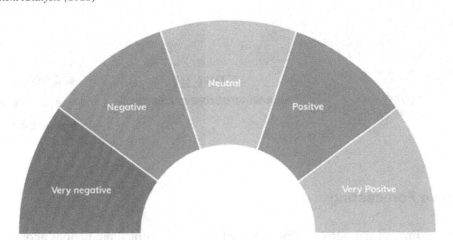

In healthcare, sentiment analysis is used to detect emotional distress or changes in patient sentiment in medical records or social media posts, aiding in early intervention and mental health support (Rad & Balas, 2020). Content creators and marketers use sentiment analysis to understand what content resonates with their audience, helping them tailor their messaging and campaigns for maximum impact (Rad et al., 2020). Sentiment analysis can be applied to financial markets to gauge investor sentiment and predict market trends (Figure 2) (Rad et al., 2022).

3.2 Coaching: At Scale

Coaching, a practice traditionally associated with one-on-one interactions and personalized guidance, is undergoing a remarkable transformation in the digital age. With the advent of Artificial Intelligence (AI) and advancements in machine learning, coaching is now poised to be delivered at scale, reaching individuals and teams with unprecedented efficiency and effectiveness. This paradigm shift brings forth a novel approach known as "Coaching—at Scale AI," revolutionizing the way individuals receive coaching, whether in the realms of personal development, professional growth, or education.

Coaching, in its traditional form, has long been recognized as a powerful method for personal and professional development (Sabti et al., 2023). Typically, it involves one-on-one sessions between a coach and a coachee, where the coach provides guidance, support, and feedback to help the individual achieve specific goals, overcome challenges, or enhance their skills. However, the reach and accessibility of traditional coaching methods have been limited by factors such as time, cost, and geographical constraints. This limitation has spurred the development of innovative approaches that leverage technology and AI to deliver coaching experiences at scale (Sharma et al., 2021a).

Figure 2. Sentiment analysis of the hotel customer
Source: Ashfaque (2023)

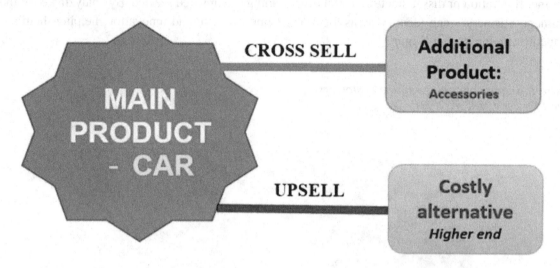

3.3 Predictive Forecasting

Predictive forecasting is a data-driven approach used to make informed predictions about future events or trends based on historical data and statistical models (Sharma et al., 2021b). It is a valuable tool for businesses, organizations, and researchers seeking to anticipate future outcomes, allocate resources efficiently, and make proactive decisions (Sharma et al., 2021c). Predictive forecasting involves several key components and methodologies (Figure 3):

Figure 3. Predictive forecasting in various domains

- Sales and Demand Forecasting: Businesses use predictive forecasting to anticipate future sales and demand for products or services, helping with inventory management and supply chain optimization.
- Financial Forecasting: Financial institutions employ predictive models to forecast stock prices, credit risk, and economic trends (Venkateswaran et al., 2023).
- Weather Forecasting: Meteorologists use advanced models to predict weather conditions, enabling timely warnings and preparedness for extreme events (Venkateswaran & Viktor, 2023).

- Energy Consumption Prediction: Utilities and energy companies use predictive forecasting to optimize energy production and distribution, reducing costs and environmental impact.
- Healthcare: Predictive models can forecast disease outbreaks, patient admissions, and healthcare resource utilization (Sharma et al., 2021d).
- Customer Churn Prediction: Businesses aim to retain customers by predicting which customers are likely to churn (leave), allowing for targeted retention efforts.
- Marketing and Personalization: Predictive analytics helps tailor marketing campaigns and recommend products to individual customers based on their preferences and behavior.
- Quality Control: Manufacturers use predictive models to identify defects in products and improve quality control processes.

4. CUSTOMER LOYALTY

Customer loyalty and Artificial Intelligence (AI) are intricately linked in today's business landscape. AI is playing a significant role in helping businesses foster and enhance customer loyalty through a range of applications and strategies. Here's how AI is influencing customer loyalty:

1. Personalized Customer Experiences:

AI-powered algorithms analyze customer data to create highly personalized experiences. By understanding individual preferences, purchase history, and behavior, AI helps businesses tailor product recommendations, marketing messages, and communication channels to resonate with each customer. Personalization fosters a deeper emotional connection, increasing loyalty.

2. Loyalty Programs Optimization:

AI helps optimize loyalty programs by analyzing member data and behavior. It can identify which rewards and incentives resonate most with customers and recommend program improvements for better engagement and retention.

3. Customer Segmentation and Targeting:

AI categorizes customers into segments based on various attributes. This enables businesses to tailor marketing strategies to different customer groups, delivering more relevant content and offers that encourage loyalty.

4. 24/7 Availability and Responsiveness:

AI-powered solutions enable businesses to be available to customers around the clock. Whether through chatbots, automated email responses, or AI-driven call centers, this accessibility and responsiveness contribute to better customer satisfaction and loyalty.

5. Product Recommendations:

AI algorithms analyze purchase history and user behavior to provide personalized product recommendations. This not only enhances the shopping experience but also drives additional sales and reinforces loyalty.

6. Customer Journey Mapping:

AI can map out customer journeys, identifying pain points and opportunities for improvement. By enhancing the overall customer experience, businesses can increase loyalty.

7. Continuous Improvement:

AI fosters a culture of continuous improvement. By providing data-backed insights and feedback loops, businesses can make iterative changes, refine strategies, and adapt to evolving customer needs, ultimately strengthening brand loyalty over time.

4.1 Business Intelligence Helps to Understand Customer Loyalty Behavior in the Following Ways

*   BI tools analyze customer data, including purchase history, behavior, and feedback, to identify patterns and trends related to loyalty.
*   BI can segment customers based on their loyalty behavior, allowing businesses to tailor strategies to different customer groups.
*   BI can use predictive models to forecast future customer behavior, including the likelihood of churn or the potential for increased loyalty.
*   BI tools can create visualizations, such as loyalty dashboards, that make it easier for decision-makers to interpret loyalty metrics and trends.

Customers show loyalty towards their preferred brands through various factors:

Quality and Consistency

Indian consumers tend to be loyal to FMCG brands known for the quality and consistency of their products. High-quality offerings build trust and credibility for a brand. Customers tend to trust brands that consistently deliver quality. Quality can lead to customer loyalty. Customers who have positive experiences with high-quality products are more likely to become repeat buyers and brand advocates.

Quality can be measured through various metrics and indicators, such as defect rates, customer complaints, product reviews and ratings, and adherence to industry standards and benchmarks. Businesses often engage in quality improvement processes to identify and rectify defects, inefficiencies, or areas where improvements can be made. Techniques like Six Sigma and Total Quality Management (TQM) are used for this purpose.

Quality assurance practices are implemented to ensure that products or services consistently meet predetermined quality standards. This may involve rigorous testing, quality control processes, and regular audits.

Consistency is essential for building trust and maintaining customer loyalty. Customers rely on a consistent experience when interacting with a brand. Inconsistencies in quality or performance can lead to dissatisfaction and erode trust. Customers may switch to competitors if they perceive inconsistency.

Consistency can be measured by tracking variations in product or service quality over time, monitoring adherence to established standards, and assessing customer feedback for fluctuations in experiences. Businesses implement various practices and processes to ensure consistency, including standard operating procedures (SOPs), employee training, quality control checks, and monitoring systems.

Pricing and Value: Brands that offer value for money and competitive pricing often enjoy loyalty among Indian customers.

Trust and Reputation: Established FMCG brands with a strong reputation for reliability and trustworthiness tend to have loyal customer bases.

Brand Familiarity: Indian consumers often stick to brands they are familiar with, especially in categories like personal care and food products.

4.2 Measuring Customer Loyalty Using BI

- Tracking customer purchase history

BI tools can track customer purchase history to identify loyal customers who consistently buy from a particular brand. One of the key functionalities of BI tools is their ability to meticulously track and analyze customer purchase history.

Customer purchase history tracking is a fundamental feature of BI tools that empower businesses to understand their customers on a deeper level. These tools collect and organize data on past purchases, including product preferences, purchase frequency, and transaction amounts. By doing so, they enable businesses to identify trends and patterns, such as seasonal buying habits or the popularity of specific products (Venkateswaran, 2023).

This historical data serves as the foundation for creating targeted marketing campaigns and personalized recommendations. For instance, if a customer frequently buys gardening supplies in the spring, a BI tool can automatically send them tailored promotions as the season approaches. This not only enhances the customer experience but also boosts sales and customer loyalty.

Moreover, BI tools allow for real-time monitoring of purchase history, enabling businesses to respond swiftly to changing consumer behaviors and market dynamics. With access to up-to-date insights, companies can make informed decisions about inventory management, pricing strategies, and product development.

4.2 Feedback From Surveys and Reviews

Leveraging feedback from surveys and reviews is a critical component of any successful business strategy. These insights provide valuable information about customer satisfaction, product performance, and areas for improvement, ultimately shaping the company's direction and enhancing customer experiences.

Surveys serve as structured mechanisms for collecting feedback. They allow businesses to pose specific questions to customers, gauging their opinions on various aspects of products or services. Surveys can be distributed through email, on websites, or within apps, providing multiple touchpoints for gathering input. Analyzing survey responses helps companies identify trends and pain points, leading to informed decision-making and strategic adjustments.

Reviews, on the other hand, offer a more organic and unfiltered perspective from customers. They are typically found on platforms like Yelp, Amazon, or social media. Companies can gain valuable insights from both positive and negative reviews, understanding what customers appreciate and where they face challenges. Engaging with reviews through responses demonstrates a commitment to customer satisfaction and can positively impact brand perception.

4.3 Monitoring Sales and Inventory

Monitoring sales and inventory is a fundamental aspect of effective inventory management for businesses of all sizes. This process involves tracking and analyzing sales data in conjunction with inventory levels to optimize operations, ensure customer satisfaction, and enhance profitability.

Sales monitoring entails keeping a close watch on all transactions and understanding how products or services are performing in the market. This includes tracking sales volume, revenue, and other relevant metrics. By doing so, businesses can identify trends, such as which products are selling well and which ones may need marketing or pricing adjustments.

Inventory monitoring involves maintaining accurate records of product quantities, replenishment schedules, and storage conditions. It's essential to strike a balance between having enough stock to meet demand without overstocking, which ties up capital and storage space. Inventory management systems help automate this process, providing real-time data on stock levels, reorder points, and product turnover rates.

By integrating sales and inventory data, businesses can make informed decisions regarding restocking, ordering, and production. This prevents stockouts, minimizes excess inventory costs, and ensures that products are readily available to meet customer demand. Additionally, it enables better cash flow management and reduces the risk of obsolete or perishable goods.

4.4 Cross-Selling and Upselling

Cross-selling and upselling represent two distinct sales strategies utilized by businesses to bolster revenue and enhance the overall customer experience. While both approaches involve suggesting additional products or services to customers, they serve different purposes and are applied in specific contexts (Figure 4).

Cross-selling revolves around recommending products or services that are related or complementary to what a customer is already purchasing. The primary objective here is to increase the total value of the customer's transaction. For instance, in the fast-food industry, cross-selling might involve offering customers the option to include a side dish or a beverage when they order a burger, thereby enhancing the overall meal experience.

Upselling, conversely, centers on encouraging customers to opt for a higher-priced version or to add premium features to the product or service they are considering (Figure 5). The core aim is to maximize the value of the customer's purchase by persuading them to invest more. An illustration of upselling occurs when a car salesperson proposes a vehicle with a higher trim level or additional amenities to a customer interested in a specific car model (Figure 6).

Figure 4. Cross-selling and upselling
Source: Gillen (2021)

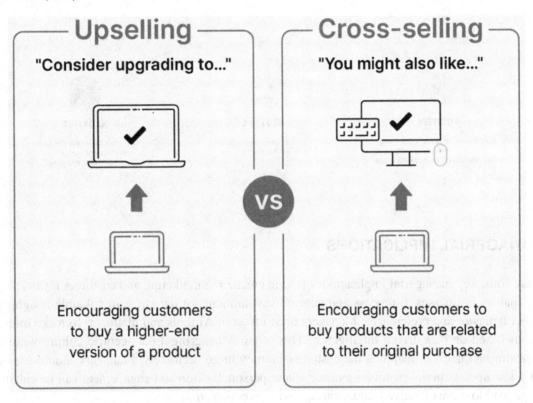

Figure 5. Illustration of upselling
Source: Surbhi (2020)

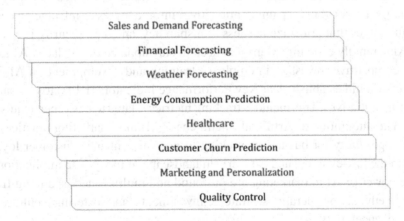

Both cross-selling and upselling are potent sales techniques that, when executed judiciously, can contribute to revenue growth and heightened customer satisfaction. These strategies hinge on a deep understanding of the customer's preferences needs, and effective communication. Successful implementation not only increases sales but also enriches the customer's buying experience by providing relevant choices and improving overall satisfaction.

Figure 6. Cross-selling and upselling

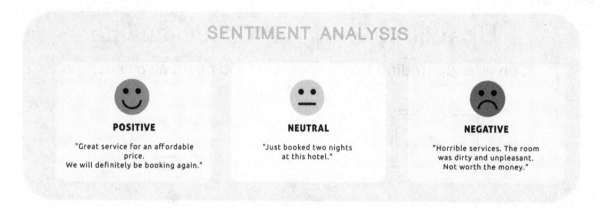

5. MANAGERIAL IMPLICATIONS

Here are some key managerial implications of AI in enhancing marketing and customer loyalty:

AI enables businesses to process and analyze vast amounts of data to gain valuable insights into customer behavior and preferences. Managers must invest in AI tools and platforms to make informed decisions based on data-driven Intelligence. This requires fostering a data-centric culture within the organization. AI helps in mapping the customer journey more accurately. Managers should use AI to identify touchpoints in the customer journey where personalization and engagement can be enhanced. This can lead to more effective lead nurturing and conversion strategies.

Deploying AI-powered chatbots and virtual assistants can improve customer service and engagement. Managers should oversee the integration of chatbots into customer support channels to handle routine inquiries and provide real-time assistance. Managers must be mindful of ethical considerations when using AI in marketing. AI algorithms can unintentionally reinforce biases or infringe on customer privacy. Developing AI guidelines that prioritize fairness, transparency, and data security is crucial.

The field of AI is rapidly evolving. Managers need to stay updated on the latest AI technologies and trends to remain competitive. Investing in employee training and development on AI-related topics is essential. Managers should establish clear Key Performance Indicators (KPIs) to measure the impact of AI-driven marketing initiatives. This includes tracking metrics related to customer acquisition, retention, and overall ROI. The integration of Artificial Intelligence (AI) into marketing practices has ushered in a transformative opportunity for businesses seeking to not only enhance customer loyalty but also to stay competitive in the fast-evolving and data-driven landscape of today. The implications for managers in harnessing the power of AI in marketing are profound and multifaceted, spanning from data-driven decision-making to ethical considerations, strategic investments, and fostering a culture of adaptability in the face of AI advancements.

AI, as a technological marvel, empowers organizations to tap into the full potential of their data. It provides a pathway to data-driven decision-making, which, in turn, can lead to the creation of more effective and personalized marketing campaigns. However, this transformation is not without its complexities, as managers must adopt a strategic approach. They must navigate ethical concerns, invest in the right AI tools and talent, and ensure that AI initiatives align seamlessly with broader business objectives.

6. CONCLUSION

AI-driven automation is another pivotal facet that managers must embrace. It streamlines marketing processes, making them more efficient and cost-effective. Automation tools can handle routine tasks, enabling marketing professionals to focus on strategic thinking and creative endeavors. This not only increases operational efficiency but also contributes to the bottom line. Managers need to recognize the strategic importance of automating routine tasks, freeing up their teams to focus on high-impact activities. Predictive analytics, powered by AI, allows businesses to forecast customer behavior, which is invaluable in marketing. It helps in understanding what customers want when they want it, and how they want it delivered. Managers need to appreciate the potential of predictive analytics in customer segmentation, allowing for the creation of more targeted campaigns that resonate with specific segments.

Beyond the transactional aspect of AI, its role in marketing extends to building lasting customer loyalty. Through AI, businesses can provide valuable, tailored experiences that resonate with individual preferences. These experiences are not just one-time interactions but ongoing relationships that are nurtured and deepened over time. Customer loyalty is a cornerstone of long-term success for any business, and AI is a tool that managers can wield to build and sustain that loyalty. However, the journey into AI in marketing is not a one-time implementation; it's a continuous process. Technology is evolving at a rapid pace, and managers need to remain agile and adaptable. They must be ready to embrace new AI advancements and integrate them into their strategies to stay at the forefront of the industry.

In conclusion, the integration of Artificial Intelligence (AI) into marketing is a transformative endeavor that opens up unprecedented possibilities for businesses. It allows for data-driven decision-making, hyper-personalized experiences at scale, streamlined marketing processes, predictive analytics, and the creation of lasting customer loyalty. Managers play a pivotal role in navigating this AI-driven landscape, from fostering a culture of data and AI literacy to addressing ethical concerns and staying agile in the face of rapid advancements. AI is not just a tool; it is a strategic imperative in the digital age, and managers who embrace it as such will be better positioned to thrive and succeed in the ever-evolving marketing landscape.

REFERENCES

Abu-Rumman, A. (2021). Effective Knowledge Sharing: A Guide to the Key Enablers and Inhibitors. In D. Tessier (Ed.), *Handbook of Research on Organizational Culture Strategies for Effective Knowledge Management and Performance* (pp. 133–156). IGI Global. doi:10.4018/978-1-7998-7422-5.ch008

Abu-Rumman, A., & Qawasmeh, R. (2021). Assessing international students' satisfaction of a Jordanian university using the service quality model. *Journal of Applied Research in Higher Education*. Advance online publication. doi:10.1108/JARHE-05-2021-0166

Al-Naif, K. L., & Al Shraah, A. E. M. (2018). Working capital management and profitability: Evidence from Jordanian mining and extraction industry sector. *IUG Journal of Economics and Business.*, 2(1), 42–60.

Al Shraah, A., Abu-Rumman, A., Alqhaiwi, L. A., & AlSha'ar, H. (2022). The impact of sourcing strategies and logistics capabilities on organizational performance during the COVID-19 pandemic: Evidence from Jordanian pharmaceutical industries. *Uncertain Supply Chain Management*, *10*(3), 1077–1090. doi:10.5267/j.uscm.2022.2.004

Al Shraah, A., Irtaimeh, H. J., & Rumman, M. A. (2013). The Strategic Human Resource Management Practices in Implying Total Quality Management (TQM): An Empirical Study on Jordanian Banking Sector. *International Journal of Management*, *4*(5), 179–190.

Alayli, S. (2023). Unravelling the Drivers of Online Purchasing Intention: The E-Commerce Scenario in Lebanon. *FMDB Transactions on Sustainable Social Sciences Letters*, *1*(1), 56–67.

Anand, P. P., Kanike, U. K., Paramasivan, P., Rajest, S. S., Regin, R., & Priscila, S. S. (2023). Embracing Industry 5.0: Pioneering Next-Generation Technology for a Flourishing Human Experience and Societal Advancement. *FMDB Transactions on Sustainable Social Sciences Letters*, *1*(1), 43–55.

Andrianto, N., Riyanto, D. Y., Riqqoh, A. K., & Fianto, A. Y. A. (2019). A conceptual framework for destination branding in jawa Timur, Indonesia. *Majalah Ekonomi*, *24*(2), 149–157. doi:10.36456/majeko. vol24.no2.a2061

Arslan, F., Singh, B., Sharma, D. K., Regin, R., Steffi, R., & Rajest, S. S. (2021). Optimization technique approach to resolve food sustainability problems. In *2021 International Conference on Computational Intelligence and Knowledge Economy (ICCIKE)*. IEEE. 10.1109/ICCIKE51210.2021.9410735

Ashfaque, Z. (2023). *Sentiment analysis with naive Bayes algorithm*. Retrieved October 25, 2023, from Medium website: https://medium.com/@zubairashfaque/sentiment-analysis-with-naive-bayes-algorithm-a31021764fb4

Atasever, M. (2023). Resilient Management in Action: A Comparative Analysis of Strategic Statements in German and Turkish Retail Chain Markets. *FMDB Transactions on Sustainable Management Letters*, *1*(2), 66–81.

Balas-Timar, D., & Lile, R. (2015). The story of Goldilocks told by organizational psychologists. *Procedia: Social and Behavioral Sciences*, *203*, 239–243. doi:10.1016/j.sbspro.2015.08.288

Demeter, E., Rad, D., & Balas, E. (2021). Schadenfreude and General Anti-Social Behaviours: The Role of Violent Content Preferences and Life Satisfaction. BRAIN. *Broad Research in Artificial Intelligence and Neuroscience*, *12*(2), 98–111. doi:10.18662/brain/12.2/194

Gillen, C. (2021, March 8). *Upselling vs. cross selling: What's the difference?* Retrieved October 25, 2023, from Zapier.com website: https://zapier.com/blog/cross-selling-vs-upselling/

Hawlitschek, F., Teubner, T., & Weinhardt, C. (2016). Trust in the sharing economy. *Die Unternehmung*, *70*(1), 26–44. doi:10.5771/0042-059X-2016-1-26

Hossain, M. S., Rahman, M. F., & Zhou, X. (2021). Impact of customers' interpersonal interactions in social commerce on customer relationship management performance. *Journal of Contemporary Marketing Science*, *4*(1), 161–181. doi:10.1108/JCMARS-12-2020-0050

Huang, M. H., & Rust, R. T. (2018). Artificial intelligence in service. *Journal of Service Research, 21*(2), 155–172. doi:10.1177/1094670517752459

Huurne, M., Ronteltap, A., Corten, R., & Buskens, V. (2017). Antecedents of trust in the sharing economy: A systematic review. *Journal of Consumer Behaviour, 16*(6), 485–498. doi:10.1002/cb.1667

Islam, J., & Rahman, Z. (2017). The impact of online brand community characteristics on customer engagement: An application of Stimulus-Organism-Response paradigm. *Telematics and Informatics, 34*(4), 96–109. doi:10.1016/j.tele.2017.01.004

Kim, K., Kim, J. W., & Lee, H. (2018). Antecedents and consequences of customer loyalty in online shopping: A case of online travel agencies. *Journal of Travel Research, 57*(4), 481–495.

Kim, M. J., Lee, C.-K., & Jung, T. (2020). Exploring consumer behavior in virtual reality tourism using an extended stimulus-organism-response model. *Journal of Travel Research, 59*(1), 69–89. doi:10.1177/0047287518818915

Ogunmola, G. A., Singh, B., Sharma, D. K., Regin, R., Rajest, S. S., & Singh, N. (2021). Involvement of distance measure in assessing and resolving efficiency environmental obstacles. In *2021 International Conference on Computational Intelligence and Knowledge Economy (ICCIKE)*. IEEE. 10.1109/ICCIKE51210.2021.9410765

Pandit, P. (2023). On the Context of the Principle of Beneficence: The Problem of Over Demandingness within Utilitarian Theory. *FMDB Transactions on Sustainable Social Sciences Letters, 1*(1), 26–42.

Paudel, P. K., Bastola, R., Eigenbrode, S. D., Borzée, A., Thapa, S., Rad, D., & Adhikari, S. (2022). Perspectives of scholars on the origin, spread and consequences of COVID-19 are diverse but not polarized. *Humanities & Social Sciences Communications, 9*(1), 1–11. doi:10.105741599-022-01216-2

Rad, D., Balas, E., Ignat, S., Rad, G., & Dixon, D. (2020). A Predictive Model of Youth Bystanders' Helping Attitudes. *Revista romaneasca pentru educatie multidimensionala-Journal for Multidimensional Education, 12*(1Sup2), 136-150.

Rad, D., & Balas, V. E. (2020). A Novel Fuzzy Scoring Approach of Behavioural Interviews in Personnel Selection. BRAIN. *Broad Research in Artificial Intelligence and Neuroscience, 11*(2), 178–188. doi:10.18662/brain/11.2/81

Rad, D., Dughi, T., & Demeter, E. (2019). The Dynamics of the Relationship between Humor and Benevolence as Values. *Revista romaneasca pentru educatie multidimensionala-Journal for Multidimensional Education, 11*(3), 201-212.

Rad, D., Egerau, A., Roman, A., Dughi, T., Balas, E., Maier, R., & Rad, G. (2022). A Preliminary Investigation of the Technology Acceptance Model (TAM) in Early Childhood Education and Care. BRAIN. *Broad Research in Artificial Intelligence and Neuroscience, 13*(1), 518–533. doi:10.18662/brain/13.1/297

Rad, D., & Rad, G. (2021). Going Agile, a Post-Pandemic Universal Work Paradigm-A Theoretical Narrative Review. *Postmodern Openings, 12*(4), 337–388. doi:10.18662/po/12.4/380

Rad, D., Rad, G., Maier, R., Demeter, E., Dicu, A., Popa, M., & Mărineanu, V. D. (2022). A Fuzzy logic modelling approach on psychological data. *Journal of Intelligent & Fuzzy Systems*, (Preprint), 1-11.

Räisänen, J., Ojala, A., & Tuovinen, T. (2021). Building trust in the sharing economy: Current approaches and future considerations. *Journal of Cleaner Production*, *279*(123724), 123724. doi:10.1016/j.jclepro.2020.123724

Ramos, J. I., Lacerona, R., & Nunag, J. M. (2023). A Study on Operational Excellence, Work Environment Factors and the Impact to Employee Performance. *FMDB Transactions on Sustainable Social Sciences Letters*, *1*(1), 12–25.

Ranchordas, S. (2014). *Does sharing mean caring? Regulating innovation in the sharing economy*. Retrieved from https://papers.ssrn.com/abstract=2492798

Roberts, M. L., Nguyen, L. D. B., Tra, M. C., & Nguyen, L. H. (2021). Artificial intelligence in personalized marketing: A systematic literature review. *International Journal of Electronic Commerce*, *25*(3), 327–364. doi:10.1080/10864415.2021.1914232

Roman, A., Rad, D., Egerau, A., Dixon, D., Dughi, T., Kelemen, G., & Rad, G. (2020). Physical Self-Schema Acceptance and Perceived Severity of Online Aggressiveness in Cyberbullying Incidents. *Journal of Interdisciplinary Studies in Education*, *9*(1), 100–116. doi:10.32674/jise.v9i1.1961

Sabti, Y. M., Alqatrani, R. I. N., Zaid, M. I., Taengkliang, B., & Kareem, J. M. (2023). Impact of Business Environment on the Performance of Employees in the Public-Listed Companies. *FMDB Transactions on Sustainable Management Letters*, *1*(2), 56–65.

Said, F. B., & Tripathi, S. (2023). Epistemology of Digital Journalism Shift in South Global Nations: A Bibliometric Analysis. *FMDB Transactions on Sustainable Technoprise Letters*, *1*(1), 47–60.

Sentiment analysis. (2022). Retrieved October 25, 2023, from Thematic website: https://getthematic.com/sentiment-analysis/

Sharma, D. K., Jalil, N. A., Regin, R., Rajest, S. S., Tummala, R. K., & Thangadurai. (2021a). Predicting network congestion with machine learning. In *2021 2nd International Conference on Smart Electronics and Communication (ICOSEC)*. IEEE.

Sharma, D. K., Singh, B., Raja, M., Regin, R., & Rajest, S. S. (2021b). An Efficient Python Approach for Simulation of Poisson Distribution. In *2021 7th International Conference on Advanced Computing and Communication Systems (ICACCS)*. IEEE.

Sharma, D. K., Singh, B., Regin, R., Steffi, R., & Chakravarthi, M. K. (2021c). Efficient Classification for Neural Machines Interpretations based on Mathematical models. In *2021 7th International Conference on Advanced Computing and Communication Systems (ICACCS)*. IEEE.

Sharma, K., Singh, B., Herman, E., Regine, R., Rajest, S. S., & Mishra, V. P. (2021d). Maximum information measure policies in reinforcement learning with deep energy-based model. In *2021 International Conference on Computational Intelligence and Knowledge Economy (ICCIKE)*. IEEE. 10.1109/ICCIKE51210.2021.9410756

Surbhi, S. (2020, February 3). *Difference between upselling and cross-selling*. Retrieved October 25, 2023, from Key Differences website: https://keydifferences.com/difference-between-upselling-and-cross-selling.html

Tambaip, B., Hadi, A. F. F., & Tjilen, A. P. (2023). Optimizing Public Service Performance: Unleashing the Potential of Compassion as an Indicator of Public Service Motivation. *FMDB Transactions on Sustainable Management Letters*, *1*(2), 46–55.

Venkateswaran, P. S. (2015). influence of information systems in Engineering Institutions at Madurai District. *International Journal of Applied Engineering Research: IJAER*, *9*, 10513–10528.

Venkateswaran, P. S. (2023). *Industry 5 - Challenges and Opportunities for business and industries*. Academic Press.

Venkateswaran, P. S., Singh, S., Paramasivan, P., Rajest, S. S., Lourens, M. E., & Regin, R. (2023). A Study on The Influence of Quality of Service on Customer Satisfaction Towards Hotel Industry. *FMDB Transactions on Sustainable Social Sciences Letters*, *1*(1), 1–11.

Venkateswaran, P. S., & Viktor, P. (2023). A Study on Brand Equity of Fast-Moving Consumer Goods with Reference to Madurai, Tamil Nadu. *FMDB Transactions on Sustainable Technoprise Letters*, *1*(1), 13–27.

Wang, C., Wang, Y., Wang, J., Xiao, J., & Liu, J. (2021). Factors influencing consumers' purchase decision-making in O2O business model: Evidence from consumers' overall evaluation. *Journal of Retailing and Consumer Services*, *61*(102565). doi:10.1016/j.jretconser.2021.102565

Chapter 4
Advancing and Methodizing Artificial Intelligence (AI) and Socially Responsible Efforts in Real Estate Marketing

Thangaraja Arumugam
ⓘD https://orcid.org/0000-0001-5496-7258
Vellore Institute of Technology, Chennai, India

R. Arun
ⓘD https://orcid.org/0000-0002-5252-1030
St. Joseph's College of Engineering, India

R. Anitha
Dr. S.N.S. Rajalakshmi College of Arts and Science, India

P. L. Swerna
Apollo Arts and Science College, India

R. Aruna
Vellore Institute of Technology, Chennai, India

Vimala Kadiresan
HELP University, Malaysia

ABSTRACT

The revolutionary effects of artificial intelligence (AI) and socially responsible marketing on the real estate market are examined in this chapter. Real estate is being redefined by changing consumer values as well as increased social and environmental consciousness. A flexible tool like artificial intelligence (AI) encourages innovation by providing data-driven insights, individualized marketing, and operational efficiencies. The concept simultaneously connects real estate transactions with significant societal and environmental contributions. The investigation starts with the key cause selection process, in which real estate professionals make choices that go beyond transactions and resonate as statements of intent with customers and communities. Forging relationships beyond typical buyer-seller interactions, creating emotionally compelling narratives becomes essential. AI boosts customer experiences, improves relationships, and synchronizes them with client values.

DOI: 10.4018/979-8-3693-0049-7.ch004

1. INTRODUCTION

The real estate sector, historically bound by physical assets and location-centric transactions, is undergoing a profound transformation at the intersection of artificial intelligence (AI) and socially responsible marketing (Jacobides et al., 2021). This shift is redefining the essence of real estate in the modern era and altering the dynamics of property transactions. Factors like square footage, price tags, and amenities, which once solely determined real estate purchases, are no longer the exclusive influencers (Rabby & Chimhundu, 2022). Today's real estate buyers represent a new generation characterized by evolving cultural values and a heightened sense of social and environmental responsibility. They seek more than just a place to reside or invest; they aspire to find homes that embody their values, contribute to positive change, and connect them to a greater purpose. The Models of artificial intelligence (AI) have been effectively applied in a variety of industries and marketplaces. The real estate market, however, often takes longer than usual to adjust to these changes.

This chapter delves into the dynamic fusion of AI and Socially responsible marketing within the real estate sector, a digital strategy poised to revolutionize the industry (Bondi et al., 2021). It explores how the combination of AI-driven marketing strategies and socially responsible marketing can not only enhance marketing efforts but also pave the way for a more meaningful and socially responsible real estate market. To produce individualized suggestions for prospective buyers or tenants, machine learning algorithms may analyse enormous volumes of data, comprising realty listings, sales history, information about demographics, and consumer preferences. These tools save people time and effort by assisting them in finding homes that match their unique needs and preferences. The digital age, marked by rapid technological advancements, has made this transformation possible. AI serves as a linchpin, providing real estate professionals with data-driven insights that inform personalized marketing strategies and streamline operational processes (Mora-Esperanza, 2004). It transcends its traditional role as a mere tool and becomes a catalyst for innovation, fundamentally reshaping how real estate professionals connect with clients and promote properties.

Concurrently, Socially responsible marketing emerges as a significant influencer, shaping the narrative of the real estate industry (Ferrell & Hochstein, 2021). CRM goes beyond conventional business objectives, urging businesses to align their operations with social or environmental goals. It fosters partnerships between companies, their clientele, and causes that share similar values. In the real estate sector, CRM serves as the bridge connecting real estate transactions with outcomes that carry significant social and environmental impacts (Bhatti et al., 2023). These platforms enable real estate professionals to engage with their communities, driving positive change and fostering stronger bonds with clients.

This chapter provides a comprehensive guide for industry professionals looking to navigate this new digital era, explaining the intricacies of integrating AI and Socially responsible marketing into real estate (Umbrello & Van de Poel, 2021). It commences with the critical step of cause selection, moves on to the art of crafting compelling narratives, explores the power of personalized marketing, delves into innovations such as virtual property tours and energy efficiency, and discusses the role of chatbots and virtual assistants in enhancing customer engagement. Additionally, it emphasizes the importance of data security, ethical AI practices, and the necessity for continuous evaluation and adaptation in this dynamic landscape (Galan-Ladero & Galera-Casquet, 2019).

In essence, this path represents the transformative potential of artificial intelligence and socially responsible marketing in the real estate industry (Pagourtzi et al., 2007). It calls upon real estate professionals, pioneers, and visionaries to embrace a future where property transactions transcend mere buying and selling, contributing to a positive impact on society and the environment. Real estate is now embracing AI and Socially responsible marketing as a digital strategy that encourages us to envision a world where each property deal represents a significant step towards a better, more compassionate future.

The real estate sector sits at the meeting point of conventional methods and the digital revolution. Real estate professionals are at a crucial crossroads where innovation, ethics, and social responsibility collide as consumer expectations and technology change. This chapter launches a thorough investigation of how Socially responsible marketing and artificial intelligence (AI) are combining to change the real estate industry. It explores the variety of ways that AI can be used to streamline processes, improve customer experiences, and align businesses with social and environmental causes that are important to their stakeholders.

The combination of artificial intelligence (AI) with Socially responsible marketing has become a dynamic strategy in an interconnected world, particularly in the real estate industry. This chapter explains how AI helps to effectively identify and promote these causes and how it plays a crucial role in bridging real estate enterprises' selected social or environmental issues. An essential component of this bridge, AI-driven analytics gives real estate companies the resources they need to identify issues that naturally match their values and appeal to their stakeholders, strengthening the sincerity of their commitment.

1.1. Artificial Intelligence (AI) in Real Estate

The real estate sector is going through a tremendous transition thanks to artificial intelligence (AI), which has historically been characterised by drawn-out and frequently complicated processes. An in-depth analysis of AI's substantial effects on the real estate sector is provided in this chapter, along with an examination of the wide range of applications it may be used for, including customer engagement and data analytics.

Leveraging AI for Data Analytics: In a time of a surplus of data, AI-driven analytics solutions enable real estate professionals to glean valuable insights from big datasets. AI improves the accuracy and speed of decision-making across a range of areas, from market trends to property values. The use of predictive modelling for property valuation: By taking into account a variety of factors and forecasting market trends, AI-driven algorithms are revolutionizing the field of property valuation. This fosters honest pricing practices and is advantageous to both buyers and sellers. Modern technologies are constantly evolving and starting to have a big impact in several different fields. The main concept is to engage with an entirely novel virtual environment while hiding the real reality. Here, we will give a quick history of each of these augmented reality technologies' development as well as an explanation of the necessary atmosphere for its creation. According to market research on AI in the real estate sector, firms can automate repetitive processes like property inspections as well as showings, which helps agents and clients save time and money. AI can assist real estate agents in making better judgments by analyzing massive amounts of data and providing market insights and forecasts on house prices, rentals, and other market trends.

The capacity of artificial intelligence in real estate to offer individualized and customized services to clients, like specialized property referrals and augmented reality tours based on their personal tastes and search history, is another advantage. The industry is now able to swiftly and precisely analyze large amounts of data and utilize that analysis to make more informed choices thanks to developments in machine learning and artificial intelligence algorithms.

Enhancing Customer Engagement through AI: AI-powered chatbots, virtual tours, and personalized recommendations are changing how clients interact with real estate listings, increasing customer engagement. The chapter examines how AI improves customer experiences by making them more interesting and educational. Streamlining Real Estate Operations: AI improves efficiency and lowers costs for real estate companies by automating repetitive operations in property management and managing property portfolios. This section explains how AI streamlines business processes for real estate firms and property owners.

The real estate sector is being profoundly changed by AI. It has become a priceless tool for real estate professionals thanks to its capacity for processing data, providing individualized experiences, and streamlining processes. The industry's efficiency, client involvement, and ethical practices will be further improved as AI technology develops, ensuring that real estate remains at the forefront of technological innovation.

1.2. Socially Responsible Marketing in Real Estate

A growing trend in the real estate sector is Socially responsible marketing, a partnership between a company and a social or environmental concern. This chapter examines the development of Socially responsible marketing, its fundamentals and relevance to the real estate industry, and how it has evolved into a crucial tactic for companies looking to not only improve their brand image but also have a significant social influence. The need to control and minimize potential environmental risks, the drive to lessen environmental consequences through evolving laws, and potential legal action are some of the elements that have helped SR problems move up the agenda of the property investment sector. Real estate businesses are one of the primary sources of social wealth; their economic benefits limit the degree of national welfare, but their competitiveness affects the overall level of national economic development. However, the accelerated growth of businesses has also resulted in a considerable economic and social environment conflict. Additionally, SR has implemented several programs and policies in response to growing public concern about social and environmental issues as well as the potential of the built environment to improve environmental quality.

The Evolution of CSR: From a corporate buzzword to a crucial component of a company's identity, corporate social responsibility (CSR) has undergone significant development. We explore the historical development of CSR in real estate and how it fits with the moral requirements of the sector.

Principles of Socially Responsible Marketing: Making donations to organizations is just one aspect of Socially responsible marketing; creating real connections with stakeholders and having a significant influence are equally important. When a business functions as a component of society, it must consider not only its own profits but also profits that are related to them, such as the realization of profits for clients, investors, and other parties, as well as the realization of a sustainable environment for all. A company's competitiveness is not solely based on cost and benefit; it can also be determined by the creativeness and value of the company, so taking on certain social obligations is not entirely an investment cost from the standpoint of the company itself. It has an effect, which is seen in the social responsibilities the corporation has taken on. The fundamental ideas that guide effective, Socially responsible marketing efforts are laid forth in this section.

The Significance in Real Estate: Real estate is uniquely positioned to have a substantial impact on society, which is why it is important. Real estate can support issues that matter to its stakeholders, whether they are community development initiatives, green building initiatives, or affordable housing activities.

In the real estate sector, socially responsible marketing has evolved from its altruistic roots to become a strategic requirement. Real estate companies may develop a strong brand identity, connect with their clients' beliefs, and make a significant contribution to societal change by partnering with causes that matter. Socially responsible marketing is more than simply a marketing tactic; it's a sign of a company's dedication to changing the world for the better.

1.3. AI Meets Socially Responsible Marketing

The chapter explores how AI can serve as a bridge between real estate businesses and their chosen social or environmental causes. It examines the role of AI in identifying and supporting these causes effectively. AI-driven analytics can help real estate companies pinpoint causes that align with their values and the interests of their stakeholders. This section explains how AI enhances cause selection. Effective cause-related marketing requires data-driven decisions. AI enables businesses to measure the impact of their Socially responsible initiatives, providing valuable insights into what works and what doesn't.

2. LITERATURE REVIEW

2.1. Real Estate in a Shift

Modern technologies are widely applied in both smart cities and the real estate sector. Intelligence has frequently been measured against technological standards (Allameh et al., 2011). Real estate is evolving and moving beyond simply valuing features like property size and price. Modern elements that go beyond conventional metrics are now having an impact on property sales as priorities in the real estate market shift (Rabby & Chimhundu, 2022). According to Thangaraja (2014), boosting consumer acceptability of IoT in real estate requires an understanding of cultural components, matching IoT solutions to these codes, and adapting approaches to shifting cultural norms. The ability to incorporate cutting-edge, disruptive technology is one of the key attributes of a "smart city" on a global scale (Gabyrs, 2014). Smart cities use a range of electronic data and cutting-edge sensors to efficiently manage their resources and assets (Cocchia, 2014). While technologies evolve and become more complicated, a city or piece of real estate is truly defined as "smart" by its capacity to incorporate new technologies as well as its tendency for innovation and openness (Parouits et al., 2014). Real estate can modify online resources to better suit the preferences of Generation Z in property research and transactions by looking at how these individuals' personality traits relate to their use of digital libraries (Thangaraja, 2022). Therefore, it is necessary to set evaluation standards for smart real estate (SRE) in order to facilitate more intelligent management and achieve the goal of the smart city. Social Network Analysis can be utilized in the real estate industry to support customized strategies for different segments and assure flexibility to match altering consumer behavior by gathering and analyzing information on customer channel preferences and their changes (Thangaraja et al., 2020).

2.2. AI in Real Estate

Ferrell et al., 2021 provide valuable insights to help firms successfully navigate and compete in the modern market. It provides helpful suggestions for thriving in today's corporate environment through effective marketing strategies. (Bondi et al., 2021) asserts that AI for social good should involve the affected communities, use the "capabilities approach" framework to assess welfare, involve community members as collaborators, and provide leading questions to respect each community's unique conception of social good. Studies define and employ structural equation modeling to examine the relationships between involvement in the real estate market, cultural traits (culture code), and the moderating role of mindfulness in decision-making processes (Thangaraja et al., 2019). (Rossini, 2000) explores the challenges of applying AI and expert systems to the real estate industry while underlining the unrealized potential of these technologies. It highlights the value of system design above relying just on cutting-edge approaches by utilizing a valuation system as a potent tool for education and training. (Viriato, 2019) focuses on how AI is revolutionizing the real estate market, especially in the prop-tech sector, and how it can transform decision-making and operations through a number of applications. It draws attention to the industry's drive toward technology adoption and the significant impacts of AI and ML. As firms hurried to adopt remote work due to the COVID-19 pandemic, cybersecurity worries increased, underscoring the urgent need for strong cybersecurity measures in this new digital landscape (Thangaraja, 2022). The author investigates how AI may enhance real estate market analysis and assessment using a three-stage methodology that uses index data to measure accuracy (Kabaivanov, 2021). The significance of government-led digitization initiatives in enhancing regulatory control in financial markets, reducing fraud, and enhancing tax collection effectiveness in order to highlight the significance of government-led digitization initiatives in enhancing regulatory control in financial markets, reducing fraud, and enhancing tax collection effectiveness (Stang, 2023), focuses on the post-2008 regulatory-driven demand for accurate real estate assessments and the role of AI and machine learning in automating and enhancing the valuation process. Tackles important knowledge gaps for appraisers and industry practitioners.

Real estate and the effects of AI, IoT, Big Data, DOI, and Blockchain, with a suggestion for an automated and integrated Real Estate Data Marketplace. It concentrates on data validation, Blockchain security, and AI analytics to ethically alter the sector, similar to tech giants like Google and Amazon (Treleaven et al., 2021). Appraisal of real estate utilizing Artificial Intelligence (AI) systems, particularly Artificial Neural Networks (ANN) and Expert Systems (ES), and case studies contrasting their prognostication ability with Multiple Regression Analysis (MRA). Additionally, it explores how hybrid technology might enhance the efficiency and precision of real estate evaluation processes (Taffee, 2006). Logistic regression can be used to predict the online purchasing preferences of rural consumers, providing useful data for marketing strategy customization (Thangaraja et al., 2020). Machine learning and artificial intelligence have the ability to radically transform the real estate sector by identifying these technologies, assessing current implementations, and predicting future disruptive implications (Conway, 2018).

Users' locations are examined in smart cities utilizing call detail records and mobility data. It uses machine learning, including a hybrid technique, to estimate real estate values and discover appreciable relationships between pricing and movement trends (Pinter, 2020). Using artificial intelligence techniques, namely the genetic algorithm model, improves the accuracy of real estate auction price projections, especially when geographic segmentation based on auction appraisal values is taken into account (Kang et al., 2020). When anticipating increased commercial possibilities, Real Estate Investment Trusts (REITs) strategically emphasize corporate social responsibility (CSR) (Chiang et al., 2019). CSR initiatives improve financial performance in real estate firms, even when excessive sustainability reporting erodes the link. Investors are drawn to initiatives that will boost future value, especially those that promote resource efficiency and environmental protection and handle causality using two-stage least squares regression (Kerscher, 2015).

The increasing use of CSR by European real estate companies, especially those that are publicly traded, suggests that investors value these efforts (Hiep et al., 2011). One should set clear investing objectives and processes, refrain from making emotional decisions, and continually review and change a real estate portfolio to maximize financial benefits and legacy-building potential (Ngoc, 2023). Tan, 2023 looks at how ethical marketing approaches have altered in the blockchain-based sharing economy. He emphasizes the need to consider all stakeholders and calls for more research to understand variations across different blockchain ecosystems. Consumers prefer longer Socially responsible Marketing initiatives, with shorter ones potentially causing discontent, according to (Chéron et al. 2012), who underline the role of campaign time in customer perception. The concept explores the potential synergies between urban development and urban greening in promoting biodiversity, but it also sheds light on challenges and legal impediments to nature-inclusive urban development (NIUD) (Mattijssen et al., 2023). Programmatic advertising is essential for real estate digital promotion in order to increase engagement and maximum return on investment in a competitive business (Thangaraja & Kiran, 2020).

2.3. Cause-Related Marketing and AI in Combination With Real Estate

There are rumors that the real estate sector is swiftly shifting from its traditional emphasis on physical assets and location-bound transactions to one that prioritizes Socially responsible marketing and artificial intelligence (AI). Growing industry adoption of socially responsible business practices is indicated by the optimization of property-related processes by AI and the incorporation of social or environmental considerations into marketing strategies by real estate enterprises using CRM (Jacobides et al., 2021). Enterprises in emerging nations must compete with international companies in their home markets to secure long-term economic success (Hiep et al., 2021). Additionally, these businesses must prioritize sustainability and social responsibility in all aspects of their operations. Gender influences customer perceptions, CRM goodwill, and product views, whereas gift amount influences non-profit benefits and CRM goodwill, with gender serving as a partial moderator (Moosmayer, 2010). CRM activities benefit customer responses to corporate CRM by fostering empathy and moral affiliation, which in turn improves consumer perceptions of CRM businesses and purchase intentions for CRM product claims (Thangaraja, 2020) & (Yang, 2018). Effective marketing and trust-building are crucial in the real estate sector, with an emphasis on factors like customer engagement and property features. Trust must be upheld in order for commercial relationships to be successful, and top-notch properties must be provided.

3. DISCUSSION AND FINDING

Throughout our exploration of the integration of AI and Socially responsible marketing in real estate—a digital approach—we've uncovered a transformative synergy that has the potential to reshape not just the real estate sector but also its role in fostering a more responsible, compassionate, and sustainable world. Our investigation commenced with the critical step of selecting a relevant cause (Varadarajan & Menon, 1988), a decision that embodies the essence of every effective Socially responsible marketing endeavor. Real estate professionals, as influential figures and community builders, found themselves at pivotal decision-making junctures. These decisions evolved into statements of intent, transcending mere real estate transactions and becoming focal points for ideals and aspirations that resonate with both clients and communities.

This foundational decision gave birth to the narrative—an impactful story that forged connections between brands and their chosen causes. Through storytelling, emotional bonds were cultivated, extending beyond traditional buyer-seller relationships. It breathed new life into Socially responsible marketing, infusing it with authenticity, emotion, and significance. In the digital age, AI has emerged as a powerful ally, optimizing marketing endeavors and enhancing customer experiences. AI became the enabler of tailored solutions, where each client interaction reflected their unique goals and values. Real estate professionals adeptly navigated the digital landscape, providing immersive experiences and sustainable solutions through AI-driven personalization, virtual property tours, and smart home integration.

AI-powered virtual assistants and chatbots continued the journey by offering round-the-clock customer support, going beyond mere query responses to deeply engage users. These digital companions assumed roles as storytellers, educators, and sources of information, strengthening the connections between businesses and their audiences (Husted & Whitehouse Jr, 2002). Donation matching programs elevated the journey's significance, amplifying contributions to chosen causes and engaging customers in the noble pursuit of social and environmental responsibility.

However, in this digital terrain, the pillars of data security and ethics remained unwavering. Real estate professionals uphold their clients' trust by adhering to stringent data privacy regulations and ethical AI practices (Seagraves, 2023). They navigated the complexities of data with integrity, ensuring that every interaction, recommendation, and contribution was underpinned by transparency and accountability. The journey culminated in a continuous cycle of measurement and adaptation. AI-powered analytics provided guidance, illuminating the path in a dynamic landscape. By evaluating the impact of their initiatives and refining their strategies, real estate professionals ensured that their contributions to society and the environment remained meaningful and relevant.

4. CONCLUSION

As we conclude this chapter, we extend an invitation to real estate professionals, innovators, and dreamers to embrace the era of integration of AI and Socially responsible marketing in real estate—a digital approach that encourages us to envision a world where every property transaction is a step toward a brighter, more compassionate future. In this future, real estate transcends its conventional boundaries, evolving into a force for positive change rather than just a business. It's a future where values and technology coexist with profit and purpose, where real estate becomes a beacon of hope in a changing world. We welcome you to the dawn of a new era in real estate, where impact and innovation walk hand in hand, shaping a world where every property transaction truly matters.

In conclusion, the integration of AI with cause-related marketing in real estate is a strategic imperative. AI serves as a bridge between technological capabilities and social responsibility, allowing companies to authentically connect with their audience and contribute to meaningful causes. It empowers real estate businesses to identify, support, and measure the impact of causes that align with their values and resonate with their stakeholders, ultimately shaping a future where each transaction is not just a business deal but also a step toward a better world.

REFERENCES

Allameh, E., Jozam, M. H., de Vries, B., Timmermans, H. J., & Beetz, J. (2011). Smart Home as a Smart Real Estate: a state of the art review. *18th International Conference of European Real Estate Society, Eindhoven, The Netherlands. ERES 2011.*

Anuradha, T. A., Jan, N. A., & Subramani, A. K. (2019). Social Media Addiction, Culture Code and Mediation Effect of Mindfulness: A Structural Equation Modelling Access. *International Journal of Recent Technology and Engineering, 8*, 1097–1102.

Arumugam, T., Jayakrishnan, B., Ranganathan, M., Kadiresan, V., & Mathai, R. (2020, October). A Social Network Analysis on Understanding Pattern of Shoppers' OmniChannel Adoption and Clustering Based on Channel Switching and Preference Attributes. *International Conference on Business Management, Innovation & Sustainability (ICBMIS).* 10.2139srn.3713754

Bhatti, H. Y., Galan-Ladero, M. M., & Galera-Casquet, C. (2023). Socially responsible marketing: A systematic review of the literature. *International Review on Public and Nonprofit Marketing, 20*(1), 25–64. doi:10.100712208-021-00326-y

Bondi, E., Xu, L., Acosta-Navas, D., & Killian, J. A. (2021, July). Envisioning communities: A participatory approach towards AI for social good. In *Proceedings of the 2021 AAAI/ACM Conference on AI, Ethics, and Society* (pp. 425-436). 10.1145/3461702.3462612

Cajias, M., & Bienert, S. (2011). Does sustainability pay off for European listed real estate companies? The dynamics between risk and provision of responsible information. *Journal of Sustainable Real Estate, 3*(1), 211–231. doi:10.1080/10835547.2011.12091823

Chéron, E., Kohlbacher, F., & Kusuma, K. (2012). The effects of brand-cause fit and campaign duration on consumer perception of Socially responsible marketing in Japan. *Journal of Consumer Marketing, 29*(5), 357–368. doi:10.1108/07363761211247479

Chiang, K. C., Wachtel, G. J., & Zhou, X. (2019). Corporate social responsibility and growth opportunity: The case of real estate investment trusts. *Journal of Business Ethics, 155*(2), 463–478. doi:10.100710551-017-3535-1

Cocchia, A. (2014). Smart and digital city: A systematic literature review. *Smart city: How to create public and economic value with high technology in urban space*, 13-43.

Conway, J. J. E. (2018). *Artificial intelligence and machine learning: current applications in real estate.* Academic Press.

El-Manaseer, S. A., Al-Kayid, J. H., Al Khawatreh, A. M., & Shamim, M. (2023). The Impact of Digital Transformation on Combating Tax Evasion (Electronic Billing System as a Model). In *Artificial Intelligence (AI) and Finance* (pp. 679–690). Springer Nature Switzerland. doi:10.1007/978-3-031-39158-3_63

Ferrell, O. C., Hartline, M., & Hochstein, B. W. (2021). *Marketing strategy.* Cengage Learning.

Gabrys, J. (2014). *Programming environments: environmentality and citizen sensing in the smart city.* . doi:10.1068/d16812

Galan-Ladero, M. M., & Galera-Casquet, C. (2019). Corporate Social Responsibility and Digital Tools: The Socially responsible Marketing Case. In Handbook of research on entrepreneurship and marketing for global reach in the digital economy (pp. 1-16). IGI Global.

Hameed, S. S., Madhavan, S., & Arumugam, T. (2020). Is consumer behaviour varying towards low and high involvement products even sports celebrity endorsed. *International Journal of Scientific and Technology Research, 9*(3), 4848–4852.

Hiep, P. M., Tien, N. H., Dana, L. P., Kuc, B. R., Van Tien, N., & Ha, V. X. (2021). Enhancing social responsibility and sustainability in real estate industry. *Turkish Journal of Computer and Mathematics Education, 12*(14), 4999–5013.

Husted, S. W., & Whitehouse, F. R. Jr. (2002). Socially responsible marketing via the world wide web: A relationship marketing strategy. *Journal of Nonprofit & Public Sector Marketing, 10*(1), 3–22. doi:10.1300/J054v10n01_02

Jacobides, M. G., Brusoni, S., & Candelon, F. (2021). The evolutionary dynamics of the artificial intelligence ecosystem. *Strategy Science, 6*(4), 412–435. doi:10.1287tsc.2021.0148

Kabaivanov, S., & Markovska, V. (2021, March). Artificial intelligence in real estate market analysis. In AIP Conference Proceedings (Vol. 2333, No. 1). AIP Publishing. doi:10.1063/5.0041806

Kang, J., Lee, H. J., Jeong, S. H., Lee, H. S., & Oh, K. J. (2020). Developing a forecasting model for real estate auction prices using artificial intelligence. *Sustainability (Basel), 12*(7), 2899. doi:10.3390u12072899

Kerscher, A. (2015). *Corporate social responsibility and the market valuation of listed real estate investment companies* (Vol. 79). Universitätsbibliothek Regensburg.

Kiran, K. U., & Arumugam, T. (2020, December). Role of programmatic advertising on effective digital promotion strategy: A conceptual framework. *Journal of Physics: Conference Series, 1716*(1), 012032. doi:10.1088/1742-6596/1716/1/012032

Mattijssen, T. J., Dijkshoorn-Dekker, M. W., Kortstee, H. J., Polman, N. B., & Snep, R. (2023). Nature-inclusive urban development: Lessons learned in three real estate projects in Dutch cities. *International Journal of Urban Sustainable Development, 15*(1), 152–171. doi:10.1080/19463138.2023.2216654

Moosmayer, D. C., & Fuljahn, A. (2010). Consumer perceptions of cause related marketing campaigns. *Journal of Consumer Marketing, 27*(6), 543–549. doi:10.1108/07363761011078280

Mora-Esperanza, J. G. (2004). Artificial intelligence applied to real estate valuation: An example for the appraisal of Madrid. *Catastro, 1*, 255–265.

Ngoc, N. M. (2023). The relevance of factors affecting real estate investment decisions for post pandemic time. *International Journal of Business and Globalisation.*

Pagourtzi, E., Metaxiotis, K., Nikolopoulos, K., Giannelos, K., & Assimakopoulos, V. (2007). Real estate valuation with artificial intelligence approaches. *International Journal of Intelligent Systems Technologies and Applications, 2*(1), 50–57. doi:10.1504/IJISTA.2007.011573

Paroutis, S., Bennett, M., & Heracleous, L. (2014). A strategic view on smart city technology: The case of IBM Smarter Cities during a recession. *Technological Forecasting and Social Change, 89*, 262–272. doi:10.1016/j.techfore.2013.08.041

Pinter, G., Mosavi, A., & Felde, I. (2020). Artificial intelligence for modeling real estate price using call detail records and hybrid machine learning approach. *Entropy (Basel, Switzerland), 22*(12), 1421. doi:10.3390/e22121421 PMID:33339406

Rabby, F., Chimhundu, R., & Hassan, R. (2022). Digital Transformation in Real Estate Marketing: A Review. *Big Data: A Road Map for Successful Digital Marketing, 39*.

Rossini, P. (2000, January). Using expert systems and artificial intelligence for real estate forecasting. In *Sixth Annual Pacific-Rim Real Estate Society Conference, Sydney, Australia* (pp. 24-27). Academic Press.

Sanjeev, M. A., Khademizadeh, S., Arumugam, T., & Tripathi, D. K. (2022). Generation Z and intention to use the digital library: Does personality matter? *The Electronic Library, 40*(1/2), 18–37. doi:10.1108/EL-04-2021-0082

Sanyal, S., Kalimuthu, M., Arumugam, T., Aruna, R., Balaji, J., Savarimuthu, A., & Patil, S. (2023). Internet of Things and Its Relevance to Digital Marketing. In *Opportunities and Challenges of Industrial IoT in 5G and 6G Networks* (pp. 138–154). IGI Global. doi:10.4018/978-1-7998-9266-3.ch007

Seagraves, P. (2023). Real Estate Insights: Is the AI revolution a real estate boon or bane? *Journal of Property Investment & Finance*. Advance online publication. doi:10.1108/JPIF-05-2023-0045

Stang, M. (2023). *Real Estate Valuation in the Age of Artificial Intelligence–Modern Machine Learning Algorithms and their Application in Property Appraisal* (Doctoral dissertation).

Sugirtha, C. M. R., Hameed, S. S., & Arumugam, T. (2020). The impact of organizational identification and employee engagement on intellectual capital assets: An empirical study. *Test Eng. Manag, 83*, 6277–6285.

Taffese, W. Z. (2006). *A survey on application of artificial intelligence in real estate industry*. In 3rd International conference on artificial intelligence in engineering and technology, Kota Kinabalu, Malaysia.

Thangam, D., Arumugam, T., Velusamy, K., Subramanian, M., Ganesan, S. K., & Suryakumar, M. (2022). COVID-19 Pandemic and Its Brunt on Digital Transformation and Cybersecurity. In Cybersecurity Crisis Management and Lessons Learned From the COVID-19 Pandemic (pp. 15-42). IGI Global.

Thangaraja, A. (n.d.). *The role of culture code in acceptance of internet of things (IoT) among FMCG consumers: A positivist approach*. Academic Press.

Treleaven, P., Barnett, J., Knight, A., & Serrano, W. (2021). Real estate data marketplace. *AI and Ethics, 1*(4), 445–462. doi:10.100743681-021-00053-4

Umbrello, S., & Van de Poel, I. (2021). Mapping value sensitive design onto AI for social good principles. *AI and Ethics, 1*(3), 283–296. doi:10.100743681-021-00038-3 PMID:34790942

Varadarajan, P. R., & Menon, A. (1988). Socially responsible marketing: A coalignment of marketing strategy and corporate philanthropy. *Journal of Marketing, 52*(3), 58–74. doi:10.1177/002224298805200306

Viriato, J. C. (2019). AI and machine learning in real estate investment. *Journal of Portfolio Management*, *45*(7), 43–54. doi:10.3905/jpm.2019.45.7.043

Yang, H. T., & Yen, G. F. (2018). Consumer responses to corporate Socially responsible marketing: A serial multiple mediator model of self-construal, empathy and moral identity. *European Journal of Marketing*, *52*(9/10), 2105–2127. doi:10.1108/EJM-07-2017-0468

Chapter 5
Unlocking the Power of Artificial Intelligence and Machine Learning in Transforming Marketing as We Know It

Thangaraja Arumugam
 https://orcid.org/0000-0001-5496-7258
Vellore Institute of Technology, Chennai, India

R. Arun
 https://orcid.org/0000-0002-5252-1030
St. Joseph's College of Engineering, India

Sundarapandiyan Natarajan
 https://orcid.org/0000-0002-1303-2947
Adithya Institute of Technology, India

Kiran Kumar Thoti
 https://orcid.org/0000-0002-6678-9425
Universiti Malaysia Kelanta, Malaysia

P. Shanthi
 https://orcid.org/0000-0002-9998-5940
SRM Institute of Science and Technology, India

Uday Kiran Kommuri
Vellore Institute of Technology, Chennai, India

ABSTRACT

Technological changes have helped the methodology of execution where we can examine the sector in addition to the manner enterprise is carried out. Productive development has facilitated correct manufacturing in large volumes. The advanced technology, together with information in analytics, smart devices, computerization, and artificial intelligence (AI), is converting the system of society and persons to interact on a basic level. The evolution and development of artificial intelligence (AI) have transformed the effectiveness of commercial enterprises globally. However, business adoption of AI-based total packages by businesses remains constrained because of a lack of know-how approximately the generation. The technology can assist the organisation in understanding the clients and permit it to target the customers better and personalize advertising and marketing movements and messages. Advertising takes the benefit of facts to big data: consumer needs research, marketplace analyses, client insights, and competition intelligence.

DOI: 10.4018/979-8-3693-0049-7.ch005

1. INTRODUCTION

The introduction of Artificial intelligence technologies has given a better rate of return on investment (ROI) for selling organization campaigns by exploiting ML, huge information problem-solving methods, and different processes towards realizing the insight interested in anticipation of the target market. The manufacturers produce additional convincing in client touch points. The fascinating online promotion provides consumer sustenance; AI makes additional customized consumer interaction, eliminating abundant speculation (Vesanen, 2007). AI is currently employed by online sellers to automate the process that was solely performed by employees; content-oriented creation, in addition to net style, is entirely beneath the extent of AI in marketing (Kiran & Arumugam, 2020). Artificial Intelligence and mechanization have entirely remodeled varied commerce aspects in promoting (Vesanen & Raulas, 2006). The commencing plan to implementation, the footprint of AI is all over in spite of the complexity and challenges related to being hooked into technology. Another viewpoint on AI holds that it constitutes predictive technology built on ML that is used to generate judgments, forecasts, and recommendations for real-world or hypothetical situations. However, ML-based AI has several drawbacks, such as the tendency to forecast the future based on historical data by identifying patterns (Adams, 2017).

For marketing and in the main online selling in the present day, the AI platform has proved to be an effective system in every business. AI platform has bridged the breach by linking information systematically in addition to tactical implementation. Modern marketers can make sure AI is a trade benefit in shaping the market scale. As Suggested by Mage Plaza, Artificial intelligence can, across the market touch point, be employed in machine learning, customer information, and different machine ideas to forecast individual activity and also in decision-making systems. The advancement in technology will control large amounts of information (Adomavicius & Tuzhilin, 2005).

Through information on the market in an exceedingly much-simplified form, marketers will additionally break it all the way down to produce tailor-made content for his or her audience. Through Artificial Intelligence, businesses can develop better promoting analytical methods in focusing on correct prospective consumers. This will allow online sellers to feed clients with accurate information on the acceptable means at the simplest time to market (Arthanari & Jambulingam, 2020). Marketers are able to instantly examine enormous quantities of marketing data from various platforms, including websites, social media, and emails. Additionally, their ability to comprehend client demands and expectations more rapidly enables them to increase campaign success and generate a return on investment (also known as ROI). As a result, marketers can focus their energy and time on tasks that are equally important or more critical. Another justification for AI's inclusion in marketing plans is the fact that, in recent decades, it has become vital for companies to understand and recognize customers' standards and preferences for both goods and services.

Artificial intelligence companies embrace installations, integrating, in addition to maintenance and backing accomplishments. The phase proposed is expanding in a major charge within the Automation markets above the predicted stage. Artificial intelligence platform consists of chipsets that are similar to Graphic Process systems, Computerised Process systems, Application-specific incorporated Circuits and Field-Programmable gate array systems. Presently, the Artificial Intelligence platform market is dominated by Graphic Process systems and Computerised Process systems for the reason that their elevated computing capability is essential for the Artificial intelligence framework (Lotz et al., 2010).

Customer journey is becoming increasingly complex. At the same time, marketing is gaining momentum at the management table, with highly record technology budgets expected to exceed those of

CIOs this year. To eliminate this further complexity and increase accountability, improvements in data analysis have more stakeholders who think that marketing can report more freely about the changing world in which they operate. Although the customer journey grows complex, the processes used to connect and analyze marketing data are changing. Big budgets and high-quality customers mean a lot of advertising technology and tools within the marketing stacks. This means that there are a variety of data sources in many integration formats - today, next month, and the foreseeable future. Data and analytics are the backbone, and marketers must look to new technological advances to make these processes as liquid and scary as possible (Amnesty International, 2018).

Artificial intelligence platform has the capability to progress data in a way that is like the human thinking process in learning, making decisions, and solving problems. Businesses now emphasize the cost of incorporating AI into their operational procedures. AI may assist businesses in a variety of ways that alter how they engage with customers, create and convey their procedures, and assess their marketing strategies (Thangaraja, 2020). Companies may experiment with using AI technology to give superior computer abilities for a significant volume of created data thanks to the development of sophisticated algorithms. Artificial Intelligence (AI) analyses business data using methods including the processing of natural language, machine learning, adaptable reading, comprehensive reading, as well as computer vision to deliver detailed information that helps decision-makers for better company management (Simon, 2019).

The Programming software organizations led the artificial intelligence platform and accounted for the growth of more than 39.10% of world revenue in 2019 (Skouras et al., 2005). The sophisticated assignment was made possible due to intelligent developments in data storage space capacity, high compute control, and similar process power to distribute high-class AI platforms to active application verticals. Artificial intelligence platform solution, which includes designing and deploying AI applications, such as those designed for the primitive, precise algebras, reference, small matric, video recorder analytical, and many sources of applications used in communication skills (Annor Antwi & Al-Dherasi, 2019). Businesses require a lot to recognize and also in analyzing optical content to gain a reasonable understanding accepted in promoting the approval of AI platforms in the predicted period (Quasim, 2015).

In this study, an elaborate discussion has been made by the researchers on the Artificial Intelligence and machine learning and background studies that emerge the collaborative approaches in marketing science.

2. CONCEPTUAL LITERATURE REVIEW

In the Forbes article, the writer says numerous companies want their organization to have Artificial Intelligence. We are discussing the neural network application, which arises like Google's Deep Mind, which is able to create associations and access definitions without depending on a pre-defined behavior algorithm. AI can support improving the precedent repetition, be able to understand and be more observant, and allow in improving skills and understanding. Many Professionals have pointed to Alan Turning because he was the first to decide if the computer is smart. Turing suggested that if computers display communication skills at the human level, we should be confident in their Intelligence. Conversion has introduced a human-level intelligence spy experiment called the Conversion test. The test gauges verbal Intelligence, conditional knowledge, as well as basic cognitive skills. AI cannot entirely replace human prediction because human assessments are still required to evaluate certain functions. Finally, to organize for a certain organization or services, ML applications still need human expertise and understanding. Therefore, ML-based AI can't entirely take the role of human Intelligence, creativity, insight, and observation. This is still agreement regarding the transformational use of AI for advances in a variety of fields, including products and services automation. This can be because of its automation capability, machine learning's predictive ability, as well as decision-making. According to the Technical Committee, stated that Artificial Intelligence and Machine Learning applications there are many categories of AI platforms. These comprise human assessment, human reasoning, logical reasoning, and logical reasoning (Chaudhury, 2020).

Frank Chen, a Venture Capitalist, has divided AI into five categories: rational consultation, information representation, scheduling and steering, language processing and sensitivity, etc. The multiplicity of automation problem and solution as well as makes the basis of AI in individual testing for presentation and accurateness of algorithm to make it more difficult to evidently describe the clear linear differences between what constitutes Artificial technology application and what does not exist". Artificial Intelligence is a technology to facilitates and enables machines to execute tasks that are based on decisions that have been left to humans in the past. It manifests itself in many ways, including machine-based learning, which can continue to improve in analysis and decisions when used most, and speech-based technology, which can understand a variety of words and different languages. Artificial Intelligence was previously a division of the commerce world and is increasing swiftly (Econsultancy, 2018).

Davenport et al., (2020) talked about how to comprehend AI's effects, particularly how it affects marketing plans and consumer behavior. The short-term as well as moderate effect of AI could prove limited, and it will function best if it complements human managers rather than replacing them, he said. Soni et al., (2019) outline two key elements that combine to make AI the fundamental technology of advanced automation. The phrase "AI Divide" and "Black AI Divide" is also defined. In order to understand the elements that contribute to the successful combination of AI and marketing, Shahid & Li, (2019). conducted a quality study in cooperation with marketing specialists from different organizations. His research has brought attention to the advantages of incorporating AI into marketing; however, technical interoperability has been a significant obstacle (Khodabandehlou & Zivari Rahman, 2017).

Overgoor et al., (2019) elaborated on engineering benchmark Processes for Data Mining structures be able to be used in improving Artificial Intelligence Solutions in selling problems. He demonstrated his thoughts with the intriguing study of mechanical score Images for Online Marketing. Ramya et al., (2019), in his research, reviewed various factors that influence consumer behavior. Products have the occasion to create an approach and promotion communication tailored to you by identifying and considering the factors that will affect their clients. Raunaque et al., (2016) study focuses on what online shoppers think about when shopping online. Her findings also include how their protection, security, and confidentiality regarding digital marketing affect digital shopping performance.

Economist (2017) introduces different varieties of prediction in addition to automation strategies that can be useful for trade forecasting. In his research, he explored other existing AI methods that seemed profitable and promising to predict business. Thangaraja (2016b) made findings on how marketing intelligence can be significantly developed. In many distributor's points, they do not outperform the competitors since they are utilized as a carrier to deliver the inventory requirements.

According to Columbus, (2018) the use of AI in conjunction with ML, Big Data, and Data Analytics will result in predictions that are more accurate than those made using any other technique. He addressed the costs and cybersecurity risks associated with AI's limitations, including their impact on power forecasts. In his research, Malhotra & Peterson, (2001) brings together academics and medical professionals to examine the problem and emerging trends that can highlight the value of marketing research.

Ajanthan, (2017) is evaluating and identifying the effects of social media marketing on product ratings with the following primary criteria: product dependability, product awareness, product image, and visual quality. Thangaraja, (2016a) is an ongoing and dynamic structure of people, tools, and processes in marketing that happens in real time. Together, they process timely, accurate, and pertinent information that marketing decision-makers can use to advance the development of their marketing strategies. Professionals accumulate and assess a lot of data on their own, but they still need to make sure that the marketing intelligence system is focused. In his research, Morgan, et al., (2019) not only points out significant issues with marketing strategy research but also offers numerous chances to generate concepts that are better in line with contemporary concerns. A research investigation on consumer experience of trade recommendations was undertaken by Shen (2014). He claims that in order to analyze marketing strategies specifically for you, academics might come up with a novel concept known as the consumer perspective (McKinsey & Company, 2013).

To determine the appropriate quality as well as indicators for a significant data marketing strategy, Kim, (2014) performed research. Using the Q approach, he concentrated on the effects of AI and the analysis of big data from a commercial standpoint. In order to spot trends in these fields, Amado et al., (2018) examined the use of big data for marketing. His research has demonstrated that there has been an increasing curiosity in big data marketing throughout time. Therefore, for instance, for Big Data to develop in the Marketing industry, business efforts must be increased. Jeya Rani & Thangaraja (2016) the marketing intelligence platform analyses how to best support the banking system and consumers in applying cutting-edge technological upgrades that various banks embrace in order to operate more effectively by luring new clients, educational institutions, and assessment processes.

Lessmann et al., (2019) concentrated on dynamical identification models. The author contends that such animals do not appropriately balance corporate aims in the typical means of flourishing. Ozcelik & Varnali, (2019) goes into detail about how recipients' psychological and behavioral interpretation affects the efficacy of internet-tailored adverts. Thangaraja (2016c) The distributors always favor social media for information gathering and order collection in order to build a marketing intelligence system that will allow the distributors to make more informed and reliable decisions. Abid et al., (2019) studied the impacts of various content components and allusions on online fan dialogues and the implications of content management. You have discussed the significance of content marketers in creating stronger online relationships.

3. PURPOSE OF AL AND ML IN MARKETING PROCESS

AI empowers marketers to increase automation, implement processes, and expand staff in such a way that it makes our lives as a workforce, consumers, and relations better. Marketing activity has been partially designed for scheduled tasks, tailored to non-legal functions, and supplemented by difficult decisions that may require workforce and equipment to build each other's strength (Arumugam et al., 2020). As managers are converted into more sophisticated in understanding technology, they are gradually experimenting with business solutions that integrate changing AI elements, optimizing and scalability. Jim Sterne says that automation, efficiency, and amplification are certain objectives of Artificial Intelligence. Nevertheless, computerization represents the most important thing for managers. It can be challenging to work with vast amounts of data and deliver insights when marketing personnel lack data science and AI competence. Enterprises should work with outside organizations to get programmers functioning properly so that data can be collected and analyzed to teach AI systems as well as enable ongoing maintenance. As ML systems take in more data, they will develop the ability to make accurate, useful decisions. Process intelligence solutions will increasingly give businesses detailed real-time insight into their processes, allowing them to track progress and make adjustments as needed. Numerous company giants have been motivated to advance into more complex and successful industries as a result of the quick adoption of developing technology, where AI has proven to be most useful. Accessibility to AI will improve an organization's ability to stay one step ahead of rivals in a number of areas.

AI contributes to the automation, implementation, and enhancement of three basic marketing processes: information collection, data analysis as well and client engagement. Today's selling relies on intellectual technology to confine user information relevant to product communication. The user benefit is, at best, help designed for the immediate needs and expectations of those who are not exposed in the long run. In the future, not only will the relationship between companies and their clients change, but artificial Intelligence will also replace company managers. The artificial intelligence assistants will be able to predict future client preferences with ease, including those related to pricing, quality, and features. As a result, marketing will resemble a competition over what to provide customers. Marketers employ AI to increase consumer demand. Customers benefit from integrated applications that take advantage of artificial Intelligence. Every purchase is tracked, along with the place where and when it was made. It might look over the information and send clients personalized marketing materials. In order to increase a customer's average purchase when they visit a neighboring shop, these notifications provide advice and discounts.

Iterative processing and algorithms that enable software to learn from patterns enable AI to gather enormous amounts of data. Each of AI's numerous subfields operates differently. Understanding how computers imitate or carry out human learning behaviors to pick up new skills or knowledge and rearrange existing structures of knowledge to continuously improve performance is the aim of machine learning (ML). AI can be helpful because people's tastes and trends are always evolving. Although some components, including personality features, don't alter over time, customer personas might. It might be much easier to organize all of this with AI automation.

Marketing gives the company a competitive edge by implementing an integrated computer automation approach. The AI marketing approach provides advantages in client micromanagement and decision-making. Data is necessary to improve the content patterns that ML systems suggest to users. Programmatic media bidding is the term for the automated process of buying and selling online advertising. These computer-based models draw on audience information, inherit ML traits, and show relevant advertisements to target audiences. The loop customization process is a continuous mechanism that provides businesses the chance to connect with clients personally and forge stronger bonds. Through a consistent feedback loop, businesses keep improving their customization procedures, creating a "good customization cycle". Christian Spindler forewarns that managers' differing views on the best customization patterns for each minute will cause considerable conflict.

3.1. Automation

All businesses manage inefficiency, which can be totally replaced by highly efficient algorithms. Companies, by tradition, do program work to decrease labor costs. Today's automated selling has become more effective than the cost-cutting machines through the increase shifting to computerization of consumer information. The company has the opportunity to not only automate but also maintain interior processes that are not visible to customers segregation, and they can send solutions that will please consumers with efficient and automated services. AI is a potent tool when used in conjunction with trustworthy market research data. This enables firms to complete a range of tasks. Target audience segmentation is a crucial element of this often-used use case. AI is noticeably quicker and more efficient than humans at this work. Companies might be able to provide more tailored offers for their consumers that they are inclined to accept if they look further. Millions of information points regarding a customer may be examined by ML to determine which days and times of the week to contact them, the recommended frequency, the content that most interest them, and which email topics, as well as headers, generate the most clicks. Using sophisticated algorithms, a website experience can be tailored. After analyzing hundreds of points of data on a single user, AI may give offers and information that are more appropriate for each type of user. Marketing is one of many industries where models for prediction may be applied.

The chatbot "TOBi" offers customized conversion recommendations + 100% compared to Vodafone's website and responds to important requests with 70% resolution. Contented automation is gradually more accountable for creating, determining, and distributing product messages. The computerized bidding method surpassed the man-made campaign with a 40% development in consumer procurement costing and an average of ten hours, which was saved monthly for each member of the team. Automated recommendation uses a prediction algorithm that will generate 35% of Amazon7 revenue and 78% of movies that are watched on Netflix TV. The algorithm can make progressive decisions on a scale. ML represents the most powerful tool for companies that are looking for good customer communication. As per Gartner, by 2020, clients will manage 27% of their business connections without personal contact.

These kinds of models are implemented into all company operations, and connecting with other systems boosts the high degrees of automation. The use of artificial Intelligence includes the capacity to comprehend and build better analytical abilities for managers. Outstanding instances of a programmed AI approach can be brought to all company units by companies like Amazon. The reputation of an item's AI-based sale forecasting approach is growing; the majority of tasks are completed without human involvement. Amazon creates a shopping list for all warehouses and updates the projected stock volumes. End users will, therefore, be more likely to recommend the popular product at the new pricing. The sales forecast will be revisited based on the outcome of this marketing campaign.

3.2. Optimization

Businesses that use artificial intelligence platforms will have to perform processes that minimize processes, decrease conversion time, and develop better output. Each advertiser can point out more opportunities to incorporate artificial Intelligence into the building brands to enhance customer attainment and maintenance practices. Artificial Intelligence allows marketers to interact with clients across all channels and will provide customized consumer trips without a significant boost in craftsmanship by reducing the amount of time spent on customer segregation and developing target campaigns, understanding technology that can significantly boost the efficiency of all sales departments.

For some marketers, optimism means focusing on strategic customer engagement efforts while minimizing non-strategy. The Disposing of emails in favor of customer contact with real-time agents, such as chatbots, is a direct step in that way. In the process of optimizing, the mechanism can assist the workforce in identifying unidentified issues and use real-time. AI-powered technologies can help with data collection, model development, testing on real customers, and model validation. Every consumer now receives personalized, relevant emails thanks to AI. Machine-learning algorithms may also help in spotting disengaged customer groups that are about to leave or go to a competitor. The study of multi-channel activities and the detection of falling consumer involvement are made easier with the help of AI-powered churn prediction. To keep consumers interested, it can send emails, push notifications, and relevant offers. When personalized content production and AI-powered churn prediction are combined, customer engagement increases, increasing lifetime value and revenue.

Although AI algorithms tend to be automated in process, their expansion, mechanism, and preparation remain a technical, highly researched, and entertaining movement. Human plays a tactical role in the continuous good planning of Artificial Intelligence systems leading through programmed programs. AI is not only "set and forget" know-how as the model is constantly programmed by hand, especially when it involves language processing. No matter how high-tech it is, there will always be a need for personal interaction to add AI technology.

3.3. Augmentation

Algorithms can help traditional teams get the most elsewhere of their selling attempts by adding up layer of expertise. For organizations, Artificial Intelligence has been added instead of performing tasks and processes without human intervention. Artificial Intelligence application is not about replacing individuals but empowering marketers to work effectively and smartly. Testing Artificial Intelligence begins with considering what individuals and machines do better. People are often able to make conceptual thinking without particular situations enhanced than the machine. They are much faster and additional accurate in information usage and make available realistic solutions in a well-defined context.

In many cases, machines improve a person's ability to draw conclusions. The functions of the communication center adopt AI to simplify decision-making. The most modern AI-enabled platform can extract the relevant piece of information through both vocal and documented conversations in concurrent to quickly understand popular issues, recommend the next finest action for agents, and predict customer chances to explode. Salesforce Einstein uses models based on rules and predictions to provide content providers with content and customer offerings. This best practice will suggest the workforce, such as free shipment, which leads to higher consumer loyalty and higher sales opportunities. With the help of AI solutions, marketers can better understand their current and potential clients, enabling them to send the appropriate message at the appropriate moment. Collecting information at each consumer interaction is the only way to create a genuinely thorough profile. By going beyond these profiles, marketers may leverage AI technology to improve marketing efforts and create more personalized content. For more creative and successful digital ads, AI can access the wealth of consumer data that is concealed in searching for keywords, social profiles, and various other online data.

Marketers employ language-based Intelligence as engagement managers, payment processors, and sales tools to improve the user experience. Instead of manually figuring out the process on their own, customers can now rely on chatbots to finish the purchase for them. With the aid of AI, it is now possible to personalize information through observation, data collection, and analysis. By assisting marketers using email campaigns, the use of technology in online advertising enables them to maximize outcomes. Among the digital marketing solutions that assist in reaching the target customer at the appropriate time and ensuring appropriate conversion tactics is email marketing.

4. CONCEPTUAL FRAMEWORK AI AND ML-BASED MARKETING MODEL

The important stages of an AI-marketing model are described in all of the marketing conceptual frameworks, which include what, how, whom, why, and outcome, and integrate machine learning in the sequential format steps throughout the marketing process (Fig. 1). In order to effectively analyze marketing goals in regards to automating, optimizing, and enhancing various relationships to search decisions for improved forecasting, expectancies, as well as personalization, managers must build an artificial intelligence plan. The array of marketing technologies has been expanded to include more than just artificial Intelligence. The first location is to consider the surroundings and sales objectives.

It seems that managing better relationships in an information and interaction progression enables organizations to predict behavior, anticipate demand, and make communication unique. Today's modern managers use user information to deliver a hyper individual customized content where each succeeding message will build on consumer interactions. This collaboration is not seen as the final phase of a customer expedition but in the planning of the future experience in a positive way and satisfying sequence. In addition, flourishing Machine Learning Companies are transforming information into seam-less communications with customers in to more automated way. This predictability, in addition to complementary experience, builds deep personal relationships with customers, enhances omnichannel consumer understanding, and drives product segregation.

Artificial Intelligence will drive for better effectiveness and usefulness of a commercial organization. These benefits of automation, efficiency, and output enhancement. That is what many organizations will expect from a cognitive system. An effective Artificial Intelligence strategy can always provide better performance just if it is processed on solid technologies (data, technology, process) and organizational (human, Capabilities, cultural) fundamentals.

Figure 1. Conceptual framework of AL and ML model in the marketing process

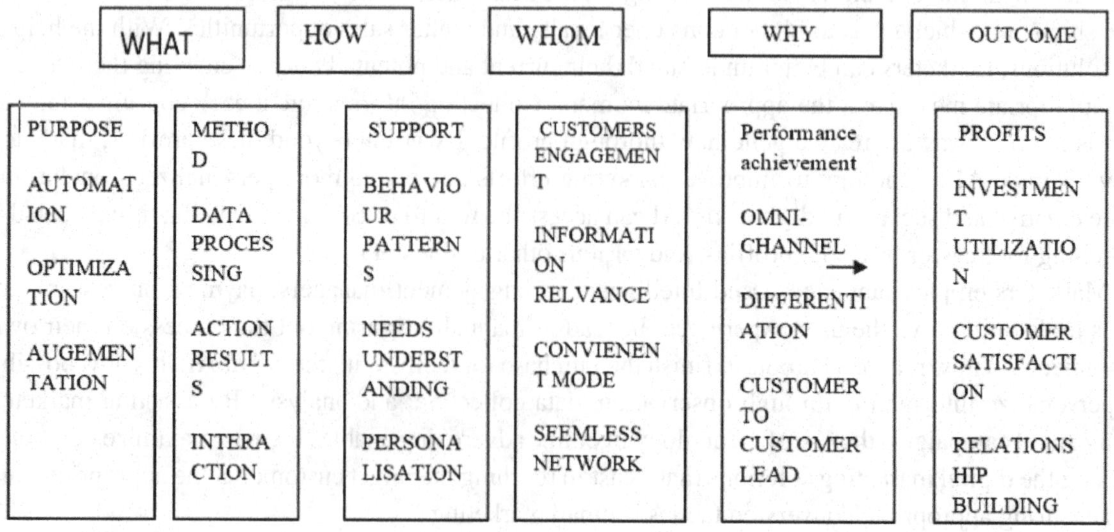

WHAT	HOW	WHOM	WHY	OUTCOME
PURPOSE	METHOD	SUPPORT	CUSTOMERS ENGAGEMENT	Performance achievement	PROFITS
AUTOMATION	DATA PROCESSING	BEHAVIOUR PATTERNS	INFORMATION RELVANCE	OMNI-CHANNEL →	INVESTMENT UTILIZATION
OPTIMIZATION	ACTION RESULTS	NEEDS UNDERSTANDING	CONVIENENT MODE	DIFFERENTIATION	CUSTOMER SATISFACTION
AUGEMENTATION	INTERACTION	PERSONALISATION	SEEMLESS NETWORK	CUSTOMER TO CUSTOMER LEAD	RELATIONSHIP BUILDING

The Marketing managers always need to tactically evaluate the selling association to reconstruct the roles as well as responsibilities for sufficiently significant in the distribution of labour between people and machines. The process will maintain the steadiness between the individual effort and the machine in injecting into all significant selling procedures and consumer journeys. The Managers as to have a proper dividing and also proper selection of the approaches to plan strategies. Considering a moment, the effect will have fully automated client service, for example, by means of chatbots, on the individual organization that runs" consumer concern". Clearly, Artificial Intelligence is not providing a better solution, and, in the expectations, when organizations become Artificial Intelligence, individual touch can still be ensured that there is an ongoing competitive advantage.

In this regard, the use of Artificial Intelligence strategies is minus about building algorithms and also has more by establishing better relations that can balance the effective strategic objective, process, and benefit of AI-driven marketing.

5. ROLE OF AL AND ML IN MODERN MARKETING

Measuring multiple marketing contributions to income growth becomes more accurate and more real-time due to statistics and machine learning applications. The significant information drives more in marketing qualified, leads qualified leads, the most excellent way in increasing the marketing campaign and improves accuracy and also profitability for pricing in some of the areas where machine learning application will transform promotion.

Today, leading marketers use machine learning techniques to better understand, anticipate, and adapt to various problems in their marketing prospects in order to solve qualitatively faster and more properly than any competitors. Understanding well-executed content while indicating eligibility for immediate closure sales is motivated by machine-learning applications that are able to learn the most effective expectations and individual customers. Machine learning takes over content selling automation, which includes leading market campaigning and goal-score, customization, and sales forecasts at a new level of accuracy and speediness.

Major sales units will rely on powerful sets in analytics as well as Performance indicators in measuring the individual progress in achieving customer goals and growth. As a machine learning application, the marketing department can make a major contribution to profit growth and fortification of customer relationships in the method.

These are the following ten methods of Artificial Intelligence and machine learning play an important role in revitalizing today and future markets:

Artificial Intelligence and Machine learning can improve customer's knowledge as well as support: The application will enable in development of active products and services. The marketing managers are leading influencers who can create and develop better strategies in order to deliver excellent customer experience. Scheduling all aspects that will attract sales and serve customers is enhanced with advertisers using machine learning software to accurately predict results.

Artificial intelligence and machine learning will be prioritized in personalized customer care and the development of better products: The advertising is very complex and has very high profits. Retailers have never been more focused on "to-do" in an area with maximizes profits and will lead to low complexity. The application sites include a Chatbot and visual assistant, profit reduction, face acknowledgment, and product recommendations.

The Real-time publicity across all the online platforms and prepared communication direction, context, and accurateness will speed up: The combined effects of this development of marketing technology will lead to increased sales performances on B2C-based retail channels. The leading generation of sales-qualified leads will increase, which could reduce the sales cycle and increase the winning rate.

The analysis reduces customer fraud using machine learning, which makes simpler risks forecast and intervention model: As a replacement for relying on the most expensive and time-consuming costs that will reduce customer behavior, most telecommunication companies and those in the highly advanced industry will turn to machine learning. The risk models help in determining how action aimed at preventing mix affects risks. The intervention models will allow the marketer to think about how the levels of interventions can influence the likelihood of valuing a customer's life.

Pricing and price flexibility are on the rise in industries with limited reserves, including airlines and hotels, which are increasingly in production and services: All retailers continue to rely on machine learning to define competitive prices, which are appropriate in context. Machine learning apps increase pricing in addition to flights, hotels, and events to cover product pricing conditions for products and services. Machine learning is used to decide price flexibility for every product, including channel category, customer segmenting, time of sale, and product location in the largely in-product price plan (Thangaraja et al.,2020).

Improving demand forecasting, assorting efficiency, and pricing: Consumer Goods and in-store marketing organizations have great opportunities for artificial intelligence applications to improve overall performance. The usage of AI applications and machine learning in all retailers' value chains will have the potential to bring about a 60% improvement in versatility and a 40% increase in digital sales by using dynamic prices.

Designing and ordering of targeting models that guide sales and marketing strategy by product lines, customer segments, and individual:

The data-driven manufacturers create as well as use propensity models in defining products and services with a high potential for purchase. The trend model is most often based on import information built into MS Excel, which makes its in-progress use consumption of time. Machine learning facilitates the design, optimization, and revenue of the sales and marketing strategies by making all the progress (Thangam et al.,2022).

Leadership accuracy is improving, leading to an increase in sales following back to early sales campaign and marketing strategy: With the usage of machine learning for getting customers and also expected listings using the relevant information through the web, the speculation model, which includes machine learning, can easily predict the relevant client profile. Every earnings rate becomes a better predictor of new potential sales volume helps in sales prioritizing in time, sales team effort, and marketing strategy. This will look interesting to see how machine learning improves sales performance

Identifying and interpreting the display of sales the specific customer segments and sub-segments using frequency cash modeling with machine learning applications has become commonplace: Using the Frequency cash model as an element of the machine learning step can be provided with accurate descriptions of the most reliable, most expensive customers.

Improving of marketing combined mix will determine what marketing offer, incentives, and program are obtainable where anticipated opportunities where other channels are another way of learning machine learning and transforming marketing. Special sale offers are created based on content, offers, and promotions. This item will be made available in a machine by using the concept of machine learning to guess the best combinations of ingredients that can lead to new sales volume. Amazon product promotions are an example of how the e-commerce website uses machine learning to increase sales and revenue for recommended products.

6. CONCLUSION

Installation and machine learning skills are essential to ensure that the company remains aggressive and well-organized in today's self-motivated environment. AL and ML have converted the existing marketing applications to increase skills as well as performs task automatically. All online transformations have been leading to a change in the focal point of processes. With the large availability of information, an innovative size for examination is made available. In-depth knowledge and classification tools have enabled a detailed customer printing and environment. This information can be used as a tool for improving customer relationship management at many levels. Employees in substantial and digital business situations have efficiency and services that can lead to better targets and customizes to the customer and their needs. Repeated information is collected, which has been used to improve customer engagement. The artificial intelligence tool is about continuing to fund switching to an additional online environment. Commerce thrives on subsisting more connected between the different services than just selling your skills.

The focus is on understanding customer desire for accessing, engagements, and customizations to improve communication between consumers and organizations. In term of automated operations and skills development, does research comes to in-depth thinking and independent mechanical practices that make the in-house marketing process effective. Particularly in the field of innovations and technology, the development of autonomous computers will be very helpful and offer innovative opportunities. The change in technology can lead to changes in customer behavior, and that means this has to have different desires and requirements. Another factor can be the limited number of employees employed in marketing programs. This will not only contribute to staff change but will also reduce personal and personal touch. Worryingly, machines do not have the capacity for good behavior and sound decisions.

Furthermore, as technology is relatively new and developing, it can have a few unintended consequences that affect not only organizations but also individuals and governments that also have an impact on the organization. Problems related to confidentiality, loss of trust, and controls are very gentle. To avoid these effects commencing the disrupting commerce successes as well as technological failures, traders will be more active in creating awareness of possible pitfalls and also incorporate various approaches to their risk analysis. At present, artificial Intelligence collects information is of customers and is used for communicating with high targets and also personalized levels. Technology is developing more and more straightforward with independent equipment.

REFERENCES

Abid, A., Harrigan, P., & Roy, S. K. (2020). Online relationship marketing through content creation and curation. *Marketing Intelligence & Planning*, *38*(6), 699–712. doi:10.1108/MIP-04-2019-0219

Adams, R. L. (2017). 10 powerful examples of artificial Intelligence in use today. *Forbes*. https://www.forbes.com/sites/robertadams/2017/01/10/10-powerful-examples-of-artificial-intelligence-in-usetoday/#2fd895e9420d

Adomavicius, G., & Tuzhilin, A. (2005). Personalization technologies: A process-oriented perspective. *Communications of the ACM, 48*(10), 83–90. doi:10.1145/1089107.1089109

Ajanthan, D. (2017). The impact of a social media marketing on customer based brand equity- A special reference to travel and tourism industry in Sri Lanka. *Trans. Asian Journal of Marketing Management Research, 6*(11), 36–46.

Amado, A., Cortez, P., Rita, P., & Moro, S. (2018). Research trends on Big Data in Marketing: A text mining and topic modeling-based literature analysis. *European Research on Management and Business Economics, 24*(1), 1–7, 24. doi:10.1016/j.iedeen.2017.06.002

Amnesty International. (2018). Machine learning, and their application for growth, Adelyn Zhou. *Slide-Share/LinkedIn.*

Annor Antwi, A., & Al-Dherasi, A. A. M. (2019) Application of Artificial Intelligence in Forecasting: A Systematic Review. SSRN *Electronic Journal.* doi:10.2139/ssrn.3483313

Arthanari, A., & Jambulingam, M. (2020). *Entertainmerce and phygital consumers–changing preferences for retail shopping destinations and retailtainment options.* Cengage learning Pvt Ltd.

Arumugam, T., Jayakrishnan, B., Ranganathan, M., Kadiresan, V., & Mathai, R. (2020). A social network analysis on understanding pattern of shoppers' OmniChannel adoption and clustering based on channel switching and preference attributes. *SSRN Electronic Journal.*

Chaudhury, D. (2020). *Artificial Intelligence influencing and transforming the marketing function.* https://talkcmo.com/featured/artificial-intelligence-influencing-and-transforming-the-marketing-function/

Columbus, L. (2018). *10 ways machine learning is revolutionizing marketing.* https://www.forbes.com/sites/louiscolumbus/2018/02/25/10-ways-machine-learning-is-revolutionizing-marketing/#701274705bb6

Davenport, T., Guha, A., Grewal, D., & Bressgott, T. (2020). How artificial Intelligence will change the future of marketing. *Journal of the Academy of Marketing Science, 48*(1), 24–42, 48. doi:10.100711747-019-00696-0

Economist. (2017). https://www.economist.com/business/2017/04/12/how-germanys-otto-uses-artificial-intelligence

Econsultancy. (2018). Vodafone's chatbot is delivering double the conversion rate of its website. *Ben Davis.* https://econsultancy.com/vodafones-chatbot-is-delivering-twice-the-conversion-rate-of-its-website/

. Jeya Rani, R., & Thangaraja, A. (2016). The role of marketing intelligence in green banking practices – A conceptual approach. *Imperial Journal of Interdisciplinary Research, 2*(9).

Khodabandehlou, S., & Zivari Rahman, M. (2017). Comparison of supervised machine learning techniques for customer churn prediction based on analysis of customer behavior. *Journal of Systems and Information Technology, 19*(1/2), 65–93. doi:10.1108/JSIT-10-2016-0061

Kim, K. Y. (2014). Business intelligence and marketing insights in an era of big data: The q-sorting approach. *KSII Transactions on Internet and Information Systems, 8*(2), 567–582. doi:10.3837/tiis.2014.02.014

Kiran, K. U., & Arumugam, T. (2020). Role of programmatic advertising on effective digital promotion strategy: A conceptual framework. *Journal of Physics: Conference Series, 1716*(1), 012032. doi:10.1088/1742-6596/1716/1/012032

Lessmann, S., Haupt, J., Coussement, K., & De Bock, K. W. (2019). Targeting customers for profit: An ensemble learning framework to support marketing decision-making. *Information Sciences*, 15–22.

Lotz, S. L., Eastlick, M. A., Mishra, A., & Shim, S. (2010). Understanding patrons' participation in activities at entertainment malls. *International Journal of Retail & Distribution Management, 38*(6), 402–422. doi:10.1108/09590551011045366

Malhotra, N. K., & Peterson, M. (2001). Marketing research in the new millennium: Emerging issues and trends. *Marketing Intelligence & Planning, 19*(4), 216–232. doi:10.1108/EUM0000000005560

McKinsey & Company. (2013). *How retailers can keep up with consumers.* https://www.mckinsey.com/industries/retail/our-insights/how-retailers-can-keep-up-with-consumers

Morgan, N. A., Whitler, K. A., Feng, H., & Chari, S. (2019). Research in marketing strategy. *Journal of the Academy of Marketing Science, 47*(1), 4–29, 47. doi:10.100711747-018-0598-1

Overgoor, G., Chica, M., Rand, W., & Weishampel, A. (2019). Letting the computers take over: Using ai to solve marketing problems. *California Management Review, 61*(4), 156–185. doi:10.1177/0008125619859318

Ozcelik, A. B., & Varnali, K. (2019). Effectiveness of online behavioral targeting: A psychological perspective. *Electronic Commerce Research and Applications, 33*, 33. doi:10.1016/j.elerap.2018.11.006

Quasim, D. R. M. D. T. (2015). Artificial Intelligence as a business forecasting and error handling tool, COMPUSOFT an International Journal of Advanced Computer Technology. *Chattopadhyay R, 4*(2), 1534–1537.

Ramya, N., & Dr Sa, A. M. (2019). Factors affecting consumer buying behaviour. *International Journal of Advanced Research, 7*(1), 563–568. doi:10.21474/IJAR01/8362

Raunaque, N., Zeeshan, Md., & Imam, A. Md. (2016). Consumer perception towards online marketing in India, International Journal of Advanced Engineering. *Management Science, 2*(8), 1236–1240.

Shahid, M. Z., & Li, G. (2019). Impact of artificial Intelligence in marketing: A perspective of marketing professionals of Pakistan, global. *Journal of Management and Business Research e Marketing, 19*(2), 26–33.

Shen, A. (2014). Recommendations as personalized marketing: Insights from customer experiences. *Journal of Services Marketing, 28*(5), 414–427. doi:10.1108/JSM-04-2013-0083

Simon, J. P. (2019). Artificial Intelligence: Scope, players, markets and geography. *Digital Policy. Regulation & Governance, 21*(3), 208–237. doi:10.1108/DPRG-08-2018-0039

Skouras, T., Avlonitis, G. J., & Indounas, K. A. (2005). Economics and marketing on pricing: How and why do they differ? *Journal of Product and Brand Management, 14*(6), 362–374. doi:10.1108/10610420510624512

Soni, N., Sharma, E. K., Singh, N., & Kapoor, A. (2019). Impact of artificial Intelligence on businesses: From research, innovation, market deployment to future shifts in business models. *Journal of Business Research*.

Thangam, D., Arumugam, T., Kommuri, U. K., Velusamy, K., Subramanian, M., Ganesan, S. K., & Suryakumar, M. (2022). COVID-19 pandemic and its brunt on digital transformation and cybersecurity. In Cybersecurity crisis management and lessons learned (pp. 15–42). IGI Global.

Thangaraja, A. (2016a). An evolution of distributors' marketing intelligence system (DMIS) among FMCG distributors: A conceptual frame work. *International Journal of Multidisciplinary Education and Research, 1*(5), 11–13.

Thangaraja, A. (2016b). Fast Moving Consumer Goods Distributors' source of Information and Marketing Intelligence System on Customer Feedback. *International Journal of Advance Research and Innovative Ideas in Education, 2*(1), 833–837.

Thangaraja, A. (2016c). The indispensability of information technology in marketing intelligence system: A conceptual approach. *International Journal for Scientific Research & Development, 4*(06), 118–121.

ThangarajaA. (2020). The veiling part of neuromarketing in developing brand preference in FMCG sector: A conceptual study. SSRN.

Vesanen, J. (2007). What is personalization? A conceptual framework. *European Journal of Marketing, 41*(5/6), 409–418. doi:10.1108/03090560710737534

Vesanen, J., & Raulas, M. (2006). Building bridges for personalization: A process model for marketing. *Journal of Interactive Marketing, 20*(1), 5–20. doi:10.1002/dir.20052

Chapter 6
Investigating Innovative Social Technology for Elevating Employee Well-Being in the Business Context

H. Hajra

Bharath Institute of Higher Education and Research, India

G. Jayalakshmi

Bharath Institute of Higher Education and Research, India

ABSTRACT

Welfare signifies the quality of life in the ecological, economic, and social environments. It is crucial as it affects employee behavior and organizational productivity. The provision of welfare amenities by employers can positively impact the workforce. For managers to achieve goals via their teams, offering necessary and desirable workplace facilities is key. Technology and industry-specific tools are instrumental in advancing employee wellness programs. With the rise of remote and hybrid work models, integrating innovative social technologies is vital to enhance employee well-being in the corporate sphere. This process involves understanding well-being, selecting appropriate technologies, protecting data privacy, managing change, evaluating program success, and fostering a culture oriented towards well-being. Goals include improving job satisfaction, encouraging a healthy work-life balance, and addressing stress and mental health issues.

INTRODUCTION

Employee welfare represents a comprehensive term encompassing many initiatives dedicated to improving the well-being, satisfaction, and development of employees within an organization. It is an umbrella term that covers a wide array of provisions and activities that extend beyond mere compensation, aiming to foster comfort, intellectual growth, social welfare, and overall happiness among the workforce (Ángeles,

DOI: 10.4018/979-8-3693-0049-7.ch006

2023). The core objective of such welfare measures is to elevate the quality of life for employees, ensuring that they feel content and valued within their work environment (Abbassy & Ead, 2020). As articulated by Todd, employee welfare is not just about meeting the bare necessities required for industry function-ing. Still, it is a concerted effort to enhance employees' physical, intellectual, and social well-being (Alabdullah et al., 2021a). Technology has revolutionized the approach to employee welfare, becoming an indispensable aspect of global operations and business management. It has granted us the ability to better understand the needs of employees, increase productivity, alleviate workloads, and foster innova-tion and creativity within the workplace (Alabdullah et al., 2021b). The global pandemic has catalyzed change, transforming how organizations approach the wellness of their employees. This transformation has been marked by the emergence of various digital platforms seamlessly integrated into the corporate world, offering new avenues for employee wellness programs.

These technological solutions are now being rapidly adopted by forward-thinking companies seek-ing to provide comprehensive and effective wellness programs that cater to the diverse needs of their employees. Such programs are not limited to the digital space but are also implemented in the physical workspace, ensuring a holistic approach to employee wellness. The aim is to create an environment where employees can professionally and personally thrive, with access to resources and support that promote their overall well-being. This strategic investment in employee welfare contributes to a hap-pier and more productive workforce. It aligns with the growing recognition of the importance of mental health, work-life balance, and the social aspect of work in today's corporate culture. Employee welfare has become a key strategic component of business operations, with technology playing a pivotal role in shaping and delivering these initiatives. Companies that prioritize the welfare of their employees are not only investing in their workforce but are also setting a new standard for the modern workplace, where the well-being of every individual is considered integral to the success and sustainability of the organization (Köseoğlu et al., 2022).

The Committee of Labour Welfare (1969) defines the scope of employee welfare as encompassing a wide range of services, facilities, and amenities. These include ensuring sufficient canteens, rest areas, recreational amenities, sanitary provisions, medical facilities, transportation arrangements for workers far from their workplaces, and various other services and amenities. Additionally, social security measures are considered an integral part of employee welfare as they contribute to improving the overall working conditions of employees.

Welfare is a comprehensive concept that encompasses the living conditions of individuals or groups in a positive relationship with their overall environment, including ecological, social, and economic as-pects. Its goal is to achieve social development through various means, such as social legislation, reform, services, work, and action. Economic welfare aims to enhance production, productivity, and development by promoting equitable distribution. Welfare measures can be classified as either mandated by law or voluntary, with legal requirements mandating employers to provide certain employee benefits beyond their wages or salaries (Ead & Abbassy, 2022).

In today's rapidly evolving business landscape, effective management is a cornerstone for the suc-cess and sustainability of all types of organizations, irrespective of their geographical roots, operational nature, or ownership structures. Organizations with varied driving forces, from profit-oriented goals to those fueled by social, religious, or philanthropic motives, share the common necessity of efficient management practices to maintain momentum and achieve continuous growth. This universality of the need for adept management underscores its role as the backbone of organizational progress, providing the strategic direction and operational oversight that propels an enterprise forward (Yeruva & Ramu, 2023).

Within the sphere of management, particular emphasis is placed on the qualitative aspects of employment, which are critical to elevating the workers' quality of life and, by extension, enhancing their productivity. These aspects include ensuring that employees receive sufficient income to meet their needs and aspirations, which acts as a motivation for improved performance. Secure working conditions are equally important, providing a safe environment that minimizes risks and health hazards and fostering a sense of well-being among the workforce. Additionally, fundamental social security benefits, such as health insurance, retirement plans, and other forms of employee assistance, contribute to a safety net that secures the livelihood of workers and their families (Ángeles, 2022).

These qualitative elements contribute to the direct benefit of employees and enhance an organization's overall operational efficiency (Ead & Abbassy, 2018). Workers who feel valued and protected are more likely to be engaged, loyal, and committed to their roles, which translates into higher levels of productivity and innovation. Consequently, organizations that prioritize these qualitative elements are not only upholding ethical and social responsibilities but strategically positioning themselves to attract and retain top talent, a key competitive advantage in the modern economy (Alabdullah & Ahmed, 2021).

The intertwining of effective management practices with the qualitative elements of employment forms a symbiotic relationship that drives employee satisfaction and organizational success. This relationship acknowledges that the welfare of the workforce is not separate from the organization's health, but rather, they are intrinsically linked (Kanaan-Jebna et al., 2022). As the global business environment becomes more complex and interconnected, the role of management in ensuring these qualitative employment standards cannot be overstated, as it is fundamental to creating a resilient and progressive organizational culture capable of navigating the challenges of the present era (Ramu & Yeruva, 2023).

Institutional structures are established to guarantee these benefits for employees within the organized sector of the economy. Efforts are actively being pursued to strengthen and expand these mechanisms as much as possible. However, most workers in the informal sector, comprising approximately 90 percent of the overall workforce, generally lack access to such benefits. It is imperative to take significant measures with a broader scope than ever before, and measures are being taken to improve the quality of working life for workers in the informal sector, including women workers. Hence, the realm of welfare is considered to have immense potential for addressing the feelings of frustration among industrial workers, alleviating their personal and family concerns, enhancing their health, providing avenues for self-expression, offering opportunities for personal excellence, and fostering a broader perspective on life.

The underlying purpose of implementing welfare programs is to foster an effective, healthy, committed, and satisfied workforce. Employee welfare holds significant importance in the realm of human resource management. According to Chambers dictionary, welfare is defined as "the state of faring or doing well, encompassing freedom from calamity and the enjoyment of health and prosperity." The characteristics of employee welfare encompass the following:

- Employee welfare encompasses a wide range of services, provisions, and amenities offered to employees to enhance their well-being and overall improvement.
- Employee welfare measures, alternatively referred to as fringe benefits and services, encompass a range of additional provisions and amenities offered to employees for their enhanced welfare and satisfaction.
- The fundamental objective is to enhance the well-being of the working class.
- Welfare measures can be categorized as either voluntary or statutory.

Agencies of employee welfare are as follows:

- The central government has established comprehensive arrangements for the well-being, security, and welfare through the Factories Act of 1948 and the Mines Act of 1952. These acts mandate the provision of facilities such as canteens, restrooms, and shelters.
- Different state governments and union territories offer welfare facilities to workers, with each government prescribing rules for worker welfare and ensuring compliance with the provisions outlined in various labor laws.
- Employers are indulged in providing facilities to employees with the logic of creating an efficient, healthy, and loyal labour force for their organization.
- In India, trade unions have made limited contributions to the welfare of workers. However, a few notable and influential unions, such as the Ahmedabad Textiles Labour Association and the Amador Sabah in Kanpur, have played a pioneering role.
- Some charitable social service organizations, like Sevasadan Society, V.M.C.A, etc., actively participate in labour welfare measures.

The following are different types of welfare services:

- The organization provides intramural facilities, including canteens, restrooms, uniforms, etc., for its employees.
- The organization extends extramural facilities outside its premises; examples include housing, education, and leave travel benefits. Concessions, interest-free loans, medical facilities, transportation facilities, etc.

Nahar Nilgiris provides various welfare facilities to their employees, such as medical allowances, free accommodation, service charges, provident fund, employee state insurance (ESI), leave allowance, traveling allowance, uniform, etc. Ways in Which Technology Provides Assistance

Enhanced employee productivity, increased flexibility, and better physical, mental, and emotional well-being can increase job satisfaction and foster employee loyalty.

Leveraging technology also empowers organizations to provide a broader and higher-quality range of healthcare services. Employee mental health significantly influences their productivity and loyalty to their employer. Numerous digital applications that offer surveys and insightful glimpses into employees' emotional well-being assist in gaining insights into their long-term mental health and day-to-day emotional states while at work. These technological tools enable organizations to understand how individuals feel about their colleagues, supervisors, subordinates, and workloads. Happiness metrics, surveys, polls, and personality and psychological assessments are employed to gauge well-being. These are crucial insights easily attainable through digital solutions for employee well-being, helping identify what contributes to workplace happiness, what causes dissatisfaction, emotional stressors, anxiety triggers, and what motivates individuals to perform better and find enjoyment in their jobs.

THE ROLE OF COMMUNICATION IN ENHANCING EMPLOYEE WELL-BEING

In today's digital age, where technology intertwines with every facet of life, communication is the cornerstone of occupational health and employee well-being. The influx of digital tools and platforms has revolutionized how workplace communities are formed and sustained, offering virtual congregations where employees can engage in meaningful dialogues about their triumphs, challenges, and the diverse factors that fuel their enthusiasm for work. These tools have transcended beyond mere productivity instruments to become crucibles for shared experiences. They enable employees to effortlessly share insights into their interactions with well-being products and narratives of their journeys through the professional sphere and beyond into the personal. As these narratives are exchanged, a rich tapestry of employee experiences is woven, providing a nuanced understanding of the workforce's dynamics. Employers, for their part, are not mere spectators in this digital arena; they are active participants who can leverage these platforms to motivate, celebrate, and reinforce the positive behaviors of their team members. By publicly recognizing the accomplishments and contributions of individuals, they not only boost morale but also set a benchmark for excellence, fostering a culture of acknowledgment and appreciation that resonates throughout the organization.

The emergence of employee communities within these online well-being platforms is a testament to the transformative power of technology in democratizing communication and making it more inclusive. These digital communities act as open forums where transparency is not just encouraged but is inherent, allowing for a free flow of information and feedback across hierarchical levels. In such an environment, employees feel heard and valued, enhancing their sense of belonging and commitment to the organization. Moreover, the data generated from these interactions offer invaluable insights into employee sentiments, serving as a barometer for the organizational climate. Employers and leaders can analyze this data to discern employee well-being, job satisfaction, and engagement patterns. It also offers a lens through which to view the collective health of the company, spotlighting areas where interventions may be necessary to bolster productivity or address underlying issues that could impede progress.

These online communities are not just about work-related discourse; they encapsulate the holistic nature of employee well-being by encompassing discussions about personal growth, work-life balance, and mental health. By providing a space where professional and personal narratives intersect, these platforms acknowledge the multifaceted nature of employees as professionals, individuals, parents, partners, and community members. This holistic approach is crucial in today's high-pressure work environments, as it underscores the importance of nurturing all aspects of an employee's life to achieve a harmonious balance, which can lead to enhanced productivity and innovation.

As these digital communities thrive, they foster an organizational culture attuned to the rhythms of their workforce, agile in their responses, and empathetic in their leadership. The interactive and collaborative nature of these platforms encourages a sense of ownership among employees, empowering them to take an active role in shaping their work environment and the culture of their organization. The collective intelligence that emerges from these shared spaces can guide strategic decisions, inform policy changes, and drive initiatives that resonate with the workforce's evolving needs. In essence, the digital transformation of workplace communication has catalyzed a cultural shift, ushering in an era of increased engagement, heightened transparency, and a deeper understanding of the human element in technology-driven workplaces.

Integrating digital tools into workplace communication has birthed vibrant communities that enhance transparency, foster a culture of recognition, and provide a holistic support system for the modern workforce. These platforms serve as microcosms of the organization, reflecting its values, ambitions, and the collective spirit of its people. They are the pulse points where the heartbeats of employee well-being and organizational health can be monitored, understood, and nurtured, ensuring that the company moves forward not as a mere collection of individuals but as a cohesive, well-informed, and empathetic community.

PROVIDING EXPERT ASSISTANCE

Many contemporary applications now offer skill enhancement opportunities through online courses and specialized online or offline coaching tailored to specific industrial subfields. Employers can leverage these digital platforms to offer employees upskilling programs, enabling them to progress within the company or excel in specific tasks or projects. Additionally, access to virtual libraries and educational resources that support employees' skill development is another valuable aspect of these training platforms. Exploring and integrating cutting-edge social technologies to boost employee well-being within the corporate landscape is an essential strategic move for contemporary enterprises. With the workforce undergoing constant transformation, coupled with the growing prevalence of remote and hybrid work setups, it becomes imperative for organizations to adjust their focus toward employee welfare. Below, we outline crucial considerations for those delving into this area:

1. Understanding Employee Well-Being: Commence by defining the multifaceted facets of well-being within your organization, encompassing physical health, mental and emotional equilibrium, job satisfaction, and work-life harmony.
2. Identifying Technological Solutions: Thoroughly research and pinpoint social technologies that have the potential to foster a positive impact on employee well-being. Examples include:
   a. Mental Health Applications: These offer tools to help employees manage stress, anxiety, and other mental health challenges.
   b. Wellness Platforms: Utilize platforms that provide fitness challenges, nutritional guidance, and stress-alleviation techniques
   c. Collaborative Tools: Implement communication and collaboration solutions that facilitate team engagement, especially within remote or hybrid work settings.
   d. Feedback and Survey Instruments: Employ tools for gathering regular employee feedback, enabling data-driven enhancements.
   e. AI-Driven Insights: Explore AI-driven platforms that provide valuable insights into employee sentiment and well-being.
3. Data Privacy and Security: When adopting social technology, prioritize safeguarding data privacy and security. Ensure employee data is handled in compliance with relevant laws and regulations, such as GDPR or HIPAA.
4. Change Management: Successful social technology integration necessitates dedicated change management efforts. Effectively communicate the benefits of these tools to employees, provide training, and offer ongoing support.

5. Well-Being Programs: Integrate technology into well-being programs that promote healthy practices, stress management, and work-life equilibrium. Encourage employees to incorporate these tools into their daily routines.

6. Measuring Impact: Establish clear key performance indicators (KPIs) to gauge the influence of social technology on employee well-being. This could involve tracking metrics such as absenteeism and employee engagement scores and adopting well-being apps.

7. Feedback Loops: Create mechanisms that enable employees to provide feedback on the efficacy of the technology and its impact on their overall well-being. Employ this feedback to iterate and refine technology solutions.

8. Personalization: Acknowledge that employees possess varying needs and preferences. Strive to personalize social technology solutions to align with individual well-being objectives.

9. Continuous Improvement: The business environment is dynamic. Continuously update and adapt your technology solutions to address evolving employee requirements and expectations.

10. Leadership Commitment: Secure endorsement and commitment from top leadership for these initiatives. Leadership support shapes the organization's culture and attitude toward employee well-being.

11. Employee Participation: Involve employees in the selection and design of well-being initiatives. Their input is invaluable in ensuring that technology solutions remain pertinent and efficacious.

12. Legal and Ethical Considerations: Be mindful of potential legal and ethical issues, such as monitoring employee well-being without their consent. Seek counsel from legal and HR experts to ensure adherence to relevant regulations.

Problem Statement: Welfare is a comprehensive term encompassing the overall well-being of individuals, including their physical, emotional, ethical, and mental aspects. The concept of welfare is subjective and varies across time, space, regions, or countries. In the context of labor welfare, it pertains to the initiatives undertaken by trade unions, employers, and various governmental and non-governmental organizations to ensure the well-being of workers. Many companies strive to meet the welfare needs of their employees by providing adequate facilities and services. This project aims to examine and evaluate the labor welfare measures implemented in Nahar Nilgiris.

Need for Study: The study explores the importance of welfare benefits in contemporary organizations. In today's dynamic work environment, it is crucial to keep employees motivated through diverse measures and initiatives. Such efforts foster employees' strong sense of affiliation and accountability towards the organization. This study needs to examine the welfare benefits offered by companies and understand their impact on employee well-being and engagement. By investigating these aspects, the study aims to gain insights into the current state of welfare benefits and their significance in creating a positive work environment at Nahar Nilgiris, Ooty.

The Scope of Study: The objective of this study is to assess the level of employee satisfaction regarding health, safety, and welfare measures provided by Nahar Nilgiris, Ooty. The scope of this research, titled "Employee Welfare Facilities," is limited to the specific location of Nahar Nilgiris in Ooty, and its findings cannot be generalized to other branches of Nahar. Identifying areas of improvement in the welfare provisions, the outcomes of this study are expected to contribute to enhancing the performance of the human resource management department.

OBJECTIVE OF STUDY

- This research examines the current welfare facilities offered to Nahar Nilgiris, Ooty employees.
- To assess the overall satisfaction level of employees regarding welfare programs.
- The aim is to establish a correlation between statutory and non-statutory welfare activities.
- This study aims to gather employees' opinions regarding providing welfare and social security benefits and assess the adequacy of these facilities.
- This study aims to determine the level of satisfaction or dissatisfaction among employees regarding various welfare and social security benefits.
- This study aims to provide suitable and meaningful recommendations to the management for enhancing welfare and social security benefits to enhance employees' overall quality of life.

The Importance of Study: This study aims to examine and comprehend the welfare measures implemented by Nahar. It seeks to assess the employees' awareness of the various facilities provided by the company. The study aims to provide valuable insights into the welfare facilities and services offered by Nahar Nilgiris, offering a comprehensive understanding of its practices. The findings of this study can assist the company in developing future strategies and practices to enhance employee motivation. The geographic focus of the study is limited to Nahar Nilgiris, Ooty.

THE LIMITATIONS OF STUDY

- Due to time constraints, the project work was limited to a sample size of 100 employees.
- Certain questions elicited incomplete or inaccurate responses from the respondents due to their inability or unwillingness to provide a comprehensive answer.
- Due to the data collection method being a questionnaire, many employees opted not to respond.
- As the respondents answered the queries based on their memory, personal bias is possible.

The Area of Study: This project, i.e., "Employee welfare in Nahar," is done under the head of "management" in Ooty, the district of Nilgiris.

REVIEW OF LITERATURE

Devina & Gupta (2012) identified welfare facilities and employee satisfaction level of welfare facilities adopted at Bosch company in Bangalore. The study reveals that the company predominantly offers welfare facilities such as medical services, a canteen, a conducive working environment, and safety measures. Additionally, it indicates that most employees express satisfaction with welfare facilities implemented by the company for their well-being.

Reenu & Panwar (2013) revealed that employees derive satisfaction from their job roles and the diverse facilities the companies provide. The workers offer their utmost support for the betterment of the company. The human resource department is responsible for managing the entire workforce within the company. Management ensures employees receive comprehensive safety, health, and welfare measures to enhance their performance and create a conducive working environment.

Shrinivas (2013) states employee welfare encompasses many services, benefits, and facilities provided to the organization's employees. This study sheds light on the concept of welfare measures and emphasizes the employees' perception of the statutory welfare measures offered by the Donimalai Iron Ore Mine in Bellary.

Abbassy (2020) states that promoting employee efficiency, health, safety, and welfare is crucial. The employer's implementation of diverse welfare measures will promptly influence the workers' health, physical and mental efficiency, alertness, morale, and overall productivity. This, in turn, contributes to heightened levels of productivity.

Gupta (2021a) concluded that communication significantly enhances employee satisfaction. Satisfied employees are known to exhibit high levels of morale. It is worth noting that satisfaction does not solely rely on welfare measures and work experience. Therefore, it is recommended that companies offer sufficient welfare measures without overburdening themselves with excessive costs in an attempt to gain a competitive advantage and proclaim themselves as the most desirable company. Other factors such as effective and transparent communication, motivating incentives, and empowering employees should also be considered to elevate employee satisfaction.

From a literature perspective, the study by Abbassy & Abo-Alnadr (2019) offers insightful findings about the welfare practices within retail stores. Their research reveals that these stores go beyond providing just intramural facilities; they also extend their reach to include extramural welfare amenities. These amenities are designed to enhance employees' health and living standards and encompass a broader spectrum of welfare, incorporating both internal workplace benefits and external support services. The study highlights that such comprehensive welfare facilities contribute significantly to the performance of the employees. When employees are well-cared for, they tend to perform their jobs more effectively, leading to increased organizational efficiency and effectiveness. The research implies a direct correlation between the welfare measures provided and the organization's overall success, suggesting that employee welfare is a matter of ethical employment practice and a strategic business consideration.

Similarly, the research by Gupta (2021b) examines the welfare activities adopted by Steel Plant, emphasizing the plant's effective working environment and the resultant boost in productivity. Their study indicates a variety of welfare schemes in place, such as medical allowances, death relief funds, insurance, and provisions for housing and transportation. Additionally, the presence of a recreation club points to the organization's commitment to its employees' social and leisure needs. This comprehensive approach to employee welfare, encompassing financial and non-financial support systems, showcases the company's dedication to creating an environment that values the holistic well-being of its workforce. These facilities, according to Nanda and Panda, are not mere perks but are instrumental in fostering an atmosphere where employees can thrive professionally and personally, thus directly contributing to the enhanced productivity of the plant.

Mert (2022) contributes to the body of literature by affirming the importance of a wide range of welfare facilities in the context of employee satisfaction and organizational productivity. They underscore the premise that providing employee welfare services is a crucial determinant of an organization's effectiveness. According to this literature, welfare measures catalyze improving job performance, ultimately driving the organization's success. These findings resonate with the growing body of research that links employee well-being with performance outcomes, suggesting that organizations that invest in comprehensive welfare programs not only enhance the quality of life for their employees but also reap the benefits of a more productive and efficient workforce.

RESEARCH METHODOLOGY

The Collection of Data: The collection of data methods employed in this study include primary data and secondary data. The data taken in this study is of a descriptive and qualitative nature, obtained through the primary data collection method.

Questionnaire Method: In this research work, a structured questionnaire is utilized to gather information from diverse employees. Additionally, some information is collected through the use of unstructured questions. The secondary data in this study is obtained through references to manuals, books, journals, and the Nahar Nilgiris' website. This information encompasses details regarding the diverse welfare facilities offered under different acts.

Analysis of Data: For this study, a sampling approach was adopted, targeting 75% of the employees employed at Nahar Nilgiris, Ooty. A sample size of 100 employees from the organization was selected using a random sampling technique.

The Technique for Data Analysis: This study analyzes data using a simple technique, specifically the percentage method. The percentage method is utilized to make comparisons between two or more criteria and describe relationships within the data. To calculate the percentage of respondents, divide the number by the total number of respondents and then multiply the result by 100. The weighted average method is:

DATA COLLECTION TOOLS

- Survey Methodology
- Fieldwork

SAMPLE DESIGN FOR THE STUDY

- **Sampling Size:** 100 Respondents
- **Sampling Unit**: Employees of Nahar Nilgiris

Analysis and Interpretation: A questionnaire survey method was employed to collect data from 100 respondents employed within the organization. Special attention was given to framing questions based on the study's objectives, primarily identifying the Labour Welfare Measures in Nahar Nilgiris. The gathered data was analyzed using the percentage method and tabulation method. Tables were prepared based on the questionnaire responses, and graphs were used to visually represent the data when necessary. The subsequent section presents the interpretations derived from the data collected.

Table 1 presents the survey results in which respondents were asked to give their opinion on a particular subject. The opinions are categorized into four levels: Excellent, Good, Satisfactory, and Poor. The data indicates the number of respondents selected for each opinion category and the corresponding percentage of the total respondents. Out of 100 respondents, half rated the subject as 'Excellent,' which is the highest approval rating. This category has the greatest number of respondents, indicating a positive reception. The 'Good' category is the second most popular opinion, with 40 respondents representing it, which accounts for 40% of the total. This suggests that a significant portion of the surveyed population found the subject favorable, but not to the extent of the 'Excellent' rating. A smaller group of 10 respondents holds the' Satisfactory' opinion, making up 10% of the total. This reflects a moderate level of acceptance or contentment with the subject.

Table 1. Opinions about overall welfare

Opinions	No. of Respondents	% of Respondents
Excellent	50	50%
Good	40	40%
Satisfactory	10	10%
Poor	0	0%
Total	100	100%

Interestingly, none of the respondents rated the subject as 'Poor,' showing no negative responses in this survey. The survey results indicate a positive overall reception, with 90% of respondents rating the subject as either 'Excellent' or 'Good,' 10% finding it 'Satisfactory,' and no negative feedback.

Interpretation: The above table reveals that 50% of the respondents feel that welfare facilities provided by the company on the whole are excellent; 40% feel it's good; 10% of them are satisfied, and none of them are dissatisfied. Figure 1 shows that the company cares for its employees. It fosters loyalty towards the organization and aids employees in working efficiently.

Table 2 appears to be a summary of survey results or an evaluation of a company's facilities and welfare provisions, where different aspects have been rated in terms of quality (Excellent, Good, Satisfactory, Poor) and then given a numerical score. The percentages at the top (40%, 35%, 0%, 0%) might correspond to the importance given to each rating category, but since there's no explicit explanation, this is a bit unclear.

Each row represents a different aspect of the company's welfare system, such as "Approach of the company towards Welfare," "Salary," "Working hours," etc. The numbers in each category (40, 32, 28, 0, etc.) probably indicate the percentage of respondents who rated that aspect in each quality category or could be the score assigned to the company by an evaluation process. The "Average" column is likely the mean score for that aspect across all categories, but it's unclear how this average was calculated. The "Weighted average" column reflects the overall quality, considering the different weights for the quality categories (possibly the percentages mentioned at the beginning). For instance, "Approach of the company towards Welfare" has a high score of "Excellent" and "Good" but none in "Poor," leading to a weighted average of 11.2.

On the other hand, the "Grievance cell" scored 100 in "Excellent" and nothing in the other categories. This may be why its weighted average is 0, suggesting that the calculation might be inverted or a table misunderstanding. Overall, this table will likely provide a quantitative assessment of the company's welfare facilities, with higher weighted averages indicating better performance in those areas. The exact methodology for calculating the averages must be clarified to fully understand the table.

Figure 1. Chart showing opinions about overall welfare activities

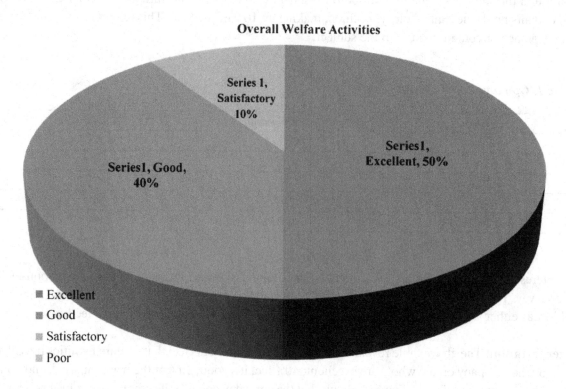

Table 2. Opinions about overall welfare activities in the weighted average method

Facility	40% Excellent	35% Good	0% Satisfactory	0% Poor	Average	Weighted Average
The approach of the Company Toward Welfare	40	32	28	0	25	11.2
Salary	56	35	9	0	25	12.25
Working hours	80	20	0	0	25	7
Leave availability	75	15	10	0	25	5.25
Transport facility	0	35	55	15	26.25	12.25
First aid and medical facilities	28	42	30	0	25	14.7
Service charges	35	23	20	22	25	8.05
Accommodation	15	60	20	5	25	21
Bonus	95	5	0	0	25	1.75
Training	75	20	5	0	25	7
Uniform	85	15	0	0	25	5.25
Comfortless in working Environment	70	30	0	0	25	10.5
Grievance cell	100	0	0	0	25	0
Overall welfare facilities	50	40	10	0	25	14

Figure 2. Visualizing employee satisfaction and areas for improvement across various company welfare facilities

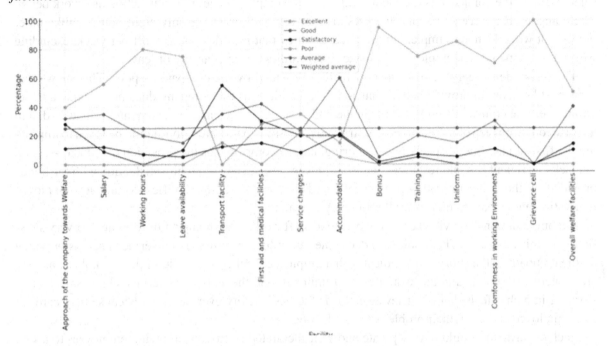

Figure 2 illustrates the distribution of ratings across various welfare facilities in a company, with each facility plotted on the x-axis and the percentage ratings on the y-axis. The categories' Excellent', 'Good,' 'Satisfactory,' 'Poor,' and 'Average' are shown as distinct lines, revealing trends and outliers in the company's welfare offerings. For instance, the 'Grievance cell' stands out with a 100% 'Excellent' rating, significantly higher than other facilities, and consequently, it has a weighted average of 0, reflecting no need for improvement. In contrast, 'Accommodation' has the highest weighted average score, indicating it is an area requiring attention despite a high 'Good' rating. 'Bonus' and 'Working hours' display strong 'Excellent' ratings, suggesting employee satisfaction in these areas.

Conversely, the 'Transport facility' appears to have a more even distribution across 'Good' and 'Satisfactory,' with a notable 'Poor' rating, suggesting mixed feelings about this service. The 'Average' line remains constant as it represents a baseline score for comparison. The 'Overall welfare facilities' score shows a balance between 'Excellent' and 'Good,' with a weighted average that indicates room for improvement. The collected data from the questionnaire has been analyzed and interpreted by creating tables and charts. The raw data from the questionnaire was organized into tables based on different questions, which served as the basis for generating charts to visually represent the collected data.

DISCUSSIONS AND FINDINGS

During the study, it was found that A significant majority of respondents exhibited awareness regarding both statutory and non-statutory Employee Welfare Facilities provided by their company. It is found that the company pays a better salary to everyone. It also provides the women a basic pay of Rs.9500, as mentioned under the government's policies. Hence, we observe that most employees have rated the salary paid by the company as excellent. This helps the employees get job satisfaction and work better. The company has three shifts, and workers are satisfied with working only eight hours, unlike other hotels that work 12 hours. Implementing a leave policy that includes one day off per week, excluding weekends, contributes to employees' satisfaction regarding the availability of leave.

The respondents feel that the transport facility provided by the company is poor. This shows that care must be taken to provide better transportation facilities as the company does not provide a travel allowance. The company's provided medicine and first aid provisions are inadequate, primarily due to the inadequate upkeep of medications and first-aid provisions. More attention should be given to improving the first-aid facilities, especially considering that the company has the provision of a doctor-on-call but lacks sufficient first-aid resources. Most employees have expressed their satisfaction with the bonus provided by the company, rating it as excellent. This positive rating significantly impacts employee motivation and enhances their overall efficiency at work.

Accommodation is provided only to the second shift workers, so many employees are not very satisfied with this approach. The employees deem the rating for the uniform and service charges provided by the company satisfactory. This indicates that employees feel comfortable in the workplace, as they are content with the quality and availability of uniforms and the associated service charges. Everyone working in Nahar feels that the grievance cell is the best facility ever provided because they care for each employee and solve their problems immediately.

Each department should have separate and well-facilitated restrooms, allowing employees to take a break and relax from their busy schedules. Workers should be provided with travel allowances, or transport facilities should be arranged for convenience. Employees should be educated about the HR department's practical workings, considering its pivotal role in any organization. Providing medical facilities is crucial to minimize absenteeism and maintain employees' overall well-being and immunization. Enhancing first aid facilities to ensure prompt and effective response to any medical emergencies is equally important. Accommodation can be given to employees other than second shift employees as well.

CONCLUSION

Technology has become critical to global business operations, enhancing employee understanding, productivity, workload management, and innovation. The pandemic has further accelerated the integration of digital platforms in workplaces, as organizations have adopted advanced tech solutions to provide comprehensive wellness programs to their employees across both digital and traditional environments to improve workforce well-being. The study highlights Nahar Nilgiris' commendable employee welfare facilities but notes there's potential for further enhancement. The recommendation is for regular welfare awareness initiatives, which are crucial in fostering employee satisfaction and, by extension, productivity. Employee contentment is central to a company's performance and market competitiveness, with employee welfare playing a key role in better outcomes and market standing. Thus, focusing on labour welfare is imperative for a company's success. Leveraging new social technologies in welfare practices can improve the work atmosphere, employee satisfaction, and the company's overall achievement. Adopting innovative social technology for employee welfare demonstrates a long-term investment in a supportive work environment, leading to increased productivity, staff retention, and overall organizational success.

LIMITATIONS

Investigating innovative social technology for elevating employee well-being in a business context presents several limitations. The rapid pace of technological evolution can render findings obsolete shortly after a study's completion, reducing the long-term applicability of the research. The diversity of business cultures and structures means that a one-size-fits-all approach is unlikely to be effective, limiting the generalizability of any single intervention. The subjective nature of "well-being" also poses a challenge, as it is influenced by a myriad of personal, cultural, and socioeconomic factors, making it difficult to measure and compare across different populations. Privacy concerns are also paramount; collecting data on employee well-being through social technology can be perceived as intrusive and may face resistance. Implementing social technologies may require significant organizational change management, and without proper strategy and support, such initiatives may fail to be adopted or even inadvertently reduce employee morale. Lastly, there is a risk that the technology could exacerbate existing inequalities if access to or the ability to utilize these tools is not evenly distributed among employees.

FUTURE SCOPE

The future scope of investigating innovative social technology for elevating employee well-being in the business context is vast and multidimensional. Integrating advanced social technologies stands at the forefront of this endeavor as organizations continue to navigate the complex interplay between employee satisfaction and productivity. In the coming years, we can anticipate a surge in the development and deployment of AI-driven platforms that analyze employee behavior and feedback in real-time, providing tailored wellness programs and interventions. Exploring virtual reality (VR) environments for stress reduction and collaborative workspaces will likely gain momentum, offering immersive experiences promoting mental health. Gamification techniques will become increasingly sophisticated, turning routine tasks into engaging challenges that boost morale and foster a culture of well-being. Additionally, the rise of wearable technology will enable continuous health monitoring, alerting employees and employers to potential burnout or health issues before they escalate. The ethical considerations surrounding privacy and data security will also evolve, necessitating robust frameworks to protect employee information while harnessing the benefits of these technologies. As we look to the future, the role of social technology in enhancing employee well-being will become a critical factor in organizational success, driving innovation in human resource strategies and workplace design.

REFERENCES

Abbassy, M. M. (2020). Opinion mining for Arabic customer feedback using machine learning. *Journal of Advanced Research in Dynamical and Control Systems*, *12*(SP3), 209–217. doi:10.5373/JARDCS/V12SP3/20201255

Abbassy, M. M., & Abo-Alnadr, A. (2019). Rule-based emotion AI in Arabic customer review. *International Journal of Advanced Computer Science and Applications*, *10*(9). Advance online publication. doi:10.14569/IJACSA.2019.0100932

Abbassy, M. M., & Ead, W. M. (2020). Intelligent Greenhouse Management System. In *2020 6th International Conference on Advanced Computing and Communication Systems (ICACCS)*. IEEE.

Alabdullah, T.T.Y., Ahmed, E.R. (2021). New Insights to Investigate the Impact of Internal Control Mechanisms on Firm Performance: A Study in Oman. *Riset Akuntansi dan Keuangan Indonesia, 6*(2).

Alabdullah, T. T. Y., Al Fakhri, I., Ahmed, E. R., & Jebna, A. K. (2021b). Empirical Study of The Influence of Board of Directors' Feature on Firm Performance. *Russian Journal of Agricultural and Socio-Economic Sciences, 11*(119), 137–146. doi:10.18551/rjoas.2021-11.16

Alabdullah, T. T. Y., Al-Fakhri, I., Ahmed, E. R., & Kanaan-Jebna, A. (2021a). Corporate Governance System and Firm Financial Performance. *Acta Scientific Computer Sciences, 4*(6), 97–103.

Ángeles, C. (2022). The legal-community obligations of the large digital service provider platforms in the metaverse era. *Cuad. Cuad. Transnational Law, 14*(2), 294–318.

Ángeles, C. (2023). The guardians of access to the metaverse. (Re)thinking the Competition Law of the European Union. *Cuad. Cuad. Transnational Law, 15*(1), 275–296.

Devina, U., & Gupta, A. (2012). Morale, Welfare measure, job satisfaction: The key mantras for gaining competitive edge. *International Journal of Physical and Social Sciences, 2*(7), 80–94.

Ead, W., & Abbassy, M. (2018). *Intelligent systems of machine learning approaches for developing E-services portals*. EAI Endorsed Transactions on Energy Web. doi:10.4108/eai.2-12-2020.167292

Ead, W. M., & Abbassy, M. M. (2022). A general cyber hygiene approach for financial analytical environment. In *Financial Data Analytics* (pp. 369–384). Springer International Publishing. doi:10.1007/978-3-030-83799-0_13

Gupta, R. K. (2021a). A study on occupational health hazards among construction workers in India. *International Journal of Enterprise Network Management, 12*(4), 325–339. doi:10.1504/IJENM.2021.119663

Gupta, R. K. (2021b). Adoption of mobile wallet services: an empirical analysis. *International Journal of Intellectual Property Management, 12*(3), 341 – 353. doi:10.1504/IJIPM.2021.10035526

Kanaan-Jebna, A., Baharudi, A. S., & Alabdullah, T. T. Y. (2022). Entrepreneurial Orientation, Market Orientation, Managerial Accounting and Manufacturing SMEs Satisfaction. *Journal of Accounting Science, 6*(1), 1–14. doi:10.21070/jas.v6i1.1590

Köseoğlu, D., Ead, S., & Abbassy, W. M. (2022). Basics of Financial Data Analytics. In *Financial Data Analytics* (pp. 23–57). Springer International Publishing. doi:10.1007/978-3-030-83799-0_2

Mert, I. (2022). *Assessment of Accounting Evaluation Practices, A Research-Based Review of Turkey and Romania. Springer Cham.* https://link.springer.com/book/10.1007/978-3-030-98486-1

Ramu, V. B., & Yeruva, A. R. (2023). Optimising AIOps system performance for e-commerce and online retail businesses with the ACF model. *International Journal of Intellectual Property Management, 13*(3/4), 412–429. doi:10.1504/IJIPM.2023.134064

Reenu, M., & Panwar, J. S. (2013). Current trends in employee welfare schemes in Udaipur Retail Sector. *International Journal of Scientific Research Review, 2*(2), 44–54.

Shrinivas, K. T. (2013). A Study on employee welfare facilities adopted at Bosch Limited, Bangalore. Bangalore. *Research Journal of Management Sciences*, 2(12), 7–11.

Yeruva, A. R., & Ramu, V. B. (2023). AIOps research innovations, performance impact and challenges faced. *International Journal of System of Systems Engineering*, 13(3), 229–247. doi:10.1504/IJSSE.2023.133013

Chapter 7
Data–Driven, Intelligent Business Learning About UPASI Services and Tea–Growers' Sustainability

H. Hajra

Bharath Institute of Higher Education and Research, India

G. Jayalakshmi

Bharath Institute of Higher Education and Research, India

ABSTRACT

The tea industry faces significant operational and financial challenges in the competitive global market, necessitating focused research to support its growth and sustainability. Access to robust data is critical for convincing management to adopt new strategies, and this study aims to provide valuable data for the industry's advancement. The United Planters Association of Southern India (UPASI), representing tea and other plantation crops in Tamil Nadu, Kerala, and Karnataka since 1893, plays a crucial role. The rich biodiversity of the Nilgiris provides an ideal environment for tea and other crops. Still, traditional farming methods often rely on inefficient information dissemination through various means, resulting in outdated or missing critical data. This gap leads to poor planning, unsustainable farming practices, environmental damage, and reduced farmer income.

INTRODUCTION

Established in 1893 during the peak of British colonial rule in India, the United Planters Association of South India (UPASI) was primarily an organization devoted to furthering the interests of British planters, with a particular focus on tea planters in South India. The founding members of UPASI, who were of foreign origin, recognized the necessity of fostering unity among planters from various regions and crops. They initiated the pyramid structure, which began with the district Planters Association of

DOI: 10.4018/979-8-3693-0049-7.ch007

India. Since its inception, the connection between UPASI (2021) and scientific research on plantation crops has been inseparable. The UPASI falls under the Ministry of Commerce. The UPASI (2021) is a crucial link between the government and the industry, playing a vital role in formulating policies for the sector. Through a Krishi Vigyan Kendra, the association runs voluntary socio-economic schemes encompassing family welfare, health education, tea cultivation, and horticulture training. Additionally, they educate small and marginal farmers on agricultural advancements and technologies (Babu, 2004).

The association's primary objectives are to disseminate knowledge of the planting and plantation industry, foster unity and concerted actions among its members in all matters concerning their collective interests and safeguard the interests of various planting industries in southern India on a global scale (Babu, 2005a). Differences that notwithstanding is the micro level of the approach of the adjustments to the changing world and its times, shifting government styles, approaches, and the changing expectations and aspirations of those connected with the planting industry in the Nilgiris contributed to the acceptance of UPASI's representative character in the region (Babu, 2005b). Currently, the UPASI Tea Research Foundation (UPASI TRF) includes the Tea Research Institute of Valparai and its six regional (Advisory) centers located in Coonoor, Gudalur, Koppa, Munnar, Meppadi, and Vandiperiyar, as mentioned earlier.

Like many others, the tea industry has significantly transformed in recent years thanks to data-driven intelligence (Ramamoorthy et al., 2012). This shift towards data-driven decision-making has provided valuable insights and strategies for businesses in the tea industry, revolutionizing how they operate and engage with consumers. By leveraging advanced analytics tools and technologies, tea companies have been able to delve deep into the nuances of their market, thereby gaining a competitive edge in an ever-evolving landscape.

One of the key learnings in this regard has been the paramount importance of personalization. Through the meticulous collection and comprehensive analysis of consumer data, tea businesses have been able to tailor their products to individual preferences, creating unique tea blends and flavors that resonate with their target audience. Gone are the days of one-size-fits-all teas; today, it's all about crafting a tea experience that feels tailor-made for each customer. This personalized approach has proven to be a game-changer in the industry, as it enhances customer satisfaction and drives brand loyalty and repeat business (Babu et al., 2007).

In the era of big data, tea companies have harnessed the power of analytics to gain a deeper understanding of customer preferences. They track everything from the types of teas customers purchase most frequently to the specific flavors and aromas they prefer (Hudson & Durairaj, 2004). This granular level of insight allows tea businesses to develop new product offerings that align precisely with their customers' tastes, ensuring a delightful and customized tea-drinking experience. For example, a tea company might use data to discover that a particular demographic of customers prefers herbal blends with floral notes and a touch of sweetness. With this knowledge, they can create a signature blend that caters to this group, increasing their market share and customer satisfaction.

Data-driven intelligence has also played a pivotal role in guiding tea companies regarding market trends. By continuously monitoring and analyzing market data, these businesses can quickly adapt to changing consumer preferences and stay ahead of the competition. For instance, when health-conscious consumers started seeking teas with functional benefits, such as immunity-boosting or stress-relief properties, data-driven insights allowed tea companies to swiftly develop and market such products. This agility in responding to trends has kept tea businesses relevant and positioned them as trendsetters in the industry.

Another critical aspect of data-driven transformation within the tea industry is optimizing the supply chain. Efficient supply chain management is essential for any business, and tea companies are no exception. Through data analytics, tea businesses can monitor and optimize every aspect of their supply chain, from sourcing tea leaves to distribution and logistics. This not only helps in cost reduction but also ensures the freshness and quality of tea products, ultimately benefiting both the company and the end consumer.

Integrating artificial intelligence (AI) and machine learning (ML) has enhanced the predictive capabilities of tea companies. By analyzing historical sales data, weather patterns, and other relevant factors, AI and ML algorithms can forecast demand more accurately, enabling businesses to plan their production and inventory management more efficiently. This predictive analytics-driven approach minimizes waste and ensures customers access their favorite teas when they want them, enhancing overall satisfaction (Kumar & Radhakrishnan, 2012).

Because of product personalization, data-driven intelligence has transformed the tea industry's marketing and customer engagement strategies. Businesses can now create highly targeted marketing campaigns by segmenting their customer base and tailoring messaging to each group's preferences. For example, a tea company may identify a segment of health-conscious consumers and launch a marketing campaign emphasizing the health benefits of their teas. Simultaneously, they may run a separate campaign for another segment of customers more interested in unique flavors and tea experiences. This level of precision in marketing increases the effectiveness of campaigns and fosters a deeper connection between the brand and its customers.

The tea industry's journey into data-driven intelligence has ushered in a new era of innovation, efficiency, and customer-centricity. Collecting, analyzing, and acting upon data has empowered tea businesses to personalize their products, adapt to market trends, optimize supply chains, and enhance customer engagement. As technology advances and data becomes even more accessible, the tea industry will likely continue transforming, offering tea enthusiasts an ever-expanding world of personalized and delightful tea experiences.

Data-driven intelligence has enabled tea companies to forecast demand accurately. Businesses can better plan their production schedules and inventory management by examining historical sales data, seasonal fluctuations, and market dynamics. This has reduced waste and cost savings, making the tea industry more sustainable and profitable.

KEY POINTS ON DATA-DRIVEN LEARNING IN THE TEA INDUSTRY

- Consumer Preferences Analysis: Data analytics help tea companies understand customer preferences. Businesses can create products that align with consumer tastes by examining data on flavor choices, tea types, and packaging preferences.
- Market Trends Forecasting: Data-driven insights enable the tea industry to stay ahead of market trends. By analyzing historical sales data and external factors, companies can anticipate shifts in demand and adjust their offerings accordingly.
- Supply Chain Optimization: Data helps in optimizing the supply chain. Tea businesses can reduce waste, cut costs, and improve efficiency by monitoring production, transportation, and inventory data.

- Quality Control: Data-driven quality control is crucial in the tea industry. Sensors and data analysis can help maintain consistent product quality, ensuring that each batch meets the desired standards.
- Customer Segmentation: Data analytics allow companies to segment their customer base. This aids in targeted marketing and product development for different demographic groups.
- Price Optimization: Businesses can use data to determine the optimal pricing strategy based on factors like production costs, market demand, and competitor pricing.
- Inventory Management: Efficient inventory management is possible through data-driven forecasting. This minimizes overstocking or understocking issues, ensuring products are readily available when needed.
- Marketing Campaigns: Data-driven insights can guide marketing campaigns. Understanding which platforms and content resonate with the target audience helps create effective marketing strategies.
- Feedback Analysis: Customer feedback and reviews can be analyzed using natural language processing and sentiment analysis to improve products and services.
- Sustainability Efforts: Data can help track and reduce the environmental footprint of tea production, making it more sustainable. This includes monitoring resource usage and waste management.
- Compliance and Quality Assurance: Data-driven tools can assist in ensuring that tea products meet regulatory and quality standards, reducing the risk of recalls and legal issues.
- Competitor Analysis: Data can be used to analyze the activities of competitors, helping businesses identify opportunities and threats in the market.
- Predictive Maintenance: For tea processing equipment, data-driven maintenance schedules can prevent breakdowns and reduce downtime, ensuring consistent production.
- Operational Efficiency: Real-time data monitoring can highlight inefficiency in the production process, allowing for timely improvements.
- Expansion and New Markets: Data analysis can identify potential regions or markets where the tea industry can expand based on consumer preferences and market demand.

ACTIVATES IN THE ASSOCIATION

The association's operations encompass economic research, market intelligence, and industrial relations. It is situated at Coonoor at Glenview. This association is working for the needs of the people and:

- Statistics
- Publications
- Reports
- Tea Research
- Events

PRODUCTS OF THE ASSOCIATION

There is a list of products taken care of by the United Planters Association of Southern India, which are as follows.

- Tea
- Coffee
- Pepper

NEED OF UPASI IN NILGIRIS

- The United Planters Association of Southern came to the Nilgiris because of the geographical condition and the atmosphere of the Nilgiri climate; there is a rich soil, i.e., The laterite soil, which is very helpful in growing tea and coffee, and it gives a rich taste for tea as well as coffee.
- To the growth of the betterment of the planters and for the betterment of the plantation sector.
- And it does need the requirements for the farmers and their children, like getting loans and scholarships, etc.
- There is a high growth of coffee, etc., and enough sufficiency to export the commodities.

THE MISSION OF THE ASSOCIATION

There are five missions of the association

- The objective is to promote, spread, and disseminate knowledge on the planting and plantation industry.
- The main objective is to encourage trade and commerce within the industry and support its overall development.
- The association's tasks include collecting, classifying, circulating, and publishing statistics and other relevant information concerning distribution, finance, employment, and various conditions.
- UPASI represents the interests of various planting industries operating in southern India.
- The objective is to foster united or coordinated action among members in all matters concerning the association.

There are five members of the United Planters Association, and they are as follows.

- Estate Members
- Small Growers Members
- Firm Members
- Association Members
- Retired Planters Members

The UPASI general meeting is scheduled to convene once a year at a designated time and location, as determined by the president. During this annual meeting, the members gather to review the annual report of the executive committee and discuss various matters relevant to the association. Before the commencement of the financial year, the United Planters Association (UPASI) holds a general meeting known as the UPASI Budget General Meeting. This meeting takes place at a specific time and location. Every year, UPASI conducts a general meeting, and it talks about the production-consumption imports and exports and, the subsidy and the benefit of the planters and the commodities section. Also, it deals with mostly the subsidies when every planter of the association and the benefit made to the planters.

ASSOCIATIONS AFFILIATED WITH UPASI

Association Before Independence

Five associations before Independence collaborated with the UPASI, which are as follows.

MPA- Mysore Planters Association: The Mysore Planters Association was started in 1864 and was associated with the South Indian Planters Association. The association was first to be founded in Mysore city, where Baba Budan made his legendary contribution to the soil of India. There will be an annual general meeting; they will tell the annual reports, the company's balance sheet, and the association's status as per the Societies Act 1860.

CPA-Codagu Planters Association: Codagu is known as Coorg in the circles during the British period. The association was started in the 1870s, and it is referred to the correspondence between Coorg planters and the government.

CTPA- Central Travancore Planters Association: It was founded in the year 1880 and the plantation of new growth space in the permanent hills and with the growing numbers of planters in the area. The scientific department of tea overall.

TPA- Travancore Planters: The TPA came in the 1880s and held its annual general meeting in Trivandrum, led by the planters working team. This is mainly producing and importing. Exporting tea, coffee, and rubber.

KDPA- Kannan Devan Planters Association: This came in the 19th century, and they were Kannan thevar in the hills. In the earlier years of the Kannan Devan Association, they first met on April 1, 1888. All these associations were associated with the United Planters Association and had played a vital role before Independence.

Currently Affiliated Association After Independence

There are 22 association members of the United Planters Association, and they are as follows.

- All India Coffee Production Merchant Association
- Annamalai Planters Association
- All Indian Coffee Cruer Association
- Association of Planters in Kerala
- Cardamom Planters association
- Central Trancore association
- Codagu planter association
- Coffee exporters association
- Kanyakumari District Planters Association
- Kannan devan Planters association
- Nelliampathhy Planters Association

- Nilgiris Small Grower Association
- The Coonoor Tea Trade Association
- Nilgiris wynaad Planters association
- Shevaroy Planters association
- The Karnataka Planters association
- The Malabar Planters Association
- The Nilgiris Bought -leaf tea manufacture association
- The Nilgiris Planters Association
- The Planters Association Tamil Nadu
- The tea Traders association Coimbatore
- Wayanad Planters association

Place of Work: There are three places of work, and they are as follows:

Nilgiris: The plantation sector in the state was, by good and large, peaceful, and they had a cardinal relationship maintained during the particular year to have a peaceful relationship with all (Table 1).

Table 1. Tea plucking basic wage, 2022-2023

Period	Tea Plucking Basic Wage
Feb/May, 2023	308.21
Oct/ Dec, 2022	310.5
July/Sep, 2022	320.7
Apr/June, 2022	500

Figure 1. A trend analysis of basic wages for tea plucking from approximately April 2022 to May 2023

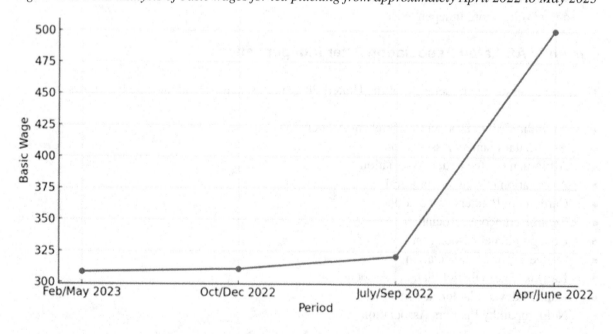

The line graph presents a trend analysis of the basic wages for tea plucking over several periods within 2022 and extending to 2023 (Figure 1). The graph illustrates a significant fluctuation in wages, with the peak observed in the second quarter of 2022 (Apr/June) at a wage of 500 units. Subsequently, there's a notable decrease in the following quarters, with the wage descending to 320.7 in the third quarter (July/Sep), then slightly dropping to 310.5 in the last quarter of the year (Oct/Dec). The first quarter of 2023 (Feb/May) witnessed the lowest wage at 308.21, indicating a potential concern for the tea plucking industry's wage trend. This visual representation is a critical tool for stakeholders to assess wage trends and make informed decisions regarding labor and financial planning within the tea industry.

Karnataka: The labor and industrial relation in the plantation industry of Karnataka was generally peaceful during 2022-2023. The Daily wages of Karnataka workers in coffee, tea, rubber, and fixed crops estates from 1-4-2022 to 31-3-2023 is Rs. 340.68. Their statistics are as follows (Table 2):

Table 2. Daily coffee kgs of the workers in Karnataka in the field

	Kodagu		Hassan
People	Arabic Coffee	Roasted Coffee	Arabic And Roasted
Adult	56 Kgs	80 Kgs	
Adolescence	46 Kgs	65 Kgs	70 Kgs

Table 3. Daily wages of the workers in Karnataka in the field

Base	Slabs Kgs	Incentive	Status
27kgs	28.37	1.05	Good
27 Kgs	15.7	1.02	Low

The job deferrals for the factory workers were 4.00 per day in Karnataka (Table 3).

Kerala: The plantation sector in the state was, by good and large, peaceful, and they had a cardinal relationship maintained during the particular year to have a peaceful relationship with all in and among these states. There were no significant changes in the labour productivity level in the state. The wages in crop wise are given below as follows (Table 4).

Table 4. Dynamics of basic wages for tea and coffee, cardamom, and rubber from April 2022 to May 2023

Period	Tea & Coffee Basic Wage	Cardamom Basic Wage	Rubber Basic Wage
Feb/May, 2023	308.21	337.21	338.21
Oct/ Dec, 2022	310.5	431.31	345.77
July/Sep, 2022	320.7	445.8	400.6
Apr/June, 2022	500	500	500

The graph presents a comparative trend analysis of basic wages for Tea and coffee, Cardamom, and rubber over four distinct periods from April/June 2022 to February/May 2023. It vividly illustrates that the basic wage for all three commodities was uniform at 500 in the earliest time block, April/June 2022. Subsequently, a divergent trend is observed. At the same time, the wages for tea, coffee, and rubber decline moderately over the subsequent periods; the basic wage for Cardamom sees a significant drop between April/June 2022 and July/Sep 2022, followed by a less pronounced decrease moving forward. Oct/Dec 2022 marks the highest discrepancy among the commodities, with Cardamom wages peaking at 431.31, contrasting with tea and coffee at 310.5. As of Feb/May 2023, the wages seem to converge somewhat, yet disparities remain evident, showcasing the volatility and variability in the wages of these commodities.

STATEMENT OF THE PROBLEM

- The tea farmers face financial problems such as wages, scholarships, etc.
- They face a high risk in the working environment in the association.
- The scholarship or scheme the farmers have applied for comes late to them.
- Some of the tea farmers are unaware of the services and the Schemes the association has provided.
- The association faces a lot of problems with the subsidies they get.

OBJECTIVES OF THE STUDY

- To have an awareness of UPSAI and its services.
- To study the needs of tea farmers
- To help them to know about UPASI services schemes and programmes
- To have a clear idea of awareness towards UPASI
- To have an idea of the schemes of UPASI

SCOPE OF THE STUDY

- To have an interest in the study of tea farmers and with their awareness,
- To know about the awareness of its tea farmers.
- To study the schemes provided by the United Planters Association to its farmers.
- To clearly understand the services given by the United Planters Association.
- To have an overall idea about tea farmers and its services, schemes, pieces of training, programmers, etc.

LIMITATIONS OF THE STUDY

- The primary data has been collected by using the questionnaires.
- The sample size was limited to 35
- The area of the study is limited to Coonoor.

REVIEW OF LITERATURE

Grifiths (1967) presents commendable research on the tea industry in India. The author's book mentions that the Indian tea industry emerged in the early 1830s. The study also revealed that the tea industry faced labor-related challenges during its early stages, further exacerbated by the emergence of multiple farmer unions.

Guha (1977) conducted a study focusing on two dimensions and the tea plantation and its economic impact. The special focus of the study was on the awareness of tea farmers. The study also dealt with certain issues, such as the working conditions of the tea farmers. This also created a major issue in the tea industry. The study also dealt with certain political developments with the tea planters.

Khawas, (2011) delved into the plight of tea workers in the hills and shed light on their impoverished conditions, particularly concerning education, sanitation, housing, and health. The research also emphasized the income, livelihood patterns, and alternative skills of the laborers working in the gardens. This study was carried out in three estates and revealed that only 1.3 percent of the tea garden population resided in houses owned by tea farmers.

Asopa, (2007) brought attention to the declining demand for Indian Tea in the global market. To remain competitive, the industry must improve production, marketing, logistics, and product forms. Additionally, the research emphasized the necessity for well-organized production and marketing systems to enable all tea growers to secure a significant place in the global market, as India is one of the major tea-producing countries.

Sarkar, (2008) explores transforming the formal labor market into an informal one within the tea industry. He identifies globalization as the main factor driving this transformation. The study reveals that due to global economic changes, tea plantations faced challenges in overcoming costs, particularly labor costs. Tea estate management adopted strategies to achieve worker flexibility and reduce expenses to address this. However, legal restrictions made it difficult to fully implement these strategies. As a result, the management of tea plantations started adopting manufacturing processes similar to those used by small tea growers. Small growers have limited liability and are only responsible for paying wages to workers as per their requirements. This practice led to a casual workforce and contributed to the shift towards an informal labor market.

Selvaraj & Gopalakrishnan, (2016) said that the industrial relations in the plantations in the Niligiri ill effect on the tea plantation of the industry regions. The study primarily focused on comparing various parameters of industrial relations in the tea industry. It used a paired sample test for its analysis. The study concluded that globalization negatively affected the tea plantation industry, rendering it vulnerable.

Ajayakumar et al., (2005) painted on the living conditions of the tea estate and the tea farmers in the Nilgiris. The study highlighted the wage composition, sanitation, health status, and literacy of workers and their family members. It also briefly covered the living conditions of the workers and their families. The study's findings showed that only 68 percent of the workers expressed satisfaction with the accommodations provided by the planters. Additionally, it was observed that only permanent workers resided in the accommodations provided by the plantation management.

Radhakrishnan et al., (2021) explored that traditional practices in tea farming have heavily relied on disseminating information through extension officers, Farmers Field Schools, mass media, or farmers sharing their own experiences. Unfortunately, vital information often reaches farmers too late or becomes outdated; sometimes, it is completely unavailable. This limited access to information has created an information gap, resulting in poor planning and farming practices, leading to environmental degradation and reduced revenues. To address this issue, tapping into existing information and communication technology can help develop an information system that promotes sustainable farming through timely access to information in the tea farming industry. This paper primarily focuses on designing such a system for the tea farming industry to advance the development of the tea industry.

Gunasundari et al., (2002) analysed that the demand for tea is witnessing a rapid rise in both domestic and international markets. Meeting this growing demand necessitates an increase in tea production in a sustainable manner. Enhancing tea productivity among existing tea farmers emerges as the most viable solution due to limited land availability and the absence of required climatic conditions.

Muraleedharan & Hudson, (2007) aim to analyze the impact of ecological aspects and the growth and efficiency, especially to its farmers. The level of the tea farmers is a little low, and the production and its source play an important role. The management has a good eradication on the level of the tea farmers. The Tea in the Nilgiris plays an important role. The awareness of tea farmers and their wages is limited, and the schemes and services are limited.

RESEARCH METHODOLOGY

This part explains the research methods used in this particular study. The method includes the data source, the study's sample size area, and the tools used for the analysis.

Data Source

- Primary Data
- Secondary Data

Sample Design

A sample of 35 respondent were taken into the study, and their data were collected for the study purpose.

Area of the Study

The area of the study was in Coonoor, the Nilgiris.

Statistical Tools Used in the Dissertation

- Sample Percentage Analysis
- Rank Analysis
- Weighted Average
- Weighted Sum Model
- Mean

Table 5. Awareness level of UPASI

Service	Highly Aware	Aware	Natural	Dis Aware	Highly Dishware	Sum	Mean	Rank
Providing Loans	13 37%)	13 (37%)	9 (26%)	0 (0%)	0 (0%)	144	4.11	5
Providing Subsidies	11 (31%)	8 (23%)	16 (46%)	0 (0%)	0 (0%)	135	3.85	7
Help From the Central Government	22 (63%)	11 (31%)	2 (6%)	0 (0%)	0 (0%)	160	4.57	3
Benefits For Farmers	11 (31%)	20 (57%)	4 (12%)	0 (0%)	0 (0%)	147	4.2	4
Awareness Programs	8 (23%)	14 (40%)	13 (37%)	0 (0%)	0 (0%)	135	3.85	7
Free Trainings	8 (23%)	8 (23%)	16 (46%)	2 (^6%)	1 (2%)	118	3.37	8
Laboratory Service	5 (14%)	18 (51%)	6 (17%)	3 (9%)	3 (9%)	170	4.85	2
Dister Relif	10 (29%)	18 (%!%)	7 (20%)	0 (0%)	0 (0%)	143	4.08	6
Other Service	8 (23%)	13 (37%)	9 (26%)	5 (14%)	0 (0%)	179	5.11	1
Providing Scholarship	18 (51%)	6 (17%)	11 (31%)	0 (0%)	0 (0%)	147	4.2	4

Source- Primary data

ANALYSIS AND INTERPRETATION

Interpretation: The majority of the Respondent belongs to the Other services group, with a 5.11 mean score and a 4.85 mean score of Respondent belonging to the Laboratory services group and a 4.57 mean score of respondents belonging to the Help from Central Government group (Table 5) and next with 4.2 mean score of the Respondents belongs to the group of benefit for farmers and providing scholarship and the Upcoming point is providing loans with 4.11mean score and the next with 4.08mean score of the Respondents belongs to Dister relief group and a group of Respondents belongs to Awareness Programs with 3.85 mean scores and the last goes to the Respondents group of Free training with 3.37 mean score.

The colorful matrix histogram vividly illustrates the levels of public awareness regarding different services (Figure 2). Each color-coded bar represents one of five awareness categories, ranging from 'Highly Awar' to 'Highly Disawar.' The distribution is shown across ten services such as 'Providin-gloans,' 'Subsidies,' and any help from the central government,' among others. The height of the bars indicates the number of responses in each category, revealing patterns in public perception. For instance, 'Help from central government' and 'Laboratory service' display a higher proportion of 'Highly Awar' responses, while 'Free Training' shows a more balanced awareness distribution. No service has many 'Dis Awar' or 'Highly Disawar' responses, indicating a general positive awareness. The histogram is a comparative tool to evaluate the effectiveness of information dissemination for each service (Table 6).

Figure 2. Spectrum of awareness: Evaluating public perception of services

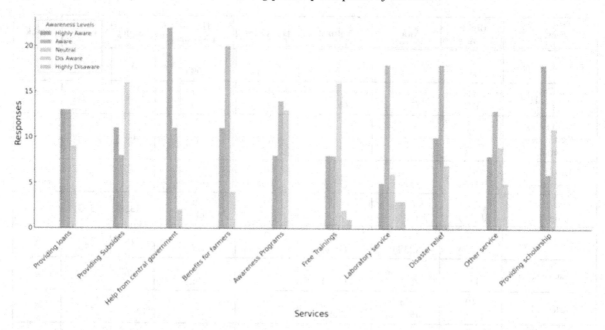

Table 6. Overall rating On UPASI

S. No.	Rating UPASI	Ranks	No of Respondent	Weighted Score	Weighted Amounted	Total Weighted Amounted	Rank
1		1 Rank	3	7	21		
		2 Rank	3	6	18		
		3 Rank	3	5	15		
	Schemes	4 Rank	10	4	40	115	
		5 Rank	3	3	9		
		6 Rank	8	2	16		
		7 Rank	5	1	5		
2		1 Rank	2	7	14		
		2 Rank	5	6	30		
		3 Rank	8	5	40		
	Training	4 Rank	8	4	32	152	
		5 Rank	10	3	30		
		6 Rank	2	2	4		
		7 Rank	2	1	2		
3		1 Rank	8	7	56		
		2 Rank	6	6	36		
	Services	3 Rank	8	5	40	165	
		4 Rank	3	4	12		
		5 Rank	3	3	9		

Table 6. Continued

S. No.	Rating UPASI	Ranks	No of Respondent	Weighted Score	Weighted Amounted	Total Weighted Amounted	Rank
		6 Rank	3	2	10		
		7 Rank	5	1	2		
4	Programs	1 Rank	8	7	56	163	
		2 Rank	8	6	48		
		3 Rank	3	5	15		
		4 Rank	5	4	20		
		5 Rank	6	3	18		
		6 Rank	2	2	4		
		7 Rank	2	1	2		
5.	Plantation		6	7	42		
		2 Rank	5	6	30		
		3 Rank	5	5	25		
		4 Rank	3	4	12	151	
		5 Rank	10	3	30		
		6 Rank	5	2	10		
		7 Rank	2	1	2		
6.		1 Rank	2	7	14		
		2 Rank	6	6	36		
		3 Rank	6	5	30		
	Members	4 Rank	5	4	20	123	
		5 Rank	2	3	6		
		6 Rank	3	2	6		
		7 Rank	11	1	11		
7.	Overall	1 Rank	2	7	14	123	
		2 Rank	6	6	36		
		3 Rank	6	5	30		
		4 Rank	5	4	20		
		5 Rank	2	3	6		
		6 Rank	3	2	6		
		7 Rank	11	1	11		

Source- Primary data

DISCUSSION AND FINDINGS

The survey results indicate the demographics and preferences of the respondents. Most respondents (69%) are male, while 54% fall into the 26 to 35 age categories. In terms of marital status, 86% of the respondents are married. Remarkably, all of the respondents (100%) are associated with the farmers and agriculturalist group, showcasing the significance of this profession among the participants.

Regarding educational backgrounds, the school group represents the majority, accounting for 83% of the respondents. Among the income groups, 27% of the respondents belong to the "10,000 above" category. Interestingly, all of the respondents (100%) come from rural areas, indicating the involvement of rural communities in the survey.

Regarding specific choices, all respondents (100%) belong to the "Yes" group for one survey aspect. Additionally, 51% of the respondents selected the "Online website" option, while 50% answered "Yes" to another question. Within the survey, most respondents (57%) are part of the Existing Members group, while 5.11% belong to another services group.

Furthermore, a significant proportion (63%) of the respondents are highly aware. In various aspects of the survey, most respondents (100%) answered "Yes," suggesting a common consensus among the participants.

The financial scheme group constitutes the majority of the respondents, making up 4.77%, while 10.4% belong to the Coffee group. Notably, once again, all of the respondents (100%) fall into the "Yes" category for certain aspects of the survey.

Overall, these survey findings offer valuable insights into the characteristics and preferences of the respondents, providing a comprehensive understanding of their demographics and opinions.

The global market for Indian Tea has experienced a decline in demand, emphasizing the need for the industry to enhance its competitiveness in various aspects. To remain viable and profitable, the Indian tea industry must improve its production processes, adopt efficient marketing strategies, streamline logistics, and diversify product offerings.

By enhancing production methods, the industry can ensure a consistent supply of high-quality tea to meet consumers' evolving preferences. Implementing advanced agricultural practices, optimizing resource utilization, and embracing sustainable farming techniques can contribute to higher productivity and better product quality.

Regarding marketing, the Indian tea industry should employ innovative approaches to reach wider international audiences and promote its unique offerings. Building strong brand identities, participating in global trade shows, and exploring digital marketing avenues are ways to gain a competitive edge.

Efficient logistics are essential for timely delivery and cost-effectiveness. Improving transportation, warehousing, and distribution networks can optimize the supply chain, reducing lead times and ensuring tea reaches international markets in its freshest state.

Furthermore, diversifying product forms can cater to a broader range of consumer preferences and create value-added offerings. This could include flavoured teas, specialty blends, or organic variants, which may attract a wider customer base and command premium prices.

By addressing these key areas of production, marketing, logistics, and product diversification, the Indian tea industry can position itself more competitively in the global market, adapt to changing demands, and revive its growth in the face of declining demand.

The study also emphasized that, as one of the major producers of Tea, India requires well-structured and organized production and marketing systems. Such systems would enable all tea growers to secure a significant and sustainable position in the global market. To achieve this, the Indian tea industry must streamline its production processes, adopt modern agricultural practices, and implement efficient marketing strategies.

By organizing and coordinating tea production, the industry can ensure consistent quality and quantity, meeting the demands of both domestic and international markets. This would also help stabilize prices and create a more predictable supply chain, benefiting both the growers and the consumers.

Moreover, a well-organized marketing system would allow Indian Tea to reach a broader range of consumers globally. This involves building strong partnerships with international buyers, exploring new market opportunities, and promoting the unique characteristics and flavours of Indian Tea.

Creating a sufficient place in the world market involves not only increasing production but also enhancing the overall reputation and recognition of Indian Tea. By adhering to high-quality standards and sustainable practices, Indian Tea can become a preferred choice among consumers worldwide, leading to increased demand and higher prices.

In summary, for India to retain its position as a chief tea producer, it is essential to establish comprehensive and well-managed production and marketing systems. This will enable tea growers to compete effectively in the global market and secure a sustainable and prominent position in the industry.

SUGGESTIONS

To promote the well-being of farmers and the agricultural sector, authorities need to consider providing more subsidies to farmers. This financial assistance can significantly alleviate the burden of production costs and encourage sustainable agricultural practices. Moreover, efforts should be made to enhance public awareness about UPASI (United Planters' Association of Southern India). Greater knowledge about UPASI's role and initiatives can foster support and engagement from various stakeholders, leading to more effective agricultural development.

Additionally, introducing family-related welfare schemes can positively impact the lives of farmers and their families. Such schemes can provide social security, healthcare, and educational benefits, contributing to the overall welfare of farming communities.

Furthermore, creating widespread awareness about the value of spices is crucial. Spices are an integral part of Indian agriculture and have significant economic potential. Farmers and consumers can benefit from increased demand and better market opportunities by promoting awareness and understanding of spices.

To drive agricultural growth, many well-designed schemes should support farmers in various aspects of their work. These schemes can encompass financial aid, technical assistance, infrastructure development, and more tailored to meet the diverse needs of farmers.

It is equally important to improve awareness among farmers regarding initiatives and services. By expanding their knowledge, farmers can better utilize the available resources and leverage UPASI's support to enhance their agricultural practices and yields.

To further aid planters, UPASI should strive to provide an extensive range of services that cater to the specific needs of farmers. These services could include training programs, access to modern technology, market linkages, and advice on sustainable practices.

Timely and adequate funding is essential for smoothly implementing agricultural schemes and initiatives. By providing funds promptly, UPASI can ensure that the intended beneficiaries receive the necessary support when they need it the most.

Increasing awareness of UPASI among urban populations can also lead to greater advocacy and support for agricultural development. Educating urban dwellers about the importance of agriculture and its impact on their lives can foster a stronger connection between rural and urban communities.

Lastly, investing in training programs for farmers and other stakeholders is crucial for capacity building and skill development. These training initiatives can empower farmers with knowledge and expertise, enabling them to effectively adapt to changing agricultural practices and market demands.

CONCLUSION

In today's tea industry, data-driven marketing has revolutionized customer engagement. Social media analytics and consumer behavior insights have enabled businesses to craft targeted campaigns, enhancing brand visibility and consumer-brand connections. This data-centric marketing approach is revolutionizing industry-client interactions. A study involving 35 respondents highlights strategic efforts in the Nilgiris, offering a spectrum of services and support that have bolstered the local tea farming community. UPASI's subsidies, awareness programs, and training initiatives are instrumental for sustainable development, demonstrating the value of data intelligence in the sector. Businesses leveraging such insights can align products with consumer preferences, improve operational efficiency, and enhance customer engagement, which is crucial in a competitive and ever-changing market.

Data analytics ensures effective marketing investments and fosters customer loyalty through personalized experiences. UPASI's model shows the significance of a supportive network for agriculture, with the prosperity of individual farmers reinforcing the industry's strength. Their approach signifies a shift towards data as a strategic imperative, influencing all business facets. This blend of data-driven marketing and comprehensive support exemplifies a global trend where data informs business strategies, consumer understanding, and market navigation. UPASI's impact in the Nilgiris is a testament to the power of data insights on both local and broader scales. At this critical point, the tea industry's future hinges on data intelligence for continued growth and leadership. The next generation of industry leaders will be those who adeptly use data to cater to global consumer demands while sustaining the farming community at the industry's heart.

LIMITATIONS

From a limitation perspective, this study faces several constraints. One key limitation is the relatively small sample size of 35 respondents, which may not adequately represent the vast and diverse tea growers and stakeholders associated with UPASI. This raises concerns about the generalizability of the findings. Additionally, the focus on a single geographical region, the Nilgiris, potentially overlooks tea growers' varied challenges and practices in other areas, limiting the study's scope. The inherent bias may arise from respondents' subjective experiences and the possibility of overestimation of UPASI's impact without a broader industry-wide comparison. Furthermore, the reliance on self-reported data can lead to discrepancies between the reported practices and actual on-ground implementation, affecting the study's accuracy. These limitations suggest that while the study provides valuable insights, its findings should be interpreted with caution, and there is a need for further research encompassing a broader spectrum of participants and regions to fully understand UPASI's role in the sustainability of tea growers.

FUTURE SCOPE

Delving into a larger and more diverse sample size across different tea-growing regions could provide a more comprehensive understanding of UPASI's impact and reveal scalable practices beneficial to the broader agricultural community. Longitudinal studies could track the long-term effects of UPASI's interventions on sustainability, offering insights into the enduring challenges and successes. Additionally, integrating advanced data analytics and machine learning could refine the assessment of UPASI's services, enabling predictive models of sustainability and resource allocation. Comparative studies with other agricultural associations could also be beneficial, identifying best practices and innovative strategies that UPASI could adopt. There's potential for exploring the interplay of economic, environmental, and social sustainability factors in tea growing, providing a multi-dimensional perspective on sustainable practices. Incorporating technological advancements such as precision agriculture and emphasizing policy influence and market trends could further illuminate paths for UPASI's evolution in supporting tea growers' sustainability. This future research could ultimately guide policy-making, drive innovation, and enhance the global competitiveness of the tea industry.

REFERENCES

Ajayakumar, K., Kumar, R., & Haridas, V. (2005). Influence of the subtending leaf on the growth of axillary bud and formation of banji bud in tea. *Indian Journal of Plant Physiology / Official Publication of the Indian Society for Plant Physiology, 10*(3), 267–272.

Asopa, V. N. (2007). *Tea industry of India the cup that cheers have tears.* IIMA-Research and Publications.

Babu, S. (2004). Tea Descriptors – Serie s-I. *Planters' Chronicle (Philadelphia, Pa.), 100*(5), 9–12.

Babu, S. (2005a). Tea descriptors: Series-2. *Planters' Chronicle (Philadelphia, Pa.), 101*(1), 12–15.

Babu, S. (2005b). Tea descriptors: Series- 3. *Planters' Chronicle (Philadelphia, Pa.), 101*(4), 27–30.

Babu, S., Saravanan, M., & Murugesan, S. (2007). Association of green leaf quality parameters in tea. *Newsletter - UPASI Tea Research Foundation, 17*(1).

Griffiths, P. (1967). *The History of the Indian Tea Industry.* Weidenfeld and Nicolson.

Guha, A. (1977). *Planteraj and swaraj: Freedom struggle and electoral politics in Assam 1820- 1947.* Delhi University Press.

Gunasundari, R., Kumar, R., & Ilango, R. V. J. (2002). Factors influencing leaf expansion time in tea. In K. Sreedharan & P. K. Kumar (Eds.), Codeword Process and Printers. Academic Press.

Hudson, J. B., & Durairaj, J. (2004). Cost control of tea cultivation. Planters'. *Chronicle (Philadelphia, Pa.), 100*(11), 8–21.

Khawas, V. (2011). Status of Tea Garden Labourers in Eastern Himalaya: A Case of Darjeeling Tea Industry. In M. Desai & S. Mitra (Eds.), Cloud, Stone and the Mind: The People and Environment of Darjeeling Hill Area (pp. 1-19). ICIMOD Online Digital Library.

Kumar, M., & Radhakrishnan, P. (2012). Tea in south India: present status and future prospects. *Souvenir. Plantation Crops Symposium*, 1–7.

Muraleedharan, N., & Hudson, J. B. (2007). Tea cultivation in south India: Agricultural policies. *Planters' Chronicle (Philadelphia, Pa.), 103*(1), 6–41.

Radhakrishnan, B., Durairaj, J., Mathew, M., Kumar, P., Udhayabahnu, K. G., Sankaranarayanan, P., & Liango, R. J. (2021). Performance of South Indian tea industry during last one decade and challenges ahead. *Bulletin of UPASI Tea Research Foundation, 56*, 3–15.

Ramamoorthy, G., Suguna, M., Kumaravadivelu, P., & Sairam, C. (2012). Intercrop in tea with medicinal plants in the Nilgiris. In Abstracts of Papers. PLACROSYMXX.

Sarkar, K. (2008). Globalization, restructuring and labor flexibility in tea plantations in West Bengal. *The Indian Journal of Labour Economics : the Quarterly Journal of the Indian Society of Labour Economics, 51*(4), 643–654.

Selvaraj, M. S., & Gopalakrishnan, S. (2016). Nightmares of an agricultural capitalist economy: Tea plantation workers in the nilgiris. *Economic and Political Weekly, 51*(18), 107–113. https://www.jstor.org/stable/44004242

UPASI Tea Research Foundation. (2021). Retrieved November 12, 2023, from Upasitearesearch.org website: http://www.upasitearesearch.org

Chapter 8
An Empirical Study on Challenges of Working From Home During COVID-19 on Work-Life Domains in the Education Sector in Bengaluru

Riya Singh

(iD) https://orcid.org/0000-0001-5281-7256

Kristu Jayanti College, India
Raji Rajan 698c9979-4017-4704-9f43-d2f4d9309ebc
Jain University, India

Nidhi Raj Gupta

(iD) https://orcid.org/0000-0002-9606-1574
Kristu Jayanti College, India

Ahmad Y. A. Bani Ahmad
Middle East University, Jordan

ABSTRACT

The chapter looks at the challenges faced by academicians at the time of COVID-19. Additionally, it examines how Bengaluru academicians reconcile work and life, as well as how this pandemic condition has affected teaching performance. Academicians are not only being challenged with teaching methodology due to the pandemic but are forced to create and innovate new ideas of teaching-learning implemented by the New Education Policy. The chapter ends with the findings on the effectiveness of WFH, quality of communication, and return to work. It concludes that although WFH created great difficulty in social interaction, which forced them to return to work, but has increased the productivity of educators in this changing phase and developed a new learning dimension in the higher education industry, even though this domain of working is feasible for several business organizations and the years to come. The COVID-19 pandemic has forced many people to work from home.

DOI: 10.4018/979-8-3693-0049-7.ch008

INTRODUCTION

The pandemic has spread around the world, attempting to test our community in many different ways and compelling individuals to reconsider a variety of practices, from their place of employment and leisure to everyday travel and duties. In addition to having an effect on the individual, it has had a negative economic and financial influence on the entire world, halting several economic sectors (Venkateswaran et al., 2023). The possibility of balancing work and personal life was hazy and frequently disputed before the pandemic (Kumar & Naachimuthu, 2023). Contrarily, COVID-19 put everyone under pressure to make a choice, and as a result, many businesses decided to experiment with functioning from home (Dawwas & Zahari, 2014). In fact, this is an unprecedented opportunity to evaluate WFH's potential as one of the next feasible options for such a congested urban setting (Akshaya & Naachimuthu, 2022).

To start with, this research aims to understand better WFH balance, including the factors that affect WFH for both men and women, as well as the effectiveness and relevance of this work schedule (Almaamari & Salial, 2022). Second, the potential effects of the WFH on academicians' life and work domains, such as versatility, motivation, and career satisfaction, will be investigated (Al-Maaitah et al., 2021).

The most obvious problem that has resulted from the situation is the need for scholars in higher education to have new, innovative skill sets (Hana et al., 2022; Said & Tripathi, 2023). This is true both for adapting to advancements in technology and using information technologies, as well as for the need to develop novel teaching techniques for new situations while juggling their personal and professional lives (Sabti et al., 2023). According to several earlier studies, a completely new constructivist strategy is necessary, along with the necessity for theatrical abilities, in order to capture the interest and focus of learners in a course subject (Mishra et al., 2020; Anand et al., 2023).

CHALLENGES FACED BY ACADEMICIANS DURING WFH

Before the pandemic, schools all around the globe were confronted with the issues of online education as they began to develop. For educational institutions, academics, parents, and students, this unanticipated presence has exacerbated certain current digital challenges while also introducing a number of new ones (Aswathi et al., 2021).

Technology investment: Schools and higher learning institutions are under great pressure to shift teaching methodology from classroom education to virtual learning, so the right kind of investment needs to be done carefully (Beshr et al., 2023). However, the institutes fail to consider whether the technology under consideration is the best fit for their specific needs. To be effective, technology must be measured against specific pedagogical outcomes. Universities and colleges that have reviewed their options will save funds on purchases that add little significance to their student's learning experiences (Hana & Naachimuthu, 2023). It is crucial to analyze educational software in order to gain the requisite experience and time to make the best choice. Distance learning tools should be relevant and should be applied within a regular classroom environment.

Academicians feel unmotivated or unsupported: Academicians had to shift towards the technology, and to a certain point, it seems to be ineffective. The educators have received support and training with ed-tech, which made academicians more confident, and also advice on blended learning models in their institution.

Collaboration from parents: In the approach of learning from home, the parents have to be more supportive during this time. They need to confirm their children have the right kind of tools to learn and encourage them to do online education.

Providing Internet security for students: It is critical for students to protect themselves from the Internet. Different devices, such as a Chrome book, need to be used correctly by students (Madhumitha & Naachimuthu, 2023). IT administrators should seek a quick, simple, and effective method of preventing pupils from accessing unsuitable or detrimental online content while also protecting devices from threats.

Dealing with distraction and studying isolation: In a real or offline classroom, it can be tough to keep students engaged and focused, and this is exacerbated even more in a virtual setting. Being unable to walk around in the classroom, teachers cannot see if students are engaged in the task at hand or distracted by online games or videos. Children require social interaction with their peers, and virtual learning causes many to feel isolated and cut off from their peers.

Post-pandemic Education: The current paradigm necessitates a new approach, which schools must take into account when designing their blended learning program. Returning to schools and colleges, students require more skills, more time, and energy to go from one place to another and understand the topics.

Teaching methodology: The shift to online teaching has been a major challenge for academicians in Bengaluru. Many were not familiar with online teaching platforms or pedagogy, and they had to quickly learn new skills. Additionally, students had varying levels of access to technology and a stable internet connection, which made it difficult to ensure that everyone was learning effectively.

Teaching performance: The pandemic has also had an impact on teaching performance. Some academicians have reported feeling overwhelmed and stressed due to the increased workload and the challenges of online teaching. This has led to some academicians feeling less confident in their teaching abilities.

ACADEMICIANS' WORK-LIFE BALANCE DURING WFH

In every industry, the concept of balancing work and personal life is a contentious and pressing subject. Many employees are working in different slots and shifts due to globalization, which is resulting in very little quality time to spend with families and friends. Researchers have paid close attention to the work and personal life balance problem in the last few decades. Women educators, in particular, face greater problems in balancing their family and professional commitments. During this lock-down phase, all members of the household are at home, and children have online classes, which makes it difficult for women to manage their accountabilities in comparison to men. The objectives of this piece are to examine the academic staff at WFH's work-life balance and the challenges of great learning and teaching via the Internet in higher education. The pandemic has also blurred the lines between work and life for academicians. With many working from home, it has been difficult to separate work time from personal time. Additionally, the increased workload due to online teaching and the need to develop new teaching materials has made it difficult for academicians to maintain a healthy work-life balance.

On the "influence of a virus breakout on life-work equilibrium, especially in the circumstances of female workers in quarantine situations," several researches have been done by Adisa et al. (2021), Möhring et al. (2021), Rodrguez-Rivero et al. (2020); Aristovnik et al. (2020). Research on how higher education professors may struggle to balance their personal and professional lives as a result of increasing levels of study tends to be paradoxical.

LITERATURE REVIEW

The purpose of WFH or working remotely is to reduce the danger of COVID-19 infestation. WFH, on the other hand, is not a fresh concept that has drawn interest from numerous institutions of philosophy throughout the years. In order to express the concept of WFH, (Nilles, 1988) coined the terms "telecommuting" and "telework" in 1973 (Messenger & Gschwind, 2016). WFH, often referred to as remote employment, teleconferencing, working remotely, teleconference, and e-working, enables employees to perform in a range of work locations, notably at home, by using cutting-edge technology to complete work-related duties (Grant et al., 2019; Gajendran and Harrison, 2007). Sethi (2020) investigates the perspectives and challenges of school teachers regarding WFH, as well as the importance of working from home.

Working from home is linked to better work performance, job satisfaction, fewer plans to quit your job, and lower levels of stress, according to empirical research (Kossek et al., 2006; Vega et al., 2015; Coenen and Kok, 2014; Contreras et al., 2020; Anderson et al., 2015; Fonner and Roloff, 2010). "The idea behind work-life balance is that work and personal well-being complement each other in displaying perfection in one's life." (Chung, Heejung, and Tanja van der, 2020; López-Igual and Rodríguez-Modroño, 2020). According to empirical studies (Kossek et al., 2006; Vega et al., 2015; Coenen and Kok, 2014; Contreras et al., 2020; Anderson et al., 2015; Fonner and Roloff, 2010), working from home is associated with greater work performance, job satisfaction, fewer plans to quit your job, and lower levels of stress.

The person will experience stress if they don't have enough assets to fulfill both their family and job obligations. Life-work balance was favorably correlated with job satisfaction, according to a prior study (Jackson and Fransman, 2018). Cohen & Liani, (2009) found that academicians in India faced challenges, such as Many academicians not having the necessary training on online teaching platforms and pedagogy. Academicians faced technical challenges such as poor internet connectivity and lack of access to devices. Academicians experienced an increased workload due to online teaching and the need to develop new teaching materials. Academicians found it difficult to maintain a healthy work-life balance while working from home.

According to research conducted by Konrad and Mangel (2000), academics in India confront issues such as experiencing feelings of isolation and feeling alienated from their colleagues and students. The increasing workload and the difficulties associated with online instruction caused academics to feel increased levels of stress and anxiety. Problems with their physical and emotional health, such as exhaustion, eye strain, and sadness, were reportedly experienced by academics. For the following four reasons, their findings and the synthesis of those findings are extremely important in the context of the new normal (van Hoek et al., 2022). The first advantage is that a synthesis will consolidate all of the data and provide an overarching picture of the present state of knowledge regarding WFH applications.

The second reason is that a recent calculation revealed that there is a 38% chance that a pandemic similar to COVID-19 will occur during a person's lifetime. Because of these factors, during COVID-19, we attempted to locate a review study that provided a synopsis of the data obtained from WFH research. In order to acquire a more comprehensive understanding of the topic and a wide range of empirical findings about WFH, this study needs to incorporate papers from a variety of countries. The empirical investigations ensure an adequate level of consistency for methodological quality, which allows for the provision of findings that fulfil internal validity.

RESEARCH METHODOLOGY

The questionnaire method was adopted for this research. The purpose of this study is to discover the difficulties academicians encounter in addition to their balance between work and life when receiving WFH from the organization.

Scope of the study: Knowing the effects of COVID-19 on academicians' stability in their professional and personal lives, as well as the WFH option offered to all intelligentsia in Bengaluru, would be useful information for all types of institutions. Through this research, various institutions can find new ways or options that can be provided to all teachers and academicians in the future so that their productivity and flexibility in work can be increased.

Data Collection: The proposed article is based on primary and secondary investigations in the area of education in Bengaluru. The data was collected from various academicians from different institutions through Google Forms, and 100 respondents responded to the survey. For data collection, a well-structured Questionnaire was used.

Questionnaires, tests, and observations were used to collect primary data. Secondary data sources include articles, research papers, journals, magazines, and weekly newspapers, among others (Alayli, 2023).

Survey Design: The sample size in this research is 100 academicians from various schools, colleges, and universities in Bengaluru representing various disciplines. During the WFH, a global epidemic in Bengaluru for a year, academicians include academic staff, freelance professors, instructors, assistant professors, associates professors, instructors, HODs, and others involved in maintaining a work-life balance. The 100 academicians were selected by random sampling method.

Statistical Technique: The hypothesis was examined after the collected data was processed using the SPSS program for Chi-Square Testing.

OBJECTIVES

- To understand the difficulties that academicians face during WFH.
- To examine academicians' work-life balance during the pandemic's WFH.
- To make recommendations for COVID-19 that would help academicians achieve a greater equilibrium between work and life.

HYPOTHESES

H0: There is no significant difference between academicians and WFH.
H0: There is no significant difference between academicians and quality personal work and life balance.
H0: There is no significant difference between academicians and those returning to the office.

DATA ANALYSIS AND INTERPRETATION

From Table 1, it is stated that 47% of academicians are in favor of working from home, 13% are not in favor of working from home, and 40% feel a mixed opinion about working from home.

Table 1. Do you prefer working from home?

	Yes	**No**	**Sometimes**
Academicians	47	13	40

Table 2. Chi-square test

	Value	**Df**	**Asymp. Sig. (2-Sided)**
Pearson Chi-Square	3.296[a]	4	.510
Likelihood Ratio	3.952	4	.412
N of Valid Cases	100		

At the level of significance defined as 0.05, with a p-value of (.510) and 4 degrees of freedom, there is no statistically significant distinction between academicians and desire for WFH, according to the findings of the analysis in Table 2 above. The p-value was less than 0; hence, the hypothesis was likewise disproved at the 0.01 level of significance. This indicates that the typical academician does not favor working from home at a 1% level of significance.

Table 3. Do you have a healthy work and life balance while working from home?

	Yes	**No**	**Sometimes**
Academicians	37	25	36

According to Table 3, 37 percent of academicians agreed that WFH helps them balance their personal and professional lives at the same time, 25 percent believe they are unable to balance their personal and professional lives, and regarding preserving a positive balance between work and private life while operating from home, 36% have conflicting views.

Table 4. Chi-square tests

	Value	Df	Asymp. Sig. (2-Sided)
Pearson Chi-Square	3.536[a]	4	.472
Likelihood Ratio	4.174	4	.383
N of Valid Cases	100		

As can be seen from Table 4's Chi-Square test result, the null assumption was not rejected at a level of significance of .472, which is higher than 0.05 (Pearson). It follows that WFH is independent of employees' vocations because the Chi-square examination does not show a significant relationship between intellectuals and a positive work-life balance as practiced by institutions.

Table 5. Do you look forward to returning to the office?

	Yes	No	Sometimes
Academicians	**55%**	**13%**	**32%**

Table 5 states that 55% of academicians are in favor of returning back to the office for efficient work and 13% are not in favor of returning to the office, and 36% have mixed opinions about returning to the office.

Table 6. Chi-square tests

	Value	Df	Asymp. Sig. (2-Sided)
Pearson Chi-Square	15.400[a]	4	.004
Likelihood Ratio	10.152	4	.038
N of Valid Cases	100		

We refuse the null hypothesis since the Chi-Square experiment's output table 6 shows a significance level of .004, which is below the level of 0.05 (Pearson). This indicates that academicians have a substantial link with going back to work, followed by institutions, according to the Chi-square test.

FINDINGS

55% of the academicians stated that during WFH, productivity in work as they had during working from institutions only, and 45% felt that during WFH, they were more productive in work. 38% of the academicians approved that they were satisfied with the quality of communication and interaction from subordinates and seniors for guidance and leadership, and 62% agreed that they were not able to connect with their leaders as and when they were in need. While they were functioning from home, 63% of academics said they found it difficult to stick to a pattern or schedule, while 27% said they could. 67% of the academicians perceived that they would not be able to take regular breaks while working from home, and 33% perceived that they would not be able to take regular breaks.

In short, we can say the eeffectiveness of Work from Home (WFH): WFH has been effective for some academicians, but it has also created challenges for others. For example, some academicians have found that it is difficult to stay focused and productive when working from home. Additionally, some academicians have reported feeling isolated and disconnected from their colleagues and students.

Quality of communication: The quality of communication between academicians and students has been affected by the pandemic. For example, some students have found it difficult to ask questions and get help from their academicians during online classes. Additionally, some academicians have found it difficult to build relationships with their students in an online environment.

Return to work: Many academicians are eager to return to work on campus, as they feel that it is the best way to teach and interact with students. However, some academicians are concerned about their health and safety, and they are hesitant to return to campus until the pandemic is under control.

Provide training and support on online teaching: Academicians should be provided with training and support on online teaching platforms and pedagogy. This will help them to teach more effectively in the online environment. Promote work-life balance: Employers should promote work-life balance for academicians. This includes setting clear expectations for work hours and providing support for academicians to take breaks and disconnect from work outside of working hours.

Support the implementation of the NEP: Employers and the government should support the implementation of the NEP by providing academicians with resources and training to develop new teaching materials and to change their teaching approaches. Invest in technology: Employers and the government should invest in technology to support online learning. This includes providing academicians with access to reliable laptops and internet connections, as well as providing students with access to devices and the Internet.

Communication plays an important role between staff members and senior subordinates. If academicians encounter technical difficulties or problems while working remotely, employers must make arrangements for meetings and interactive sessions using Zoom, Google Meet, and other tools rather than sending emails to make them feel more at ease. Academicians should think and plan their work before starting the day. Important work, including their household chores and unexpected work or calls from the employer. Academicians should set up a WFH-friendly workspace in their homes.

CONCLUSION

In this pandemic, the current study addresses the needs of intellectuals and their perspectives while working from home. WFH option followed by various institutions during the lock-down situation has created an impact on the academicians' work-life, and it was being seen from the research that WFH would be a better alternative if we have the knowledge of all updated applications and technology to use to make WFH better. This Pandemic situation has completely changed the working patterns of all intellectuals and it was determined that institutions should divide the work so that WFH and office work could continue. The COVID-19 pandemic has had a significant impact on academicians in Bengaluru, India. Academicians have faced a number of challenges, including teaching methodology, work-life balance, teaching performance, and the implementation of the NEP. However, academicians have shown great resilience and innovation in adapting to the new learning environment. The study concludes that WFH has created some challenges for academicians, such as difficulty in social interaction and the need to return to work. However, WFH has also increased the productivity of educators in this changing phase and developed a new learning dimension in the higher education industry. Even though this domain of working is feasible for several business organizations and the years to come, academicians are eager to return to work on campus, as they feel that it is the best way to teach and interact with students.

REFERENCES

Adisa, T. A., Aiyenitaju, O., & Adekoya, O. D. (2021). The work-family balance of British working women during the COVID-19 Pandemic. *Journal of Work-Applied Management, 13*(2), 241–260. Advance online publication. doi:10.1108/JWAM-07-2020-0036

Akshaya, A., & Naachimuthu, K. P. (2022). Locavorism to Enhance Environmental, Social, & Economic Well-being. *Indian Journal of Agriculture Business, 8*(1), 25–33.

Al-Maaitah, T. A., Tha'er Majali, M. A., & Almaaitah, D. A. (2021). The Impact of COVID-19 on the Electronic Commerce Users Behavior. *Journal of Contemporary Issues in Business and Government, 27*(1), 772–783.

Alayli, S. (2023). Unravelling the Drivers of Online Purchasing Intention: The E-Commerce Scenario in Lebanon. *FMDB Transactions on Sustainable Social Sciences Letters, 1*(1), 56–67.

Almaamari, Q. A., & Salial, M. M. (2022). Influence of Job Satisfaction, Effective Teamwork and Social Media on Employee's Performance in Bahraini Telecommunication Sector. *Specialusis Ugdymas, 1*(43), 2063–2070.

Anand, P. P., Kanike, U. K., Paramasivan, P., Rajest, S. S., Regin, R., & Priscila, S. S. (2023). Embracing Industry 5.0: Pioneering Next-Generation Technology for a Flourishing Human Experience and Societal Advancement. *FMDB Transactions on Sustainable Social Sciences Letters, 1*(1), 43–55.

Anderson, A. J., Kaplan, S. A., & Vega, R. P. (2015). The impact of telework on emotional experience: When, and for whom, does telework improve daily affective well-being? *European Journal of Work and Organizational Psychology, 24*(6), 882–897. doi:10.1080/1359432X.2014.966086

Aristovnik, A., Keržič, D., Ravšelj, D., Tomaževič, N., & Umek, L. (2020). Impacts of the COVID-19 Pandemic on Life of Higher Education Students: A Global Perspective. *Sustainability (Basel), 12*(20), 8438. doi:10.3390u12208438

Aswathi, P., Sangavi, P., Naachimuthu, K. P., & Krishna, T. (2021). *Proceedings of the ICSSR Sponsored Webinar on Human Behavior and Environmental Sustainability*. Academic Press.

Beshr, B., Muhammad, S. K., Alaghbari, M. A., & Albo-Aainain, M. I. (2023). The mediating role of empowering workers in the relationship between the entrepreneurial orientation and operational performance of Bahraini family businesses. *Resmilitaris, 13*(1), 1331-1341.

Chung, H., & van der Lippe, T. (2020). Flexible working, work-life balance, and gender equality: Introduction. *Social Indicators Research, 151*(2), 365–381. doi:10.100711205-018-2025-x PMID:33029036

Coenen, M., & Kok, R. A. W. (2014). Workplace flexibility and new product development performance: The role of telework and flexible work schedules. *European Management Journal*, *32*(4), 564–576. doi:10.1016/j.emj.2013.12.003

Cohen, A., & Liani, E. (2009). Work-family conflict among female employees in Israeli hospitals. *Personnel Review*, *38*(2), 124–141. doi:10.1108/00483480910931307

Contreras, F., Baykal, E., & Abid, G. (2020). E-leadership and teleworking in times of COVID-19 and beyond: What we know and where do we go. *Frontiers in Psychology*, *11*, 590271. doi:10.3389/fpsyg.2020.590271 PMID:33362656

Dawwas, M., & Zahari, I. (2014). Testing the Relationship between Human Resource Practices and Turnover Intention in a non-Western context of the Palestine. *Journal of Advanced Social Research*, *4*(4), 10–22.

Fonner, K. L., & Roloff, M. E. (2010). Why Teleworkers are More Satisfied with Their Jobs than are Office-Based Workers: When Less Contact is Beneficial. *Journal of Applied Communication Research*, *38*(4), 336–361. doi:10.1080/00909882.2010.513998

Gajendran, R. S., & Harrison, D. A. (2007). The good, the bad, and the unknown about telecommuting: Meta-analysis of psychological mediators and individual consequences. *The Journal of Applied Psychology*, *92*(6), 1524–1541. doi:10.1037/0021-9010.92.6.1524 PMID:18020794

Grant, C. A., Wallace, L. M., Spurgeon, P. C., Tramontano, C., & Charalampous, M. (2019). Construction and initial validation of the E-Work Life Scale to measure remote e-working. *Employee Relations*, *41*(1), 16–33. doi:10.1108/ER-09-2017-0229

Hana, M., & Naachimuthu, K. P. (2023). A Comprehensive Model on Rejection Sensitivity. *South India Journal of Social Sciences*, *21*(19), 19–31.

Hana, M., Vishnupriya, S., & Naachimuthu, K. P. (2022). Restorative Effect of Direct and Indirect Nature Exposure - A Systematic Review. *International Journal of Scientific Research*, *11*(5), 10–15.

Jackson, L. T. B., & Fransman, E. I. (2018). Flexi work, financial well-being, work–life balance and their effects on subjective experiences of productivity and job satisfaction of females in an institution of higher learning. *Suid-Afrikaanse Tydskrif vir Ekonomiese en Bestuurswetenskappe*, *21*(1). Advance online publication. doi:10.4102ajems.v21i1.1487

Konrad, A. M., & Mangel, R. (2000). The impact of work-life programs on firm productivity. *Strategic Management Journal*, *21*(12), 1225–1237. doi:10.1002/1097-0266(200012)21:12<1225::AID-SMJ135>3.0.CO;2-3

Kossek, E. E., Lautsch, B. A., & Eaton, S. C. (2006). Telecommuting, control, and boundary management: Correlates of policy use and practice, job control, and work–family effectiveness. *Journal of Vocational Behavior*, *68*(2), 347–367. doi:10.1016/j.jvb.2005.07.002

Kumar, A., & Naachimuthu, K. P. (2023). Market Potential for Shawarma Outlet in Coimbatore - An Analysis. *South India Journal of Social Sciences*, *XXI*(1), 130–140.

López-Igual, P., & Rodríguez-Modroño, P. (2020). Who is teleworking and where from? Exploring the main determinants of telework in Europe. *Sustainability (Basel), 12*(21), 8797. doi:10.3390u12218797

Madhumitha, D., & Naachimuthu, K. P. (2023). Emotional Regulation among the Members of LGBTQ+ Community. *Education and Society, 47*(2), 34–45.

Messenger, J. C., & Gschwind, L. (2016). Three generations of Telework: New ICTs and the (R)evolution from home office to virtual office. *New Technology, Work and Employment, 31*(3), 195–208. doi:10.1111/ntwe.12073

Mishra, L., Gupta, T., & Shree, A. (2020). Online teaching-learning in higher education during lockdown period of COVID-19 pandemic. *International Journal of Educational Research Open, 1*(100012), 100012. doi:10.1016/j.ijedro.2020.100012 PMID:35059663

Möhring, K., Naumann, E., Reifenscheid, M., Wenz, A., Rettig, T., Krieger, U., … Blom, A. G. (2021). The COVID-19 pandemic and subjective well-being: longitudinal evidence on satisfaction with work and family. *European Societies, 23*(sup1), S601–S617. doi:10.1080/14616696.2020.1833066

Nilles, J. M. (1988). Traffic reduction by telecommuting: A status review and selected bibliography. *Transportation Research Part A, General, 22*(4), 301–317. doi:10.1016/0191-2607(88)90008-8

Rodríguez-Rivero, R., Yáñez, S., Fernández-Aller, C., & Carrasco-Gallego, R. (2020). Is it time for a revolution in work–life balance? Reflections from Spain. *Sustainability (Basel), 12*(22), 9563. doi:10.3390u12229563

Sabti, Y. M., Alqatrani, R. I. N., Zaid, M. I., Taengkliang, B., & Kareem, J. M. (2023). Impact of Business Environment on the Performance of Employees in the Public-Listed Companies. *FMDB Transactions on Sustainable Management Letters, 1*(2), 56–65.

Said, F. B., & Tripathi, S. (2023). Epistemology of Digital Journalism Shift in South Global Nations: A Bibliometric Analysis. *FMDB Transactions on Sustainable Technoprise Letters, 1*(1), 47–60.

Sethi, S., & Saini, N. K. (2020). COVID-19: Opinions and Challenges of School Teachers on WFH. *Asian Journal of Nursing Education and Research, 10*(4), 532–536. doi:10.5958/2349-2996.2020.00115.9

Vega, R. P., Anderson, A. J., & Kaplan, S. A. (2015). A within-person examination of the effects of telework. *Journal of Business and Psychology, 30*(2), 313–323. doi:10.100710869-014-9359-4

Venkateswaran, P. S., Singh, S., Paramasivan, P., Rajest, S. S., Lourens, M. E., & Regin, R. (2023). A Study on The Influence of Quality of Service on Customer Satisfaction Towards Hotel Industry. *FMDB Transactions on Sustainable Social Sciences Letters, 1*(1), 1–11.

Chapter 9
Leveraging MIS Technologies for Preserving India's Cultural Heritage on Digitization, Accessibility, and Sustainability

A. Sabarirajan
PSNA College of Engineering and Technology, India

Latha Thamma Reddi
https://orcid.org/0009-0005-6338-7972
DXC Technology, USA

Sandeep Rangineni
https://orcid.org/0009-0003-9623-4062
Pluto TV, USA

R. Regin
SRM Institute of Science And Technology, India

S. Suman Rajest
https://orcid.org/0000-0001-8315-3747
Dhaanish Ahmed College of Engineering, India

P. Paramasivan
Dhaanish Ahmed College of Engineering, India

ABSTRACT

Written documents, inscriptions, and artefacts have been left behind by India's long and eventful past, providing a wealth of essential information about the country's cultural legacy. India's history spans many millennia, making it one of the world's oldest civilizations. However, given the fragile nature of these old materials and their widespread distribution across the world, preserving and gaining access to them can be a difficult and time-consuming endeavour. This study investigates the application of management information system (MIS) technologies with the goal of enhancing digital archiving and preservation techniques for India's immense cultural heritage in order to overcome the challenges described above. The research endeavours to provide solutions to problems that arise in relation to the maintenance and accessibility of historical documents and artefacts by centering its attention on digitalization, data management, and cloud storage.

DOI: 10.4018/979-8-3693-0049-7.ch009

1. INTRODUCTION

The history of India extends back over many centuries and include a great number of written records, inscriptions, and artefacts that provide light on the country's rich cultural past (Tripathi & Al-Shahri, 2023). However, the delicate character of historical materials, in conjunction with their geographical dispersion, provides considerable hurdles to both the preservation of these resources and their accessibility (Ocoró et al., 2023). This study investigates the potential for Management Information System (MIS) technologies to revolutionise digital archiving and preservation strategies, thereby ensuring that India's cultural heritage will be preserved for future generations (Vashishtha & Dhawan, 2023). This research was conducted to address the challenges that have been mentioned (Ahmad & Sharma, 2020).

The process of digitising historical records is going to be the primary focus of this investigation (Srinivas et al., 2023). The procedure entails the application of cutting-edge imaging techniques, Optical Character Recognition (OCR), and data validation in order to guarantee the correct reproduction of tangible historical records while maintaining the original documents' authenticity and integrity (Priscila et al., 2023). This shift from physical to digital formats not only improves the long-term preservation of these delicate items but also makes it easier for scholars, historians, and the general public to gain access to a greater amount of information (Vashishtha & Kapoor, 2023).

The lifespan and accessibility of digitised historical records are dependent on effective data management and storage practises being put into place (Venkateswaran & Viktor, 2023). This chapter examines the significance of effective data organisation, the generation of metadata, and quality control techniques in order to facilitate effective retrieval and to guarantee the integrity of the data (Kuragayala, 2023). Cloud-based preservation solutions are being considered as a potential perfect platform for safely preserving India's historical archives due to their scalability, accessibility, and redundancy (Venkateswaran et al., 2023). This research investigates the design and development of user-friendly interfaces with the objective of simplifying the process of searching for and navigating through historical documents in the interest of increasing user accessibility (Said & Tripathi, 2023). These user interfaces improve the overall user experience, which in turn encourages increased involvement with India's cultural legacy, which in turn fosters a deeper understanding and appreciation of the country's past (Tambaip et al., 2023).

However, the preservation of India's cultural heritage through digitization gives rise to legal and ethical considerations (Ramos et al., 2023). This chapter critically examines the implications of copyright, intellectual property, and ethical concerns related to digitization and data sharing. A delicate balance must be struck between the principles of open access and responsible preservation, taking into account the rights and responsibilities of all stakeholders involved.

2. LITERATURE REVIEW

Cultural heritage, encompassing both tangible and intangible expressions, has gained prominence since the mid-20th century, spurred by organizations like UNESCO, which articulated its definition during the 1972 Convention for the Protection of World Cultural and Natural Heritage. This definition, acknowledging the evolving nature of cultural heritage, reflects changes in conservation paradigms influenced by global developments (Vecco, 2010 & UNESCO). Heritage knowledge, the legacy inherited from the past, is transmitted through oral tradition and written mediums such as songs, poems, and philosophical ideas (Graham, 2002 & Akhlak et al., 2020). To safeguard these resources and make them accessible to a broader audience, digitization emerges as a pivotal method (María et al., 2023).

Preservation, the deliberate act of conserving cultural heritage for posterity, finds application in historical museums, cultural centers, research, and education (Logan, 2007). Across nations, concerns about safeguarding and transmitting cultural and intangible heritages to new generations have led to the adoption of information and communication technologies (ICTs) for effective preservation and dissemination. These tools facilitate showcasing traditional sites (Jara et al., 2015; Manzhong, 2017), imparting a nation's cultural richness (Tan & Wu, 2016; Zhu et al., 2017), disseminating region-specific symbols (Zhang et al., 2015; Huang & Chen, 2019), and digitally protecting intangible heritage (Liu, 2015; Zhao, 2017).

Hari Krishna et al. (2023) present a study that highlights the ethical dimensions of artificial intelligence in business research; the chapter provides a foundation for ethical considerations that are vital when deploying technology for preserving cultural artifacts and traditions. The work of Bhanushali et al. (2022) investigate the importance of data analysis and interpretation, which can be translated to the digitization and analysis of cultural artifacts. The study conducted by Ramesh Kumar et al. (2022) explores the impact of training and development and the chapter's insights into training and development have relevance in the context of skill development and capacity-building for heritage conservation efforts.

Venkateswaran et al. (2018) propose a Technology Acceptance Model for automobile purchase decisions. While the focus is on the automobile industry, the concept of technology acceptance is transferable to the cultural heritage domain, where user-friendly and accessible digitization platforms play a crucial role.

India, boasting an extensive and ancient collection of manuscripts, confronts the challenge of preserving these resources scattered across the nation in various heritage institutions and personal holdings (Tripathi, 2021). The imperative to identify, document, preserve, and provide research community access underscores the need for proper archiving. Many of these invaluable resources currently face degradation and potential extinction due to inadequate preservation measures.

3. RESEARCH METHODOLOGY

The research adopts qualitative and quantitative techniques to comprehensively address the objectives of the study. The qualitative aspect will involve in-depth interviews and focus group discussions with experts in digital archiving, cultural heritage preservation, and MIS technologies and the general public (Żywiołek et al., 2022). The qualitative data was collected through purposive sampling, selecting knowledgeable experts in the field. Semi-structured interviews and focus group discussions will be conducted to explore their insights, experiences, and opinions regarding the use of MIS technologies in cultural heritage preservation. The qualitative data will provide rich, contextual information to complement the quantitative findings.

The qualitative data collected from interviews and focus group discussions are transcribed and thematically analyzed (Pandit, 2023). Thematic analysis, introduced by Braun and Clarke (2006), emerges as a powerful tool for identifying, organizing, and describing recurring frames within collected data (Batool et al., 2023). This approach allows for the exploration of diverse perspectives among research participants, often yielding unforeseen insights. Thematic analysis centers on identifying recurrent themes, thus furnishing a comprehensive overview of key outcomes derived from qualitatively coded interview texts. The thematic analysis will involve identifying recurring patterns, themes, and insights, helping to draw meaningful conclusions from the qualitative data.

4. FINDINGS AND SUGGESTIONS

The provided data consists of responses to a questionnaire related to cultural heritage preservation and the use of Management Information Systems (MIS) technologies for this purpose. The responses are grouped into several sections, each containing multiple questions and corresponding answers. The analysis aims to extract common themes, insights, and perspectives from these responses. The survey data analysis reveals several key themes and insights regarding the understanding of cultural heritage preservation and its intersection with Management Information Systems (MIS) technologies (Table 1).

Table 1. Understanding of cultural heritage preservation and MIS technologies

Section I	Questions Focused	Key Themes	Mentions	Proportion
Understanding of Cultural Heritage Preservation and MIS Technologies	· Can you describe your understanding of cultural heritage preservation and its importance? · In your opinion, how can Management Information Systems (MIS) technologies contribute to cultural heritage preservation?	Social Cohesion and Understanding	41	34%
		Future Generations and Education	24	20%
		Research and Tourism	31	25%
		Identity and National Pride	12	10%
		Definition of Cultural Heritage	14	11%

Social Cohesion and Understanding (34%): A significant proportion of respondents emphasize the role of cultural heritage preservation in fostering social cohesion and enhancing understanding among diverse communities. This indicates recognition of heritage as a unifying force that promotes inclusivity and mutual respect.

Future Generations and Education (20%): A notable number of participants acknowledge the significance of cultural heritage preservation in providing educational opportunities for future generations. This suggests a prevailing sentiment that preserving heritage through MIS technologies can serve as a valuable educational resource, enriching the learning experiences of young individuals (Anand et al., 2023).

Research and Tourism (25%): A considerable portion of respondents recognize the potential of MIS technologies in facilitating research and boosting tourism through cultural heritage preservation. This highlights the belief that digital platforms and systems can attract scholarly interest and attract visitors, thereby contributing to economic growth (Tucmeanu et al., 2022).

Identity and National Pride (10%): A smaller yet notable percentage of respondents emphasize the connection between cultural heritage preservation and fostering a sense of identity and national pride. This suggests that preserving heritage through MIS technologies can reinforce a nation's unique cultural identity and evoke a sense of collective pride.

Definition of Cultural Heritage (11%): A distinct segment of participants engages with the concept of defining cultural heritage. This underscores the importance of clarifying what constitutes cultural heritage in a contemporary context, possibly indicating ongoing discussions and evolving perspectives within the field (Table 2).

Table 2. Use of MIS technologies in cultural heritage preservation

Section II	Questions Focused	Key Themes	Mentions	Proportion
Use of MIS Technologies in Cultural Heritage Preservation	· Have you had any personal experience or involvement in utilizing MIS technologies for cultural heritage preservation projects? If yes, could you provide an example? · What types of MIS technologies have you come across in the context of cultural heritage preservation? · How do you perceive the effectiveness of MIS technologies in documenting and safeguarding cultural heritage? Please provide examples to illustrate your viewpoint.	Digitization and Preservation	42	34
		Remote Monitoring	34	28
		Virtual Reality (VR)	27	22
		Big Data Analytics	19	16

The analysis of responses pertaining to the utilization of Management Information Systems (MIS) technologies in cultural heritage preservation reveals several key themes and insights:

Digitization and preservation (34%): A substantial proportion of respondents have engaged with MIS technologies for digitizing and preserving cultural heritage. This indicates a prevailing trend in leveraging digital tools to create digital archives, replicas, or representations of cultural artifacts, sites, and traditions. Participants cite instances where MIS technologies have been employed to convert physical artifacts into digital formats, ensuring their longevity and accessibility.

Remote Monitoring (28%): A noteworthy segment of participants acknowledges the role of MIS technologies, particularly remote monitoring systems, in cultural heritage preservation. This highlights the practicality of remote sensing, data collection, and real-time monitoring in safeguarding vulnerable heritage sites, artworks, and artifacts. Respondents emphasize the value of continuous surveillance to prevent damage or theft.

Virtual Reality (VR) (22%): A considerable number of respondents express familiarity with MIS technologies like Virtual Reality (VR) for cultural heritage preservation. This suggests an appreciation for immersive experiences that enable users to explore historical sites, artifacts, and cultural contexts. Examples provided by participants highlight the use of VR to engage audiences and convey the significance of heritage.

Big Data Analytics (16%): A notable proportion of participants recognize the potential of Big Data Analytics within the context of cultural heritage preservation. This underscores the use of advanced data processing techniques to analyze vast amounts of information related to heritage sites, artworks, and historical data. Participants believe that such analyses can yield valuable insights for conservation and management strategies (Table 3).

Table 3. Challenges and opportunities

Section III	Question Focused	Key Themes	Mentions	Proportion
Challenges and Opportunities	· Based on your experiences, what are some of the challenges or obstacles associated with implementing MIS technologies in cultural heritage preservation? · Are there any specific cultural or ethical considerations that need to be addressed when using MIS technologies for heritage preservation? · From your perspective, what potential opportunities or innovative approaches do MIS technologies bring to enhance cultural heritage preservation efforts?	Technical Expertise	46	38%
		Cultural Sensitivities	37	30%
		Standardization	22	18%
		Data Sharing and Consistency	17	14%

In Table 3, the focus is on addressing challenges and opportunities related to the implementation of Management Information Systems (MIS) technologies in the context of cultural heritage preservation. The content presents key themes and provides a breakdown of mentions and proportions for various aspects.

Challenges and Opportunities: The section begins by posing questions about challenges and obstacles associated with integrating MIS technologies into cultural heritage preservation. It seeks to understand the difficulties faced in this endeavor. Additionally, it prompts exploration of potential opportunities and innovative approaches that MIS technologies can offer to enhance efforts in safeguarding cultural heritage.

Technical Expertise: The data reveals that technical expertise is a prominent theme, mentioned 46 times, making up 38% of the content. This suggests that having the necessary technical skills and knowledge is crucial for successfully implementing MIS technologies in cultural heritage preservation.

Cultural Sensitivities: Cultural sensitivities emerge as another significant theme, with 37 mentions (30% of the content). This indicates that respecting and addressing cultural values, beliefs, and practices is a critical consideration when using MIS technologies for heritage preservation.

Standardization: Standardization is highlighted as a key concern, mentioned 22 times (18% of the content). This implies that establishing consistent protocols and frameworks for utilizing MIS technologies is important to ensure effective cultural heritage preservation.

Data Sharing and Consistency: The theme of data sharing and consistency is mentioned 17 times. While not as dominant as other themes, this aspect still holds importance (14% of the content). It suggests that maintaining accurate and accessible data, along with ensuring its uniformity, is a factor to be reckoned with.

The distribution of mentions and proportions among these key themes provides insight into the different aspects that influence the integration of MIS technologies into cultural heritage preservation efforts. The focus on technical expertise, cultural sensitivities, standardization, and data management underscores the multifaceted nature of the challenges and opportunities in this domain.

Table 4 of the content delves into the subject of collaborations and stakeholder involvement in the context of integrating Management Information Systems (MIS) technologies into cultural heritage preservation. The section focuses on key themes, providing insights through mentions and proportions of these themes.

Table 4. Collaborations and stakeholder involvement

Section IV	Question Focused	Key Themes	Mentions	Proportion
Collaborations and Stakeholder Involvement	· How do you think collaboration among different stakeholders (e.g., local communities, experts, and government bodies) can impact the successful integration of MIS technologies in cultural heritage preservation? · What recommendations would you provide to improve the integration and effectiveness of MIS technologies in cultural heritage preservation initiatives?	The importance of collaboration	39	32%
		The role of local communities	42	34%
		The role of experts.	26	21%
		The role of government bodies	11	9%
		Challenges and benefits of collaboration	4	3%

Importance of Collaboration: The content begins by addressing the significance of collaboration among various stakeholders, such as local communities, experts, and government bodies. It seeks to explore how working together can impact the successful implementation of MIS technologies in cultural heritage preservation. This theme is emphasized with 39 mentions, constituting 32% of the content. This suggests that collaboration is seen as a vital factor in the effective use of MIS technologies for preserving cultural heritage.

The Role of Local Communities: The role of local communities is a central theme, with 42 mentions (34% of the content). This indicates that involving and engaging local communities in heritage preservation efforts is considered crucial. Their participation is likely seen as instrumental in ensuring the relevance and sustainability of MIS technology integration.

The Role of Experts: The theme of the role of experts is highlighted with 26 mentions (21% of the content). This implies that the insights and expertise of professionals in the field play a significant role in guiding the successful incorporation of MIS technologies for cultural heritage preservation.

The Role of Government Bodies: Government bodies' role is discussed with 11 mentions (9% of the content). This suggests that governmental support and involvement are recognized as important for creating an enabling environment and implementing policies that facilitate the integration of MIS technologies in heritage preservation.

Challenges and Benefits of Collaboration: Although a smaller proportion, the content briefly touches on the challenges and benefits of collaboration, mentioned 4 times (3% of the content). This implies that while collaboration brings advantages, there may also be obstacles that need to be navigated.

Overall, Section IV underscores the vital role of collaboration among stakeholders, particularly local communities and experts, in the successful integration of MIS technologies for cultural heritage preservation. It acknowledges the influence of government bodies and briefly addresses potential challenges and benefits arising from collaborative efforts.

Table 5 of the data focuses on future trends and recommendations regarding the utilization of Management Information Systems (MIS) technologies for cultural heritage preservation. This section provides insights into anticipated developments and suggested actions, which are categorized by key themes, along with their mentions and proportions.

Increased Use of AI: With 20 mentions (16% of the content), the theme of increased use of Artificial Intelligence (AI) stands out. This suggests a strong anticipation that AI technologies will play a more prominent role in enhancing cultural heritage preservation efforts, possibly through tasks like data analysis, pattern recognition, and automation (Mohsan et al., 2022).

Table 5. Future trends and recommendations

Section V	Question Focused	Key Themes	Mentions	Proportion
Future Trends and Recommendations	· In your opinion, what future trends do you anticipate in the use of MIS technologies for cultural heritage preservation? · What recommendations would you provide to improve the integration and effectiveness of MIS technologies in cultural heritage preservation initiatives?	Increased use of AI	20	16%
		VR and AR	12	10%
		Big data	11	9%
		Increased funding	19	16%
		Improved training	20	16%
		Standardized guidelines	14	11%
		Cultural sensitivity	15	12%
		Continued research and development	11	9%

VR and AR: Virtual Reality (VR) and Augmented Reality (AR) are mentioned 12 times (10% of the content). This implies an expectation that these immersive technologies will gain significance in bringing cultural heritage experiences to life, offering interactive and engaging ways for audiences to connect with heritage sites (Khan et al., 2023).

Big Data: The theme of big data is mentioned 11 times (9% of the content). This indicates a recognition of the potential of large-scale data collection and analysis to provide valuable insights for effective cultural heritage preservation strategies.

Increased Funding: The need for increased funding is highlighted with 19 mentions (16% of the content). This suggests that securing adequate financial resources is considered essential for the successful integration and sustainability of MIS technologies in heritage preservation initiatives.

Improved Training: The importance of improved training is emphasized with 20 mentions (16% of the content). This signifies the belief that enhancing the skills and knowledge of individuals involved in heritage preservation will contribute to more effective use of MIS technologies.

Standardized Guidelines: Standardized guidelines are mentioned 14 times (11% of the content). This points to the recognition that having clear and consistent protocols for the use of MIS technologies is important for maintaining quality and integrity in cultural heritage preservation efforts.

Cultural Sensitivity: Cultural sensitivity is mentioned 15 times (12% of the content). This highlights the awareness of the need to address cultural considerations and respect local values when implementing MIS technologies in heritage preservation.

Continued Research and Development: The theme of continued research and development is mentioned 11 times (9% of the content). This suggests an understanding that ongoing innovation and exploration will be necessary to keep pace with evolving technologies and cultural preservation needs.

Overall, Section V indicates a forward-looking perspective, anticipating a greater role for AI, VR, and AR in cultural heritage preservation. It emphasizes the importance of funding, training, guidelines, and cultural sensitivity while also recognizing the need for ongoing research and development to shape the future of MIS technologies in this domain (Table 6).

The provided content presents key themes and their corresponding mentions along with proportions in response to a question focused on experiences, opinions, or insights related to the use of Management Information Systems (MIS) technologies in cultural heritage preservation. The responses highlight various aspects of improving the effectiveness and impact of MIS technologies in this domain.

Table 6. Additional insights

Section VI	Question Focused	Key Themes	Mentions	Proportion
Additional Insights	Is there anything else you would like to share about your experiences, opinions, or insights related to the use of MIS technologies in cultural heritage preservation?	Increased Funding	20	16%
		Enhanced Training	19	16%
		Uniform Standards	16	13%
		Collaborative Approach	15	12%
		Cultural and Ethical Considerations	14	11%
		Continued Research and Development	11	9%
		Global Accessibility	13	11%
		Educational Outreach	14	11%

Increased funding (16%): A significant portion of the respondents emphasized the need for increased funding in the field of cultural heritage preservation using MIS technologies. This indicates that financial support is crucial to facilitate the development and implementation of advanced technologies for safeguarding cultural heritage.

Enhanced training (16%): The respondents recognize the importance of providing enhanced training to individuals involved in cultural heritage preservation. This suggests a consensus that training programs should be designed to equip professionals with the necessary skills to effectively utilize MIS technologies for preserving cultural artifacts and sites.

Uniform Standards (13%): The mention of uniform standards suggests a concern for establishing consistent guidelines and protocols for using MIS technologies in cultural heritage preservation. This standardization could ensure that efforts are aligned and that data and methodologies are compatible across various projects.

Collaborative approach (12%): The emphasis on a collaborative approach highlights the recognition that successful cultural heritage preservation requires partnerships and cooperation among various stakeholders. This approach could involve collaboration between different organizations, experts, and communities.

Cultural and Ethical Considerations (11%): The acknowledgment of cultural and ethical considerations indicates a thoughtful approach to using MIS technologies in cultural heritage preservation. Respondents likely discussed the importance of respecting cultural sensitivities and ethical principles in the integration of technology.

Continued Research and Development (9%): The recognition of the need for continued research and development reflects an understanding that the field of MIS technologies in cultural heritage preservation is evolving. This suggests a desire for ongoing innovation and improvements in the technology and methodologies used.

Global Accessibility (11%): The mention of global accessibility suggests an awareness of the importance of ensuring that MIS technologies are accessible and applicable across different regions and cultural contexts. This aligns with the broader goal of making cultural heritage preservation efforts inclusive and widely beneficial.

Educational outreach (11%): The emphasis on educational outreach indicates recognition of the role of public awareness and education in cultural heritage preservation. This likely involves initiatives to inform and engage the public in the importance of using MIS technologies for safeguarding cultural heritage.

In summary, the responses provided in the content highlight several key themes that are crucial for the effective use of MIS technologies in cultural heritage preservation. These themes encompass financial support, training, standardization, collaboration, cultural considerations, research and development, global accessibility, and educational outreach. Respondents express a comprehensive understanding of the multifaceted aspects involved in leveraging technology for the preservation of cultural heritage.

5. SUGGESTIONS FOR ENHANCING MIS TECHNOLOGIES IN CULTURAL HERITAGE PRESERVATION

Increased Funding: Allocate more resources to support the implementation and maintenance of MIS technologies, enabling broader access and improved infrastructure.

Enhanced Training: Develop comprehensive training programs to equip professionals with the technical skills required for effective use of MIS technologies.

Uniform Standards: Establish consistent guidelines for digitization, cataloging, and preservation of cultural artifacts to ensure quality and coherence across projects.

Collaborative Approach: Foster collaboration among stakeholders, including local communities, experts, and government bodies, ensuring culturally sensitive and efficient use of MIS technologies.

Cultural and Ethical Considerations: Prioritize addressing cultural and ethical aspects in MIS technology implementation, including respect for beliefs, privacy, and sensitivities.

Continued Research and Development: Support ongoing research to leverage technological advancements for enhancing cultural heritage preservation.

Global Accessibility: Extend access to MIS technologies, especially in developing regions, promoting wider community engagement.

Educational Outreach: Utilize MIS technologies for educational purposes, creating interactive resources to raise public awareness and appreciation for heritage preservation.

6. CONCLUSION

The literature underscores the evolving nature of cultural heritage preservation, spurred by organizations like UNESCO (1072) and fueled by the rapid advancement of information and communication technologies. Preservation efforts are integral to ensuring the transmission of heritage knowledge to future generations. The case of India's manuscripts highlights the urgency of preserving tangible cultural heritage through effective digitization and archiving strategies. The responses from participants highlight a deep appreciation for the role of cultural heritage preservation in fostering social cohesion, education, research, national pride, and tourism. The understanding of MIS technologies' potential to digitize, monitor, and create an immersive experience resonates with the participants' perspectives. The integration of MIS technologies in heritage preservation holds immense promise, from digitizing artifacts for protection and accessibility to employing big data analytics for impact assessment.

Challenges such as data security, technical expertise, and cultural sensitivities are recognized. It is evident that the involvement of local communities, experts, and government bodies is crucial for the successful integration of MIS technologies. Collaborative efforts not only enrich the preservation process but also ensure cultural authenticity. As future trends unfold, participants foresee AI, VR, AR, and expanded big data analytics playing pivotal roles in cultural heritage preservation. Their recommendations emphasize the need for funding, training, uniform standards, collaboration, and continued research to harness the full potential of MIS technologies. Overall, the insights gathered highlight the transformative power of MIS technologies and the collective commitment to preserving and promoting cultural heritage for generations to come.

REFERENCES

Ahmad, A., & Sharma, S. (2020). Sustainable digital preservation and access of heritage knowledge in India: A review. *DESIDOC Journal of Library and Information Technology*, *40*(5), 321–325. doi:10.14429/djlit.40.05.15822

Anand, P. P., Kanike, U. K., Paramasivan, P., Rajest, S. S., Regin, R., & Priscila, S. S. (2023). Embracing Industry 5.0: Pioneering Next-Generation Technology for a Flourishing Human Experience and Societal Advancement. *FMDB Transactions on Sustainable Social Sciences Letters*, *1*(1), 43–55.

Batool, K., Zhao, Z.-Y., Irfan, M., & Żywiołek, J. (2023). Assessing the role of sustainable strategies in alleviating energy poverty: An environmental sustainability paradigm. *Environmental Science and Pollution Research International*, *30*(25), 67109–67130. doi:10.100711356-023-27076-0 PMID:37103699

Bhanushali, M. M., Narang, P., Sabarirajan, A., & Turai, A. K., S. K., & U, K. S. (2022). Human Resource Management based Economic analysis using Data Mining. In *Proceedings of the 2022 3rd International Conference on Intelligent Engineering and Management (ICIEM)* (pp. 872-876). 10.1109/ICIEM54221.2022.9853202

Braun, V., & Clarke, V. (2006). Using thematic analysis in psychology. *Qualitative Research in Psychology*, *3*(2), 77–101. doi:10.1191/1478088706qp063oa

Graham, B. (2002). Heritage as knowledge: Capital or culture? *Urban Studies (Edinburgh, Scotland)*, *39*(5-6), 1003–1017. doi:10.1080/00420980220128426

Hari Krishna, S., Madala, R., Ramya, P., Sabarirajan, A., Dobhal, D., & Sapate, S. (2023). Ethically Governed Artificial Intelligence Based Innovative Business Research in Finance and Marketing System. In *Proceedings of the 2023 Eighth International Conference on Science Technology Engineering and Mathematics (ICONSTEM)* (pp. 1-7). 10.1109/ICONSTEM56934.2023.10142352

Huang, Y.-C., & Chen, Y.-J. (2019). Digital Image Design Research of Popular Culture Exhibition. *Proceedings of the International Conference on Signal and Image Processing*. 10.1109/SIPROCESS.2019.8868467

Jara, A. J., Sun, T. Y., Song, H., Bie, T. R., Genooud, D., & Bocchi, Y. (2015). Internet of Things for Cultural Heritage of Smart Cities and Smart Regions. *Proceedings of the IEEE 29th—International Conference on Advanced Information Networking and Applications Workshops*. 10.1109/WAINA.2015.169

Khan, M. A., Kumar, N., Mohsan, S. A. H., Khan, W. U., Nasralla, M. M., Alsharif, M. H., & Ullah, I. (2023). Swarm of UAVs for network management in 6G: A technical review. *IEEE Transactions on Network and Service Management, 20*(1), 741–761. doi:10.1109/TNSM.2022.3213370

Kuragayala, P. S. (2023). A Systematic Review on Workforce Development in Healthcare Sector: Implications in the Post-COVID Scenario. *FMDB Transactions on Sustainable Technoprise Letters, 1*(1), 36–46.

Liu, X. (2015). Research on the Service Platform to Realize Unified Retrieval and Revelation of Digital Cultural Resources. *Proceedings of the 8th International Symposium on Computational Intelligence and Design.* 10.1109/ISCID.2015.239

Manzhong, L. (2017). The Application of Virtual Reality Technology in the Preservation of Mining and Metallurgy Culture in Huangshi Region. *Proceedings of the 2017 IEEE International Conference on Information, Communication and Engineering.* 10.1109/ICICE.2017.8479067

María, J. J. L., Polo, O. C. C., & Elhadary, T. (2023). An Analysis of the Morality and Social Responsibility of Non-Profit Organizations. *FMDB Transactions on Sustainable Technoprise Letters, 1*(1), 28–35.

Mohsan, S. A. H., Othman, N. Q. H., Khan, M. A., Amjad, H., & Żywiołek, J. (2022). A comprehensive review of micro UAV charging techniques. *Micromachines, 13*(6), 977. doi:10.3390/mi13060977 PMID:35744592

Ocoró, M. P., Polo, O. C. C., & Khandare, S. (2023). Importance of Business Financial Risk Analysis in SMEs According to COVID-19. *FMDB Transactions on Sustainable Management Letters, 1*(1), 12–21.

Pandit, P. (2023). On the Context of the Principle of Beneficence: The Problem of Over Demandingness within Utilitarian Theory. *FMDB Transactions on Sustainable Social Sciences Letters, 1*(1), 26–42.

Priscila, S. S., Rajest, S. S., Tadiboina, S. N., Regin, R., & András, S. (2023). Analysis of Machine Learning and Deep Learning Methods for Superstore Sales Prediction. *FMDB Transactions on Sustainable Computer Letters, 1*(1), 1–11.

Ramesh Kumar, V., Selvaraj, M., Venkateswaran, P. S., Sabarirajan, A., Shatila, K., & Agarwal, V. (2022). The impact of training and development programs on employees' performance: The case of Lebanese SMEs. *International Journal of Intellectual Property Management, 12*(3).

Ramos, J. I., Lacerona, R., & Nunag, J. M. (2023). A Study on Operational Excellence, Work Environment Factors and the Impact to Employee Performance. *FMDB Transactions on Sustainable Social Sciences Letters, 1*(1), 12–25.

Said, F. B., & Tripathi, S. (2023). Epistemology of Digital Journalism Shift in South Global Nations: A Bibliometric Analysis. *FMDB Transactions on Sustainable Technoprise Letters, 1*(1), 47–60.

Srinivas, K., Velmurugan, P. R., & Andiyappillai, N. (2023). Digital Human Resources and Management Support Improve Human Resources Effectiveness. *FMDB Transactions on Sustainable Management Letters, 1*(1), 32–45.

Tambaip, B., Hadi, A. F. F., & Tjilen, A. P. (2023). Optimizing Public Service Performance: Unleashing the Potential of Compassion as an Indicator of Public Service Motivation. *FMDB Transactions on Sustainable Management Letters, 1*(2), 46–55.

Tan, X., & Wu, C. Y. X. (2016). Chinese Traditional Visual Cultural Symbols Recognition Based on Convolutional Neural Network. *Proceedings of the International Conference on Measuring Technology and Mechatronics Automation.*

Tripathi, D. S. (2021). *Guidelines for digitisation of archival material.* National Mission for Manuscripts. https://www.yumpu.com/en/document/view/33206162/standards-for-digitization-national-mission-for-manuscripts

Tripathi, S., & Al-Shahri, M. (2023). Problems and Prospects on the Evolution of Advertising and Public Relations Industries in Oman. *FMDB Transactions on Sustainable Management Letters, 1*(1), 1–11.

Tucmeanu, E. R., Tucmeanu, A. I., Iliescu, M. G., Żywiołek, J., & Yousaf, Z. (2022). Successful management of IT projects in healthcare institutions after COVID-19: Role of digital orientation and innovation adaption. *Healthcare (Basel), 10*(10), 2005. doi:10.3390/healthcare10102005 PMID:36292452

UNESCO. (1972). *Convención Sobre la Protección del Patrimonio Mundial, Cultural y Natural.* UNESCO.

UNESCO. (n.d.). *What is Intangible Cultural Heritage?* Retrieved from https://ich.unesco.org/en/what-is-intangible-heritage-00003

Vashishtha, E., & Dhawan, G. (2023). Comparison of Baldrige Criteria of Strategy Planning and Harrison Text. *FMDB Transactions on Sustainable Management Letters, 1*(1), 22–31.

Vashishtha, E., & Kapoor, H. (2023). Implementation of Blockchain Technology Across International Healthcare Markets. *FMDB Transactions on Sustainable Technoprise Letters, 1*(1), 1–12.

Vecco, M. (2010). A definition of cultural heritage: From the tangible to the intangible. *Journal of Cultural Heritage, 11*(3), 321–324. doi:10.1016/j.culher.2010.01.006

Venkateswaran, P. S., Sabarirajan, A., Arun, B., Muthupandian, T., & Manimaran, D. S. (2018). Technology Acceptance Model for Making Decision to Purchase Automobile in Coimbatore District. *International Journal of Mechanical Engineering and Technology, 9*(11), 1608–1613.

Venkateswaran, P. S., Singh, S., Paramasivan, P., Rajest, S. S., Lourens, M. E., & Regin, R. (2023). A Study on The Influence of Quality of Service on Customer Satisfaction Towards Hotel Industry. *FMDB Transactions on Sustainable Social Sciences Letters, 1*(1), 1–11.

Venkateswaran, P. S., & Viktor, P. (2023). A Study on Brand Equity of Fast-Moving Consumer Goods with Reference to Madurai, Tamil Nadu. *FMDB Transactions on Sustainable Technoprise Letters, 1*(1), 13–27.

Zhang, G., Wang, J., Huang, W., Yang, Y., Su, H., Yue, Y., Zhai, Y., Liu, M., & Chen, L. (2015). A Study of Chinese Character Culture Big Data Platform. *Proceedings of the International Conference on Cloud Computing and Big Data.* 10.1109/CCBD.2015.18

Zhu, Z., Fan, M., Sun, C., & Long, R. (2017). Cultural symbiosis: Chu Culture and Course Teaching of Interface Design-A Case Study on a Chinese Bestiary. *Proceedings of the 2017 7th International Workshop on Computer Science and Engineering*.

Żywiołek, J., Tucmeanu, E. R., Tucmeanu, A. I., Isac, N., & Yousaf, Z. (2022). Nexus of transformational leadership, employee adaptiveness, knowledge sharing, and employee creativity. *Sustainability (Basel)*, *14*(18), 11607. doi:10.3390u141811607

Chapter 10
A Quality Perspective and Its Importance to Business Competitiveness on Human Resource Information Systems

N. Geethanjali
PSNA College of Engineering and Technology, India

Kishore Kandepu
Oberon IT Inc., USA

Seema Bhakuni
Doon Group of Institutions, India

P. Paramasivan
Dhaanish Ahmed College of Engineering, India

C. Satheesh
Dhaanish Ahmed College of Engineering, India

J. Rahila
Dhaanish Ahmed College of Engineering, India

ABSTRACT

Human resource information system (HRIS) is a human resource management (HRM) tool that allows an employer to design and manipulate a complete human sources method through records generation. The rising hyper-competitive generation over the previous few years has enhanced the need for maintaining records and inventions in human resource control for competitiveness. The revolution in the records era is absolutely and swiftly redefining the way matters are completed in almost every subject of human activity. Human assets and records generation are two factors that many corporations are looking to make use of as strategic weapons to compete. Human resource generation or human aid facts methods shape the interplay between human resource control and data technology. There has been a sizable increase within the wide variety of companies collecting, storing, and reading records regarding their human assets through using human aid data systems.

DOI: 10.4018/979-8-3693-0049-7.ch010

1. INTRODUCTION

A human resource information system, often known as an HRIS, is a piece of software that provides assistance to HRM operations by way of the generation of records. One of the most important functions of any organisation is providing assistance to individuals (Shibly, 2011). The use of HRIS as a means to accumulate information into key components leads to an increase in the productive capacity of an organisation (Alayli, 2023). In order to easily see and change employee standing in accordance with the organisational hierarchy, the HR records structures have been developed to be both flexible and obvious to HR managers and senior management (Atasever, 2023). This strategy provides HR professionals with the data they need to manage personnel databases (Bourini, 2011).

HRIS can help with long-range planning by providing data for hard workforce planning and delivery and demand forecasts. It can also help with staffing by providing statistics on same employment, separations, and applicant qualifications. Finally, it can help with improvement by providing data on education application fees and trainee work performance (Kadhim & Sadikmohamadtaqi, 2012). The performance of this software is improved because to its remarkable statistics (Kuragayala, 2023). The Human Resource Information System (HRIS) provides further assistance to payback programmes, earnings predictions, pay budgets, and hard work/employee members of the family by providing statistics on contract negotiations and employee assistance (Anand et al., 2023). It is necessary to have a quality assurance plan and procedures in place during the information collection process for HRIS in order to carry out these HRM activities. (Mara et al., 2023) The value of something is increased when its quality, whether it be in terms of human resources (HR) or materials.

Reliable data are the foundation for decisions that can garner consensus. This information must be accurate, trustworthy, presented in the correct time frame, and comprehensive. A correct, methodical, and scientific approach to determining human resource activities is provided by the features of an HRIS (Nagarajan & Naachimuthu, 2021). The data friendliness of HRIS provides assistance that is accurate, up to date, and condensed when making routine and recurring decisions about human resources. In this chapter, the most beneficial aspect of the Human Information system is discussed (Figure 1).

Figure 1. Human resource information systems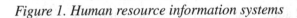

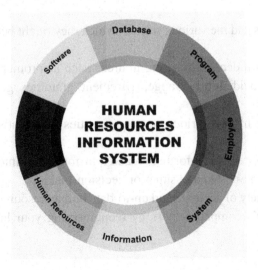

The recent years have seen the emergence of a hypercompetitive era, which has extended the requirement for records structures and eras in human aid control in order to maintain competitiveness (Naachimuthu et al., 2022). Systems of facts provide important contributions to the enhancement of organisational performance and the development of specialists in human resources (Shifana & Naachimuthu, 2022). In today's globally competitive business market, organisations frequently implement data structures and statistics technologies in an effort to improve the human resource management tool (Ramos et al., 2023). In conjunction with the development of data systems and technology, the introduction of Human Resource Information Structures (HRIS) has resulted in a major improvement in the capacity to satisfy factual requirements (Pandit, 2023). The Human Resource Information System (HRIS) is an integration of the traditional field of human resource management, specifically its major human resource activities and strategies, with the field of record generation (Priyadarshini & Naachimuthu, 2020). Experts in the field of human resources in the current world need precise and up-to-date information on a variety of topics, including recruiting, selection, education, advancement, repayment, productiveness, quality of life, and attrition rate, amongst others (Savya & Naachimuthu, 2022).

HRIS provides a great deal of assistance in the management of all procedures, activities, records, and information that are necessary to manage human resources in a modern workplace (Phoek et al., 2023). It addresses all facets of human resource management and functions as an integrated application that is required to collect, document, save, control, provide, manipulate, and present statistics regarding human assets (Ocoró et al., 2023). The purpose of this chapter is to provide information on the role and significance of HRIS in the direction of increasing business competitiveness (Sabti et al., 2023). The preceding chapter also emphasises the requirement for HRIS as well as its components, advantages, and capabilities (Padmapriya & Naachimuthu, 2023).

HRIS

A human resource records system, often known as an HRIS, is a mechanism that makes use of information technology in order to achieve effective management of various human resource characteristics and programmes (Priscila et al., 2023). It is a computerised device that typically consists of a records base or an inter-associated information base, and it is used to record staff and the precise details on their employment (Gill and Johnson, 2010). The following is a list of additional incentives for the installation of HRIS.

- A framework of policies and the various ways in which they might be applied in relation to human capital.
- Providing assistance with decision-making in areas such as promotions, transfers, nominations, setting the personnel provident price range, retirement, gratuities, go away tour concessions, and earned leave pay.
- Providing the government and various statutory entities with statistical information and filing required returns.
- The process of gathering relevant information and transforming it into facts and knowledge for the purpose of advancing time-tested and superior decision-making.
- Developing a wider variety of accurate and up-to-date human resource-related reports in real time.
- Increase your company's competitiveness by reengineering your human resource management strategies and functions.

- Increasing the happiness of workers by transferring responsibility for human aid services in a more timely and appropriate manner.
- provides a comprehensive records picture as a single, all-inclusive data base; this enables organisations to give structural connection across all of their teams and sports as well as increase the pace at which information transactions take place.

2. COMPONENTS OF HRIS

HRIS has major 3 purposeful components, as shown below (Figure 2).

Figure 2. Components of human aid records systems

Input: The enter function provides the capabilities essential to getting helpful information about human resources entered into the HRIS. It is the process of entering information about employees into the HRIS. Once the essential information has been acquired, the records must next be entered into the system, which necessitates the utilisation of specific strategies and procedures (Vashishtha & Dhawan, 2023). Edit tables are a useful tool for determining whether or not the information should be used (Sudheer & Naachimuthu, 2022). These tables include authorised values, which are used to guide the automated checks that are performed on the data (Said & Tripathi, 2023). The edit tables should be able to be easily changed and replaced by the tool, and the tool should have this functionality. The technology available today makes it possible to scan and store authentic photographs of company records, together with signatures and handwritten annotations (Saxena et al., 2023).

The actual updating of the data that has been saved in the various methods is the responsibility of the records renovation and data protection feature (Sri et al., 2022). These records need to be added to the system as changes occur in the statistics pertaining to human resources; as new information is added to the system, it is considerably more frequently applicable to keep the previous records in the form of historical data (Vashishtha, & Kapoor, 2023). After the statistics have been entered into the HRIS, it revises the base of statistics and adds new records to it (Venkateswaran, & Viktor, 2023).

Because the majority of people who use HRIS aren't concerned with gathering, modifying, and updating human resource information, the output function of HRIS is the one that gets the most attention. This is because most people who use HRIS are more concerned about the data and reports that are being used by the structures (Tripathi & Al-Shahri, 2023). In order to produce valuable output for users of laptops, HRIS approaches must first do necessary calculations and then format the display (Srinivas et al., 2023).

A human resource information system (HRIS) is a computerised tool that facilitates the processing of information concerning human resource management. A well-designed human resource information system (HRIS) serves as a responsible choice and an instrument that is intended to fulfil the needs of the company in terms of manpower statistics (Tambaip et al., 2023).

Quality of data is described by the level of information, the set of techniques to acquire this type of information, and the level of accuracy (Venkateswaran et al., 2023). For information to be matched for use, it must be free of duplications, misspellings, omissions, and useless variations, and need to agree to a described shape (Chapman, 2005).

Quality of Data

- Accurate
- Precise
- Appropriateness
- Totality
- Reliability and Relevance

The degree to which the statistics accurately reflect reality is one measure of the accuracy of the information. Accuracy is defined as the degree to which measured values, observations, or estimates of the actual or actual fee are close to the true value. Precise is a term that relates to the reliability of a brand in generating the same results every time. The availability of information at the time it is necessary is what is meant by "appropriateness." The term "totality" indicates that all records that are eligible are covered. The lack of apparent conflicts, as well as the degree of internal validity and reliability, are both components of the concept of relevance. These characteristics are important additions to HRIS in the field of HRM. The coverage of a good enough statistics base for decision-making techniques, development of diffusion software, education, training, advertising, career making plans, verbal exchange, evaluation of operating abilities of personnel', and complying working claims with individual abilities are therefore the fundamental causes of HRIS.

3. HRIS IN QUALITY PERSPECTIVE

Alam, (2017) investigates the role of MIS in enhancing decision-making through improved employee capabilities. Venkateswaran et al. (2018) propose a technology acceptance model that provides insights into technology acceptance and decision-making processes that can be extended to MIS utilization for informed decision-making.

The concept of first-class human resources records follows a hierarchical structure. Records of employees, control of facts, and access to experts are the three tiers that make up the hierarchy. Making sure that the appropriate person makes use of the relevant data in a timely manner is the primary challenge that arises in the process of managing and generating information. Measures of high-quality statistics centre on the output that is produced by a device in addition to the fee utility or relative relevance that is assigned to it by the user. (DeLone and colleagues' 2014 study). The most important qualities of information are tremendous, and they include exactness, precision, forex, timeliness of production, reliability, completeness, concision, format, and relevance (Obeidat, 2012). Quantification of the system's overall performance characteristics This principle refers back to the specifics of the technical interface for the facts system (DeLone et al., 2014). The following analysis describes the high-quality characteristics of important records, which can be used in determining the nature of the data.

Raw Data Regarding Human Resources It is likely that it will be hard to draw valuable information from the concept of data that is of substandard first-class. Therefore, information should be correct, comprehensive, and limited in scope.

Statistics control: From the raw statistics, accurate and compiled statistics are accumulated. These facts are used to research exclusive factors consistent with the requirements. This fact provides first-rate outcomes and a fundamental platform for useful human resource records devices.

Information accession: The consequences provided by using statistics evaluation enable to establishment of a whole HRIS. Consequently, decision-making, policy implementation, and knowledge sharing grow to be smooth in the enterprise.

In this particular setting, the goal shifted to the development of a conceptual framework for determining how utilisation and usefulness are impacted by HRIS statistics. Statistics system designs discovered that success is a property of the perceived pleasantness of the information that is given by utilising the system (Sabherwal et al., 2006; Delone et al., 2014). This finding was made in relation to a number of different variables (Figure 3).

Figure 3. HRIS In quality perspective

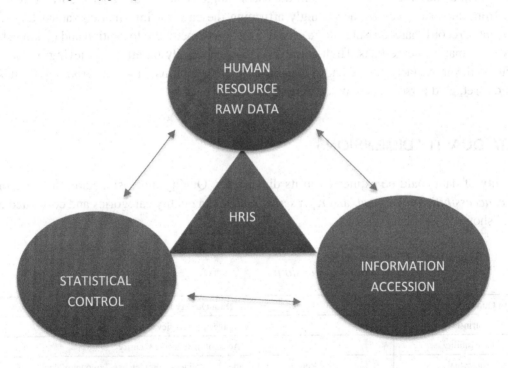

In this particular setting, the goal shifted to the development of a conceptual framework with the intention of comparing the influence of the quality of HRIS statistics on consumption and value. Records system models demonstrated, among other variables, that success is a characteristic of the perceived pleasantness of the data provided by the device. This was found to be the case regardless of the other variables (Sabherwal et al., 2006; Delone et al., 2014). Companies who want to get the most out of their investments in human resource information systems have to make sure they keep detailed records of the various quality improvement projects they undertake. This could ensure that the process is implemented appropriately and create exceptionally high-quality information that can be used for processing and decision-making. Additionally, this may result in an advantage gained by aggressive behaviour. In addition, study could be carried out in order to comprehend.

- Aspects crucial to the accomplishment of successful HRIS data quality programmes,
- Factors that influence the level of customer satisfaction with HRIS,
- Dedication and focus are the drivers for HRIS control responsibilities.
- The impact that having a supervisor trained in HRIS has on agencies.

Venkateswaran P.S. et al. (2018) propose a Technology Acceptance Model for automobile purchase decisions. While the focus is on the automobile industry, the concept of technology acceptance is transferable to the cultural heritage domain, where user-friendly and accessible digitization platforms play a crucial role.

Facts first-rate, either perceived or actual, have been determined to persuade persistent device utilization and user pride (Wu & Wang, 2006). Information usage and user satisfaction are regarded as primary records system achievement measures from the users" angle (Hong et al., 2008). Further, records are derived from uncooked records, accordingly affirming the case for information satisfactory control. Consequently, record characteristics play a crucial function in method information and making effective choices in Human resource facts. High-quality HRIS is especially based on achieving organizational goals due to the above facts quoted and spoken. Due to the fact human aid is a corporation's maximum treasured asset, glad personnel are preconditions for happy patrons.

4. DATA QUALITY DIMENSIONS

The quality of data could be explicated in its dimensions. Quality dimensions are four categories of *intrinsic, accessibility,* c*ontextual,* and *representational*. Data quality categories and correlated dimensions are shown in the table 1 below:

Table 1. Data quality categories and dimensions

Data Quality Category	Data Quality Dimension
Intrinsic	Accuracy, objectivity, believability, reputation
Accessibility	Accessibility, access security
Contextual	Relevancy, value-added, timeliness, completeness, amount of data
Representational	Interpretability, ease of understanding, concise representation, consistent representation.

In the above table, all categories may be described in the following ways.

Intrinsic: complete and actual information continually provides a real base for evaluation. These statistics pleasant category is involved with factors that include correctness and believability.

Accessibility: The use of records is an issue of safety too. Accessibility refers to the benefit of getting admission in addition to statistics safety. This saves us from unfair ways.

Representational: A whole and concise interpretation and generalization of the result make analysis extra vast and treasured. This dimension refers to the convenience of remodeling records into beneficial facts.

Raw data stored in Human resource information devices should meet these excellent necessities on the way to add value to the enterprise. Bad data satisfaction will have a bad impact on user attitudes toward the records systems and anticipated benefits (Swartz, 2007). A maximum of the agencies select the records' great dimensions and related measurement thresholds based totally on their business context, necessities, tiers of hazard, and so forth. Its miles stated that each dimension is in all likelihood to have a one-of-a-kind weighting, and so that it will achieve a correct degree of the pleasantness of facts, the enterprise will need to decide how an awful lot each size contributes to the quality of the facts as a whole.

5. IMPLEMENTATION OF HUMAN RESOURCE INFORMATION SYSTEM

The effective implementation of HRIS requires reengineering of business approaches, which isn't always smooth to adapt by using the human resource department. The usefulness of an HRIS is difficult for its customers. There are styles of HRIS users:

- HR specialists who deal with HR functions, and
- The ultimate beneficiary of HRIS.

Those are customers who decide the adoption of HRIS. It is very important to view the implementation of HRIS as a whole to ensure information integrity. The implementation of HRIS encountered several demanding situations that affected its recognition through its users, some of which include:

- Customs: Organizational tradition encourages undertaking HRIS on facts control, facts processes, and statistics use.
- Statistics series mode: To make sure the collection of first-class records moves from a series of mixture records to centers-degree and body of workers-stage statistics
- Improvement of quality efforts: A right method has to exist in business enterprise to improve records exceptional if it isn't always as much as expected.
- Adoption: hobby to Adopting new records management technology and procedures.
- Adjustments: coping with everyday modifications within the human resource facts required as consistent with the process.
- Update: well-timed and reliable information on HRIS ought to be updated from time to time.

Furthermore, Ruel (2004) of their paper identified six environmental characteristics that affect HRIS implementation; these are competition, technological development, HRM nation of art, hard work marketplace, societal developments, and governmental regulation. Apart from those factors, it's stated that in a transnational agency, the HRIS is inspired by factors such as institutional and cultural host-USA environment (Dowling et al., 2008). The general implementation of HRIS will be effective till its satisfaction will be able and valuable.

Preference of HRIS

HRIS helps in recording and analyzing personal and business enterprise records and documents, which include worker handbooks, emergency evacuation, and safety strategies (Fletcher, 2005). It also enables the organizations to preserve a correct, entire, and up-to-date information base that may be retrieved from reviews and manuals.

HRIS benefits may be systematized in line with Kovach et al., 1999).

- Increase competitiveness by enhancing useful human resource operations.
- Ability to put in force several exceptional operators to human useful resources.
- Shift the focal point from the operational (transaction) human resource data to strategic human resource statistics.
- Encompass personnel as a lively part of the HRIS.
- Reengineering the complete human aid department.

Krishna and Bhaskar, (2011) summarized the benefits of HRIS, as referred to in Figure 4.

Figure 4. The benefits of HRIS

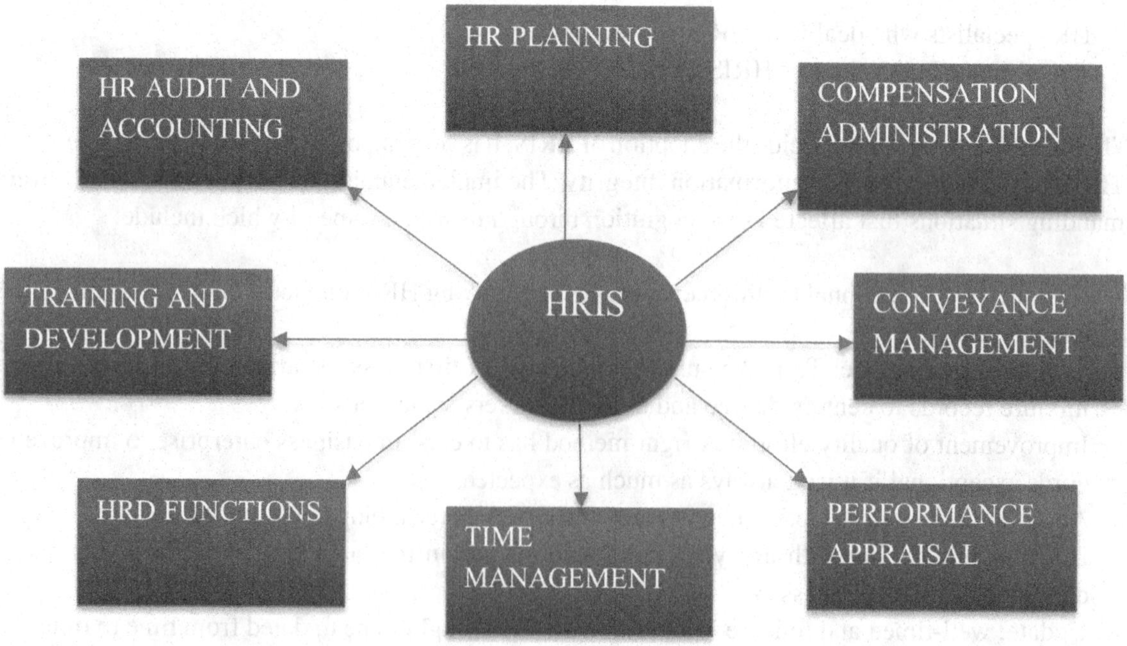

HRIS benefits can be categorized as follows:
  ◦ Advantages for top management
  ◦ Advantages for the HR department
  ◦ Advantages for staff

Advantages for top management include an Increase in normal choice-making performance. Cost lowering and higher manipulation of budget. A clean, imaginative, and prescient enterprise that includes commercial enterprise transparency. Sharp perception into the process of hiring and firing employees, on the mixture degree.

Advantages for the HR department include Ownership of a single record base of all personnel within the enterprise with all essential data and possibilities of different reviews. Removal of chapter and forms that are a great deal slower and with a higher chance of errors. The capability to update information bases in real-time, on the idea of all adjustments, which is of excessive importance to domestically different groups. Reduce mistakes that might be due to human issues. Stepped forward control tool by the regulation. Elimination or discount of redundancy in the system. Standardization of enterprise tactics.

Advantages for personnel: Saves time (Time management). The possibility of unbiased entry to records, which often way operating in one software window. 24/7 records availability. Increasing the body of workers' morale. Automated monitoring and reminder of enterprise responsibilities and events. Encouraging personnel to make decisions and tasks on the idea of facts acquired in the HRIS. The ability to attend inner education guides via the web and the improvement of private abilities and knowledge.

6. CONCLUSION

HRIS is achieved and influenced by HRIS delight, which is influenced by the aid of perceived HRIS satisfaction, perceived HRIS ease of use, and perceived HRIS usefulness. HRIS statistics is defined as "fitness to be used" for selection and coverage making. Accuracy, timeliness, consistency, precision, completeness, and relevance are all measures of information pleasant. Right high-quality HRIS assists the HR branch in making the HRM manner less difficult, faster, less expensive, and greater effective, as well as it advantages the corporation to more fulfillment. The data exceptional of HRIS makes it more treasured by customers by offering them updated, entire, and designated facts to assist their decisions and supplying them with smooth to recognize information that is relevant to their work.

The combination of Human assets and information technology known as HRIS is being implemented by many corporations as strategic weapons toward the rebellion commercial enterprise competitiveness. From the above-noted discussion, it can be concluded that HRIS can be a business enterprise-wide choice support system that helps to achieve both strategic and operational goals. Corporations are increasingly shifting beyond guiding human resource tools nowadays by way of computerizing character human resource responsibilities, installing HRIS and the usage of the internet and intranet use of its human sources, and preserving competitiveness in its market.

HRIS can be visible as a backbone of the organization and vital in assembling the desires of all stakeholders within the enterprise. HRIS permits effectiveness and performance and promotes competitiveness in a few companies. As a result, HRIS needs to be driven through strategic vision, and it has to be applied as an open system in which record generation allows verbal exchange freely among integrated features. Consequently, comprehensive and effective HRIS needs to be pushed by using the organization's imaginative and prescient cost and tradition. Ultimately, the chapter has enlightened the strategic role and significance of HRIS, especially toward business competitiveness. But future studies ought to bear in mind what makes a successful implementation of HRIS.

REFERENCES

Alam, J. (2017). Human resource information system: A quality concept. *International Journal of Advanced Research*, 5(9), 1423–1427. doi:10.21474/IJAR01/5462

Alayli, S. (2023). Unravelling the Drivers of Online Purchasing Intention: The E-Commerce Scenario in Lebanon. *FMDB Transactions on Sustainable Social Sciences Letters*, 1(1), 56–67.

Anand, P. P., Kanike, U. K., Paramasivan, P., Rajest, S. S., Regin, R., & Priscila, S. S. (2023). Embracing Industry 5.0: Pioneering Next-Generation Technology for a Flourishing Human Experience and Societal Advancement. *FMDB Transactions on Sustainable Social Sciences Letters*, 1(1), 43–55.

Atasever, M. (2023). Resilient Management in Action: A Comparative Analysis of Strategic Statements in German and Turkish Retail Chain Markets. *FMDB Transactions on Sustainable Management Letters*, 1(2), 66–81.

Bourini, F. (2011). Investigating the Relationship between Human Resource Information System and Strategic Capability among Employees). *Journal of Advanced Social Research*, 6(3).

Chapman, A. (2005). *Principles of data quality, version 1.0*. Global Biodiversity Information Facility.

DeLone, W., McLean, E., & Sedera, D. (2014). Future of information systems success: Opportunities and challenges. In Computing Handbook, Third Edition (pp. 70-1-70–19). Chapman and Hall/CRC.

Dowling, P. J., Festing, M., & Engle, A. D. (2008). *International Human Resource Management - Managing people in a multinational context*. Cengage Learning.

Fletcher, P. (2005). *From Personnel Administration to Business Driven Human Capital Management: The Transformation of the role of HR in the digital age*. Jossey-Bass.

Gill, J., & Johnson, P. (2010). *Research methods of managers*. Sage Publications Limited.

Hong, S., Kim, J., & Lee, H. (2008). „Antecedents of user-continuance in information systems: Towards and integrative view". *Journal of Computer Information Systems*, 48(3), 1–13.

Kadhim, R., & Sadikmohamadtaqi, B. (2012). Prototyping A Hospital Human Resource Information System). *International Journal of Independent Research and Studies*, 1(1).

Kovach, K. A., & Cathcart, C. E. Jr. (1999). Human resource information systems (HRIS): Providing business with rapid data access, information exchange and strategic advantage. *Public Personnel Management*, 28(2), 275–282. doi:10.1177/009102609902800208

Krishna, C. Y. S., & Bhaskar, S. V. (2011). Assessment of support and benefits of HRIS in medium-scale textile industries. *International Journal of Research in Economics & Social Sciences*, 1(2), 48–57.

Kuragayala, P. S. (2023). A Systematic Review on Workforce Development in Healthcare Sector: Implications in the Post-COVID Scenario. *FMDB Transactions on Sustainable Technoprise Letters*, 1(1), 36–46.

María, J. J. L., Polo, O. C. C., & Elhadary, T. (2023). An Analysis of the Morality and Social Responsibility of Non-Profit Organizations. *FMDB Transactions on Sustainable Technoprise Letters*, 1(1), 28–35.

Naachimuthu, K. P., Ganga, S., & Mathiyoli, P. M. (2022). Psychosocial Impact of COVID-19 Lockdown. *IAHRW International Journal of Social Sciences Review*, *10*(1), 52–59.

Nagarajan, G., & Naachimuthu, K. P. (2021). Positive Emotions and Experiences of Trans Men and Trans Women - A Grounded Theory Approach. *International Journal of Early Childhood Special Education*, *14*(2), 6430–6447.

Obeidat, B. (2012). The Relationship between Human Resource Information System (HRIS) Functions and Human Resource Management (HRM) Functionalities). *Journal of Management Research*, *4*(4). Advance online publication. doi:10.5296/jmr.v4i4.2262

Ocoró, M. P., Polo, O. C. C., & Khandare, S. (2023). Importance of Business Financial Risk Analysis in SMEs According to COVID-19. *FMDB Transactions on Sustainable Management Letters*, *1*(1), 12–21.

Padmapriya, P., & Naachimuthu, K. P. (2023). Social and Philosophical Construction of Emotions in Bhagavad Gita & Plutchik Wheel of Emotions. *Journal of the Asiatic Society of Mumbai*, *XCVI*(27), 22–36.

Pandit, P. (2023). On the Context of the Principle of Beneficence: The Problem of Over Demandingness within Utilitarian Theory. *FMDB Transactions on Sustainable Social Sciences Letters*, *1*(1), 26–42.

Phoek, S. E. M., Lauwinata, L., & Kowarin, L. R. N. (2023). Tourism Development in Merauke Regency, South Papua Province: Strengthening Physical Infrastructure for Local Economic Growth and Enchanting Tourist Attractions. *FMDB Transactions on Sustainable Management Letters*, *1*(2), 82–94.

Priscila, S. S., Rajest, S. S., Tadiboina, S. N., Regin, R., & András, S. (2023). Analysis of Machine Learning and Deep Learning Methods for Superstore Sales Prediction. *FMDB Transactions on Sustainable Computer Letters*, *1*(1), 1–11.

Priyadarshini, N. S., & Naachimuthu, K. P. (2020). Ancient and Modern Conception to Virtues: Comparing Naaladiyar and Positive Psychology. In *International Conference on Multi Facets of Sacred Literature* (pp. 1–12). Academic Press.

Ramos, J. I., Lacerona, R., & Nunag, J. M. (2023). A Study on Operational Excellence, Work Environment Factors and the Impact to Employee Performance. *FMDB Transactions on Sustainable Social Sciences Letters*, *1*(1), 12–25.

Sabherwal, R., Jeyaraj, A., & Chowa, C. (2006). Information system success: Individual and organizational determinants. *Management Science*, *52*(12), 1849–1864. doi:10.1287/mnsc.1060.0583

Sabti, Y. M., Alqatrani, R. I. N., Zaid, M. I., Taengkliang, B., & Kareem, J. M. (2023). Impact of Business Environment on the Performance of Employees in the Public-Listed Companies. *FMDB Transactions on Sustainable Management Letters*, *1*(2), 56–65.

Said, F. B., & Tripathi, S. (2023). Epistemology of Digital Journalism Shift in South Global Nations: A Bibliometric Analysis. *FMDB Transactions on Sustainable Technoprise Letters*, *1*(1), 47–60.

. Savya, N., & Naachimuthu, K. P. (2022). Psychosocial Determinants of Name Dropping: A Conceptual Framework. *Madhya Bharti - Humanities and Social Sciences, 83*(14), 1–12.

Saxena, D., Khandare, S., & Chaudhary, S. (2023). An Overview of ChatGPT: Impact on Academic Learning. *FMDB Transactions on Sustainable Techno Learning*, *1*(1), 11–20.

Shibly, A. (2011). Human Resources Information Systems Success Assessment). *Australian Journal of Basic and Applied Sciences*, *6*(4).

Shifana, F., & Naachimuthu, K. P. (2022). Elements of Holistic Human Development in Naanmanik-kadigai: A Hermeneutic Study. *Journal of Positive School Psychology*, *6*(4), 2218–2231.

Sri, G. P., Jayapriya, J., Poornima, T., & Naachimuthu, K. P. (2022). Hermeneutics of Iniyavai Naarpadhu and Inna Naarpadhu. *Journal of Positive School Psychology*, *6*(8), 4358–4368.

Srinivas, K., Velmurugan, P. R., & Andiyappillai, N. (2023). Digital Human Resources and Management Support Improve Human Resources Effectiveness. *FMDB Transactions on Sustainable Management Letters*, *1*(1), 32–45.

Sudheer, V., & Naachimuthu, K. P. (2022). Effect of JPMR on State-Trait Anxiety Among Young Female Adults During COVID-19 Pandemic Lockdown. *International Journal of Health Sciences*, *6*(55), 1192–1202. doi:10.53730/ijhs.v6nS5.8848

Swartz, N. (2007). Data management problems widespread". *Information Management Journal*, *41*(5), 28–30.

Tambaip, B., Hadi, A. F. F., & Tjilen, A. P. (2023). Optimizing Public Service Performance: Unleashing the Potential of Compassion as an Indicator of Public Service Motivation. *FMDB Transactions on Sustainable Management Letters*, *1*(2), 46–55.

Tripathi, S., & Al-Shahri, M. (2023). Problems and Prospects on the Evolution of Advertising and Public Relations Industries in Oman. *FMDB Transactions on Sustainable Management Letters*, *1*(1), 1–11.

Vashishtha, E., & Dhawan, G. (2023). Comparison of Baldrige Criteria of Strategy Planning and Harrison Text. *FMDB Transactions on Sustainable Management Letters*, *1*(1), 22–31.

Vashishtha, E., & Kapoor, H. (2023). Implementation of Blockchain Technology Across International Healthcare Markets. *FMDB Transactions on Sustainable Technoprise Letters*, *1*(1), 1–12.

Venkateswaran, P. S., Sabarirajan, A., Arun, B., Muthupandian, T., & Manimaran, D. S. (2018). Technology Acceptance Model for Making Decision to Purchase Automobile in Coimbatore District. *International Journal of Mechanical Engineering and Technology*, *9*(11), 1608–1613.

Venkateswaran, P. S., Singh, S., Paramasivan, P., Rajest, S. S., Lourens, M. E., & Regin, R. (2023). A Study on The Influence of Quality of Service on Customer Satisfaction Towards Hotel Industry. *FMDB Transactions on Sustainable Social Sciences Letters*, *1*(1), 1–11.

Venkateswaran, P. S., & Viktor, P. (2023). A Study on Brand Equity of Fast-Moving Consumer Goods with Reference to Madurai, Tamil Nadu. *FMDB Transactions on Sustainable Technoprise Letters*, *1*(1), 13–27.

Wu, J.-H., & Wang, Y.-M. (2006). Measuring ERP success: The ultimate users' view. *International Journal of Operations & Production Management*, *26*(8), 882–903. doi:10.1108/01443570610678657

Chapter 11
A Study on Management Information Systems and Its Role in Decision Making

M. Sriramkumar
PSNA College of Engineering and Technology, India

Rosario Huerta-Soto
Universidad Cesar Vallejo, Peru

Jenny Elizabeth Vega-García
Universidad Cesar Vallejo, Peru

P. Paramasivan
Dhaanish Ahmed College of Engineering, India

J. Rahila
Dhaanish Ahmed College of Engineering, India

S. Manikandan
Dhaanish Ahmed College of Engineering, India

ABSTRACT

The management information system deals with processes going through computer data and is integrated with other methods to deliver information faster and more efficient way to support decision-making and other administrative tasks. The function of MIS in organizational decision-making is the primary subject of this chapter. How decisions are made in an organization utilizing MIS, what problems the organization runs into throughout this process, and some suggestions to solve these problems are covered. It offers a concise explanation of how MIS enhances decision-making. The areas of health and customization have been affected by the rapid advancement of information technology and telecommunications. At all levels of management, from the top to the lowest, the highest quality judgments can be achieved with the best alignment of various technologies. The ability of information technology to organize accurate and pertinent data offers significant prospects for quick and effective fraud that improves the standard of decision-making.

DOI: 10.4018/979-8-3693-0049-7.ch011

1. INTRODUCTION

A Management Information System (MIS) stands as a cornerstone in the realm of modern organizational management, revolutionizing the way businesses operate and strategize in an increasingly complex and data-driven world (Arslan et al., 2021). Rooted in the power of technology, MIS serves as a pivotal tool that empowers managers to navigate the intricacies of organizational functioning with efficiency, precision and informed decision-making (Ogunmola et al., 2021). In this era of digitization and information proliferation, MIS emerges as a comprehensive and computerized framework that orchestrates the collection, processing, storage, and dissemination of data, metamorphosing raw information into actionable insights that fuel decision-making across diverse echelons of an organization (Figure 1).

Figure 1. Management information systems

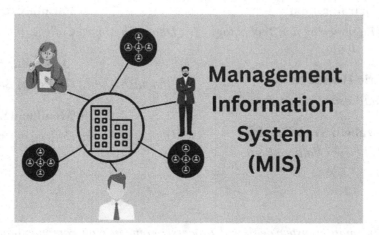

At its core, the fundamental essence of an MIS is to furnish managers with the requisite tools and resources to seamlessly orchestrate, evaluate, and direct multifarious facets of an organization's operations (Sharma et al., 2021). Whether it pertains to financial intricacies, human resources dynamics, sales and marketing strategies, or intricacies of inventory management, MIS adroitly aligns itself to the distinct functional areas within an organizational ecosystem, underscoring its adaptive and versatile nature (Sharma et al., 2021a). This agility grants organizations the dexterity to fine-tune their MIS to their specific operational needs, allowing for tailored and pertinent insights that drive effective and agile decision-making (Sharma et al., 2021b).

MIS plays a crucial role in training by providing the necessary data and insights to design targeted and effective training programs (Sharma et al., 2021c). Through MIS, organizations can identify skill gaps, performance trends, and areas requiring improvement (Gupta, 2021). This data-driven approach ensures that training efforts are aligned with actual organizational needs, optimizing the allocation of resources and maximizing the impact of training initiatives (Balasudarsun et al., 2022))

An organization's competitive edge is forged through the crucible of efficiency, productivity, and strategic acumen, and in this regard, MIS emerges as a catalyst for transformative change (Gupta, 2021a). By streamlining convoluted processes and engendering a culture of data-driven insights, MIS paves the way for heightened efficiency and a renewed competitive edge (Gupta, 2022). The dynamic interplay between technology and management knits together a tapestry of strategic foresight, culminating in decisions that are not only prudent but also grounded in empirical evidence (Batool et al., 2023). This symbiosis between data and decision-making propels organizations toward achieving their objectives with precision and alacrity (Figure 2).

Figure 2. Types of management information systems
Source: www.wharftt.com

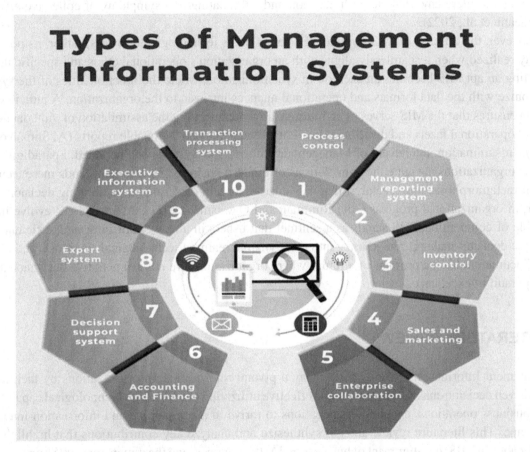

The salient attribute that underscores MIS's indispensability lies in its ability to bestow organizations with swifter access to mission-critical data, underpinning timely and informed decisions. The modern business landscape is an arena of rapidity, where decisions are often akin to ephemeral opportunities that require swift and judicious responses (Mohsan et al., 2022). MIS steps into this breach by serving as a sentinel of information, ensuring that the managerial echelons are armed with the requisite insights to navigate through the maelstrom of options and determine the most sagacious course of action. From allocating resources for investments to the intricacies of recruitment, from the nuances of supply chain management to gauging market dynamics, MIS unfurls a panoply of data-driven insights that form the bedrock of informed decisions (Żywiołek et al., 2022).

Decision-making, in its essence, is the crucible where an organization's trajectory is forged, and MIS emerges as the linchpin in this transformative process. The fabric of an organization's efficiency is interwoven with the quality of its decisions, and MIS threads through this fabric with precision (Al Shraah et al., 2022). By furnishing timely, accurate, and pertinent information, MIS enables decision-makers to traverse the labyrinthine corridors of options, thereby illuminating the path forward (Abu-Rumman, 2021). From top-tier executives shaping strategic paradigms to middle management optimizing operational efficiency and frontline personnel honing tactical strategies, MIS envelops the entire spectrum of managerial hierarchy, shaping each decision and culminating in a symphony of collective efficacy (Tucmeanu et al., 2022).

However, the efficacy of MIS does not rest solely on its technological prowess; rather, its potential is fully realized when it seamlessly aligns with an organization's operational ethos and specific needs. Selecting an apt MIS becomes an exercise in synchronization, where the functionalities of the system harmonize with the data formats and operational nuances intrinsic to the organization. A judicious selection ensures that the MIS serves as an intuitive ally, orchestrating the assimilation of vital data from myriad operational facets and distilling it into comprehensible and actionable reports (Al Shraah et al., 2013). In summation, the advent of Management Information Systems has heralded a paradigm shift in how organizations navigate the convolutions of modern business. Its role transcends mere technology; it metamorphoses into a catalyst that galvanizes data into discernment, facilitating decisions that underpin organizational progress (Abu-Rumman and Qawasmeh, 2021). As businesses evolve in the crucible of competition, MIS stands as a sentinel that ushers in a new era of informed, efficient, and strategic decision-making. The journey into this dynamic realm of technological symbiosis and managerial acumen holds the promise of a future where organizations are not just adaptive but visionary in their pursuit of excellence.

2. LITERATURE REVIEW

Management Information Systems (MIS) play a pivotal role in modern organizations by facilitating data-driven decision-making processes. The effective utilization of MIS aligns technological capabilities with business operations, enabling organizations to thrive in a competitive and information-intensive landscape. This literature review aims to synthesize and analyze key contributions that highlight the significance of MIS, the alignment of business and MIS strategies, and the dimensions of IS success. The role of Management Information Systems (MIS) in decision-making has garnered significant attention due to its potential to enhance the strategic capabilities of organizations.

Bhanushali et al. (2022) delve into Human Resource Management and economic analysis using data mining techniques; their study contributes to the understanding of data-driven approaches that underlie effective decision-making in organizational settings. Hari Krishna et al. (2023) present research on ethically governed artificial intelligence-based innovative business practices; their insights into ethical considerations highlight the importance of ethical dimensions in decision-making processes involving MIS.

Kumar et al. (2022) investigate the role of MIS in enhancing decision-making through improved employee capabilities. Venkateswaran et al. (2018) propose a technology acceptance model that provides insights into technology acceptance and decision-making processes that can be extended to MIS utilization for informed decision-making.

A Management Information System (MIS) plays a crucial role in the realm of online purchases, ensuring efficient and effective management of various processes involved in e-commerce transactions. MIS leverages technology and data to streamline online purchase operations, enhance customer experiences, and inform strategic decision-making (Balasudarsun et al., 2022)

Technological advancements, as highlighted by Asemi et al., (2011) have transformed the financial sector, necessitating innovative financial solutions driven by MIS for efficient and cost-effective transactions. Gabriel, (2013) further explores the diversity of the review genre in IS studies, while Hamza, (2016) adapts economics' stylized facts to tackle knowledge accumulation challenges in a heterogeneous environment. Hari Krishna et al., (2023) identified six dimensions of IS success, including information quality, system quality, use, user satisfaction, individual impact, and organizational impact. Hari Krishna et al., (2023) conducted a meta-analysis of empirical studies to explore relationships within the is success model at the individual level, contributing to a deeper understanding of these dimensions. Laudon & Laudon, (2010) used a multi-dimensional technique to analyze is success studies, further enriching the literature. Shannon and Weaver's framework provides insight into MIS at different levels. The technical level focuses on the efficiency and propriety of the system, while the semantic level pertains to the intended meaning of information propagation (Khan et al., 2023). The effectiveness level explores the impact of information on the receiver, shedding light on the multifaceted nature of MIS's role (Tripathi, 2011).

This literature review has highlighted the critical role of MIS in facilitating timely and effective decision-making within organizations. The alignment of business and MIS strategies, as well as the exploration of dimensions of is success, further emphasizes the importance of integrating technological capabilities with organizational objectives. As organizations continue to navigate a rapidly changing environment, the insights provided by this review underscore the ongoing relevance and significance of MIS in driving success and competitive advantage.

Choosing a specific course of action in response to dangers and opportunities is the process of decision-making (Manikandan & Amsaveni, 2016). An individual, group, or organization can be more effective when good decisions are made; on the other hand, the reverse is true when bad decisions are made. Every organization's members make decisions that either help it develop, succeed, or fail. According to Daft, decisions can be dangerous and unpredictable without results.

3. NEED FOR MIS

In the landscape of organizational management, clarity regarding requirements assumes paramount importance across all echelons of managerial strata. Precise delineation of factors such as requisite information, available data types, stakeholders' profiles, and other pertinent elements is indispensable. It is within this context that Management Information Systems (MIS) ascend as a foundational pillar, meticulously designed and orchestrated to propel organizations toward optimized operational efficacy and strategic prowess (Figure 3).

The multifaceted role of MIS finds its nucleus in a coherent alignment with an array of imperatives driven by the compelling need for comprehensive organizational functionality (Khaled Lafi Al-Naif and Ata, 2018). Several compelling reasons underscore the establishment and adept management of MIS within organizations:

Figure 3. Need for management information systems (MIS)

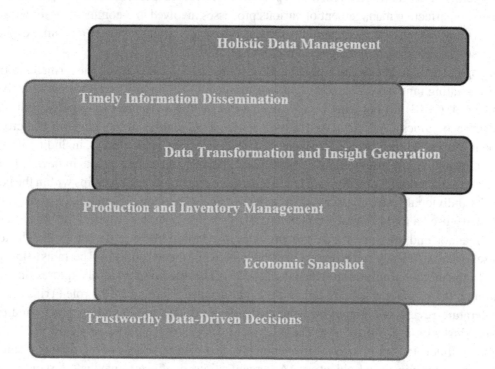

Holistic Data Management: MIS stands as the veritable custodian of diverse functional areas' data within an organization. By meticulously curating and managing data emanating from every facet, MIS establishes an intricate lattice of organized information reservoirs that serve as the wellspring for informed decision-making.

Timely Information Dissemination: The hallmark of MIS lies in its expeditious and accurate information dissemination capabilities. With inherent agility, MIS ensures that crucial information reaches the relevant stakeholders promptly, fostering a real-time flow of insights that underscore agile and astute decision-making.

Data Transformation and Insight Generation: At the core of MIS's mission lies the transformative potential of data. By harnessing collected data, MIS embarks on a transformative journey, meticulously processing and crystallizing raw data into actionable insights that underpin effective decision-making.

Production and Inventory Management: Within the dynamic realm of organizational operations, the ability to access real-time production and inventory information emerges as a linchpin. MIS engenders an environment where such vital information is readily accessible, offering a panoramic view that guides efficient production and inventory management strategies.

Economic Snapshot: Akin to a compass navigating the organization through the tempestuous seas of the business world, MIS provides a precise compass bearing on the company's present economic landscape. This panoramic insight equips decision-makers with the discernment necessary to steer the organization toward fiscal health and strategic advantage.

Trustworthy Data-Driven Decisions: An unmistakable facet of MIS lies in its capacity to expedite the translation of trusted data into actionable decisions. By seamlessly integrating reliable data sources, MIS empowers decision-makers with the ability to swiftly implement strategies grounded in empirical evidence.

At the core of this paradigm lies the quintessence of an information system, a dynamic framework poised to ensure that managers wield access to pertinent information precisely when exigencies demand it. This architectural marvel operates as a conduit, ensuring that decision-makers are equipped with a rich tapestry of knowledge, one that fuels the complex process of drawing insights from data, inferencing from knowledge, and culminating in decisions that orchestrate the attainment of organizational objectives.

Within the intricate landscape of managerial responsibilities, the assimilation and translation of colossal data reserves metamorphose into an indispensable mandate. MIS, in this context, assumes the role of a virtuoso orchestrator, deftly conducting the symphony of data into harmonious melodies of meaningful insights. The imperatives of MIS mirror the intrinsic worth of information itself, ranking on par with tangible assets such as financial resources, physical infrastructure, and human capital. The bedrock of organizational resilience and strategic success lies in the interplay between managerial acumen and the transformative potential of MIS. This synthesis illuminates the pivotal role that MIS occupies, emerging not only as a conduit for information but as an indispensable guardian of the organization's trajectory. As the modern business landscape navigates through ever-shifting tides, MIS emerges as the beacon that navigates organizations toward competitive eminence and enduring sustainability.

4. CONCEPT OF DECISION MAKING

The process of making a decision is a mental activity that entails picking one course of action to pursue out of a number of potential options. Every human being must face the daily challenge of making decisions. This is a rule that cannot be broken in any way. The act of making decisions is both a routine and a systematic procedure in corporate organisations. Profits are the consequence of decisions that are effective and successful, whereas losses are the result of actions that are ineffective and failed. As a consequence of this, the process of making decisions at the corporate level is the most crucial part of any firm. During the course of a decision-making process, we settle on a single path of action after considering a number of potential options. The process of reaching a choice can incorporate a wide variety of instruments, approaches, and points of view.

4.1 Dynamic Decision Making

Dynamic decision-making, also known as DDM, is a form of synergetic decision-making that involves the involvement of interdependent systems and takes place in an environment that shifts over time as a result of the actions taken by the decision-makers in the past or of events that are beyond their control. These decisions are made in the moment and require a higher level of sophistication. Observing how people utilise their expertise to govern the dynamics of the system and recording the best decisions made as a result is what's meant to be understood by the term "dynamic decision-making."

4.2 Sensitivity Analysis

Sensitivity analysis is a crucial tool utilized in various fields to assess the robustness and reliability of models, predictions, and decisions. This analytical technique involves systematically altering input variables or parameters within a model and observing the resulting changes in the output. Its primary objective is to understand how uncertainties or variations in input values impact the final outcomes, aiding in better decision-making and risk management.

In finance, sensitivity analysis plays a pivotal role in assessing investment portfolios. By adjusting variables such as interest rates, inflation rates, or asset returns, analysts can gauge the portfolio's response to different market scenarios. This enables investors to make informed choices to optimize returns while minimizing potential losses.

In engineering, sensitivity analysis is employed to assess the performance of complex systems. Engineers manipulate factors like material properties, environmental conditions, or design parameters to evaluate how these variations influence a system's reliability, safety, or efficiency. This process helps engineers identify critical components and potential failure points, facilitating the creation of more resilient designs.

In healthcare, sensitivity analysis proves valuable in medical research and decision-making. By altering variables like patient demographics, treatment protocols, or disease progression rates, researchers can assess the robustness of clinical models. These assists healthcare professionals in tailoring treatments and predicting potential outcomes, thus enhancing patient care and medical interventions.

Sensitivity analysis also extends its utility to environmental studies, where it aids in understanding the potential impacts of various factors on ecological systems. By manipulating variables such as pollutant levels, habitat changes, or climate factors, scientists can predict how ecosystems might respond to different stressors, informing conservation strategies and environmental policies.

5. DECISION SUPPORT FOR THE MANAGEMENT INFORMATION SYSTEM

A new kind of working environment that is based on computer-mediated communication has been created as a result of the creative solutions that contemporary technology makes available to businesses, corporations, and other scientific institutions. This sets us apart from our other coworkers and affords us greater freedom, simpler approaches to resolving business challenges, greater invention, and improved teamwork, among other benefits.

Analytical models are utilised by DSS in order to make use of the summarised data, as well as any exceptions, patterns, or trends that may be present. A decision support system is one that assists in the process of decision-making but does not necessarily provide a decision on its own. In order to identify problems, devise solutions, and settle on a course of action, those in charge of making decisions assemble usable information from raw data, papers, personal expertise, and/or business models.

5.1 Programmed Decision

Programmed decision-making is utilized to find a solution or conclusion and includes decisions that already have a strategy or regulation in place. In other words, managers have made similar decisions in the past, and the process is repetitive and conventional. They adhere to predefined norms and formal patterns. Examples of programmed decisions include generating weekly work plans for part-time employees, making decisions about employees who arrive late for work, and replenishing office supplies.

The application of programmed decisions is not restricted to resolving simple issues such as vacation policies or other problems of a similar nature; rather, they are also utilised to address more complex concerns, such as the kinds of tests that a doctor must perform before performing major surgery on a diabetic patient.

5.2 Programmed Decision

Non-programmed choices are one-of-a-kind. They are frequently ill-conceived, one-time decisions. Traditionally, approaches such as judgment, intuition, and creativity have been used to deal with them.

Recently, decision-makers have turned to heuristic problem-solving approaches, in which logic, common sense, and trial and error are utilized to address problems that are too huge or complex to be solved using quantitative or automated procedures.

5.3 Group Decision Making

Dynamic decision-making refers to the process of making choices in situations characterized by uncertainty, complexity, and changing conditions. Unlike static decision-making, which occurs in stable and well-defined environments, dynamic decision-making involves adapting and responding to evolving circumstances. This approach is essential in various contexts, such as business, military strategy, healthcare, and everyday life, where decisions must account for the dynamic nature of the environment.

In the realm of business, dynamic decision-making is crucial for staying competitive in rapidly changing markets. Companies need to adjust their strategies, product offerings, and operational plans based on shifting consumer preferences, technological advancements, and market trends. This agility allows them to seize opportunities, mitigate risks, and maintain relevance in an ever-evolving business landscape.

Military operations also heavily rely on dynamic decision-making. Commanders and soldiers must adapt their tactics and responses in real time to changing battlefield conditions, enemy movements, and unexpected developments. The ability to make swift and informed decisions can be the difference between success and failure in complex and fluid combat scenarios.

In healthcare, dynamic decision-making is evident in medical diagnosis and treatment. Doctors must consider a patient's evolving symptoms, test results, and medical history to make accurate and timely decisions about treatments and interventions. Medical professionals constantly assess and adjust their approaches based on new information and the patient's changing condition.

Even in everyday life, individuals engage in dynamic decision-making. Choosing the best route for a commute, deciding what to cook for dinner based on available ingredients, or managing personal finances in a fluctuating economy all require adapting choices to changing circumstances.

Effective dynamic decision-making often involves utilizing real-time data, scenario planning, and predictive models to anticipate potential outcomes. It also requires a balance between flexibility and consistency, as decisions need to be adjusted without compromising overall objectives.

6. MIS Model

A management information system (MIS) is a computerised database of financial data that is set up and designed to generate regular reports on operations for all levels of management within a company. These reports are distributed to the various levels of management within the company. Additionally, particular reports may often be received from the system in a straightforward manner. The primary objective of the management information system (MIS) is to supply managers with feedback on their own performance in order to enable top management to monitor the entirety of the organisation. In order to determine whether or not objectives are being met, the MIS will frequently make comparisons between "actual" data and "planned" outcomes and results from the prior year.

The Management Information System collects data sent in by the various departments and operations of the company. Some of the data are recorded by hand at regular intervals, while others are entered automatically by check-out counters that are connected to computers. The built-in query languages of the system are utilised in order to retrieve various routine reports, which are then preprogrammed to either run on demand or at predetermined intervals. The display functions of the system are used by managers to monitor progress at desk-side personal computers that are networked to the management information system (MIS). Numerous highly developed technologies, which also present it, are utilised in order to keep an eye on how successful the company's stock is.

7. CONCLUSION

When it comes to making decisions regarding your company's future, you should constantly weigh the relevance of both positive and negative business outcomes, with an emphasis on the former. By acting in this manner, the company will have a better chance of avoiding significant losses while also maintaining its steady growth. Sometimes, it appears simple to postpone making decisions, especially if you experience significant conflict as a result of a difficult choice. The only way to maintain control over your time and professional life, though, is to make choices and accept the results. MIS also plays a vital part in providing decision-makers with a vast array of well-organized possibilities from which they may choose their preferred solutions. This helps to ensure that the results of any decisions made will nearly always be positive. In point of fact, this is the primary reason why a large number of decision-makers embrace the utilisation of MIS technologies when confronted with challenging business decisions. According to a well-known premise of management information systems (MIS), making intelligent choices guarantees that the business choices you make will, in the long run, result in success. In actuality, it is for this reason that many decision-makers favor the use of MIS tools when making difficult business decisions. The fact that our companies have access to reliable decision-making processes guarantees that they will produce decisions that are economically viable. According to the explanation that was provided before, management information systems (MIS) centre their attention on information, whereas decision support systems (DSS) centre their attention on decision-making.

REFERENCES

Abu-Rumman, A. (2021). Effective Knowledge Sharing: A Guide to the Key Enablers and Inhibitors. In D. Tessier (Ed.), *Handbook of Research on Organizational Culture Strategies for Effective Knowledge Management and Performance* (pp. 133–156). IGI Global. doi:10.4018/978-1-7998-7422-5.ch008

Abu-Rumman, A. & Qawasmeh, R. (2021). Assessing international students' satisfaction of a Jordanian university using the service quality model. *Journal of Applied Research in Higher Education*. doi:10.1108/JARHE-05-2021-0166

Al-Naif, K. L., & Al Shraah, A. E. M. (2018). Working capital management and profitability: Evidence from Jordanian mining and extraction industry sector. *IUG Journal of Economics and Business.*, *2*(1), 42–60.

Al Shraah, A., Abu-Rumman, A., Alqhaiwi, L. A., & AlSha'ar, H. (2022). The impact of sourcing strategies and logistics capabilities on organizational performance during the COVID-19 pandemic: Evidence from Jordanian pharmaceutical industries. *Uncertain Supply Chain Management*, *10*(3), 1077–1090. doi:10.5267/j.uscm.2022.2.004

Al Shraah, A., Irtaimeh, H. J., & Rumman, M. A. (2013). The Strategic Human Resource Management Practices in Implying Total Quality Management (TQM): An Empirical Study on Jordanian Banking Sector. *International Journal of Management*, *4*(5), 179–190.

Arslan, F., Singh, B., Sharma, D. K., Regin, R., Steffi, R., & Rajest, S. S. (2021). Optimization technique approach to resolve food sustainability problems. In *2021 International Conference on Computational Intelligence and Knowledge Economy (ICCIKE)*. IEEE. 10.1109/ICCIKE51210.2021.9410735

Asemi, A., Safari, A., & Zavareh, A. A. (2011). The Role of Management Information System (MIS) and Decision Support System (DSS) for Manager's Decision Making Process. *International Journal of Business and Management*, *6*(7). Advance online publication. doi:10.5539/ijbm.v6n7p164

Balasudarsun, D., Sathish, D., Venkateswaran, D., Byloppilly, D. R., Devesh, S., & Naved, D. M. (2022). Predicting consumers' online grocery purchase intention within middle-class families. *Webology*, *19*(1), 3620–3642. doi:10.14704/WEB/V19I1/WEB19239

Batool, K., Zhao, Z.-Y., Irfan, M., & Żywiołek, J. (2023). Assessing the role of sustainable strategies in alleviating energy poverty: An environmental sustainability paradigm. *Environmental Science and Pollution Research International*, *30*(25), 67109–67130. doi:10.100711356-023-27076-0 PMID:37103699

Bhanushali, M. M., Narang, P., Sabarirajan, A., & Turai, A. K., S. K., & U, K. S. (2022). Human Resource Management based Economic analysis using Data Mining. In *Proceedings of the 2022 3rd International Conference on Intelligent Engineering and Management (ICIEM)* (pp. 872-876). 10.1109/ICIEM54221.2022.9853202

Gabriel, J. M. O. (2013). Management Information Systems and Corporate Decision-Making: A Literature Review. *International Journal of Management*, *2*(3).

Gupta, R. K. (2021). A study on occupational health hazards among construction workers in India. *International Journal of Enterprise Network Management*, *12*(4), 325–339. doi:10.1504/IJENM.2021.119663

Gupta, R. K. (2021a). Adoption of mobile wallet services: an empirical analysis. *International Journal of Intellectual Property Management, 12*(3), 341 – 353. doi:10.1504/IJIPM.2021.10035526

Gupta, R. K. (2022). Utilization of Digital Network Learning and Healthcare for Verbal Assessment and Counselling During Post COVID-19 Period. *Technologies Artificial Intelligence and the Future of Learning Post-COVID, 19*, 117–134.

Hamza, A. (2016). Impact of Management Information System (MIS) on Managers' Decision in Industrial Companies in India. *International Journal of Management, 7*(4), 172–178.

Hari Krishna, S., Madala, R., Ramya, P., Sabarirajan, A., Dobhal, D., & Sapate, S. (2023). Ethically Governed Artificial Intelligence Based Innovative Business Research in Finance and Marketing System. In *Proceedings of the 2023 Eighth International Conference on Science Technology Engineering and Mathematics* (pp. 1-7). 10.1109/ICONSTEM56934.2023.10142352

Khan, M. A., Kumar, N., Mohsan, S. A. H., Khan, W. U., Nasralla, M. M., Alsharif, M. H., & Ullah, I. (2023). Swarm of UAVs for network management in 6G: A technical review. *IEEE Transactions on Network and Service Management, 20*(1), 741–761. doi:10.1109/TNSM.2022.3213370

Kumar, V. R., Selvaraj, M., Venkateswaran, P. S., Sabarirajan, A., Shatila, K., & Agarwal, V. (2022). The impact of training and development programs on employees performance: The case of Lebanese SMEs. *International Journal of Intellectual Property Management, 12*(3), 368. doi:10.1504/IJIPM.2022.124646

Laudon, K., & Laudon, J. (2010). *Managing the digital firm with management information systems* (11th ed.). Pearson Prentice Hall.

Manikandan, M., & Amsaveni, N. (2016). Management Information System Research Output: A Scientometric Study. *Global Journal of Library and Information Science, 5*(1), 21–27.

Mohsan, S. A. H., Othman, N. Q. H., Khan, M. A., Amjad, H., & Żywiołek, J. (2022). A comprehensive review of micro UAV charging techniques. *Micromachines, 13*(6), 977. doi:10.3390/mi13060977 PMID:35744592

Ogunmola, G. A., Singh, B., Sharma, D. K., Regin, R., Rajest, S. S., & Singh, N. (2021). Involvement of distance measure in assessing and resolving efficiency environmental obstacles. In *2021 International Conference on Computational Intelligence and Knowledge Economy (ICCIKE)*. IEEE. 10.1109/ICCIKE51210.2021.9410765

Sharma, D. K., Jalil, N. A., Regin, R., Rajest, S. S., Tummala, R. K., & Thangadurai. (2021). Predicting network congestion with machine learning. In *2021 2nd International Conference on Smart Electronics and Communication (ICOSEC)*. IEEE.

Sharma, D. K., Singh, B., Raja, M., Regin, R., & Rajest, S. S. (2021a). An Efficient Python Approach for Simulation of Poisson Distribution. In *2021 7th International Conference on Advanced Computing and Communication Systems (ICACCS)*. IEEE.

Sharma, D. K., Singh, B., Regin, R., Steffi, R., & Chakravarthi, M. K. (2021b). Efficient Classification for Neural Machines Interpretations based on Mathematical models. In *2021 7th International Conference on Advanced Computing and Communication Systems (ICACCS)*. IEEE.

Sharma, K., Singh, B., Herman, E., Regine, R., Rajest, S. S., & Mishra, V. P. (2021c). Maximum information measure policies in reinforcement learning with deep energy-based model. In *2021 International Conference on Computational Intelligence and Knowledge Economy (ICCIKE)*. IEEE. 10.1109/ICCIKE51210.2021.9410756

Tripathi, K. P. (2011). Decision Making as a Component of Problem Solving. *International Journal of Information Technology and Management Information System*, *1*(1), 55–59.

Tucmeanu, E. R., Tucmeanu, A. I., Iliescu, M. G., Żywiołek, J., & Yousaf, Z. (2022). Successful management of IT projects in healthcare institutions after COVID-19: Role of digital orientation and innovation adaption. *Healthcare (Basel)*, *10*(10), 2005. doi:10.3390/healthcare10102005 PMID:36292452

Venkateswaran, P. S., Sabarirajan, A., Arun, B., Muthupandian, T., & Manimaran, D. S. (2018). Technology Acceptance Model for Making Decision to Purchase Automobile in Coimbatore District. *International Journal of Mechanical Engineering and Technology*, *9*(11), 1608–1613.

Żywiołek, J., Tucmeanu, E. R., Tucmeanu, A. I., Isac, N., & Yousaf, Z. (2022). Nexus of transformational leadership, employee adaptiveness, knowledge sharing, and employee creativity. *Sustainability (Basel)*, *14*(18), 11607. doi:10.3390u141811607

Chapter 12
A Study of the Analysis of the Blockchain Messaging Apps Market

Anusha Thakur

(iD) https://orcid.org/0000-0001-8761-2250

University of Petroleum and Energy Studies, India

ABSTRACT

Distributed ledger and blockchain technologies have revolutionized the way businesses imagine and operate across organizational boundaries. Non-repudiation plays a vital role in communications to overcome disputes and establish trust. The incorporation of blockchain-based messaging enables the usage of a decentralized network of nodes, surmounting the conventional methods. Key market players are emphasizing accessing partnerships with technology-based companies, thereby bolstering its regional demand over the forecast period. This chapter focuses on market analysis and forecasting for the forecast period of 2021–2030 in terms of revenue. Further, the chapter briefly focuses on the determinants such as drivers, restraints, and opportunities impacting the market for blockchain messaging apps in different applications and end-user segments.

INTRODUCTION

The Blockchain-based platforms have traversed the disillusionment channel of the hype cycle and are headed to boost productivity. The technology focuses on changing the conduct of businesses across organizational boundaries, which includes transforming the brand, copyrights, professional certifications, provenance, along with other digital and tangible assets (Henry, 2021).

The privacy risks of message interception by authoritarian governments or law enforcement are momentous, even if they are limited to specific countries or certain people. The impact of messaging apps from outside of work has pervaded via offices, predominantly those permitting an encryption level.

DOI: 10.4018/979-8-3693-0049-7.ch012

With the increasing awareness of people for their privacy rights, it has become pivotal for messaging applications to move towards end-to-end encryption (E2EE), to cater to the changing security and privacy concerns of the users (Singh, 2021). Encryption, or even the supposition that encryption exists, enables speech to move freely without apprehension about the messages being read, intercepted, or used for non-intended purposes by the sender (Bronfman, 2021).

In today's scenario, the messaging platforms depend on client-to-server communication, wherein, an exclusive ID is given to a strand, and stored in a centralized database. With the growing concern in terms of the user's ownership of data rights and their freedom of speech, blockchain-enabled messaging systems pose to be the right solution. Incorporation of the blockchain technology augments the building of decentralized applications in a way, not done before. The usage of blockchain-based messaging offers newer ways and advantages to communicate, unlike conventional methods.

It thereby becomes intriguing for technology developers to develop systems that are operationally flexible and useful as their corresponding items while catering to issues such as increasing transactional costs. With the help of the decentralized network of nodes to the way of messages, blockchain-based messaging apps be secure with lesser chances of being tampered with.

Research Questions

RQ 1: Need for blockchain messaging apps?
RQ 2: What are the market estimates and forecasts for blockchain messaging apps in terms of revenue for the forecast period 2021 - 2030?
RQ 3: What are the factors, and challenges, boosting and hindering the market for blockchain messaging apps respectively?
RQ 4: Which application segment dominated the market?
RQ 5: Which end-user segment accounted for the largest market share?
RQ 6: What are the solutions adopted by the key market players?

Purpose of the Article

This article contemplates the projected market size with a global analysis of regional segments, application types, and end-user segments. It focuses on different factors bolstering and hindering the market growth of blockchain messaging apps. The paper also focuses on the key growth opportunities paving the way for the application of these technologies among businesses. In addition to these, prospects of this concept, with a brief description of competitive strategic solutions and initiatives adopted by the new entrants and existing players have also been illustrated.

Key Findings in the Research

The increasing smartphone penetration and usage of the internet, has led to a significant rise in the number of messaging platforms and users, thereby driving the overall market demand. Various benefits offered by the technology such as tamper-proof data storability, and flexibility of high crypto trading, are also expected to contribute to the rising demand for blockchain-based messaging apps.

The study is a market research-based study that defines and analyses blockchain technology applications in the data privacy and messaging apps market. The article presents an in-depth description of the market study and a wide range of statistics for the segments based on application, end-user, and regional segments for the forecast period of 2021-2030.

LITERATURE REVIEW

The archetype shift demanded by the blockchain's principle of decentralization envisions a subsequent migration to the trust-to-trust principle from the end-to-end principle (Ali, 2017). This decentralization facet forms the base of blockchain-based systems and paves the way for consensus and distributed trust (Hassan, 2020). To cater to the mass surveillance of discussions by large corporations and government agencies, several major messaging platforms nowadays, are emphasizing on the integration of end-to-end encryption to their protocols. The process of end-to-end encryption is an exceptional way of implementing a secure messaging protocol with additional security features (K. Cohn-Gordon, 2020), such as future secrecy (Marlinspike, 2013).

Using technologies such as Blockchain poses to test the status quo of the vital trust structure prevailing in the Internet, on the way to an accentuated principle of trusted auditability, confidentiality, transparency, and decentralization. Integration of blockchain technology in the messaging platforms surmounts the limitations of conventional messaging application systems, thereby completely revolutionizing the processes.

NEED FOR BLOCKCHAIN MESSAGING APP

With the increasing dependency of people on the internet, the implementation of a secure and safe encryption model has gained significant traction. One of the key focus areas of the companies is the need for data security, easy-to-implement systems, and privacy systems seeking to maintain the data confidentiality of the organization.

Messaging apps are one of the vital tools for everyday use in communication systems. The advent of Web3 has led to an increase in the array of decentralized applications and services operating without a centralized server (John, 2022).

The messaging apps nowadays are engaged in incorporating blockchain technology to facilitate the communication process between users via blockchain-based transactions. This can be attributed to the decentralized end-to-end structure and solutions that blockchain-based apps possess and offers. In addition to this, these technological apps also use many autonomous nodes and offer better security, unlike centralized servers. Blockchain technology augments the ways of doing business in terms of better efficiency and security. Sending public keys, for instance, over the blockchain eradicates the requirement for a central server and the possibility of third-party vulnerable attacks.

The growing demand for instant and confidential messages has bolstered the demand for encrypted messaging apps. The inclusion of blockchain is thereby, expected to completely revolutionize the security of the communication process among the users (Harris, 2018). In today's scenario, several platforms have entered the market, catering to the changing scenario and messaging environment. The key market players emphasize on strategic planning such as mergers & acquisitions, collaborations, and partnerships to mark their global presence for the messaging app solutions.

MARKET PLAYERS OF BLOCKCHAIN MESSAGING APPS

Solana Foundation

The Solana Foundation, based in Zug, Switzerland, is a non-profit foundation, devoted to the security, adoption, and decentralization of the Solana ecosystem. The foundation focuses on structuring the protocols into the most censorship-resistant network (Foundation, Solana Foundation, n.d.). In addition to, it also emphasizes on the implementation of decentralized technologies for the public betterment (Foundation, Solana Foundation, 2023).

Initiatives

- *Open Source:* The foundation emphasizes on developing an open-source community to spur the advancement of a robust system of financial services and products to help access the Solana network.
- *Decentralization:* Increasing the network by counting more validator nodes and increasing the super minority via the delegations.
- *Staking:* This includes simplifying staking by offering open-source reference implementations, grants, and community support.

Solutions

Secretum: Secretum is the pioneer of blockchain messaging apps, which uses the Solana (SOL) blockchain, wherein, user identification or a centralized server is not present. Secretum users connect via the crypto wallet address, instead of the mobile numbers. The communication process uses the blockchain transactions of SER tokens to exchange messages, and files as well as conduct video calls in seconds. The technology influences the Proof-of-Stake (PoS) consensus mechanism by setting in motion the network traffic via the stakers of the SER badge. The communication process among the users is encoded and reposited on the decentralized nodes as a replacement for using a centralized server.

Status

Status is an innovative Ethereum-based blockchain messenger, that provides users with several blockchain features. The messaging app offers features such as a secure Web3, a crypto wallet, and a keycard with cutting-edge technology. The technology is designed to promote the sovereignty of individuals, protect the right to secure, and private conversations, as well as allow the free flow of information.

Solutions

V1.13 Release - Socks, Spam, and Keycard: In April 2021, Status announced the latest version of mobile with UI improvements and the latest features to increase control over the messaging experience.

WIP Activity Center: This latest release presents the latest "activity center" in which the latest group chats and chat invitations appear, where acceptance or request decline can be taken care of. It also offers better control over and prevents invitations from spamming the chat feed.

Accept Posts from Contacts Only: The feature also provides enhanced privacy and control, thereby setting a privacy policy to safeguard the group chat and private messages received from contacts only.

Delivery Validation for Confidential Groups: The messages referred to within the confidential groups will be marked as complete with a dual check mark, even if received by at least one of the members. The feature is expected to bring the app nearer to feature parity with other typical messengers, in spite, of the distributed architecture of the mobile application.

Keycard Updates: The keycard can be easily reset, with the change of the PUK and PIN as well. In addition to this, an additional keycard can be used as a backup to the prevailing one.

Improvements and Bugfixes: This version offers bug fixes and several improvements that endure to enhance the app into an intuitive all-in-one and a simple messenger, and browser.

V1.12 Release - Keycard on iOS, Crypto Onramps, and More: In March 2021, Status v1.12 announced the introduction of several features, that keep the app updated with the current scenario, and make it more entertaining.

Keycard iOS Integration: Keycard, a cold storage hardware wallet is intended to secure the private keys offline with greater security. With the introduction of this version, an extra layer of security gets added to the accounts, transactions, and assets for both iOS and Android.

Easier Access to Crypto Onramps: The version emphasizes on to add seamless crypto onramps into the product invented. Onramps offered include LocalCryptos, Transak, Ramp, Wyre, and Moonpay, from the wallet tab. These options enable the purchase of crypto all from inside Status.

Enhanced messaging: Bringing the app nearer to highlight parity with the mainstream v1.12, and web2 chat giants consisting of "sent" message validations in 1:1 private message (GmbH, 2021).

V1.7 Release - iOS Notifications, Mentions, Nicknames & More: In September 2020, Version 1.7 announced the introduction of an innovative approach to iOS notifications with the mention on both Android and iOS. Both mentions as well as the iOS notifications are monitored actively and are in beta. With the inclusion of new features, the sending of transactions has become way easier.

Re-introducing Status Desktop – Beta v0.1.0: In September 2020, the status Desktop returns as beta v0.1.0 to offer secure and private communication on Linux, Windows, and Mac.

Cyber Dust

Cyber Dust, headquartered in Los Angeles, California, US, was founded in 2014, to offer its users an innovative, confidential, and secure means of communication. The messages on this app are never cached or saved to the hard drive and disappear in 30 seconds from the random-access memory of the device (Nededog, 2015). This pseudonymous app is the classical form of messaging app, engaged in connecting the users via their mobile contact numbers.

Solutions

Cyber Dust offers enhanced protection of the assets via stealth search, watchdog, and encrypted messenger. The messaging app is a suite of digital security tools to identify theft protection, thereby, enabling seamless web search, and confidential communication. The messages communicated via the app are end-to-end encrypted, wherein, no one owes the authority to view the contents of the message apart from the receivers and senders.

This messaging app is acknowledged for its "dusting" feature, which mechanically deletes the texting history after 24 hours. It also enables the users to delete the messages after reading, with no storage or record of the same anywhere.

In addition, to this, Dust offers an integrated stealth search feature which offers an anonymous web browsing feature, with no non-essential data being downloaded, and concluding a digital mark on the web.

Market Drivers Bolstering the Blockchain Messaging App Market

Rising Consumer Demand for Confidentiality in Messaging Apps

Consumers nowadays are largely emphasizing on privacy and autonomy, from NFTs and decentralized finance to Signal Messenger and DuckDuckGo, in conducting or collaborating the businesses (Buhler, 2021). The convergence of the rising demand for privacy and the increasing supply of user-friendly private tech has led to an unparalleled prospect for businesses with a vision of enhanced confidentiality online experiences.

Shadow IT, cloud migration, and business changes augment complexities to the diversified attack surface. Launching elementary safety principles such as proactive threat detection, multi-factor authentication, and regular user education, with at least a solid recovery and backup plan, is one of the vital aspects of any business. Robust multi-layered methods such as back-up and password policies, augment the protection of sensitive data and mitigate the related risks in an organization.

With the upcoming ways of working, becomes essential and critical for small and medium-sized businesses (SMBs) and enterprises to balance their usage with enhanced access and security, thereby, preventing security breaches, data loss disasters, and regulatory compliance issues (Wood, 2021). Hence, several big tech platforms strive building to decentralized products with the inclusion of high-end privacy-related features.

Market Challenges Hindering the Blockchain Messaging App Market

High Cost Related to Blockchain Messaging Apps

The costs of building a blockchain app are dependent on varied factors, such as types of blockchain, complexity, app features, along other technology stacks. The cost of blockchain-based apps can be calculated via different specific numbers, examples, and factors (LeewayHertz, 2023). A few factors to be catered to, while considering the implementation of the blockchain-based app can be illustrated as (tejaswipkle, 2023):

- *Size of the App development agency:* The small-size companies charge less in comparison to large and medium-sized companies have higher cost estimates owing to their focus on maintaining standard portfolios.
- *Level of Decentralization:* With a low level of decentralization, the process is expected to be less expensive and simple, while with a higher degree of decentralization, the process is expected to be expensive and complicated.

Opportunities in the Blockchain Messaging App Market

Embracing Web 3.0

With the applications becoming more interactive and engaging, the need for messaging apps is increasingly witnessing a surge in demand. In the evolution of the internet, Web 3.0 is the well-thought-out, next stage, and is expected to be possibly a bigger paradigm shift in comparison to the era of Web 2.0. Web 3.0 is an idea built upon the concepts of openness, decentralization, and better operator utilities in every application field (from VR/metaverse applications to gaming to messaging to digital assets trading).

It integrates different technologies such as the semantic web, machine learning, AI, and blockchain, for generating newer versions of the internet, thereby allowing decentralized interaction and communication among different applications and users. Hence, the concept of Web 3.0 has the potential to introduce several value developments for businesses in diversified areas (Weston, 2022).

The probable Web 3.0 applications for negotiating with several use cases emphasize on establishing the conceptual grounds for attempting the usage of web3 apps. The impact of Web 3.0 is unparalleled, of given its reach and size of the possible niche segments such as (Lama, 2022):

- Nearly 3 billion people across the world use messaging apps, with an average of approximately 145 billion messages being sent every day.
- Predictions illustrate that the metaverse segment is expected to reach nearly $1.54 trillion by 2030, which is a tenfold surge over its current value.
- The financing of crypto assets is nearly $2 trillion, from less than $200 billion in 2019.
- Digital tokens, and Non-Fungible Tokens (NFTs), representing the specific work of a metaverse element, image, or art, and whose rights are documented on the blockchain witnessed an increase in trading volumes.

The concept accentuates the evolution of an equal and open network with comparable rights for everyone to take part in the network. In addition, it also assures interoperability, decentralization, permissionless, secure, and self-governing networks for businesses. Hence, Web 3.0 is expected to be the fundamental change for consumers to concerning privacy and security issues (Chernikova, 2021).

RESEARCH METHODOLOGY

The study offers an analysis of determinants impacting the blockchain messaging app market, with a key focus on market sizing and forecasts over the projected period. The research focuses on different market drivers, trends, challenges, opportunities, regulatory policies, and strategies impacting market growth over the forecast period. The forecast analysis will be in terms of revenue at the global, and regional levels, with the key trends varying for 2021-2030 (projected period)

Research Objectives

The objectives of the research study can be illustrated as:

- To study the evolution of blockchain messaging app technology, with a major focus on recent technological trends in the market.
- To identify the factors boosting the growth of the blockchain messaging app market across different end-user verticals over the forecast period.
- To emphasize on the future aspects, challenges, and implications of this technology in the market
- To examine the factors such as mergers & acquisitions, R&D solutions, and collaborations among the key market players in the global blockchain messaging app market.

  Inclusions:

- Application segment based on Message, and Payment
- End-user segment by Business, and Individual
- Regional segmentation based on North America, Europe, Asia Pacific, Latin America, and Middle East & Africa

Scope of the Study

The article considers the current scenario of the global blockchain messaging app market along with the key market forces for the forecast period of 2021 - 2030. The article emphasizes on anticipating market change by assigning weightage to market forces (drivers, restraints, opportunities). Further, the study focuses on regional as well as segment revenue for assessing the overall market scenario. It further emphasizes on competitive strategies and market share analysis as well.

The enclosed aspects comprise of market size and estimates of the blockchain messaging app market in terms of revenue over the projected period; as well as segmentation based on, regions covering North America, Europe, Asia Pacific, and the Rest of the World (RoW). This helps in determining the overall size of the market over the forecasted period in terms of revenue, getting insights about the factors that are engaged in propelling the market, along with the factors restraining its growth and development. The given statistics are consequently attained from secondary sources via various company annual reports, investor documents, journals, and statistics published by various market leaders. The data can be analyzed owing to the below-mentioned factors:

- Demand and supply estimates
- Market developments and trends.
- Future aspects and opportunities offering insights on product innovation, commercialization as well as expansion in different regions.

The data has been categorized based on varied parameters such as region, application, and end-user segment. Methodologies to study the gathered data can be illustrated as:

- **Top-Down Approach:** The data are collected for the global scenario and are then separated into different entities (which include application type/region/end-user, in this case, it is based on regional analysis).
- **Bottom-Up Approach:** The data are collected and estimated for regional segments and are then combined to obtain the global numbers. The data are then forecasted based on different market trends, and initiatives for over the forecast period of 2021 to 2030. The bottom-up method helps gain holistic information and understand current and future market scenarios of the same, thereby enabling the companies to accordingly strategize their plans and policies.

FINDINGS AND MARKET ANALYSIS

Global Analysis

The blockchain messaging app market was valued at $21.09 million in 2021, and is expected to witness a surge in its growth rate over the forecast period. The market is expected to be valued at $545.06 million in 2030. The growth of the market can mainly be attributed to its distributed end-to-end encryption technology offering high-end security to the users. In addition to this, growing awareness among users regarding the exploitation of privacy has also favorably impacted blockchain messaging app's market demand. Advancements in Web 3.0 also pave the way for several opportunities impacting the adoption of the blockchain messaging apps market.

Exhibit 1

Figure 1. Global blockchain messaging apps market 2021-2030 ($ million)
(Secondary Sources)

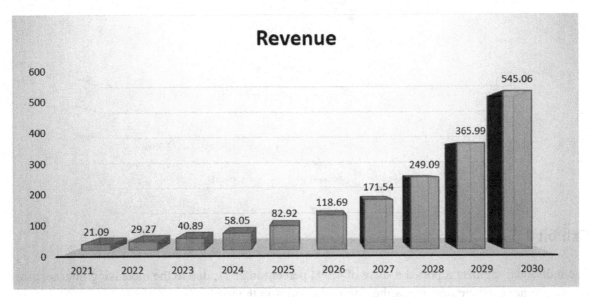

Application Analysis

On the basis, of the application types, the market can be categorized into payment and message types. The message segment dominated the market with a market share of nearly 72.09 percent. The key players across the world, are engaged in introducing messaging apps for seamless and confidential exchange of texts.

Exhibit 2

Blockchain-based payment systems are decentralized systems working on a blockchain network. The payment segment emphasizes on facilitating, processing, and validating the transactions made in a business, on a distributed ledger system or blockchain technology. The segment witness substantial growth owing to the rising traceability and simplified processes.

End-use Analysis

End-use segments can be categorized into individual, and business. The business segment accounted for the market share of approximately 57.06 percent of the overall market. This can mainly be attributed to the advantages offered by blockchain messaging apps such as decentralized communication, and ease of usage, leading to high-privacy processes in businesses.

Figure 2. Application segment analysis of global blockchain messaging apps market (In terms of market share)
(Secondary Sources)

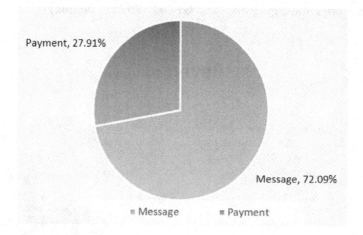

Exhibit 3

The individual segment reported a share of 42.94 percent in 2021, due to the increasing internet usage and smartphone penetration across the different regions in the world.

Regional Analysis

The market can be categorized into regions of North America, Europe, Asia Pacific, Latin America, and Middle East & Africa. Europe accounted for the market share of nearly 32.83 percent of the overall market. The Asia Pacific region accounted for significant growth owing to the increasing adoption of new technologies and growing digitalization across the regions.

Figure 3. End-use analysis of global blockchain messaging apps market (In terms of market share)
(Secondary Sources)

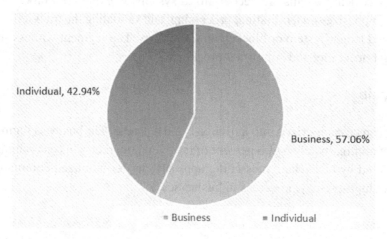

Exhibit 4

North America accounted for nearly 33.65 percent of the total share in 2021, thereby witnessing considerable growth. The increasing adoption of blockchain technology and the legalization of cryptocurrency in the region boosts the market growth. In addition to this, the market players in the region are engaged in introducing apps and offering secured communication platforms to individuals.

The Middle Eastern and Latin American regions are expected to witness considerable growth over the forecast period, owing to the increasing internet and smartphone proliferation. Increasing collaborations and partnerships between technology and the key market players also contribute favorably to the growth of the market globally.

Figure 4. Geographical analysis of global blockchain messaging apps market in 2021 ($ million)
(Secondary Sources)

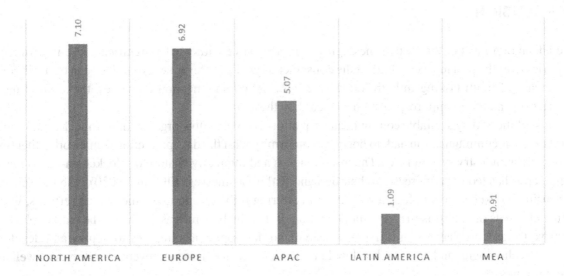

DISCUSSION

The blockchain messaging app market is anticipated to witness a substantial market growth over the forecast period. This chapter contemplates the current state of the global blockchain messaging apps market with a major emphasis on different determinants (market drivers, opportunities, challenges in implementation, and trends) impacting the market growth. It offers a comprehensive analysis of both the supply as well as demand side of the market.

Key Takeaways

The key vendors nowadays are increasingly emphasizing on developing customer-centric solutions and platforms for their business segments in order to increase profit margins and sales. Further, the businesses also intend to focus on strategizing the future research plans and models along with their implications on the same. The chapter emphasizes on the economic contribution of blockchain messaging apps along with different models and intermediaries.

- On the basis, of the end-user segment, the business segment dominated the market.
- The message segment accounted for a majority share of 72.09 percent on the basis of the blockchain messaging apps application types.
- North America will continue its market dominance during the forecast period.
- APAC is expected to witness considerable growth in demand for the blockchain messaging apps market during the forecast period.
- The vendor landscape of the blockchain messaging apps market is expected to be fragmented. Some of the few leading vendors include Cyber Dust, Telegram, Status, Solana Foundation, and Crypviser.

CONCLUSION

The adaptation rates of the instant messaging platforms have witnessed a significant rise in different countries over the past few years both at the consumer as well as enterprise levels. This can be attributed to the ease of multi-tasking in both formal and informal communication processes, the secured user experience, and the prompt response time offered by these.

Most of the widely available communication platforms do not allow organizations to scale, track, and regulate, their communication and do not offer conformity with the data protection frameworks, thereby posing cross-industry system risks. The instantaneous and interactive nature of blockchain-based messaging apps has led to an increase in their demand within businesses (Ellewala, 2020). The messenger apps using blockchain technology are engaged in offering fully decentralized messaging services, with secure channels of enterprise-level communication. It thereby becomes essential for the market players to strive towards implementing different research and development initiatives to deploy and develop efficient technologies and cater to the global product and service demand, revenue strategies as well as pricing trends.

To conclude this, the proposed article intends to offer an outline for blockchain messaging apps market data and forecasts based on applications, end-users, and regions. The main purpose of this article is to analyze a wide range of indicators and statistics contributing to the prospects and dynamics of the market strategically.

REFERENCES

Academy, M. (2022, December 6). *Exploring Blockchain-Based Messaging Apps.* Retrieved from Moralis Academy: https://academy.moralis.io/blog/exploring-blockchain-based-messaging-apps

Ali, M. (2017). *Trust-to-Trust Design of a New Internet* [PhD dissertation]. Princeton University.

Bronfman, J. (2021, April 15). *How Do Messaging Apps Respond to Privacy?* Retrieved from Common Sense Media: https://www.commonsense.org/education/articles/tell-me-about-it-how-do-messaging-apps-respond-to-privacy

Buhler, K. (2021, November 18). *The Rising Consumer Demand for Data Privacy and Autonomy*. Retrieved from Sequoia Capital: https://www.sequoiacap.com/article/the-rising-consumer-demand-for-data-privacy-and-autonomy/

Chernikova, A. (2021, December 11). *Why More and More Companies Are Embracing Web 3.0*. Retrieved from Entrepreneur Media, LLC: https://www.entrepreneur.com/science-technology/why-more-and-more-companies-are-embracing-web-30/397262

Cohn-Gordon, K., Cremers, C., Dowling, B., Garratt, L., & Stebila, D. (2020). A Formal Security Analysis of the Signal Messaging Protocol. *Journal of Cryptology*, *33*(4), 1914–1983. doi:10.100700145-020-09360-1

Ellewala, U. P. (2020). Secure Messaging Platform Based on Blockchain. *2020 2nd International Conference on Advancements in Computing (ICAC)*. 10.1109/ICAC51239.2020.9357306

Foundation, S. (2023). *Solana Foundation*. Retrieved from https://solana.com/news/announcing-the-formation-of-the-solana-foundation

Foundation, S. (n.d.). *Solana Foundation*. Retrieved from https://solana.com/

Gmb, H. S. R. (2021, March 22). *News & Announcements: V1.12 Release - Keycard on iOS, Crypto Onramps, and More*. Retrieved from Status Research & Development GmbH: https://our.status.im/v1-12-release-keycard-on-ios-crypto-onramps-and-more/

Harris, R. (2018, April 3). *A Blockchain Messaging Platform That's Unstoppable*. Retrieved from App Developer Magazine: https://appdevelopermagazine.com/a-blockchain-messaging-platform-that%27s-unstoppable/

Hassan, F. A. (2020). *Blockchain and the Future of the Internet: A Comprehensive Review*. https://arxiv.org/pdf/1904.00733.pdf

Henry, W. a. (2021, December 7). *Blockchain: Ready for Business*. Retrieved from Tech Trends 2022, Deloitte Insights: https://www2.deloitte.com/us/en/insights/focus/tech-trends/2022/blockchain-trends.html

Jagati, S. (2022, February 1). *Blockchain-based Decentralized Messengers: A Privacy Pipedream?* Retrieved from Cointelegraph: https://cointelegraph.com/news/blockchain-based-decentralized-messengers-a-privacy-pipedream

John, C. (2022, October 28). *Why Social Media and Messaging Apps on Blockchain May be a Better Option*. Retrieved from India Today: https://www.indiatoday.in/opinion-columns/story/why-social-media-messaging-apps-on-blockchain-may-be-a-better-option-opinion-2290395-2022-10-28

Lama, S. (2022, April 4). *Secretum: The Messaging App of Web 3.0 Era*. Retrieved from BeInNews Academy: https://beincrypto.com/secretum-the-messaging-app-of-the-web-3-0-era/

LeewayHertz. (2023). *How To Determine the Cost of Blockchain Implementation*. Retrieved from LeewayHertz: https://www.leewayhertz.com/cost-of-blockchain-implementation/

Marlinspike, M. (2013, November 26). *Advanced Cryptographic Ratcheting*. Retrieved from Signal: https://signal.org/blog/advanced-ratcheting/

Nededog, J. (2015, May 27). *Mark Cuban's Cyber Dust is Producing its First Original Web Series*. Retrieved from Business Insider: https://www.businessinsider.in/mark-cubans-cyber-dust-is-producing-its-first-original-web-series/articleshow/47436464.cms

Singh, R. C. (2021). Blockchain-Enabled End-to-End Encryption for Instant Messaging Applications. In *IEEE 23rd International Symposium on a World of Wireless, Mobile and Multimedia Networks (WoW-MoM) 2022, Belfast* (pp. 501-506). IEEE.

tejaswipkle. (2023). *How Much Does It Cost to Develop Blockchain Apps?* Retrieved from geeksforgeeks: https://www.geeksforgeeks.org/how-much-does-it-cost-to-develop-blockchain-apps/

Weston, G. (2022, September 30). *Top 10 Web3 Applications You Must Know*. Retrieved from 101 Blockchains: https://101blockchains.com/top-web3-applications/

Wood, S. (2021, June 4). *The Security Implications for Private Messaging Apps*. Retrieved from TechRadar: https://www.techradar.com/news/the-security-implications-for-private-messaging-apps

Chapter 13
Unleashing Business Potential:
Harnessing OpenStreetMap for Intelligent Growth and Sustainability

Munir Ahmad

https://orcid.org/0000-0003-4836-6151

Survey of Pakistan, Pakistan

ABSTRACT

The economic value of green spaces and their enormous potential can positively impact both community development and business growth. This chapter explored the value of OSM data especially green space data for business development. Strategic investment in parks and other green spaces has positive effects on the environment as well as the economy. Integration of OSM data with other essential datasets can provide businesses with useful tools for utilizing green spaces. OSM improves client segmentation, market analysis, and distribution channels, promoting sustainable business practices. OSM can also help in developing revenue strategies, discovering competitors, and optimizing logistics. When used in business growth, OSM green space data offers a variety of alternatives, from site selection to eco-friendly campuses, eco-tourism, and conservation projects. Additionally, OSM data encourages civic participation, ecological regrowth, and eco-aware consumer marketing.

INTRODUCTION

Organizational progress and achievement heavily rely on the pivotal role of business development. This multifaceted domain encompasses a diverse array of strategies, initiatives, and processes aimed at broadening a company's market footprint, elevating its performance, and fostering enduring expansion. While the sphere of business development is expansive, it can be distilled into several central themes and areas of concentration. One prominent facet is e-business development, delving into how enterprises can secure competitive advantages through the adoption of e-commerce strategies (Phan, 2003). The facet is digital business development. Numerous industrial enterprises leverage digital technology to revolutionize their

DOI: 10.4018/979-8-3693-0049-7.ch013

business strategies and venture into novel, creative offerings (Sjödin et al., 2020). These digital-driven business models often incorporate service components into tangible products, enabling companies to deliver tailored solutions (Kohtamäki et al., 2020).

Sustainable business development stands as another notable sphere of interest. It revolves around the incorporation of sustainability principles into business methodologies and routines. Scholars have underscored the significance of sustainable practices, innovation, and forward-thinking leadership in shaping a sustainable future for enterprises (Rainey, 2006). The exploration of governance structures and external business development endeavors is equally vital. Researchers delved into how diverse governance models and the relevance of external business development pursuits can affect a company's innovative performance. This spotlights the role of governance frameworks in propelling innovation within organizations (Keil et al., 2008).

Furthermore, the correlation between the development of small businesses and the tourism sector revealed the intricate interplay between tourism and the growth of local enterprises in different regions as noted by Page et al., (1999). Another area of interest involves the factors that can influence women in business development within developing countries as asserted by Hossain et al., (2009). This investigation explored the distinct challenges and opportunities encountered by women in the business arena, emphasizing that business development is shaped by a variety of factors, including those specific to gender.

In today's highly competitive environment, businesses are actively exploring creative strategies to secure a competitive advantage and achieve sustainable growth, especially in the data-driven era where knowledge is paramount. Spatial data refers to information concerning the physical location and attributes of objects or phenomena on the Earth's surface (Rajabifard & Williamson, 2001). Analyzing spatial data can empower business innovators to glean a profound understanding of the possibilities and challenges within specific geographic regions, enabling them to formulate strategies for sustainable entrepreneurship and growth. The utilization of spatial data has gained prominence due to its potential to provide valuable insights into market trends (Argiolas, 2014; Li & Kao, 2022), consumer behavior (Widaningrum et al., 2020), and resource allocation (Shang et al., 2021). Spatial data can be integrated with sustainable development and entrepreneurship to promote sustainability in the economy, environment, and society through data-driven opportunities and inclusive practices (Ahmad, 2023).

OpenStreetMap (OSM) is a collaborative mapping project, that provides an open and freely available dataset and can be a useful resource for businesses (Wiki, 2023b). The incorporation of OSM data has the potential to completely alter how businesses handle numerous crucial areas of their operations. For instance, OSM data can revolutionize market research by giving businesses more insights into demographics, consumer preferences, and behaviour. Businesses can use OSM data to find untapped markets and strategically plan their market entry or expansion (Dupre, 2020). OSM has a vital role in promoting sustainable progress encompassing the realms of the economy, environment, and society (Ahmad & Ali, 2023). OSM data is also very important for location planning. Based on variables like accessibility, closeness to potential customers, and local infrastructure, businesses can use OSM data to locate viable places for their operations. This data-driven strategy can optimize location selection and improve decision-making to match the company's goals (Baganz et al., 2020).

Additionally, OSM data can enable companies to more accurately define their target consumers. Businesses can learn more about consumer preferences, geolocation trends, and regional demand patterns by superimposing OSM data with customer databases. This specific data enables focused marketing initiatives and tailored client interactions (Rifat et al., 2012). OSM data is essential for supply chain and logistics optimization in addition to market analysis and location planning. Businesses can optimize transportation routes, shorten delivery times, and cut transportation costs by using OSM data with other databases. The supply chain domain can benefit from the accurate and timely information provided by OSM (Weise & Mostaghim, 2022).

To this effect, the primary objective of this chapter is to bridge the gap between the valuable resource of OSM data and its application in business development, with a specific focus on green spaces. To achieve this goal, the chapter is structured logically, moving from general concepts to more specific and targeted applications. The initial sections provide essential background information, emphasizing the value of both OSM data and green spaces independently. Subsequently, the chapter narrows its focus to demonstrate how OSM and green spaces can be effectively integrated for business development. The organization of the chapter is as follows:

To begin with, section two provides a comprehensive review of the overall value of OSM for business development. It delves into the various ways OSM data can be harnessed by businesses to gain a competitive edge, optimize market analysis, identify customer segments, and improve sales and distribution channels. This section serves as the foundation for understanding the broader potential of OSM in driving business growth. Section three delves into the economic value of green spaces. Drawing insights from numerous studies, this section highlights the substantial benefits that green spaces offer to both communities and businesses. It explores how investing in parks and green areas not only contributes to environmental well-being but also results in tangible economic advantages. Understanding the value of green spaces is crucial to appreciating the impact of incorporating OSM green space data in business development.

Moving forward, section four expands on the applications of OpenStreetMap beyond business development, with a particular focus on green infrastructure. This section sheds light on how OSM has been instrumental in various studies related to green infrastructure planning, ecological conservation, and sustainable practices. Examining these diverse applications of OSM strengthens the case for its incorporation into business development strategies.

Section five constitutes the core of this chapter, it specifically investigates the use of OSM green space data for business development purposes. It explores how businesses can capitalize on this valuable data to make informed decisions in site selection, planning, and design processes. By strategically choosing locations near green spaces, businesses can enhance their appeal and promote employee well-being, fostering a positive impact on both the environment and their workforce. Furthermore, section six outlines the best practices for effectively utilizing OSM data in business development initiatives. These practices encompass data collection, analysis, and integration strategies that optimize the potential of OSM green space data. Understanding the best practices ensures that businesses can harness the full benefits of OSM for their development plans. Finally, the last section serves as the concluding remarks for this chapter.

BUSINESS DEVELOPMENT USING OSM

OSM offers essential spatial data and geographic information, presenting numerous possibilities for businesses to streamline their operations, enhance their market targeting, and make well-informed decisions. Key aspects of leveraging OSM for business growth and maintaining a competitive edge are summarized in Figure 1 and presented as follows:

Market Analysis

It refers to a thorough investigation of the market to discover market trends, consumer preferences, and the competitive environment. The location of retail stores can play a significant role in determining their sales dynamics and overall success in a competitive market (Formánek & Sokol, 2022). OpenStreetMap data can be used for market analysis, by extracting information about the amenities and infrastructure that already exist in a specific location. Businesses can evaluate the prospective client base, find market gaps, and learn more about the distribution of competitors by analyzing the OSM data in combination with other non-spatial information. For instance, OSM data can be used by a retail business to pinpoint locations with a high concentration of competitors' businesses or those with fewer of a particular sort of store. A competitive strategy can be created using this information to assist in discovering market opportunities.

Customer Segmentation

It enables dividing up the target market into segments based on its behaviour, psychography, and demographics. This makes it easier to target particular client segments with marketing initiatives, product development, and customer engagement tactics. The market can be segmented based on geographic variables by fusing OSM data with demographic data. This can help in locating particular places with higher populations of potential clients who fit desired characteristics. For example, Macdonald et al., (2022) created clear and organized maps and categories for retail areas in the UK, including town centers, high streets, and other shopping areas. by using geocoded retail location data from the Valuation Office Agency (VOA) and OSM.

Sales and Distribution Channels

It refers to figuring out the best ways to reach and sell to customers. This includes direct sales, alliances, e-commerce platforms, distributors, or a mix of channels that are in line with the target market and maximize reach. Finding the best sites for sales and distribution channels can be supported by OSM data. Businesses can identify the most advantageous locations to set up physical storefronts, warehouses, or distribution centers by examining population density data from various official sources and transportation infrastructure data from OSM.

For example, de Abreu e Silva & Alho, (2017) investigated the connections between perceived problems with urban freight delivery parking and a range of influencing factors, including characteristics of commercial establishments, distribution channels, delivery operations, and the perceived issues themselves (such as vehicles obstructing others, inadequate loading/unloading bays, and instances of illegal parking). This study used data from diverse sources such as parking records, the OpenStreetMap repository for spatial data, the Portuguese National Statistics Institute for relevant statistical data, and the City Council's retail establishments' census.

Logistics and Supply Chain Optimization

For businesses involved in logistics and supply chain operations, OSM data can be valuable for optimizing routes, determining efficient delivery networks, and minimizing transportation costs. By leveraging the road network and transportation data available in OSM, businesses can analyze different route options, estimate travel times, and identify potential bottlenecks. For example, utilized OpenStreetMap data to extract road networks, including traffic signals to model time-dependent transport times to simulate supply chain scenarios in the city of Winnipeg (Gutenschwager et al., 2019). This can lead to improved operational efficiency and cost savings (Slind, 2023).

Strategic Partnerships

It denotes identifying and establishing strategic partnerships with other businesses that can enhance or complement products. This may result in increased customer reach, resource sharing, and chances for both parties to thrive. OSM data can be used to locate possible business partners in particular regions. For instance, analyzing OSM data can assist in locating companies or organizations with established logistics skills in the target locations if someone is seeking a distribution partner.

Revenue Generation

It refers to creating a detailed revenue model that details the company's expected revenue generation. This may include pricing tactics, subscription models, one-time sales, licencing, or other revenue streams pertinent to a company. OSM data can offer insights into the market demand and prospective client base in several sectors. Based on variables like competitiveness, population density, and amenities offered in a specific place, pricing strategies can be developed using this information. For example, zur Heiden & Winter, (2021) noted that cities with successful retail centers, where the amount of money spent on shopping is high compared to the number of residents, are defined by their central location and concentrated shopping areas. The success of these centers is not reliant on particular types of shops, but rather on their overall layout and accessibility.

Marketing and Promotion

It enables the development of a thorough marketing strategy to increase awareness, develop brand equity, and attract customers. This can include advertising, content marketing, social media, public relations, and other online and offline marketing methods. Rifat et al., (2012) noted that location-based advertising (LBA) using OSM data is an effective marketing channel in Bangladesh that provides personalized and targeted advertisements to consumers based on their real-world location, offering benefits to both customers and marketers. By finding locations with a larger concentration of potential clients, OSM data can help in targeting marketing initiatives. Businesses can find good spots for outdoor advertising, sponsorships, or focused online marketing efforts by analyzing OSM data in combination with other market-related data.

Customer Acquisition and Retention

It refers to implementing strategies to acquire new customers and retain existing ones. Lead creation, client relationship management, loyalty programmes, and exceptional customer service are all included in this. OSM data can assist in understanding the proximity of customers to business locations or distribution channels. By combining OSM data with demographic and socio-economic data, businesses can gain insights into the characteristics and preferences of the population in a specific area. This information can be used to develop targeted customer acquisition strategies, tailored marketing campaigns, and convenient customer service options.

Operational Execution

Making sure that business operations, such as production, shipping, quality assurance, and customer service, are carried out efficiently and effectively. This contributes to operational excellence and provides a great client experience. The road network, transport infrastructure, and points of interest can be extracted from OSM data to determine effective routes, increase operational efficiency, and optimize logistics and supply chain operations.

Performance Measurement

It enables establishing metrics and key performance indicators (KPIs) to monitor the development of the businesses and their success. This makes it possible to make decisions based on data and to modify plans in light of performance insights. The performance of various business sites or distribution networks can be monitored using OSM data. Businesses can assess the effectiveness of their business development initiatives in certain locations by looking at data on foot traffic, consumer density, or transit patterns.

Continuous Improvement

It refers to emphasizing a culture of learning and progress. Growth and innovation can be boosted by routinely analyzing and improving business development strategies in response to client input, market developments, and internal evaluations. OSM data can include historical or real-time information regarding alterations in amenities, infrastructure, or population density. This enables companies to make data-driven decisions for ongoing improvement and adjust their plans in response to changing market conditions. For example, Viana et al., (2019) examined the historical contributions of OSM data to generate multi-temporal LULC maps with high thematic accuracy, especially for larger features in rural areas.

Risk Assessment and Business Continuity

OpenStreetMap data can be utilized for risk analysis and business continuity planning in addition to business development. Businesses can determine how vulnerable their operations are to natural disasters and make appropriate plans by combining data on natural features like rivers, mountains, and flood zones. This may entail choosing safer sites for crucial facilities or putting in place backup plans to maintain operations in case of calamities. For example, Rest & Hirsch, (2022) evaluated how susceptible important home health care (HHC) assets are to disasters and underscored the significance of emergency readiness for HHC services. The study used OSM transportation data to determine the best routes for handling emergencies through a COVID-19 case study.

Figure 1. OSM for business development

Market Analysis	Customer Segmentation
Strategic Partnerships	Sales and Distribution Channels
Revenue Generation	Logistics and Supply Chain Optimization
Marketing and Promotion	Customer Acquisition and Retention
Operational Execution	Performance Measurement
Continuous Improvement	Risk Assessment and Business Continuity

ECONOMIC VALUE OF GREEN SPACES

Public and private sectors that invest in parks and green areas can gain in several ways beyond the environmental perspective. Numerous studies have emphasized the benefits of such investments for economic growth, enhanced property values, improved local businesses, and boosts in the overall quality of life in a community (Conway et al., 2010; David et al., 2022; Forest, 2008; Jabbar et al., 2022; Springwater, 2021). As a result, the market may drive a shift toward green infrastructure (Tony, 2011).

Urban open spaces have been found to generate job prospects due to their place value, promoting community growth and economic prosperity (Forest, 2008; Jennings et al., 2017). Businesses that prioritize good landscaping also benefit greatly since customers identify them with providing high-quality products and services. Customers are consequently frequently prepared to spend more for goods supplied by stores with attractive landscaping (Forest, 2008). Beyond only pleasing to the eye, attractive landscaping makes businesses more visible, bringing in customers and locals. This, in turn, promotes a sense of communal pride and helps people's opinions of the region as a whole to be favourable (Forest, 2008).

Green infrastructure has an impact on regional initiatives in addition to local community projects. For instance, it is projected that since its beginning, Philadelphia's Green City, Clean Waters green infrastructure initiative has created close to a thousand job possibilities (SBNGP, 2019). Similar to this, Chester County's commitment to protecting open spaces has shown substantial economic benefits, amounting to $238 million yearly, while also producing close to 1,800 jobs in industries including park maintenance, agriculture, and tourism (David et al., 2022). Additionally, according to David et al., (2022), Chester County's open space approach has resulted in significant property value growth, adding $1.65 billion in extra value to the area. Moreover, the corresponding tax revenues produced annually total around $27.4 million.

Green infrastructure has positive effects on businesses' financial success in addition to economic advantages. Dan Burden, (2006) suggested that businesses situated on streets with trees can experience a 12% increase in their income compared to those without trees. Furthermore, having mature tree canopies along streets gives companies the chance to charge a premium of 8–12% for their goods and services, thus enhancing their financial situation (Dan Burden, 2006)

When taken as a whole, these studies show the green infrastructure's revolutionary potential, making it an appealing option for both communities and enterprises. Integrating green spaces and sustainable practices into urban development can result in economic growth and a higher quality of life for locals and visitors alike.

OPENSTREETMAP FOR GREEN INFRASTRUCTURE

OpenStreetMap is a crowd-sourced, open-content map of the entire world, created and maintained by volunteers. With a mission to encourage innovative uses of map data and provide an alternative to conventional map providers, OpenStreetMap fosters community mapping efforts where volunteers survey and enhance geographical information using wiki-style software. The project offers diverse map editing tools and invites contributions from developers and translators. Established in 2004 by Steve Coast, the OpenStreetMap Foundation was founded in 2006 to support the growth and distribution of free geospatial data, without controlling the data itself. Emphasizing global collaboration, OpenStreetMap continues to evolve, striving to provide accessible and freely available geospatial data for everyone to utilize and share (Wiki, 2023b).

Many studies investigated the use of OSM data to support the analysis of green infrastructure in several ways. For example, OpenStreetMap data was utilized to quantify the extent of green infrastructure present in 184 European cities as part of the CCM coverage (Kumar & Vuilliomenet, 2021). Moreover, in another study, OSM was employed to create an inventory of ecosystems that actively support green infrastructure (O. Klimanova et al., 2021). Additionally, the accessibility of green spaces to green infrastructure in China is assessed by extracting green space data from the OSM platform (Ma et al., 2023).

Land use categories were derived from OpenStreetMap data to identify and classify agricultural lands and green areas (O. A. Klimanova & Illarionova, 2020). Similarly, landmark information, including details about streets, parking lots, industrial and commercial buildings, as well as public parks, was retrieved from OpenStreetMap (Arthur & Hack, 2022). In another study, data sourced from OpenStreetMap was employed to identify and delineate parks based on their geometries and attribute descriptions, which encompassed designations like parks, playgrounds, and protected areas (Venter et al., 2020).

Ludwig et al., (2021) analyzed land use parcels obtained from OSM data and specifically focused on the city of Dresden, Germany. Utilizing OSM for analyzing urban green spaces, Texier et al., (2018) discovered that the OSM dataset closely resembles the official cadaster-based approaches, like UrbIS in Brussels. Moreover, it is worth noting that the OSM data might not comprehensively represent municipal commonages or city green belts located on the outskirts of smaller cities. Despite this limitation, the researchers were unable to obtain alternative, higher-quality data that provides national coverage as noted by Venter et al., (2020). The literature concerning the utilization of OpenStreetMap data for analyzing green infrastructure and green spaces is extensive. Table 1 provides a summary of selected studies, including details such as the country of focus, the scope of analysis conducted in each study, and the specific tags or keys employed.

As evident from Table 1, the mentioned studies encompassed a diverse range of green space tags, providing valuable insights into the examination of green infrastructure and its various applications across different regions.

Table 1. Selected studies on OSM for green spaces

Tags/Keys	Values	Country	Analysis	Reference
Natural	wood, tree_row, tree, scrub, heath, grassland, fell, shrub	Europe	Correlation between green infrastructure and the cultural vibrancy	(Kumar & Vuilliomenet, 2021)
Landuse	allotments, farmland, farmyard, flowerbed, forest, meadow, orchard, vineyard, cemetery, grass, greenhouse_horticulture, plant_nursery, recreation_ground, normali_green			(Kumar & Vuilliomenet, 2021)
Leisure	garden, nature_reserve, park			(Kumar & Vuilliomenet, 2021)
Landuse	farmland	Russia	Quality of green infrastructure	(O. Klimanova et al., 2021)
Vegetation	wood			(O. A. Klimanova & Illarionova, 2020)
Landuse	forest, orchard, grass, meadow, village_green, recreation_ground, garden, park, allotments, cemetery			(O. A. Klimanova & Illarionova, 2020)
Not Mentioned	park, playground, and protected area	South Africa	Distribution of green spaces	(Venter et al., 2020).
Land use	forest; recreation ground, grass, meadow, orchard, greenfield, village green, and vineyard	Belgium	Spatial dimensions of urban green spaces	(Texier et al., 2018)
Leisure	common, dog park, garden; golf course; nature reserve; park and pitch			(Texier et al., 2018)
Natural	scrub; fell; grassland; heath; moor and wood.			(Texier et al., 2018)

OSM GREEN SPACES FOR BUSINESS DEVELOPMENT

With the growing awareness of sustainable practices and environmental responsibility among businesses, the integration of green spaces from OSM data is gaining prominence as a valuable tool for boosting business development. Figure 2 outlined the key aspects of harnessing OSM green spaces to drive business growth and maintain a competitive advantage, as presented below:

Site Selection and Planning

OSM data offers a wealth of geospatial information, including details on various locations, infrastructure, and amenities in a given area. OSM data holds promising potential for supporting data-driven business research and expanding the possibilities for site selection (Baumbach et al., 2019). The location, scope, and character of green spaces, parks, and nature reserves are all well-represented by OSM data. Businesses can use this information to make well-informed decisions regarding suitable locations for their businesses that are close to green spaces.

A business can reap several advantages from being strategically located next to green spaces, which will help both the company and its staff. Being close to green spaces can improve the appeal of businesses, bringing in eco-aware clients and helping to create a livelier and healthier urban environment. Companies can use green spaces' appeal to entice additional customers and clients (Djanogly, 2018). Customers can have a great eating experience amidst the splendour of nature at a restaurant or café that is close to a park or nature reserve. Similar to how restaurants and shops near parks may foster a welcoming and peaceful environment for customers, increasing loyalty and repeat business.

Enhancing Employee Well-Being

Employee well-being, stress reduction, and job satisfaction have all been linked to access to green spaces. Employers can use OSM data to find workplaces or campuses that are close to parks or other green spaces. Numerous studies have been carried out recently to highlight the importance of being close to green spaces. For instance, Kardan et al., (2015)'s study discovered that people who lived nearer to green spaces reported lower levels of stress and a greater sense of well-being. This study emphasizes the beneficial effects that green spaces can have on the mental health of local populations.

Additionally, a study by MacKerron & Mourato, (2013) that looked at the connection between green spaces and people's happiness found a favourable association between having access to natural areas and feeling satisfied with one's life in general. These results offer empirical proof of the importance of green spaces in fostering pleasure and well-being.

Choosing Pollution-Resilient Locations

OSM data can be combined with pollution-related datasets to reveal information on the degree of noise, air quality, and other environmental aspects that have a direct bearing on people's ability to live or work in a certain area. By using this information, businesses can choose areas with low pollution levels, reducing the environmental impact of their activities. A healthier and more sustainable workplace can be created for both employees and the community by choosing locations with good air quality and less noise pollution.

For several reasons, choosing a site for a business in a low-pollution area is essential. High pollution levels, especially air pollution, have been associated with some respiratory and cardiovascular conditions that result in absenteeism and lower productivity at work. Businesses may avoid regions with poor air quality and maintain a healthier and more engaged staff by analyzing OSM data along with pollution information. Several real-world studies have been carried out recently to show the necessity of choosing low-pollution zones for enterprises. For instance, a study by Chang et al., (2019) that looked at the effect of air pollution on worker productivity found that exposure to dirty air caused employees to have poorer levels of productivity and cognitive performance. This study emphasizes how crucial it is to pick areas with excellent air quality if you want to keep a highly productive team. A study by (Clark et al., 2014) also looked at the connection between pollution exposure and community health. According to the study, communities living in polluted locations had greater incidences of respiratory ailments and poorer overall quality of life. In line with the company's dedication to social welfare, choosing to locate a firm in a low-pollution region has positive effects on not only the health and happiness of the neighborhood's residents but also on those of the employees.

Businesses can discover possible risks related to pollution-prone locations with the help of OSM data. For instance, businesses in sectors like food processing or healthcare that depend on clean air and water can avoid areas with a history of pollution problems to protect their operations and reputation from potential impact.

Sustainable Energy Solutions for Businesses

Significant opportunity exists for lowering energy needs and improving sustainability through the integration of green spaces into business development. According to research (Fan et al., 2019; Gomez-Martinez et al., 2021) areas close to green spaces tend to use less energy. For example, Liu et al., (2022) noted that green spaces in the Beijing Metropolitan Area play a crucial role in mitigating the urban heat island effect and improving the thermal environment in summer for surrounding communities. Similarly, Semenzato & Bortolini, (2023) argued that the presence of urban green spaces, particularly trees, can effectively mitigate the urban heat island effect and reduce air temperatures in cities.

OSM's extensive database of green spaces can allow businesses to identify locations that benefit from the natural cooling effect, reduced heat island effect, and improved air quality associated with such areas. Thus, by selecting sites near green spaces, businesses can tap into these benefits and lower their overall energy consumption. Moreover, data from OSM's green spaces can be combined with knowledge of renewable energy sources and energy-efficient construction. Businesses can choose locations close to green areas that support sustainable building methods and make use of renewable energy sources. The addition of solar panels, green roofs, or other energy-saving measures can not only lessen the company's carbon footprint but also result in long-term cost savings due to decreased energy usage (Nations, 2018; Osman et al., 2023).

Sustainable Business Campus Design

OSM green spaces data can help in designing ecologically friendly layouts for larger-scale developments like corporate campuses or industrial parks. Businesses can design environmentally responsible and visually pleasing layouts that encourage sustainability and improve the general well-being of the campus environment (Lindemann-Matthies & Brieger, 2016).

The aesthetic appeal that green spaces bring is one of the main benefits of incorporating them into campus design (Djanogly, 2018). Businesses can make the campus into a welcoming and peaceful setting that promotes a sense of harmony with nature by putting green spaces strategically, such as gardens, parks, and green belts. In addition to improving the visual appeal, having more vegetation around improves the mood and enjoyment of all stakeholders.

Beyond aesthetics, green areas are essential for fostering biodiversity on campus. The data on green areas in OSM can be used to locate the best spots to grow native trees, shrubs, and plants that will attract a variety of birds, insects, and other species. The development's eco-friendliness is further enhanced by adding bike lanes and pedestrian walkways inside the campus. OSM data can be used to find ideal routes for walkability (Bartzokas-Tsiompras, 2022) that encourage active commuting for workers. Supporting a better lifestyle for employees while reducing carbon emissions and traffic congestion is achieved by encouraging walking and bicycling (Frank et al., 2010).

Eco-Tourism and Hospitality

There is a rising focus on eco-friendly practices and sustainability in the dynamic environment of the tourism and hospitality industries. Businesses in these industries can provide clients with distinctive and ecologically responsible experiences by analyzing and using OSM data on green spaces. Businesses can better develop ecotourism projects, outdoor activities, and housing alternatives that are not only accessible to natural attractions but also help to preserve these pristine ecosystems by making use of OSM's extensive database of green areas.

Companies can design itineraries that transport visitors to magnificent natural monuments and offer possibilities for wildlife observation, hiking, and sustainable outdoor excursions by using and mapping OSM data on green spaces, parks, and nature reserves. In addition to fostering a closer relationship with nature, this strategy also raises visitors' awareness of environmental issues and motivates them to support conservation initiatives (Buckley, 2012).

Additionally, using OSM green area data enables hospitality businesses to carefully choose locations for eco-friendly lodging options. In addition to improving the entire guest experience, this proximity also lessens the need for resource-intensive developments, reducing the ecological impact of these businesses (Q. Liu et al., 2022).

Economic and Community Development

Green space data from OSM can support launching community and economic development programmes. Local companies and governments can make strategic plans to promote local events, outdoor festivals, and leisure pursuits using this useful geographical information.

Finding the best spots for neighbourhood gatherings and outdoor celebrations can be benefited from OSM green space data. Parks, gardens, and nature preserves identified in the OSM database can provide excellent venues for organizing gatherings, markets, concerts, and cultural celebrations. Local governments can encourage community involvement and promote a feeling of shared identity and pride among citizens by using these green areas for events.

Additionally, making investments in parks and community events helps to promote a positive view of the area, which attracts tourists and possible investors. Communities that exhibit a dedication to sustainable development and environmental care can gain a competitive edge in attracting businesses (Ye et al., 2021).

Ecological Conservation and Restoration

The data on green spaces in OSM can be a useful resource for companies looking to implement ecological conservation and habitat restoration projects. Businesses can identify crucial regions that need habitat restoration or conservation initiatives by using this geospatial information, paving the path for a more sustainable future. Businesses can learn more about ecologically significant locations and spot areas that might be at risk of environmental hazards or degradation by mapping green spaces, nature reserves, and natural ecosystems.

The prioritization of conservation initiatives can be supported by the integration of OSM green space data with restoration plans. Businesses may make sure that their efforts are focused on regions where they can have the biggest positive influence on biodiversity conservation by taking a variety of criteria into account, such as the size of the area, the richness of species, and the degree of degradation (Bottrill & Pressey, 2012). A deeper appreciation for the environment among visitors and locals alike can be fostered by conservation initiatives and habitat restoration, which can also open up opportunities for ecotourism, teaching, and research (Fischer & Lindenmayer, 2007).

Green Advertising and Branding

Businesses are realizing the benefits of implementing eco-friendly practices and integrating sustainability into their branding and advertising initiatives in an era where consumer behaviour is being increasingly influenced by environmental consciousness. With the use of OSM green space data, businesses can emphasize their dedication to green spaces and appeal to environmentally-conscious consumers.

A company's green reputation can be boosted by using OSM data in marketing initiatives, which also has the potential to attract a growing market of environmentally conscious consumers. Businesses can use this data in their marketing materials and communication strategies by mapping and analyzing the data regarding green spaces and nature reserves close to their location. It sends a clear message about the company's environmental responsibility and dedication to sustainable practices when it emphasizes its proximity to green places in marketing, website content, and social media posts (Garg, 2015).

However, Baumbach et al., (2019) also indicated that the majority of marketing strategies adopted by the selected developers in Poznań can be categorized as "Greenwashing" (GW), while only a small number of properties showcased characteristics of "Nature-based Solutions" (NbS).

Research and Analysis

OSM green space data emerges as a useful resource for researchers and analysts in the fields of urban planning and public health research. This extensive dataset can offer vital insights into the connection between urban environments, green areas, and public health, helping businesses and local governments to make decisions based on the best available facts.

OSM green space data can support the comparison of various cities and areas. With varied demographics, land-use patterns, and socioeconomic considerations, researchers can spot trends and patterns in the existence of green spaces in metropolitan regions. Such comparison research can provide important new information about how green spaces can help mitigate urban problems and improve overall urban livability. Businesses and local governments can be guided towards constructing more sustainable and health-promoting urban environments by understanding the positive effects of green spaces on physical and mental health as well as community well-being (WHO, 2016).

Figure 2. OSM green spaces for business development

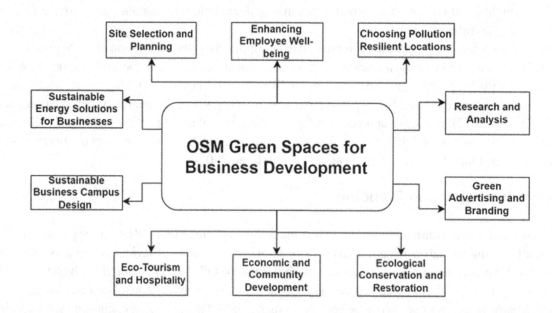

MANAGERIAL AND THEORETICAL IMPLICATIONS

The integration of OpenStreetMap green spaces for business development has several significant managerial and theoretical implications:

Managerial Implications

OSM green space data can help businesses make informed decisions about where to establish or expand their operations. By considering factors like proximity to green spaces, businesses can enhance their employees' well-being, attract talent, and potentially improve productivity.

Understanding the availability of green spaces near their operations can enable businesses to plan recreational activities or wellness programs for employees. This can contribute to improved employee satisfaction and reduced absenteeism.

Businesses can use OSM green space data to plan their infrastructure more efficiently. For example, they can take advantage of existing green spaces for recreational areas, reducing the need for extensive and costly in-house facilities.

Incorporating green spaces into business development can allow companies to align with CSR principles. By contributing to the preservation and maintenance of nearby green areas, businesses can demonstrate their commitment to environmental sustainability and social well-being, enhancing their reputation (Porter & Kramer, 2011).

Leveraging OSM green space data, businesses can differentiate themselves in the market. They can highlight their commitment to green initiatives and sustainable practices, attracting environmentally conscious consumers who prefer eco-friendly products and services (Makower & Pike, 2008).

Theoretical Implications

The utilization of green spaces as a resource in business development can align the business with the principles of environmental resource theory. This theory suggests that businesses should consider the environmental context in which they operate to ensure long-term sustainability.

OSM green space data integration can resonate with the principles of social ecology, which emphasize the interconnectedness of human society and the natural environment. By incorporating green spaces into their development strategies, businesses acknowledge the importance of a harmonious coexistence with the environment.

Businesses embracing green spaces for development can demonstrate commitment to stakeholder theory, which recognizes that organizations should consider the interests of all stakeholders, including the community and the environment, not just the consumer. This approach may enhance long-term sustainability and corporate reputation.

BEST PRACTICES FOR UTILIZING OSM DATA

To make the most of OpenStreetMap data, it is essential to approach its usage with careful consideration and a commitment to best practices that prioritize accuracy, relevance, and ethical conduct. Here are some recommended practices for maximizing the benefits of OSM data:

- Respect the OSM Community and Licencing: OpenStreetMap was created through collaboration by a large international contributor community. Respect their efforts and abide by the OSM data usage policy and licensing terms. Give proper attribution and adhere to the ODbL (Open Database License) when using OSM data in applications or projects.
- Stay Updated: The community updates OSM data frequently. Update your dataset frequently to guarantee that you have access to the most recent data. It's important to stay current because changes to highways, landmarks, and other geographic characteristics can happen regularly.
- Use APIs and Tools: To access and manipulate OSM data, use the OpenStreetMap APIs (Application Programming Interfaces) and tools. These APIs offer dependable data access and are made to withstand heavy usage.
- Understand Data Size and Scope: OSM data can be huge and resource-intensive to handle. Keep in mind the scope and size of the data you require for your particular use case. To retrieve the necessary information, download an extract from websites such as GeoFabrik, HOTOSM, and Overpass Turbo (LearnOSM, 2016).
- Understand Data Tags and Categories: To categorize various feature types (such as roads, buildings, and parks), OSM data is organized using tags (Wiki, 2023a). Understanding the OSM tagging system will let you accurately retrieve the precise data you require.
- Combine OSM Data with Other Sources: To improve your study or application, think about combining OSM Data with other geographic data sources. Comprehensive insights can be obtained by combining OSM data with information from reputable government sources or other geographic databases.

- Verify Data Accuracy: Although OSM data is useful, it is crucial to ensure that it is accurate, especially when used in crucial decision-making procedures. When feasible, cross-reference OSM data with other reliable sources to ensure the accuracy of the information.
- Contribute back to OSM: If you find inaccuracies or out-of-date information in OSM data during your study, think about making updates or corrections to the data and giving something back to the OSM community. Participating actively in the community improves the data for all users.
- Consider Data Privacy and Security: When using OSM data, be Aware of Data Privacy and Security Issues. Avoid exposing sensitive or personal information about people using OSM data, and make sure data protection laws are followed.
- Support OSM: If your company uses OSM data, think about providing donations or resources to the project. The OSM community can be sustained and expanded through contributions to the OpenStreetMap Foundation or the provision of server resources for data hosting.

CONCLUSION

Green areas have a significant economic value to influence both community development and business growth. In addition to improving environmental well-being, investing in parks and other green spaces has several positive economic effects. Businesses that proactively use green infrastructure and include sustainable practices in their development plans stand to earn competitive advantages and improve their overall performance.

OSM data can be employed to boost businesses in several ways. Improved market analysis, client segmentation, and improved sales and distribution methods can all result from using OSM in business development. OSM can also help to develop revenue creation plans, discover potential alliances, and optimize supply chain and logistical operations. Businesses can target particular client categories and concentrate on customer acquisition and retention efforts by using OSM for marketing and promotion.

The possibilities for using green areas from OSM data in business growth are numerous and extensive. Businesses can choose locations near green spaces to increase their appeal and foster employee well-being by making informed decisions regarding site selection and planning. By choosing low-pollution areas, a better working environment can be developed. Furthermore, businesses can pursue sustainable energy solutions, design eco-friendly campuses, and explore eco-tourism and hospitality opportunities to align with environmental values and attract eco-conscious consumers.

By finding appropriate locations for events and encouraging community engagement, OSM green space data can also help with economic and community development. Additionally, it can support ecological preservation and restoration initiatives, allowing corporations to give priority to conservation efforts and encourage environmental responsibility. Employing OSM data in marketing and branding can improve a business's reputation as being environmentally friendly and attract customers who care about the environment.

OSM green space data provides important insights for academics and analysts on the relationship between urban settings, green spaces, and public health. Comparing cities and regions with different socioeconomic and demographic characteristics can reveal important insights about the benefits of green spaces on overall urban livability and community well-being.

Future research can concentrate on developing green infrastructure and sustainable practices that are tailored to particular business types and industries. Understanding the unique needs and benefits of different businesses can lead to more targeted and effective strategies. Measuring the success and impact of these activities can be supported by the creation of standardized performance criteria for the integration of green spaces into corporate development. Businesses will be able to evaluate their success and make data-driven decisions by establishing clear metrics.

REFERENCES

Ahmad, M. (2023). *Spatial Data as a Catalyst to Drive Entrepreneurial Growth and Sustainable Development*. doi:10.4018/978-1-6684-9843-9.ch004

Ahmad, M., & Ali, A. (2023). Mapping the Future of Sustainable Development Through Cloud-Based Solutions: A Case Study of OpenStreetMap. In Promoting Sustainable Management Through Technological Innovation (pp. 153–176). IGI Global. doi:10.4018/978-1-6684-9979-5.ch011

Argiolas, M. (2014). Surveying housing market supply affordability using a spatial data mining approach. *WIT Transactions on Ecology and the Environment, 191*, 125–137. Advance online publication. doi:10.2495/SC140111

Arthur, N., & Hack, J. (2022). A multiple scale, function, and type approach to determine and improve Green Infrastructure of urban watersheds. *Urban Forestry & Urban Greening, 68*, 127459. Advance online publication. doi:10.1016/j.ufug.2022.127459

Baganz, G., Proksch, G., Kloas, W., Lorleberg, W., Baganz, D., Staaks, G., & Lohrberg, F. (2020). Site Resource Inventories-A Missing Link in the Circular City's Information Flow. *Advances in Geosciences, 54*, 23–32. Advance online publication. doi:10.5194/adgeo-54-23-2020

Bartzokas-Tsiompras, A. (2022). Utilizing OpenStreetMap data to measure and compare pedestrian street lengths in 992 cities around the world. *European Journal of Geography, 13*(2), 127–141. Advance online publication. doi:10.48088/ejg.a.bar.13.2.127.138

Baumbach, S., Rubel, C., Ahmed, S., & Dengel, A. (2019). Geospatial customer, competitor and supplier analysis for site selection of supermarkets. *ACM International Conference Proceeding Series, Part F148261*. 10.1145/3318236.3318264

Bottrill, M. C., & Pressey, R. L. (2012). The effectiveness and evaluation of conservation planning. In Conservation Letters (Vol. 5, Issue 6). doi:10.1111/j.1755-263X.2012.00268.x

Buckley, R. (2012). Sustainable tourism: Research and reality. In Annals of Tourism Research (Vol. 39, Issue 2). doi:10.1016/j.annals.2012.02.003

Chang, T. Y., Zivin, J. G., Gross, T., & Neidell, M. (2019). The effect of pollution on worker productivity: Evidence from call center workers in China. *American Economic Journal. Applied Economics, 11*(1), 151–172. Advance online publication. doi:10.1257/app.20160436

Clark, L. P., Millet, D. B., & Marshall, J. D. (2014). National patterns in environmental injustice and inequality: Outdoor NO2 air pollution in the United States. *PLoS One, 9*(4), e94431. Advance online publication. doi:10.1371/journal.pone.0094431 PMID:24736569

Conway, D., Li, C. Q., Wolch, J., Kahle, C., & Jerrett, M. (2010). A spatial autocorrelation approach for examining the effects of urban greenspace on residential property values. *The Journal of Real Estate Finance and Economics*, *41*(2), 150–169. Advance online publication. doi:10.100711146-008-9159-6

Dan Burden. (2006). *Urban Street Trees*. https://www.walkable.org/download/22_benefits.pdf

David, R., Steve, W., Melissa, W., & John, L. (2022). *Green Infrastructure Financing*. https://icma.org/sites/default/files/2022-05/Final%20Financing%20Green%20Infrastructure.pdf

de Abreu e Silva, J., & Alho, A. R. (2017). Using Structural Equations Modeling to explore perceived urban freight deliveries parking issues. *Transportation Research Part A, Policy and Practice*, *102*, 18–32. Advance online publication. doi:10.1016/j.tra.2016.08.022

Djanogly, H. (2018). Why Going Green Can Have a Positive Impact on Attracting Customers. *Customer-Think*. https://customerthink.com/why-going-green-can-have-a-positive-impact-on-attracting-customers/

Dupre, D. (2020). Urban and socio-economic correlates of property prices in dublin's area. *Proceedings - 2020 IEEE 7th International Conference on Data Science and Advanced Analytics, DSAA 2020*. 10.1109/DSAA49011.2020.00070

Fan, H., Yu, Z., Yang, G., Liu, T. Y., Liu, T. Y., Hung, C. H., & Vejre, H. (2019). How to cool hot-humid (Asian) cities with urban trees? An optimal landscape size perspective. *Agricultural and Forest Meteorology*, *265*, 338–348. Advance online publication. doi:10.1016/j.agrformet.2018.11.027

Fischer, J., & Lindenmayer, D. B. (2007). Landscape modification and habitat fragmentation: A synthesis. In Global Ecology and Biogeography (Vol. 16, Issue 3). doi:10.1111/j.1466-8238.2007.00287.x

Forest, M. (2008). *The Economic Value of Green Infrastructure*. http://www.greeninfrastructurenw.co.uk/resources/The_Economic_Value_of_Green_Infrastructure.pdf

Formánek, T., & Sokol, O. (2022). Location effects: Geo-spatial and socio-demographic determinants of sales dynamics in brick-and-mortar retail stores. *Journal of Retailing and Consumer Services*, *66*, 102902. Advance online publication. doi:10.1016/j.jretconser.2021.102902

Frank, L. D., Sallis, J. F., Saelens, B. E., Leary, L., Cain, L., Conway, T. L., & Hess, P. M. (2010). The development of a walkability index: Application to the neighborhood quality of life study. In British Journal of Sports Medicine (Vol. 44, Issue 13). doi:10.1136/bjsm.2009.058701

Garg, A. (2015). Green Marketing for Sustainable Development: An Industry Perspective. *Sustainable Development (Bradford)*, *23*(5), 301–316. Advance online publication. doi:10.1002d.1592

Gomez-Martinez, F., De Beurs, K. M., Koch, J., & Widener, J. (2021). Multi-temporal land surface temperature and vegetation greenness in urban green spaces of Puebla, Mexico. *Land (Basel)*, *10*(2), 155. Advance online publication. doi:10.3390/land10020155

Gutenschwager, K., McLeod, R. D., & Friesen, M. R. (2019). From Openstreetmap and Cell Phone Data to Road Network Simulation Models. *Proceedings - Winter Simulation Conference, 2019-December*. doi:10.1109/WSC40007.2019.9004833

Hossain, A., Naser, K., Zaman, A., & Nuseibeh, R. (2009). Factors influencing women business development in the developing countries: Evidence from Bangladesh. *The International Journal of Organizational Analysis, 17*(3), 202–224. Advance online publication. doi:10.1108/19348830910974923

Jabbar, M., Yusoff, M. M., & Shafie, A. (2022). Assessing the role of urban green spaces for human well-being: a systematic review. In GeoJournal (Vol. 87, Issue 5). doi:10.100710708-021-10474-7

Jennings, V., Baptiste, A. K., Osborne Jelks, N., & Skeete, R. (2017). Urban green space and the pursuit of health equity in parts of the United States. *International Journal of Environmental Research and Public Health, 14*(11), 1432. Advance online publication. doi:10.3390/ijerph14111432 PMID:29165367

Kardan, O., Gozdyra, P., Misic, B., Moola, F., Palmer, L. J., Paus, T., & Berman, M. G. (2015). Neighborhood greenspace and health in a large urban center. *Scientific Reports, 5*(1), 11610. Advance online publication. doi:10.1038rep11610 PMID:26158911

Keil, T., Maula, M., Schildt, H., & Zahra, S. A. (2008). The effect of governance modes and relatedness of external business development activities on innovative performance. In Strategic Management Journal (Vol. 29, Issue 8). doi:10.1002mj.672

Klimanova, O., Illarionova, O., Grunewald, K., & Bukvareva, E. (2021). Green infrastructure, urbanization, and ecosystem services: The main challenges for Russia's largest cities. *Land (Basel), 10*(12), 1292. Advance online publication. doi:10.3390/land10121292

Klimanova, O. A., & Illarionova, O. I. (2020). Green infrastructure indicators for urban planning: Applying the integrated approach for Russian largest cities. *Geography, Environment, Sustainability, 13*(1), 251–259.

Kohtamäki, M., Parida, V., Patel, P. C., & Gebauer, H. (2020). The relationship between digitalization and servitization: The role of servitization in capturing the financial potential of digitalization. *Technological Forecasting and Social Change, 151*, 119804. Advance online publication. doi:10.1016/j.techfore.2019.119804

Kumar, V., & Vuilliomenet, A. (2021). Urban nature: Does green infrastructure relate to the cultural and creative vitality of European cities? *Sustainability (Basel), 13*(14), 8052. Advance online publication. doi:10.3390u13148052

Le Texier, M., Schiel, K., & Caruso, G. (2018). The provision of urban green space and its accessibility: Spatial data effects in Brussels. *PLoS One, 13*(10), e0204684. Advance online publication. doi:10.1371/journal.pone.0204684 PMID:30332449

Learn, O. S. M. (2016). *OpenStreetMap Data.* https://learnosm.org/en/osm-data/

Li, X., & Kao, C. (2022). Spatial Analysis and Modeling of the Housing Value Changes in the U.S. during the COVID-19 Pandemic. *Journal of Risk and Financial Management, 15*(3), 139. Advance online publication. doi:10.3390/jrfm15030139

Lindemann-Matthies, P., & Brieger, H. (2016). Does urban gardening increase aesthetic quality of urban areas? A case study from Germany. *Urban Forestry & Urban Greening, 17*, 33–41. Advance online publication. doi:10.1016/j.ufug.2016.03.010

Liu, Q., Browne, A. L., & Iossifova, D. (2022). A socio-material approach to resource consumption and environmental sustainability of tourist accommodations in a Chinese hot spring town. *Sustainable Production and Consumption*, *30*, 424–437. Advance online publication. doi:10.1016/j.spc.2021.12.021

Liu, W., Zhao, H., Sun, S., Xu, X., Huang, T., & Zhu, J. (2022). Green Space Cooling Effect and Contribution to Mitigate Heat Island Effect of Surrounding Communities in Beijing Metropolitan Area. *Frontiers in Public Health*, *10*, 870403. Advance online publication. doi:10.3389/fpubh.2022.870403 PMID:35586004

Ludwig, C., Hecht, R., Lautenbach, S., Schorcht, M., & Zipf, A. (2021). Mapping Public Urban Green Spaces Based on OpenStreetMap and Sentinel-2 Imagery Using Belief Functions. *ISPRS International Journal of Geo-Information*, *10*(4), 251. Advance online publication. doi:10.3390/ijgi10040251

Ma, Y., Brindley, P., & Lange, E. (2023). From Modelling and Analysis of Accessibility of Urban Green Space to Green Infrastructure Planning: Guangzhou as a Case Study. In Adaptive Urban Transformation: Urban Landscape Dynamics, Regional Design and Territorial Governance in the Pearl River Delta, China (pp. 249–266). Springer.

Macdonald, J. L., Dolega, L., & Singleton, A. (2022). An open source delineation and hierarchical classification of UK retail agglomerations. *Scientific Data*, *9*(1), 541. Advance online publication. doi:10.103841597-022-01556-3 PMID:36057644

MacKerron, G., & Mourato, S. (2013). Happiness is greater in natural environments. *Global Environmental Change*, *23*(5), 992–1000. Advance online publication. doi:10.1016/j.gloenvcha.2013.03.010

Makower, J., & Pike, C. (2008). Strategies for the green economy : opportunities and challenges in the new world of business. In Strategies.

Nations, U. (2018). *Renewable energy sources cut carbon emissions, efficiently increase electricity output worldwide, delegates say in second committee.* https://press.un.org/en/2018/gaef3501.doc.htm

Osman, A. I., Chen, L., Yang, M., Msigwa, G., Farghali, M., Fawzy, S., Rooney, D. W., & Yap, P. S. (2023). Cost, environmental impact, and resilience of renewable energy under a changing climate: A review. *Environmental Chemistry Letters*, *21*(2), 741–764. Advance online publication. doi:10.100710311-022-01532-8

Page, S. J., Forer, P., & Lawton, G. R. (1999). Small business development and tourism: Terra incognita? *Tourism Management*, *20*(4), 435–459. Advance online publication. doi:10.1016/S0261-5177(99)00024-2

Phan, D. D. (2003). E-business development for competitive advantages: A case study. *Information & Management*, *40*(6), 581–590. Advance online publication. doi:10.1016/S0378-7206(02)00089-7

Porter, M. E., & Kramer, M. R. (2011). Creating Shared Value. *Harvard Business Review*, 89.

Rainey, D. L. (2006). Sustainable business development: Inventing the future through strategy, innovation, and leadership. In *Sustainable Business Development*. Inventing the Future Through Strategy, Innovation, and Leadership. doi:10.1017/CBO9780511617607.015

Rajabifard, A., & Williamson, I. P. (2001). Spatial data infrastructures: concept, SDI hierarchy and future directions. *Proceedings of GEOMATICS*, 10. https://doi.org/10.1.1.9.1919

Rest, K. D., & Hirsch, P. (2022). Insights and decision support for home health care services in times of disasters. *Central European Journal of Operations Research, 30*(1), 133–157. Advance online publication. doi:10.100710100-021-00770-5 PMID:34366709

Rifat, M. R., Moutushy, S., & Ferdous, H. S. (2012). A Location Based Advertisement scheme using OpenStreetMap. *Proceeding of the 15th International Conference on Computer and Information Technology, ICCIT 2012*, 423–428. 10.1109/ICCITechn.2012.6509801

SBNGP. (2019). *The Economic, Social, and Environmental Case for Green City, Clean Waters: An Update.* https://www.sbnphiladelphia.org/wp-content/uploads/2021/04/SBN-GCCW-Report-071219.pdf

Semenzato, P., & Bortolini, L. (2023). Urban Heat Island Mitigation and Urban Green Spaces: Testing a Model in the City of Padova (Italy). *Land (Basel), 12*(2), 476. Advance online publication. doi:10.3390/land12020476

Shang, S., Du, S., Du, S., & Zhu, S. (2021). Estimating building-scale population using multi-source spatial data. *Cities (London, England), 111*, 103002. Advance online publication. doi:10.1016/j.cities.2020.103002

Sjödin, D., Parida, V., Jovanovic, M., & Visnjic, I. (2020). Value Creation and Value Capture Alignment in Business Model Innovation: A Process View on Outcome-Based Business Models. *Journal of Product Innovation Management, 37*(2), 158–183. Advance online publication. doi:10.1111/jpim.12516

Slind, T. (2023). *How to Bring Location Services to Your Company and Customers.* https://www.locana.co/how-to-bring-location-services-to-your-company-and-customers/

Springwater. (2021). *The economic value of parks and green spaces.* http://www.springwaterpcd.org/the-value-of-parks-and-recreation

Tony, M. (2011, August). *How do we put a value on green infrastructure?* Built Environment; The Guardian. https://www.theguardian.com/sustainable-business/value-green-infrastructure-spaces

Venter, Z. S., Shackleton, C. M., Van Staden, F., Selomane, O., & Masterson, V. A. (2020). Green Apartheid: Urban green infrastructure remains unequally distributed across income and race geographies in South Africa. *Landscape and Urban Planning, 203*, 103889. doi:10.1016/j.landurbplan.2020.103889

Viana, C. M., Encalada, L., & Rocha, J. (2019). The value of OpenStreetMap historical contributions as a source of sampling data for multi-temporal land use/cover maps. *ISPRS International Journal of Geo-Information, 8*(3), 116. Advance online publication. doi:10.3390/ijgi8030116

Wang, J., Rienow, A., David, M., & Albert, C. (2022). Green infrastructure connectivity analysis across spatiotemporal scales: A transferable approach in the Ruhr Metropolitan Area, Germany. *The Science of the Total Environment, 813*, 152463. doi:10.1016/j.scitotenv.2021.152463 PMID:34952053

Weise, J., & Mostaghim, S. (2022). A Scalable Many-Objective Pathfinding Benchmark Suite. *IEEE Transactions on Evolutionary Computation, 26*(1), 188–194. Advance online publication. doi:10.1109/TEVC.2021.3089050

WHO. (2016). *Urban green spaces and health.* WHO.

Widaningrum, D. L., Surjandari, I., & Sudiana, D. (2020). Discovering spatial patterns of fast-food restaurants in Jakarta, Indonesia. *Journal of Industrial and Production Engineering, 37*(8), 403–421. Advance online publication. doi:10.1080/21681015.2020.1823495

WikiO. (2023a). *Tags.* https://wiki.openstreetmap.org/wiki/Tags

Wiki, O. (2023b). *About OpenStreetMap.* https://wiki.openstreetmap.org/wiki/About_OpenStreetMap

Ye, C., Zhao, Z., & Cai, J. (2021). The Impact of Smart City Construction on the Quality of Foreign Direct Investment in China. *Complexity, 2021,* 1–9. Advance online publication. doi:10.1155/2021/5619950

zur Heiden, P., & Winter, D. (2021). Discovering Geographical Patterns of Retailers' Locations for Successful Retail in City Centers. *Innovation Through Information Systems: Volume I: A Collection of Latest Research on Domain Issues,* 99–104.

Chapter 14
An Overview of the Management of Stakeholders Following COVID–19

Anjali Motwani
Jain University, India

Mariam Mathen
Jain University, India

Y. P. Sai Lakshmi
Sri Venkateswara College of Engineering, India

Biswaranjan Senapati
https://orcid.org/0000-0002-0717-5888
Parker Hannifin Corp., USA

ABSTRACT

This study's objective is to investigate the various categories of stakeholders and propose strategies for efficiently managing those stakeholders regarding the potential dangers and difficulties that may be encountered by the organization while attempting to manage them throughout COVID-19. In general, the management of stakeholders is a ubiquitous activity, and businesses should adhere to an effective and efficient structure to perform this role. This chapter aimed to investigate whether there are any novel or original approaches to managing stakeholders, as well as to provide some potential solutions to the challenges of doing so during this pandemic. In addition, the authors tried to shed some light on the crucial relationship between stakeholder management and business reputation. According to the results, more research is needed to provide novel insights into stakeholder management. A manager or project manager can utilize the results from this article in several ways.

DOI: 10.4018/979-8-3693-0049-7.ch014

1. INTRODUCTION

Stakeholders and stakeholder management: Stakeholders play a vital role in the organization's existence (Köpsel et al., 2021). A stakeholder is a person, an individual, or a group that can positively or negatively influence or affect the organization (Leach, 2002). A stakeholder can be defined as an individual, group, or organization that may affect, be affected by, or perceive themselves to be affected by a project's decision, activity, or outcome (Parent & Deephouse, 2007).

Organizing, monitoring, and enhancing your connections with your stakeholders is known as stakeholder management (Angeline et al., 2023). It entails methodically identifying stakeholders, assessing their requirements and expectations, and preparing and implementing various tasks to engage with them (Rajest et al., 2023a). Using a good stakeholder management strategy, you can coordinate your interactions and evaluate the quantity and quality of your relationships with different stakeholders (Post et al., 2002).

Today's Stakeholders are becoming more aware of corporate actions' significance and effects on the environment and society (Rajest et al., 2023b). Stakeholders have the power to praise or condemn corporations (Regin et al., 2023; Köseoğlu et al., 2022). This encourages businesses to partner with and include stakeholders in their decision-making (Vashishtha & Dhawan, 2023). Therefore, a stakeholder-based approach can assist businesses in permanently changing their corporate behavior (Srinivas et al., 2023). This includes Improved reputation and branding, Improved accountability to and assessments from the investment community, Improved employee commitment, Decreased vulnerability through stronger relationships with communities, and Stronger financial performance and profitability (e.g., through eco-efficiency) (Abbassy, 2020).

The projects taken up by the organizations are failing because they cannot meet the stakeholders' expectations (Abbassy & Ead, 2020). Also, the companies are not taking any initiative to know the reasons behind the failure (Ead & Abbassy, 2022). If the companies can formulate strategies according to the categories of the stakeholders to identify their expectations of the organization, then to a large extent, they can be successful in their projects or activities (Abbassy & Abo-Alnadr, 2019).

Categories of Stakeholders

Stakeholders can be classified into two groups:

- Internal or Primary Stakeholders
- External or Secondary Stakeholders

Internal Stakeholders: are those stakeholders who are within the organization. Internal stakeholders include employees, shareholders, managers, and the board of directors.

Employees: Employees have a stake in the business and rely on sound business decisions because they directly impact those decisions.

Investors: They are investing their hard-earned money to get a reasonable rate of return. Hence, they are very much interested in the functioning of the business (Priscila et al., 2023).

BOD and Managers: Top executives mainly focus on the department's functioning and business activities. Because it has an impact on the other stakeholders, too (Phoek et al., 2023).

External or Secondary Stakeholders are those outside the organization and not directly impacted by the project. These stakeholders include suppliers, customers, creditors, clients, intermediaries, government, competitors, and society (Hussain & Alam, 2023).

Customers: Customers are the end-users of the product or service of the organization. The organization should try to meet their expectations ethically.

Government: The government collects taxes from businesses based on their profitability or turnover, which is the government's revenue. The organizations should also comply with all legal and statutory norms.

Society: A company, an organization, or a business provides job opportunities and various infrastructural facilities for the betterment of society.

Creditors: The organization benefits the creditors with their credit scores, their new contracts, and liquidity.

Suppliers: The suppliers will benefit only if the business's products and services are in high demand. So, they are very much interested in the success of the project or business.

Figure 1. Organizational performance depends on stakeholder management

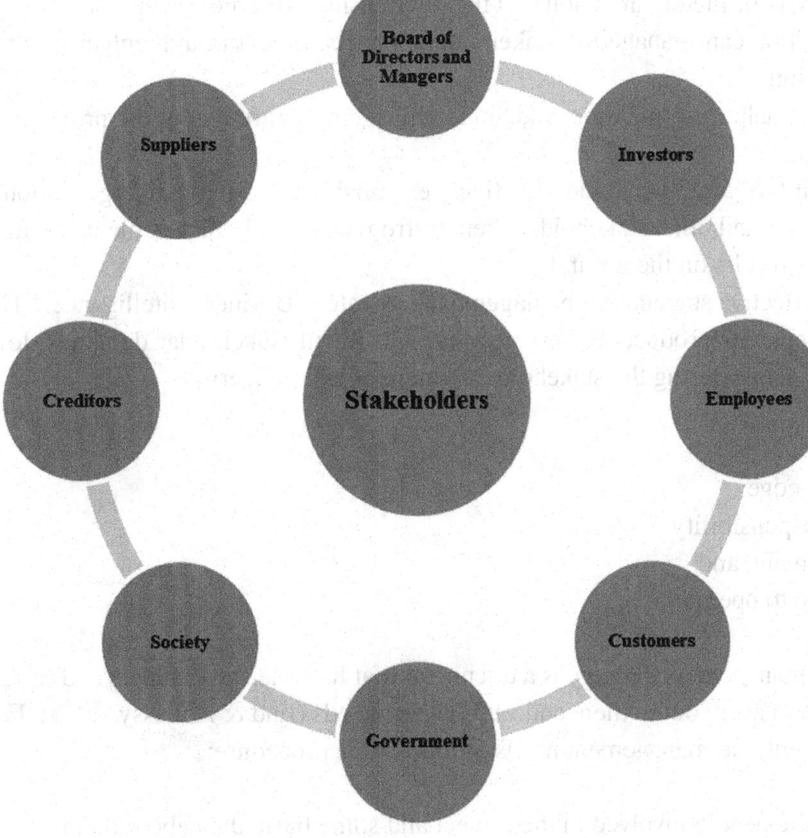

Stakeholder management is critical to the organization's success, so it is considered the critical success factor (Figure 1). Stakeholder management focuses on all stakeholders' influences on the activities. Organizations should take serious effort in developing and maintaining relationships with the stakeholders (Mitchell et al., 1997). Previous studies state that most businesses or projects fail due to a lack of involvement from individuals directly or indirectly related to the same (Singh et al., 2023). This situation can be controlled by improving relationships with the stakeholders because it directly impacts the businesses or projects. Involvement helps in getting proper support and contribution from the related parties.

Regardless of the type or category of stakeholders, the following attributes remain common: influence, connection, power, and irreplaceability.

Stakeholder management is considered to be a complex process because the roles, views, and perceptions differ from individual to individual and group to group. Hence, the organization must deploy an effective mechanism for managing the stakeholders.

An effective mechanism of stakeholder management strategy can help the organizations in different ways:

- It avoids or resolves conflicts between various stakeholders.
- It helps the organization to get more support from key stakeholders.
- It enhances the quality of the communication between the stakeholders, and hence, it will increase the productivity of the organization and the relationship with the stakeholders.
- The organization can manage the stakeholders' expectations through enhanced productivity and communication.
- The strategies help us to monitor stakeholder engagement throughout the project.

Businesses that recognize the value of actively establishing and maintaining relationships with the affected communities and other stakeholders benefit from better risk management, stronger stakeholder support, and better results on the ground.

Additionally, effective stakeholder management generates "Business Intelligence." The corporation can develop concepts for products or services that will fulfill stakeholder demands, lower costs, and maximize value by considering the stakeholders' interests and concerns.

- Credibility
- Competitive edge
- Corporate responsibility
- risk management, and
- social license to operate

A stakeholder management strategy is a document that lists the stakeholders and the approaches the company will take to reach out to them and satisfy their needs (Ead & Abbassy, 2018). For the preparation of this document, the management needs to follow this procedure;

- A list of all the people involved in the project and some basic data about them.
- An interest or power matrix or stakeholder map.
- Prioritization of stakeholders is included.

- A communication strategy for stakeholders.
- A section outlining the various stakeholder management tactics to be used in various situations, like conflict resolution or project status reporting methods.

2. REVIEW OF LITERATURE

The term stakeholder was first appeared in the management literature in 1963. Stakeholder means any group or individual who can affect or is affected by the achievement of the organization's objectives. From that period onwards, stakeholders are considered indispensable to any activities, projects, or businesses. Stakeholders should be managed appropriately because they are the critical success factors in project management (Yang et al., 2009). For this, they have to maintain a cordial relationship between the project management and the stakeholders (Ward & Chapman, 2008), and the management should identify the various factors or attributes that influence the stakeholder management (Srinivasan & Dhivya, 2020). Also, the companies could manage their activities or businesses fruitfully with the help of stakeholder management by maintaining social distancing and lockdowns.

Which stakeholder groups should be given priority has also been a topic of much discussion. Stakeholder and shareholder objectives are now acknowledged to be complementary rather than competitive (Berman et al., 1999). When stakeholder theory was first proposed, it was considered antithetical to the shareholder perspective. However, since then, the issue has developed. One strategy entails categorizing stakeholders, ranking them according to importance, and forging mutually beneficial connections with the most significant ones. According to Hart & Sharma (2004), most organizations still focus on well-known, prominent, or strong groups to maintain their competitive advantages. Instead of focusing exclusively on the demands of the most important or influential stakeholders, an alternate approach to stakeholder management also considers the needs of many other stakeholders. Hart and Sharma (2004) elaborated on this idea. They proposed that organizations may want to seek outside of conventional stakeholder networks, such as, for example, fringe stakeholders, to manage disruptive change and gain expertise to build competitive inventiveness.

Capon & Mintzberg, (1996) claim that organizations make decisions by engaging in official and informal negotiations with the many stakeholders. As coalition membership changes, member interactions alter, and goals are attained or not, the organization's goals adapt and change through time.

This pandemic helped the healthcare sectors deliver and manage their services (Folayan et al., 2021). Different strategies and reporting tools, such as Wrike, will help the management control the challenges the stakeholders pose. Also, they should deploy a proper stakeholder analysis process to determine the different stakeholder categories and rank them according to their positive or negative influence.

According Nguyen et al., (2018) to this study, stakeholder analysis, stakeholder influence, stakeholder management strategies, and stakeholder engagement were considered the different themes related to Stakeholder management. According to the article, social network analysis is useful for examining the intricacy of stakeholder interrelationships in the context of CPs. Stakeholder analysis and stakeholder engagement methodologies effectively tackle environmental complexity (involving various stakeholders, a changing policy and regulatory environment, and a changing natural environment) projects.

The results demonstrate how stakeholder management is increasingly interwoven into corporate operations and how the rise of the internet, social networking, and big data has pressured companies to develop new tools and techniques for managing stakeholders online. To sum up, synthesizing the data with the created framework enables comprehension of many research strands and provides directions for further Study (Pedrini & Ferri, 2019).

According to the Study, the clients and end users were the most significant project stakeholders. Additionally, this research allowed the researcher to propose a process for managing stakeholders: plan, identify, analyze, communicate, act, and follow up. The management can meet the stakeholders' interests with this (Dohnalova & Zimola, 2014)

One of the key success criteria for boosting a company's competitiveness at the moment is stakeholder relationship management. The influence of stakeholder groups and their impact on an undertaking must now be considered to maintain the enterprise's long-term stability. Due to these factors, corporate strategy should include managing an organization's business relationships with its stakeholders. The enterprise's stakeholders should be identified and examined using the right approaches, processes, and tools to discover alternate possibilities of their impact on the enterprise. An organization should take advantage of stakeholder engagement opportunities while identifying and thwarting any possible risks (Henriques & Sadorsky, 1999).

In their Study, Graves et al., (2000) emphasized the significance of stakeholder connections in "built-to-last" businesses. The stakeholders most important to the effective realization of the vision are maintained in good relationships by the values-driven, visionary businesses. By offering them a pleasant working environment, they encourage high morale and effective work from their staff. Businesses can gain their trust by offering customers goods or services that meet or exceed their expectations. The issues are dealt with collaboratively and amicably right from the beginning by the communities.

Reink Goodijk (2002) has made a few observations about some aspects. According to him, management that is aware and prudent knows the value of managing relationships with funding sources and involving stakeholders. Relationship management and stakeholder engagement both require an open mind and a willingness to consider a variety of signals, changes, and problems while simultaneously striving to strike a balance between the various interests involved and deliver solutions.

3. OBJECTIVES

- To understand the means of effective management of stakeholders
- To study the challenges faced in managing stakeholders.
- To recognize new/innovative methods of stakeholder management
- To suggest remedies for better stakeholder management in current times.
- To understand the relation between stakeholder management and corporate reputation.

4. DATA ANALYSIS AND INTERPRETATION

The article focuses on understanding the new ways and means of stakeholder management post-Covid-19 era. The paper lists the challenges faced by industries from a bird's eye view. The study is based on secondary data available from various sources. The study also focuses on various means of managing stakeholders in the digitized era through various digital techniques.

The study is purely based on secondary data and previous research works. The scope of the study is limited because a smaller number of research works were only available regarding stakeholder management. The study considers only the concept of stakeholder management and corporate reputation. Other concepts like stakeholder capitalism, stakeholder engagement, etc, were not considered in this paper.

Scope: The scope of the research is to understand the changes enforced by the technology and changing patterns of stakeholder management and the challenges created by the pandemic.

Figure 2. Effective stakeholder management

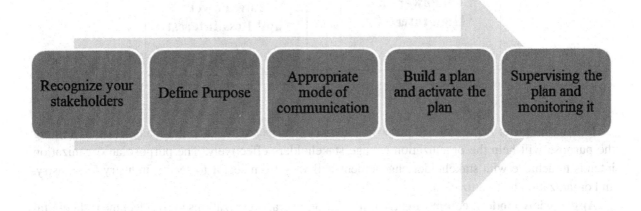

Recognizing the stakeholders helps find ways to deal with and prioritize them (Figure 2). Every stakeholder is important as it can affect the business, so managing stakeholders is an art. There is a simple way of managing stakeholders; "Stakeholder Mapping." Stakeholder mapping involves visualizing all the different parties involved in or impacted by the project. The different stakeholder groups' motivations and objectives should be depicted in this visual tool and who they are. When assessing the impact and motivation of project stakeholders, stakeholder mapping is essential. With the right stakeholder map, you can avoid hurdles more successfully. Knowing how to categorize and manage stakeholders will impact the outcome of your project.

Power Interest Grid

High power and high interest: These stakeholders are the most important for any organization (Figure 3). Any company needs to keep these stakeholders happy as they have high power to affect them.

High powerless interest: Such stakeholders are also important to an organization, and the organization needs to try to keep them content.

Low power and high interest: These stakeholders are important, as they need to be kept well informed and keep communicating with them. Moreover, these can be very beneficial as they provide helpful details.

Low power and less interest: These are the least important, with negligible interest in the organization.

Figure 3. Power interest grid

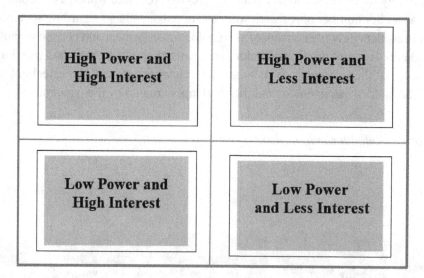

Define Purpose: A pre-defined purpose is the key to effective stakeholder management. Defining the purpose will help the organization engage stakeholders effectively. The purpose an organization intends to achieve with stakeholder engagement will vary from sector to sector, industry to industry, and organization to organization.

Appropriate mode of communication: In this digital era, organizations must select the right digital tool to communicate with their stakeholders. According to stakeholder mapping in the power interest grid, stakeholders should be segregated, and appropriate channels and tools of communication should be devised. The effectiveness of the communication channel plays a vital role in building the relationship between the company and the stakeholders. Also, this will help in resolving the conflicts of the stakeholders.

Build a plan and activate the plan: For each stakeholder's effective management, a specific plan needs to be developed and executed. Planning a proper level of communication will lead to better management of stakeholders. Along with an effective plan, effective execution is equally important. Key points to consider for effective communication:

- Communicating in their matter of interest
- Gaining information
- Managing the expectations
- Involving stakeholders as part of the decision-making process

Supervising the Plan and Monitoring It

Maintaining the plan is the most difficult part of any management process. Monitoring on a timely basis becomes even more crucial for stakeholders with power and interest in the organization. Keeping an update and adding a subordinate plan if the need arises. Taking feedback from stakeholders from time to time to improve the overall Stakeholder management.

Challenges in Stakeholder Management

Different opinions: Many stakeholders might have colliding opinions, which may affect an organization's decision-making.

Contending priorities: Each stakeholder comes with a distinct set of objectives that need to be fulfilled by an organization, so one needs to prioritize them, which in turn is challenging for any organization.

Scarce Resource: The pressure to satisfy stakeholders is high, and the resources are always scarce.

Contrasting data and Decision-making: The data needs to be available to all stakeholders for appropriate decision-making, but as per different stakeholders, opinions may differ, which may have divergent decision suggestions.

Cognizance of the Organization and Ongoing Interest: If the organization is aware of the current trends and interests of the stakeholders, it can match up to the needs of all, but in reality, it is a difficult task to accomplish by any organization.

Innovative methods of adopting Technology: Adopting new ways of technology to satisfy stakeholders and to keep upskilling them is a big challenge for organizations to cope with.

Innovative Methods of Stakeholder Management

- Concentration on stakeholders that have a key position
- Notifying stakeholders and valuing their involvement
- Customizing the approach to the specific stakeholder need.
- Modifying the process of importing feedback to specific stakeholder groups.
- Consistently presenting data.
- Focusing on Brand recognition as it has a strong effect on stakeholders' receptiveness
- Use of easy adoptive Technology to empower and engage Stakeholders
- Social Media Marketing and Advertising for better engagement
- Social Networking: Twitter, Facebook, and Blogs for conveying information in a correct way and at a lesser cost

Suggestions to Enhance Stakeholder Management

- Moderate/minimize conflict and enhance stakeholder participation
- Ensure that most stakeholders are at benefitting end and the decisions are transparent and justifiable
- Create and focus on activities that build towards specific recommendations that assist quality online engagement.
- Creating and engaging in dialogue, reflections, and guidance on how to cope with challenges post-COVID-19.
- Enable discussion and learning on how to employ and promote effective stakeholder management

5. DISCUSSION AND FINDINGS

The term "corporate reputation" describes how a company is perceived by its constituents, including its customers, shareholders, and the general public. It is influenced by the business's operations, products, and stakeholder communications. External factors like market trends and media coverage also influence it. Due to its ability to increase trust, customer loyalty, and staff happiness, as well as financial success and perks like better stock prices and increased revenue, a company's reputation can be one of its most important assets. In addition to their potential to create wealth, good business reputations are essential since their intangible nature makes replicating them by rival companies much more difficult.

Even though the idea of corporate reputation was originally considered burdensome and essentially academic, it is today a renowned, well-known asset among a company's assets. A change in stakeholders' interactions with enterprises has made it a significant driver of company value. Per advancements in communications technology, the significance of a company's reputation has become increasingly recognized. There is more connectivity than ever before. News of a company's triumphs or failures is available to stakeholders in real time. With much-increased scrutiny of corporate conduct both before and after reputation crises, hyper-openness makes it difficult to hide failures. As a result of the growth of social media, there is now a true media anarchy where customers can interact with and criticize the acts of businesses directly, even adding tags to their marketing communications.

The organisation is influenced both directly and indirectly by its stakeholders, particularly with regard to the reputation of the business. When viewed through the lens of standardised criteria of corporate reputation, the connection between stakeholders and the business is immediately apparent. According to the research that was done on the concept of corporate reputation, the interactions that stakeholders have with the company have a substantial impact on how the general public perceives corporate reputation (Helm, 2007; Puncheva, 2008; Omar et al., 2009; Peloza et al., 2012). As a consequence of this connection, a number of researchers have investigated the significance of stakeholders for the reputation of businesses (Neville et al., 2005; Hillenbrand & Money, 2007; Capriotti, 2009). Visualizing the many different groups that are either a part of the project or are affected by it is what is meant by the term "stakeholder mapping." This graphical instrument needs to make the identities, goals, and motivations of the stakeholders very clear.

According to Neville et al (2005)'s research, it is expected that when a company is dependent on its stakeholders, those stakeholders would have an effect not only on the organization's financial performance but also on its reputation. The stakeholders currently possess the organization's necessary resources, which are currently in their possession. According to the argument presented by Krstic (2014), the link between stakeholders and the organisation can both positively and negatively affect profit, tenacity, relationships, and corporate reputation. The organization's reputation is put at danger whenever there is an imbalance in the interactions that take place between the organisation and its stakeholders and whenever there is a lack of responsibility, openness, and accountability.

To reduce reputational risk, increase resource availability, solve arising problems, achieve organizational goals, facilitate specific business processes, and enhance product and service quality, stakeholders and the organization must work together (Krstic, 2014). To build a solid reputation, an organization must be able to manage input from stakeholders and participate in subtle interactions (Dickinson-Delaporte et al., 2010) based on two-way communication (Krstic, 2014).

Long-term commitments between an organisation and its various stakeholders can assure that a performance will be effective even in the midst of a crisis (Dickinson-Delaporte et al., 2010). According to Jones (1995) and Hillenbrand & Money (2007), the cornerstone for an organization's sustained success is a mutual trust between the institution and its stakeholders. According to Hillenbrand and Money (2007), the establishment of trustworthy ties between an organisation and its stakeholders is necessary for the sustained success of a firm. In order to maintain a positive firm reputation, future financial performance, and sustainability, all three are dependent on responsible behaviour in interpersonal interactions. These findings are consistent with those that were discovered by Capriotti (2009), who discovered that the accountability and transparency of the media had a positive effect on the perceptions that stakeholders had of the organisation. The author argued that businesses that are seen favorably by their stakeholder groups have stronger corporate reputations.

6. CONCLUSION

Stakeholders are the critical success factor of any project or business. They should be given due importance based on the outcome of stakeholder analysis. Not only that, they should be properly informed about the concerned projects. This paper highlights the various innovative strategies organizations can use to manage stakeholders. These innovative strategies and tools are developed per the recent advancements in technology. Stakeholders played a vital role in managing the activities of various organizations fruitfully during the COVID-19. It is evident from the previous studies that the stakeholders played a remarkable role in the healthcare sector. The stakeholders' effective participation helped the companies overcome the challenges and threats - the pandemic period.

This paper helps researchers to get an overview of stakeholder management, strategies, and the challenges faced by the organization. This study offers some new perspectives on the stakeholder management process. The stakeholders are the most crucial factor in determining whether a project succeeds or fails. Second, the reviews demonstrate that all stakeholder groups are equally capable of destabilizing the project and creating issues. Third, the findings suggest that more work should be done to offer fresh perspectives on stakeholder management. A manager or project manager can apply the findings from this article in several ways. We generally contend that project managers should focus more on the stakeholders and be more externally focused. Thanks to the stakeholder management plan, the project manager will better understand which stakeholders to prioritize.

FUTURE RESEARCH WORKS

In the course of this research, only a few ideas pertaining to the management of stakeholders were taken into consideration. For the purpose of determining the connection between stakeholder management and company reputation, just a cursory examination of the various types of published research was carried out. Using not only a method of quantitative empirical research but also qualitative research, future research works may be able to shed further light on the issues related to stakeholder management, stakeholder engagement, and stakeholder capitalism, as well as the various sets of software and AI tools that can be used in the better management of stakeholders. This research may be conducted using both qualitative and quantitative research methods.

REFERENCES

Abbassy, M. M. (2020). Opinion mining for Arabic customer feedback using machine learning. *Journal of Advanced Research in Dynamical and Control Systems*, *12*(SP3), 209–217. doi:10.5373/JARDCS/V12SP3/20201255

Abbassy, M. M., & Abo-Alnadr, A. (2019). Rule-based emotion AI in Arabic customer review. *International Journal of Advanced Computer Science and Applications*, *10*(9). Advance online publication. doi:10.14569/IJACSA.2019.0100932

Abbassy, M. M., & Ead, W. M. (2020). Intelligent Greenhouse Management System. In *2020 6th International Conference on Advanced Computing and Communication Systems (ICACCS)*. IEEE.

Angeline, R., Aarthi, S., Regin, R., & Rajest, S. S. (2023). Dynamic intelligence-driven engineering flooding attack prediction using ensemble learning. In *Advances in Artificial and Human Intelligence in the Modern Era* (pp. 109–124). IGI Global. doi:10.4018/979-8-3693-1301-5.ch006

Berman, S. L., Wicks, A. C., Kotha, S., & Jones, T. M. (1999). Does stakeholder orientation matter? The relationship between stakeholder management models and firm financial performance. *Academy of Management Journal*, *42*(5), 488–506. doi:10.2307/256972

Capon, N., & Mintzberg, H. (1996). The rise and fall of strategic planning. *Academy of Management Review*, *21*(1), 298. doi:10.2307/258641

Capriotti, P. (2009). Economic and social roles of companies in the mass media. The impact media visibility has on businesses' being recognized as economic and social actors. *Business & Society*, *48*(2), 225–242. doi:10.1177/0007650307305724

Dickinson-Delaporte, S., Beverland, M., & Lindgreen, A. (2010). Building corporate reputation with stakeholders: Exploring the role of message ambiguity for social marketers. *European Journal of Marketing*, *44*(11/12), 1856–1874. doi:10.1108/03090561011079918

Dohnalova, Z., & Zimola, B. (2014). Corporate Stakeholder Management", Procedia - Social and Behavioral Sciences 110. *Procedia: Social and Behavioral Sciences*, *110*, 879–886. doi:10.1016/j.sbspro.2013.12.933

Ead, W., & Abbassy, M. (2018). *Intelligent systems of machine learning approaches for developing E-services portals*. EAI Endorsed Transactions on Energy Web. doi:10.4108/eai.2-12-2020.167292

Ead, W. M., & Abbassy, M. M. (2022). A general cyber hygiene approach for financial analytical environment. In *Financial Data Analytics* (pp. 369–384). Springer International Publishing. doi:10.1007/978-3-030-83799-0_13

Folayan, M. O., Brown, B., Haire, B., Babalola, C. P., & Ndembi, N. (2021). Considerations for stakeholder engagement and COVID-19 related clinical trials' conduct in sub-Saharan Africa. *Developing World Bioethics*, *21*(1), 44–50. doi:10.1111/dewb.12283 PMID:32798320

Goodijk, R. (2002). Partnership at corporate level: The meaning of the stakeholder model. *Journal of Change Management*, *3*(3), 225–241. doi:10.1080/714042537

Graves, S., Sandra, B., & Waddock, A. (2000). Beyond Build to Last... Stakeholder Relations in "Built to Last" Companies. *Business and Society Review, 105*(4), 393–418. doi:10.1111/0045-3609.00090

Hart, S. L., & Sharma, S. (2004). Engaging fringe stakeholders for competitive imagination. *IEEE Engineering Management Review, 32*(3), 28–28. doi:10.1109/EMR.2004.25105

Helm, S. (2007). One reputation or many? Comparing stakeholders' perceptions of corporate reputation. *International Journal (Toronto, Ont.), 12*(3), 238–254.

Henriques, I., & Sadorsky, P. (1999). The relationship between environmental commitment and managerial perceptions of stakeholder importance. *Academy of Management Journal, 42*(1), 87–99. doi:10.2307/256876

Hillenbrand, C., & Money, K. (2007). Corporate responsibility and corporate reputation: Two separate concepts or two sides of the same coin? *Corporate Reputation Review, 10*(4), 261–277. doi:10.1057/palgrave.crr.1550057

Hussain, S., & Alam, F. (2023). Willingness to Pay for Tourism Services: A Case Study from Harappa, Sahiwal. *FMDB Transactions on Sustainable Management Letters, 1*(3), 105–113.

Jones, T. M. (1995). Instrumental stakeholder theory: A synthesis of ethics and economics. *Academy of Management Review, 20*(2), 404–437. doi:10.2307/258852

Köpsel, V., de Moura Kiipper, G., & Peck, M. A. (2021). Stakeholder engagement vs. social distancing-how does the Covid-19 pandemic affect participatory research in EU marine science projects? *Maritime Studies, 20*(2), 189–205. doi:10.100740152-021-00223-4 PMID:35300281

Köseoğlu, D., Ead, S., & Abbassy, W. M. (2022). Basics of Financial Data Analytics. In *Financial Data Analytics* (pp. 23–57). Springer International Publishing. doi:10.1007/978-3-030-83799-0_2

Krstic, N. (2014). Stakeholder management from the business perspective. *Megatrend Revija, 11*(2), 165–182. doi:10.5937/MegRev1402165K

Leach, W. D. (2002). Surveying Diverse Stakeholder Groups. *Society & Natural Resources, 15*(7), 641–649. doi:10.1080/08941920290069245

Mitchell, R. K., Agle, B. R., & Wood, D. J. (1997). Toward a theory of stakeholder identification and salience: Defining the principle of who and what really counts. *Academy of Management Review, 22*(4), 853. doi:10.2307/259247

Neville, B. A., Bell, S. J., & Menguc, B. (2005). Corporate reputation, stakeholders and the social performance - financial performance relationship. *European Journal of Marketing, 39*(9), 1184–1198. doi:10.1108/03090560510610798

Nguyen, T. S., Mohamed, S., & Panuwatwanich, K. (2018). Stakeholder management in complex project: Review of contemporary literature. *Journal of Engineering, Project, and Production Management, 8*(2), 75–89. doi:10.32738/JEPPM.201807.0003

Omar, M., Williams, R. L. Jr, & Lingelbach, D. (2009). Global brand market-entry strategy to manage corporate reputation. *Journal of Product and Brand Management, 18*(3), 177–187. doi:10.1108/10610420910957807

Parent, M. M., & Deephouse, D. L. (2007). A case study of stakeholder identification and prioritization by managers. *Journal of Business Ethics*, 75(1), 1–23. doi:10.100710551-007-9533-y

Pedrini, M., & Ferri, L. M. (2019). Stakeholder management: A systematic literature review. *Corporate Governance (Bradford)*, 19(1), 44–59. doi:10.1108/CG-08-2017-0172

Peloza, J., Loock, M., Cerruti, J., & Muyot, M. (2012). Sustainability: How stakeholder perceptions differ from corporate reality. *California Management Review*, 55(1), 74–97. doi:10.1525/cmr.2012.55.1.74

Phoek, S. E. M., Lauwinata, L., & Kowarin, L. R. N. (2023). Tourism Development in Merauke Regency, South Papua Province: Strengthening Physical Infrastructure for Local Economic Growth and Enchanting Tourist Attractions. *FMDB Transactions on Sustainable Management Letters*, 1(2), 82–94.

Post, J. E., Preston, L. E., & Sachs, S. (2002). Managing the extended enterprise: The new stakeholder view. *California Management Review*, 45(1), 6–28. doi:10.2307/41166151

Priscila, S. S., Rajest, S. S., Tadiboina, S. N., Regin, R., & András, S. (2023). Analysis of Machine Learning and Deep Learning Methods for Superstore Sales Prediction. *FMDB Transactions on Sustainable Computer Letters*, 1(1), 1–11.

Puncheva, P. (2008). The role of corporate reputation in the stakeholder decision-making process. *Business & Society*, 47(3), 272–290. doi:10.1177/0007650306297946

Rajest, S. S., Singh, B., Obaid, A. J., Regin, R., & Chinnusamy, K. (2023b). Advances in artificial and human intelligence in the modern era. *Advances in Computational Intelligence and Robotics*. Advance online publication. doi:10.4018/979-8-3693-1301-5

Rajest, S. S., Singh, B. J., Obaid, A., Regin, R., & Chinnusamy, K. (2023a). Recent developments in machine and human intelligence. *Advances in Computational Intelligence and Robotics*. Advance online publication. doi:10.4018/978-1-6684-9189-8

Regin, R., Khanna, A. A., Krishnan, V., Gupta, M., Bose, R. S., & Rajest, S. S. (2023). Information design and unifying approach for secured data sharing using attribute-based access control mechanisms. In Recent Developments in Machine and Human Intelligence (pp. 256–276). IGI Global.

Singh, M., Bhushan, M., Sharma, R., & Cavaliere, L. P. L. (2023). An Organized Assessment of the Literature of Entrepreneurial Skills and Emotional Intelligence. *FMDB Transactions on Sustainable Management Letters*, 1(3), 95–104.

Srinivas, K., Velmurugan, P. R., & Andiyappillai, N. (2023). Digital Human Resources and Management Support Improve Human Resources Effectiveness. *FMDB Transactions on Sustainable Management Letters*, 1(1), 32–45.

Srinivasan, N. P., & Dhivya, S. (2020). An empirical study on stakeholder management in construction projects. *Materials Today: Proceedings*, 21, 60–62. doi:10.1016/j.matpr.2019.05.361

Vashishtha, E., & Dhawan, G. (2023). Comparison of Baldrige Criteria of Strategy Planning and Harrison Text. *FMDB Transactions on Sustainable Management Letters*, 1(1), 22–31.

Ward, S., & Chapman, C. (2008). Stakeholders and uncertainty management in projects. *Construction Management and Economics*, *26*(6), 563–577. doi:10.1080/01446190801998708

Yang, J., Shen, G. Q., Ho, M., Drew, D. S., & Chan, A. P. C. (2009). Exploring critical success factors for stakeholder management in construction projects. *Journal of Civil Engineering and Management*, *15*(4), 337–348. doi:10.3846/1392-3730.2009.15.337-348

Chapter 15
Emerging Digitalization Trends in Human Resource Management

Usha Prabhu
ⓘ https://orcid.org/0000-0001-6219-5358
Jain University, India

Y. Fathima
Jain University, India

N. Sathyanarayana
ⓘ https://orcid.org/0000-0002-4185-7751
Jain University, India

Madireddi S. S. V. Srikumar
Jain University, India

Luigi Pio Leonardo Cavaliere
University of Foggia, Italy

ABSTRACT

New technology has transformed how organizations function in recent decades. With recent advancements, companies may work faster and more efficiently. Human resources departments profited since they have several duties that touch internal and external clients. Electronic human resource management (e-HRM) uses the latest web-based and computer-based technologies, including artificial intelligence, machine learning, and deep learning applications, to conduct human resource management activities. These tools make human resource professionals' tasks easier and allow them to focus on strategic work rather than paperwork. Digital human resource management (DHRM) has moved to recruiting, career management, training and development, performance management, and pay. This chapter examines information technology (IT), digital human resource management, planning, and decision-making.

DOI: 10.4018/979-8-3693-0049-7.ch015

1. INTRODUCTION

The pandemic has changed the way people think about everything. To be at the top, the HR industry needs to come up with a model that works, increases both flexibility and efficiency, maximizes productivity, and cost-benefit analysis to be done by the organization. Almost every day, HR changes its structure to keep up with changes in technology (Akrich, 1992). If business leaders take the right steps and use the right methods, it should have a positive effect on daily operations and, in turn, on the employees (Stanton & Coovert, 2004). Disruptive factors that have an impact on employees' personal and professional lives have been shaking the global economy continuously. From our point of view, the following are the most important HRM trends for 2022 and beyond (Eller et al., 2020).

The human resource management industry has seen a substantial transformation in recent years. From a flexible work paradigm to an all-encompassing approach to employee well-being, 2022 will be the year in which future HR trends will contribute to the HR sector transformation. What parts of the future of the human resources industry provide cause for optimism? And what developments should we watch for? This chapter will provide insights into what to anticipate from the industry and how it will affect the work, the worker, and the workplace (Hawking et al., 2004). In recent years, HR departments at many different types of businesses have benefited from the incorporation of various technological solutions. Through the use of social media, mobile apps, data analytics, and cloud storage, businesses may better optimize their human resources using the digital HR paradigm. Data analytics, simulation tools, and modernized education platforms are all top goals for HR technology.

2. DECENTRALIZED HUMAN RESOURCES: THE RISE OF MODERN MANAGEMENT APPROACHES

According to Anyim et al., (2011) poll, significant staff turnover means revamping traditional methods of finding new employees. As a result, HR departments continue to prioritize adaptability, digitalization, and hybrid work arrangements.

According to the analysis by Bell et al., (2006), HR departments should decentralize in favour of a "hyperlocal model," in which managers take on the responsibility of communicating directly with their teams. They went on to say that standard methods of management appraisal and advancement should be revised as well (Townsend & Bennett, 2003). Companies should not promote "task managers" to upper management roles but rather people who have demonstrated their ability to lead and coach others. When planning for human resource technology in 2022, keep in mind the following:

- Managerial assessment metrics should be reviewed, and managers should be encouraged to grow in areas other than operational competence.
- Don't accept the premise that management knows best.
- Managers should be given more resources and information. Increase productivity by using the correct technological resources to identify and train managers more effectively.

Digitalization might be described as the changes resulting from the application of digital technology to every facet of human civilization (Stolterman & Fors, 2004; Bondarouk & Rul, 2009). Digital technologies are altering the old methods of HRM service delivery within enterprises. There is a significant possibility that digitalizing HRM will contribute to an increase in overall corporate success (Hooi, 2006).

The research shows that no one, all-encompassing concept of digitalization exists. Indeed, the vast majority of writers use this word without explaining its significance to the reader. Instead of defining digitalization, they present it by focusing on its most important effects on people and businesses. Evseeva, et al., (2019) result of the investigation show that there is no precise definition of digitalization. The majority of writers employ this phrase as though the reader is capable of understanding it without needing an explanation. Instead of providing definitions, they only highlight the most important effects that digitalization would have on society at large and businesses to introduce the word (Indermun, 2014).

Kristoff et al. (2018), digitalization is defined by the ways in which people interact with and make use of digital technologies. Others see digitization as a process rather than a static state.

Bhatnagar & Sandhu, (2005) espouse a similar view of digitalization as a process, describing digital HR transformation as a "process of transitioning to digital HR to achieve greater levels of automation and data-driven decision making. Business evolution is made possible by technological advancements".

Osipova (2019) added to the examination of this word by suggesting that its meaning might be construed either narrowly or liberally. In the first instance, digitalization is shifted from analog to digital, so this is consistent with that of the other writers. Osipova (2019), digitization is a long-term process that incorporates both strategic & technological improvements. Abdali (2019) argues that digitalization necessitates the alignment of processes, practices, and organizational culture with new digital technologies that need to modify the model of the business (Kossek, 1987).

In order to stay competitive, Das and Sureshkrishna (2019) assert that enterprises must be willing to accept new technology. In this context, digitization is seen as a necessity, a development that enterprises cannot avoid. Nevertheless, the author's discussion of digitalization highlights a number of features that appear critical to defining it. As a process, digitalization is (1) dynamic and adaptable; (2) user-friendly; (3) centered on the client; (4) motivated by data; (5) a vehicle for teamwork; and (6) crucial to the survival of businesses. Therefore, we argue in this research that digitalization entails more than just the use of technological resources inside an organization. Instead, it entails making use of these resources to revamp the company's basic operating principle and its long-term goals (Hunt, 2014).

Bondarouk et al., (2009) looked at the implications for the workplace of using digital technology for both training and hiring. Digital recruiting and training, or HR operations, have been emphasized by the authors as having a beneficial influence performance of the employee. Florea and Badea (2013) dug into the matter, noting the pros and cons of various recruitment strategies. In contrast, some writers have sought to investigate the effects of digital transformation on HR managers to learn more about the difficulties digitalization poses for them (Das and Sureshkrishna, 2019).

Das and Sureshkrishna (2019) state that digitization has resulted in widespread social change and has far-reaching consequences for human resource management (HRM) professionals and their businesses. Bondarouk et al., (2016) research proved this as well. Human resource managers are seen as seeing digitization as a never-changing process. Human resource managers face a recursive set of implications from digitalization since the former is a necessary condition for the latter to materialize.

Employee productivity was analyzed by Fedorova et al. (2019), who looked at the effects of digitization. They noted that this success contributed to less time spent on mundane chores and fewer mistakes made by humans.

3. DIGITAL LEARNING, TRAINING, AND DEVELOPMENT

Digital Learning (DL) platforms are one example of the increased access to education made possible by the Internet. Through it, firms may facilitate employee learning and development, streamline processes, and increase file sharing and resource accessibility. Learning on the job inspires workers to take initiative and advance in their careers. There will be further momentum in this direction in 2022. In addition to that, we'd like to draw attention to two more significant HR technology developments that have emerged this year (Grant & Newell, 2013).

- Create a database for storing and organizing your information. HR software allows managers to keep training and orientation materials in one place, as reported by Finances Online.
- Add focus on health and happiness to your learning and development initiatives. By prioritizing and managing knowledge in your company, you can assist your staff in zeroing in on what's most important, avoiding information overload, lower stress levels, and boosting morale and productivity (McDonnell & Heard, 2023).

3.1. Technology That Elevates Hybrid Working

Hybrid work arrangements are preferred by both employees and employers, according to several polls. When asked if they would stay in their current jobs if they were obliged to return to the office full-time due to the COVID-19 outbreak, 34% of professionals who are currently working from home claimed they would look for new employment.

Organizations using hybrid work models will need to progress in three ways.

- **People**. HR professionals will continue to look for ways to facilitate communication and collaboration between in-office and remote workers.
- **Places**. There will be a rise in the use of analytical platforms that provide information to teams about the worth of commercial real estate in various markets around the country, as well as about the accessibility of locations, potential avenues for collaboration, and other factors.
- **Scheduling**. The need for tools that facilitate long-term planning and the fulfilment of obligations and constraints will persist well beyond 2022.

3.2. Conformity With the D&I, DEI, and DEI&B

With the advent of the hybrid work age, corporations have easier access to a wider pool of qualified and varied workers without having to relocate them. Over the past two years, the concept of diversity and inclusion has evolved significantly, revealing that the original "diversity and inclusion" (D&I) model is insufficient in a prejudiced society. Diversity, equality, and inclusion are on the rise in the business world (DEI). Nevertheless, diversity, equality, and inclusion alone are not sufficient to provide a workplace that motivates employees to give their best and is well-suited to the 21st-century workplace. The DEI is joined with the employee's workplace affiliation to form the DEI&B. Workers no longer consider their jobs to be satisfying pursuits. As a result of the epidemic, people are starting to place more importance on having a reason for living, achieving their goals, and feeling good about themselves (Figure 1).

The AIHR research identifies the following as key areas where HR technology will be trending in 2022 to boost morale in the workplace:

- Develop a two-way communication approach, increase continuous listening, and use their information to inform future messaging.
- Permit regular communication between managers and staff.

Figure 1. Diversity, equity, inclusion, and belonging (DEIB) at organizations
Source: Author's contributions based on the study

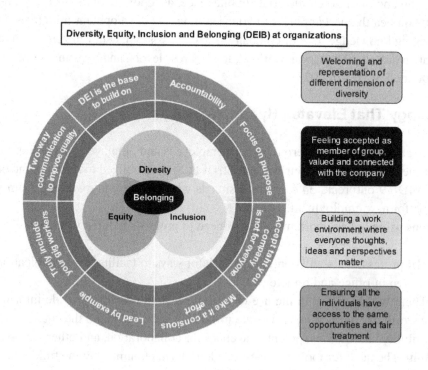

3.3. Tech Development for the Human Well-Being

An excessive work schedule can significantly increase the risk of cardiovascular illnesses, according to the results of a new study published by the National Centre for Biotechnology Information. (NCBI). In addition, working too much hinders efficiency and raises the possibility of developing mental health issues encompassing despair and anxiety. Thus, in 2022, mental health and resilience will be more than simply trendy terms (Lepak & Snell, 1998). Businesses should make significant financial investments to enhance employee well-being and make sure they are prepared to take on new challenges and explore new possibilities (Emerging Markets, 2021). In 2022, these well-being sectors would be the main emphasis of HR technology innovations, according to Selection Software Review:

- Create a feeling of safety for them. Create a culture where everyone feels comfortable voicing their opinions during discussions about their jobs and careers without fear of censure.
- Policy creation for stress management. Policies that allow employees to arrange their working hours and downtime include employee assistance programs and flexible work schedules (Lepak et al., 2005).

4. HUMAN RESOURCE INTEGRATION

Today, the success of an organization depends a lot on how well HRM and business strategy work together. Getting the development system and the control system to work together is hard. However, the coordination gives the business an edge over its competitors. The process of bringing together the goals of an organization is the integration function of HRM. The integration Function of HRM brings together all the things that a company does to manage its employees. So that they can be willing to work and do a good job for the best results. However, integration requires giving employees financial or non-financial incentives to work hard. Create a company culture that encourages a good balance between work and life, where managers don't fear harsh criticism, and where holidays and paid time off can be used in different ways (Figure 2).

Figure 2. Human resource integration proposed framework
Source: Author's contributions based on the study

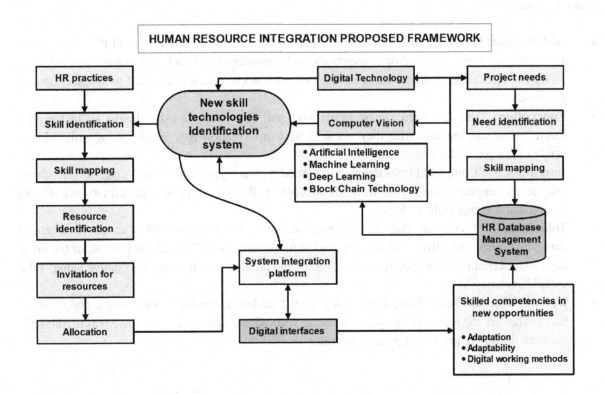

"Through a variety of use cases, blockchain technology will be immediately integrated into the HR department, therefore increasing transparency and trust." Mercer Company.

The Morgan Philips Group predicts that by 2022, the Blockchain will have altered several trends in human resources technology. Examples of Blockchain's security features include the ability to encrypt internal networks so that data may be safely shared across departments and corporations. Using this method, hiring managers may verify details about prospective workers, such as their academic and professional credentials. Incorporating blockchain technology will allow human resources managers to do the following:

- **Standardization**. Blockchain makes it easier for talent departments to work together and gives programmers advice on how to improve their work. This enhances the effectiveness of HR processes.
- **Trust**. To prevent unauthorized access, blockchain registries use a key-based system, so only those with the right credentials may access the records. The Trusted Global Network for HR Data is one such initiative that would make it easier for interested parties to get the data they need.
- **Security**. Human resources departments that use Blockchain technology can safely store and manage massive volumes of sensitive information about the firm and its personnel.

Blockchain makes it possible for people who don't know each other to interact in a way that can be trusted. It does this by utilising a combination of five design features that together authenticate users, validate transactions, and preserve this data in a way that is both immutable and resistant to tampering.

Even though early attempts at a "blockchain" lacked all five components, to be considered a blockchain, they must now:

- **Distribution:** Nodes are machines that are part of the blockchain network and that are running a program designed to monitor transactions and guarantee the Blockchain's business rules are followed. The ledger is stored in its entirety on each node, and it is updated as transactions are processed.
- **Encryption:** Data has been stored safely and partially anonymously, thanks to technology. Contributors can regulate who they are and what information they need, giving only what is needed for a particular transaction.
- **Immutability:** Completed transactions are signed with a cryptographic key given a time stamp, and record-keeping additions are made in the correct. Records can't be changed unless everyone agrees that it's important to do so.
- **Tokenization:** Tokens are digital representations of real-world assets like "money," "a unit of data," or "a user's identity," and they are traded for one another. Through the process of tokenization, a blockchain may be used to both represent and facilitate the trading of a "native value" (also called "currency").
- **Decentralization:** As a result, most nodes are not under the command of a single organization, and neither are the rules. Since transactions are verified and approved by a consensus method, the network doesn't require a single administrator.

4.1. Existing and Emerging Technologies Enable Blockchains

Several new and old technologies, like encryption and peer-to-peer connections, make it possible for Blockchain to have these features. However, current systems can't handle the volume and speed expected in a blockchain era. The following are already considered essential abilities:

- **Decentralized apps (DApps):** Distributed-ledger applications are those that securely store their technology, including data, instructions, and logs of operations.
- **Terms and Conditions (T&C) for Distributed Businesses:** Trust mechanisms for automated use in non-business transactions and communications.
- **Smart contracts:** Business processes are programs or protocols that help, check, or carry them out.
- **Smart resources:** Digital representations of physical assets that computer programs can control.

Using blockchains will significantly alter existing operating models or corporate processes, and to construct new commercial, social, and other governing paradigms, businesses will need to combine existing technology in unique ways and acquire new capabilities.

4.2. Blockchain With HR

Think about the implications of these tools and abilities for the way in which companies engage with talent in the actual world.

Envision launching your company's next major strategic initiative with the help of a blockchain that integrates all of the company's operations, from in-house employees to external contractors and suppliers, as well as all of the cross-departmental communications, approvals, pilots, stage-gate reviews, budgetary authorizations, etc.

The right people may be authorized and hired at each necessary process stage without the need for phone calls, emails, or mountains of paper. Actions will flow automatically and transparently down the chain, and users will only have access to the data and tools they need for as long as they need them.

4.3. Most Promising HR-Related Use Cases

Technology relating to Blockchain experiments conducted utilizes only a subset of the characteristics that make Blockchain special, and hence only a subset of its potential value. Nevertheless, these early applications of Blockchain in human resources provide a taste of what's to come:

- **Human resources data detectives:** HR departments are increasingly becoming data-driven, with a focus on analyzing brilliant employees to guarantee a high-performance workforce. Human Resources Data Detectives use cutting-edge big data tools to assist in closing the gap. A Human Resources Data Detective will gather, examine, and research information about employees from a variety of systems, including but not limited to Human Resource Information Systems, Human Capital Management systems, Time and Attendance systems, and Learning Management Systems.
- **Data security and access for employees:** Numerous confidential details about employees are accessible to employers. On a blockchain, records may be encoded and written in a manner that

renders them immutable. This is especially important for sensitive information like medical problems or past performance. However, these documents can also be made accessible to authorized users using a token if necessary.

- **Smart contracts for people who work on a temporary or contract basis:** A smart contract gives everyone involved rights and obligations that can't be changed. HR contracts that can't be changed can, for example, Once the work has been completed successfully by the employees, the money should be released automatically from escrow. This makes it easier for workers to get paid and helps companies keep their cash flow steady.

- **HR Facilitators**: During the COVID-19 outbreak, HR managers learned the importance of putting the health and safety of their staff, clients, and neighbors first, thanks to the work of the facilitators. Now more than ever, HR departments must manage the incorporation and participation of a remote workforce. It is the facilitator's job to make sure that everyone has access to the tools they need to perform at their highest level and that they have a genuine connection to the company as a whole.

- **The Role of the Algorithm Auditor** is becoming increasingly important as artificial intelligence (AI) becomes more integrated into daily life and leads to more informed business decisions. In order to be effective, AI must adhere to all applicable laws and uphold the company's core principles. Business success relies on algorithms, but their application must be morally sound to maintain a competitive edge.

- **Keeping rules and laws:** A "right to be forgotten" under laws like the General Data Protection Regulation gives workers the legal recourse to have their personal information deleted. (GDPR) of the European Union (EU), which allows them to do so by destroying the encryption key. HR will benefit from blockchain technology to ensure that employees maintain control over their personal information even as rules become more stringent.

- **Benefits and pay:** Transactions that are encrypted and saved on the Blockchain as data that cannot be changed are more trustworthy. This makes auditing and reporting on compliance easier. Payees will no longer have to use middlemen like banks to get their money. Also, banks will no longer be able to change the value of transactions by trading fiat (government-issued) currencies, which changes the value of those currencies.

4.4. Direct Access to External Talent

There are already ways to pay gig economy workers and other temporary workers in real time using blockchain technology. Payroll aggregators, banks, and currencies based on fiat are not required under this system. But that's not all that HR and workers can get out of these innovations; they could also make it easier to find talent.

So far, the best way to use Blockchain in HR is to handle payroll. Key transactions are encrypted and saved on the Blockchain as data that can't be changed. Vendor key management service saves the information needed (so a key can't be extracted using just one component), and a hash protects sensitive payroll data. This innovative method of payment also allows for the hiring and payment of workers in places with restricted payment channels or nations with unstable fiat currencies.

When using a blockchain, transactions may be completed instantly and, if wanted, using any cryptocurrency accepted worldwide. This will open up access to pools of talent that have been out of reach in the past due to factors like location or the inability to verify an applicant's credentials.

Employers will also be able to hire the two billion people who don't have bank accounts. Workers in the gig economy can get paid without going through third parties like banks or freelance management services. Employers can keep a copy of the payment records that can't be changed. This is useful for auditing and staying in compliance.

4.5. Action Plan for CHROs to Take on Blockchain

HR leaders can take short-, medium-, and long-term steps to make sure the HR function is in a good place to track and take advantage of how Blockchain changes. When planning your strategy, you should think about the following:

- **Strategy:** Meet with stakeholders from your function and IT to talk about how Blockchain could change the way you work and figure out how it fits into the current and future business models for your function and the whole company. Look for ways that Blockchain can strengthen or improve your functional value proposition in a way that no other technology can. Choose a realistic way to adopt Blockchain based on how it can be used strategically or tactically to improve core functional processes.
- **Capabilities:** People who are proficient in and educated about the technological components and capabilities that make Blockchain feasible are in high demand as a result of the many upcoming organizations that are beginning to investigate and invest in the technology behind Blockchain. However, there are not enough experienced people who are familiar with blockchain technology and how it may be utilized to create new chances in the company. Establish the foundations as quickly as you can, and start working with outside talent or assisting your staff members as soon as feasible to develop their talents.

5. DIGITAL TRANSFORMATION IN HR

Digital transformation in the office has no limits. It has spread to many different industries and places of work. Now, it's time for HR to change to digital. The tough job market is pushing companies to change how they handle human resources. Digital HR strategy that includes tools for automation, employee engagement, and keeping an eye on analytics are needed by organizations. The way companies work on the inside is changing because of the digital transformation of human resources. The days of HR tasks being done by hand and on paper are over. In their stead are forward-thinking digital technologies, HR teams, and strategies that are centered on the future. In its most basic form, HR digital transformation is the process of utilizing digital tools and strategies for human resources to improve the experience of workers as well as the performance of operational processes via the use of data-driven and automated procedures. The following are some frequent applications of digital transformation that may be found in the human resources digital strategy of an organization: Automation, HR chatbots, People analytics, AI-driven recruitment approaches, onboarding software, on-demand training, and performance review by a robot system are all examples of areas that have been revolutionized by automation (Fig.3).

Figure 3. Framework for digital transformation in HR
Source: Author's contributions based on the study

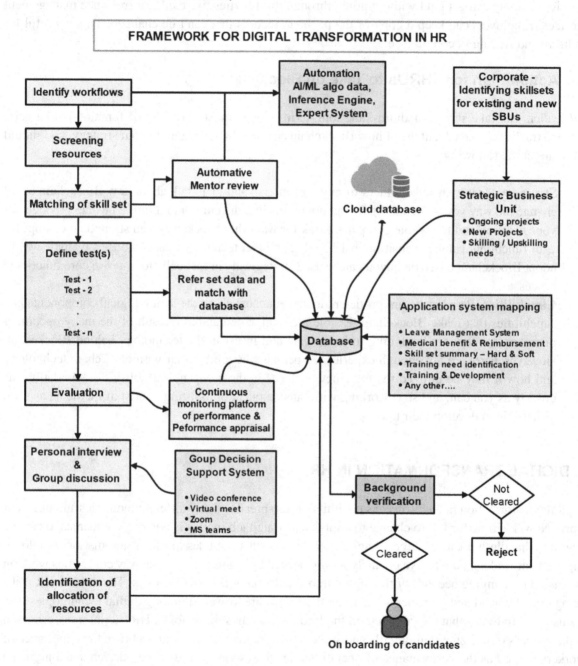

5.1. Digital Transformation Trends for 2023

People Analytics to Data Literacy: People analytics have improved recently. HR teams might use data on recruiting, retention, motivation, and development. The need for people analytics will increase in 2022. Businesses want a framework to comprehend the data and apply its conclusions throughout the company.

HR Digital Transformation Talent Acquisition and Retention: People analytics have improved recently. HR teams might use data on recruiting, retention, motivation, and development. The need for people analytics will increase in 2022. Businesses want a framework to comprehend the data and apply its conclusions throughout the company.

- A candidate's résumé is screened using an applicant tracking system (ATS), which also generates requests for interviews. Language support, monitoring of pre-screening questions and replies, and automatic evaluation of resumes are some of the additional features that may be available.
- Maintaining a pool of passive applicants that can be brought in for consideration quickly is made possible by candidate relationship management.
- HR may get suggestions about future and existing applicants from current workers using employee referral software.

5.2. Digitized HR Processes

Artificial intelligence (AI): According to Gartner, up from 17 percent the year before, almost 30% of firms plan to utilize an AI solution as a supplement to their HR technology. Hyper Automation: As AI develops, a wider range of jobs will be able to be automated. AI chatbots, for instance, may significantly improve the employee experience by giving staff members the information and data they require. To enhance customer service, cut labour costs, and transfer responsibility for managing regular transactions from HR to workers, managers, and job seekers, HR executives implement systems for employee and manager self-service, abbreviated as ESS and MSS, respectively. Self-service technologies are expected to continue their upward trend, with examples including digital assistants and chatbots that are driven by artificial intelligence.

5.3. Diversity, Equity, and Inclusion

It has been demonstrated that diversity, equity, and inclusion (DEI) promote employee engagement, boost productivity, and draw top talent. DEI is a key engine for growth and workers. DEI is also being made available to HR executives, who must incorporate it to improve their modern workplace culture.

"By 2022, more people-centric platforms will have developed inclusive-by-design technologies, enabling workers to self-identify in the digital workplace rather than be limited by assumptions about their gender, pronouns, and legal names." – Danielle Brown, chief people officer – Gusto.

AI may eliminate adjectives from job candidate profiles, preventing unintentional bias in hiring. AI systems that track worker diversity across many KPIs are also predicted to grow.

5.4. HR Management Software for Digital Transformation

Hiring, onboarding, scheduling, compliance, and benefits are just some of the HR processes that may run more efficiently with the right technological infrastructure in place. Automation is facilitating HR procedures by decreasing potential bottlenecks, boosting productivity, and concurrently enhancing employee satisfaction. Software for human resources management that is widely used includes Monday. com, QuickBooks, Paycor, and Gusto.

5.5. HR Technologies (HR Tech)

The phrase "HR tech" refers to all the technology that human resources personnel use to enhance organizational operations. We anticipate that HR technology will be helpful in the following areas in 2022 and beyond:

- As more cloud-based HR technology outsourcing suppliers include payroll services in their digital HR offerings, particularly for SMBs, payroll solutions are diversifying. The importance of other aspects of the digital revolution, such as attendance software, is also rising.
- Travel and expense management: Expense and travel management services are used by HR departments to maintain tabs on trip expenditures, pay vendors, and pay employees through integration with payroll. Additionally, some businesses use expenditure report software to give management a snapshot of their spending through automated analytics and reporting.
- Engagement of employees: Engagement of employees Platforms and applications that utilize a variety of strategies to keep employees engaged in their work are increasingly using HR technology. These include gamification strategies, communication systems that let businesses share information and employees engage, and mobile applications with social media-like posting and commenting features.
- Performance management solutions: Since new automated processes may now monitor employee performance, traditional annual evaluations are starting to feel a little dated.
- Benefits administration is evolving, including more than simply health and disability insurance, vacation time, and sick days, in part due to digitalization. Corporate wellness is expanding its range of services by fusing internet technology with human components like wellness coaches and exercise programs. As a result, several businesses in the human resources technology industry have developed software specifically aimed at getting their workers to take part in health and wellness programs.
- Technology for learning: HR technology suppliers are moving corporate training and education programs to interactive online platforms. Software for learning management (LMS) may be used to personalize training courses and monitor employee development. Students may also use interactive tools through an LMS, including discussion boards, video conferencing, and threaded conversations.
- HR analytics: Human resource analytics, often known as people analytics, is the practice of utilizing information on employees as a means of enhancing vital company functions. Managers of human resources may benefit from HR analytics leaders because they have access to data-driven insights that enhance talent management, streamline administrative tasks, and boost morale.

5.6. Facilitating a Remote and Hybrid Workforce

Since remote and hybrid employment is not going away, it is more difficult to maintain compliance when there are scattered workers in different cities, states, or even foreign nations. Recognizing this, HR technology products like Oyster are assisting businesses in adapting to remote and hybrid workplaces by helping to create locally compliant contracts, communicate employment conditions, and maintain consolidated, secure, and accessible paperwork.

6. HR TECH FOR DIGITAL TRANSFORMATION IN 2023 AND BEYOND

These advancements are what are driving the digital change in human resources (HR), but it is essential to bear in mind that this transformation is more about people than it is about technology. To guarantee strong user acceptance, IT executives and HR teams must include important stakeholders in the solution-sourcing procedure. Innovative solutions must be developed through a rigorously collaborative approach, including important stakeholders.

The digital revolution of HR is, in short, a permanent development. As the world around them grows increasingly digital, HR executives are watching in awe, and it's about time. Moreover, the HR department can face the current trends in digital transformation head-on and offer the business a digital edge by working with vendors and workers to discover solutions that benefit everyone.

Solis distinguishes six stages of digital transformation:

- This one is very self-explanatory: business as usual.
- Digital literacy and creativity are actively promoted within the company via several experiments.
- Formalized: This is the point where the issue has significance to the corporate world. However, this is not always the case, which is unfortunate. If it is not important to the business, leadership should not promote it.
- Strategic - People are becoming more conscious of the need to work together. The collaboration of their efforts and thoughts results in the production of novel strategic roadmaps.
- Converged: A specialized digital transformation team is created at this point to direct the company's strategy and daily operations.
- Innovative and adaptable - The phrase "business as usual" has been replaced with "digital transformation," and a new ecosystem is now being constructed.

6.1. Human Capital: Futuristic Workforce in HR

In 2015, the United States of America came up with the Sustainable Development Goals and issued a worldwide appeal to all of the countries that are a part of its alliance to devise a strategy to end poverty, safeguard the environment, and guarantee that people will be able to live in peace and prosperity by the year 2030. Innovation has emerged as one of the primary drivers of modern economic growth and wealth, resulting in Industry 5.0. The Industrial Revolution, which took place in the 18th century in England and saw the replacement of the guild system with the factory system, is crucial to highlighting the transition phase from Industry 1.0 to Industry 5.0. This process extended to other nations and was subsequently adopted. In Industry 2.0, the manufacturing sector changed. This revolution was characterized as a time of economic expansion with rising business productivity (mass production) and a sharp increase in unemployment as robots took the position of factory workers. The digital revolution, also known as Industry 3.0, began in the 1980s of the 20th century with the automation of memory-programmable controllers and computers' usage of integrated circuit chips and digital logic; related technologies included computers, digital cellular phones, and the Internet. As a result of the digital revolution, technology is getting digitized. The term "Industry 4.0" refers to the fusion of physical assets with cutting-edge technologies, including AI, IoT, robotics, 3D printing, cyber-physical systems (CPS), cyber security, and cloud storage. Industry 4.0 concentrated on enhancing process efficiency. Supply chains are designed and managed as resilient, sustainable, and human-centric systems using a mix of organizational concepts and technological advancements known as "industry 5.0."

Disruptive forces that have an impact on both social and professional life are constantly altering the world economy. People's daily tasks, tools, and organizational procedures will all alter significantly as strong competition for human tacit knowledge increases. Rewarding and keeping employees will be a major problem for the firm. There are possibilities and hazards to navigating the shifting HR landscape. Businesses may perform better by automating operations to decrease mistakes, improve quality and speed, and, in certain cases, achieve achievements that are beyond what is humanly achievable. Routine work might be changed by automation; this could affect everyone from miners and gardeners to commercial bankers, fashion designers, and CEOs. Organizations need creative, efficient, and effective solutions to meet the ever-changing requirements of conducting business, such as adaptability, 24/7 global access, speed, and precision. The HR digital revolution has already begun and is progressing rapidly. Because they recognize they must disrupt or be disrupted, leading organizations have begun constructing entirely new work environments.

6.2. Digital Transformation: Effect on HR

When human resources are digitized, it will affect every aspect of the modern workplace, from the nature of the labor to the nature of the careers available to workers to the knowledge and expectations of both employers and employees. Workers want more than simply a paycheck; they want to feel interested in their jobs and the success of their company. The culture of a group is crucial to achieving both engagement and digital transformation. How can a business adapt its culture to the digital age? To do this, it has transformed into something astute, modern, and open. It's automated, faster, and more dynamic than manual methods; it makes use of social media; it provides consumer-grade technologies that are ready to use, and it's speedier. It's immensely important that it's become a way of life for the people who work there. The moment is right to welcome digital transformation. Let's take a step back and examine how HR has changed over the past ten years. We can see that the emphasis on automation has resulted in repeated, simpler HR procedures that seem outmoded, fragmented, and disconnected. Automation is not the same as digital transformation. Beyond automation, digital transformation develops an all-in workforce strategy that increases worker diversity, improves company agility, and makes better use of intelligent services.

The HR and IT sectors are being upended by rapid organizational transformation. Investors seeking the next big thing in technology put a lot of money into human resources (HR) technologies in 2016. The number of HR technology deals has been on the rise in recent years and is only expected to rise more in the future. Medium-sized enterprises have been a primary target of the sector's expanding influx of capital, which has mostly been utilized to fund the development of comprehensive HR solutions. The shift from desktop to mobile computing, the advent of analytics and AI, the popularity of video social recruiting, and the widespread adoption of wearable technology are all factors in the evolution of the modern workplace.

HR should benefit over the long term. "HR is not HR" will be the new HR catchphrase. By using more interactive, self-service-oriented feedback loop methodologies with continuous program revisions, HR will be forced to change its perspective from one of planning and implementing programs. A fresh vision for what the employee experience may and should be will arise from this, increasing employee buy-in and adoption. From the boardroom to the front lines, these developments will surely influence HR.

Beyond automation, digital transformation delivers an all-in strategy with increased business agility, intelligent services, and the talent of a varied workforce. Any digital transformation must acknowledge the fact that technology cannot create the culture or engage personnel on its own. Because Millennials will make up the majority of the workforce in the future, creating meaningful work will be much more crucial than in the past. If the job they are doing or the information on the applications they use is not exciting, relevant, or inspiring, employees will be reluctant to adopt new technology. Employees need to understand that they can shape the future by being given the freedom to innovate.

7. EMERGING FUTURE OF THE WORKFORCE

With five distinct generations represented in the workforce, a dramatic rise in contingent employees, and the development of global talent pools, the workforce of the future will continue to diversity. Even though these modifications make HR more difficult, new technology is improving strategic planning and administration of relevant HR tasks. To accomplish business goals with more simplicity, global relevance, and a style that is engaging rather than intimidating to Millennials, Baby Boomers, unions, contract employees, executives everyone HR must continuously develop new methods as the workforce develops (Fig.4).

- During the digital transition, upskilling this heterogeneous workforce is essential, and leaders have a crucial role to play in fostering cultural change. Six digital competencies that the future workforce, particularly leaders, should master. To appeal to a workforce that is varied in terms of culture, age, and capabilities, HR must create innovative strategies to accomplish business goals that are simpler to implement globally and more relevant locally.
- Utilize technology as an enabler: Just as smartphones altered how we live and work, we must accept that new technologies will continue to alter virtually every aspect of our lives, both at home and at work. Accept it sooner rather than later when wearable virtual reality devices, avatars, and self-driving vehicles start to appear in the workplace.
- Accept disruption: It is truer than ever that "change is the only constant." Adapt to change. Change now has a different character than it did in the past, and it is happening more quickly than before. Since many things are less linear, this leads to a higher lack of predictability, the introduction of new factors that we are unfamiliar with, and ambiguous cause-and-effect correlations. The situation is worse. Accept the chaos and organize it.
- Utilize information technology: For better and quicker outcomes, use social media frequently. Following the Paris attacks, hundreds of safe locations for citizens to stay were organized on Twitter in just one hour, as opposed to months without social media. Utilize this talent.
- Gain proficiency in iteration: The majority of HR initiatives that used to take a long time to establish were developed at the top of the firm and were finally "rolled out" to employees. Projects now often grow over time with ongoing feedback from others and progress fast through the phases of

development, rather than waiting for a solution that is 100 percent flawless before deciding on a rollout strategy, which might take too much time in this fast-paced corporate environment. Good project management is still crucial. Learn how to iterate and become accustomed to making modest, gradual changes.

- Don't waste the crowd: Don't feel like you have to do everything as a leader. According to Steve Jobs, "We recruit brilliant people so they can tell us what to do.

- Examine what is beneath: This delicate balance between data and intuition has never changed and will never change. The challenge in the digital age is to find methods to mix science, data, and art -the human aspect. Given that we will have access to more data for evaluation and will still be expected to make decisions that affect employees, we will be forced to reconcile these two factors in our daily work and dig deeper to make superior conclusions.

In the digital future, these six digital talents will be beneficial to us as individuals, leaders, and workers. Leaders need to improve in these abilities.

Figure 4. Dynamic changes in future workforce
Source: Author's contributions based on the study

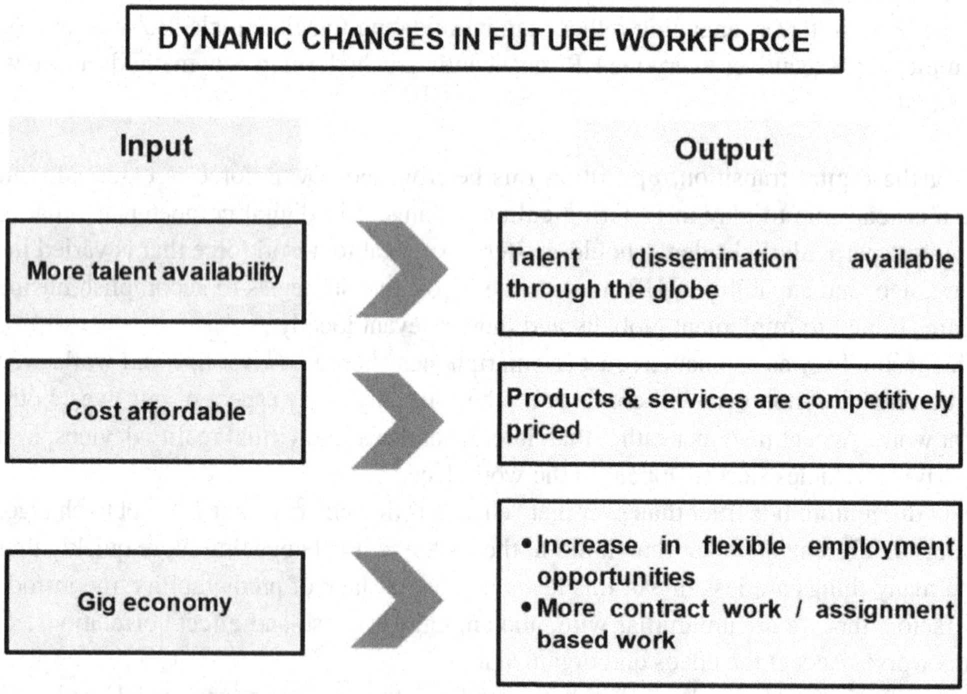

DYNAMIC CHANGES IN FUTURE WORKFORCE

Input	Output
More talent availability	Talent dissemination available through the globe
Cost affordable	Products & services are competitively priced
Gig economy	• Increase in flexible employment opportunities • More contract work / assignment based work

8. REIMAGINATION OF WORK

Consumer-grade tools are a basic need since employees' expectations of their companies have advanced more quickly than businesses. To recruit and keep the greatest personnel for the future, new methods are essential. The moment has come to rebuild and redefine employment. Through improved visibility throughout the business, successful team and enterprise cooperation, and the abolition of several manual chores and repetitive procedures, innovations will have an impact on how we operate in real-time. Significant HR alterations have already been seen. 360-degree performance management, talent acquisition, and the emergence of HR analytics are three areas that are changing. Big changes will continue to occur.

Continuous Performance Management

- Presently, in the cloud with digital capabilities, ratings are being done away with, and continuous feedback and goal systems enable strong data, performance assessment, and improved decision-making approaches.
- Tools like talks, game elements, and team management will be added to future projects, as well as development plans, personality tests relevant to employment titles, and annual performance reviews.

Social Talent Acquisition

- Recruitment and talent acquisition are now challenging. Finding the finest talent, employer branding, and application management are still fronts in the talent battle.
- Future: Using relationship management technology, quick, thorough recruiting systems will concentrate on the applicant experience. Wearables powered by artificial intelligence will offer experiences like exploring factories and offices as well as places related to corporate culture. Candidates will be picked up for interviews by autonomous vehicles, avatars will assist with onboarding, and assessments of potential will forecast success in upcoming positions up until retirement.

Rise of People Analytics

- Organizations are replacing HR data warehouses with sophisticated analytics, reporting dashboards, and predictive models.
- Future analytics will use cognitive processing and natural language systems to evaluate patterns in email, communication, and performance used to predict employee behavior, the correlation of performance and conduct with succession, and the anticipation of future security and safety infractions.

9. CONCLUSION

A significant number of workers place a high value on working for a company that is either at the forefront of digital innovation or that is well-equipped with advanced technological resources. The digital workplace, which promotes productivity and creativity by combining culture, employee engagement, and the technology they use in their professions, will result in a distinct experience for employees. This is because the digital workplace will combine these factors. This not only reduces obstacles to communication but also improves the working environment for all of the staff members. The new digital experience, in its purest form, comprises supporting transformation and incorporating newly developed technology into one's regular job duties. Businesses that have been able to successfully transform their HR departments through the use of digital technology are more likely to report strong financial performance, make investments in increasing diversity at all levels, and develop succession plans. Productivity will improve in the future because to advances in technology; HR directors cannot ignore this trend because it is so important. Now more than ever, human resources need to embrace the digital revolution, be at the forefront of HR innovation, and involve people.

REFERENCES

Abdali, M. (2019). *The strategic use of digital learning solutions: An HRM perspective* (Doctoral dissertation).

Akrich, M. (1992). *Shaping technology/building society: Studies in sociotechnical change.* MIT Press.

Anyim, F. C., Ikemefuna, C. O., & Mbah, S. E. (2011). Human resource management challenges in Nigeria under a globalized economy. *International Journal of Economics and Management Sciences, 1*(4), 1–11.

Bell, B. S., Lee, S. W., & Yeung, S. K. (2006). The impact of e-HR on professional competence in HRM: Implications for the development of HR professionals. *Human Resource Management, 45,* 295–308.

Bhatnagar, J., & Sandhu, S. (2005). Psychological empowerment and organisational citizenship behaviour (OCB) in "IT" managers: A talent retention tool. Indian Journal of Industrial Relations, 449–469.

Bondarouk, T., Ruël, H., & van der Heijden, B. (2009). e-HRM effectiveness in a public sector organization: A multi-stakeholder perspective. *International Journal of Human Resource Management, 20*(3), 578–590. doi:10.1080/09585190802707359

Bondarouk, T., Schilling, D., & Ruël, H. (2016). eHRM adoption in emerging economies: The case of subsidiaries of multinational corporations in Indonesia: E-HRM Adoption in Emerging Economies. *Canadian Journal of Administrative Sciences / Revue Canadienne Des Sciences de l Administration, 33*(2), 124–137. doi:10.1002/cjas.1376

Bondarouk, T. V., & Ruël, H. J. M. (2009). Electronic Human Resource Management: Challenges in the digital era. *International Journal of Human Resource Management, 20*(3), 505–514. doi:10.1080/09585190802707235

Das, S., & Sureshkrishna, G. (2019). Challenges of digitalization for HR Professionals: An Exploratory Study. *International Journal of Innovative Researchin Technology, 6*(1).

Eller, R., Alford, P., Kallmünzer, A., & Peters, M. (2020). Antecedents, consequences, and challenges of small and medium-sized enterprise digitalization. *Journal of Business Research, 112,* 119–127. doi:10.1016/j.jbusres.2020.03.004

Emerging Markets. (2021). Retrieved November 4, 2023, from Msci.com website: https://www.msci.com/our-solutions/index/emerging-markets

Evseeva, O., Kalchenko, O., Evseeva, S., & Plis, K. (2019). Instruments of human resource management based on the digital technologies in Russia. In *Proceedings of the International Conference on Digital Technologies in Logistics and Infrastructure (ICDTLI 2019).* Paris, France: Atlantis Press. 10.2991/icdtli-19.2019.29

Fedorova, A., Zarubina, A., Pikulina, Y., Moskovskikh, A., Balandina, T., & Gafurova, T. (2019). Digitalization of The Human Resource Management: Russian Companies Case. In *International Conference on Education, Social Sciences and Humanities* (pp. 1227–1230). Academic Press.

Florea, V. N., & Badea, M. (2013). Acceptance of new Technologies in HR: E-Recruitment in Organizations. In *Proceedings of the European Conference on Information Management & Evaluation* (pp. 344–352). Academic Press.

Grant, D., & Newell, S. (2013). Realizing the strategic potential of e-HRM. *The Journal of Strategic Information Systems*, *22*(3), 187–192. doi:10.1016/j.jsis.2013.07.001

Hawking, P., Stein, A., & Foster, S. (2004). E-HR and employee self-service: A case study of a Victorian public sector organisation. *Issues in Informing Science and Information Technology*, *1*, 1017–1026. doi:10.28945/795

Hooi, L. W. (2006). Implementing e-HRM: The readiness of small and medium sized manufacturing companies in Malaysia. *Asia Pacific Business Review*, *12*(4), 465–485. doi:10.1080/13602380600570874

Hunt, C. (2014). *Transforming talent management: The impact of social and digital tech.* Academic Press.

Indermun, V. (2014). Importance of human resource management practices and the impact companies face in relation to competitive challenges. *Singaporean Journal of Business Economics and Management Studies*, *2*(11), 125–135. doi:10.12816/0006786

Kossek, E. E. (1987). Human resources management innovation. *Human Resource Management*, *26*(1), 71–92. doi:10.1002/hrm.3930260105

Kristoff, H., Hoen, B. T., Adrian, L., & Stang, V. (2018). *Digitalization & HR.* Academic Press.

Lepak, D. P., Bartol, K. M., & Erhardt, N. L. (2005). A contingency framework for the delivery of HR practices. *Human Resource Management Review*, *15*(2), 139–159. doi:10.1016/j.hrmr.2005.06.001

Lepak, D. P., & Snell, S. A. (1998). Virtual HR: Strategic human resource management in the 21st century. *Human Resource Management Review*, *8*(3), 215–234. doi:10.1016/S1053-4822(98)90003-1

McDonnell, A., & Heard, C. (2023). *Centralize your RFP Process With Olive.* Retrieved November 4, 2023, from Olive Technologies website: https://olive.app

Osipova, O. (2019). Digital trasformation of personnel management services. In *International Conference on Digital Technologies in Logistics and Infrastructure (ICDTLI2019).* Atlantis Press.

Stanton, J. M., & Coovert, M. D. (2004). Turbulent waters: The intersection of informationtechnologyandhuman resources. *Human Resource Management*, *43*(2), 121–125. doi:10.1002/hrm.20010

Stolterman, E., & Fors, A. C. (2004). Information technology and the good life. In *Information Systems Research* (pp. 687–692). Springer US. doi:10.1007/1-4020-8095-6_45

Townsend, A. M., & Bennett, J. T. (2003). Human resources and information technology. *Journal of Labor Research*, *24*(3), 361–363. doi:10.100712122-003-1000-7

Chapter 16
Emotional Intelligence and Job Performance in the IT Sector on the Mediating Effect of Occupational Role Stress

Manne Neelima Chaudhary
iD https://orcid.org/0000-0002-5066-488X
Jain University, India

Sheetal V. Hukkeri
Jain University, India

B. Vanitha
Government First Grade College, India

G. Srinivas
Jain University, India

M. Nirmala
iD https://orcid.org/0000-0002-5066-488X
Jain University, India

ABSTRACT

This research observes the connection between the major components such as emotional intelligence (EI), employee job performance (JP), and organisational role stress (ORS). There has been previous research that has been carried out pertaining to EI and JP. However, there have been a very limited number of studies where a third variable has mediated emotional intelligence and job performance variables. There are even fewer studies wherein organisational role stress has been considered as a mediator. Most of the studies pertaining to emotional intelligence have been carried out in the Western context, and very few Indian studies exist. The information technology (IT) sector is considered one of the most rapidly growing sectors in India, and there is very limited research on the EI of Indian employees in the IT sector; hence, the same has been covered in this study. The current study is descriptive, as the variables under investigation are continuous.

DOI: 10.4018/979-8-3693-0049-7.ch016

1. INTRODUCTION

With the changing market economy, organisations are facing diverse changes and challenges. In this highly volatile and uncertain business environment, organisations can only rely upon their human resources to create better performance by becoming more adaptable to this new VUCA (volatile, uncertain, complex & ambiguous) world. For several decades, there have been a lot of studies carried out by various researchers and behaviourists on the factors that can lead to a person's success in their life. The traditional Intelligence or Intelligence Quotient (IQ) of an individual was one of the success factors identified. However, in addition to those, certain other factors such as "leadership", "Self-confidence", "adaptability", and "interpersonal skills" also were identified that help an individual achieve success in life. These additional factors identified had no association with the IQ of an individual and were distinct and helped in the actual dealing of individual emotions and this led to the concept of EI.

In the words of Goleman (1998) said that EI is defined as the ability to sense, understand, value and effectively apply the power of emotions as a source of human energy, information, trust, creativity and influence. EI essentially is a mixture of both the emotions and intellect of an individual. The capability of an individual to recognise, evaluate and manage their emotions can be termed as EI. There have been umpteen numbers of studies that have been carried out by various researchers in the domain of EI. Most of the studies that have been carried out in the organisational context have found that employees who have high EI tend to be more aware of their emotions as well as those of others working along with them, and they would also be capable of expressing and controlling their emotions. EI enables individuals to think out of the box and creatively and also helps them overcome different problems and challenges with the help of emotions. EI is not about being emotional but being smart in dealing with individual emotions as well as the other individual's emotions. As per Goleman (1995), emotional intelligence is one of the most significant traits that leads to success at work and hence, many companies have resorted to training their employees in the field of emotional intelligence. These companies believe that training their employees to regulate their emotions and those of others better can lead to better performance at work (Cobero et al., 2006).

Salovey and Mayer (1990) carried out the initial seminal work on Emotional intelligence, post which there have been many more researchers who have carried forward the work on EI in various domains such as management, medical research, psychology, etc. As per Salovey & Mayer (1990), "EI is the ability to monitor one's own and others' feelings and emotions, to discriminate among them and to use this information to guide one's thinking and actions". The researchers stated that employees who had a high emotional quotient were more self-aware about their emotions, which could be anger, anxiety, unhappiness, etc. and hence were also capable of regulating those emotions into more favourable emotional states such as motivation, enhanced creativity, etc.

As per the latest NASSCOM report (2020), it was found that in India, it is the Information Technology (IT) sector that has and is continuing to contribute the most to the Indian GDP as well as establish the presence of India in the International context. The IT sector has played a big part in the lives of people by providing employment and also helping employees working in the IT sector to enhance their standard of living (Gupta et al., 2015). To further enhance the contribution made by the IT sector in India, it becomes imperative to enhance the JP of the employees working in the IT sector, which can result in the enhancement of overall organisational performance, thereby contributing to the further growth of the sector (Dhani & Sharma, 2016). There is cutthroat competition in the IT sector, and hence, IT companies must work continuously towards enhancing the employees' performance and productivity in the organisation. Therefore, many programmes and interventions have been regularly carried out by IT companies. One such important intervention programme carried out by all IT organisations is to enhance the emotional quotient of their employees.

There are five basic components of emotional intelligence, which are mentioned below.

- Self-Awareness: It can be considered as an individual's capacity to recognise and understand their moods, motivations and emotions. Basically, self-awareness implies that when confronted with a critical disparity that will take a great deal of steady and centred work, essentially forget it and stick to staying away from self-assessment on this specific inconsistency.
- Self-regulation: It is the extent to which one can alter their emotions and behaviour depending upon the situation. It is not about hiding one's true emotions, but it is about expressing the emotions at the appropriate place and time.
- Social skills: It is a very important aspect of emotional intelligence, which helps people bond and build rapport and meaningful relationships with others. Employees benefit a lot by building a strong rapport with their co-workers.
- Empathy: It deals with one's ability to understand the emotions and feelings of other individuals. It is not just about identifying other individual's emotions but also responding to such emotions. Empathetic people also tend to be good at influencing social relationships, particularly in the workplace environment. People can build their empathy by sharing their own emotions with others, being a good listener, and trying to be more open to conversations.
- Motivation: Emotionally intelligent Individuals tend to be motivated intrinsically rather than extrinsically. They are not just motivated by things such as money, fame, recognition, etc., but also tend to seek out internal rewards and, tend to be more goal-oriented and have a greater need for achievement.

2. LITERATURE REVIEW

2.1. EI and Job Performance

There have been various studies that have been carried out revolving around EI and JP of employees in various industries. In one study conducted by Shahhosseini et al. (2012) on the impact of EI on the JP of individuals working in organisations, a substantial positive association was seen between the variables mentioned as EI on JP and JP on EI. Another study was carried out by Kidwell (2011), which was a workplace investigation on EI; the study found that EI could be linked to every aspect of employee performance at the workplace. Similar studies in the field of higher education also found that there is a strong, significant connection between factors of EI and JP. A greater degree of significant positive association was found between EI factors and JP of the faculty members working in higher educational institutions (Jyoti, 2016). Another study focused on EI, organisational commitment and job satisfaction and found that EI significantly influenced organisational commitment and employee job satisfaction of working employees. There have also been numerous studies that have been carried out on the antecedents of job performance. Many factors such as "motivation", "perceived supervisory support", "organisational support", "communication", "mindfulness", "organisational culture", "financial rewards", and "emotional intelligence" have been found to have a noteworthy significant influence on JP of employees working across diverse industries (Armstrong, 2012).

Some of the studies have concluded that just as workers need to put in physical effort for manual labour, similarly, service sector employees such as the ones working in the IT sector need EI as the basic skill for performing well on their jobs (Mastracci & Hsieh, 2016). There have been studies that have concluded that when employees who have a high emotional quotient are better at perceiving their emotions as well as other individual's and also are better at managing their emotions and hence tend to display optimistic emotions and decrease the display of undesirable emotions, especially at the workplace (Chen et al., 2019). Another study by Kidwell et al. (2011) conducted on sales employees found that there was a major association and influence of the EI of these personnel on their performance, and it was also concluded in the study that employees with a higher EI tend to have higher salaries and are also better at customer retention.

Hence, the following hypothesis is framed: H_1: Emotional Intelligence positively influences the JP of employees in the IT sector.

2.2. Occupational Role Stress (ORS)

Stress at the office is an increasing substance of concern for the employees as well as the organisations. Many aspects of the workplace trigger occupational stress among employees, such as lack of job security, poor satisfaction with the job, lack of freedom, heavy workload, etc. These factors could cause ill effects on the employees' health and their well-being. There could be many physical as well as emotional responses which could be triggered as a result of stress at the workplace, and most of these responses could be harmful to the individual employees. Whenever the job-related demands tend to be on the higher end, and the degree of control that an employee has over these job-related demands is relatively low, it leads to stress.

As per Lu et al. (2008), occupational stress results in some of the most complicated health issues and hence, many researchers are carrying out studies pertaining to occupational stress in the fields of "psychology" and "medical sciences" as well. Occupational stress, which can also be termed as job stress, can be defined as "the experience of negative emotional states such as "frustration", "worry", "anxiety" and "depression attributed to work-related factors". There have been several studies that have been carried out by many scholars in the recent past that have identified drastic negative consequences of occupational stress. Some of these negative consequences are reduced employee productivity, reduced job satisfaction and higher turnover intentions of employees. It is, therefore, essential for the employees as well as the organisations to realise the presence of stress and the factors which are resulting in that stress and take measures to overcome those stressors.

Another study by Tănăsescu (2013) was carried out in the banking sector. As per this study, it was found that the individual employees who faced a moderate level of occupational stress at the workplace experienced "Role Stagnation", "Role Inadequacy", "Role Erosion", and "Role Overload". Many studies have carried out studies pertaining to organisational role stress as both a predictor as well as an outcome variable. There are many reasons for employees to perceive work stress in the organisation. Stress can result from the resources, opportunities and demands placed on the employees at the workplace by the employer or their supervisor. Such stress can result in emotional, physical and behavioural issues in the employees. Many studies have found a noteworthy negative influence of work stress on the employees' JP, irrespective of the industry or the country in which an employee works.

2.3 Mediating Role of Organisational Role Stress

Many researchers, as listed above, have found a noteworthy positive association between EI and JP of the employees. There have been a few studies that have tried to understand the influence of EI on Organizational Role Stress (ORS), and many such studies have found a significant association between EI and ORS. Hence, concluded that individuals with a greater extent of EI tend to have a lesser amount of organisational role stress (Desti & Shanthi, 2015). Certain other studies found that when employees are capable of identifying their own emotions and also good at positively expressing those emotions tend to suffer much less from ORS and also face all job demands more calmly as compared to those employees who have difficulty in identifying their own emotions and expressing of those emotions (Ranasinghe et al., 2017). In addition to studies trying to determine the impact of EI on ORS, there have also been studies that have been carried out to examine the role of ORS on the JP of employees in diverse sectors. In most of these studies, a significant negative association was found between ORS and the job performance of employees (Ahmed & Ramzan, 2013). Therefore, the following hypotheses are framed:

H_2: Emotional Intelligence negatively influences organisational role stress.
H_3: Occupational role stress negatively influences the JP of individual employees.
H_4: Occupational Role Stress mediates the association between EI and JP of employees in the IT sector

3. STUDY OBJECTIVES

The study objectives are as follows:

- To measure the level of EI, JP and ORS among IT employees.
- To understand the association between EI, ORS, and job performance.
- To determine the influence of EI on ORS, ORS on JP and EI on JP.
- To identify the mediating effect of ORS between EI and Job performance.

4. CONCEPTUAL FRAMEWORK

Based on the literature, the following conceptual model was developed (Figure 1).

4.1. Data Collection Measures

The research instrument comprised four different sections. The first section comprised demographic questions. The second section measured the employee job performance of employees and the scale used was the 25-item Job Performance scale developed by Tănăsescu (2013). The third section comprised items to measure Occupational Role Stress, and the scale used was the 25-item ORS scale developed by Ahmed & Ramzan (2013). The fourth section measured Emotional Intelligence, and the scale used was a 16-item EI scale developed by Wong and Law (2002). All the items in the scale, as mentioned earlier, used a 5-point Likert scale.

Figure 1. Conceptual model

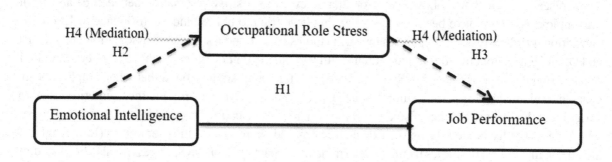

4.2. Research Design

The current research study is descriptive, as the variables under investigation are continuous, and the data is quantitative. Standard and reliable instruments were used to measure the variables under investigation. These research instruments were administered to 200 IT sector employees across Bangalore. The questionnaire was shared both in person as well in the form of a Google form whose link was shared with over 500 IT employees. The response rate was 40 per cent. The data obtained was analysed using the SPSS package.

5. RESULTS

The sample distribution comprised 64.5 per cent males and 35.5 per cent females. Nearly 30 per cent were married, and 70 per cent were single. Almost 37.5 per cent were between the age clusters of 20 to 25 years, 32.5 per cent of them were between 26 and 30 years, and 30 per cent of them were above 30 years. More than 70 per cent held a bachelor's degree while 30 per cent of them held a master's degree."

5.1. Reliability of Standardised Instruments

The reliability of the scales was determined through the Cronbach alpha test of reliability and the Kaiser-Meyer-Olkin (KMO) value test. From the below Table 1, it can be seen that the scales adopted for measuring the variables are reliable."

Table 1. Reliability test

Construct	Reliability Value (α)	KMO Value
EI	0.967	0.873
JP	0.868	0.857
ORS	0.798	0.802

5.2. Hypotheses Testing

Objective 1: To Measure the Level of EI, ORS, and JP of IT Sector Employees

From the above Figure 2, it can be comprehended that the EI level of IT sector employees is very high; however, their ORS is also high, but their job performance is moderate.

Figure 2. Mean score of EI, ORS, and JP of IT sector employees

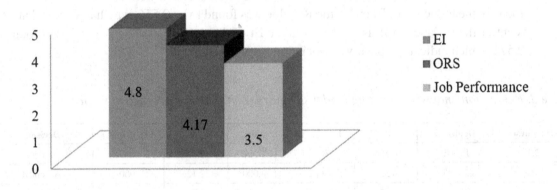

Objective 2: To Understand the Association Between EI, ORS, and JP of Employees in the IT Sector

The Correlation Table 2 indicates that there is a noteworthy significant positive association between EI and JP of the IT sector employees, which implies that the higher the emotional quotient of the employees greater their job performance. However, a noteworthy negative correlation was found between EI and ORS, which implies that when the emotional quotient of the employees increases, they perceive lesser organisational role stress. In addition to this, there was also a significant negative association between ORS and JP, which implies that when employees perceive lesser ORS in the workplace, the greater will be their job performance. Pearson's correlation coefficients were found to be significant at a 1 per cent significance level.

Objective 3: To Determine the Influence of EI on ORS, ORS on JP and EI on Job Performance

Regression analysis was used to understand the influence of EI on ORS, ORS on JP and EI on Job performance (Table 3).

Table 2. Correlation between EI, ORS, and JP of IT employees

	EI	ORS	JP
EI	1		
ORS	-.423**	1	
JP	.456**	-.370**	1

"** Correlation is significant at 0.01 level."

- To determine the influence of EI on ORS, the R^2 value was found to be 0.324, which indicates that 32.4 per cent of the variance in ORS is attributed to the EI of the employees. The Beta (β) was found to be - 0.285, which indicates a negative association between EI and ORS.
- To understand the influence of ORS on JP, the R^2 value was found to be 0.228, which indicates that 22.8 per cent of the variance in JP is attributed to the ORS of the employees. The Beta (β) was found to be - 0.471, which indicates a negative association between ORS & JP.
- To identify the influence of EI on JP, the R^2 value was found to be 0.556, which indicates that 55.6 per cent of the variance in JP is attributed to the EI of the employees. The Beta (β) was found to be 0.571, which indicates a positive association between EI & JP.

Table 3. Regression analysis indicating model summary, ANOVA, and coefficient values

Hypotheses	Depiction	R^2	F (ANOVA)	Sig.	T	Sig. (Coeff.)	Decision
H1	EI→JP	0.556	86.831	.000	17.657	.000	Accepted
H2	EI→ORS	0.324	140.468	.000	22.126	.000	Accepted
H3	ORS→JP	0.228	109.302	.000	12.559	.000	Accepted

Objective 4: To Identify the Mediating Effect of ORS Between EI and JP

H4: ORS mediates the association between EI and JP of employees in the IT sector.

The goodness-of-fit index of the model investigating the mediator role of organizational role stress between EI and JP is as follows: $\chi2/df$ (chi-square/degrees of freedom) is 3.043 (p= .001), lower than 5, which indicates a good fit. The "RMSEA" is .0141, which is in the range of 0.05–0.10, indicating thereby a good fit; the normal fit index (NFI) is .958, "CFI" is .983, "GFI" is .963, which all are in the range of 0.90–0.99, reflecting thereby good fit again. (Figure 3) As a result, it can be determined that the created model does fit well and that it can be used to test the mediation. "The analysis results of the direct, indirect effect and the total effect of the mediator on the dependent variable have been shown in Table 4. All the values in the table are standardized beta coefficients.

Figure 3. Structural model path diagram developed for model

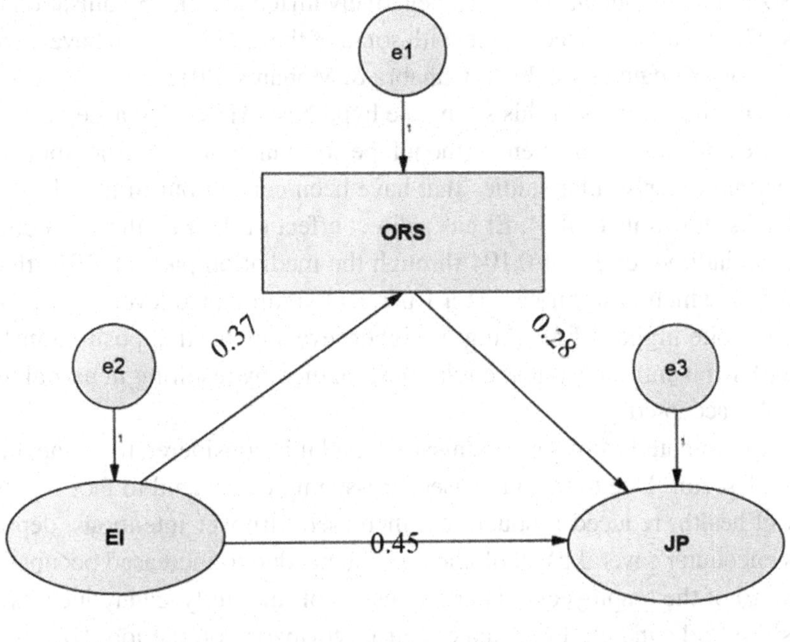

Table 4. Standardized coefficients of mediator role of ORS between EI and JP

Variables	B	Direct Effect	Indirect Effect	Total Effect	Decision
ORS←EI	.366**	.45**	.104**	.554**	Partial mediation
JP←EI	.455**				
JP← ORS	.281**				

**At 1% significance level

From Table 4, it is clear that emotional intelligence affects organizational role stress (β =.366, p < .01), organizational role stress affects job performance (β =.281, p < .01), and Emotional Intelligence affects job performance (β =.455, p > .01). "To identify the mediating effect of ORS, both the direct and indirect effects were computed". "It is evident from Table 4 that the direct path coefficient is .45 is significant. By including the mediator, the standardized path coefficient decreases to 0.104, which is significant, thereby indicating a partially mediated effect on the relationship between EI & JP. The hypothesis H4 is accepted."

6. DISCUSSIONS

The above structural model has analysed the relationships between the investigating variables, namely emotional intelligence, organisational role stress and job performance of IT sector employees. As per the findings of the study, hypothesis H1 is accepted, indicating that EI positively influences the JP of employees in the IT sector. This is in line with a few other studies that have been conducted and found similar results (Dhani & Sharma, 2017; Wu, 2011). Furthermore, as per the findings of this study, hypothesis H2 is also accepted, indicating that EI negatively influences the organisational role stress of IT sector employees. This result is in accordance with some of the studies which have also obtained similar results in the IT sector (Yamani et al., 2014; Chhabra & Mohanty, 2013).

In accordance with the findings of this study, the hypothesis H3 is also accepted, indicating that organisational role stress negatively influences the job performance of IT sector employees. This finding is supported by certain other similar studies that have been carried out in the IT sector (Ajayi, 2018; Yang et al., 2021). As shown in Table 4, EI has a direct effect of 0.45 on the JP of employees in the IT sector. It also has an indirect effect of 0.104 through the mediation path of ORS, thereby resulting in a total effect of 0.554, which is significant at a 1 per cent significance level. Thus, a partial mediation can be observed. Despite higher EI resulting in higher levels of JP, this positive influence is reduced when the mediator ORS is introduced in the relationship, thereby resulting in partial mediation. Hence, hypothesis H4 is also accepted.

Stress cannot be eliminated from any organisation, and it is considered to be inevitable in a growing sector such as the IT sector. Due to this increased stress, employees tend to face lots of negative repercussions such as ill health, reduced productivity, increased turnover intentions, depression, etc. Most of the employees encounter several psychological problems due to increased occupational stress at the organisations. The EI of the employees, as per the results of this study, can reduce the negative aspects of occupational stress and can help to enhance their performance on the job. HR managers of various organisations tend to recruit candidates with high levels of EI to improve employee job performance (Chia, 2005).

As per many of the studies that have been carried out, there is a strong association between the occupational stress faced by employees and their satisfaction with the job that they are working on. Most of the studies have found that reduced occupational stress leads to higher job satisfaction and vice-versa. However, employees with higher EI can mitigate the negative aspects of occupational stress to a certain extent and can lead to enhancement in the performance of the employees. Many stress-relieving practices such as yoga, meditation, workouts and other techniques of relaxation can help individual employees minimise the stress that they are encountering at the workplace. This study has a few implications relevant to employees working in service sector organisations such as IT companies. The Emotional Intelligence of employees can help them in their job role and career roles as well as help in making an employee an effective team player. Secondly, self-awareness and self-regulation are important for employees to maintain their cool while working in a highly volatile and competitive sector such as the IT sector.

Emotional management tactics or strategies can help employees develop a better bonding or rapport with their co-workers and their managers. From the study, it was found that EI generally has a positive influence on the JP of employees; therefore, IT companies can use this as a tool to further enhance employee job performance through EI intervention or training programmes. The employer can also assess the emotional quotient of the candidates before recruiting them into their organisations, as their EI level can predict their future level of performance in the organisation. Organisational role stress tends to reduce the employee's job performance; hence, the employers/ top management should try and reduce the unrealistic job demands that are imposed on the employees in the organisations.

7. CONCLUSION

This study concludes by reiterating the significant findings of the study. From the results, it was found that the emotional Intelligence of IT employees can result in significantly higher job performance. IT employees who possess a greater amount of self-awareness and are able to manage their and others' emotions better will have a greater probability of good performance in the organisation as compared to those who lack self-awareness and self-regulation of emotions. A good EI intervention or training programme must be regularly provided to all the IT employees by their organisations in order to enhance the employee job performance further. The current study, Emotional Intelligence and Job Performance, on the mediating effect of occupational role stress and the related study, is more important to learn in detail as it has a high impact on any organisation. The variables such as emotional intelligence, job performance and occupational role stress can be learned individually to gain more knowledge in this area. In any organisation, the role of emotional intelligence can help the employees in their job role career roles. Also, it supports making an employee an effective team player. Also, self-awareness and self-regulation are significant to maintain their comfortable working in a highly volatile and competitive sector. Emotional management tactics or strategies can help employees develop a better bonding or rapport with their co-workers and their managers.

REFERENCES

Ahmed, A., & Ramzan, M. (2013). Effects of job stress on employees' job performance a study on banking sector of Pakistan. *IOSR Journal of Business and Management, 11*(6), 61–68. doi:10.9790/487X-1166168

AjayiS. (2018). Effect of stress on employee performance and job satisfaction: A case study of Nigerian banking industry. Available at SSRN 3160620. doi:10.2139/ssrn.3160620

Armstrong, M. (2012). *A handbook of human resource management practice*. Kogan.

Chen, K. Y., Chang, C. W., & Wang, C. H. (2019). Frontline employees' passion and emotional exhaustion: The mediating role of emotional labor strategies. *International Journal of Hospitality Management, 76*, 163–172. doi:10.1016/j.ijhm.2018.05.006

Chhabra, B., & Mohanty, R. P. (2013). Effect of emotional Intelligence on work stress–a study of Indian managers. *International Journal of Indian Culture and Business Management, 6*(3), 300–313. doi:10.1504/IJICBM.2013.053104

Chia, Y. M. (2005). Job offers of multi-national accounting firms: The effects of emotional intelligence, extra-curricular activities, and academic performance. *Accounting Education, 14*(1), 75–93. doi:10.1080/06939280042000229707

Cobero, C., Primi, R., & Muniz, M. (2006). Inteligencia emocional e desempenho no trabalho: Um estudo com MSCEIT, BPR-5 e 16PF. *Cadernos de Psicologia e Educação Paideia, 16*(35), 337–348. doi:10.1590/S0103-863X2006000300005

Desti, K., & Shanthi, R. (2015). A study on emotional intelligence at workplace. *European Journal of Business and Management, 7*, 147–154.

Dhani, P., & Sharma, T. (2016). Emotional intelligence; history, models and measures. *International Journal of Science Technology and Management, 5*(7), 189-201.

Dhani, P., & Sharma, T. (2017). Effect of Emotional Intelligence on Job Performance of IT employees: A gender study. *Procedia Computer Science, 122*, 180–185. doi:10.1016/j.procs.2017.11.358

Goleman, D. (1995). *Emotional Intelligence.* Bantam Books.

Goleman, D. (1998, March). The emotionally competent leader. *The Healthcare Forum Journal, 41*(2), 36–38. PMID:10177113

Gupta, S. D., Raychaudhuri, A., & Haldar, S. K. (2015). Information technology sector in India and gender inclusivity. *Gender in Management.*

Jyoti, J. (2016). Impact of Demographic Variables on Emotional Intelligence: A Study among the Employees of Private Sector Banks in Madhya Pradesh, India. *Research Journal of Management Science., 5*(10), 20–24.

Kidwell, J. (2011). Book Review: Ecological Hermeneutics: Norman C. Habel and Peter Trudinger, Exploring Ecological Hermeneutics, (Atlanta: Society of Biblical Literature, 2008. $24.95. pp. 183. ISBN: 978-1-58983-346-3). *The Expository Times, 122*(11), 563–563. doi:10.1177/00145246111220110107

Lu, L., Kao, S.-F., Chang, T.-T., Wu, H.-S., & Cooper, C. L. (2008). Work/Family Demands, Work Flexibility, Work/Family Conflict, and Their Consequences at Work: A National Probability Sample in Taiwan. *International Journal of Stress Management, 15*(1), 1–21. doi:10.1037/1072-5245.15.1.1

Mastracci, S., & Hsieh, C. W. (2016). Emotional Labor and Job Stress in Caring Professions: Exploring Universalism and Particularism in Construct and Culture. *International Journal of Public Administration, 39*(14), 1–9. doi:10.1080/01900692.2015.1068327

Ranasinghe, P., Wathurapatha, W. S., Mathangasinghe, Y., & Ponnamperuma, G. (2017). Emotional intelligence, perceived stress and academic performance of Sri Lankan medical undergraduates. *BMC Medical Education, 17*(1), 41. Advance online publication. doi:10.118612909-017-0884-5 PMID:28219419

Salovey, P., & Mayer, J. D. (1990). Emotional Intelligence. *Imagination, Cognition and Personality, 9*(3), 185–211. doi:10.2190/DUGG-P24E-52WK-6CDG

Shahhosseini, M., Silong, A. D., Ismaill, I. A., & Uli, J. N. (2012). The role of emotional intelligence on job performance. *International Journal of Business and Social Science, 3*(21).

Tănăsescu, R.-I., & Leon, R. (2013). Emotional intelligence, occupational stress and job performance in the Romanian banking system: A case study. *Management Dynamics in the Knowledge Economy, 7*(3), 322–335. doi:10.25019/MDKE/7.3.03

Wong, C. S., & Law, K. S. (2002). The effects of leader and follower emotional intelligence on performance and attitude: An exploratory study. *The Leadership Quarterly, 13*(3), 243–274. doi:10.1016/S1048-9843(02)00099-1

Wu, Y.-C. (2011). Job stress and job performance among employees in the Taiwanese finance sector: The role of emotional intelligence. *Social Behavior and Personality, 39*(1), 21–31. doi:10.2224bp.2011.39.1.21

Yamani, N., Shahabi, M., & Haghani, F. (2014). The relationship between emotional intelligence and job stress in the faculty of medicine in Isfahan University of Medical Sciences. *Journal of Advances in Medical Education & Professionalism*, 2(1), 20. PMID:25512914

Yang, S. Y., Chen, S. C., Lee, L., & Liu, Y. S. (2021). Employee stress, job satisfaction, and job performance: A comparison between high-technology and traditional industry in Taiwan. The Journal of Asian Finance. *Economics and Business*, 8(3), 605–618.

Chapter 17
The Role of Sustainable Leadership in Ensuring Long-Term Success

M. Beena

Jain University, India

Patcha Bhujanga Rao

iD https://orcid.org/0000-0003-4736-8497

Jain University, India

Vijaya Bhaskar Reddy Meegada

iD https://orcid.org/0009-0000-9132-3742

Sreenivasa Institute of Technology and Management Studies, India

ABSTRACT

Sustainable development is a novel interdisciplinary field of study. The field of sustainable leadership is an innovative approach to effective leadership that was recently created to resolve issues associated with sustainable development. Before incorporating sustainable development into a company's strategy, the company's senior executives must first integrate sustainability into daily operations. Even though leaders play a crucial role in bringing about change, there is still a lack of knowledge about leadership and its relationship to sustainable practices; therefore, additional research is required to demonstrate this. There is a gap in the literature between sustainable practices, sustainability performance, and IT employees' leadership skills. In response, a survey questionnaire was created to collect data, and structural equation modeling (SEM) was used to examine the moderating influence of IT managers' leadership abilities on the relationships between sustainable practices and sustainability performance.

DOI: 10.4018/979-8-3693-0049-7.ch017

1. INTRODUCTION

The rapid pace of change in modern business contexts has resulted in a surge in complexity. Businesses, if they wish to survive in the face of mounting public, government, and NGO pressure in the wake of financial scandals, bankruptcies, and natural disasters, will need to incorporate ever-greater degrees of complexity into their operations (Siddiquei et al., 2021). Sustainable leadership (SL) promotes the use of management practices backed by empirical evidence as part of an all-encompassing approach to corporate leadership that prioritizes social and environmental responsibility without sacrificing financial success (Smith & Sharicz, 2011). Sustainable leadership practices include positive labor relations, a shared vision, a commitment to social responsibility, and the treatment of employees with respect (Suriyankietkaew & Avery, 2016).

The literature on sustainable leadership is still in its infancy; hence, there is an urgent need to grow this area of study further (Burawat, 2019). The majority of current managerial researchers feel that organizational learning is essential for long-term success. Learning at the organizational level reveals social, economic, and environmental views that should be taken into account while realigning a company's processes and structures (Soana, 2011). It is defined by a dedication to procedure, a priority on collaboration, and a concentration on the basics of business and its aims (Subramanyam, 1983).

Throughout the years, the concept of sustainability has gained significant attention in various fields, including business, architecture, and environmental science (Srinivas et al., 2023; Mert, 2022). As the world faces mounting challenges related to climate change, resource depletion, and social inequality, the need for sustainable practices has become more urgent than ever before (Xiao & Watson, 2019). In this study, we aim to explore the impact of sustainable performances on businesses, societies, and the environment (Vashishtha & Kapoor, 2023). By examining the strategies, outcomes, and implications of sustainable performances, we seek to contribute to the growing body of knowledge on sustainable development and shed light on the potential benefits and challenges associated with adopting sustainable practices (Ying et al., 2020).

The principle behind sustainable performance is to fulfil existing obligations without sacrificing the capacity of succeeding generations to do the same for themselves (Templier & Paré, 2015). This is known as "filling present requirements without compromising future generations' capacity to fulfil their own obligations." Within the context of commercial enterprises, "sustainable performance" refers to a range of activities, including environmental stewardship, social responsibility, and the ability to remain economically viable (Saxena et al., 2023). It goes beyond merely complying with regulations and aims to integrate sustainability into fundamental company processes rather than just complying with legislation (Phoek et al., 2023). This includes lowering carbon emissions, preserving natural resources, promoting ethical labour practises, and making a good impact on the communities in which the company operates (Singh et al., 2023). By acting in this manner, companies can not only lessen the harm they cause to the environment and society but also improve their reputations and increase the amount of money they make over the long run (Ocoró et al., 2023).

Understanding the approaches taken by companies in order to attain sustainable performance is one of the primary focuses of this research. Companies will implement a variety of strategies, which may include collaborating with stakeholders or making changes to their internal operations (Vashishtha & Dhawan, 2023). Some companies, for instance, reduce the amount of trash produced by their manufacturing procedures by implementing recycling programmes, investing in renewable energy sources, and cutting back on waste disposal (Sudheer & Naachimuthu, 2022). Others form collaborations with suppliers, non-governmental organisations (NGOs), or governments in order to tackle issues of sustainability together (Tripathi & Al-Shahri, 2023). By analysing these approaches, it will be possible for us to gain comprehension of the various routes leading to sustainability and to recognise the best methods that are responsible for producing observable and gratifying results (Priyadarshini & Naachimuthu, 2020).

In addition, the purpose of this research is to examine the effects that sustainable performances have had on businesses, societies, and the natural environment. Although sustainable business practises are frequently accompanied by greater expenses, there is the possibility that doing so could result in additional benefits such as an improved reputation, increased customer loyalty, and less operational risks. In addition, sustainable performances have a wider impact on society as a whole by supporting economic growth, enhancing living conditions, and advancing social equality. It is possible to provide factual evidence of the positive consequences of sustainable performances by quantifying and analysing these outcomes (Kuragayala, 2023). This can encourage more businesses to adopt and support sustainable practises (Younas & Ali, 2021).

However, it is essential to acknowledge the potential challenges and limitations of sustainable performance. Some businesses may face barriers in terms of financial constraints, lack of awareness, or resistance to change (Ur Rehman et al., 2023; Sri et al., 2022). The adoption of sustainable practices may also require significant investments in technologies, staff training, or supply chain modification. Moreover, sustainability is a complex and multidimensional concept that requires continuous monitoring, evaluation, and improvement. Therefore, this study aims to identify and address these challenges, providing recommendations and insights into how businesses can effectively navigate the path toward sustainable performance.

Overall, this study on the impact of sustainable performances seeks to contribute to the ongoing dialogue on sustainability and its relevance in various fields. By exploring the strategies, outcomes, and implications of sustainable performances, we hope to inspire businesses, policymakers, and individuals to prioritize sustainable practices, leading to a more environmentally conscious, socially equitable, and economically prosperous future.

1.1 Research Question

In this study, we have narrowed our attention to methods that are tailored to the problem of long-term growth and change. These methods are not all there is. They were picked because of the obvious impact they would have on long-term viability and systemic shifts.

To address the current issue facing capitalism, Alt et al., (2015) have made a concerted effort to improve transformational leadership qualities. The necessity to alter the economic system as a whole is something that Gerard et al., (2017), who also takes a holistic leadership stance, has emphasized. What it takes for executives to push sustainability initiatives within organizations is something Mainali et al., (2018) investigated. These three perspectives, transformational leadership, systems thinking, and emotional intelligence, each comes from a unique academic background, which will deepen the comparison. An organization's view of sustainability shifts from a compliance issue to a strategic opportunity as it raises the bar and finds new ways to use sustainability to gain a competitive edge, and as a result, it uses long-term metrics to evaluate its success in this area through leadership practices (Shifana & Naachimuthu, 2022). Therefore, the sustainability leader needs to be good at seeing ahead and assessing long-term sustainability trends, as well as finding new possibilities and devising strategies to reposition the organization so that it can take advantage of them.

2. LITERATURE REVIEW AND HYPOTHESIS DEVELOPMENT

Survival demands a departure from "business as usual," an approach that puts shareholders' short-term financial objectives ahead of stakeholders' long-term interests. Sustainability has been identified by top corporations as the next business "mega-trend" that will significantly impact the companies' capacity to remain competitive in the future, much like information technology, globalization, and the quality movement before it. According to Moradi et al., (2022), a sustainable business model is the only model worthy of legitimacy.

It is this idea that, according to NRBV framework advocates, best characterizes how a business might profit from its existing resources. This management theory stresses the value of a company's strategic assets and core competencies in laying the groundwork for sustainable competitive advantages. However, the NRBV framework cannot be used by businesses that factor in environmental considerations (Zhao & Zhou, 2019). In many cases, it is impossible for contemporary firms to address sustainability concerns without taking environmental conditions into account. Access to resources and capacities that encourage environmentally sustainable economic activity is a source of competitive advantage, according to NRBV theory. When responding to the external environment, organizations with unique resources need to take bold steps to address the environmental concerns of their diverse stakeholder groups. Companies can gain an advantage by capitalizing on their leaders' scarcity, individuality, worth, and irreplaceability. Iqbal & Piwowar-Sulej, (2022) explain that "sustainable leadership" takes into account the organization as a whole and promotes the incorporation of social, economic, and environmental factors. The definition of NRBV theory reveals that this investigation made use of this source (Savya & Naachimuthu, 2022).

A dynamic skill relies on the ability to create, collect, integrate, disseminate, and use several types of information. In the context of knowledge-based dynamic capacities, organizational learning comprises both the creation of new data and the organization of previously collected information into a common knowledge base. Learning organizations place a premium on knowledge creation and utilization, which in turn drives superior performance. Therefore, the presence of organizational learning increases the likelihood that an organization's flexible ability will meet the requirements of a diverse variety of stakeholders. As a result, dynamic capability is an essential concept that connects the dots between institutional knowledge and sustained achievement.

According to Iqbal & Piwowar-Sulej, (2022) sustainable leaders create a culture where employees feel safe to talk to each other and exchange ideas. As a result, a psychologically secure workplace is a key factor in effective employee learning. Benyamin et al., (2006) note that sustainable leaders are those who prioritize innovation, foresight, growth, morality, openness to sharing knowledge, and responsibility to society and the natural world. According to Mahdi & Almsafir, (2014), having a common vision for the future of the organization is beneficial to its growth. Additionally, sustainable leaders promote open communication and data flow inside their organizations. Some evidence suggests (Santos-Vijande et al., 2012; Sattayaraksa & Boon-itt, 2016; Seddighi & Mathew, 2020). that managers see unions as a drag on production, which has led to union avoidance, suppression, and substitution. Some research (Gill, 2009) suggests that unions' advocacy for High-Performance Work Practices (HPWP) can make a business more competitive. In order to solve social problems, shared value solutions can be implemented (Porter, 2019).

Iris employees are able to grow professionally, learn from one another, and help the company succeed when they are led by people who are committed to the long haul and who exude authenticity and integrity in all that they do. For long-term success in achieving development goals, authentic leadership is essential, and this is where a learning organization comes in. Moral leadership, according to Saleem et al. (2020), however, is insufficient to motivate people to take environmentally friendly measures. When some variables operate as mediators, the impact of ethical and sustainable leadership on pro-environmental behavior among workers is magnified. Therefore, for ethical leaders to influence employee behavior, factors like employee passion for protecting the environment and motivation are required (Peng et al., 2021; Saleem et al., 2020). However, as has been made abundantly obvious, this viewpoint only extended to the activities of employers while on the job (Figure 1).

By using their experience, resources, and management skills, businesses may take the lead in social change through shared value, surpassing the capabilities of even the most well-intentioned governmental and social sector organizations. In this approach, consumers' faith in businesses can be restored. Consequently, the following hypothesis is proposed for this investigation:

2.1 Research Objectives

- To study the factors affecting sustainable performance
- To determine the impact of sustainable leadership practices on sustainable performance

2.2. Research Hypothesis

- H: Sustainable leadership practices significantly influence the sustainability performance of SMEs.
- H1: The effectiveness of sustainability strategies is profoundly influenced by labour relations.
- H2: The success of an organization's sustainability efforts is dramatically affected by how much it values its personnel.
- H3: When people work together toward a common goal, sustainability gains traction.

Figure 1. Framework of the study

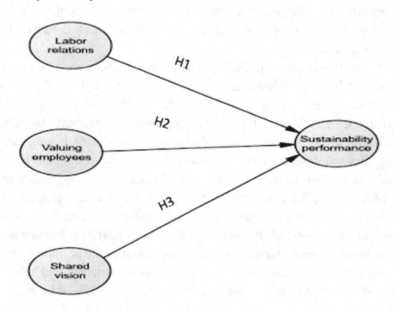

3. RESEARCH METHODOLOGY

The study drew on empirical data collected from a representative cross-section of SMEs in Bangalore. The survey's respondents were all firm owners or executives with a deep awareness of their organizations' inner workings, and they were chosen at random. The semi-structured questionnaire consists of two parts: questions about the respondents and the company and questions concerning the study variables. Participants were asked to rate their level of agreement or disagreement on a scale from 5 (strongly agree) to 1 (strongly disagree). Out of a total of 280 questionnaires submitted by respondents, only 268 samples were chosen for further analysis due to the elimination of data with missing values during the data screening procedure (Al-Maaitah et al., 2021a).

The metrics used in the scale were derived and modified from earlier research. Pham & Kim, (2019) chose variables for use in assessing company sustainability performance. Iqbal & Piwowar-Sulej, (2022), and Suriyankietkaew & Avery, (2016) provided the basis for the development of scales to measure sustainable leadership practices. SPSS and AMOS version 26 were used to perform descriptive and inferential statistical tests on the data (Al-Maaitah et al., 2021b). The data in Tables 1 and 3 are described using descriptive statistics.

The research used EFA (Exploratory factor analysis) to figure out how the data on the measures were organized, and then they used CFA to check the reliability and validity of the constructed variables. At last, we used Structural Equation Modelling (SEM) to put our study hypotheses to the test.

Factor analysis: A preliminary factor analysis was carried out to check that the selected scale items were loaded appropriately with a factor loading score that was greater than 0.5 and that there was no evidence of any cross-loading. The Kaiser–Meyer–Olkin (KMO) value is used to determine whether or not an existing sample size is sufficient for additional research. Bartlett's Test of Sphericity reveals that factor analysis is useful for our data because it has a high value of KMO (0.889) and a low value of significance (0.05). Principal Component Analysis (PCA) was performed using the Promax Rotation Method Kaiser Normalization on the 13 elements. Having Eigen values that are more than one is one of the criteria for factor extraction, and this leads to the discovery of four factors that together explain 81.79 percent of the total variance.

The mean value of the SME owners' and managers' evaluation of the company's sustainability performance is 4.47, well above the neutral threshold of 3. Respondents are in agreement with the role of sustainable leadership practises and the performance of their firm if the mean values for labour relations (M=4.24), valuing employees (M=4.30), and shared vision (M=4.38) are all close to agreement.

You can see the relationship between the independent factors and the dependent variables in table 2. All substantial positive correlations with performance show that better sustainability performance may be achieved by SMEs with more adoption of sustainability leadership methods.

Cronbach's alpha, a measure of internal consistency, is presented in table 3 to conclude our analysis of the research variables. The alpha value for all four factors is greater than 0.7, meeting the minimum criteria for reliability.

Table 1. Details of respondents from selected SMEs (N=268)

Measures	Items	Frequency	Percentage
Gender	Male	147	55
	Female	121	45
Age	Below 24	2	0.74
	25-30	48	18
	30-35	78	29.1
	35-40	112	41.7
	40 & above	28	10.4
Education	Secondary	1	0.03
	Undergraduate	134	52.2
	Postgraduate	92	34.3
	Others	41	15.29
Type of business	Micro	53	20
	Small	97	36
	Medium	118	44
Industry	Food and beverages	31	11.5
	Durables, consumer electronics, and machinery	67	25
	Chemicals, pharmaceutical, and plastics	18	6.7
	Textile, leather, and clothing	21	7.8
	Other manufacturing	131	48.8

Source: Primary survey

4. TEST HYPOTHESES USING SEM

In order to determine whether or not there is a causal connection between the research constructs, the study does a structural equation modelling (SEM) analysis and applies the maximum likelihood technique. The purpose of this study was to evaluate the effect that three exogenous variables (also known as independent variables) have on the performance of endogenous dependent variables that are concerned with sustainability. A crucial ratio value of 1.96 and a p-value that is less than 0.05 at the 5 percent level of significance are the criteria that are used to determine whether a study hypothesis should be accepted or rejected.

The results of our path analysis and the tests of our hypothesis are displayed in Table 4. We present the standardized route coefficient together with the accompanying p-value for each association that we find. The conclusion that can be drawn from looking at Table 4 as well as Figure 2 is that the standardized path coefficient () of labour relations to performance is positive and significant, with a value of 0.315 and a significance level of 0.000. Because the p-value is less than 0.05 and the CR is more than 1.96, it can be concluded that hypothesis H1 is correct.

Table 2. Factor loadings of variables

Factor	Items	Item Loadings
Labor relations	LR1: High-performance work is easier to implement when unions and managers have good relations with their workers.	0.861
	LR2: The unionized workplace with strong employee connections is expected to outperform those with weaker ties between management and workers, as well as non-unionized workplaces.	0.872
	LR3: trust among workers and continuity within teams will be impacted.	0.890
Valuing employees	VE1: Adding to society's well-being is a great way for businesses to boost their bottom line.	0.764
	VE2: Many opportunities to meet unmet needs, increase efficiencies, distinguish products, and grow markets are made possible by strengthening the ties between business success and societal progress.	0.862
	VE3: Company profits, workers and their families enjoy better health, and society as a whole reaps the rewards of reduced sick days and increased output.	0.765
	VE4: In all sectors of public policy, the idea of value creation should direct spending.	0.839
Shared vision	SV1: Businesses' capacity to share a common vision helps speed up their progress toward environmental management competence.	0.849
	SV2: A shared vision establishes standards for conduct and recommends the kinds of learning that employees should prioritize.	0.761
	SV3: managers delegate authority by conveying the company's vision to its employees, who then bear a portion of the burden of making those aims a reality.	0.844
Sustainability performance	SP1: Leadership in your company strikes a healthy balance between profit and doing good.	0.761
	SP2: When a mistake is made that has an impact on sustainability, your organization's management makes it official.	0.801
	SP3: Your company's leadership is open to fixing problems that could compromise sustainability.	0.838

Table 3. Data correlation, Cronbach's alpha, mean, standard deviation

	Labor Relations	Valuing Employees	Shared Vision	Sustainability Performance
Reliability (Alpha value)	0.921	0.882	0.879	0.856
Mean	4.2388	4.2985	4.3818	4.4776
Standard deviation	.90231	.76436	.81938	.69831
Labor relations	1	.387**	.444**	.532**
Valuing employees	.387**	1	.420**	.515**
Shared vision	.444**	.420**	1	.491**
Sustainability Performance	.532**	.515**	.491**	1

Note: ** indicates at the.01 level of significance, a correlation exists (2-tailed)

Having a value of 0.355, a CR value of 5.370, and a p value of 0.000 (p less than 0.05) indicates that the influence of valuing employees on the performance of SMEs is positive and significant. This provides adequate evidence to accept hypothesis H2. Shared vision had a similar beneficial effect on the performance of SMEs, with a value of 0.239 and a significance level of 0.000. Because the p-value for this link is lower than 0.05, we can conclude that it is significant; as a result, hypothesis H3 was supported by this data. The data also showed that the influence of valuing employees has more of an effect on performance compared to other sustainable leadership practices, as the standardized regression value is greater for valuing employees. This was shown to be the case when the findings were analyzed.

The value of the coefficient of determination (R2) is 0.534, which indicates that three sustainable leadership practises can explain 53.4 percent of the variations in sustainability performance. These practises are labour relations, valuing employees, and having a shared vision for the organization's future. CMIN/df = 2.742, RMSEA = 0.068, CFI = 0.947, NFI = 0.925, and AGFI = 0.853 are the values that represent the fit indices of the measurement model. Based on the findings, it appears that the structure model well predicts and interprets the data.

Figure 2. Casual model

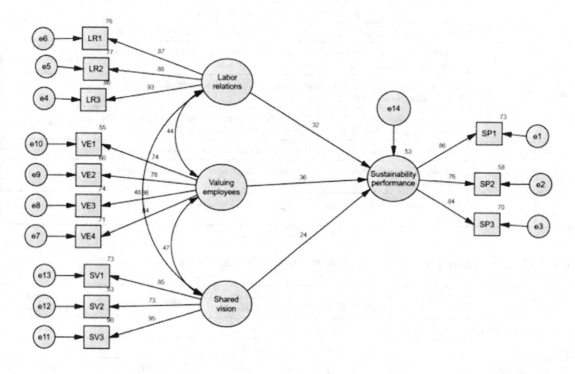

Table 4. Path coefficients of the structural model

Hypo-theses	Outcome Variables		Causal Variables	SE.	CR.	P	Path Coefficient	Result
H1	Sustainability Performance	←	Labor relations	.050	4.946	***	.315	Accepted
H2	Sustainability Performance	←	Valuing employees	.060	5.370	***	.355	Accepted
H3	Sustainability Performance	←	Shared vision	.051	3.708	***	.239	Accepted

Note: SE; Critical ratio, Path Coefficient, and Standard Error Probability of significance (p) and standardised regression weights. *** indicates p<0.000.

5. DISCUSSION AND IMPLICATIONS

The purpose of this study was to investigate the ways in which adopting sustainable leadership practises affects the success of a selection of small and medium-sized firms (SMEs) in the city of Bangalore. The following further explanations of the study's findings can be found in this section:

The research substantiated all of the leadership behaviours that lead to enduring performance in their respective organisations. The findings revealed that the performance of the company may be improved by implementing sustainable leadership methods such as positive labour relations, employee appreciation, and a shared vision. The findings are in line with those of other studies which have shown that improving a company's performance in terms of sustainability can be accomplished by placing a greater emphasis on its employees.

The most important managerial consequence for CEOs, business owners, and managers is to become aware of vital sustainable leadership behaviours that boost performance. Students can improve their prospects of long-term success in business by developing the skills necessary to become great leaders and managers through participation in activities such as these. These principles of sustainable leadership offer the best possible framework for preserving approaches of effective leadership.

Comparing different leadership styles and conducting research on efficient and environmentally responsible company operations are two examples of activities that might demonstrate how future leaders will need to make considerable adjustments to their way of thinking. Some schools of thought in economics are aligned with consciousness-based approaches. These include schools of thought that point out the deficiencies of more conventional schools of thought (such as supply and demand, market equilibrium, and rationality) by arguing that these conventional schools of thought ignore important psychological, social, and ecological factors.

Unlike other leadership methods, which begin with the perspective of the leaders or the status quo of their organisation, SL is predicated on an appreciation of the transformative and disruptive changes that occur within the context of modern business and society. This is in contrast to other leadership techniques, which begin with the viewpoint of the leaders. Therefore, in order to get ready for the enormously transformative and sustainable journey that lies ahead, future leaders will need to adopt strategies that enable them to discover and adopt new mindsets, beliefs, and attitudes, as well as build the required skill set. This is necessary in order to prepare for the journey.

6. CONCLUSION

In a nutshell, the interplay between leadership awareness and the particulars of the given situation, both in the present and in the past, is the secret to attaining long-term success in the process of corporate transformation. This is true both in the present and in the past. Because it recognises the relationship between context, consciousness, and continuity as the foundation for sustained leadership development, SL provides a new context and purpose for the connected, creative, and collective leadership qualities. This allows SL to give these qualities a new context and purpose. To validate the SL model in actual business environments and to precisely describe each of the SL leadership qualities, additional research is required. The current study is collecting data from small and medium-sized businesses that are located in Bangalore. This research may be expanded to include findings from other parts of the county.

REFERENCES

Al-Maaitah, D. A., Tha'er Majali, M. A., & Almaaitah, T. A. (2021a). The role of leadership styles on staffs job satisfaction in public organizations. *Journal of Contemporary Issues in Business and Government*, *27*(1), 772–783.

Al-Maaitah, T. A., Tha'er Majali, M. A., & Almaaitah, D. A. (2021b). The Impact of COVID-19 on the Electronic Commerce Users Behavior. *Journal of Contemporary Issues in Business and Government*, *27*(1), 772–783.

Alt, E., Díez-de-Castro, E. P., & Lloréns-Montes, F. J. (2015). Linking employee stakeholders to environmental performance: The role of proactive environmental strategies and shared vision. *Journal of Business Ethics*, *128*(1), 167–181. doi:10.100710551-014-2095-x

Benyamin, B., Uhl-Bien, M., Marion, R., Seers, A., Orton, J. D., & Schreiber, C. (2006). Complexity leadership theory: An interactive perspective on leading in complex adaptive systems. *Emergence*, *8*, 2–12.

Burawat, P. (2019). The relationships among transformational leadership, sustainable leadership, lean manufacturing, and sustainability performance in Thai SMEs manufacturing industry. *International Journal of Quality & Reliability Management*, *36*(6), 1014–1036. doi:10.1108/IJQRM-09-2017-0178

Gerard, L., McMillan, J., & D'Annunzio-Green, N. (2017). Conceptualising sustainable leadership. *Industrial and Commercial Training*, *49*(3), 116–126. doi:10.1108/ICT-12-2016-0079

Gill, C., & Meyer, D. (2013). Union presence, employee relations and high-performance work practices. *Personnel Review*, *42*(5), 508–528. doi:10.1108/PR-07-2011-0117

Iqbal, Q., & Piwowar-Sulej, K. (2022). Sustainable leadership in higher education institutions: Social innovation as a mechanism. *International Journal of Sustainability in Higher Education*, *23*(8), 1–20. doi:10.1108/IJSHE-04-2021-0162

Kuragayala, P. S. (2023). A Systematic Review on Workforce Development in Healthcare Sector: Implications in the Post-COVID Scenario. *FMDB Transactions on Sustainable Technoprise Letters*, *1*(1), 36–46.

Mahdi, O. R., & Almsafir, M. K. (2014). The role of strategic leadership in building sustainable competitive advantage in the academic environment. *Procedia: Social and Behavioral Sciences*, *129*, 289–296. doi:10.1016/j.sbspro.2014.03.679

Mainali, B., Luukkanen, J., Silveira, S., & Kaivo-oja, J. (2018). Evaluating synergies and trade-offs among sustainable development goals (SDGs): Explorative analyses of development paths in south Asia and sub-Saharan Africa. *Sustainability (Basel)*, *10*(3), 815. doi:10.3390u10030815

Mert, I. (2022). *Assessment of Accounting Evaluation Practices, A Research-Based Review of Turkey and Romania. Springer Cham*. https://link.springer.com/book/10.1007/978-3-030-98486-1

Moradi, S., Ansari, R., & Taherkhani, R. (2022). A systematic analysis of construction performance management: Key performance indicators from 2000 to 2020. *Civil Engineering (Shiraz)*, *46*(1), 15–31. doi:10.100740996-021-00626-7

Ocoró, M. P., Polo, O. C. C., & Khandare, S. (2023). Importance of Business Financial Risk Analysis in SMEs According to COVID-19. *FMDB Transactions on Sustainable Management Letters, 1*(1), 12–21.

Peng, J., Chen, X., Zou, Y., & Nie, Q. (2021). Environmentally specific transformational leadership and team pro-environmental behaviors: The roles of pro-environmental goal clarity, pro-environmental harmonious passion, and power distance. *Human Relations; Studies towards the Integration of the Social Sciences, 74*(11), 1864–1888. doi:10.1177/0018726720942306

Pham, H., & Kim, S.-Y. (2019). The effects of sustainable practices and managers' leadership competences on sustainability performance of construction firms. *Sustainable Production and Consumption, 20*, 1–14. doi:10.1016/j.spc.2019.05.003

Phoek, S. E. M., Lauwinata, L., & Kowarin, L. R. N. (2023). Tourism Development in Merauke Regency, South Papua Province: Strengthening Physical Infrastructure for Local Economic Growth and Enchanting Tourist Attractions. *FMDB Transactions on Sustainable Management Letters, 1*(2), 82–94.

Porter, M. E., & Kramer, M. R. (2019). Creating shared value: How to reinvent capitalism-and unleash a wave of innovation and growth. In *Managing Sustainable Business* (pp. 323–346). Springer Netherlands. doi:10.1007/978-94-024-1144-7_16

Priyadarshini, N. S., & Naachimuthu, K. P. (2020). Ancient and Modern Conception to Virtues: Comparing Naaladiyar and Positive Psychology. In *International Conference on Multi Facets of Sacred Literature* (pp. 1–12). Academic Press.

Saleem, M., Qadeer, F., Mahmood, F., Ariza-Montes, A., & Han, H. (2020). Ethical leadership and employee green behavior: A multilevel moderated mediation analysis. *Sustainability (Basel), 12*(8), 3314. doi:10.3390u12083314

Santos-Vijande, M. L., López-Sánchez, J. Á., & Trespalacios, J. A. (2012). How organizational learning affects a firm's flexibility, competitive strategy, and performance. *Journal of Business Research, 65*(8), 1079–1089. doi:10.1016/j.jbusres.2011.09.002

Sattayaraksa, T., & Boon-itt, S. (2016). CEO transformational leadership and the new product development process: The mediating roles of organizational learning and innovation culture. *Leadership and Organization Development Journal, 37*(6), 730–749. doi:10.1108/LODJ-10-2014-0197

Savya, N., & Naachimuthu, K. P. (2022). Psychosocial Determinants of Name Dropping: A Conceptual Framework. *Madhya Bharti - Humanities and Social Sciences, 83*(14), 1–12.

Saxena, D., Khandare, S., & Chaudhary, S. (2023). An Overview of ChatGPT: Impact on Academic Learning. *FMDB Transactions on Sustainable Techno Learning, 1*(1), 11–20.

Seddighi, H. R., & Mathew, S. (2020). Innovation and regional development via the firm's core competence: Some recent evidence from North East England. *Journal of Innovation & Knowledge, 5*(4), 219–227. doi:10.1016/j.jik.2019.12.005

Shifana, F., & Naachimuthu, K. P. (2022). Elements of Holistic Human Development in Naanmanikkadigai: A Hermeneutic Study. *Journal of Positive School Psychology, 6*(4), 2218–2231.

Siddiquei, A., Asmi, F., Asadullah, M. A., & Mir, F. (2021). Environmental-specific servant leadership as a strategic tool to accomplish environmental performance: A case of China. *International Journal of Manpower*, *42*(7), 1161–1182. doi:10.1108/IJM-07-2020-0350

Singh, M., Bhushan, M., Sharma, R., & Cavaliere, L. P. L. (2023). An Organized Assessment of the Literature of Entrepreneurial Skills and Emotional Intelligence. *FMDB Transactions on Sustainable Management Letters*, *1*(3), 95–104.

Smith, P. A. C., & Sharicz, C. (2011). The shift needed for sustainability. *The Learning Organization*, *18*(1), 73–86. doi:10.1108/09696471111096019

Soana, M.-G. (2011). The relationship between corporate social performance and corporate financial performance in the banking sector. *Journal of Business Ethics*, *104*(1), 133–148. doi:10.100710551-011-0894-x

Sri, G. P., Jayapriya, J., Poornima, T., & Naachimuthu, K. P. (2022). Hermeneutics of Iniyavai Naarpadhu and Inna Naarpadhu. *Journal of Positive School Psychology*, *6*(8), 4358–4368.

Srinivas, K., Velmurugan, P. R., & Andiyappillai, N. (2023). Digital Human Resources and Management Support Improve Human Resources Effectiveness. *FMDB Transactions on Sustainable Management Letters*, *1*(1), 32–45.

Subramanyam, K. (1983). Bibliometric studies of research collaboration: A review. *Journal of Information Science*, *6*(1), 33–38. doi:10.1177/016555158300600105

Sudheer, V., & Naachimuthu, K. P. (2022). Effect of JPMR on State-Trait Anxiety Among Young Female Adults During COVID-19 Pandemic Lockdown. *International Journal of Health Sciences*, *6*(55), 1192–1202. doi:10.53730/ijhs.v6nS5.8848

Suriyankietkaew, S., & Avery, G. (2016). Sustainable leadership practices driving financial performance: Empirical evidence from Thai SMEs. *Sustainability (Basel)*, *8*(4), 327. doi:10.3390u8040327

Templier, M., & Paré, G. (2015). A framework for guiding and evaluating literature reviews. *Communications of the Association for Information Systems*, *37*. Advance online publication. doi:10.17705/1CAIS.03706

Tripathi, S., & Al-Shahri, M. (2023). Problems and Prospects on the Evolution of Advertising and Public Relations Industries in Oman. *FMDB Transactions on Sustainable Management Letters*, *1*(1), 1–11.

Ur Rehman, Z., Shafique, I., Khawaja, K. F., Saeed, M., & Kalyar, M. N. (2023). Linking responsible leadership with financial and environmental performance: Determining mediation and moderation. *International Journal of Productivity and Performance Management*, *72*(1), 24–46. doi:10.1108/IJPPM-12-2020-0626

Vashishtha, E., & Dhawan, G. (2023). Comparison of Baldrige Criteria of Strategy Planning and Harrison Text. *FMDB Transactions on Sustainable Management Letters*, *1*(1), 22–31.

Vashishtha, E., & Kapoor, H. (2023). Implementation of Blockchain Technology Across International Healthcare Markets. *FMDB Transactions on Sustainable Technoprise Letters*, *1*(1), 1–12.

Xiao, Y., & Watson, M. (2019). Guidance on conducting a systematic literature review. *Journal of Planning Education and Research*, *39*(1), 93–112. doi:10.1177/0739456X17723971

Ying, M., Faraz, N. A., Ahmed, F., & Raza, A. (2020). How does servant leadership foster employees' voluntary green behavior? A sequential mediation model. *International Journal of Environmental Research and Public Health*, *17*(5), 1792. doi:10.3390/ijerph17051792 PMID:32164222

Younas, A., & Ali, P. (2021). Five tips for developing useful literature summary tables for writing review articles. *Evidence-Based Nursing*, *24*(2), 32–34. doi:10.1136/ebnurs-2021-103417 PMID:33674415

Zhao, H., & Zhou, Q. (2019). Exploring the impact of responsible leadership on organizational citizenship behavior for the environment: A leadership identity perspective. *Sustainability (Basel)*, *11*(4), 944. doi:10.3390u11040944

Chapter 18
Wise Apply on a Machine Learning–Based College Recommendation Data System

Jyoti P. Kanjalkar
https://orcid.org/0000-0002-4064-7189
Vishwakarma Institute of Technology, India

Gaurav N. Patil
Vishwakarma Institute of Technology, India

Gaurav R. Patil
Vishwakarma Institute of Technology, India

Yash Parande
Vishwakarma Institute of Technology, India

Bhavesh Dilip Patil
Vishwakarma Institute of Technology, India

Pramod Kanjalkar
Vishwakarma Institute of Technology, India

ABSTRACT

This chapter presents a college recommendation system using machine learning with the features of branch, caste, location, and fees. The system aims to provide personalized recommendations to students based on their preferences and past academic performance. The dataset used in the study consists of information about various colleges, including their location, fees, available branches, and the percentage of students belonging to different castes. The system uses a combination of machine learning algorithms, including decision trees and random forests, to provide accurate and efficient recommendations. The Adaboost algorithm is used to find colleges with similar features to the student's preferences, while decision trees and random forests are used to make predictions based on past data. The proposed system is evaluated using metrics such as accuracy, precision, recall, and F1 score. The results show that the system provides highly accurate and personalized recommendations to students.

DOI: 10.4018/979-8-3693-0049-7.ch018

1. INTRODUCTION

Machine learning, or ML, is a subfield of AI concerned with teaching computers to learn new skills without being explicitly programmed to do so (Girase et al., 2017). The goal of machine learning is to give computers the ability to learn from experience and steadily improve their results (Jain et al., 2018). It's useful for solving difficult problems, making accurate predictions, and spotting trends (Singh et al., 2020). Machine learning is a rapidly evolving field with applications in various industries, from healthcare and finance to marketing and cybersecurity (Sharma et al., 2019). As technology advances, machine learning continues to play a crucial role in automating tasks, extracting insights from data, and enabling intelligent decision-making (Tian et al., 2019).

When an algorithm is trained on a labelled dataset, also known as "supervised learning," the output label for each input data point is known beforehand (Abdullahi et al., 2023). The purpose of supervised learning is to train an algorithm to accurately predict or classify data it has never seen before by exposing it to examples of that data and its expected outcomes (the inputs) (Angeline et al., 2023). Supervised learning is a foundational concept in machine learning and is widely used in various fields due to its ability to make predictions based on labeled data (Anand et al., 2023). It forms the basis for many practical applications and continues to be an active area of research and development (Rajasekaran et al., 2023).

Unsupervised learning is a type of machine learning where the algorithm is given unlabelled data and must find patterns, relationships, or structures within the data on its own (Rajest, et al., 2023a). Unlike supervised learning, there are no predefined output labels to guide the learning process. The goal of unsupervised learning is often to explore the hidden structure within the data or to group similar data points together (Rajest, et al., 2023b). Unsupervised learning is a powerful approach for exploring and understanding the underlying structure of data (Regin et al., 2023). It is particularly useful when the data lacks labeled examples or when the objective is to uncover hidden patterns or relationships (Sivapriya et al., 2023).

In the machine learning paradigm known as Reinforcement Learning (RL), an agent learns to make decisions by seeing and responding to its surroundings (Sohlot et al., 2023). The agent learns the best course of action through repeated exposure to feedback in the form of incentives and punishments. Human and animal learning processes serve as inspiration for reinforcement learning. Key components and concepts of reinforcement learning include:

Agent: The entity that makes decisions and takes actions in an environment. The goal of the agent is to maximize its cumulative reward over time.

Environment: The external system with which the agent interacts. The agent's actions cause a change in the environment, which in turn affects the agent.

State: A representation of the current situation or configuration of the environment. The state provides the context for the agent's decision-making process.

Action: The set of possible moves or decisions that the agent can take in a given state. Actions influence the state of the environment.

Reward: A numerical signal that the environment provides to the agent as feedback after it takes an action in a certain state. The reward indicates the immediate benefit or cost associated with the action.

Policy: The strategy or mapping from states to actions that the agent follows to make decisions. The objective is to learn a strategy that maximises future rewards.

Value Function: The value function predicts how much the agent stands to gain over time if they begin in a given state and implement a certain policy. It aids the agent in weighing the relative attractiveness of potential future situations.

Exploration and Exploitation: Balancing exploration (trying new actions to discover their effects) and exploitation (choosing actions that are known to yield high rewards) is a crucial challenge in reinforcement learning.

Markov Decision Process (MDP): A mathematical framework that formalizes the reinforcement learning problem. It includes states, actions, transition probabilities, rewards, and the discount factor.

Q-Learning and Policy Gradient Methods: Q-Learning: A model-free reinforcement learning algorithm that learns a state-action value function (Q-function) without requiring a model of the environment.

Policy Gradient Methods: These methods directly learn the policy by optimizing the parameters of a parameterized policy.

Deep Reinforcement Learning: Deep Q-Networks (DQN): Combining reinforcement learning with deep neural networks to handle high-dimensional state spaces.

Policy Gradient with Neural Networks: Using neural networks to represent the policy and train it to maximize the expected cumulative reward.

Applications: Many different fields have found success with implementing reinforcement learning, such as:

- Game playing (e.g., AlphaGo, Atari games).
- Robotics and autonomous systems.
- Traffic signal optimization.
- Finance (e.g., algorithmic trading).
- Natural language processing.

Reinforcement learning is suitable for scenarios where an agent learns through interaction with an environment and can adapt its behavior based on feedback. While it has shown remarkable success in various domains, challenges such as sample inefficiency, exploration strategies, and generalization to different environments remain active areas of research in reinforcement learning. In this Chapter, we have proposed a college recommendation system that considers four critical factors: location, caste, fee, and branch based on a student's percentiles. This system is designed to help students find the best colleges that match their preferences and budget while also considering their academic performance.

The branch is a vital aspect when choosing a college. Some students have a clear idea of the field they want to pursue, while others may be more flexible. The recommendation system provides a list of colleges based on the student's branch preferences, ensuring that they have the necessary resources and faculty to excel in their chosen field. Caste is another significant factor in college selection, especially in India, where it is a critical determinant of social status. The system considers the student's caste and provides a list of colleges that are more inclusive and provide equal opportunities for all students. Location is a crucial factor when choosing a college. Some students may prefer colleges in their hometown or state, while others may be more interested in colleges located in big cities or remote areas. The recommendation system considers the student's location preferences and provides a list of colleges in that area.

Finally, fees are an important consideration for many students and families. The recommendation system takes into account the student's budget and provides a list of colleges that are affordable based on their percentile.

2. LITERATURE REVIEW

College recommendation systems using machine learning have been the subject of numerous research papers in recent years. In this literature survey, we will review some of the latest and most significant research papers on college recommendation systems using machine learning.

Wang & Shi, (2016) compared two significant machine learning methods in this work. Paper displays different statistics based on the result of both techniques. They started by putting the Random forests prediction method into practise. This model displays an accuracy of around 80%, meaning that about 80 out of 100 anticipated results were accurate. Adaboost was the second algorithm put into practise. The Adaboost algorithm-trained model has an accuracy of about 90%. The system is Windows 7, and Python is used for the software. The resources utilized for training the model and testing the results are as follows. The result of the article reveals that the AdaBoost method is considerably more efficient and reliable \s than Random forests while dealing with the admission prediction \s process utilizing machine learning.

The authors of this study, Hamid et al., came up with a one-of-a-kind design for a college entrance hybrid recommender that was built on data mining methods and knowledge discovery principles. This was done in order to address the issues associated with college admissions prediction. This system's high performance is the result of the combined efforts of its two cascade hybrid recommenders and its college predictor. Both of these components work together. The initial recommender is the one who decides which paths students in the preparatory year will take. At the same time, the second recommender chooses which students will be admitted to the specialised college based on how well they performed on the preparation year exams. Using historical data on students' GPAs and admissions to the institution, this software makes predictions about which universities are most likely to be attended. It takes into consideration the academic credentials, history, and student records of the applicant, in addition to college entrance requirements. After that, it makes a prognosis on the likelihood of a student enrolling in university colleges. A high rate of accurate prediction is a benefit, but another advantage is flexibility. This is because the system can anticipate potential schools that meet the student's profile as well as suitable track channels in which the students should enrol. The students' replies favourably increasing as long as they are assigned to the most appropriate institution that fits their demands is one way to achieve trustworthiness. This is necessary for the achievement of trustworthiness.

Shiksha.com (2021): This web-based tool offers direction and answers to questions regarding schooling. They created a predictor for colleges that uses student data as input and presents the potential colleges based on the institutions' requirements. The application most likely trains the model's data mining algorithm using cut-offs from prior years. Instead of using scores, the website presents a list of institutions based on rankings. The filters are only available for choosing branches and colleges, and the website's created list cannot be exported.

Kumari et al., (2019) provides an overview of the college recommendation system architecture and the data sources used in the system, including publicly available college admissions data and user-generated data. The system uses a range of machine learning techniques, including decision trees, random forests, and gradient boosting, to predict a student's chances of admission to specific colleges based on their academic profile, extracurricular activities, and demographic information. Using a range of databases, a comparative analysis of machine learning algorithms such as Decision Tree, Random Forest, and Adaboost is undertaken. Breast cancer, iris, and wine were all loaded from the sklearn dataset API into the example database. The comparison revealed that the Adaboost algorithm outperformed the other two methods. The Ensemble AdaBoost Classifier from Python's scikit-learn module is used to classify the data. The approach is being developed for various colleges in the Mumbai region. The model has been previously trained and saved in pickle format. The cached pickle is loaded as a model during prediction and can be utilized for prediction. This increases the College Recommendation system's time efficiency.

Pande & Chetty, (2018) have presented an intensive survey of Capsule Network (CapsNet) based approaches for several applications. Pande & Chetty, (2019) and Pande & Chetty, (2021) use CapsNet for leaf categorization. This approach can also be employed for an effective college recommendation system as it not only learns the features, but also identifies the relationships among the learned features and upholds them throughout the network.

3. PROPOSED METHODOLOGY

Shiksha.com is a proprietary program. The system contains filers depending on cost structure, review grades, castes/categories, and college locations that were not included in the previous application. The College Recommendation System displays the distance of the college from the user's location and allows the user to export the list of colleges selected using the application.

The study involves the use of a machine learning algorithm on a data collection of college cut-off lists from previous years. The data set was manually gathered from the state-level engineering admissions website. The data set was pre-processed in order for machine learning methods to be applied. Pre-processing involves transferring data from.pdf to.csv format and categorizing data into characteristics (year, branch, category, score) and class labels (admission). Data pre-processing also includes dealing with null values in the dataset. A Python-based framework called Streamlit is used to build the web application, which renders web pages. Streamlit, which is an open-source Python framework, makes it simple to build and distribute stunning, personalized online applications for data science and machine learning. The user interface and Python variables may be combined using the Streamlit framework. For the project's implementation, the model provides the algorithms that were employed. The user interface and its style are rendered via the template's HTML and CSS pages. Controlling the application's flow is the view. It co-ordinates the interface's functions.

In this paper, we have compared three algorithms, namely Decision Tree, Random Forest, and Adaboost. Algorithms that we worked on are:

Decision Tree: According to our knowledge, Decision trees are a popular algorithm used in recommendation systems because they can handle both categorical and continuous data, can be easily interpreted, and can handle high-dimensional feature spaces. Decision trees can be combined with ensemble methods, such as Random Forests, which can improve the accuracy and robustness of the recommendation system. However, decision trees can be prone to overfitting, where they become too complex and start memorizing the training data rather than learning general patterns that can be applied to new data. This can lead to poor performance on new data, which is a critical requirement for recommendation systems.

Random Forest: Random Forest is commonly used in recommendation systems due to its ability to handle high-dimensional data and capture complex non-linear relationships between features. Random forest is also useful in handling missing data values and noisy data, which is common in real-world recommendation scenarios. It can also handle large datasets efficiently and can be easily parallelized to speed up training. But if the data is very sparse, with many missing values, or if the feature space is very large, then it may be difficult for a random forest to capture all the complex interactions between features. In such cases, other techniques, such as matrix factorization or deep learning models, may be more suitable.

AdaBoost (Adaptive Boosting) is a machine learning algorithm that can be used in recommendation systems to improve their performance by combining multiple weak learners into strong learners. In a recommendation system, AdaBoost can be used to identify and weigh the most relevant features (e.g., user behavior, item properties, contextual information) to make personalized recommendations for each user. This can result in better generalization performance, especially when dealing with high-dimensional data sets. Also, we have used Google Maps Distance Matrix API that provides information about the distance and travel time between multiple locations. This API fetches the co-ordinates of the user's location and college location, giving out the distance. After comparing all the algorithms, we conclude that Adaboost works with the highest accuracy (95.677892), while random forest and Decision Tree stand at 94.876223 & 92.222567, respectively.

4. PROPOSED SYSTEM

The project also includes the creation of an Excel file, which the student may use as a reference for making the decision. The Excel file is built depending on the student's preferences. The student gets access to a set of filters that he or she may use to narrow down the list of colleges. Branch, Fee structure, Caste/Category, and distance of the institution from the student's location are among the criteria that the student can have in the Excel file of colleges (Table 1).

Table 1. Proposed system

Article Referred	No of the Factors Considered	Parameters Evaluated
College Admission Predictor Php	1	Percentile
College Admission Predictor and Smart List Generator	4	Percentile, Caste, Branch, Year
MHT-CET College Predictor, Shisksha	3	MHT-CET Score, State, Gender
College Admission Prediction Using Ensemble Machine Learning Models	2	Percentile, Location
Proposed system	5	Percentile, Caste, Branch, Location, Fees

5. RESULTS AND DISCUSSION

We give an interface where the user may pick choices after building the web app. The diagrams below explain how the web app works.

In Figure 1 and Figure 3, the panel on the left screen asks for different parameters the user wants in the list of colleges. The main screen asks for inputs like percentile, caste, branch, and fees according to the option selected in the panel.

Figure 1. Home page of the proposed system

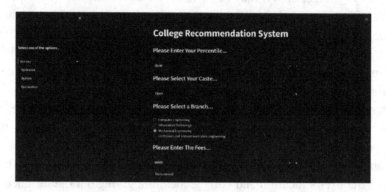

Figure 2. Output list of colleges with the selected parameters

Clg Code	College Name	Branch	Open	Fees
1105	Prof. Ram Meghe Institute of Technology & Research, Amravati	Mechanical Engineering	78.2630	55000
1012	Government College of Engineering,Yavatmal	Mechanical Engineering	73.9094	40000
1114	Sipna Shikshan Prasarak Mandal College of Engineering & Technology, Amravati	Mechanical Engineering	44.7581	54000
1117	Janata Shikshan Prasarak Mandal's Babasaheb Naik College Of Engineering, Pusad	Mechanical Engineering	43.4222	35000
1105	Prof. Ram Meghe Institute of Technology & Research, Amravati	Mechanical Engineering	42.6019	55000
1121	Shri Hanuman Vyayam Prasarak Mandals College of Engineering & Technology, Amravati	Mechanical Engineering	29.4873	50000
1116	Shri Shivaji Education Society's College of Engineering and Technology, Akola	Mechanical Engineering	16.8663	35000
1107	P. R. Pote (Patil) Education & Welfare Trust's Group of Institution(Integrated Campus), Amravati	Mechanical Engineering	15.0473	42000
1119	Paramhansa Ramkrishna Maunibaba Shikshan Santha's , Anuradha Engineering College, Chikhali	Mechanical Engineering	7.0736	32000
1120	Jawaharlal Darda Institute of Engineering and Technology, Yavatmal	Mechanical Engineering	3.2697	41000

Figure 2 is the output that we get after clicking on the recommend button. The output shows the list of colleges that the user is eligible for. The above output includes the name and codes of the colleges, the branch selected by the user, the cut-off percentile according to the selected caste, and the academic fee college charges.

The above figure 4 shows the output list along with the location feature. It gives the distance between the user's location and the college in km, along with the branch selected and cut-off percentiles.

Decision Tree Algorithm

One of the most common types of algorithms used in machine learning, a Decision Tree can be applied to both classification and regression work. It's a model that looks like a tree, and each node in it indicates a decision that's based on the importance of a different aspect. Nodes in the tree structure reflect decisions or tests on features, branches indicate the outcomes of these tests, and leaves represent the final anticipated output. The tree structure consists of nodes, branches, and leaves (class or value).

Figure 3. The screen displayed when we select the "by location" option

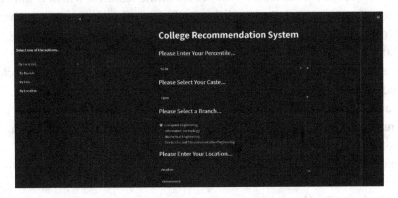

Figure 4. Output list with location feature

Clg Code	College Name	Branch	Open	Distance
1101	Shri Sant Gajanan Maharaj College of Engineering,Shegaon	Computer Engineering	90.4090	270.02875
1101	Shri Sant Gajanan Maharaj College of Engineering,Shegaon	Computer Engineering	90.4090	270.02875
1012	Government College of Engineering,Yavatmal	Computer Engineering	84.6386	430.82708
1105	Prof. Ram Meghe Institute of Technology & Research, Amravati	Computer Engineering	83.3519	370.40153
1114	Sipna Shikshan Prasarak Mandal College of Engineering & Technology, Amravati	Computer Engineering	76.0781	370.40153
1120	Jawaharlal Darda Institute of Engineering and Technology, Yavatmal	Computer Engineering	68.4657	430.82708
1107	P. R. Pote (Patil) Education & Welfare Trust's Group of Institution(Integrated Campus), Amravati	Computer Engineering	68.2279	370.40153
1128	Prof Ram Meghe College of Engineering and Management, Badnera	Computer Engineering	67.4741	380.78206
1121	Shri Hanuman Vyayam Prasarak Mandals College of Engineering & Technology, Amravati	Computer Engineering	66.4468	370.40153
1119	Paramhansa Ramkrishna Maunibaba Shikshan Santha's , Anuradha Engineering College, Chikhali	Computer Engineering	55.7162	577.64609

Decision Tree Structure

Root Node: The topmost node in the tree, which represents the initial decision or test on a specific feature.
Internal Nodes: Nodes in the middle of the tree that represent subsequent decisions or tests on features.
Branches: Connections between nodes, representing the outcomes of decisions or tests.
Leaves: Terminal nodes at the bottom of the tree that represent the final predicted output (class or value).

Decision Making

At each internal node, a decision is made based on the value of a specific feature. The tree branches into different paths based on the possible outcomes of the decision.

Training the Decision Tree: A labelled dataset is used to train the Decision Tree, and for each data point in the dataset, features and a label are associated with it (class or value). The dataset is divided into subsets by the algorithm on the basis of the values of the features, which results in the creation of decision nodes. The objective is to do splits in such a way that the resulting subsets are consistent with regard to the labels.

Splitting Criteria: The decision on which feature to split on and what values to use for the split is determined by a splitting criterion. Common criteria include Gini impurity (for classification) and mean squared error (for regression).

Stopping Criteria: The process of creating decision nodes and splits continues until a certain stopping criterion is met. This could be the maximum depth of the tree, the minimum number of samples in a leaf, or other criteria.

Prediction: To make predictions for a new data point, it traverses the tree from the root node to a leaf, following the decisions based on the features of the data point. The predicted output is the label associated with the leaf node.

Advantages: Decision Trees are easy to understand and interpret, making them a popular choice for explaining machine learning models to non-experts. They require minimal data pre-processing, such as normalization or scaling. They can handle both numerical and categorical data.

Disadvantages: Overfitting is a risk when using decision trees, and this risk increases with the depth and complexity of the tree. When a model "overfits," it means that it has captured noise that was present in the training data. They are prone to being affected by quite little shifts in the data. It's possible that Decision Trees won't work very well with datasets that have an uneven distribution of classes.

Ensemble Methods: To address overfitting, ensemble methods like Random Forests are often used. Random Forests build multiple Decision Trees and combine their predictions to improve accuracy and generalization.

Random Forest Algorithm: Random Forest is an algorithm for ensemble learning that is predicated on the idea of constructing a large number of decision trees during training and then outputting the class, which is either the mode of the classes (classification) or the mean prediction (regression) of the individual trees. Random Forest can be used for both classification and regression. It is a widely used and potent algorithm that is famous for the robustness and high accuracy it possesses.

Applications

Random Forest is used in a variety of applications, including:

Random Forest:
- ○ Classification: Identifying spam emails, diagnosing diseases, and image classification.
- ○ Regression: Predicting housing prices, stock prices, and other continuous variables.
- ○ Feature Importance Analysis: Determining the importance of features in a dataset.

Challenges:
- ○ Random forests might not perform well on very high-dimensional and sparse datasets.
- ○ The interpretability of a Random Forest model can be challenging due to the complexity of the ensemble.

Adaboost Algorithm

AdaBoost, short for Adaptive Boosting, is an ensemble learning algorithm designed to improve the performance of weak learners (usually decision trees) and create a strong classifier. It was introduced by Yoav Freund and Robert Schapire in 1996. AdaBoost works by iteratively giving more weight to misclassified samples, allowing subsequent weak learners to focus on the previously misclassified data points. AdaBoost is a powerful and versatile algorithm that has been successfully applied to various machine-learning tasks. It is especially useful when combined with weak learners that perform slightly better than random chance.

Applications

AdaBoost is commonly used in:

- Binary Classification: Spam detection, face detection, and medical diagnosis.
- Multi-Class Classification: Image recognition, handwriting recognition.

Challenges

- Sensitive to Noisy Data: AdaBoost can be sensitive to outliers and noisy data.
- Overfitting: While AdaBoost tends to generalize well, it can still overfit if the weak learners are too complex or if there is too much noise in the data.

The field of artificial intelligence (AI) known as machine learning (ML) focuses on the creation of statistical models and algorithms that provide computers the ability to carry out tasks without being explicitly programmed to do so. Machine learning is a subset of AI. The primary objective of the field of machine learning is to develop methods by which computers may acquire knowledge from data and gradually enhance their capabilities. It is a strong instrument for identifying patterns, developing hypotheses, and finding solutions to difficult situations. Learning by machine is a rapidly developing topic that is finding applications in a wide range of industries, including healthcare, finance, marketing, and cybersecurity, among others. Machine learning is continuing to play an important part in the automation of processes, the extraction of insights from data, and the facilitation of intelligent decision-making as technology continues to progress.

6. CONCLUSION

The present admission procedure at schools for higher studies is a stressful process that necessitates extensive research to choose the finest possible college. As a result of failing to conduct the necessary research, the student may be admitted to a less suitable college. This procedure should be simplified by developing an application that caters to the need to do the necessary analysis and output the most suited college. The web application has an easy-to-use interface. It needs the user to enter certain required information and presents the student with the likelihood of admission to the college. The student can also obtain a list of institutions based on the criteria specified, which can be utilized for application in the admissions process. While it is a user's option which institution is best suited to him or her, this program makes it easier for a user to choose from a large number of educational organizations where they wish to establish their career based on their preferences.

REFERENCES

Abdullahi, Y., Bhardwaj, A., Rahila, J., Anand, P., & Kandepu, K. (2023). Development of Automatic Change-Over with Auto-Start Timer and Artificial Intelligent Generator. *FMDB Transactions on Sustainable Energy Sequence*, *1*(1), 11–26.

Anand, P. P., Sulthan, N., Jayanth, P., & Deepika, A. A. (2023). A Creating Musical Compositions Through Recurrent Neural Networks: An Approach for Generating Melodic Creations. *FMDB Transactions on Sustainable Computing Systems*, *1*(2), 54–64.

Angeline, R., Aarthi, S., Regin, R., & Rajest, S. S. (2023). Dynamic intelligence-driven engineering flooding attack prediction using ensemble learning. In *Advances in Artificial and Human Intelligence in the Modern Era* (pp. 109–124). IGI Global. doi:10.4018/979-8-3693-1301-5.ch006

Girase, S., Powar, V., & Mukhopadhyay, D. (2017). A user-friendly college recommending system using user-profiling and matrix factorization technique. In *2017 International Conference on Computing, Communication and Automation (ICCCA)*. IEEE. 10.1109/CCAA.2017.8229779

Hamid, A., Ragab, M., Fatah, A., Mashat, S., & Khedra, A. M. (2012). Hybrid Recommender System for Predicting College Admission. In *12th International Conference on Intelligent Systems Design and Applications (ISDA)* (pp. 107–113). Academic Press.

Jain, V., Gupta, M., Kevadia, J., & Shinde, P. K. (2018). College Recommendation System. *International Journal of Engineering Research & Technology (Ahmedabad)*, *5*(01).

Kumari, K., Kataria, M., Limbani, V., & Soni, R. (2019). CAPSLG: College admission predictor and smart list generator. SSRN *Electronic Journal*. doi:10.2139/ssrn.3370798

Pande, S., & Chetty, M. S. R. (2018). Analysis of Capsule Network (Capsnet) Architectures and Applications. *Journal of Advanced Research in Dynamical and Control Systems*, *10*(10), 2765–2771.

Pande, S., & Chetty, M. S. R. (2019). Bezier Curve Based Medicinal Leaf Classification using Capsule Network. *International Journal of Advanced Trends in Computer Science and Engineering*, *8*(6), 2735–2742. doi:10.30534/ijatcse/2019/09862019

Pande, S. D., & Chetty, M. S. R. (2021). Fast medicinal leaf retrieval using CapsNet. In *Advances in Intelligent Systems and Computing* (pp. 149–155). Springer Singapore.

Rajasekaran, N., Jagatheesan, S. M., Krithika, S., & Albanchez, J. S. (2023). Development and Testing of Incorporated ASM with MVP Architecture Model for Android Mobile App Development. *FMDB Transactions on Sustainable Computing Systems*, *1*(2), 65–76.

Rajest, S. S., Singh, B., Obaid, A. J., Regin, R., & Chinnusamy, K. (2023b). Advances in artificial and human intelligence in the modern era. *Advances in Computational Intelligence and Robotics*. Advance online publication. doi:10.4018/979-8-3693-1301-5

Rajest, S. S., Singh, B. J., Obaid, A., Regin, R., & Chinnusamy, K. (2023a). Recent developments in machine and human intelligence. *Advances in Computational Intelligence and Robotics*. Advance online publication. doi:10.4018/978-1-6684-9189-8

Regin, R., Khanna, A. A., Krishnan, V., Gupta, M., Bose, R. S., & Rajest, S. S. (2023). Information design and unifying approach for secured data sharing using attribute-based access control mechanisms. In Recent Developments in Machine and Human Intelligence (pp. 256–276). IGI Global.

Sharma, V., Trehan, T., Chanana, R., & Dawn, S. (2019). StudieMe: College Recommendation System. In *2019 3rd International Conference on Recent Developments in Control, Automation & Power Engineering (RDCAPE)*. IEEE.

Shiksha.com. (2021). *Higher Education in India*. Retrieved November 14, 2023, from Shiksha.com website: https://www.shiksha.com

Singh, M., Sohani, P., Desai, J., Sharma, N. K., Chitte, P., & Gite, S. (2020). A Novel Approach for Colleges Recommendation for Admission Seekers Using Decision Tree. Ramrao Adik Institute of Technology.

Sivapriya, G. B. V., Ganesh, U. G., Pradeeshwar, V., Dharshini, M., & Al-Amin, M. (2023). Crime Prediction and Analysis Using Data Mining and Machine Learning: A Simple Approach that Helps Predictive Policing. *FMDB Transactions on Sustainable Computer Letters*, *1*(2), 64–75.

Sohlot, J., Teotia, P., Govinda, K., Rangineni, S., & Paramasivan, P. (2023). A Hybrid Approach on Fertilizer Resource Optimization in Agriculture Using Opposition-Based Harmony Search with Manta Ray Foraging Optimization. *FMDB Transactions on Sustainable Computing Systems*, *1*(1), 44–53.

Tian, Y., Zheng, B., Wang, Y., Zhang, Y., & Wu, Q. (2019). College library personalized recommendation system based on hybrid recommendation algorithm. *Procedia CIRP*, *83*, 490–494. doi:10.1016/j.procir.2019.04.126

Wang, Z., & Shi, Y. (2016). Prediction of the Admission Lines of College Entrance Examination based on Machine Learning. In *2nd IEEE International Conference on Computer and Communications* (pp. 332–335). IEEE.

Chapter 19
The Role of Talent Management to Accomplish Its Principal Purpose in Human Resource Management

Srinivas Kolachina
ⓘ https://orcid.org/0000-0002-9310-8218
Koneru Lakshmaiah Education Foundation, India

Pavan Kumar Rayapudi
Koneru Lakshmaiah Education Foundation, India

Swarna Sumanth
Koneru Lakshmaiah Education Foundation, India

S. Suman Rajest
ⓘ https://orcid.org/0000-0001-8315-3747
Dhaanish Ahmed College of Engineering, India

Venkat Rama Chowdary Godavarthi
Koneru Lakshmaiah Education Foundation, India

Nasir Abdul Jalil
Universiti Teknologi PETRONAS, Malaysia

ABSTRACT

Talent management is the constant system that includes attracting and retaining high-quality employees who have developed skills, professional planning, and interest in growth. This management continuously motivates the employees to improve their tasks and performances. The dependent variable measures the bundles of human resource management practices recruitment, performances, staffing, training, and developmental compensation. The independent variables of human resources are talent retention, career management, employee training, and talent attraction, while the dependent variables are employee engagement for growth in management. Talent management defines talent development as the work or efforts that were learned and the employee's improvement to continue the organizational performance. In order to understand the impact more clearly, a survey has been done on 65 employees taken on a random basis. The use of 13 questions was taken into consideration. The responses collected are then put into SPSS software to analyze the results using the proper testing method.

DOI: 10.4018/979-8-3693-0049-7.ch019

1. INTRODUCTION

Human Resources (HR) and Talent Management are crucial components in organizations aiming to maximize their performance and profitability (Akshaya & Naachimuthu, 2022). HR encompasses a range of functions dedicated to managing and developing human capital within an organization, while Talent Management focuses specifically on attracting, retaining, and developing high-potential employees. This professional draft will explore the role of HR and Talent Management in driving organizational success and optimizing profitability (Tambaip et al., 2023). Effective HR practices play a vital role in aligning the workforce with the organization's strategic goals. HR professionals are responsible for workforce planning, ensuring that the right talent is in place to meet current and future needs. Through strategic recruitment and selection processes, HR identifies and attracts candidates who possess the skills, knowledge, and attributes required for success in specific roles (Ramos et al., 2023).

Once talented individuals are brought on board, HR's role extends to employee onboarding, training, and development. By providing comprehensive induction programs and ongoing learning opportunities, HR ensures that employees are equipped with the necessary skills and knowledge to excel in their positions. Effective training and development initiatives not only enhance individual employee performance but also contribute to overall organizational productivity and profitability. Furthermore, HR plays a critical role in fostering employee engagement. Engaged employees are more committed, motivated, and productive, leading to improved organizational performance. HR professionals implement strategies to create a positive work environment, promote open communication, recognize and reward employee achievements, and provide avenues for career growth. By nurturing a culture of engagement and empowerment, HR drives employee satisfaction, retention, and, ultimately, organizational profitability (Naachimuthu et al., 2022).

Talent Management, as a subset of HR, focuses specifically on identifying and nurturing high-potential individuals within the organization. Through effective talent management practices, organizations can capitalize on their most valuable assets - talented employees - to maximize business outcomes. Talent Management encompasses various processes such as talent identification, succession planning, career development, and performance management (Rajest et al., 2023a). By implementing talent management initiatives, organizations can identify individuals with the potential to become future leaders. Through mentorship programs, job rotations, and targeted development plans, HR professionals provide talented employees with the necessary support and opportunities to grow their skills and knowledge. This strategic investment in talent not only enhances individual performance but also cultivates a pipeline of capable leaders who can drive the organization toward sustainable growth and profitability (Vashishtha & Dhawan, 2023).

Moreover, HR and Talent Management go hand in hand in creating a culture of continuous improvement. HR professionals facilitate performance management systems that establish clear performance expectations, provide regular feedback, and link individual goals to organizational objectives (Venkateswaran et al., 2023). By aligning performance management with talent management initiatives, HR professionals ensure that high-potential individuals receive the necessary guidance and recognition for their contributions, thus motivating them to continue excelling in their roles (Nagarajan & Naachimuthu, 2021). Talent Management is the constant system that includes attracting and retaining high-quality employees who have developed skills, professional planning, and interest in growth (Anand et al., 2023). This management continuously motivates the employees to improve their tasks and performances (Padmapriya & Naachimuthu, 2023). The main purpose of this Talent management is to create a good, skilled, and motivated workforce who'll able to work with any company in this long journey. In human resources, Talent management is how the employees recruit and engage in the job and develop a workforce (Aswathi et al., 2021).

Rethinking Talent Management: Applying Just-in-Time Principles to Develop and Retain Talent

Peter Cappelli, A Management Professor at Wharton School, has authored an article published in Harvard Business Review about a novel way to look at Talent Management, which he names the Talen on Demand Framework. Let us have a brief glance at the same (Alayli, 2023).

Traditional talent management approaches have often struggled to keep pace with the dynamic demands of the modern business landscape (Kumar & Naachimuthu, 2023). However, by drawing inspiration from supply chain management principles, organizations can adopt a talent-on-demand framework akin to just-in-time manufacturing. This approach enables companies to effectively anticipate talent needs, reduce bottlenecks, and adapt to evolving demands (Sri et al., 2022). By embracing four key principles Make and Buy to Manage Risk, Adapt to Uncertainty in Talent Demand, Improve Return on Investment in Developing Employees, and Preserve the Investment by Balancing Employee-Employer Interests companies can revolutionize their talent management strategies and optimize their workforce capabilities (Srinivas et al., 2023).

Principle 1: Manage Risk by Making and Buying

In the past, organizations aimed to develop all their leaders internally, resulting in talent shortages and inefficiencies (Kuragayala, 2023). Today, the approach must be more balanced. While internal talent development remains cost-effective and less disruptive, external hiring can provide faster and more responsive solutions. To strike the right balance, organizations should abandon the notion of accurately predicting talent demand and instead embrace short-term simulations and forecasting (Shifana & Naa Chimuthu, 2022). By utilizing sophisticated software and collaborating with operational executives, companies can make informed decisions on the optimal mix of internal development and external hiring to mitigate risks and meet talent needs efficiently (Sudheer & Naachimuthu, 2022).

Principle 2: Adjust to Talent Demand Uncertainty

Similar to how supply chain managers shorten their time horizon for demand forecasts, talent managers can benefit from shorter and more responsive forecasts (María et al., 2023). For instance, splitting a new cohort of hires into smaller groups that join the organization at different times can alleviate the pressure to find numerous roles all at once (Angeline et al., 2023). By forecasting demand in shorter periods throughout employees' careers, organizations can improve accuracy and better coordinate developmental assignments (Sabti et al., 2023). Additionally, breaking down long training programs into discrete parts with their own forecasts reduces redundancy in training investments and enhances the adaptability of talent management strategies (Saxena et al., 2023).

Principle 3: Increase ROI on Employee Development

Historically, companies considered their expensive development programs as unavoidable costs of doing business (Tripathi & Al-Shahri, 2023). However, the changing dynamics of the talent pool, characterized by decreased loyalty and increased market mobility, present opportunities to lower training costs and improve return on investment (ROI) (Kumar et al., 2023). One approach is to engage employees in sharing the costs of their own development (Venkateswaran et al., 2023). This can be achieved by encouraging employees to take on voluntary learning projects in addition to their regular work (Pandit, 2023). Another effective strategy is to retain employees for a predictable period, such as through contracts that require repayment of training costs if they leave early (Vashishtha & Kapoor, 2023). Moreover, companies can maintain ties with former employees by investing in small efforts to keep them connected, benefiting from their updated skills and potential returns in the future (Hana & Naachimuthu, 2023).

Principle 4: Balance Employee-Employer Interests to Protect Investment

While talent portability empowers employees to make career decisions based on their preferences, it also presents challenges for employers seeking to retain and develop their top talent. To improve retention rates and align employee and employer interests, organizations have transitioned from the traditional chess-master model to internal job boards (Hana et al., 2022). These boards enable employees to explore and apply for internal openings, fostering greater autonomy in career management (Rajest et al., 2023b). By empowering employees with job mobility within the organization, companies can reduce turnover and improve employee satisfaction (Ocoró et al., 2023). By adopting a talent-on-demand framework inspired by just-in-time manufacturing and supply chain management principles, organizations can revolutionize their talent management strategies. Embracing the four key principles discussed Make and Buy to Manage Risk, Adapt to Uncertainty in Talent Demand, Improve Return on Investment in Developing Employees, and Preserve the Investment by Balancing Employee-Employer Interests enables organizations to anticipate talent needs, optimize development efforts, reduce costs, and enhance employee retention.

Aims

The study's purpose is to find the impact on Human resources due to the development of Talent Management taken as a main criterion in internal organization operations data admixture.

Research Objectives

RO 1: To evaluate the development of the training process management in human resource
RO 2: To know the generate the talent management for improving the development of human resources
RO 3: To understand the retention process for employment in human resource
RO 4: To keep the safety in the workplace in human resource

Research Questions

RQ 1: What questions to ask when developing the training program?
RQ 2: How can the talent management process be improved?

RQ 3: What should be done to retain the employees?
RQ 4: What are the objectives of the employee retention questionnaire

2. LITERATURE REVIEW

Talent management is a multidisciplinary field that has been widely explored and researched by numerous authors. Below is a literature review highlighting the key contributions of various authors in the field of talent management:

The dependent variable measures the bundles of human resource management practices recruitment, performances, staffing, training, and developmental compensation (Priscila et al., 2023). As stated by Kravariti & Johnston (2020), Company performance of human resources is a variable that is dependent and measured by job or service quality, technological innovation, and sales management growth (Atasever, 2023). The independent variables of human resources are talent retention, career management, employee training, and talent attraction, while the dependent variables are employee engagement for growth in management (Said & Tripathi, 2023). However, Liker, (2021) specifies that Essentially, the independent variable is the input while the dependent variable is the output.

Figure 1. Important role of human resource (Liker, 2021)

Figure 1 shows that Talent Management uses independent variables to access sales, expenses, profitability, performances, and more. Workforce planning is the system or process of analyzing, planning workforce supply, forecasting, marketing demand, and assessing gaps to ensure that any organization has the right employees with the correct professional skills in the right places at the correct time to fulfill their intention (Savya & Naachimuthu, 2022).

Talent management is developing the industries, appropriate atmosphere at service, effective performances, and potential talent for growing productivity and learning. As stated by Claus (2019), Talent management aims at engaging and retaining efficient and high-performing employees, while performance management targets setting the performance objective, activities, and aims according to the management planning and performances. Talent management wants constructive feedback, career goals, aims, and opportunities to achieve success by providing mental, physical, and emotional support and encouragement. Employee motivation strategies are engaged, interest in their responsibilities, and processes are put in place to keep the employees inspired.

Figure 2. Creation of motivation level by talent management (Mattis, 2018)

Figure 2 states different processes of Creation of motivation level by Talent Management, which undertakes its development process. However, (Mattis, 2018) specifies that Talent resource motivates employees to provide clearance about any expectation, regular recognition, praise, a clear understanding, and a caring attitude with respect.

Michaels et al., (2001), which is considered a landmark in talent management literature. They emphasize the importance of identifying, attracting, developing, and retaining top talent in organizations. They argue that talent is a critical source of competitive advantage and provides practical strategies for managing talent effectively.

In a book titled "Talent Is Overrated" by Colvin, (2008) challenges the traditional notion that talent is innate and instead argues that deliberate practice and focused effort are the primary drivers of exceptional performance. He explores the concept of deliberate practice and its implications for talent development and suggests that talent management should focus on providing opportunities for deliberate practice rather than solely relying on natural abilities.

Berger & Berger, (2010) edited a book titled "The Talent Management Handbook." This comprehensive handbook, first published in 2004 and updated in subsequent editions, provides a compilation of articles by multiple authors covering various aspects of talent management. It includes chapters on talent acquisition, performance management, leadership development, succession planning, and employee engagement. The book offers a wealth of practical strategies, tools, and case studies for implementing effective talent management practices.

Conaty & Charan, (2010) published a book named "The Talent Masters" in 2010, which presents insights from interviews with top executives from various companies known for their talent management practices. Conaty and Charan (2010) emphasize the importance of developing a talent mindset throughout the organization and provide practical guidance on talent assessment, development, and succession planning.

Iles et al., (2010). explored various aspects of Talent Management in her research work titled "Talent Management and HRM in Multinational Companies in Beijing: Definitions, Differences, and Drivers." This research article, published in 2010, explores the definitions, differences, and drivers of talent management in multinational companies (MNCs) operating in Beijing. Iles et al., (2010) discussed the challenges faced by MNCs in talent management and examines the influence of cultural factors on talent management practices. The study provides valuable insights into the complexities of talent management in a global context.

Singh et al., (2023) investigated the impact of talent management practices on employee engagement in two different organizations in 2014 in one of their research works. Their study reveals that organizations with robust talent management programs have higher levels of employee engagement. They emphasize the role of talent management in creating opportunities for employee development and growth, which in turn foster engagement and commitment.

In 2020, a research article titled "Talent Management: A Critical Review" by McDonnell & Wiblen, (2020) provide a critical review of the talent management literature. The authors analyze the definitions, theoretical foundations, and key themes in talent management research. They highlight the need for a more holistic and integrated approach to talent management and call for further research to bridge the gap between theory and practice.

Phoek et al., (2023) explored the effectiveness of Talent Management in connection with employee motivation and engagement. They examined the relationship between talent management effectiveness, employee motivation, and engagement. Their study suggests that effective talent management practices positively influence employee motivation and engagement, leading to improved organizational performance. The authors highlight the importance of creating a supportive and engaging work environment to enhance talent management outcomes.

Priyadarshini & Naachimuthu, (2020), analyzed the relationship between talent management practices and business performance. Their research shows a positive association between talent management and financial performance, highlighting the strategic value of effective talent management. The authors emphasize the importance of aligning talent management practices with organizational goals and continuously evaluating their impact on business outcomes.

Tambe et al., (2019) discussed the implications of digital transformation on talent management. They highlight the importance of HR's role in adapting talent management strategies to the digital age, including leveraging technology for talent acquisition, development, and engagement. The authors suggested that organizations need to embrace digital platforms and tools to effectively manage talent in the evolving digital landscape.

Hana et al., (2022) explore the relationship between talent management, job embeddedness, employee engagement, and retention in their research work published in 2022. Their study finds that talent management practices positively impact job embeddedness, which in turn enhances employee engagement and reduces turnover intentions. The authors emphasize the significance of talent management in creating a sense of belonging and commitment among employees.

As stated by Liker (2021), Talent Management keeps focusing on the activities and processes used to notify the key position, the development of high potential, high-performing employees to fulfill the roles of the company, and the constant management of such workers with the differentiated architecture of human resources. Talent management defines talent development as the work or efforts that were learned and the employee's improvement to continue the organizational performance results in good productivity; however, Gallardo-Gallardo et al., (2018) this management focuses on the candidates with natural strengths, effective in the required services, and motivations.

These are just a few examples of the extensive literature available on talent management. The field continues to evolve as researchers and practitioners explore new perspectives, theories, and strategies to effectively attract, develop, and retain talent in organizations.

3. METHODOLOGY

The study conducted by Duggan et al., (2020) aimed to investigate the importance of human resources and the impact of talent management on it. To gain a clearer understanding of this impact, a survey was conducted among 65 randomly selected employees. Liker (2021) mentions that the survey consisted of 13 questions, which were designed to gather data on various aspects of talent management. The responses collected from the survey were then analyzed using the SPSS software, employing appropriate testing methods such as hypothesis testing and demographic analysis.

Conducting a primary survey is an essential step in research as it allows researchers to gather data directly from different sources. By including responses from various individuals, the survey aims to increase the information and knowledge available on the topic of talent management in human resources. This comprehensive approach enhances the overall quality of the research and provides a broader perspective on the subject matter.

The researcher followed a sequential approach to conducting the research, ensuring that each step was carried out in a systematic manner. This includes designing the survey questionnaire, collecting responses, and analyzing the data using quantitative analysis methods. Quantitative analysis provides a structured strategy to understand and interpret the data gathered, allowing the researcher to explore various topics and questions in detail.

By employing appropriate research methods and data analysis techniques, the study aimed to uncover the major impacts of talent management on the human resources department. The use of hypothesis testing helps to validate or refute specific assumptions or claims, providing valuable insights into the relationship between talent management practices and human resources outcomes (Regin et al., 2023). Additionally, demographic analysis allows for a deeper understanding of how different factors, such as age, gender, or experience, may influence the perceptions and experiences of employees in relation to talent management.

The study conducted a primary survey to investigate the importance of human resources and the impact of talent management. The survey included 13 questions and gathered responses from 65 randomly selected employees. The collected data was then analyzed using SPSS software, employing hypothesis testing and demographic analysis methods. By following a sequential research approach and utilizing quantitative analysis, the study aimed to provide detailed insights into the relationship between talent management and human resources, contributing to the overall knowledge and understanding of this topic.

Hypothesis Testing

Hypothesis 1

H1: Talent management greatly influences the role of Human resources
H0: Talent management doesn't have any influence on the role of Human resources

Hypothesis 2

H1: Management criteria decide the development of Human resources
H0: Management Criteria do not decide the development of Human resources

Hypothesis 3

H1: Workforce planning develops the productivity of human resources
H0: Workforce planning doesn't have any development of Human resource

Demographic Data: Age

The maximum percentage of the respondents is from the age of 15 to 35 as 23.08% of them are in this group of age as the respondents know about the market more in detail. The respondents between the ages of 35 and 50 are 38.46%, and the others who are between the ages of 50 and 60 are 38.46% (Figure 3).

Figure 3. Age analysis (SPSS)

What is your age?

		Frequency	Percent	Valid Percent	Cumulative Percent
Valid	Between 15 to 35	15	23.1	23.1	23.1
	Between 35 to 50	25	38.5	38.5	61.5
	Between 50 to 60	25	38.5	38.5	100.0
	Total	65	100.0	100.0	

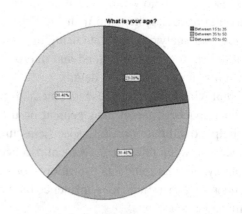

Gender

30.77% are male respondents, and the female respondents are 53.85% and 15.38 % prefer not to say their gender (Figure 4).

Figure 4. Gender analysis (SPSS)

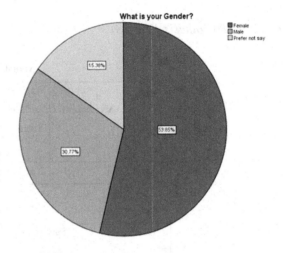

What is your Gender?

		Frequency	Percent	Valid Percent	Cumulative Percent
Valid	Female	35	53.8	53.8	53.8
	Male	20	30.8	30.8	84.6
	Prefer not say	10	15.4	15.4	100.0
	Total	65	100.0	100.0	

Monthly Income

30.77% of respondents have an income above 50000, 7.69% of respondents have an income between 10000 to 25000, 30.77% of the respondents have an income between 25000 and 35000, and lastly, 30.77% of respondents have between 35000 to 50000 approx (Figure 5).

Figure 5. Analysis of monthly income (SPSS)

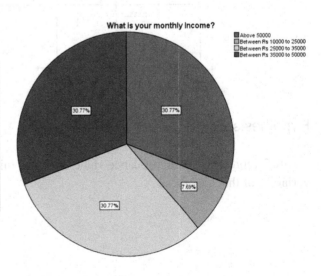

What is your monthly Income?

		Frequency	Percent	Valid Percent	Cumulative Percent
Valid	Above 50000	20	30.8	30.8	30.8
	Between Rs 10000 to 25000	5	7.7	7.7	38.5
	Between Rs 25000 to 35000	20	30.8	30.8	69.2
	Between Rs 35000 to 50000	20	30.8	30.8	100.0
	Total	65	100.0	100.0	

Descriptive Analysis

Hypothesis 1

The significance value of regression analysis represented in Figure 6 is 0, which represents the variables of this hypothesis are correlated.

Figure 6. Hypothesis 1 (SPSS)

Model Summary[b]

Model	R	R Square	Adjusted R Square	Std. Error of the Estimate	Change Statistics					Durbin-Watson
					R Square Change	F Change	df1	df2	Sig. F Change	
1	.431[a]	.186	.173	2.86417	.186	14.359	1	63	.000	2.545

ANOVA[a]

Model		Sum of Squares	df	Mean Square	F	Sig.
1	Regression	117.795	1	117.795	14.359	.000[b]
	Residual	516.820	63	8.203		
	Total	634.615	64			

Coefficients[a]

Model		Unstandardized Coefficients		Standardized Coefficients	t	Sig.
		B	Std. Error	Beta		
1	(Constant)	3.171	2.076		1.527	.132
	IV1	.659	.174	.431	3.789	.000

Hypothesis 2

Figure 7 represents the significance value of 0, and this represents the strong relationship between the variables of this hypothesis.

Figure 7. **Hypothesis 2** *(SPSS)*

Model Summary[b]

Model	R	R Square	Adjusted R Square	Std. Error of the Estimate	Change Statistics					Durbin-Watson
					R Square Change	F Change	df1	df2	Sig. F Change	
1	.656[a]	.431	.422	2.39449	.431	47.684	1	63	.000	2.181

ANOVA[a]

Model		Sum of Squares	df	Mean Square	F	Sig.
1	Regression	273.400	1	273.400	47.684	.000[b]
	Residual	361.215	63	5.734		
	Total	634.615	64			

Coefficients[a]

Model		Unstandardized Coefficients		Standardized Coefficients	t	Sig.
		B	Std. Error	Beta		
1	(Constant)	4.875	.925		5.272	.000
	IV2	.811	.117	.656	6.905	.000

Hypothesis 3

This hypothesis has a significance value of 0, and this value is ideal if it is below 0.005 (Figure 8). This means the different variables are strongly related to each other.

4. DISCUSSION

Talent management is a critical aspect of human resource management that focuses on developing and leveraging the skills, abilities, and potential of employees to drive organizational success and foster economic growth. It encompasses various practices such as staffing plans, workplace policies, recruitment, selection, training, and performance improvement. The ultimate goal of talent management is to align the capabilities and aspirations of employees with the strategic objectives of the organization.

According to Arif et al., (2019), Human Resources is a comprehensive system that encompasses the entire employee lifecycle, from hiring and employing individuals to training, compensating, and developing their functions within the organization. In this context, talent management plays a crucial role in

Figure 8. **Hypothesis 3** *(SPSS)*

Model Summary[b]

Model	R	R Square	Adjusted R Square	Std. Error of the Estimate	Change Statistics					Durbin-Watson
					R Square Change	F Change	df1	df2	Sig. F Change	
1	.656[a]	.431	.422	2.39449	.431	47.684	1	63	.000	2.181

ANOVA[a]

	Model	Sum of Squares	df	Mean Square	F	Sig.
1	Regression	273.400	1	273.400	47.684	.000[b]
	Residual	361.215	63	5.734		
	Total	634.615	64			

Coefficients[a]

	Model	Unstandardized Coefficients		Standardized Coefficients	t	Sig.
		B	Std. Error	Beta		
1	(Constant)	4.875	.925		5.272	.000
	IV2	.811	.117	.656	6.905	.000

ensuring that the right individuals are recruited and selected for positions that best match their skills and potential. It also involves providing continuous training and development opportunities to enhance their performance and contribute to their professional growth.

Managers at all levels have a role to play in talent management. They are responsible for identifying and nurturing talent within their teams, providing guidance and support, and creating a conducive work environment that encourages employee growth and engagement. This is in line with McDonnell & Wiblen, (2020) perspective that every manager has a role in human resource management.

One of the key practices within talent management is the talent review, as highlighted by Duggan et al., (2020). Talent reviews are meetings where company leaders discuss and evaluate employees' performance, potential, and readiness for future positions. These discussions enable leaders to identify high-performing employees, recognize their contributions, and provide them with opportunities for growth and advancement. Talent reviews also facilitate the identification of leadership potential and help in succession planning, ensuring that the organization has a pipeline of talented individuals ready to assume key roles.

Effective talent management is built on fostering positive relationships between leaders and employees. Leaders who actively engage with their team members can influence and inspire them to deliver improved performance and service quality. By recognizing and rewarding high performers, talent management encourages a culture of excellence and motivates employees to strive for continuous improvement.

Furthermore, talent management involves developing strategies and programs that cater to employees at different levels of the organization. This includes identifying potential leaders, providing them with the necessary training and development opportunities, and aligning their skills and capabilities with the leadership requirements of the organization.

To summarize, Talent management is a comprehensive approach to human resource management that focuses on hiring, developing, and leveraging the potential of employees. It involves various practices such as staffing plans, workplace policies, recruitment, selection, training, and performance improvement. Talent management recognizes high performers, fosters positive relationships between leaders and employees, and aims to align individual capabilities with organizational objectives. By investing in talent management, organizations can create a motivated and skilled workforce that drives economic growth and enhances overall business performance.

5. CONCLUSION

Human resource management (HRM) is an essential function within any organization, as it aligns workforce levels with the company's requirements and ensures the long-term engagement and satisfaction of employees. HRM involves effectively managing and deploying the organization's human capital to propel it towards its goals. By optimizing employee performance, HRM supports the strategic objectives and initiatives of the organization. One crucial aspect of HRM is talent management, which encompasses various activities such as recruitment, employee selection, onboarding, training, and skills development. Talent management aims to identify and attract individuals with the right skills and potential to contribute to the organization's success. It involves creating an environment that fosters growth and learning, providing employees with the necessary resources and opportunities to excel in their roles. The research on talent management of human resources entails a comprehensive examination of the various factors that influence the effective management of talent. This research process involves determining the key elements and strategies necessary for recruiting, retaining, and developing a high-performing workforce. By understanding these factors, organizations can create robust talent management programs that attract top talent, enhance employee engagement, and align individual goals with organizational objectives.

REFERENCES

Akshaya, A., & Naachimuthu, K. P. (2022). Locavorism to Enhance Environmental, Social, & Economic Well-being. *Indian Journal of Agriculture Business*, *8*(1), 25–33.

Alayli, S. (2023). Unravelling the Drivers of Online Purchasing Intention: The E-Commerce Scenario in Lebanon. *FMDB Transactions on Sustainable Social Sciences Letters*, *1*(1), 56–67.

Anand, P. P., Kanike, U. K., Paramasivan, P., Rajest, S. S., Regin, R., & Priscila, S. S. (2023). Embracing Industry 5.0: Pioneering Next-Generation Technology for a Flourishing Human Experience and Societal Advancement. *FMDB Transactions on Sustainable Social Sciences Letters*, *1*(1), 43–55.

Angeline, R., Aarthi, S., Regin, R., & Rajest, S. S. (2023). Dynamic intelligence-driven engineering flooding attack prediction using ensemble learning. In *Advances in Artificial and Human Intelligence in the Modern Era* (pp. 109–124). IGI Global. doi:10.4018/979-8-3693-1301-5.ch006

Arif, S., Zainudin, H. K., & Hamid, A. (2019). Influence of Leadership, Organizational Culture, Work Motivation, and Job Satisfaction of Performance Principles of Senior High School in Medan City. *Budapest International Research and Critics Institute-Journal (BIRCI-Journal), 2*(4), 239-254.

Aswathi, P., Sangavi, P., Naachimuthu, K. P., & Krishna, T. (2021). *Proceedings of the ICSSR Sponsored Webinar on Human Behavior and Environmental Sustainability*. Academic Press.

Atasever, M. (2023). Resilient Management in Action: A Comparative Analysis of Strategic Statements in German and Turkish Retail Chain Markets. *FMDB Transactions on Sustainable Management Letters, 1*(2), 66–81.

Berger, L., & Berger, D. (2010). *The Talent Management Handbook: Creating a sustainable competitive advantage by selecting, developing, and promoting the best people*. McGraw Hill Professional.

Claus, L. (2019). HR disruption Time already to reinvent talent management. *Business Research Quarterly, 22*(3), 207–215. doi:10.1016/j.brq.2019.04.002

Colvin, G. (2008). *Talent is overrated: What really separated world-class performers from everybody else*. Penguin.

Conaty, B., & Charan, R. (2010). *The talent masters: Why smart leaders put people before numbers*. Random House Digital.

Duggan, J., Sherman, U., Carbery, R., & McDonnell, A. (2020). Algorithmic management and app-work in the gig economy: A research agenda for employment relations and HRM. *Human Resource Management Journal, 30*(1), 114–132. doi:10.1111/1748-8583.12258

Gallardo-Gallardo, E., Thunnissen, M., & Scullion, H. (2020). Talent management: Context matters. *International Journal of Human Resource Management, 31*(4), 457–473. doi:10.1080/09585192.2019.1642645

Hana, M., & Naachimuthu, K. P. (2023). A Comprehensive Model on Rejection Sensitivity. *South India Journal of Social Sciences, 21*(19), 19–31.

Hana, M., Vishnupriya, S., & Naachimuthu, K. P. (2022). Restorative Effect of Direct and Indirect Nature Exposure - A Systematic Review. *International Journal of Scientific Research, 11*(5), 10–15.

Iles, P., Chuai, X., & Preece, D. (2010). Talent Management and HRM in Multinational companies in Beijing: Definitions, differences and drivers. *Journal of World Business, 45*(2), 179–189. doi:10.1016/j.jwb.2009.09.014

Kravariti, F., & Johnston, K. (2020). Talent management: A critical literature review and research agenda for public sector human resource management. *Public Management Review, 22*(1), 75–95. doi:10.1080/14719037.2019.1638439

Kumar, A., & Naachimuthu, K. P. (2023). Market Potential for Shawarma Outlet in Coimbatore - An Analysis. *South India Journal of Social Sciences*, *21*(1), 130–140.

Kumar, S. A., Rajest, S. S., Aravind, B. R., & Bhuvaneswari, G. (2023). Virtual learning styles based on learning style detection. *International Journal of Knowledge and Learning*, *1*(1), 10057158. Advance online publication. doi:10.1504/IJKL.2023.10057158

Kuragayala, P. S. (2023). A Systematic Review on Workforce Development in Healthcare Sector: Implications in the Post-COVID Scenario. *FMDB Transactions on Sustainable Technoprise Letters*, *1*(1), 36–46.

Liker, J. K. (2021). *Toyota way: 14 management principles from the world's greatest manufacturer*. McGraw-Hill Education.

María, J. J. L., Polo, O. C. C., & Elhadary, T. (2023). An Analysis of the Morality and Social Responsibility of Non-Profit Organizations. *FMDB Transactions on Sustainable Technoprise Letters*, *1*(1), 28–35.

Mattis, J. (2018). *National Defense Strategy of the United States of America*. Department of Defense Washington United States.

McDonnell, A., & Wiblen, S. (2020). *Talent management: A research overview*. Routledge. doi:10.4324/9780429342301

Michaels, E., Handfield-Jones, H., & Axelrod, B. (2001). *The war for talent*. Harvard Business Press.

Naachimuthu, K. P., Ganga, S., & Mathiyoli, P. M. (2022). Psychosocial Impact of COVID-19 Lockdown. *IAHRW International Journal of Social Sciences Review*, *10*(1), 52–59.

Nagarajan, G., & Naachimuthu, K. P. (2021). Positive Emotions and Experiences of Trans Men and Trans Women - A Grounded Theory Approach. *International Journal of Early Childhood Special Education*, *14*(2), 6430–6447.

Ocoró, M. P., Polo, O. C. C., & Khandare, S. (2023). Importance of Business Financial Risk Analysis in SMEs According to COVID-19. *FMDB Transactions on Sustainable Management Letters*, *1*(1), 12–21.

Padmapriya, P., & Naachimuthu, K. P. (2023). Social and Philosophical Construction of Emotions in Bhagavad Gita & Plutchik Wheel of Emotions. *Journal of the Asiatic Society of Mumbai*, *XCVI*(27), 22–36.

Pandit, P. (2023). On the Context of the Principle of Beneficence: The Problem of Over Demandingness within Utilitarian Theory. *FMDB Transactions on Sustainable Social Sciences Letters*, *1*(1), 26–42.

Phoek, S. E. M., Lauwinata, L., & Kowarin, L. R. N. (2023). Tourism Development in Merauke Regency, South Papua Province: Strengthening Physical Infrastructure for Local Economic Growth and Enchanting Tourist Attractions. *FMDB Transactions on Sustainable Management Letters*, *1*(2), 82–94.

Priscila, S. S., Rajest, S. S., Tadiboina, S. N., Regin, R., & András, S. (2023). Analysis of Machine Learning and Deep Learning Methods for Superstore Sales Prediction. *FMDB Transactions on Sustainable Computer Letters*, *1*(1), 1–11.

Priyadarshini, N. S., & Naachimuthu, K. P. (2020). Ancient and Modern Conception to Virtues: Comparing Naaladiyar and Positive Psychology. In *International Conference on Multi Facets of Sacred Literature* (pp. 1–12). Academic Press.

Rajest, S. S., Singh, B., Obaid, A. J., Regin, R., & Chinnusamy, K. (Eds.). (2023b). Advances in Computational Intelligence and Robotics *Advances in artificial and human intelligence in the modern era.* doi:10.4018/979-8-3693-1301-5

Rajest, S. S., Singh, B., Obaid, J. A., Regin, R., & Chinnusamy, K. (Eds.). (2023a). Recent developments in machine and human intelligence. Advances in Computational Intelligence and Robotics. doi:10.4018/978-1-6684-9189-8

Ramos, J. I., Lacerona, R., & Nunag, J. M. (2023). A Study on Operational Excellence, Work Environment Factors and the Impact to Employee Performance. *FMDB Transactions on Sustainable Social Sciences Letters*, 1(1), 12–25.

Regin, R., Khanna, A. A., Krishnan, V., Gupta, M., Bose, R. S., & Rajest, S. S. (2023). Information design and unifying approach for secured data sharing using attribute-based access control mechanisms. In Recent Developments in Machine and Human Intelligence (pp. 256–276). IGI Global.

Sabti, Y. M., Alqatrani, R. I. N., Zaid, M. I., Taengkliang, B., & Kareem, J. M. (2023). Impact of Business Environment on the Performance of Employees in the Public-Listed Companies. *FMDB Transactions on Sustainable Management Letters*, 1(2), 56–65.

Said, F. B., & Tripathi, S. (2023). Epistemology of Digital Journalism Shift in South Global Nations: A Bibliometric Analysis. *FMDB Transactions on Sustainable Technoprise Letters*, 1(1), 47–60.

Savya, N., & Naachimuthu, K. P. (2022). Psychosocial Determinants of Name Dropping: A Conceptual Framework. *Madhya Bharti - Humanities and Social Sciences, 83*(14), 1–12.

Saxena, D., Khandare, S., & Chaudhary, S. (2023). An Overview of ChatGPT: Impact on Academic Learning. *FMDB Transactions on Sustainable Techno Learning*, 1(1), 11–20.

Shifana, F., & Naachimuthu, K. P. (2022). Elements of Holistic Human Development in Naanmanikkadigai: A Hermeneutic Study. *Journal of Positive School Psychology*, 6(4), 2218–2231.

Singh, M., Bhushan, M., Sharma, R., & Cavaliere, L. P. L. (2023). An Organized Assessment of the Literature of Entrepreneurial Skills and Emotional Intelligence. *FMDB Transactions on Sustainable Management Letters*, 1(3), 95–104.

Sri, G. P., Jayapriya, J., Poornima, T., & Naachimuthu, K. P. (2022). Hermeneutics of Iniyavai Naarpadhu and Inna Naarpadhu. *Journal of Positive School Psychology*, 6(8), 4358–4368.

Srinivas, K., Velmurugan, P. R., & Andiyappillai, N. (2023). Digital Human Resources and Management Support Improve Human Resources Effectiveness. *FMDB Transactions on Sustainable Management Letters*, 1(1), 32–45.

Sudheer, V., & Naachimuthu, K. P. (2022). Effect of JPMR on State-Trait Anxiety Among Young Female Adults During COVID-19 Pandemic Lockdown. *International Journal of Health Sciences*, 6(55), 1192–1202. doi:10.53730/ijhs.v6nS5.8848

Tambaip, B., Hadi, A. F. F., & Tjilen, A. P. (2023). Optimizing Public Service Performance: Unleashing the Potential of Compassion as an Indicator of Public Service Motivation. *FMDB Transactions on Sustainable Management Letters*, 1(2), 46–55.

Tambe, P., Cappelli, P., & Yakubovich, V. (2019). Artificial intelligence in human resources management: Challenges and a path forward. *California Management Review*, *61*(4), 15–42. doi:10.1177/0008125619867910

Tripathi, S., & Al-Shahri, M. (2023). Problems and Prospects on the Evolution of Advertising and Public Relations Industries in Oman. *FMDB Transactions on Sustainable Management Letters*, *1*(1), 1–11.

Vashishtha, E., & Dhawan, G. (2023). Comparison of Baldrige Criteria of Strategy Planning and Harrison Text. *FMDB Transactions on Sustainable Management Letters*, *1*(1), 22–31.

Vashishtha, E., & Kapoor, H. (2023). Implementation of Blockchain Technology Across International Healthcare Markets. *FMDB Transactions on Sustainable Technoprise Letters*, *1*(1), 1–12.

Venkateswaran, P. S., Singh, S., Paramasivan, P., Rajest, S. S., Lourens, M. E., & Regin, R. (2023). A Study on The Influence of Quality of Service on Customer Satisfaction Towards Hotel Industry. *FMDB Transactions on Sustainable Social Sciences Letters*, *1*(1), 1–11.

Venkateswaran, P. S., & Viktor, P. (2023). A Study on Brand Equity of Fast-Moving Consumer Goods with Reference to Madurai, Tamil Nadu. *FMDB Transactions on Sustainable Technoprise Letters*, *1*(1), 13–27.

APPENDIX

Survey Questions

- What is your Gender?
- What is your age?
- What is your monthly income?
- DV: Human Resources
- Employee management requires proper strategies to have more organizational development.
- Human Resource development needs proper training and motivation skills to be included.
- Leadership skills with proper implementation strategies make the internal environment more effective.
- IV1: Talent Management
- Employee engagement largely depends on the process of strategic implementation.
- Talent management creates more positive scope in the case of setting goals and overall tracking.
- Personnel are more motivated to work on their internal development
- IV2: Management Criteria
- Management is more responsible for the level of motivation in the employees.
- Competencies and goal tracking are the larger tools to recognize the skills of an employee.
- IV3: Workforce Planning
- Proper Alignment with the adherence to strategic tools makes the workforce have a larger level of dedication.
- Workforce planning needs more development processes with the help of risk consultancy.

Chapter 20
A Perspective on Cross–Border Aspects of Insolvency and Implications for Resolution Plans and Recovery

T. Shenbagavalli
Jain University, India

R. Ravichandran
Jain University, India

V. Rakesh
Jain University, India

N. Sathyanarayana
iD https://orcid.org/0000-0002-4185-7751
Jain University, India

ABSTRACT

The relevance of data in India's socio-economic development has been defined in several policy documents in the digital economy. Using Indian law to regulate a contract creates major concerns, which can sometimes compromise it as a negotiating chip in cross-border agreements. As previously stated, Indian courts can revoke foreign arbitral verdicts if they determine that the arbitrators misapplied Indian law. As a result, a party to a contract governed by Indian law risked falling victim to the "public policy" fallacy. This will reduce the interest of foreign investors and create more cross-border issues. Many countries have modified the UNCITRAL model law to avoid such situations according to their requirement. Even the Indian government recently introduced MAP effective from May 6; the same model law was modified to give faster resolution in cross-border disputes under sections 64 and 65 of the Insolvency, Restructuring, and Dissolution Act 2018.

DOI: 10.4018/979-8-3693-0049-7.ch020

1. INTRODUCTION

The Concept of Cross border insolvency has been gaining quite an importance in the current global scenario, with many countries vying for FDI into their economy while at the same time trying to leverage their local insolvency laws to recover the maximum possible outstanding dues for the financial system, The issue has become more complex with a variety of regulations rules, and local court jurisdictions involved which is a vital role in deciding the fate of resolution plans which the industries and sectors in an economy need, on a timely basis. In this context, one can say the climate facilitated by the regulations in a country for cross-border insolvency may, to some extent, be regarded as a determining factor in the volume of FDI flowing into a country. In the Digital world, the globalization of business markets creates many changes in the economic system. Due to these system changes, a lot of cross-border trade has increased. As a byproduct of globalization's growth in commerce, numerous advancements are backed by a plethora of FDI through business, all governed by an FDI policy. Since 2017, the sectoral limitations for the single brand retail trade sector under the automatic method have been raised from 49% to 100% (FDI allocated for trading 6%, 100% of equity inflow from April 2021 to March 2022). In the defense sector, the automatic route in dealing with some revision has been increased from 49% to 74%, and the new category of Digital media can have up to 26%, and other sectors like the service sector, 16%, Computer software and hardware 15%, Telecommunication 6%. Even though the Indian government announced a Liberalized Industrial policy in 1990, the business entities follow multiples spiral jurisdiction (Figure 1).

Figure 1. Cross-border issues

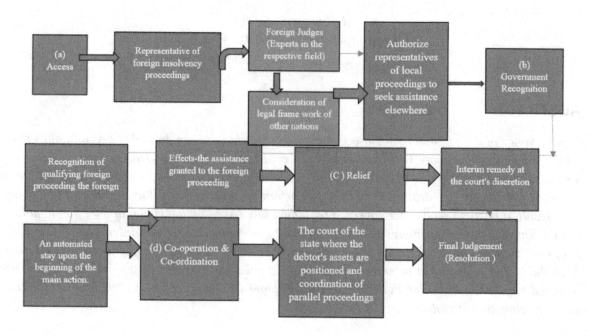

India is a developing country; the Indian government properly regulates the cash inflow through cross-border business through RBI, FEMA, and SEBI, as well through GAAR regulations, the Companies Act of 2013 & under sections from 90 to 90AS, and relevant sections of Income Tax Act, as governing the Cross -border income and asset flows namely section-9(1), transfer pricing provisions and IT rules related to that namely Rule 10-11 of IT rules. Foreign corporations invest in India to benefit from India's growth story. This growth of cross-border business develops not only the business but also the number of issues to bankruptcy and insolvency across borders; if appropriate changes are made to the relevant legislation's potential resolution, applicants across the borders can also help the Indian regime.

Issues Related to the Nature of Supervision

- Cross border-trade (b) Cross border banking (c) Cross border flow of funds.
- Cross-border bankruptcy relief to the potential resolution of applicants only for Tax and not for default penalty and fees.

Issues relating to information sharing: The absence of reciprocity while sharing the information between the supervisors and the information flow makes it difficult to access qualified information about cross-border.

Suggested Changes in Approach and Methods of Supervision

The aspect of cross-border in the context of insolvency is indeed critical today as it opens us to the various investors from outside the country also looking for investment, and with India going to the trillion dollar economy club, the key aspects of resolution of obtaining a resolution plan demand a separate approach. In this frame of prism, we need to view the effectiveness of the resolution plans, which perhaps can be improved if the investors and interested parties from overseas are also allowed. The implications are impacted through the legal framework of the following regulatory bodies, which need a single-window approach (Figure 2).

Figure 2. Cross-border bankruptcy and insolvency

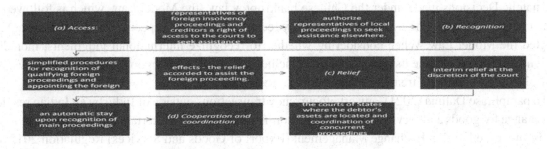

This paper examines the past experiences obtained from the context of IBC regarding resolution plans involving cross-border insolvency and looks at possible changes in RBI regulations, SEBI, Companies Act 2013. The IBC code and the outcomes obtained in the past. It also proposes to suggest recommendations for the future way the regulators need to take care of and how the ecosystem can evolve in this regard.

2. REVIEW OF LITERATURE

A detailed review of the literature has been made to find out the research gap and to identify the issues related to this study. To resolve the cross-border controversy, Singapore has taken the step to adopt the UNCITRAL Model Law for debt restructuring, along with their jurisdiction allowing foreign counsel international judges those who are eminent based on their respective zones to work together with Singapore counsel to facilitate the process to get resolved in a smooth way within the stipulated period. For example, Zipmex operates in Thailand, Indonesia, Singapore, and Australia. It acts as a platform to exchange digital currency and offers a wide range of currency options, high liquidity, and world-class experience, helping investors maximize their earnings for smoothened and efficient trading for institutional and privatized traders. The availability of mode 24/7 for the benefit of the investors in BTC, ETH, COMP & many more, but also navigate token (ZMT)) Decentralized finance -The Vault Group's payments have recently applied for moratorium protection. Three Arrows Capital's foreign agents applied for recognition in Singapore of liquidation proceedings initiated in the British Virgin Islands.

Chinese bankruptcy judgment pursuing recognition overseas: The first is the Chinese bankruptcy judgment case of Guangdong International Trust & Investment Company (GITIC). Before EBL2006, the case was recognized in Hong Kong in 1999. A Chinese court recognized this Chinese bankruptcy judgment, which was rejected by the Hong Kong litigation and assets seizure of local creditors; the court instructed the creditor to register the claim with the liquidator in China.

According to Zhang (2022), the second incident occurred after the EBL 2006 was enacted and involved the bankruptcy reorganization of Zhejiang to point Photovoltaic Co., Ltd. in China in 2014. In contrast to Chinese courts, the New Jersey court recognized the bankruptcy and awarded relief under Chapter 15 of the American Bankruptcy Code on the sole basis that it was fair to do so because the American creditor would have otherwise taken undue advantage of the situation. The local creditor's attempt to seize the firm's U.S. holdings was thus frustrated. Unjust practices persist in many Chinese courts, unfortunately. Decisions made under the Chinese bankruptcy law (the Model Law, which is followed by many countries besides China) are generally easily recognized abroad, especially in countries that have adopted the Model Law. When considering whether to recognize international judgments, including foreign bankruptcy judgments, several nations, including the United Kingdom, the United States, and Australia, do not require a treaty or the presence of reciprocity.

To paraphrase Dalmia (2021), any cryptocurrency transactions outside of India by an Indian resident in exchange for goods and services rendered by a non-resident are almost certainly considered exports of goods under the Foreign Exchange Management (Export of Goods and Services) Regulation 2015 and the Master Directions on Export of Goods. According to these regulations, any exports must be received in full through authorized banking channels, and any set-off import payments must only be paid through a mechanism made possible by a bank. This means that international swap is out of the question and that Indian citizens can only send Bitcoin outside through regulated financial institutions. The Enforcement Directorate of FEMA routinely conducts raids on cryptocurrency exchanges in India due to these businesses' prevalence of violations of foreign exchange legislation. In conclusion, an Indian citizen or permanent resident conducting cryptocurrency trading with a foreign national infringes Indian foreign exchange regulations. The legal framework for virtual currencies in India is still in its infancy. The rule promotes and regulates Bitcoin transactions at home and abroad.

3. OBJECTIVES

- To study the IBC in resolving cross-border Bankruptcy and Insolvency through past cross-border bankruptcy and insolvency cases.
- To Study the issues and implications that are impacted through the legal framework of regulatory bodies.
- Discuss the legislative provision affecting.
- To examine the possibility of a single cell to reduce and resolve cross-border issues.

3.1. Research Gap

The literature review specified a gap in the field of study to give early resolution in Cross-Border disputes with a Modified Law, Article 9 with multinational jurisdiction.

3.2. Statement of Problem

The insolvency and bankruptcy code (IBC) was enacted on May 28, 2016, against the backdrop of rising non-performing loans, with the intent of establishing a consolidated framework for the insolvency proceedings of joint stock companies, partnership firms, and individuals to address NPA issues in two different ways. The evident shift on the side of debtors toward decisive decision-making to prevent company disasters foreshadows a process through which financially troubled corporations will be rehabilitated. The evident change in debtors' decision-making to avert business collapses a system by which financially challenged corporate entities are rehabilitated and returned to full vigor. According to the World Bank's Ease of Doing Business Report, the average time required to settle bankruptcy in India is more than four years.

4. METHODOLOGY OF STUDY

Facts and information are systematically collected from the Cross-Border issue cases. This exploratory study is presented to draw inferences that may be based on collected data based on real judgment cases related to cross-border issues. The methodology includes sources of data and analysis of data.

4.1 Sources of Data

The analysis is based only on secondary data from judgment cases involving cross-border concerns and the legal framework followed by regulatory agencies such as RBI, FEMA, SEBI, IBC, and Tax relief cases. In addition, further essential information was gathered from various periodicals, publications, etc. All of them serve as secondary data.

4.2 Framework of the Analysis

The authors propose to examine the past literature in this regard, particularly in the context of the IBC regulatory prism, and look at past studies and gleanings. The data source will be mainly secondary, using IBBI data, past cases of NCLT in this regard, issues that arose in these cases, and implications in terms of SEBI, RBI regulations, Companies Act 2013, and IBC. The study is an exploratory study aimed at looking at the various aspects that have a bearing on the success or otherwise of the IBC cases. Reference is also linked to PMLA-related actions, which may slow down the flow of investors' money into the Indian sector if effective steps are not taken to assure or assuage the investor interests and suitable protection is given to them. In addition, the major legal consultants and the Big Four – Deloitte, E&Y, PWC, and KPMG – will be consulted regarding the global practices utilized elsewhere in cross-border bankruptcy resolution. From the legal perspective, the views of professional firms are more critical as it has major implication in terms of recommendations being put out by them as they are the main advisors to foreign investors who look forward to investing in India, and hence, their views and perspectives are becoming critical. A review of their views, findings, and suggestions is expected to give us practical and feasible possibilities to implement the recommendations and help take the resolution plans forward suitably.

The cases of IBBI involving cross-border resolution proposals are also examined and commented upon. All these, we believe, will help us present an effective framework to be proposed in this paper. FEMA and RBI are also looked at from the point of taxation, and suitable recommendations are proposed.

5. DATA ANALYSIS

Examining prior international bankruptcies and insolvencies to learn about the IBC's effectiveness in this area: Jet Airways has been struggling financially since filing for bankruptcy in the Netherlands in 2018. In this case, Jet Airways (India) Ltd. vs. State Bank of India and Anr. The trustee appointed by the Noord-Holland District Court, Trade, Subdistrict, and Insolvency, learned about the Indian insolvency case and notified the NCLT over the concurrent action for the same firm. The NCLT declared the Dutch proceedings invalid since the current IBC regulations in India do not provide for a cross-border insolvency procedure.

The case was taken in a new direction when an appeal was filed with the NCLAT, making the Jet Airways Case a prototypical example of how to use international insolvency procedures in India. To ensure cooperation and coordination between the two parallel procedures to maximize the value of the bankrupt corporation, the NCLAT sought an agreement between the Indian Resolution Professional and the Dutch Trustee. This established a cross-border insolvency protocol between the two court-appointed authorities, which the NCLAT eventually authorized. Since Jet Airways is a company incorporated in

India and operates mostly out of its headquarters there, it was decided that India would serve as the company's COMI. The Jet Airlines case, India's first international insolvency proceeding, has cleared the path for new cross-border insolvency laws in India (IBC: Idea, Impressions and Implementation, 2022)

The Mumbai bench of the National Company Law Tribunal (bankruptcy court) approved the Twin Star Technologies buyout offer in June of last year after receiving approval from the Committee of Creditors of Videocon (called Resolution Plan under bankruptcy law).

BoM and IFCI appealed that judgment before the NCLAT, which overturned the NCLT decision on Wednesday because the IBC had not been followed."

A two-member bench consisting of Jarat Kumar Jain and Ashok Kumar Mishra declared that the approval of the takeover plan was not in compliance with Section 31 of the Code and voided the Resolution Plan authorized by the Committee of Creditors (CoC) and Adjudicating Authority (NCLT). It remanded the case to the CoC to complete the procedure in compliance with the Code's requirements. This indicates that the CoC would solicit new bids for Videocon unless a higher court contested and overturned the NCLAT judgment. "We know the order, which will postpone Videocon's resolution. We expect the formal order and will take the necessary steps afterward. Gopal Jain, an advocate for Twin Star, said commenting on the order on the company's behalf.

On June 8, the National Company Law Tribunal (NCLT) approved the bankrupt Videocon Industries' resolution, clearing the way for Anil Agarwal's Twin Star Technologies to purchase the oil company's consumer durables. The thirteen businesses that make up the Videocon group that Twin Star Technologies offered Rs 2,962 crore for are Videocon Industries, Videocon Telecom, Evans Fraser & Co, Millennium Appliances India, Applicomp, Electro world Digital Solutions, Techno Kart India, Techno Electronics, Century Appliances, Value Industries, PE Electronics, CE India, and Sky Appliances. There was opposition from smaller financial institutions like Bank of Maharashtra, IFCI, Morgan Securities, SIDBI, and ABG Shipyard, but backing from larger financial institutions. The National Company Law Appellate Tribunal (NCLAT) has delayed enforcement of the decision since July when dissenting creditors appealed (PTI, 2022).

To Study the issues and implications that are impacted through the legal framework of regulatory bodies: In the landmark judgment of the above case, "To investigate how the legislative structure of regulatory agencies influences the problems and repercussions."

This landmark decision by the constitution SC bench of India on whether specific software might fall within the definition of goods under the state's sales tax law. The majority opinion of the court held that the word Goods used in the Constitution of India is very wide, and it covers all kinds of immovable property, regardless of whether tangible or intangible, and a transaction stipulating the sale under the relevant acts. In his dissenting opinion, Justice Sinha outlined a three-pronged test to determine whether or not a piece of software could be considered a commodity. Even though FEMA does not clearly define goods, this ruling is not strictly about cryptocurrencies or their definition under FEMA, but it does provide important interpretive guidelines. Going ahead, it's clear that cryptocurrencies are immaterial despite being created, promoted, and kept on actual servers.

One may bring, sell, transmit, transfer, deliver, store, and process these items. Bitcoin and Ethereum, two examples of cryptocurrencies, serve some functions, such as a medium of exchange, a means of making micropayments, and the backbone of decentralized apps. These characteristics, as well as the demand for cryptocurrencies, are indicative of their usefulness. As the nature of cryptocurrencies most closely resembles that of products under FEMA, they should be designated as such.

Following FEMA, "Any instrument which may be utilized to establish a financial responsibility" qualifies as currency. Cryptocurrencies are not specified by name or location among the mentioned groups. Currency notes refer to and include both coins and paper money. In addition, the RBI responded to an RTI request by stating that cryptocurrencies are not treated as money by the RBI under FEMA. For these reasons, the FEMA does not consider cryptocurrency to be "Currency" since (1) it does not fall under the definition of currency in section (h) of the FEMA, and (2) the RBI has not notified cryptocurrency as a currency.

Section 2(n) of the FEMA defines foreign exchange as "foreign currency". For FEMA, Section 2(m) defines "foreign currency" as any currency apart from Indian currency. Nevertheless, cryptocurrencies are not recognized as foreign money or forex under FEMA.

Discuss the legislative provisions affecting the success of cross-border resolution plans and recovery. To examine the possibility of a single cell to reduce and resolve cross-border issues.

The Insolvency, Restructuring, and Dissolution Act (IRDA) was introduced and has the following features.

- International Judges (Along with a panel of Singapore Judges, well-experienced international judges having eminent membership of respective jurisdiction.
- Foreign Law (To solve submission issues, the SICC allowed questions of foreign Law, and foreign lawyers can directly make submissions on the areas of foreign Law)
- Joinder of third parties (They increase the power of SICC to join third parties' action even if they are not part of an SICC jurisdiction agreement, Which tends to involve different parties such as
- debtors, creditors, and asset owners.)
- Enforceability (Judgement and order will be enforceable in the other jurisdiction, increasing the recognition of Singapore court's judgments and orders by the foreign courts.)

The past and current legislative framework of China's Cross-Border Insolvency Law: China did not have cross-border ad hoc insolvency legislation until 2006, when the EBL 2006 was issued. Preceding the EBL 2006, corporate insolvency was driven based on the concentration of two prominences. Then how are these cases disseminated by the Chinese government proceeding with the EBL 2006. They adhered to three legal principles that promote cross-border insolvency cooperation.

The first is civil and commercial judicial aid treaties. In the following instances, if a foreign bankruptcy seeks recognition or enforcement in China, the Chinese court may approve:

- If there is no link between China and the foreign jurisdiction where, the procedure is unlatched based on treaties or inter-mutual agreements.
- If the recognition violates China's public interest.
- If the recognition contravenes the legal interests of Chinese creditors.
- Other essential considerations that Chinese courts recognize must be taken into account.

Typically, Chinese courts, it would seem, are opposed to international judgment recognition concerns, such as foreign bankruptcy judgment judgments. This bitterness may be viewed in two distinct ways.

Many Chinese jurisdictions have always been considerably adverse because of this bitterness effect on foreign judgment resolution issues, including cross-border issues judgment decisions. After Enterprise Bankruptcy Law (EBL 2006), Article 5 contains two boundaries: The outbound transnational insolvency asserted that a Chinese insolvency case connected to a company's assets and had a global impact. If a foreign company's assets are located in China, a foreign insolvency judgment might be recognized and implemented in China (Table 1).

Table 1. FDI inflow status of China from 2011 to 2021

Years	FDI Inflows in Billion US $
2011	123.99
2012	121.07
2013	23.91
2014	128.5
2015	135.58
2016	133.71
2017	136.32
2018	138.31
2019	141.23
2020	149.34
2021	180.96

Figure 3. FDI inflow status of China from 2022 to 2021 FDI inflows in billion US $

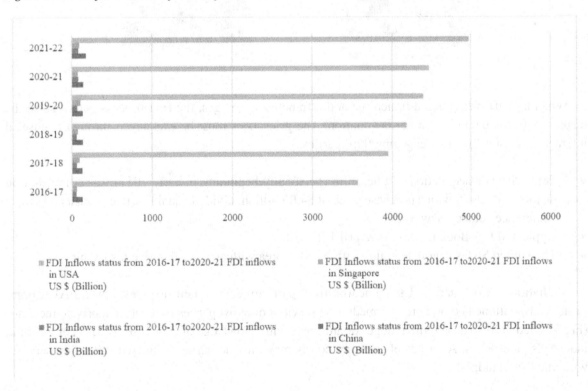

■ FDI Inflows status from 2016-17 to2020-21 FDI inflows in USA US $ (Billion)

■ FDI Inflows status from 2016-17 to2020-21 FDI inflows in Singapore US $ (Billion)

■ FDI Inflows status from 2016-17 to2020-21 FDI inflows in India US $ (Billion)

■ FDI Inflows status from 2016-17 to2020-21 FDI inflows in China US $ (Billion)

The mentioned boundaries helped to increase the FDI inflow in the previous year by 181 US billion $. Rate approximately more than 21% (Figure 3). The above chart implies that even during the COVID-19 times, the inflows to China were higher, and India was the lowest, implying perhaps a lack of trust and uncertainty surrounding the business climate in India in the minds of the investor community from abroad.

The legal framework of the USA in cross-border resolutions: The legal framework in the US for cross-border resolutions of insolvency is founded on informal negotiation, Conciliation, mediation, and arbitration, with litigation being an approach taken only as a last resort. A prevalence of a healthy ecosystem in this regard helps better and early resolution of cross-border insolvency in the US context (Figure 4).

Figure 4. USA cross-border resolution legal framework

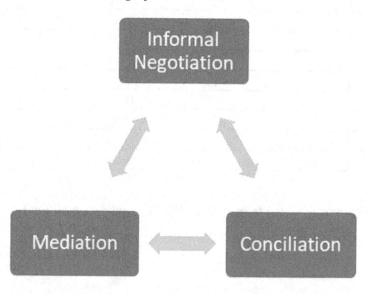

When a conflict between a franchisee and a franchisor emerges, the first process is to resolve the dispute with the help of informal negotiation. The grievances must be exchanged through counseled interaction sessions without engaging third parties.

- Walt Disney's acquisition of Lucasfilm (personally beginning in early 2011) was completed on October 30, 2013, with a purchase price of $4.05 billion, divided equally between cash and shares (Reference source- New York Times).
- Apple and U S Book publishers -April 12, 2012.
- The United States negotiated talks with North Korea with erratic, secretive leadership.

Mediation & Conciliation: Uses a neutral third party to resolve their disputes. Several ADR organizations (mentioned below) provide mediation services or assist parties in locating a private mediator (Fig.5). Mediators may be retired judges or attorneys with knowledge of franchise conflicts or a certain industry's enterprises. Alternatively, certain courts may provide parties with free mediation services with magistrate judges.

Figure 5. Information negotiation

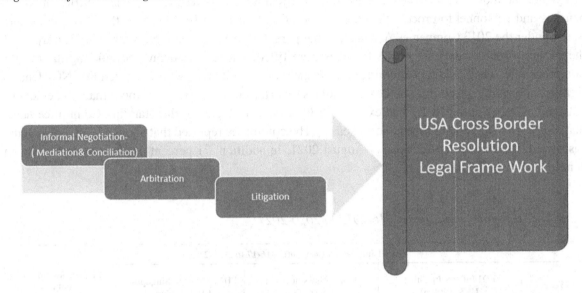

Arbitration: Several well-known venues for alternative cross-border conflict resolution provide arbitral proceedings and maybe mediator services. Among these establishments is the International Centre for Dispute Resolution (ICDR), the international branch of the American Arbitration Association, the International Chamber of Commerce (ICC), JAMS, the London Court of International Arbitration (LCIA), the Hong Kong International Arbitration Centre (HKIAC), the Singapore International Arbitration Centre (SIAC), and the World Intellectual Property Organization (WIPO), which specializes in franchise disputes (Frank, 2021).

6. DISCUSSION

The following laws and regulations primarily govern cross-border transactions in India: the Companies Act 2013; (ii) the SEBI (Substantial Acquisition of Shares and Takeovers) Regulations 2011; (iii) the Competition Act 2002; (iv) the Insolvency and Bankruptcy Code 2016; (v) the Department of Industrial Policy and Promotion (DIPP); (vi) the Income Tax Act 1961; (vii) the Transfer of Property Act 1882; ((Pathak, 2022).

Suppose any cross-border issues require any resolution again, they have to fulfill the requirement of the Indian Jurisdiction, which has a spiral regulatory body, particularly to meet the requirement of FDI inflows; the following comparison table 2 gives the status of inflows from 2016 to 2021, Cross – Border Dispute resolutions will reduce the interest of. The following Table 2 proves that India has to take steps to increase the inflow of FDI for national development.

For nearly 20% of incidents for which final reports have been presented, an average of 431 days is required (Fig. 6). For the other 80% of instances where a liquidation order has been issued, 46% of cases have been continuing for above 2 years, 23% between 1 to 2 years, and 13% for > 270 days and < one year. Even in cases of voluntary liquidation, delays are frequent. As of December 2021, 34 percent of continuing IBC voluntary liquidation cases have been ongoing for over two years, 18 percent between 1 to 2 years, and more than 270 days and less than one year. One cause of the delays is insufficient NCLT benches and personnel to process the cases. In addition to hearing IBC matters, the NCLT considers issues under the 2013 Companies Act, such as mergers. For instance, as of November 2021, only 45 of the 64 authorized vacancies for NCLT judges were filled. This causes delays in initiating the resolution procedure. The Standing Committee on Finance for 2020-21 further emphasized that NCLT has a significant backlog. According to the committee's report, as of May 31, 2021, more than 70 percent of outstanding cases at the NCLT had exceeded 180 days. The Report of the Standing Committee notes that the NCLT takes a long time to accept cases. The committee reported that about 13,740 bankruptcy cases were pending with NCLTs as of August 2021. In addition, 71 percent of these cases have been pending for over 180 days.

Table 2. FDI inflows status from 2016-2017 to 2020-2021

FDI Inflows Status From 2016-17 to 2020-21				
Year	FDI Inflows in China US $ (Billion)	FDI Inflows in India US $ (Billion)	FDI Inflows in Singapore US $ (Billion)	FDI Inflows in the USA US $ (Billion)
2016-17	133.71	55.6	65.36	3560
2017-18	136.32	61.96	99.21	3950
2018-19	138.31	62	81.18	4180
2019-20	141.23	74.39	111.48	4400
2020-21	149.34	81.97	74.75	4470
2021-22	180.96	83.57	99	4980

Figure 6. FDI inflows

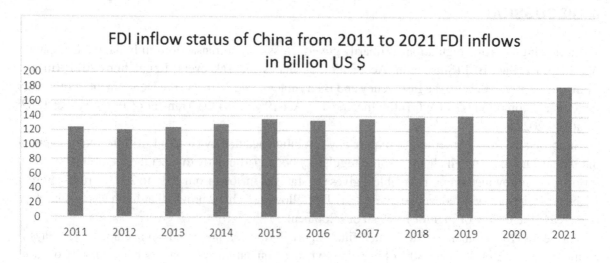

Insolvency and Bankruptcy Code: A Successful Journey In addition, there are several minor procedural and uncontested matters requiring NCLT approval, including: "(a) Replacement of Interim Resolution Professional (IRP) with RP; (b) Extension of CIRP from 180 days to 270 days; (c) Exclusion of period; and (d) Admission of CD into liquidation and appointment of a Liquidator, etc." These approvals may take a long time because the NCLT is concerned with sanctioned strength, which can cause unnecessary delays in the admission and/or liquidation procedures (IBC: Idea, Impressions, and Implementation, 2022). The functional structure of IBC: To give cross-border dispute resolution, the following percent structure has to be made some changes to be made (Figures 7 and 8).

Figure 7. Present framework of cross- border dispute resolution

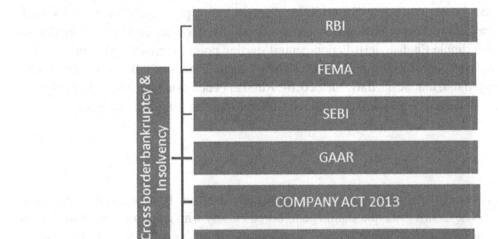

Figure 8. Proposal for the new framework for cross-border disputes to get a faster resolution

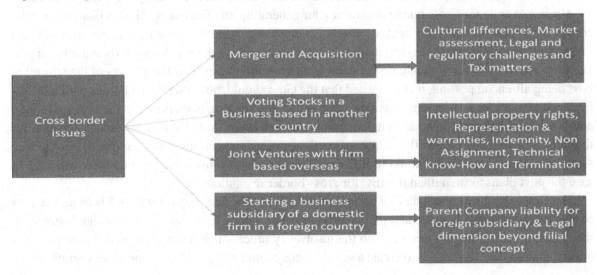

The judgments have been issued expeditiously, particularly in comparison to conventional courts; parties may have foreign legal representatives or arbitrators (this is highly restricted in traditional courts and should be increased), those who are experts in the concerned field. As per Article 9, Two judges from each party. The third Judge acts as the neutral, who will act as the presiding arbitrator of the tribunal. Foreign law decisions are based on legal arguments rather than expert testimony. Parties might agree to restrict or modify appeal rights, allowing rulings to be more final and definitive, and Parties are permitted to ignore regulations governing evidence.

To provide settlement of cross-border conflicts, its clause In order to provide opportunity, a business agreement in numerous fields must be amended. The parties have a real chance to address any disagreements via mediation before initiating litigation or arbitration, and the agreement provides for a binding conclusion if mediation fails. It is an alternative to the separate clause with a multi-tiered conflict resolution procedure: cross-border that allows for resolving disputes via dispute resolution methods, such as negotiation and mediation. This provision has been developed from a separate clause on mediation to give local counsel a simple English, jurisdiction-neutral starting point for cross-border transactions. Periodically updated jurisdiction-specific drafting notes give useful information for Brazil, China, France, Germany, Hong Kong, India, Indonesia, Italy, Mexico, the Russian Federation, Singapore, South Africa, South Korea, Spain, the United Arab Emirates, and the United Kingdom (England and Wales).

7. FINDINGS

The study's findings indicate that the following steps must be taken to ensure better and earlier resolution in cross-border cases. The COMI principle should be followed closely with legal support for mediation and conciliation over arbitration and court processes. A nudge given to businesses to resolve cross-border insolvencies will create a favorable ecosystem. Foreign courts' judgment should be accepted, and any legal subterfuges used by Indian business houses to stall the proceedings on enforcement of the foreign court's judgment should not be supported. Mediation and conciliation are to be taken as primary compared to arbitration, and effective ADR mechanisms are to be given more thrust to release the pressure on an already clogged judicial system. This will lower the cost of obtaining a decree by investors, enhance the quality of resolution plans, and increase the trust levels for the investor community in the Indian scenario.

A separate code for Cross border insolvency for generating an effective resolution plan can also be considered so that the necessary centralization of approvals, conditions, and eligibility requirements are met on time with a lower haircut -and reduce the approvals levels at the regulator courts and other appellate authorities – which only increase the delay in the resolution process. The powers of the sovereign govt being all-encompassing, it is suggested that the Govt should, after due consultations with industry leaders and legal luminaries, immediately issue suitable notifications mentioning the various foreign courts whose judgments can be accepted for enforcement in India, provided there are adequate assets for the same in Indian jurisdiction (the Chinese court's approach can certainly be looked at in this specific situations). Suitable amendment to the IBC code for cross-border insolvencies to be made effective in case the govt plans to strengthen the IBC for cross-border resolution plans.

The Govt, along with the Judiciary, should co-opt a list of foreign judges for NCLT hearing in Cross border cases to be also in the panel, particularly when the case involves assets in a foreign country, so that their views can duly be factored into the insolvency process resolution plan and enforcement can happen in time. The Govt needs to create a suitable ecosystem for this by issuing necessary notifications or amendments to various acts like the Companies Act 2013, IBC code 2016, RBI FEMA regulations, etc. This will enrich the quality of judgments arising from the process, reduce the cost of haircuts, and make the business house more accountable while submitting resolution plans. A separate clause on setting up a cell and a few provisions for fast-track enforcement of foreign court's judgment or order should be useful in reducing the time delays, provided the IBC contains a suitable clause to that effect. With the heavy delays in IBC and lack of suitable strength judges in NCLT, the IBC process has lost much of its merits, with institutions and financial creditors taking a heavy haircut. These must change if a successful resolution plan for cross-border insolvency is desired.

Group insolvency clause must be introduced in the IBC code by suitable amendments as then the tendency of business houses to bankrupt one unit and start another will be curbed. Personal guarantees given by promoters and other directors involved should immediately be invoked and put in a trust or an escrow once the companies they were directors earlier have declared bankruptcy. This will give a chance to prosecute directors and promoters, go after their assets, and protect the estate from bankruptcy without much loss of time and value. Many NCLT /Court judgments, in recent times, also provide for the same. The temptation for the Judiciary to intervene and give a stay is to be resisted, particularly when involving a foreign court judgment under arbitration or recognition of insolvency proceeding commencement. A case in point could be the stay granted by Delhi HC on the SIAC arbitration tribunal in the Future group takeover by Amazon and the single-member bench of SIAC granting its judgment in favor of Amazon, which was vacated only by the Supreme Court.

SEBI regulation relating to IPO (ICDR 2018) as amended (wef January 14, 2022) on the objects of IPO issue, conditions related to the utilization of fund proceeds, lock-in period, etc. can be relaxed in case of the cross border resolution plan is approved by the NCLT and by the court and the same can be filed with SEBI. Sebi can also come out with special exemptions (safe harbor clauses) in certain cases involving Cross border insolvency where funds are proposed to be raised from overseas markets, provided the investor in the resolution plan is an already approved entity in the investor country under the monitoring arrangement or a registered entity in the homeland -with a foreign regulator (e.g., SEC-UK, FSA-UK, MAS-Singapore, etc.). This will give much-needed flexibility and release the delays associated with the compliance process.

Exchange and sharing of information networks for corporates with layered subsidiaries in Tax haven jurisdictions (e.g., BVI, Isle of Man, etc.) have caused considerable agony and delay in resolution in cross-border cases. To the tax information network where countries share their data with other members on a bilateral basis, India too should arrange to quickly sew up agreements to exchange information in financial defaults of cross-border cases. This will curb the tendency to hide the details of beneficiaries, which are located in Tax havens, with opaque regulations and other non-cooperating jurisdictions, making it more difficult for authorities to trace the assets and their linkage to their real owners and bring them to the bankruptcy court. Different subsidiaries hold the assets in a jurisdiction with which India has no information-sharing agreements.

The urge and tendency of certain Govt departments, particularly those related to the Enforcement directorate, are invoking the provisions related to FEMA and PMLA – and Show cause notices issued to the intermediaries and banks, which may be vitiating the ecosystem and investors may develop cold feet in the process. As long as the related investor is controlled or registered with a regulator in the investor country – no adverse inferences need to be drawn. In the case of Sterling SEZ Infrastructure Ltd, the National Company Law Appellate Tribunal (NCLAT) reaffirmed on April 13, 2021, that rules and actions under the Insolvency and Bankruptcy Code (IBC) would take precedence over other laws and actions, such as the attachment of property by the Enforcement Directorate (ED) under the Prevention of Money Laundering Act (PMLA). In the Indian scenario, this is a peculiar feature and may further delay the resolution process, as the investor may be unwilling to invest funds due to a higher level of uncertainties, which can best be avoided to the extent possible.

8. CONCLUSION

The effectiveness of cross-border insolvency impacts the inflow of FDI and ease of doing business in India, and hence, the Govt of India and the respective regulators need to take note of these aspects urgently to avoid further haircuts in future insolvency cases. Higher haircuts may also imply that the resolution plans on offer are too infructuous, or investors are not confident about the economic future of the country and the financial strength of the particular entity in a future date. These, in turn, will fetch lower realization for assets under the block, which may create a vicious cycle of higher haircuts and lower realization, which must be avoided by all m means. It is expected that unless these measures are quickly implemented, the haircuts are likely to go further north and create a damaging impact on the bank's balance sheet and may call for urgent and heavy doses of fresh capital injections. Consequently, the cross-border insolvency resolution plans will take a downward plunge below the liquidation values. Therefore, the Cross-border insolvency framework needs to be strengthened further. A higher level of engagement with other overseas regulator quasi govt- bodies and govt to a level of cooperation as to how they handle the cross-border cases at their end may well help Indian regulators in the process, and it would wise enough to share their information, experiences and collaborate more frequently to enable factor the resultant outcomes into effective policy-making framework for the Cross-Border Insolvency cases arising in India. The committee has to be framed to review the performance of IBC. The review committee has framed with the representatives of RBI, SEBI, MCA, EIU, CBDTT, and supreme court judges because of faster recovery and reduced the Air cuts to get resolution.

REFERENCES

Dalmia, V. P. (2021). *Cross border transactions: Cryptocurrency and foreign exchange management act (FEMA)*. Retrieved November 2, 2023, from Vaish Associates Advocates website: https://www.mondaq.com/india/fin-tech/1023148/cross-border-transactions-cryptocurrency-and-foreign-exchange-management-act-fema

Frank, M. J. (2021). *Approaches to resolving cross-border disputes between franchisee and franchisor*. Retrieved November 2, 2023, from Lexology website: https://www.lexology.com/library/detail.aspx?g=2d45293e-179e-4338-933a-72e5c13e283f

IBC Idea, Impressions and Implementation (2022). Retrieved November 2, 2023, from Gov.in website: https://ibbi.gov.in/uploads/whatsnew/b5fba368fbd5c5817333f95fbb0d48bb.pdf?cv=1

Pathak, S. K. (2022). *Role of sebi: Cross border merger, takeover code*. Retrieved November 2, 2023, from Ijirl.com website: https://ijirl.com/wp-content/uploads/2022/03/ROLE-OF-SEBI-CROSS-BORDER-MERGER-TAKEOVER-CODE.pdf

PTI. (2022). Videocon Group insolvency: NCLAT junks Anil Agarwal-led firm's takeover, calls for fresh bids. *The New Indian Express*. Retrieved from https://www.newindianexpress.com/business/2022/jan/05/videocon-group-insolvency-nclat-junks-anil-agarwal-led-firms-takeover-calls-for-fresh-bids-2403388.html

Zhang, Z. (2022). Globalized cross-border insolvency law: The roles played by China. *European Business Organization Law Review*, *23*(3), 735–780. doi:10.100740804-021-00222-2

Chapter 21
A Study on Pink Tax Price Disparity of Gender Variation With Specific Reference to Comestible Goods

T. Shenbagavalli
Jain University, India

Vidya Chandrasekar
Jain University, India

Nompi Raj
Jain University, India

ABSTRACT

The Pink Tax is an additional sum of money that is paid daily by women for comparable or comparable-in-value edible products. Specifically, the Pink Tax is a tax on pink products. There are a lot of people who either don't comprehend the justification for the presence of this tax in society or have a limited awareness of it. It is often referred to by the name "hidden tax." While the Pink Tax is not a legitimate form of taxation, it does still exist. The regulations that prevent price discrimination based on gender are only present in a select number of state and municipal governments, but the federal government does not have any such laws. The objective of this study is to bring attention to a tax that frequently isn't focused on within the day-to-day activities of women, to investigate the price differences between commodities in which women pay a higher amount compared to men for the same product, and to investigate the reason why female products are so expensive.

DOI: 10.4018/979-8-3693-0049-7.ch021

1. INTRODUCTION

The term "pink tax" describes gender-based price discrimination wherein women frequently pay more than males for comparable goods and services that are only distinguishable by the color of the product and its packaging (Alabdullah et al., 2021a). Knowledge of this price disparity in both wealthy and poor nations (Alabdullah & Ahmed, 2021). According to a poll, as many as 67% of Indian citizens have never ever heard of the pink tax. Gendered pricing first came to light as a result of the GST's reduction from 18% to 12% (Alabdullah et al., 2021b). In many categories of goods and services, from toys for young children to medical assistance equipment for the elderly, this so-called tax, which causes a price difference between generic or gender products with their female-targeted counterparts, can be seen (Al-Maaitah et al., 2021a).

A razor for males costs Rs. 180, while its pink counterpart, or the female's version, costs Rs. 250, a startling difference of Rs. 70 for just a change in the product's colour, according to one study (Al-Maaitah et al., 2021b). Similar to this, a basic t-shirt costs Rs. 305 for males and Rs. 359 for women. Women may also pay up to 92 percent extra for the same garments to be dry-cleaned (Gupta, 2021a). A study by the New York City Department of Consumer Affairs that examined the pricing of hundreds of items from cradle to cane came to the conclusion that there is a 7% overall discrepancy in product costs and also that women consumers paid increased costs in 30 of the 35 product categories (Almaamari & Salial, 2022).

The average annual cost of the pink tax for a woman is $2,135. A woman by the age of 35 pays an astounding sum of $47,000 under the pretense of this "gender tax," according to the official website of Beat the Pink Tax (Saxena et al., 2023). In addition to the gender pay difference, women also have additional financial burdens. Despite the 12% tax on feminine hygiene products being eliminated in India in 2018, Following a protest and a petition with 4,00,000 signatures against the 12% GST, temporary finance minister Piyush Goyal announced it in 2018. Similar to the pink tax, the salary disparity continued to exist even in industrialized nations like the United States as of 2018, reaching as high as 19 percent in India (Almaamari, 2022). As a result of Gupta's (2021b) income and higher expenditure, women are doubly disadvantaged simply because of their gender.

2. REVIEW OF LITERATURE

According to the information presented on NYC.gov, which was outlined by Zelniker (2018) in his research. The following table provides a visual representation of the variance in the percentages of the prices.

Table 1. Variance in percentages of the prices

Details	Male (₹)	Female (₹)
clothes cost 4% more than boys' clothing	100	100+4=104
Women pay 7% more than men for accessories such as tote bags and watches.	100	100+7=107
13% more for personal care such as deodorant	100	100+13=113

These differences cannot be justified due to the fact that companies are simply taking more resources from women while paying them a lower wage, despite the fact that there has been no change in the direct or indirect cost of the materials or manufacturing involved in the production of these goods, which are produced in a manner that is not significantly dissimilar to the production process that is used for producing items that are comparable to those produced for men (Zelniker, 2018; Tripathi & Al-Shahri, 2023).

Aguiar & Hurst (2005) said that the higher tax of 28% (Former Luxury Tax pre-GST) is not directly imposed on pink tax while levying tax inclusion at the time of price fixation. "Due to the fact that many feminine hygiene products, in particular these products, are considered disposable goods, a tax is in effect. Although this tax is more well-known in society and frequently provokes resentment, not much has been done to get rid of it. One of the goals of selective consumption taxes is to discourage consumption that is not wanted, however this is not the only aim of these taxes (Vashishtha & Kapoor, 2023). Always gendered pricing discreteness in consumer goods, sometimes known as the "pink tax," is commonplace. This phenomenon is pervasive. A recent report that was recently commissioned by New York City found that gendered price variations manifest in approximately 60 percent of products and that, given a gendered differential, women's product is 233 percent more likely to bear the premium (Mara et al., 2023). This finding was found in a recent report that was commissioned by New York City. It is important to note that there have been some attempts made to reduce the severity of this economic punishment. In 1995, the state of California passed a law that made it illegal to discriminate based on a person's gender when setting prices. More recently, in April 2019, Representative Jackie Speier of California introduced the Pink Tax Repeal Act in the House of Representatives of the United States of America. Outside of the United States, there have been initiatives made to address product-specific pink taxes, primarily on feminine hygiene products in Canada, Colombia, Germany, India, and Kenya. These countries include Canada, Kenya, and India (Kuragayala, 2023).

According to one estimate from California lawmakers regarding "hygiene feminine goods, women pay $20 million a year in California alone as a result of the luxury VAT on these products," As a result, the pink tax is not an actual tax in the eyes of the law (Srinivas et al., 2023). Because it cannot be used to raise money for government-sponsored economic growth, it is not payable to the government. Because it only draws certain products and services, this hidden tax might be interpreted as a selective consumption tax. The last legal instance of gender discrimination in the United States may be the fees attached to clothing, shoes, and swimsuits as they enter the country's ports. "Whether it's an oil change or dry cleaning, women frequently pay more for services that are comparable to those provided to males. Given that the majority of goods sold individually, depending on gender, are essentially the same quality aside from packaging, this is challenging. Gendered goods that are fundamentally distinct, such as those that deal with certain aspects of health, ignore quality similarities. This tendency first appears in girls when they are young."

Pink did not become a "girly" colour until after World War II (Stamberg, 2014). The "cost of being female," which results from societal cultural standards, can be used to further differentiate consumer price disparity. These underlying biases, for instance, frequently result in the undervaluation of female aptitude, which also influences the conditions around the economic gap that women encounter (Sayers, 2012). Women have suffered from severe economic inequality throughout history (Priscila et al., 2023). Women in ancient Egypt had the same financial rights as men, including the ability to own property (Mcgee & Moore, 2014).

As per India's concern, there is a remuneration gap between men and women in the system of wages. The present Tax system of GST under the luxury tax bracket is 28%, which will increase the selling price. Furthermore, it was proved by Dinerman (1989) in his study with the reference to sales tax. The same concept was given by Alara Efsun (2018). The disparity of female consumer they are in a binding position to pay more for their indispensable items.

Selective consumption taxes aim to do many things, one of which is discourage wasteful spending (Vashishtha & Kapoor, 2023). The "pink tax," or the practise of charging a higher premium for women's or younger people's versions of the same product, is extremely common. New York City commissioned a study that indicated that women's items are 233 percent more likely to be priced more than men's (Mara et al., 2023) due to the existence of a gendered disparity in pricing. It's worth noting that some work has been done to lessen the financial hit. In 1995, California passed a law that made it illegal to charge different sexes for the same goods or services. Jackie Speier, a representative from California, introduced the Pink Tax Repeal Act in the House of Representatives in April of 2019. Efforts have been made to reduce pink taxes in Canada, Colombia, Germany, India, and Kenya, all of which are outside the United States (Kuragayala, 2023).

Ayres and Siegelman (1995) found that women and black men paid much greater markups for automobiles than white males, providing evidence of racial and gender discrimination in negotiating for new cars (Mert, 2022a).

Goldberg (1996) and Tregouet (2015) have both investigated this situation in more detail, while Castillo et al. (2012) have found systematic disparities between men's and women's taxi price bargaining stages. "Fitzpatrick (2017), in the context of haggling for anti-malarial medications, evidence of gender price discrimination (Vashishtha & Dhawan, 2023). These studies show that women are subjected to price discrimination, but they fail to identify the mechanism by which this happens when dealing with commodities with straightforward take-it-or-leave-it list prices or the significance of varying consumer preferences across different product categories".

Aguiar and Hurst (2005) use survey data to demonstrate that consumption patterns among people stay relatively constant as they approach retirement while highlighting differences in consumption sources (such as eating out, producing things at home, etc.) for both genders. "Aguiar and Hurst 2007 While not specifically focusing on gender differences, their findings on the price returns of time spent shopping have significant implications for understanding the differences in prices paid by men and women. These findings include the substitution elasticity between shopping and home production, the willingness to engage in price shopping or to take advantage of deals, and the willingness to engage in price shopping".

Moretti (2013) has shown that Price indices that are distinctive to a population have significant effects on real wage disparities. Nowadays, estimates of the gender wage gap that take into account variations in qualifications range from 10% to 20%. By lowering women's purchasing power, an overall pink tax on female consumption worsens these disparities (Srivastava & Roychoudhury, 2020). Furthermore, according to accounting principles, the Pink Tax's existence also draws attention to disparities between men's and women's overall consumption and savings rates. Women's real wages are lower, and they may have fewer opportunities to save for their lifetimes and spend since they pay more on average for their individual consumption bundles (Yeruva & Ramu, 2023).

Stevens and Shanahan (2017) found that the Pink Tax results in women spending more than men for comparable products. This is especially true for products marketed specifically to women. Some estimates place the annual cost to female consumers in the United States due to gender-based pricing at over $1400. Pink taxes provide a higher price on products aimed at women just because they are associated with the colour pink (Ocoró et al., 2023) and not because the goods themselves are pink. Pink and blue being designated for different genders is a relatively new idea (Srivastava & Roychoudhury, 2021). Prior to the 20th century, pink and blue were interchangeable nursery hues, and babies were typically dressed in white on a regular basis (Paoletti, 2012). For ladies of the period, blue was favored over other colors because of its dainty appearance, which was deemed more acceptable for the then-perceived inferior gender (Kanaan-Jebna et al., 2022).

Brand & Gross's (2020) research on Gender-Based Pricing through Human-Computer interaction reveals a gender-specific difference in recommender systems. They employed Quantile Regressions and Amazon's data to determine the range of prices for the most popular items. The findings indicated that there was a gender bias in the premiums that were recommended. Product recommendations for women typically show a bigger premium than those for men, even if a premium relative to the viewed product is levied for both sexes (about 5 percent more at the median, ceteris paribus). Price at entry and product demand (measured by sales rank) are two factors that can affect this (Mert, 2022b).

More recently, Rousille (2021) connects nearly all of the gender pay gap among IT industry employees to variations in interviewee wage demands, highlighting the possible contribution of bargaining power differences to gender inequality.

3. OBJECTIVES OF THE STUDY

- The primary goal of this research is to study the public awareness of Pink Tax.
- It also expresses their views on whether the Pink Tax encourages gender inequality.
- To analyze why female products are so expensive

3.1. Research Methodology

The study is exploratory in nature. The basic data was gathered using a structured online survey that asked a series of questions to better understand people's perceptions of the pink tax. The survey is presented here, as well as in the analysis and appendices. Respondents were questioned about their thoughts on the pink tax and how it will affect them. They were specifically asked if they believe women pay more for their products than men do and if it promotes gender inequality. A total of 50 responses were included in the sample.

4. DATA ANALYSIS AND INTERPRETATION

4.1. Sources of the Data

This research paper is based on primary data where we got responses from individuals through Google Forms. Here are the responses that we received:

In the following step, PFF cancellation is applied to get rid of the most significant components of the stator current spectra. The frequency spectrum of stator current under all bearing situations following PFFC is depicted in Figure 1. The Wiener filter effectively removes the contribution of fault frequencies, but the FFT has trouble differentiating between crucial frequencies and other frequencies. In order to estimate the fault frequencies, an S-transform based spectrum analysis is performed.

4.2. Graphical Representation and Analysis of Data

To study the public awareness of the Pink Tax.

Figure 1 depicts the percentage gender distribution of those who responded to our questionnaire, revealing that females account for 72 percent of the total population, with men accounting for the remainder of 28%.

Table 2. Response based on gender

Value	Frequency	Percentage
Female	36	72%
Male	14	28%

Figure 1. Response based on gender

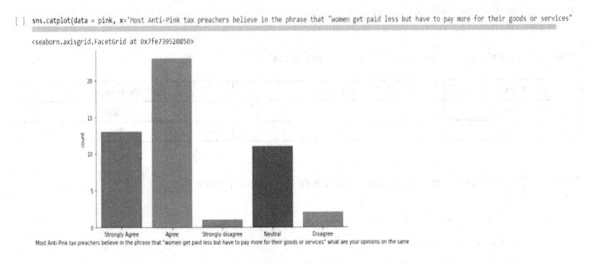

```
[ ] sns.catplot(data = pink, x='Most Anti-Pink tax preachers believe in the phrase that "women get paid less but have to pay more for their goods or services"
```
```
<seaborn.axisgrid.FacetGrid at 0x7fe739520850>
```

Figure 2 briefs the female products' status of expense, and we got a resounding yes. 96 percent of those polled thought they had to pay more. This clearly indicates that this is a problem that affects the majority of people rather than just one or two.

Table 3. Awareness of the pink tax

Values	Frequency	Percentage
Yes	48	96%
No	2	4%

Figure 2. Awareness of the pink tax

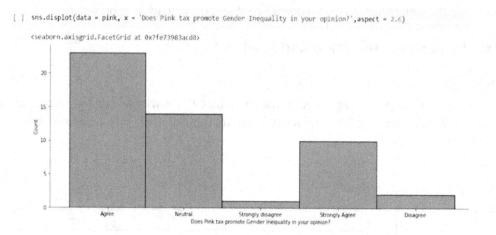

Figure 3 demonstrates that people are not even aware of it, implying that serious awareness or campaigning is required to make women aware that they are paying more for their products. Out of 50 respondents, 60% of women are not aware of this additional cost, which is paid while buying their products (Phoek et al., 2023).

Table 4. To analyze the expense of the female products

Values	Frequency	Percentage
Yes	33	66%
No	17	34%

Figure 3. To picture-out analysis of the expense of the female product

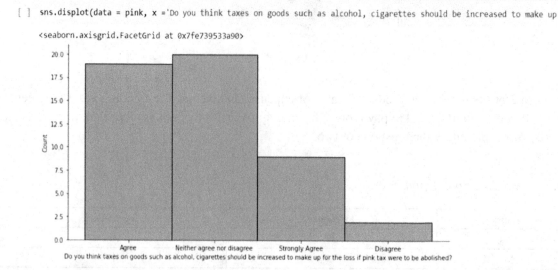

4.3. Support the Additional Charge for Female Products

Furthermore, a simple question was posed to see if people supported the Pink Tax or not, and the majority of people (80 percent) said no. Despite the fact that it is not feasible, women are tied to paying additional charges for their usage items, leaving them with no other alternative.

Figure 4 demonstrates, based on the 50 samples regarding the additional charges paid for pink products are not even aware of it, implying that serious awareness or campaigning is required to make women aware that they are paying additional charges for their products.

Table 5. To analyze the additional expense of the female products

Values	Frequency	Percentage
Yes	40	80%
No	10	20%

Figure 4. To picture the additional expense of the female products

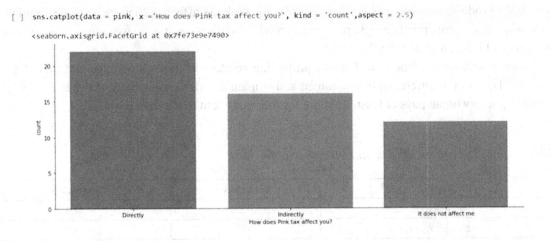

Figure 5 demonstrates, based on the 50 samples' responses online regarding the additional charges paid for the hidden tax products, whether it affects the interest of the customer while buying the products. Nearly 44% of the respondents are affected directly, 32% are indirectly, and around 24% do not get any changes.

Table 6. Pink tax affects the interest of buying the hidden tax product

Values	Frequency	Percentage
Directly	22	44%
Indirectly	16	32%
It does not affect me	12	24%

Figure 5. To give the status about the interest of buying the hidden tax product

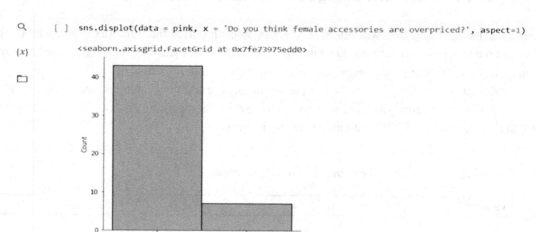

The next question was about how the Pink Tax affects the famine customer financially at the time of buying the product. According to the graph above, the pink tax affected 76 percent of the population in some way (44 percent directly and 32 percent indirectly). While the rest, who we assume are non-working women, said it had no effect on them.

Figure 6 demonstrates the Pink Tax was promoting gender inequality among people, and 66 percent said yes. The price indifference between men and women clearly demonstrates the presence of gender inequality, as a woman pays at least 7% more for the same item that a man pays.

Table 7. Pink Tax affected the famine customer financially

Values	Frequency	Percentage
Agree	23	46%
Strongly Agree	10	20%
Disagree	2	4%
Strongly Disagree	1	2%
Neutral	14	28%

The Data Analysis and Data Visualization of the data that we acquired from the primary source, which is the questionnaire, the analysis using Python programming and presented the results in the slides below

Figure 7 $_{(p1)}$ depicts the amount of individuals who are aware of the Pink Tax is shown above. More than 30 out of 50 individuals had never heard of the pink tax, and just a handful have heard of it. This demonstrates that there is a significant lack of awareness. People should be aware that women pay more for their products than men do. We created the graph using Python's data visualization function, the plot () method, and the seaborn package.

Figure 6. Opinion about the promotional gender inequality

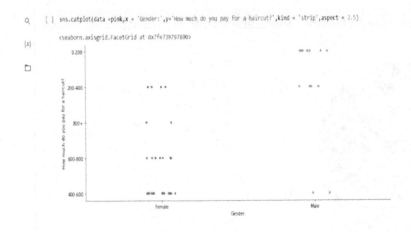

Figure 7. (p1)

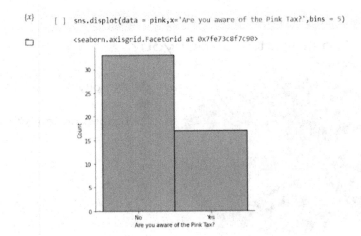

Figures 8 and 9 are picturing the count for the number of people who think female accessories are very expensive. Almost 85% of the people who responded said that female products are costly. Due lack of literacy about tax, many are clueless about this hidden tax. This additional tax is collected from the female customer. These products are not unique when compared to the merits of a man's products. All female customers are experiencing price disparity in the pattern of gender pricing, and this price variation intends to increase this concept study inherently significant (Ramu & Yeruva, 2023).

Figure 10 shows the way in which the pink tax affects the people. Almost 50% of the people have said that it affects them directly. Around 25% of the people have opted for indirect effectiveness. This proves that the Pink Tax affects everyone in some or the other way.

Figure 8. (p2)

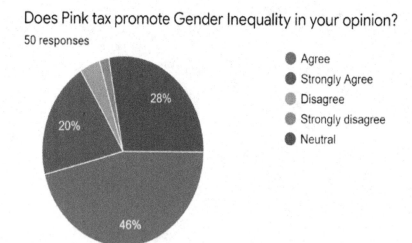

Does Pink tax promote Gender Inequality in your opinion?
50 responses

● Agree
● Strongly Agree
● Disagree
● Strongly disagree
● Neutral

Figure 9. (p3)

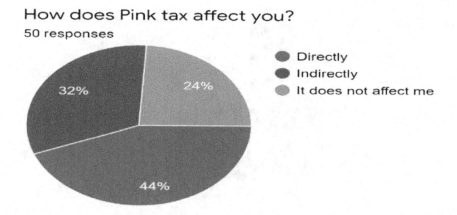

How does Pink tax affect you?
50 responses

● Directly
● Indirectly
● It does not affect me

In order to compare the prices between men's and women's products and services, we constructed a strip plot that helps us to see the prices paid by each gender. By seeing the above plot, we can get to know that most of the women pay around Rs.600 for their haircut, while the majority of the men pay only Rs.200 on average. The differences in the pricing can be clearly seen here. Some women also pay around Rs.800 for a haircut, which is really very expensive.

All these jesters, to fulfill the expectation from the mass media to improvise their personalities, many young women are using pick products. Women are conditioned to think that buying these pink goods with their names on them is the only way to be accepted and that their natural appearance won't be good enough. Female clients continue to use it as a result of public and friend feedback. Women experience unstated pressure in their daily lives to meet society's standards for attractiveness. Women frequently think that their success is closely related to how they look. These expectations are closely related to gender pricing because women are conditioned from an early age to buy pink things in order to appear feminine.

Figure 10. (p4)

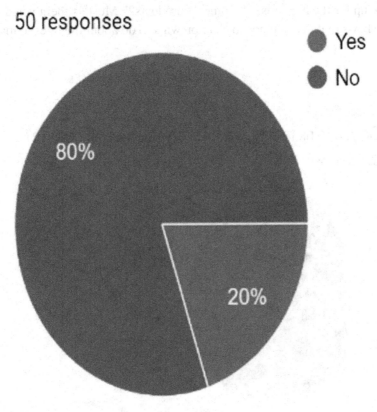

Do you support Pink Tax?

50 responses

Yes
No

80%

20%

Figure 11. (p5)

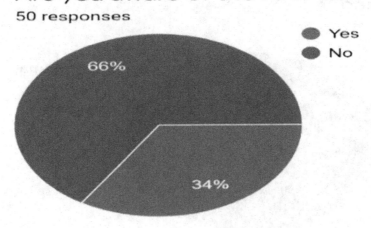

Are you aware of the Pink Tax?

50 responses

Yes
No

66%

34%

Figure 11 depicts people's views on whether they think the pink tax promotes gender inequality. Most of the people agree on this, while some of them are not able to take a stand on one opinion, so they have opted for neutral. This shows that people are not very clear and aware of the pink tax concept.

There was also no clear answer to the question, 'Do you think the rate of alcohol or cigarettes should be increased to make up for the high cost of women's products?'. Most of them voted for neither agree nor disagree, which shows that they are not so clear on what to do about the rates to make it up (Figures 12 and 13).

Figure 12. (p6)

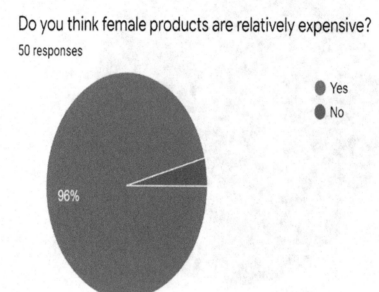

Do you think female products are relatively expensive?
50 responses

96%

● Yes
● No

Figure 13. (p7)

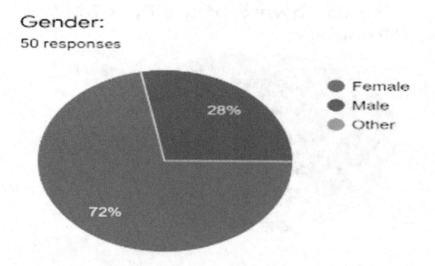

Gender:
50 responses

28%

72%

● Female
● Male
● Other

5. DISCUSSION

We may now be able to explain why the pink tax persists by looking at past economic differences between men and women. Even if many overt forms of discrimination have been eradicated, women continue to be subjected to economic disadvantages as a result of the hidden feminine tax as well as other consumption levies directed specifically at women. For instance, additional feminine taxes in the form of sales tax (pre-GST) on tampons and other feminine items contribute to an economic imbalance of female customers. These taxes are levied on feminine hygiene products by making women pay more than males for things that are already marketed to their specific gender.

In addition, the compensation that they receive contributes to the gap that exists between men and women in terms of salaries, as does occupational segregation based on gender, which is a factor that has led to earnings inequalities (Dinerman,1989). The "cost of being female," which derives from the cultural expectations of society, is another factor that may be used to differentiate the price differences between consumer goods. For instance, these deep-seated biases frequently result in the underestimation of women's potential, which further contributes to the conditions that underlie the economic disparities that exist between women and men (Sayers, 2012). sociocultural standards contribute to the perpetuation of the phenomenon known as the "pink tax" due to the fact that they are associated with the overall cost of belonging to the feminine gender. The rationale behind why retailers charge male and female customers differently. A few key reasons companies attribute to this are:

- To designate product
- To designate Retail Women are less price-elastic

As indicated by the comments we obtained from people, there is a lack of awareness regarding the pink tax. Sixty-six percent of those who responded to our survey had no idea what the pink tax was. People had the misconception that products marketed for women were more expensive, which was supported by the fact that 98 percent of respondents agreed with this assertion. A little less than half of them (46 percent) concurred that there is a clear correlation between the Pink Tax and increased gender disparity. On the other hand, 28 percent of them preferred to maintain their impartiality and did not voice any view, which is evidence of their lack of awareness. According to our research, the majority of those polled are women. Forty-four percent of those polled stated that the Pink Tax will directly affect them. The remaining 32 percent of those polled believe that it has an indirect impact on them as a result of this. Despite this, it is estimated that around 76% of the population will be impacted by the Pink Tax in some form.

In the year 2004, Kenya did away with the value-added tax that was previously placed on menstrual products. It is the first nation in the world to abolish the supplementary tax. In the year 2015, the national goods and services tax in Canada was removed from the category of menstruation products. In the year 2018, the government of Australia passed a law that will reduce ten percent of the GST tax that is currently placed on feminine goods. The tax of 5% that had been placed on menstrual products in Columbia has been eliminated. The United Kingdom (UK) has proposed that 5 percent of the value-added tax will be eliminated in the year 2021. However, the Indian government has eliminated the Goods and Services tax of 12% that was applied to period items. In spite of the fact that the government has removed a certain proportion of the tax, the corporations continue to raise prices according to the demand for the product's design and colour.

6. CONCLUSION

It is crucial for customers to acknowledge the efforts of businesses that are actively trying to stray from the standard. Businesses need to be aware of this awareness and shift in consumer preferences because it will affect their pricing and marketing strategies. For instance, Burger King has already started a public campaign to oppose the pink tax. The subscription razor manufacturer Billie offers a referral discount known as "The Pink Tax Refund" as part of its campaign against the gender tax. Taking an active role in the battle against patriarchy and making money by acting as change agents rather than continuing to be exploiters is the way forward for corporations. We must first dispel the ingrained, harmful stereotypes of women as naïve, sensitive, and obedient to all illogical standards if we are to change the way society treats women financially. And it is our responsibility to actively engage in the struggle against oppression and to inspire others to follow suit. We are hoping that someday, all of the ladies who shop for deals won't have to rely on the men's department's year-round sales.

REFERENCES

Aguiar, M., & Hurst, E. (2005). Consumption versus expenditure. *Journal of Political Economy, 113*(5), 919–948. doi:10.1086/491590

Aguiar, M., & Hurst, E. (2007). Life-cycle prices and production. *The American Economic Review, 97*(5), 1533–1559. doi:10.1257/aer.97.5.1533

Al-maaitah, D. A., Tha'er Majali, M. A., & Almaaitah, T. A. (2021a). The role of leadership styles on staff job satisfaction in public organizations. *Journal of Contemporary Issues in Business and Government, 27*(1), 772–783.

Al-maaitah, T. A., Tha'er Majali, M. A., & Almaaitah, D. A. (2021b). The Impact of COVID-19 on the Electronic Commerce Users Behavior. *Journal of Contemporary Issues in Business and Government, 27*(1), 772–783.

Alabdullah, T.T.Y., & Ahmed, E.R. (2021). New Insights to Investigate the Impact of Internal Control Mechanisms on Firm Performance: A Study in Oman. *Riset Akuntansi dan Keuangan Indonesia, 6*(2).

Alabdullah, T. T. Y., Al Fakhri, I., Ahmed, E. R., & Jebna, A. K. (2021b). Empirical Study of The Influence of Board of Directors' Feature on Firm Performance. *Russian Journal of Agricultural and Socio-Economic Sciences, 11*(119), 137–146. doi:10.18551/rjoas.2021-11.16

Alabdullah, T. T. Y., Al-Fakhri, I., Ahmed, E. R., & Kanaan-Jebna, A. (2021a). Corporate Governance System and Firm Financial Performance. *Acta Scientific Computer Sciences, 4*(6), 97–103.

Alara Efsun, Y. (2018). *Pink Tax, and the Law: Discriminating Against Women Consumers*. Academic Press.

Almaamari, Q. A., Ali, B. M., & Almeer, S. (2022). Factors influencing organizational performance at petroleum products distribution company in Yemen. *Specialusis Ugdymas, 1*(43), 2071–2083.

Almaamari, Q. A., & Salial, M. M. (2022). Influence of Job Satisfaction, Effective Teamwork, and Social Media on Employee's Performance in Bahraini Telecommunication Sector. *Specialusis Ugdymas*, *1*(43), 2063–2070.

Ayres, I., & Siegelman, P. (1995). Race and gender discrimination in bargaining for a new car. *The American Economic Review*, 304–321.

Brand, A., & Gross, T. (2020). Paying the pink tax on a blue dress-exploring gender-based price-premiums in fashion recommendations. In *Human-Centered Software Engineering: 8th IFIP WG 13.2 International Working Conference* (Vol. 2020, pp. 190–198). Eindhoven, The Netherlands: Springer International Publishing. 10.1007/978-3-030-64266-2_12

Castillo, M., Petrie, R., Torero, M. A., & Vesterlund, L. (2012). Gender differences in bargaining outcomes: A field experiment on discrimination. SSRN *Electronic Journal*. doi:10.2139/ssrn.2087134

Dinerman, M. (1989). Book Reviews : Women's Quest for Economic Equality. By Victor R. Fuchs. Cambridge, MA: Harvard University Press, 1988, 171 pp., $18.95, paper. *Affilia*, *4*(3), 82–84. doi:10.1177/088610998900400310

Fitzpatrick, A. (2017). Shopping while female: Who pays higher prices and why? *The American Economic Review*, *107*(5), 146–149. doi:10.1257/aer.p20171127

Goldberg, P. K. (1996). Dealer price discrimination in new car purchases: Evidence from the consumer expenditure survey. *Journal of Political Economy*, *104*(3), 622–654. doi:10.1086/262035

Gupta, R. K. (2021a). A study on occupational health hazards among construction workers in India. *International Journal of Enterprise Network Management*, *12*(4), 325–339. doi:10.1504/IJENM.2021.119663

Gupta, R. K. (2021b). Adoption of mobile wallet services: an empirical analysis. *International Journal of Intellectual Property Management, 12*(3), 341 – 353. doi:10.1504/IJIPM.2021.10035526

Kanaan-Jebna, A., Baharudi, A. S., & Alabdullah, T. T. Y. (2022). Entrepreneurial Orientation, Market Orientation, Managerial Accounting, and Manufacturing SMEs Satisfaction. *Journal of Accounting Science*, *6*(1), 1–14. doi:10.21070/jas.v6i1.1590

Kuragayala, P. S. (2023). A Systematic Review on Workforce Development in Healthcare Sector: Implications in the Post-COVID Scenario. *FMDB Transactions on Sustainable Technoprise Letters*, *1*(1), 36–46.

María, J. J. L., Polo, O. C. C., & Elhadary, T. (2023). An Analysis of the Morality and Social Responsibility of Non-Profit Organizations. *FMDB Transactions on Sustainable Technoprise Letters*, *1*(1), 28–35.

Mcgee, S., & Moore, H. (2014). *Women's rights and their money: a timeline from Cleopatra to Lilly Ledbetter*. Lilly Ledbetter.

Mert, I. (2021a). Analyzing the Sustainability of the Accounting Valuation Practices in Romania during the Adaptation Period to the European Union. *Revista Argentina de Clínica Psicológica*, *30*(1), 787–798.

Mert, I. (2021b). The Effects of the Qualitative Parameters of Internal Auditing Works on the Preferences of Investment Funds' Analysts. *Economic Alternatives*, (1), 60–71.

Mert, I. (2022a). *Assessment of Accounting Evaluation Practices, A Research-Based Review of Turkey and Romania. Springer Cham.* https://link.springer.com/book/10.1007/978-3-030-98486-1

Mert, I. (2022b). Investigation Techniques, Methods, Types, and Increasing Impact of Forensic Accounting in Digital Period. *Maliye ve Finans Yazıları*, (118), 13–32. doi:10.33203/mfy.1084274

Moretti, E. (2013). Real Wage Inequality. American Economic Journal. *American Economic Journal. Applied Economics*, *5*(1), 65–103. doi:10.1257/app.5.1.65

Ocoró, M. P., Polo, O. C. C., & Khandare, S. (2023). Importance of Business Financial Risk Analysis in SMEs According to COVID-19. *FMDB Transactions on Sustainable Management Letters*, *1*(1), 12–21.

Paoletti, J. B. (2012). Pink and Blue: Telling the Boys from the Girls in America. *America.*

Phoek, S. E. M., Lauwinata, L., & Kowarin, L. R. N. (2023). Tourism Development in Merauke Regency, South Papua Province: Strengthening Physical Infrastructure for Local Economic Growth and Enchanting Tourist Attractions. *FMDB Transactions on Sustainable Management Letters*, *1*(2), 82–94.

Priscila, S. S., Rajest, S. S., Tadiboina, S. N., Regin, R., & András, S. (2023). Analysis of Machine Learning and Deep Learning Methods for Superstore Sales Prediction. *FMDB Transactions on Sustainable Computer Letters*, *1*(1), 1–11.

Ramu, V. B., & Yeruva, A. R. (2023). Optimising AIOps system performance for e-commerce and online retail businesses with the ACF model. *International Journal of Intellectual Property Management*, *13*(3/4), 412–429. doi:10.1504/IJIPM.2023.134064

Rousille, N. (2021). *The Central Role of the Ask Gap in Gender Pay Inequality.* Academic Press.

Saxena, D., Khandare, S., & Chaudhary, S. (2023). An Overview of ChatGPT: Impact on Academic Learning. *FMDB Transactions on Sustainable Techno Learning*, *1*(1), 11–20.

Sayers, R. C. (2012). The cost of being female: Critical comment on block. *Journal of Business Ethics*, *106*(4), 519–524. doi:10.100710551-011-1017-4

Srinivas, K., Velmurugan, P. R., & Andiyappillai, N. (2023). Digital Human Resources and Management Support Improve Human Resources Effectiveness. *FMDB Transactions on Sustainable Management Letters*, *1*(1), 32–45.

Srivastava, D. K., & Roychoudhury, B. (2020). Words are important: A textual content based identity resolution scheme across multiple online social networks. *Knowledge-Based Systems*, *195*, 105624. doi:10.1016/j.knosys.2020.105624

Srivastava, D. K., & Roychoudhury, B. (2021). Understanding the Factors that Influence Adoption of Privacy Protection Features in Online Social Networks. *Journal of Global Information Technology Management*, *24*(3), 164–182. doi:10.1080/1097198X.2021.1954416

Stamberg, S. (2014). Girls Are Taught To 'Think Pink. In ' But That Wasn't Always So. Academic Press.

Stevens, J. L., & Shanahan, K. J. (2017). Structured abstract: Anger, willingness, or clueless? Understanding why women pay a pink tax on the products they consume. In *Creating Marketing Magic and Innovative Future Marketing Trends* (pp. 571–575). Springer International Publishing. doi:10.1007/978-3-319-45596-9_108

Tregouet, T. (2015). Gender-based price discrimination in matching markets. *International Journal of Industrial Organization, 42*, 34–45. doi:10.1016/j.ijindorg.2015.05.007

Tripathi, S., & Al-Shahri, M. (2023). Problems and Prospects on the Evolution of Advertising and Public Relations Industries in Oman. *FMDB Transactions on Sustainable Management Letters, 1*(1), 1–11.

Vashishtha, E., & Dhawan, G. (2023). Comparison of Baldrige Criteria of Strategy Planning and Harrison Text. *FMDB Transactions on Sustainable Management Letters, 1*(1), 22–31.

Vashishtha, E., & Kapoor, H. (2023). Implementation of Blockchain Technology Across International Healthcare Markets. *FMDB Transactions on Sustainable Technoprise Letters, 1*(1), 1–12.

Yeruva, A. R., & Ramu, V. B. (2023). AIOps research innovations, performance impact and challenges faced. *International Journal of System of Systems Engineering, 13*(3), 229–247. doi:10.1504/IJSSE.2023.133013

Zelniker, N. (2018). *Pink tax' means women still pay more for goods and services*. Academic Press.

Chapter 22
Big Data in Driving Greener Social Welfare and Sustainable Environmental Management

Thangaraja Arumugam
(iD) https://orcid.org/0000-0001-5496-7258
Vellore Institute of Technology, Chennai, India

V. Vinayagalakshmi
(iD) https://orcid.org/0000-0003-0075-6222
Vellore Institute of Technology, India

K. M. Ashifa
Istanbul Nisantasi University, Turkey

Uday Kiran
Vellore Institute of Technology, India

S. Ramya
(iD) https://orcid.org/0009-0000-1275-748X
Vellore Institute of Technology, India

ABSTRACT

The emergence of big data (BD) has opened up new opportunities for addressing social and environmental challenges. This chapter examines the potential of BD to drive green social welfare and sustainable environmental management. The chapter highlights how big data can be used to develop new approaches for monitoring and managing natural resources and addressing social issues such as poverty and inequality. It explores how big data can be used to promote sustainable development, from enhancing resource efficiency to improving disaster management. The chapter also discusses challenges associated with using big data for social welfare and sustainable development, including privacy concerns and improved data quality. Ultimately, the chapter concludes that big data has the potential to transform our approach to sustainable development but that a coordinated effort is required to ensure that it is used effectively and responsibly.

DOI: 10.4018/979-8-3693-0049-7.ch022

1. INTRODUCTION

The quotes deficit the power of big data. The developments in digital technology have enabled the gathering of vast amounts of data on people's behaviors and preferences, primarily through social media and online activities. As a result, tremendous amounts of digitized trace data have accumulated. This has led to the development of methods for analyzing this data, which has become a lucrative enterprise. However, concerns about privacy and the potential misuse of personal information have also arisen, leading to calls for increased regulation and transparency in data collection and use.

The large amount of data collected on individuals through digital means has numerous practical applications in different sectors. Advertisers, insurers, and bankers utilize this data to improve their services and gain market insights. The concept of "big data" is used to describe the process of managing and analyzing vast amounts of data. There isn't a universally accepted definition, and most people concur that big data refers to extremely vast and complex data collections that need specialized analysis and processing methods and technology.

Data-intensive science is represented by the branch of big data known as scientific big data, which has traits including complexity, comprehensiveness, global reach, and strong information and communication technology integration (Halevi & Moed, 2012). Despite its growing significance in research, its theories, approaches, and models are rarely applied. External characteristics of scientific big data include objective natural processes and objects, disparate data quantities across fields, and significant levels of uncertainty, dimensionality, and computing complexity. Understanding its internal workings and how to use it in research is crucial. The Chinese government has funded scientific big data research to foster public welfare research and create service centers for scientific big data applications to deal with national security challenges and economic and social growth (Guo et al. 2014).

The impact of big data analytics on enterprises has already been significant, with a range of innovative applications being developed. The possibilities are endless, from online to offline commerce to proactive customer support and IoT-equipped autos. Big data is so disruptive that it's transforming how we approach decision-making across various fields. Big data is used to discover information dissemination patterns, crime, diseases, etc. Location analytics is only one example of how this is being done. And it's evident how big data can completely renovate how we live, effort, and play, given its wide range of applications in fields like technology and science, smart health and well-being, security, and public safety. Companies are increasingly utilizing big data to gather information and build knowledge to achieve social and environmental sustainability. The emergence of this era of open information has prompted a sense of urgency in developing sustainable environmental management. However, despite calls from both internal and external stakeholders, the concept of environmental sustainability in business remains a topic of debate.

Executives may face challenges in meeting the increasing environmental demands and adjusting their operations accordingly. To address these challenges and create sustainable value, scholars and practitioners have suggested utilizing big data as an emerging tool for generating practical ideas. Research studies by authors including Keeso (2014) and Song et al. (2018) provide examples of these concepts.

Schoech et al. (2002) proposed utilizing knowledge management systems to build a collective knowledge repository for social workers that various agencies can access. Nevertheless, challenges in technology and expenses have hindered the implementation of such systems. Integrating information electronically across multiple agencies to establish a harmonized system is known as interoperability.

Big data techniques are currently being utilized in various businesses, including the welfare sector in North America and, more significantly, in New Zealand and Australia. These efforts seek to compile information from many sources and use cutting-edge analytical techniques to promote the use of evidence in decision-making. Recent research has demonstrated the value of big data as an additional data source and analytical tool for investigating social welfare policies and practices, particularly for analyzing large and longitudinal datasets. Despite recent technological improvements, environmental protection and social welfare have slowly adopted the digital information age. Much debate in the social sciences has been ignited by the potential of big data projects to offer new perspectives on the preparation and distribution, including aiming for societal amenities by utilizing information from numerous databases across government and non-governmental organizations. The practical difficulties of deploying big data operations in the field and their potential effects on effectiveness have not yet been fully investigated.

Scholars have different viewpoints regarding the application of big data for social welfare and environmental management, with some saying that issues with high dimensionality, security, and privacy may limit its advantages. Despite this, big data practice has been fuelled by the growing trend of companies and attention to environmental management. By considering several BD competencies, including leadership, client relations, technology, and culture, this study intends to examine the effects of big information on the association among executive quality for service welfare and sustainable environmental management.

This chapter is divided into four key components to help it accomplish its objectives. The study setting is introduced in the first section, emphasizing big data's value to the environment and social welfare. The theoretical foundations for big data, service well-being, and environmental management are presented in the second section. Case studies are presented in the third section to show how big data may be used to generate and promote service welfare. The fourth and last section will focus on case studies that show how big data is used to develop and assist environmental management. The chapter ends with suggestions for additional study on this crucial subject.

2. LITERATURE REVIEW

2.1 Defining Big Data

The concept of big data is relatively recent, and its historical origins are somewhat ambiguous. It likely began early in discussions held at Silicon Graphics Inc. (SGI) during the mid-1990s, but it gained significant prominence around 2011. The current buzz around big data can be attributed to the marketing efforts of top technology companies, notably IBM, which invested in promoting the specialized analytics market. Over time, the definitions of big data have evolved rapidly, leading to some degree of confusion. Some definitions focused on big data, while others attempted to elucidate what it can achieve, as revealed in a Harris Interactive online survey of 154 C-suite global executives conducted in April 2012 on behalf of SAP (Beaver et al., 2010). Big data encompasses an extensive array of data characterized by high volume, high velocity, and heterogeneity. Effectively processing this data demands creative and cost-effective techniques, with the ultimate goal of enhancing comprehension and decision-making.

As per the Tech America Foundation's Federal Big Data Commission findings in 2012, big data pertains to substantial amounts of swiftly moving, intricate, and diverse information assets. These assets demand sophisticated methods and technologies for their capture, storage, distribution, management, and analysis.

The trio of Volume, Variety, and Velocity represents three key dimensions of challenges within data management (Gandomi & Haider, 2015).

- **Volume:** Big data sizes are quantified in terms of multiple terabytes and petabytes, with volume indicating the quantity of data involved. Over half of the 1144 people who participated in an IBM study in the middle of 2012 said they thought datasets larger than one terabyte were big data. Big data volumes are defined in terms of time and data type, with future thresholds changing due to expanding storage capabilities and the demand for various data management solutions. As the size of datasets might change, it is impossible to determine a particular criterion for huge data volumes because the industry also affects these parameters.
- **Variety:** Technology advancements have enabled businesses to employ organized, semi-structured, and unstructured data, referred to as variety in big data. Five percent of all data is structured, tabular, and unorganized for analysis. Text, photos, audio, and video are all unstructured data types. Organizations can now use data in business operations thanks to new data management technologies and analytics, such as facial recognition for store visits and clickstream data for online merchants.
- **Velocity:** Velocity refers to the speed at which data is generated and processed. The surge in data creation, driven by digital devices such as smartphones and sensors, has made real-time analytics and data-driven decision-making indispensable. For instance, Wal-Mart and other businesses conduct over a million transactions every hour, creating data for tailored offers and increased consumer value. Big data technologies are needed for real-time intelligence because traditional data management systems cannot handle enormous data flows.

As a key feature of big data, Oracle highlights that value often exhibits a low-value density, implying that the initial data received usually possesses limited value in proportion to its volume. Nonetheless, a substantial value can be discerned by examining substantial quantities of similar data. These aspects of big data are crucial for effective data management and analysis.

Big data limitations are determined by a company's size, industry, and location, all of which change over time. Because these dimensions are interdependent, changes in one can impact the others. In any business or social endeavor, a critical "three-V tipping point" exists beyond which traditional data management and analysis methods prove inadequate for prompt intelligence. The future should be marked by an equilibrium both businesses and society seek.

2.2 Big Data Analytics

When properly applied to decision-making, big data is helpful. In order to do this, organizations require effective procedures that can transform massive amounts of data into insightful information. Data management and analytics are the first two steps in drawing insights from large data. Data management refers to the procedures and tools used to collect, store, and prepare data. Analytics, conversely, refers to the techniques used to analyze and derive valuable insights from vast quantities of data. "extracting insights" from big data can be seen as an overarching process, with big data analytics serving as a component within it. In this article, we introduce a pertinent selection of big data analytics tools and briefly discuss analytical approaches for both structured and unstructured data within big data.

Text analytics: Within the realm of text analytics, information is derived from textual data through the application of statistical analysis, computational linguistics, and machine learning techniques. Information extraction (IE), summarization, question-and-answer (QA), and sentiment analysis are techniques (Jiang, 2012). IE collects structured information from unstructured text, whereas QA responds to inquiries in natural language. Sentiment analysis examines opinionated material using methodologies broken down into subgroups at the document, phrase, and aspect levels. These methods improve a company's overall business operations by assisting with consumer sentiment analysis and decision-making.

Audio analytics: In order to enhance customer experience, assess agent effectiveness, and pinpoint service or product problems, consumer call centers and the healthcare industry utilize a technology called audio analytics, sometimes known as voice analytics (Patil, 2010). It can handle irate callers, offer real-time feedback, and analyze live calls. It assists with medical condition diagnosis and treatment, analyses baby cries and manages massive volumes of data from speech-driven clinical documentation systems.

Video analytics: Video analytics, or video content analysis, is used for monitoring, inspecting, and extracting valuable information from video streams. This method is commonly utilized in automated security and surveillance systems and retail settings for marketing and operational management purposes (Brown et al., 2011). Retail allows for the organization of multimedia data to enable easy searching and retrieval, aiding retailers in identifying missed opportunities. Server-based and edge-based are the two methods used in video analytics. When analyzing content, edge-based architecture applies analytics at the system's edge rather than routing video to a central server.

Social media analytics involves examining data from social media platforms, encompassing structured and unstructured information, and emphasizes analytics based on content and structure. Nodes and edges, which stand in for users and connections, are used to model the structure of social networks (Aggarwal, 2011). The visualization of massive networks, identification of human behavioral patterns, and prediction of emergent features are all made possible by community discovery, social influence analysis, and link prediction. These strategies are useful in marketing, the www, biology, security, and recommendation systems.

Predictive analytics: To forecast future results across several disciplines, predictive analytics uses historical and present data. Moving averages, linear regression, regression, and machine learning algorithms are some of the methods (Fan et al., 2014). The heterogeneity, noise build-up, incidental endogeneity of big data, and spurious correlation, which can result in false positives and jeopardize the reliability of statistical methods, make it difficult to develop new statistical methods for big data.

2.3 Big Data in Social Welfare

In "Truth About Big Data," Becker states that there are no entirely novel data quality concerns in Big Data analytics ventures (Becker et al., 2015). It is a scientific, cultural, and intellectual context that relies on the interaction of technology, mythology, and analysis. It has given rise to many utopian and dystopian languages, identified as important ethical concerns (Boyd & Crawford, 2012).

The use of data can be influenced by the perspectives and values of individuals conducting the research by considering the politics and subjectivities involved with the help of big data to prevent biases from being reinforced and to encourage fair use (Gillingham & Graham, 2017). For big data to favorably influence evidence-based policy and practice, q several traditional practical issues must be resolved. Above all, we require fresh critical perspectives on big data that start doubting its veracity as a naturalized representation of social reality (Crawford et al., 2014). As part of his theoretical contribution to the scientific dialogue surrounding Big Data employs three main methodologies. The fundamental features of Big Data are first exposed. Second, we provide solutions that prove Big Data can be managed. Here, we outline some potential approaches to Big Data. Third, our research showed that Big Data can lead to beneficial results, such as a higher return on investment (Pospiech & Felden, 2015). According to a study by Qasim Ali Nisar, public hospitals prioritize big data management more than commercial hospitals to help make effective decisions and improve environmental performance (Nisar). The many driving factors of big data such as economic sustainability, social uncertainty, and environmental concerns. However, research by Gangwar, Mishra, and Kamble shows that economic sustainability holds more weight than social and environmental sustainability, as reflected in their index values.

2.4 Big Data in Environmental Management

Environmental management is a complex field that requires large amounts of data to make informed decisions (Stankov, 2020). In current eons, the propagation of big data has transformed how environmental management is conducted, making it possible to accumulate and investigate huge amounts of information. Big data refers to vast, intricate data sets that cannot be processed using conventional methods (Song et al., 2018). It is characterized by its volume, velocity, and variety, which make it difficult to store, analyze, and visualize. Environmental management is the processes and techniques used to protect, conserve, and restore the natural environment.

Many systems and tools have been created to manage and evaluate large data in environmental management. Geographic Information Systems (GIS) is a tool used to manage, analyze, and visualize spatial data. It has become an important tool in environmental management, letting users map and analyze environmental data (Antenucci et al., 1991). Remote sensing is a method used to gather data from a remote location, often satellites or aircraft. It is an important tool in environmental management, allowing users to collect data on large areas quickly and efficiently (Chi et al., 2016).

Developing algorithms that can learn from data and predict the future is known as "machine learning," a subset of artificial intelligence. Environmental management lets users analyze and predict environmental trends and patterns (Sun et al., 2019). Implementing big data for environmental sustainability and conservation is concentrated on managing climate change, natural resource utilisation, and biodiversity. The authors emphasize the significance of big data in various fields, especially when it originates to anticipating and minimizing the properties of climate change (Cai & Li, 2019). Big data in environmental monitoring and management, considering the usage of big data in monitoring biodiversity, water quality, and air quality. Big data can potentially enhance environmental monitoring and management, particularly in creating new monitoring methods and enhancing data analysis (Zhu et al., 2017).

3. THE DATA-DRIVEN REVOLUTION FOR SOCIAL GOOD: EMPOWERING SOCIAL WELFARE WITH BIG DATA

With the growth of technology and the accessibility of enormous data, social welfare agencies are exploring ways to use big data to improve their services and programs. "Randy Bean, the creator of New Vantage, wrote an article for Forbes titled 'Another Side of Big Data: Big Data for Social Good' in which he suggests that big data can serve a purpose beyond simply speeding up learning and commercial insights" (Gillingham, 2019). Big data in social welfare can help agencies identify current social problems in our society, such as healthcare problems, cyberbullying, urban planning, and natural disasters (Madyatmadja et al., 2022). Big data is presently used in social welfare in many ways:

- **Predictive analytics:** Social welfare agencies can leverage big data to detect patterns and trends related to social issues such as child abuse, poverty, and homelessness.
- **Resource allocation:** By analyzing social indicators such as poverty and unemployment data, social welfare agencies can leverage big data to allocate their resources more effectively to areas and populations that require it the most.
- **Artifice discovery:** Big data can be used to detect fraud in social welfare programs, such as Medicaid and food stamp programs. With these large datasets, agencies can identify fraud patterns and intervene to prevent them.
- **Program evaluation:** Social welfare agencies can use big data to evaluate the effectiveness of their programs by analyzing the outcomes of these programs. The data-driven approach enables agencies to identify which programs produce positive results and which need improvement.

3.1 From Insights to Action: Using Big Data to Drive Social Change

Big data practice in societal welfare has the potential to produce a variety of advantages. (Pastorino, et al, 2019), Including:

- **Improved decision-making**: Social welfare organizations can utilize BD to acquire useful evidence about the requirements of the communities they cater to. By analyzing vast datasets, these organizations can recognize recurring patterns and trends that aid in formulating effective decision-making strategies.
- **Enhanced program design**: Big data enables social welfare agencies to design programs tailored to the communities' unique needs.
- **Optimized service delivery:** By utilizing data analytics, agencies can pinpoint areas where services are most needed and allocate resources accordingly, resulting in more effective service delivery.

3.2 The Dark Side of Big Data: Challenges in Using Data for Social Welfare

"In their article 'Big Data for Social Innovation' published in the Stanford Social Innovation Review magazine, Kevin C. Desouza and Kendra L. Smith discuss several concerns that need to be addressed for big data to be useful in social work". The major issues they highlight are the lack of agency communication and the reluctance to share raw data. The authors emphasize the importance of overcoming these barriers to effectively leverage big data for social innovation (Schneider & Seelmeyer, 2019). The other challenges they addressed such as:

- **Data Quality:** Data quality can be a challenge in social welfare, as data is often collected from multiple sources and may be incomplete or inconsistent.
- **Resource Constraints:** Enacting big data analytics can be an exclusive, needful, and important outlay in technology, infrastructure, and people. This could be a task for social welfare agencies with limited resources.

- **Technical Proficiency:** Effectively analyzing big data demands specific technical competencies and expertise. Numerous social welfare organizations may lack the resources or personnel to analyze and utilize big data.
- **Regulatory Compliance:** Social welfare agencies are subject to various regulatory requirements, including "data protection laws and regulations". With the help of big data, we must comply with these regulations, which can be complex and time-consuming.

3.3 The Fine Line: Balancing Ethical and Privacy Concerns With Big Data in Social Welfare

The help of big data in social welfare can provide many benefits, but it also raises ethical and privacy concerns that must be addressed to protect the rights of individuals.

One major concern is the potential for bias and discrimination. Big data algorithms can perpetuate existing biases and reinforce discriminatory practices, leading to unfair treatment of certain groups. To address this concern, social welfare agencies must ensure that data is collected and analyzed in a fair and unbiased way, with diverse datasets and multiple perspectives incorporated into the analysis process. Another concern is the privacy and confidentiality of personal information.

Big data in social welfare may contain sensitive information, such as health records, income, and employment history. Individuals have a right to know how their data is collected, used, and stored. To address this concern, social welfare agencies must ensure that all data is anonymized or de-identified before it is analyzed to protect the privacy of individuals while still allowing for meaningful analysis (Kshetri, 2014). Informed consent is another important ethical consideration.

Individuals should have the right to know how their data is collected and used and provide informed consent before their data is collected. Social welfare agencies must communicate transparently with individuals about collecting, storing, and using their data. Finally, data security is a significant concern (Loebbecke & Picot, 2015). Social welfare data is subject to security risks, such as cyberattacks and data breaches. Social assistance organizations must respond to this by putting strong security measures in place to safeguard the data from unwanted access and misuse, such as encryption, firewalls, and access limits.

While big data can bring significant benefits to social welfare, it is important to address the ethical and privacy concerns associated with its use (Philip & Graham, 2017). Social welfare agencies must ensure that data is collected and analyzed fairly and unbiasedly, that individuals are informed and provide informed consent, and that data is protected from unauthorized access or misuse.

3.4 Case Studies

- In the aftermath of natural disasters like hurricanes, earthquakes, or floods, timely and effective response is crucial to save lives and relieve affected communities. During Hurricane Harvey in 2017, the American Red Cross used big data and analytics to track social media posts, online maps, and weather data to identify areas where help was most needed. This information helped them deploy resources, such as emergency supplies and personnel, to the most affected areas, improving the efficiency of their response efforts (Wan & Zhu, 2020).
- The Los Angeles Homeless Services Authority (LAHSA) uses big data and predictive analytics to identify individuals most likely to become homeless based on previous homeless history, income, employment, and health data. This information helps them allocate resources, such as housing

vouchers, job training, and case management services, to individuals at risk of homelessness and prevent them from becoming homeless (Lorenzo, 2021).

- The United States Department of Agriculture (USDA) uses big data and analytics to analyze the income and demographic data of participating school students to identify those eligible for free or reduced-price meals. This information helps schools and districts effectively target and enroll eligible students in nutrition assistance programs, ensuring adequate nutrition and supporting their overall health and well-being (Dohlman et al., 2022).

4. GREENING THE GLOBE: BIG DATA'S IMPACT ON ENVIRONMENTAL MANAGEMENT DEVELOPMENT

Big data has grown important as a tool for environmental management, giving decision-makers access to more thorough and precise data to address difficult environmental problems. (Kong et al., 2020). Examples of current and future use of big data in environmental management are shown below:

- **Climate modeling:** Big data can enhance climate modeling, allowing scientists to correctly forecast future climate change effects. For instance, the European Center for Medium-Range Weather Predictions uses big data to run high-resolution models of future climatic conditions.
- **Monitoring environmental conditions:** Big data enables real-time environmental monitoring. For instance, the "National Oceanic and Atmospheric Administration" (NOAA) makes use of big data to track and monitor hurricanes, typhoons, and other meteorological events.
- **Managing natural resources:** Big data can be used to manage natural resources more efficiently. For example, the Forest Service uses big data to identify areas at risk of wildfire and prioritize resources for mitigation efforts.
- **Wildlife conservation:** Big data can be used to track wildlife populations and movements, enabling better conservation efforts. For example, the Wildlife Conservation Society uses big data to monitor the movements of elephants in Africa and identify areas where they are at risk of poaching.
- **Air and water quality monitoring:** Real-time monitoring of the quality of the air and water is possible with big data. Big data is used, for instance, by the City of Chicago to measure emissions from industrial plants and monitor air quality.
- **Waste management:** Big data can improve waste management by identifying areas where waste is generated and developing more efficient disposal and recycling systems.

4.1 The Power of Big Data for A Green Future: How Environmental Management Can Benefit

The vast amounts of data generated by environmental sensors, satellites, and citizen science initiatives can provide valuable insights into our planet's health and help us make more informed decisions to protect it (Runting et al., 2020). Hence, the potential benefits of using big data in environmental management include:

- **Improved resource management:** Big data can help managers make more informed decisions about natural resource management. Through large volumes of data, managers can identify trends and patterns that inform more efficient and sustainable use of resources.
- **More accurate monitoring and assessment:** Big data can provide more comprehensive and accurate information about environmental conditions. This can enable managers to identify and respond to emerging issues more quickly and effectively.
- **Better decision-making:** Big data can inform more evidence-based decision-making by providing more comprehensive and accurate information. This can help ensure that decisions are based on data rather than assumptions or guesswork.

4.2 The Complexities of Utilizing Big Data in Environmental Management

Environmental sensors and monitoring systems provide excessive data, which must be analyzed using cutting-edge technological techniques and knowledge. (Lucivero, 2020). Hence, the several complexities of using big data in environmental management include:

- **Data quality and reliability:** Big data is only valuable if it is of good quality and reliability. However, data quality can vary widely, and managers must ensure their data is accurate and relevant.
- **Data privacy and security:** Environmental data can be sensitive and must be protected to ensure it is not misused or disclosed inappropriately.
- **Technical capacity:** Analyzing big data requires technical expertise and specialized software and infrastructure. Managers must ensure they have the technical capacity to analyze and interpret the data they collect.
- **Cost:** The collection and analysis of big data can be expensive. Managers must ensure that the benefits of using big data outweigh the costs.

4.3 Navigating Ethical and Environmental Concerns in Big Data for Environmental Management

the help of big data in environmental management is becoming increasingly important as decision-makers seek more comprehensive and accurate information to address complex environmental challenges (Dubey et al., 2019). The potential benefits of using big data in environmental management include improved resource management, more accurate monitoring and assessment, and better decision-making. One of the key benefits of using big data in environmental management is the ability to improve resource management. By analyzing large volumes of data, managers can identify trends and patterns that inform more efficient and sustainable use of resources (Etzion & Aragon-Correa, 2016). For example, big data can identify areas at risk of wildfire and prioritize resources for mitigation efforts or optimize the placement of renewable energy infrastructure to maximize energy output and minimize environmental impacts.

Big data can also provide more comprehensive and accurate information about environmental conditions, enabling managers to identify and respond to emerging issues more quickly and effectively (Song et al., 2017). For example, big data can monitor air and water quality in real time or track wildlife populations and movements, enabling better conservation efforts. Finally, big data can inform more evidence-based decision-making by providing decision-makers with more comprehensive and accurate information. This can help ensure that decisions are based on data rather than assumptions or guesswork (Corbett, 2018). For example, big data can inform climate modeling, enabling scientists to predict the future impacts of climate change more accurately and inform policy decisions.

However, the help of big data in environmental management also presents several challenges, such as data quality and reliability, data privacy and security, technical capacity, and cost. Addressing these challenges is crucial to ensure that big data is used responsibly and sustainably. Overall, with help of big data in environmental management presents both opportunities and challenges. By addressing ethical and environmental concerns and adopting sustainable and responsible practices, managers can ensure that big data is used to benefit both the environment and society.

4.4 Big Earth Data Analysis

Big Earth data analysis and mining are essential for proving the worth of huge data and efficiently utilizing it. However, due to their complexity, high correlation, and noise, conventional strategies like divide-and-conquer and scale-change are challenging. Traditional spatiotemporal data mining techniques like spatial autoregressive models and machine learning have heavy processing demands and frequent I/O operations. There is an urgent need for automated methods rooted in intelligent reasoning theory to improve data mining and facilitate scientific discoveries within the vast realm of Earth data (Guo, H, 2017).

The "CASEarth" project, initiated by the Chinese Academy of Sciences (CAS) as part of their Strategic Priority Research Programme (SPRP), focuses on conducting comprehensive research using a wealth of Earth data. The project promotes multidisciplinary, cross-scale scientific investigations, rekindling interest in large-scale Earth studies. By approaching major scientific challenges from a systematic and all-encompassing perspective, CASEarth seeks to deepen our understanding of the Earth's intricate system (Gibb et al., 2022). At its core, the project aims to establish an international hub for advancing big earth data science, with three central objectives.

First, it aspires to create the world's leading platform for big earth data. Second, it aims to pioneer global infrastructure capable of handling extensive Earth data. Finally, it seeks to develop a decision support system. CASEarth distinguishes itself through three key methods: advancing scientific knowledge, driving technological innovation, and supporting governmental decision-making. As part of this initiative, a high-precision cloud service platform for Big Earth Data will be established. This platform will introduce novel approaches and paradigms for making scientific discoveries using extensive data. Furthermore, it will provide real-time decision support by harnessing large-scale Earth data (Guo et al., 2017).

Knowledge-based economies and big data represent a critical frontier that reshapes our daily lives and enhances our global comprehension. This paradigm relies on correlations and cutting-edge methodologies, which drive the expansion of various fields. A subset of this extensive data, known as big Earth data, introduces a novel dimension to Earth sciences research and can potentially bring about a revolutionary shift in the discipline. A pressing need exists to confront the scientific challenge of integrating Earth system models with diverse forms of big Earth data. To address this challenge, the Chinese Academy of Sciences' Strategic Priority Research Programme, in collaboration with domestic and international scientists, is dedicated to establishing a global center specializing in the science of big earth data.

4.5 Case Studies

- The Beijing Municipal Environmental Monitoring Center in China uses big data and Internet of Things (IoT) technologies to collect and analyze data from thousands of air quality monitoring stations. The data includes information on various air pollutants, meteorological conditions, and traffic patterns. By analyzing this data, the center can identify pollution hotspots, track changes in air quality, and make data-driven decisions to mitigate air pollution, such as implementing traffic control measures, adjusting industrial emissions, and issuing health advisories (Kumar et al., 2019).

- The South Florida Water Management District (Wanvestraut, 2020) in the United States uses big data and remote sensing technologies to collect and analyze data from sensors placed in water bodies, weather stations, and other sources. The data includes information on water levels, water quality, evapotranspiration, and rainfall. By analyzing this data, the district can make informed decisions on water allocation, flood control, and water quality management, which helps protect water resources and ensure sustainable water management practices.

- The SMART (Spatial Monitoring and Reporting Tool) program developed by the Wildlife Conservation Society (Conservancy, 2021) uses big data and satellite technologies to track the movement of endangered species, such as elephants, rhinos, and tigers. The data includes information on animal locations, movements, behaviors, and threats such as poaching and habitat loss. By analyzing this data, conservationists can identify areas where animals are at risk, deploy resources to prevent poaching, and implement conservation measures to protect endangered species and their habitats.

5. CONCLUSION

In summary, businesses use big data to create sustainable business plans that align with environmental sustainability. Due to growing pro-environmental attitudes, businesses are shifting from traditional, environmentally harmful operating procedures to more expensive, eco-friendly alternatives. Big data provides effective solutions that balance environmental concerns with cost and profitability, especially in the face of competition and sustainability challenges. Big data analytics are also used to assess sustainable development goals and predict potential environmental hazards, indicating a promising future for an environment-centric big data revolution.

It is important to prioritize the development of regional open data platforms that can facilitate the mobilization of data for achieving global goals. To prevent the misuse of big data, additional research must be conducted. Although algorithms have been developed to assist in decision-making and prioritize assistance for those most in need in the social welfare sector, the practical applications of these algorithms have lacked dependability and real-world applicability. Generating trustworthy data is a major obstacle to the further adoption of big data technologies in this sector, and fresh ideas are needed to develop and apply information systems in social welfare organizations. Policymakers, managers, practitioners, and service consumers should not be intimidated by the amount of data, the complexity of algorithms, or the computational power required for big data. Experts referenced in the chapter suggest that collaboration and discussion about data collection, classification, and use are essential and that algorithmic accountability must be at the forefront of any big data initiatives.

To effectively utilize big data in the social welfare sector, stakeholders must come together and discuss what information is needed, how to collect it, classify it, and use it to train algorithms. Algorithmic accountability should serve as the foundation for these developments, and professionals from both the data science and social welfare fields should collaborate to explore the potential benefits of big data approaches. Independent research should support and ensure the transparency of big data development, implementation, and use in social welfare organizations. While there is a growing body of research on creating algorithms, little is known about their application in social welfare settings and how practitioners would respond to algorithmic decision-support tools. While big data initiatives in social welfare are still in their early stages, concerns about vulnerability and accuracy may slow their progress, leading to reconsidering investment in the field.

REFERENCES

Aggarwal, C. C. (2011). *An introduction to social network data analytics.* Springer US. doi:10.1007/978-1-4419-8462-3

Antenucci, J. C., Brown, K., Croswell, P. L., Kevany, M. J., & Archer, H. (1991). *Geographic Information Systems: a guide to the technology* (Vol. 115). Van Nostrand Reinhold.

Baesens, B., Bapna, R., Marsden, J. R., Vanthienen, J., & Zhao, J. L. (2016). Transformational issues of big data and analytics in networked business. *Management Information Systems Quarterly, 40*(4), 807–818. doi:10.25300/MISQ/2016/40:4.03

Beaver, D., Kumar, S., Li, H. C., Sobel, J., & Vajgel, P. (2010). Finding a needle in haystack: Facebook's photo storage. *9th USENIX Symposium on Operating Systems Design and Implementation (OSDI 10).*

Becker, D., King, T. D., & McMullen, B. (2015, October). Big data, big data quality problem. In *2015 IEEE International Conference on Big Data (Big Data)* (pp. 2644-2653). IEEE. 10.1109/BigData.2015.7364064

Boyd, D., & Crawford, K. (2012). Critical questions for big data: Provocations for a cultural, technological, and scholarly phenomenon. *Information Communication and Society, 15*(5), 662–679. doi:10.1080/1369118X.2012.678878

Brown, B., Bughin, J., Byers, A. H., Chui, M., Dobbs, R., Manyika, J., & Roxburgh, C. (2011). *Big data: The next frontier for innovation, competition, and productivity.* McKinsey Global Institute.

Cai, L., Qi, Y., Wei, W., Wu, J., & Li, J. (2019). mrMoulder: A recommendation-based adaptive parameter tuning approach for big data processing platform. *Future Generation Computer Systems, 93,* 570–582. doi:10.1016/j.future.2018.05.080

Chen, H., Chiang, R. H., & Storey, V. C. (2012). Business intelligence and analytics: From big data to big impact. *Management Information Systems Quarterly, 36*(4), 1165–1188. doi:10.2307/41703503

Chi, M., Plaza, A., Benediktsson, J. A., Sun, Z., Shen, J., & Zhu, Y. (2016). Big data for remote sensing: Challenges and opportunities. *Proceedings of the IEEE, 104*(11), 2207–2219. doi:10.1109/JPROC.2016.2598228

Conservancy, N. (2021). Wildlife Conservation Society. *WORLD (Oakland, Calif.).*

Corbett, C. J. (2018). How sustainable is big data? *Production and Operations Management, 27*(9), 1685–1695. doi:10.1111/poms.12837

Crawford, K., Gray, M. L., & Miltner, K. (2014). Big Data| Critiquing Big Data: Politics, ethics, epistemology| special section introduction. *International Journal of Communication, 8*, 10.

Dohlman, E., Hansen, J., & Boussios, D. (2022). *USDA Agricultural Projections to 2031 (No. 323859).* United States Department of Agriculture.

Dubey, R., Gunasekaran, A., Childe, S. J., Papadopoulos, T., Luo, Z., Wamba, S. F., & Roubaud, D. (2019). Can big data and predictive analytics improve social and environmental sustainability? *Technological Forecasting and Social Change, 144*, 534–545. doi:10.1016/j.techfore.2017.06.020

El-Gayar, O., & Fritz, B. D. (2006). Environmental management information systems (EMIS) for sustainable development: A conceptual overview. *Communications of the Association for Information Systems, 17*(1), 34. doi:10.17705/1CAIS.01734

Etzion, D., & Aragon-Correa, J. A. (2016). Big data, management, and sustainability: Strategic opportunities ahead. *Organization & Environment, 29*(2), 147–155. doi:10.1177/1086026616650437

Fan, J., Han, F., & Liu, H. (2014). Challenges of big data analysis. *National Science Review, 1*(2), 293–314. doi:10.1093/nsr/nwt032 PMID:25419469

Gandomi, A., & Haider, M. (2015). Beyond the hype: Big data concepts, methods, and analytics. *International Journal of Information Management, 35*(2), 137–144. doi:10.1016/j.ijinfomgt.2014.10.007

Gangwar, H., Mishra, R., & Kamble, S. (2023). Adoption of big data analytics practices for sustainable development in the e-commerce supply chain: A mixed-method study. *International Journal of Quality & Reliability Management, 40*(4), 965–989. doi:10.1108/IJQRM-07-2021-0224

Gibb, R. G., Purss, M. B., Sabeur, Z., Strobl, P., & Qu, T. (2022). Global reference grids for big earth data. *Big Earth Data, 6*(3), 251–255. doi:10.1080/20964471.2022.2113037

Gillingham, P. (2019). Big data in social welfare. In *Big Data* (pp. 245–263). Edward Elgar Publishing. doi:10.4337/9781788112352.00016

Gillingham, P., & Graham, T. (2017). Big data in social welfare: The development of a critical perspective on social work's latest "electronic turn". *Australian Social Work, 70*(2), 135–147. doi:10.1080/03 12407X.2015.1134606

Graham, T. (2014). Technologies of choice: the structural shaping of choice on the World Wide Web. *Challenging Identities, Institutions and Communities: Refereed Proceedings of the TASA 2014*, 1-13.

Guo, H. (2017). Big Earth data: A new frontier in Earth and information sciences. *Big Earth Data, 1*(1-2), 4–20. doi:10.1080/20964471.2017.1403062

Guo, H., Liu, Z., Jiang, H., Wang, C., Liu, J., & Liang, D. (2017). Big Earth Data: A new challenge and opportunity for Digital Earth's development. *International Journal of Digital Earth, 10*(1), 1–12. doi:10.1080/17538947.2016.1264490

Guo, H., Wang, L., Chen, F., & Liang, D. (2014). Scientific big data and digital Earth. *Chinese Science Bulletin, 59*(35), 5066–5073. doi:10.100711434-014-0645-3

Halevi, G., & Moed Dr, H. F. (2012). The evolution of big data as a research and scientific topic: Overview of the literature. *Research Trends, 1*(30), 2.

Jee, K., & Kim, G. H. (2013). Potentiality of big data in the medical sector: Focus on how to reshape the healthcare system. *Healthcare Informatics Research, 19*(2), 79–85. doi:10.4258/hir.2013.19.2.79 PMID:23882412

Jiang, J. (2012). Information extraction from text. *Mining text data*, 11-41.

Keeso, A. (2014). *Big data and environmental sustainability: a conversation starter*. Smith School of Enterprise and the Environment. Working Paper Series, (14-04).

Kong, L., Liu, Z., & Wu, J. (2020). A systematic review of big data-based urban sustainability research: State-of-the-science and future directions. *Journal of Cleaner Production, 273*, 123142. doi:10.1016/j.jclepro.2020.123142

Kshetri, N. (2014). Big data's impact on privacy, security, and consumer welfare. *Telecommunications Policy, 38*(11), 1134–1145. doi:10.1016/j.telpol.2014.10.002

Kumar, S., Tiwari, P., & Zymbler, M. (2019). Internet of Things is a revolutionary approach for future technology enhancement: A review. *Journal of Big Data, 6*(1), 1–21. doi:10.118640537-019-0268-2

Loebbecke, C., & Picot, A. (2015). Reflections on societal and business model transformation arising from digitization and big data analytics: A research agenda. *The Journal of Strategic Information Systems, 24*(3), 149–157. doi:10.1016/j.jsis.2015.08.002

Lorenzo, C. (2021). *Los Angeles Homeless Services Authority (LAHSA) Homelessness Prevention Program Evaluation* [Doctoral dissertation]. California State University, Northridge.

Lucivero, F. (2020). Big data, big waste? A reflection on the environmental sustainability of big data initiatives. *Science and Engineering Ethics, 26*(2), 1009–1030. doi:10.100711948-019-00171-7 PMID:31893331

Madyatmadja, E. D., Hiererra, S. E., Sembiring, D. J. M., Karya, S., & Pristinella, D. (2022, August). Social Media in Business Intelligence as a Solution Toward Social Problems: A Systematic Literature Review. In *2022 International Conference on Information Management and Technology (ICIMTech)* (pp. 505-510). IEEE. 10.1109/ICIMTech55957.2022.9915261

Nisar, Q. A., Nasir, N., Jamshed, S., Naz, S., Ali, M., & Ali, S. (2021). Big data management and environmental performance: Role of big data decision-making capabilities and decision-making quality. *Journal of Enterprise Information Management, 34*(4), 1061–1096. doi:10.1108/JEIM-04-2020-0137

Pastorino, R., De Vito, C., Migliara, G., Glocker, K., Binenbaum, I., Ricciardi, W., & Boccia, S. (2019). Benefits and challenges of Big Data in healthcare: An overview of the European initiatives. *European Journal of Public Health, 29*(Supplement_3), 23–27. doi:10.1093/eurpub/ckz168 PMID:31738444

Patil, H. A. (2010). "Cry Baby": Using Spectrographic Analysis to Assess Neonatal Health Status from an Infant's Cry. *Advances in speech recognition: Mobile environments, call centers and clinics*, 323-348.

Philip, G., & Graham, T. (2017). *Big Data in Social Welfare: The Development of a Critical Perspective on Social Work's Latest*. Electronic Turn.

Pick, J. B., Turetken, O., Deokar, A. V., & Sarkar, A. (2017). Location analytics and decision support: Reflections on recent advancements, a research framework, and the path ahead. *Decision Support Systems*, *99*, 1–8. doi:10.1016/j.dss.2017.05.016

Pospiech, M., & Felden, C. (2015, October). Towards a big data theory model. In *2015 IEEE International Conference on Big Data (Big Data)* (pp. 2082-2090). IEEE. 10.1109/BigData.2015.7363990

Runting, R. K., Phinn, S., Xie, Z., Venter, O., & Watson, J. E. (2020). Opportunities for big data in conservation and sustainability. *Nature Communications*, *11*(1), 2003. doi:10.103841467-020-15870-0 PMID:32332744

Schneider, D., & Seelmeyer, U. (2019). Challenges in using big data to develop decision support systems for social work in Germany. *Journal of Technology in Human Services*, *37*(2-3), 113–128. doi:10.1080/15228835.2019.1614513

Schoech, D., Fitch, D., MacFadden, R., & Schkade, L. L. (2002). From data to intelligence: Introducing the intelligent organization. *Administration in Social Work*, *26*(1), 1–21. doi:10.1300/J147v26n01_01

Song, M., Cen, L., Zheng, Z., Fisher, R., Liang, X., Wang, Y., & Huisingh, D. (2017). How would big data support societal development and environmental sustainability? Insights and practices. *Journal of Cleaner Production*, *142*, 489–500. doi:10.1016/j.jclepro.2016.10.091

Song, M. L., Fisher, R., Wang, J. L., & Cui, L. B. (2018). Environmental performance evaluation with big data: Theories and methods. *Annals of Operations Research*, *270*(1-2), 459–472. doi:10.100710479-016-2158-8

Stankov, I. (2020, September). Environmental management information systems. In *2020 12th Electrical Engineering Faculty Conference (BulEF)* (pp. 1-7). IEEE. 10.1109/BulEF51036.2020.9326021

Sun, A. Y., & Scanlon, B. R. (2019). How can Big Data and machine learning benefit environment and water management: A survey of methods, applications, and future directions. *Environmental Research Letters*, *14*(7), 073001. doi:10.1088/1748-9326/ab1b7d

Wan, Y., & Zhu, Q. (2020). The IT Challenges in Disaster Relief: What We Learned From Hurricane Harvey. *IT Professional*, *22*(6), 52–58. doi:10.1109/MITP.2020.3005675

Wanvestraut, R. (2020). *South Florida Water Management District Utility Rate Survey*. Academic Press.

Ward, J. S., & Barker, A. (2013). *Undefined by data: a survey of big data definitions*. arXiv preprint arXiv:1309.5821.

Zhu, C., Zhou, H., Leung, V. C., Wang, K., Zhang, Y., & Yang, L. T. (2017). Toward big data in green city. *IEEE Communications Magazine*, *55*(11), 14–18. doi:10.1109/MCOM.2017.1700142

Chapter 23
Embracing the Future of Retail With Virtual Try-On Technology

Rupayan Roy

Department of Fashion Technology, National Institute of Fashion Technology, Kannur Campus, Kannur, India

Swetha Ramakrishnan

Department of Fashion Technology, National Institute of Fashion Technology, Kannur Campus, Kannur, India

ABSTRACT

This chapter provides an overview of virtual try-on technology and its potential impact on the retail industry. It defines the technology and its various types, including AR, VR, and 3D modeling. The chapter also discusses the benefits of virtual try-on technology, including improved customer engagement, reduced return rates, and increased sales. However, the chapter also explores the limitations of the technology, such as technical constraints and cost barriers. Privacy and ethical considerations are also discussed. The chapter examines the future of virtual try-on technology, particularly the potential impact of emerging technologies such as 5G, AI, and AR/VR. It emphasizes the need for retailers to invest in this technology and prioritize user experience to stay competitive and meet changing consumer needs. Overall, this chapter provides a comprehensive overview of virtual try-on technology and its significance in the digital age of retail.

1. INTRODUCTION

Over the past few decades, there has been a tremendous revolution in the retail sector, driven by changes in customer behaviour and technological improvements (Shankar et al., 2021). The emergence of e-commerce has completely changed the game by allowing customers to shop whenever they want, from anywhere. To deliver a pleasurable shopping experience that rivals the in-store experience, for example, has proven to be a new challenge for retailers as a result of this shift (Arora and Verma, 2019).

DOI: 10.4018/979-8-3693-0049-7.ch023

Introducing virtual try-on. Retailers looking for fresh approaches to communicate with customers and give them a more engaging and dynamic shopping experience are increasingly implementing this cutting-edge technology. Customers can virtually try on things, such as apparel or accessories, in a simulated setting without having to make physical contact. To give users a realistic and dynamic experience, it makes use of a variety of approaches, including augmented reality (AR), virtual reality (VR), and 3D modelling (Bonetti et al., 2019, Dacko, 2017, Liu11 et al., 2018). The Figure 1 shows the market shear of AR in Retail.

Figure 1. AR in retail market research report 2022-2028
Source: Alam et al. (2022)

The capacity of virtual try-on to address a number of difficulties faced by retailers is the reason for its rising popularity. First off, by giving customers a more engaging and immersive experience with the product, it improves consumer engagement and happiness. Secondly, it can reduce return rates and associated costs by allowing customers to make more educated purchasing decisions (Violante et al., 2019). Finally, because technology enables customers to more clearly perceive the product and its features, virtual try-on can result in higher sales and revenue.

Virtual try-on does have some restrictions and difficulties, though. This article will examine the potential of virtual try-on technology and its implications on the future of retail management. Technical constraints and economic obstacles may prevent its adoption, while user experience issues and ethical and privacy concerns may also surface (Xi et al., 2022). The article's thesis is that businesses may improve customer experiences, lower return rates, and boost sales by utilising virtual try-on technology, which is a game-changer. The essay will go into greater detail about the advantages and drawbacks of virtual try-on, the effects it has had on the retail sector, and the potential and difficulties it brings for merchants. By the end of this essay, readers will have a better grasp of how virtual try-on technology may help shops stay competitive and fulfil the changing needs of consumers in the digital age.

2. THE CURRENT STATE OF RETAIL MANAGEMENT

2.1 Overview of Traditional Retail Practices

Our economy has relied heavily on retail for many years. Customers would physically visit a store, look around the merchandise, and then make a purchase. In order to draw customers, retailers have to place their stores in busy places and outfit them with eye-catching visual marketing displays. Since then, the retail sector has seen substantial change. Retailers must increasingly compete with online merchants that provide a convenient, hassle-free buying experience due to the growth of e-commerce. In order to compete in the online market and improve client engagement, many brick-and-mortar companies have been forced to invest in digital technologies (Chan, 2013).

2.2 Challenges Faced by Brick-and-Mortar Stores in the Digital Age

The loss of foot traffic is one of the main problems facing brick and mortar retailers in the digital age. Physical establishments are finding it more and more challenging to draw customers as people increasingly purchase online. Sales have decreased as a result, which can be difficult for small and medium-sized retailers (Keels, 2021). The requirement to give clients a smooth omnichannel experience presents another difficulty. Customers increasingly demand a consistent experience across all platforms, including online, mobile, and physical stores, thanks to the growth of e-commerce. In order to analyse customer interactions across channels and deliver individualised advice and offers, merchants must invest in digital technologies (Rigby, 2011).

Brick and mortar stores also struggle with managing logistics and inventory. They must make sure that the appropriate products are available at the appropriate times in the appropriate quantities. A sophisticated inventory management system that can monitor sales data and modify inventory levels appropriately is needed for this. They must also make sure they can effectively handle order fulfilment, shipping, and refunds (Ricker and Kalakota, 1999). Customer satisfaction is an issue for traditional brick-and-mortar retailers as well. Customers today want a convenient and personalised buying experience with quick checkout, free delivery, and simple returns thanks to the growth of e-commerce. Retailers must make technological investments to enable them to offer these services while also maintaining clean, well-maintained stores with knowledgeable and amiable staff (Zimmermann et al., 2023, Duarte et al., 2018).

For brick-and-mortar stores, the COVID-19 pandemic has brought yet another set of difficulties. Sales have been significantly damaged by store closings and decreased foot traffic, and safety concerns have raised the demand for sanitization and social isolation measures (Pantano and Willems, 2022). Many retailers are making investments in digital technologies to help them overcome these obstacles and improve customer engagement and the omnichannel experience. For instance, several businesses offer clients virtual try-on experiences using augmented reality (AR) and virtual reality (VR) technologies. Other people are offering tailored advice and customer assistance utilising chatbots and artificial intelligence (AI) (Elnahla and Neilson, 2021).

Ultimately, the old retail model is up against formidable obstacles in the digital era. Brick-and-mortar retailers must invest in digital solutions that help them manage inventory and logistics, improve consumer engagement, offer a seamless omnichannel experience, and create a positive shopping experience. Those who can effectively overcome these obstacles will be in a good position to compete in the dynamic retail environment.

3. VIRTUAL TRY-ON: DEFINITION AND TYPES

With the help of a computer or mobile device, shoppers may virtually try on things thanks to a relatively new technology called virtual try-on. Particularly in the fashion and cosmetics sectors, it has grown in popularity recently. Virtual try-on technology creates a realistic, interactive experience that enables customers to see how a product will look on them before making a purchase using augmented reality (AR), virtual reality (VR), and 3D modelling (Lee et al., 2022, Feng and Xie, 2019).

3.1 Explanation of What Virtual Try-On Is and How It Works

A digital image of a product is placed over a real-time video or picture of the customer to create a virtual try-on. This gives the buyer a real-time preview of how the product will appear on them. To produce a realistic, interactive experience, the technology combines computer vision, machine learning, and 3D modelling (Hilken et al., 2018). Customers normally need to download a mobile app or visit a website that offers virtual try-on capabilities in order to use virtual try-on technology. In order to build a digital avatar or model, they must next submit a photo or video of themselves. The buyer can next peruse a variety of products and select those they want to virtually try on (Plotkina and Saurel, 2019).

The virtual try-on technology places a digital representation of the product over the customer's avatar or model when they choose a product. The user can then pan and zoom the avatar or model to view how the item appears from various perspectives. They can also alter the product's size, style, or colour to see how it appears in other configurations (Liu et al., 2020).

3.2 Overview of Different Types of Virtual Try-On Technologies

Virtual try-on solutions come in a variety of forms, and each one takes a distinct approach to giving clients a genuine, engaging experience (Merle et al., 2012). The following are some of the most popular virtual try-on technologies:

3.2.1 Augmented Reality (AR)

AR is a technology that superimposes digital data on the physical world. The usage of augmented reality (AR) in virtual try-on involves superimposing a digital representation of a product over a real-time video or photograph of the customer. To ensure that the digital representation of the product is perfectly aligned with the client's body, AR technology uses computer vision and machine learning to accurately track the location and movements of the customer (Tawira and Ivanov, 2023).

The fashion and beauty sectors make extensive use of augmented reality (AR), which enables clients to digitally try on apparel, accessories, and makeup. A mobile app is often used to access AR virtual try-on technology, which records a live video of the user using the device's camera (Wang et al., 2022).

3.2.2 Virtual Reality (VR)

With the use of AR, digital data can be superimposed on the physical world. With regard to virtual try-on, augmented reality (AR) is used to superimpose a digital image of a product over a real-time video or image of the consumer. Computer vision and machine learning are used in augmented reality (AR) to precisely track the position and motion of the client, ensuring that the digital representation of the product is appropriately aligned with the customer's body (Daassi and Debbabi, 2021).

Customers may virtually try on clothing, accessories, and makeup thanks to the widespread usage of augmented reality (AR) technology in the fashion and beauty sectors. The majority of the time, a smartphone app is used to access AR virtual try-on technology, which captures a live video of the user (Bonetti et al., 2019) via the device's camera.

3.2.3 3D Modeling

With the aid of technology, three-dimensional digital objects can be generated. A digital representation of the product is created using 3D modelling for virtual try-ons and can be superimposed over a live video or an image of the customer. The fashion and beauty sectors make extensive use of 3D modelling technology to produce digital representations of attire, accessories, and cosmetics. The creation of virtual try-on experiences that let customers see how a product will look on them before making a purchase can then be done using these digital models (Javornik, 2016).

Figure 2. Virtual try-on technology

a) Picture to Upload by consumer

b) Source Picture (Product)

c) Virtually constructed (blended) image of the consumer

The subject of virtual try-on technology is quickly developing and altering how consumers buy for goods. Virtual try-on technology is assisting in bridging the gap between online and offline retail by giving customers a realistic, interactive experience that allows them to virtually try on products (Kim and Forsythe, 2008). Virtual try-on will certainly be used in even more creative ways in the retail sector as technology advances and becomes more widely available as shown in Figure 2. Virtual try-on technology, whether it be through augmented reality, virtual reality, or 3D modelling, is influencing the future of retail management and enabling customers to have a more personalised and interesting shopping experience (Chylinski et al., 2020, Boardman et al., 2020).

4. BENEFITS OF VIRTUAL TRY-ON FOR RETAILERS

The use of virtual try-on technology to improve the shopping experience for customers is quickly gaining favour in the retail sector. Virtual try-on technology is changing the way that merchants connect with their customers by enabling shoppers to virtually try on things prior to making a purchase. It also offers a number of benefits to retailers. We will examine some of the major advantages of virtual try-on technology for merchants in this paper (Hwangbo et al., 2020).

4.1 Improved Customer Engagement and Satisfaction

Virtual try-on technology helps merchants increase consumer engagement and satisfaction, which is one of its main advantages. Virtual try-on technology aids in establishing a more emotional bond between customers and products by giving them a more realistic, interactive purchasing experience. Retailers may see an increase in client loyalty and return business as a result (Hwangbo et al., 2020).

The frustration that customers frequently experience when making online purchases is further lessened by the use of virtual try-on technology. For instance, buyers who purchase for apparel online frequently worry about how a certain item will fit or appear on them. By enabling clients to digitally try on apparel and see how it will look on their body type, virtual try-on technology offers a solution to this issue (Baytar and Ashdown, 2015). Virtual try-on technology can help merchants strengthen their relationships with their customers and eventually boost their bottom line by delivering a more enjoyable, rewarding shopping experience.

4.2 Reduced Return Rates and Associated Costs

For retailers, a key advantage of virtual try-on technology is that it lowers return rates and related expenses. Customers are more likely to return a product if it doesn't live up to their expectations when they are unclear of how it will fit or appear (Sahoo et al., 2018). Retailers may incur considerable expenses as a result, such as shipping and restocking costs, as well as a reduction in sales. Virtual try-on technology gives customers a more accurate idea of how a thing will fit and appear, which lowers the percentage of returns. This may lessen the quantity of goods returned, which will ultimately minimise the costs incurred by retailers (Gallino and Moreno, 2018).

4.3 Increased Sales and Revenue

Virtual try-on technology can also aid retailers in boosting sales and revenue. Virtual try-on technology can aid in boosting the likelihood that a purchase will be made by giving customers a more interesting and gratifying shopping experience (Zhang et al., 2019). Customers who utilised virtual try-on technology, for instance, were found to be 60% more likely to make a purchase than those who did not, according to a study by Avametric. The same survey also discovered that customers who used virtual try-on technology had an average order value that was 35% greater than those who did not (Tawira and Ivanov, 2023). These results imply that virtual try-on technology can be a useful tool for businesses to increase sales and revenue, and that it is an investment that is worthwhile for retailers trying to expand their business.

4.4 Examples of Successful Implementation by Major Retailers

Virtual try-on technology has already been successfully used by a number of large retailers. For instance, utilising augmented reality technology, the beauty retailer Sephora allows clients to virtually test on makeup via their smartphone. Customers can do this instead of physically trying on things to see how different makeup hues will look on their skin tone (Tan et al., 2022).

Another illustration is the eyewear company Warby Parker, which allows clients to virtually test on glasses via their website. This gives buyers a better idea of how various frames will seem on their facial features and gives a more accurate portrayal of how the glasses will fit and appear in real life (Bodhani, 2012). These examples show how businesses in a range of industries can successfully deploy virtual try-on technology and how it can offer major advantages to both retailers and customers.

The retail sector is fast changing thanks to virtual try-on technology, which also benefits merchants in a number of ways. Virtual try-on technology is assisting shops to stay competitive in the digital age by enhancing consumer engagement and satisfaction, lowering return rates and related expenses, and increasing sales and revenue (Berman and Pollack, 2021, Singh, 2022). Virtual try-on technology has developed into a useful tool for merchants aiming to satisfy the changing demands and expectations of their customers as e-commerce becomes more and more important and there is a growing demand for more interactive and personalised shopping experiences (Blázquez, 2014). Future developments in virtual try-on solutions are probably going to be considerably more sophisticated as technology develops, thus boosting its possibilities and benefiting businesses even more (Varadarajan et al., 2010).

Overall, merchants have found virtual try-on technology to be a worthwhile investment, and those who have done so successfully have seen notable increases in customer engagement, satisfaction, and sales. As a result, it is anticipated that in the upcoming years, virtual try-on technology will spread throughout the retail sector and continue to play a significant role in determining the future of retail management.

5. CHALLENGES AND LIMITATIONS OF VIRTUAL TRY-ON

The retail sector could undergo a change thanks to virtual try-on technology, which would provide customers a more engaging and dynamic buying experience. Virtual try-on, however, is not without its difficulties and restrictions, much like any new technology (Lau et al., 2019; Song et al., 2020). We will examine some of the main drawbacks and restrictions of virtual try-on technology in this article, including technical constraints and financial barriers, issues with and concerns about the user experience, and ethical and privacy issues.

5.1 Technical Limitations and Cost Barriers

The technical constraints that come with virtual try-on technology are one of its key drawbacks. It can be a difficult procedure that takes a lot of time and resources to produce realistic virtual representations of items (Violante and Vezzetti, 2014). For other businesses, especially smaller ones with tighter budgets, this may not be practical due to hefty development costs and a drawn-out implementation procedure. The accuracy of technologies used for virtual try-ons presents another technical difficulty. Virtual try-ons can provide consumers a general notion of how a product would seem on them, but they are not necessarily an exact portrayal (Kim and LaBat, 2013). There is still some room for error in terms of how closely the virtual product can be matched to the real product because variations in body shape, size, and skin tone can alter how a product appears in a virtual environment (Koritnik et al., 2008).

Another obstacle to virtual try-on technology is cost. Virtual try-on technology implementation can be expensive, especially for smaller stores who do not have the funds to purchase the required hardware and software (Qasem, 2021, Xi et al., 2022). The overall cost of the technology may also be increased by continuous upkeep expenses, updates, and the requirement to continually enhance the virtual try-on experience.

5.2 User Experience Challenges and Concerns

Assuring a great user experience using virtual try-on technology is another difficulty. The technology's usability is one of the primary issues. Customers could find it challenging to use the virtual try-on interface or to comprehend how it works. Customers may become frustrated as a result and stop utilising the virtual try-on feature altogether (Qasem, 2021; Wolfinbarger and Gilly, 2001). The quality of the virtual try-on experience is another issue with user experience. Although technology for virtual try-ons has advanced significantly in recent years, there are still limitations to the level of accuracy and depth that can be accomplished. Customers may be very put off by poor virtual product representations, which could ultimately result in lower sales and consumer satisfaction (Gu et al., 2014).

5.3 Ethical and Privacy Considerations

With regard to virtual try-on technology, there are additional ethical and privacy issues to consider. Use of client data is one of the primary issues. Customers who use virtual try-on technology must provide a photo of themselves, which might cause privacy and data security problems. Retailers must make sure that they are clear about how consumer data is handled and maintained and that they have adequate data protection safeguards in place (Feng et al., 2019; Pearson and Benameur, 2010).

The potential for virtual try-on technology to encourage unhealthy body image norms is another ethical problem. Virtual try-on technology might unintentionally foster harmful body image norms and unattainable beauty standards by giving clients a virtual depiction of how a product would look on them (Mears, 2010). Retailers need to be aware of this and make sure that their virtual try-on equipment isn't spreading harmful messages about body image.

The development of virtual try-on technology has the potential to revolutionise the retail sector by giving consumers a more engaging and dynamic shopping experience. Virtual try-on does, however, have its difficulties and limitations, much like any new technology (Pachoulakis and Kapetanakis, 2012, De et al., 2019). Virtual try-on technology adoption may be hampered by technical constraints, financial constraints, user experience issues, and ethical and privacy concerns, among other factors.

Retailers must make the appropriate investments in skills and money to provide high-quality virtual try-on experiences in order to overcome these difficulties and constraints. This entails purchasing the required gear and software in addition to engaging qualified developers and designers who can produce accurate virtual representations of products. Retailers must also put the user experience first and take measures to make sure that their virtual try-on platforms are simple to use and give accurate product representations.

When deploying virtual try-on technology, merchants must also take ethical and privacy concerns into account. Retailers must, for instance, make sure that they get the proper consent from customers before collecting and using their personal data, such as photos or biometric data. Retailers must also put in place the necessary security measures to guard against theft and unauthorised use of this data (Varadarajan et al., 2010).

Retailers must also take into account the possible effects of virtual try-on technology on retail industry jobs. Virtual try-on technology has the potential to boost productivity and cut expenses, but it also has the potential to eliminate jobs for traditional retail positions like sales assistants and fitting room attendants (Ogunjimi et al., 2021). Retailers must therefore weigh the advantages of virtual try-on technology against any potential consequences it may have on their staff and take action to counteract any unfavourable outcomes.

Virtual try-on technology has many advantages for both shops and customers, but it also has drawbacks and limitations. However, businesses can successfully deploy virtual try-on technology to improve their business processes and offer a greater customer experience by carefully considering these variables and investing in the appropriate resources and skills (Chircu and Kauffman, 2000).

6. THE FUTURE OF VIRTUAL TRY-ON IN RETAIL MANAGEMENT

The retail sector is being rapidly transformed by the introduction of virtual try-on technology, which offers both customers and businesses a number of advantages. In order to stay competitive and satisfy changing consumer demands, merchants must stay abreast of new developments in virtual try-on as technology develops (Kim et al., 2017).

6.1 Emerging Technologies and Innovations

The application of augmented reality (AR) and virtual reality (VR) technologies is one of the most interesting breakthroughs in virtual try-on technology. The Figure 3 represents the the block diagram of the working principle of virtual try-on technology. Consumers can interact with products in a more lifelike and engaging way using AR and VR technologies, which let them fully immerse themselves in a virtual environment (Ekmeil et al., 2021). Because AR technology enables users to superimpose virtual images over actual situations, it is especially well-suited for virtual try-on applications. For instance, a customer may use the camera on their smartphone to place a virtual pair of glasses on their face and see how they would seem on them in real-time. Contrarily, virtual reality (VR) technology produces a fully immersive virtual world that may be utilised to replicate the sensation of trying on clothing. For instance, a customer may test out various furniture arrangements in a virtual living room or try on clothes in a virtual dressing room using a VR headset (Oh et al., 2004).

Aside from machine learning algorithms, which can be used to enhance the accuracy and realism of virtual try-on experiences, other emerging technologies in virtual try-on include 3D scanning and modelling, which enables retailers to create extremely accurate and detailed virtual representations of products.

Figure 3. Block diagram for the working principle of virtual try-on

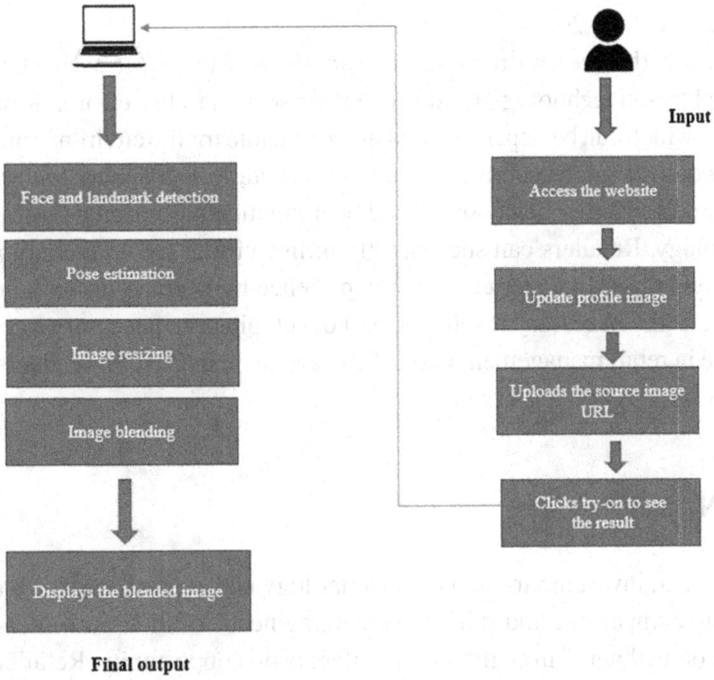

6.2 Potential Impact on the Retail Industry and Consumer Behavior

The retail sector and consumer behaviour could be dramatically impacted by the adoption of virtual try-on technology. Virtual try-on technology can boost customer engagement and happiness by giving customers a more participatory and engaging shopping experience, which will enhance sales and revenue for merchants (Mnyakin, 2020).

By enabling customers to preview how things will appear and fit before making a purchase, virtual try-on technology can also aid in lowering return rates and related costs. This may result in more assured purchasing choices and fewer returns, which may cost businesses money (Gallino and Moreno, 2018).

Additionally, the use of virtual try-on technology could alter how customers browse for goods. Consumers may start to demand virtual try-on capabilities when making purchases either online or in-person as virtual try-on technology becomes more common and advanced (Yaoyuneyong et al., 2014).

6.3 Opportunities for Retailers to Stay Competitive and Meet Changing Consumer Needs

Retailers must continue to invest in virtual try-on technology and stay current with new trends and advances in order to remain competitive and fulfil the changing needs of their customers. Retailers have the chance to use virtual try-on technology as part of their omnichannel initiatives (Yemenici, 2022). Retailers may give their customers a seamless and uniform purchasing experience by enabling virtual try-on capabilities across all channels, including online, mobile, and in-store.

Utilizing virtual try-on technology to customise the shopping experience for their clients is another chance for merchants. Retailers might, for instance, recommend things based on a customer's past purchases or likes and then give them the option to virtually put them on before making a purchase (Blázquez, 2014; Pereira et al., 2022).

Finally, by decreasing the need for real product samples and the waste associated with returns, merchants can use virtual try-on technology to improve their sustainability efforts. Retailers can lessen the need for real samples, which can be expensive and unsustainable for the environment, by adopting virtual try-on technology to deliver more accurate product representations (Papahristou and Bilalis, 2016).

The retail sector and consumer behaviour could be dramatically impacted by the quickly developing virtual try-on technology. Retailers can successfully utilise virtual try-on technology to improve their business operations and offer a greater customer experience by keeping up with new developments in technology, investing in the necessary resources, and developing the necessary knowledge. Virtual try-on has a bright future in retail management and offers several chances for merchants to stay competitive and satisfy their customers' evolving wants.

7. CONCLUSION

Retailers must continue to invest in virtual try-on technology and keep up with new trends and advances if they want to remain competitive and fulfil the changing needs of their customers. The use of virtual try-on technology in omnichannel initiatives by retailers is one opportunity. Retailers may offer smooth and standardised shopping experiences for their customers by enabling virtual try-on capabilities across all channels, including online, mobile, and in-store. Retailers can also give their customers a more tailored buying experience by utilising virtual try-on technology. Retailers may, for instance, recommend things based on past purchases or preferences of a customer and then let the buyer virtually try those products on before making a purchase. The requirement for real product samples and waste from returns can both be decreased by shops using virtual try-on technology to improve their sustainability efforts. Retailers can cut back on the need for real samples, which can be expensive and environmentally unsustainable, by adopting virtual try-on technology to deliver more accurate product representations.

Virtual try-on technology is advancing quickly and has the potential to have a big impact on both consumer behaviour and the retail sector. Retailers can successfully utilise virtual try-on technology to improve their business operations and offer a greater customer experience by keeping up with new developments in technology, investing in the necessary resources, and developing the essential skills. Virtual try-on has a promising future in retail management and offers several chances for businesses to remain competitive and adapt to changing consumer demands.

REFERENCES

Arora, S., & Verma, A. (2019). M-commerce: Crusader for "Phygital" retail. In M-Commerce (pp. 163-182). Apple Academic Press.

Baytar, F., & Ashdown, S. (2015). An exploratory study of interaction patterns around the use of virtual apparel design and try-on technology. *Fashion Practice*, *7*(1), 31–52.

Berman, B., & Pollack, D. (2021). Strategies for the successful implementation of augmented reality. *Business Horizons*, *64*(5), 621–630. doi:10.1016/j.bushor.2021.02.027

Blázquez, M. (2014). Fashion shopping in multichannel retail: The role of technology in enhancing the customer experience. *International Journal of Electronic Commerce*, *18*(4), 97–116. doi:10.2753/JEC1086-4415180404

Blázquez, M. (2014). Fashion shopping in multichannel retail: The role of technology in enhancing the customer experience. *International Journal of Electronic Commerce*, *18*(4), 97–116. doi:10.2753/JEC1086-4415180404

Boardman, R., Henninger, C. E., & Zhu, A. (2020). Augmented reality and virtual reality: new drivers for fashion retail? *Technology-Driven Sustainability: Innovation in the Fashion Supply Chain*, 155-172.

Bodhani, A. (2012). Shops offer the e-tail experience. *Engineering & Technology*, *7*(5), 46–49. doi:10.1049/et.2012.0512

Bonetti, F., Pantano, E., Warnaby, G., & Quinn, L. (2019). Augmenting reality: Fusing consumers' experiences and interactions with immersive technologies in physical retail settings. *International Journal of Technology Marketing*, *13*(3-4), 260–284. doi:10.1504/IJTMKT.2019.104592

. Bonetti, F., Pantano, E., Warnaby, G., Quinn, L., & Perry, P. (2019). Augmented reality in real stores: empirical evidence from consumers' interaction with AR in a retail format. *Augmented reality and virtual reality: The power of AR and VR for business*, 3-16.

Chan, J. P. (2013). *The promise of digital technology in brick and mortar retail* [Doctoral dissertation]. Massachusetts Institute of Technology.

Chircu, A. M., & Kauffman, R. J. (2000). Limits to value in electronic commerce-related IT investments. *Journal of Management Information Systems*, *17*(2), 59–80. doi:10.1080/07421222.2000.11045645

Chylinski, M., Heller, J., Hilken, T., Keeling, D. I., Mahr, D., & de Ruyter, K. (2020). Augmented reality marketing: A technology-enabled approach to situated customer experience. *Australasian Marketing Journal*, *28*(4), 374–384. doi:10.1016/j.ausmj.2020.04.004

Daassi, M., & Debbabi, S. (2021). Intention to reuse AR-based apps: The combined role of the sense of immersion, product presence and perceived realism. *Information & Management*, *58*(4), 103453. doi:10.1016/j.im.2021.103453

Dacko, S. G. (2017). Enabling smart retail settings via mobile augmented reality shopping apps. *Technological Forecasting and Social Change*, *124*, 243–256. doi:10.1016/j.techfore.2016.09.032

De Regt, A., & Barnes, S. J. (2019). V-commerce in retail: nature and potential impact. *Augmented reality and virtual reality: The power of AR and VR for business*, 17-25.

Duarte, P., Silva, S. C., & Ferreira, M. B. (2018). How convenient is it? Delivering online shopping convenience to enhance customer satisfaction and encourage e-WOM. *Journal of Retailing and Consumer Services, 44*, 161–169. doi:10.1016/j.jretconser.2018.06.007

Ekmeil, F. A. R., Abumandil, M. S. S., Alkhawaja, M. I., Siam, I. M., & Alaklouk, S. A. A. (2021, March). Augmented reality and virtual reality revolutionize rusiness transformation in digital marketing tech industry analysts and visionaries during Coronavirus (COVID 19). *Journal of Physics: Conference Series, 1860*(1), 012012. doi:10.1088/1742-6596/1860/1/012012

Elnahla, N., & Neilson, L. C. (2021). *The stressors faced by retail workers during the COVID-19 pandemic*. Academic Press.

Feng, Y., & Xie, Q. (2019). Privacy concerns, perceived intrusiveness, and privacy controls: An analysis of virtual try-on apps. *Journal of Interactive Advertising, 19*(1), 43–57. doi:10.1080/15252019.2018.1521317

Gallino, S., & Moreno, A. (2018). The value of fit information in online retail: Evidence from a randomized field experiment. *Manufacturing & Service Operations Management, 20*(4), 767–787. doi:10.1287/msom.2017.0686

Gu, B., & Ye, Q. (2014). First step in social media: Measuring the influence of online management responses on customer satisfaction. *Production and Operations Management, 23*(4), 570–582. doi:10.1111/poms.12043

Hilken, T., Heller, J., Chylinski, M., Keeling, D. I., Mahr, D., & de Ruyter, K. (2018). Making omnichannel an augmented reality: The current and future state of the art. *Journal of Research in Interactive Marketing, 12*(4), 509–523. doi:10.1108/JRIM-01-2018-0023

Hwangbo, H., Kim, E. H., Lee, S. H., & Jang, Y. J. (2020). Effects of 3d virtual "try-on" on online sales and customers' purchasing experiences. *IEEE Access : Practical Innovations, Open Solutions, 8*, 189479–189489. doi:10.1109/ACCESS.2020.3023040

Javornik, A. (2016). Augmented reality: Research agenda for studying the impact of its media characteristics on consumer behaviour. *Journal of Retailing and Consumer Services, 30*, 252–261. doi:10.1016/j.jretconser.2016.02.004

Keels, G. N. (2021). *Brick-and-Mortar Retail Stores Disappearing in the Digital Age: Marketing Strategies for Sustainability* [Doctoral dissertation]. University of Maryland University College.

Kim, D. E., & LaBat, K. (2013). Consumer experience in using 3D virtual garment simulation technology. *Journal of the Textile Institute, 104*(8), 819–829. doi:10.1080/00405000.2012.758353

Kim, H. Y., Lee, J. Y., Mun, J. M., & Johnson, K. K. (2017). Consumer adoption of smart in-store technology: Assessing the predictive value of attitude versus beliefs in the technology acceptance model. *International Journal of Fashion Design, Technology and Education, 10*(1), 26–36. doi:10.1080/17543266.2016.1177737

Kim, J., & Forsythe, S. (2008). Adoption of virtual try-on technology for online apparel shopping. *Journal of Interactive Marketing, 22*(2), 45–59. doi:10.1002/dir.20113

Koritnik, T., Bajd, T., & Munih, M. (2008). Virtual environment for lower-extremities training. *Gait & Posture, 27*(2), 323–330. doi:10.1016/j.gaitpost.2007.04.015 PMID:17596945

Lau, K. W., & Lee, P. Y. (2019). Shopping in virtual reality: A study on consumers' shopping experience in a stereoscopic virtual reality. *Virtual Reality (Waltham Cross), 23*(3), 255–268. doi:10.100710055-018-0362-3

Lee, H., Xu, Y., & Porterfield, A. (2022). Antecedents and moderators of consumer adoption toward AR-enhanced virtual try-on technology: A stimulus-organism-response approach. *International Journal of Consumer Studies, 46*(4), 1319–1338. doi:10.1111/ijcs.12760

Liu, X., Sohn, Y. H., & Park, D. W. (2018). Application development with augmented reality technique using Unity 3D and Vuforia. *International Journal of Applied Engineering Research, 13*(21), 15068-15071.

Liu, Y., Liu, Y., Xu, S., Cheng, K., Masuko, S., & Tanaka, J. (2020). Comparing VR-and AR-based try-on systems using personalized avatars. *Electronics (Basel), 9*(11), 1814. doi:10.3390/electronics9111814

Mears, A. (2010). Size zero high-end ethnic: Cultural production and the reproduction of culture in fashion modeling. *Poetics, 38*(1), 21–46. doi:10.1016/j.poetic.2009.10.002

Merle, A., Senecal, S., & St-Onge, A. (2012). Whether and how virtual try-on influences consumer responses to an apparel web site. *International Journal of Electronic Commerce, 16*(3), 41–64. doi:10.2753/JEC1086-4415160302

Mnyakin, M. (2020). Investigating the Impacts of AR, AI, and Website Optimization on Ecommerce Sales Growth. *ResearchBerg Review of Science and Technology, 3*(1), 116–130.

Ogunjimi, A., Rahman, M., Islam, N., & Hasan, R. (2021). Smart mirror fashion technology for the retail chain transformation. *Technological Forecasting and Social Change, 173*, 121118. doi:10.1016/j.techfore.2021.121118

Oh, H., Yoon, S. Y., & Hawley, J. (2004). What virtual reality can offer to the furniture industry. *Journal of Textile and Apparel. Technology and Management, 4*(1), 1–17.

Pachoulakis, I., & Kapetanakis, K. (2012). Augmented reality platforms for virtual fitting rooms. *The International Journal of Multimedia & Its Applications, 4*(4), 35–46. doi:10.5121/ijma.2012.4404

Pantano, E., Pedeliento, G., & Christodoulides, G. (2022). A strategic framework for technological innovations in support of the customer experience: A focus on luxury retailers. *Journal of Retailing and Consumer Services, 66*, 102959. doi:10.1016/j.jretconser.2022.102959

Pantano, E., & Willems, K. (2022). *Retail in a New World: Recovering from the Pandemic that Changed the World*. Emerald Group Publishing. doi:10.1108/9781801178464

Papahristou, E., & Bilalis, N. (2016). A new sustainable product development model in apparel based on 3D technologies for virtual proper fit. In *Sustainable Design and Manufacturing 2016* (pp. 85–95). Springer International Publishing. doi:10.1007/978-3-319-32098-4_8

Pereira, A. M., Moura, J. A. B., Costa, E. D. B., Vieira, T., Landim, A. R., Bazaki, E., & Wanick, V. (2022). Customer models for artificial intelligence-based decision support in fashion online retail supply chains. *Decision Support Systems*, *158*, 113795. doi:10.1016/j.dss.2022.113795

Plotkina, D., & Saurel, H. (2019). Me or just like me? The role of virtual try-on and physical appearance in apparel M-retailing. *Journal of Retailing and Consumer Services*, *51*, 362–377. doi:10.1016/j.jretconser.2019.07.002

Pruitt, J., & Adlin, T. (2010). *The persona lifecycle: keeping people in mind throughout product design*. Elsevier.

Qasem, Z. (2021). The effect of positive TRI traits on centennials adoption of try-on technology in the context of E-fashion retailing. *International Journal of Information Management*, *56*, 102254. doi:10.1016/j.ijinfomgt.2020.102254 PMID:33106720

Ricker, F., & Kalakota, R. (1999). Order fulfillment: the hidden key to e-commerce success. *Supply Chain Management Review, 11*(3), 60-70.

Rigby, D. (2011). The future of shopping. *Harvard Business Review*, *89*(12), 65–76.

Sahoo, N., Dellarocas, C., & Srinivasan, S. (2018). The impact of online product reviews on product returns. *Information Systems Research*, *29*(3), 723–738. doi:10.1287/isre.2017.0736

Shankar, V., Kalyanam, K., Setia, P., Golmohammadi, A., Tirunillai, S., Douglass, T., Hennessey, J., Bull, J. S., & Waddoups, R. (2021). How technology is changing retail. *Journal of Retailing*, *97*(1), 13–27. doi:10.1016/j.jretai.2020.10.006

Singh, N. (2022). Sustainable artificial intelligence tool strategy and customer experience in eye wear retail chain stores. *Journal of Contemporary Issues in Business and Government*, *28*(4), 935–951.

Song, H. K., Baek, E., & Choo, H. J. (2020). Try-on experience with augmented reality comforts your decision: Focusing on the roles of immersion and psychological ownership. *Information Technology & People*, *33*(4), 1214–1234. doi:10.1108/ITP-02-2019-0092

Tan, Y. C., Chandukala, S. R., & Reddy, S. K. (2022). Augmented reality in retail and its impact on sales. *Journal of Marketing*, *86*(1), 48–66. doi:10.1177/0022242921995449

Tawira, L., & Ivanov, A. (2023). Leveraging personalization and customization affordances of virtual try-on apps for a new model in apparel m-shopping. *Asia Pacific Journal of Marketing and Logistics*, *35*(2), 451–471. doi:10.1108/APJML-09-2021-0652

Tawira, L., & Ivanov, A. (2023). Leveraging personalization and customization affordances of virtual try-on apps for a new model in apparel m-shopping. *Asia Pacific Journal of Marketing and Logistics*, *35*(2), 451–471. doi:10.1108/APJML-09-2021-0652

Varadarajan, R., Srinivasan, R., Vadakkepatt, G. G., Yadav, M. S., Pavlou, P. A., Krishnamurthy, S., & Krause, T. (2010). Interactive technologies and retailing strategy: A review, conceptual framework and future research directions. *Journal of Interactive Marketing*, *24*(2), 96–110. doi:10.1016/j.intmar.2010.02.004

Violante, M. G., & Vezzetti, E. (2014). Implementing a new approach for the design of an e-learning platform in engineering education. *Computer Applications in Engineering Education*, 22(4), 708–727. doi:10.1002/cae.21564

Violante, M. G., Vezzetti, E., & Piazzolla, P. (2019). How to design a virtual reality experience that impacts the consumer engagement: The case of the virtual supermarket. *International Journal on Interactive Design and Manufacturing*, 13(1), 243–262. doi:10.100712008-018-00528-5

Wang, Y., Ko, E., & Wang, H. (2022). Augmented reality (AR) app use in the beauty product industry and consumer purchase intention. *Asia Pacific Journal of Marketing and Logistics*, 34(1), 110–131. doi:10.1108/APJML-11-2019-0684

Xi, N., Chen, J., Gama, F., Riar, M., & Hamari, J. (2022). The challenges of entering the metaverse: An experiment on the effect of extended reality on workload. *Information Systems Frontiers*, 1–22. doi:10.100710796-022-10244-x PMID:35194390

Xue, L., Parker, C. J., & McCormick, H. (2019). A virtual reality and retailing literature review: Current focus, underlying themes and future directions. *Augmented Reality and Virtual Reality: The Power of AR and VR for Business*, 27-41.

Yaoyuneyong, G., Foster, J. K., & Flynn, L. R. (2014). Factors impacting the efficacy of augmented reality virtual dressing room technology as a tool for online visual merchandising. *Journal of Global Fashion Marketing*, 5(4), 283–296. doi:10.1080/20932685.2014.926129

Yemenici, A. D. (2022). Entrepreneurship in the world of Metaverse: Virtual or real? *Journal of Metaverse*, 2(2), 71–82. doi:10.57019/jmv.1126135

Zhang, T., Wang, W. Y. C., Cao, L., & Wang, Y. (2019). The role of virtual try-on technology in online purchase decision from consumers' aspect. *Internet Research*, 29(3), 529–551. doi:10.1108/IntR-12-2017-0540

Zimmermann, R., Mora, D., Cirqueira, D., Helfert, M., Bezbradica, M., Werth, D., Weitzl, W. J., Riedl, R., & Auinger, A. (2023). Enhancing brick-and-mortar store shopping experience with an augmented reality shopping assistant application using personalized recommendations and explainable artificial intelligence. *Journal of Research in Interactive Marketing*, 17(2), 273–298. doi:10.1108/JRIM-09-2021-0237

Chapter 24
The Role of Renewable Energy Consumption in Promoting Sustainability and Circular Economy:
A Data-Driven Analysis

Lucio Laureti
Lum University Giuseppe Degennaro, Italy

Alessandro Massaro
Lum University Giuseppe Degennaro, Italy

Alberto Costantiello
Lum University Giuseppe Degennaro, Italy

Angelo Leogrande
Lum University Giuseppe Degennaro, Italy

ABSTRACT

In this chapter, the authors investigate the role of "renewable energy consumption" in the context of circular economy. They assume that the consumption of renewable energy is a proxy for the development of circular economy. They use data from the environmental, social, and governance (ESG) dataset of the World Bank for 193 countries in the period 2011-2020. They perform several econometric techniques (i.e., panel data with fixed effects, panel data with random effects, pooled ordinary least squares [OLS], weighted least squares [WLS]). The results show that "renewable energy consumption" is positively associated among others to "cooling degree days" and "adjusted savings: net forest depletion" and negatively associated among others to "greenhouse gas (GHG) net emissions/removals by land use change and forestry (LUCF)" and "mean drought index." Furthermore, they perform a cluster analysis with the application of the k-Means algorithm and find the presence of four clusters. Finally, they compare eight different machine-learning algorithms to predict the value of renewable energy consumption.

DOI: 10.4018/979-8-3693-0049-7.ch024

INTRODUCTION

In the following chapter we analyze the role of renewable energy consumption in the context of the circular economy with attention to environmental sustainability. The reasons that prompted us to tackle this analysis consist on the one hand in the empirical evidence of the existence of climate change (Nordhaus, 2013) and on the other hand in the international economic policies that increasingly push states to invest in the green economy. Finally, it is necessary to consider the role of economic science, which has always warned about the negative externalities generated in connection with pollution (Pigou, 1920). Certainly, there is a link between economic growth and environmental pollution that has characterized the historical development of capitalism (McGuire, 2020), (Hanlon, 2020). Even in Europe, at the origins of capitalism, pollution generated by industrialization destroyed rivers (Whelan, et al., 2022), forests, polluted cities and destroyed entire populations. Awareness about the need to introduce green oriented policies into capitalism is therefore not just a trend of generation Z (Hurrelmann & Albrecht, 2021) but rather a real long-term need either in Western civilization either in global civilization (Meadows, Meadows, Randers, & Behrens, 2018).

Renewable energies have received public and private financial support either in developing and industrialized countries (Mazzucato & Semieniuk, 2018). However, there are many doubts about the possibility of relying totally on the energy efficiency of renewables. In fact, many countries that have a high GDP-growth rate continue to pollute. The use of non-renewable forms of energy and the related CO_2 production are inextricably and positively associated to economic growth. It is therefore difficult to propose to newly industrialized, poor and underdeveloped countries, especially in Asian, a transition to renewable energy without losing at least partially the ability to growth in terms of GDP. In fact, the need to escape from poverty, underdevelopment, ignorance, and hunger could overshadow the environmental and renewables issues in many low-income countries.

Furthermore, the current state of technological knowledge does not allow for the creation of renewables that can fully replace non-renewable energies. However, it is very probable that in a medium-long term it will be possible to increase the efficiency of renewables. In this regard, the issue of energy storage plays a crucial role. Furthermore, new discoveries in the physical field could lead to the knowledge of new energies, such as dark energies, connected to dark matter, which could open up absolutely new and unpredictable energy scenarios. It is therefore probable that investments in green-tech can make renewable energies much more advanced and efficient in the future, creating the conditions for a reduction in the use of non-renewables.

Certainly, in the scientific literature presented in the chapter, the idea of the existence of the Environmental Kuznets Curve-EKC is often promoted. The EKC is a type of curve that describes the transition to a more sustainable economy through the increase of per capita income. The EKC curve is an inverted U-shaped curve. In the beginning, per capita income and pollution grow together to a maximum. Beyond the maximum point, the further growth of per capita GDP generates a reduction in pollution. The EKC is not free from criticism and skepticism. At an ideal level it could be understood as a theoretical reference. But, it is also true that, many highly developed countries, such as the USA for example, have levels of pollution and CO_2 emissions that are still very high despite the growth of the GDP. It is therefore clear that the application of the EKC is not a historical necessity, but rather the consequence of environmental economic policies.

The chapter proceeds as follows: the second section contains the strategy of the applied methodology, the third section presents a brief analysis of the literature, the fourth section contains the results of the econometric analysis, the fifth section shows the clustering analysis, the sixth section presents the promotional activities that can be implemented for improve sustainability, the seventh section contains the analysis of machine learning algorithms and the predictions, the eighth section shows the suggestions for government policies based on process mining, the ninth section presents the limitations, implications and further research, the tenth section contains the discussion, the eleventh section concludes.

LITERATURE REVIEW

A brief analysis of the scientific literature related to renewable energy consumption is presented below. The analysis highlights contradictory results. In fact, some results highlight the role of renewable energy consumption for the reduction of pollution from CO_2 emissions, others show how it is not possible to identify a clear impact of renewable energy in the sense of economic growth. However, the studies presented consider both developing and industrialized countries. It is more difficult for developing countries to access renewable energy while remaining on the path of economic growth. In fact, at present it seems that it is not possible for a country to grow without polluting. The use of renewable energies, on the other hand, tends to be an objective of economic policy especially for middle-high income countries for more ethical-moral than economic-financial reasons.

Renewable energy is positively associated to economic growth only in low middle-income countries (Narayan & Doytch, 2017). Political instability at national level reduces renewable energy consumption (Shafiullah, Miah, Alam, & Atif, 2021). There is a negative relationship between renewable energy consumption and trade openness in developing countries (Zeren & Akkuş, 2020), even if in the case of OECD 35 countries renewable energy consumption and trade openness are positively associated (Zhang, Zhang, Lee, & Zhou, 2021). Financial development end economic growth improve the renewable energy usage in the case of India; on the one side there is a bidirectional causality between renewable energy usage and economic growth while on the other side there is unidirectional relationship between financial development and renewable energy (Eren, Taspinar, & Gokmenoglu, 2019). The relationship between economic growth and renewable energy consumption is unidirectional in EU countries (Radmehr, Henneberry, & Shayanmehr, 2021). The increase in energy consumption is positively associated to economic growth, with no distinction between renewable and non-renewable energy consumption (Tugcu & Topcu, 2018). There is a positive relationship between renewable energy consumption and globalization (Padhan, Padhang, Tiwari, Ahmed, & Hammoudeh, 2020). Advancement in technology and quality of governance have positive effects on renewable energy consumption in Sub-Sahara African countries (Baye, et al., 2021). Renewable energy consumption promotes sustainability in EU countries (Alola, Bekun, & rkodie, 2019). Renewable energy consumption, through its impact on energy prices, has a positive effect on the reduction of CO_2 emission in G7 countries (Ike, Usman, Alola, & Sarkodie, 2020). An increase in banking performance can improve the level of renewable energy consumption (Amuakwa-Mensah & Näsström, 2022). Gender diversification promotes the adoption of renewable energy consumption at corporate level (Atif, Hossain, Alam, & Goergen, 2021).

There exist a positive relationship between renewable energy consumption and the reduction of CO_2 in Pakistan (Zhang, Wang, & Wang, 2017), (Naz, et al., 2019) . Economic complexity improves the level of renewable energy consumption (Can & Ahmed, 2022). It is not clear if renewable energy consumption improves economic growth, even if it seems that non-renewable energy consumption generates GDP growth, at least in South America Countries (Deng, Alvarado, Toledo, & Caraguay, 2020). Empirical analysis shows that renewable energy consumption has no effect on the reduction of CO_2 emissions, in the case of Turkey, due to a low GDP per capita according to EKC (Pata, 2018). An increase in GDP per capita generates an improvement in renewable energy consumption for many Latin America Countries, as predicted in EKC (Anser, Hanif, Alharthi, & Chaudhry, 2020). Renewable energy consumption is positively associated to international trade in the short run, as in the case of Tunisia (Brini, Amara, & Jemmali, 2017). In the case of low per capita income, such as Ghana, the increase in renewable energy consumption is positively associated in the long-run with the level of financial development (Kwakwa, 2020).

Renewable energy consumption has no significant impact on economic growth in the case of Algeria (Amri, 2017) and of 15 West African countries (Maji, Sulaiman, & Abdul-Rahim, 2019). Financial development increases renewable energy consumption with positive effects on the reduction of CO_2 emissions (Khan, Khan, & Binh, 2020). There is no Granger causality between renewable energy consumption and economic growth in a set of seven European countries (Li & Leung, 2021). Renewable energy consumption reduces environmental degradation (Usman, Alola, & Sarkodie, 2020). There is a positive relationship between renewable energy consumption and economic growth in EU countries (Smolović, Muhadinović, Radonjić, & Đurašković, 2020). Renewable energy consumption is positively associated to economic growth in African countries (Qudrat-Ullah & Nevo, 2021). Renewable energy consumption and globalization have positive effects on the reduction on CO_2 emissions in Argentina, a country for which EKC holds (Yuping, et al., 2021). Renewable energy consumption has a twofold impact on trade competitiveness i.e. positive for OECD countries and negative for non-OECD countries (Ilechukwu & Lahiri, 2022).

THE ECONOMETRIC MODEL FOR THE ESTIMATION OF THE RENEWABLE ENERGY CONSUMPTION

We have used Panel Data with Random Effects, Panel Data with Fixed Effects, WLS, and Pooled OLS to estimate the value of renewable energy consumption in 193 countries for the period 2011 and 2020. We have estimated the following equation:

Equation 1. Estimation of Renewable Energy Consumption

Renewable Energy Consumption$_{it}$

$$= a_1 + b_1 \left(CoolingDegreeDays \right)_{it} + b_2 \left(AdjustedSavingsNetForestDepletion \right)_{it}$$

$$+ b_3 \left(AgricultureForestryAndFishing \right)_{it} + b_4 \left(AgriculturalLand \right)_{it}$$

$$+b_5 \left(PM2.5AirPollution\right)_{it} + b_6 \left(RenewableElectricityOutput\right)_{it} + b_7 \left(ForestArea\right)_{it}$$

$$+b_8 \left(EnergyUse\right)_{it} + b_9 \left(EnergyImports\right)_{it} + b_{10} \left(AccessToElectricity\right)_{it}$$

$$+b_{11} \left(FossilFuelEnergyConsumption\right)_{it} + b_{12} \left(AdjustedSavingsNaturalResourcesDepletion\right)_{it}$$

$$+b_{13} \left(CO_2Emissions\right)_{it} + b_{14} \left(Maximum5dayRainfall25yearReturnLevel\right)_{it}$$

$$+b_{15} \left(GHGnetEmissions / RemovalsbyLUCF\right)_{it} + b_{16} \left(MeanDroughtIndex\right)_{it}$$

Where i=139 and t=[2011;2020]
The value of Renewable Energy Consumption is positively associated to:

- *Cooling Degree Days:* it is a measurement designed to quantify the energy demand needed to cool buildings. It is the number of degrees that the average temperature of a day is above 18°C **(WB, Cooling Degree Days, s.d.)** . There is a positive relationship between renewable energy consumption and the increase in days that have an average temperature above 18 degrees. This relationship can be better understood considering that the countries that have the greatest consumption of renewable energy are African or South Asian countries which therefore necessarily have a high number of days with a temperature above 18 degrees. Furthermore, the fact that the temperature is above 18 degrees leads to an increase in the use of air conditioning systems and therefore to an increase in the consumption of renewable energy.

- *Adjusted savings: net forest depletion-ANSFD:* is calculated as the product of unit resource rents and the excess log harvest over natural growth (WB, Adjusted savings: net forest depletion (current US\$), s.d.). There is a positive relationship between the growth of renewable energy consumption and the net depletion of forests. Specifically, it can be noted that countries that have a high level of renewable energy consumption also have a high performance in terms of adjusted savings net forest depletion. This condition is because the countries that have higher levels of renewable energy consumption are almost all African countries where there is also a significant deforestation activity. The variable adjusted savings net forest depletion (% of GNI), summarized in the acronym ASNFD, has a value that varies from a minimum of 0.00 units up to a maximum value of 15.94. If we consider the top five countries by value of renewable energy consumption, then we have the following results in terms of ASFND: Congo, Dem. Rep. with 8.96, Somalia with 14.16, Uganda with 7.58, Gabon with 2.44 units and Ethiopia with 5.50 units. This result is paradoxical since, on the one hand, the increase in renewable energy consumption produces advantages in terms of CO_2 reduction, while on the other hand, deforestation increases CO_2 (Figure 1).

Figure 1. Relationship between renewable energy consumption-REC and ANSFD

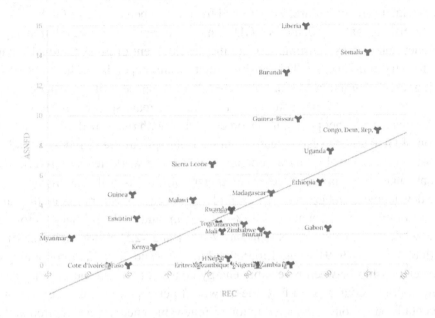

Figure 2. Relationship between ANSFD and REC at world level
Source: World Bank

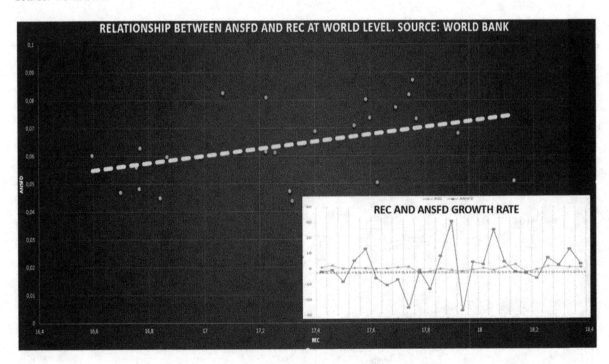

- *Agriculture, forestry, and fishing, value added-AFF*: considers the value of the gross domestic product deriving from agriculture, forestry and fishing as a percentage of GDP (WB, Agriculture, forestry, and fishing, value added (% of GDP), n.d.). There is a positive relationship between the value of renewable energy consumption and the development of gross national product from agriculture, forestry and fisheries. This positive relationship depends on the fact that the countries with the highest consumption of renewable energy are countries with low per capita income, i.e. African countries. Many African countries have a large primary sector in terms of GDP compared to countries that have higher per capita incomes. In fact, with the growth of per capita income, the distribution of GDP among sectors tends to move from agriculture to industry, and subsequently from industry to services. In African countries, which are world leaders in terms of renewable energy consumption, the primary sector component of GDP is still very high due to the lack of economic development and growth. For example, in the case of Sierra Leone the value of renewable energy consumption is equal to 75.44% with an amount of the primary sector on GDP equal to 58.15%, while the same values for Chad are 77.79% and 42.59%, for Mali 76.64% and 37.31%, Niger with 80.83% and 36.91%, and Liberia with 87.24% and 36.44% . Economic growth should invert the relationship between renewable energy consumption and the primary sector in terms of GDP, for African countries. In fact, the growth of per capita income is energy intensive, and therefore entails on the one hand a reduction of renewable energy consumption and on the other hand, a specialization by sector oriented towards industry and services (Figure 3).

Figure 3. Relationship between REC-renewable energy consumption and AFF-agriculture, forestry, and fishing

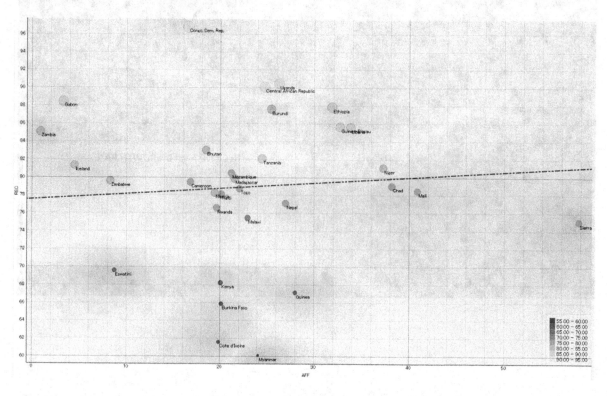

- *Agricultural Land:* considers the value of agricultural land with respect to the share of arable land, with permanent crops and permanent pastures. Arable land includes land defined by the FAO as land under temporary crops, temporary grassland for mowing or grazing, market land or market gardens, and land temporarily fallow. Lands abandoned due to cultivation shifts are excluded from agricultural land. Land under permanent crops is land planted with crops that use the land for long periods and do not need to be replanted after each harvest, such as cocoa, coffee, and rubber. Permanent pasture is land used for five or more years for forage, including natural and cultivated crops (WB, Agricultural land (% of land area), n.d.). There is a positive relationship between the value of land cultivated for agricultural purposes and the value of renewable energy consumption. This relation indicates that the development of renewable energy makes possible to reduce the prices of energy supply for agricultural enterprises by improving their production capacity and causing the expansion of agricultural firms and farms.

- *PM2.5 air pollution, mean annual exposure:* considers the population's weighted exposure to environmental pollution from PM2.5. Such exposure is defined as the average level of exposure of a nation's population to concentrations of airborne particles measuring less than 2.5 microns in aerodynamic diameter, which are capable of penetrating deeply into the respiratory tract and causing serious damage to health. Exposure is calculated by weighting the average annual concentrations of PM2.5 by population in urban and rural areas (WB, PM2.5 air pollution, mean annual exposure (micrograms per cubic meter), n.d.). There is a positive relationship between the value of renewable energy consumption and the value of exposure to environmental pollution from PM2.5. If we look at the data, it is possible to verify that countries that have high levels of renewable energy consumption also have high levels of PM 2.5 air pollution. For example, Nepal which has a renewable energy consumption value of 77.39% also has a PM2.5 air pollution value of 99.73, and the corresponding values for Niger are 80.83% and 94.05, for Cameroon it is 79.41% and 72.79, for Nigeria it is 81.40% and 71.79 and for Chad it is 77.79% and 66.02. The countries that have low levels of PM2.5 are the War and deforestation generate PM 2.5 air pollution in many countries that are world leaders in renewable energy consumption (Figure 4).

- *Renewable electricity output:* calculates the share of electricity generated by renewable energy plants in the total electricity generated by all types of plants (WB, Renewable electricity output (% of total electricity output), n.d.). There is a positive relationship between the value of renewable energy production and the value of renewable energy consumption. This relationship may appear tautological in nature. The possibility for companies and organizations to consume renewable energy also depends on the production capacity installed at the country level. Developing countries tend to be more oriented towards renewable energy both from the point of view of production and from the point of view of consumption, also because this type of energy is more convenient from an economic point of view than using traditional coal, gas or oil fired energy systems (Mukhtarov, Mikayilov, Maharramov, Aliyev, & Suleymanov, 2022), (Shah, Hiles, & Morley, 2018), (Khan, Yasmeen, Shakoor, Khan, & Muhammad, 2017). From this derives the possibility of creating a green turnaround at the global level, which is precisely induced by reasons of economic convenience and not only by ideological reasons regarding the climatic effects of the western-style capitalist industrial system. From a strictly numerical point of view, considering the data of the World Bank it is possible to verify that countries that are top leaders in renewable energy consumption also have very high levels in terms of renewable energy output. For example, the Congo Dem. Rep. has a value of renewable energy consumption equal to 96.24% and renewable energy output equal to 99.82, the corresponding values for the Central African Republic are 91.26% and 99.42%, Uganda 90.22% and 92.95%, Gabon 89.88% and 43.74%. Therefore, it is evident in the data that the countries that have greater renewable energy production capacity are also the countries that have greater renewable energy consumption capacity (Figure 5).

Figure 4. Relationship between REC and PM2.5 air pollution

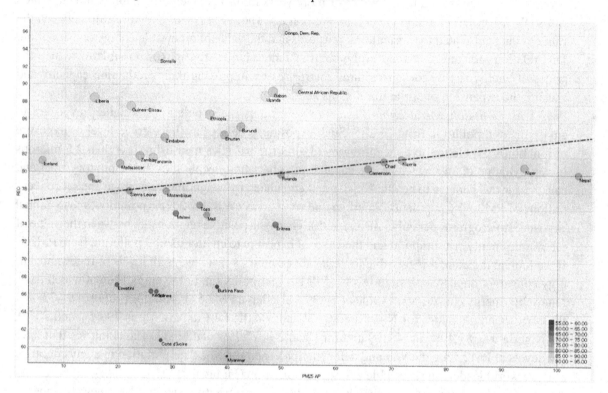

- *Forest area:* describes land under natural woodland or planted trees of at least 5 meters in situ, whether productive or not, and excludes woodland in agricultural production systems and trees in urban parks and gardens (WB, Forest area (% of land area), n.d.). There is a positive relationship between the value of renewable energy consumption and the value of forest area. Forest area does not take into consideration the land endowment that can be exploited for economic reasons through forestry or timber harvesting. There is therefore a positive relationship between the value of renewable energy consumption and the value of forest areas that cannot be exploited economically.

- *Energy Use:* refers to the consumption of primary energy before transformation into other end-use fuels, equal to domestic production plus imports and changes in stocks, minus exports and fuels supplied to ships and aircraft engaged in international transport (WB, World Bank, n.d.). There is a positive relationship between the value of energy consumption and the value of energy use. The growth in energy use is relevant especially for developing countries. In fact, one of the reasons that explain the gap between high-income countries and low per capita income countries is due to the growth in energy consumption. In this sense, the growth of the consumption of renewable energy increases the consumption of energy at a quantitative level. However, the growth in the consumption of renewable energy also affects the improvement of the energy mix at the country level, creating the conditions for greater sustainability of the newly industrialized economic systems.

Figure 5. Relationship between renewable energy consumption-REC and renewable energy output-REO

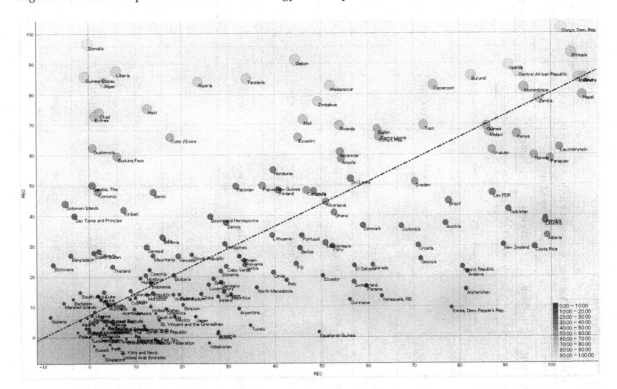

The value of Renewable Energy Consumption is negatively associated to:

- *Net Energy Imports:* are estimated as energy consumption minus production, both measured in oil equivalents. A negative value indicates that the country is a net exporter. Energy consumption refers to the use of primary energy before transformation into other end-use fuels, equal to domestic production plus imports and inventory changes, minus exports and fuels supplied to ships and aircraft engaged in international shipping (WB, Energy imports, net (% of energy use), n.d.). There is a negative relationship between the value of net energy imports and the value of renewable energy consumption. As a result, the growth in the value of renewable energy consumption improves energy autonomy and independence at the country level. It therefore follows that the growth in the consumption of renewable energy has a positive impact in reducing imports, above all of oil, making countries less sensitive to exogenous oil shocks.

Table 1. Econometric estimation to evaluate the value of renewable energy consumption

		Econometric Estimation to Evaluate the Value of Renewable Energy Consumption								
		Pooled OLS		Fixed Effects		Random Effects		WLS		Average
		Coefficient	p-Value	Coefficient	p-Value	Coefficient	p-Value	Coefficient	p-Value	
	Constant	0.134603		0.864397		0.782813		-0.927839		0.2134935
A2	Access to electricity (% of population)	-0.0835935	***	-0.0801385	***	-0.0805122	***	-0.0642803	***	-0.077131125
A3	Adjusted savings: natural resources depletion (% of GNI)	-0.202787	***	-0.186089	***	-0.188005	***	-0.285265	***	-0.2155365
A4	Adjusted savings: net forest depletion (% of GNI)	2.50274	***	2.43591	***	2.44311	***	2.98075	***	2.5906275
A5	Agricultural land (% of land area)	0.399825	***	0.407253	***	0.406575	***	0.379098	***	0.39818775
A6	Agriculture, forestry, and fishing, value added (% of GDP)	0.499634	***	0.483336	***	0.485011	***	0.52613	***	0.49852775
A11	CO_2 emissions (metric tons per capita)	-0.987779	***	-0.894552	*	-0.905014	***	-0.897511	***	-0.921214
A13	Cooling Degree Days (projected change in number of degree Celsius)	7.95296	**	6.36222	*	6.55062	**	13.1092	***	8.49375
A17	Energy imports, net (% of energy use)	-0.0135271	**	-0.0140287	**	-0.0139805	**	-0.0155368	***	-0.014268275
A19	Energy use (kg of oil equivalent per capita)	0.00229778	***	0.00215669	***	0.00217334	***	0.0018323	***	0.002115028
A22	Forest area (% of land area)	0.251868	***	0.22458	***	0.227616	***	0.243401	***	0.23686625

continues on following page

Table 1. Continued

		Econometric Estimation to Evaluate the Value of Renewable Energy Consumption								Average
		Pooled OLS		Fixed Effects		Random Effects		WLS		
		Coefficient	p-Value	Coefficient	p-Value	Coefficient	p-Value	Coefficient	p-Value	
A23	Fossil fuel energy consumption (% of total)	-0.194452	***	-0.191801	***	-0.192157	***	-0.166195	***	-0.18615125
A25	GHG net emissions/ removals by LUCF (Mt of CO_2 equivalent)	-7.17613	***	-6.88342	***	-6.91556	***	-6.46297	***	-6.85952
A37	Maximum 5-day Rainfall. 25-year Return Level (projected change in mm)	-2.95262	**	-2.79825	**	-2.81559	**	-2.72424	***	-2.822675
A38	Mean Drought Index (projected change. unitless)	-98.0934	***	-93.4056	***	-93.9537	***	-110.218	***	-98.917675
A46	PM2.5 air pollution. mean annual exposure (micrograms per cubic meter)	0.297817	***	0.278347	***	0.280443	***	0.264457	***	0.280266
A56	Renewable electricity output (% of total electricity output)	0.279309	***	0.276429	***	0.276683	***	0.271142	***	0.27589075

- *Access to electricity:* is the percentage of the population that has access to electricity. Electrification data is collected from industry, national surveys and international sources. Access to electricity is particularly crucial for human development as electricity is, in practice, indispensable for some basic activities, such as lighting, refrigeration and the operation of household appliances, and cannot be easily replaced by others forms of energy. Individuals' access to electricity is one of the clearest and most unbiased indicators of a country's state of energy poverty (WB, Access to electricity (% of population), n.d.). There is a negative relationship between the value of access to electricity and the value of renewable energy consumption. Countries in which the consumption of renewable energy is more widespread are generally countries with a low-medium per capita income which therefore tend to have problems in accessing electricity.

- *Fossil fuel energy consumption:* includes coal, oil, and natural gas-based products. Fossil fuels are non-renewable resources because they take millions of years to form and reserves are depleted much faster than new ones are created (WB, Fossil fuel energy consumption (% of total), n.d.). There is a negative relationship between the value of renewable energy consumption and the value of fossil fuel energy consumption. This negative relationship shows the presence of a substitution effect between the value of renewable energy consumption and the value of fossil fuel energy consumption. In this sense, a zero-sum game condition is determined between the two sources of energy consumption. The fact that there is a growth in the consumption of renewable energy structurally improves the quality of the composition of the energy mix basket, creating the conditions for a more sustainable economy that is more oriented to circular economy.

- *Adjusted savings: natural resources depletion:* considers the depletion of natural resources as the sum of the net depletion of forests, energy depletion and mineral depletion. Net forest depletion is the unit resource rent multiplied by the excess harvest of timber in excess of natural growth. Energy depletion is the ratio between the value of the stock of energy resources and the remaining life of the reserve, limited to 25 years. It covers coal, crude oil and natural gas. Mineral depletion is the ratio of the value of the mineral resource stock to the remaining life of the reserve, limited to 25 years. Covers tin, gold, lead, zinc, iron, copper, nickel. silver, bauxite and phosphate (WB, Adjusted savings: natural resources depletion (% of GNI), n.d.). There is a negative relationship between the value of natural resource depletion and the value of renewable energy consumption. This report highlights the fact that the growth of renewable energy consumption helps the country in completing the transition to a green energy system and reduces dependence on traditional energy sources. The consumption of renewable energy therefore improves the possibility of preserving natural resources at the country level.

- CO_2 *emissions:* are those deriving from the combustion of fossils and the production of cement. They include carbon dioxide produced during the burning of solid, liquid and gaseous fuels and gas flaring (WB, CO2 emissions (metric tons per capita), s.d.). There is a negative relationship between the value of carbon dioxide emissions and the value of renewable energy consumption. This relationship turns out to be because the consumption of renewable energies makes it possible to significantly reduce carbon dioxide emissions, creating the conditions for an improvement in the environmental condition. Economic policies aimed at the production of green energy are a necessary complement to environmental economic policies. It is therefore possible to improve the condition of the environment through the implementation of energy economic policies capable of reducing carbon dioxide emissions.

- *Maximum 5-day Rainfall, 25-year Return Level:* a 25-year yield level of 5-day cumulative precipitation is the maximum amount of precipitation over a 5-day period that can be expected once in an average 25-year period. Infrequent precipitation events are often referred to as events of some return level. It is possible for two or more events of that magnitude to occur in much shorter intervals. However, such events would only occur once every 25 years in the long run. The maximum precipitation accumulated over a 5-day period represents a proxy for medium-severity floods induced by prolonged and heavy rainfall, relevant for infrastructure, agricultural productivity and disaster risk management (WB, Maximum 5-day Rainfall, 25-year Return Level (projected change in mm), n.d.). There is a negative relationship between the value of renewable energy consumption and the aggressiveness of rainfall. The growth in the consumption of renewable energy can improve the overall climatic condition at a country level by reducing the aggressiveness of meteorological phenomena, which can destroy or even damage crops and create hydrogeological instability.

- *GHG net emissions/removals by LUCF:* considers changes in atmospheric levels of all greenhouse gases attributable to forestry and land use change activities (WB, GHG net emissions/removals by LUCF (Mt of CO2 equivalent), n.d.). There is a negative relationship between the value of the variation of the change in atmospheric levels of greenhouse gases and the value of the consumption of renewable energy. The consumption of renewable energy, also through its production, reduces the use of land aimed at emitting gas. The result is therefore an overall improvement in the environmental and climatic condition at country level with the possibility of structurally reducing pollution deriving from emissions. Furthermore, the cultural change that the consumption of renewable energy generates in the population and in the industrial system has a relevant rule in reducing pollution.

- *Mean Drought Index:* is an average drought index, calculated for a 12-month period, found to be closely related to the impacts of drought on ecosystems, crops and water resources. The indicator is designed to account for both rainfall and potential evapotranspiration in determining drought (WB, Mean Drought Index (projected change, unitless), n.d.). There is a negative relationship between the value of the average drought index and the value of the consumption of renewable energy. The value of precipitation is positively associated with an improvement in climatic conditions, a reduction in the increase in temperature, a green economic policy orientation, and a set of effects and economic policies that make it possible to avoid extreme weather phenomena such as drought or excessive rainfall.

CLUSTER ANALYSIS WITH K-MEANS ALGORITHM OPTIMIZED WITH THE ELBOW METHOD

In this section, we propose a cluster analysis using the k-Means algorithm optimized with the Elbow Method (Thorndike, 1953) (Figure 6). For the cluster analysis, we have used the interval period 2010-2019. We have 189 countries since four of the original 193 countries have missing data and cannot be processed in the cluster analysis. The composition of each clusters is reported in the Appendix. We found the presence of four clusters (Figure 7).

Figure 6. Cluster analysis with k-means algorithm optimized with the elbow method

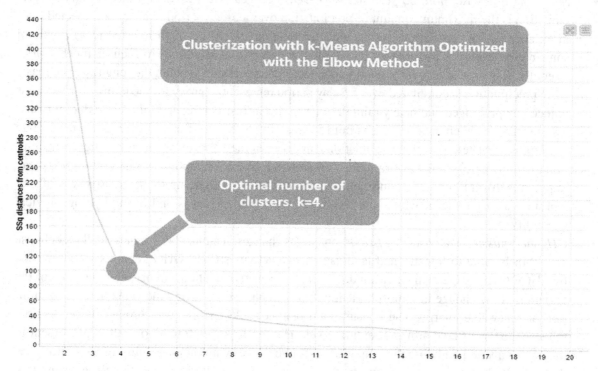

Figure 7. The structure of the clusters

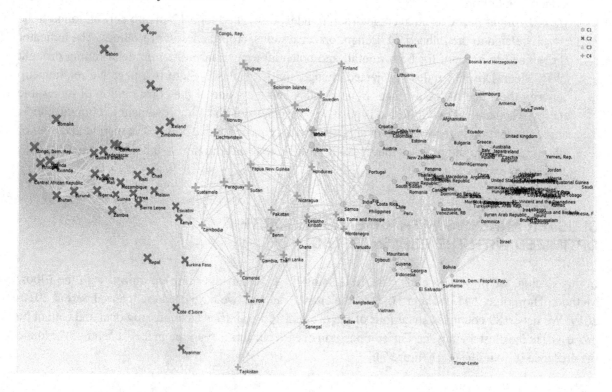

We can consider the level of median to generate an order of clusters. Considering the value of the median, it results that the value of Cluster 2-C2 is equal to an amount of 80.12 units, followed by Cluster 4-C4 with a median equal to a value of 49.29, followed by Cluster 1-C1 with a value of the median equal to an amount of 26.025, and by Cluster 3-C3. The following ordering therefore derives. i.e. C2>C4>C1>C3 (Figure 8 and Figure 9).

Figure 8. A map of countries based on renewable energy consumption

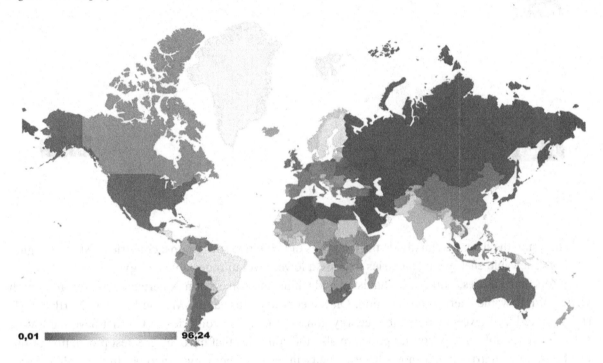

We will focus our attention only on the first of the clusters or C2 and on the last of the clusters or C3.

Analysing the countries of C2, we can see that these are countries that are part of the African continent and in particular of central and sub-Saharan Africa. In particular, Congo Dem. Rep. is the first country for value of renewable energy consumption with a value of 96.24%, followed by Somalia with a value of 95.03%, and by the Central African Republic with an amount equal to 91.26%. The last countries belonging to C2, i.e. the dominant cluster, are Burkina Faso with a value of 64.85%, followed by the Ivory Coast with a value of 62.46 and Myanmar with a value of 57 .85%. It therefore follows that the countries belonging to C2 have a Renewable Energy Consumption-REC value between 96.24 for Congo, up to a value of 57.85 for Myanmar.

C3 is the cluster with the lowest value of renewable energy consumption. Considering the countries of C3 in a ranking, it is possible to verify that Bulgaria is in first place with a value of renewable energy consumption equal to 19.34%, followed by Afghanistan and Greece with a value equal to 18.51%. In the middle of the table are Jordan with a value of 8.17%, followed by Dominica with a value of 8.05% and Belarus with a value of 7.83%, Qatar. Saudi Arabia and Brunei Darussalam close the ranking.

Figure 9. The geographical representation of the composition of each clusters

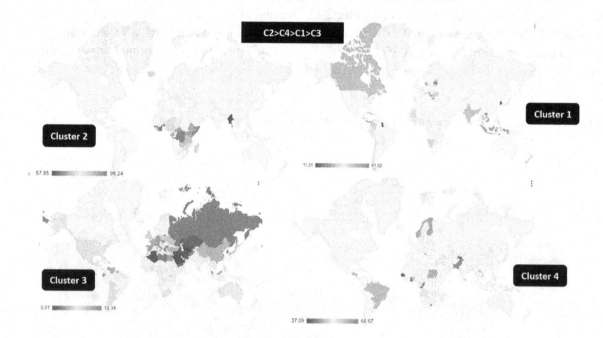

Analysing the data, we can divide the countries of C3 in two sub-groups: countries that use a higher level of renewable energy and countries that use a lower level of renewable energy.

European countries, Turkey, Afghanistan and China and some Latin American countries have high values of renewable energy consumption. On the contrary, Russia, the Middle East and Northern Africa have reduced levels of renewable energy consumption. The countries in C3 that have the lowest values of renewable energy consumption are also the countries that have the greatest production of oil. Furthermore, countries in C3 shows heterogeneity in terms of per capita income. In fact, while European countries have high values in terms of per capita income, other countries, such as the countries of Northern Africa and the countries of Latin America, have lower per capita incomes. The participation in C3 cannot be defined neither from a strictly geographical point of view, neither from an economic point of view. Given the heterogeneity of the countries in C3, it follows that the reduced value of renewable energy consumption is the product of energy choices rather than the result of initial economic and geographical conditions (Figure 10).

MACHINE LEARNING AND PREDICTIONS

In the following section we apply a machine learning analysis to predict the future value of renewable energy consumption. Specifically, eight different machine learning algorithms are compared in terms of performance. The predictive performance of the algorithms is evaluated on the basis of the following elements, namely the R-squared and the following statistical errors, namely:

Figure 10. Representation of C2 and C3

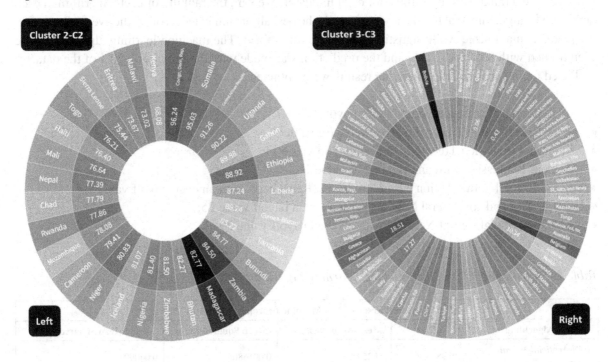

The formula of R-Squared

$$R^2 = 1 - \frac{SumSquaredRegression}{TotalSumOfSquares} = 1 - \frac{\sum(y_i - \widehat{y_i})^2}{\sum(y_i - \overline{y_i})(y_i - \overline{y_i})} \tag{2}$$

The formula of mean average error:

$$MAE = \frac{\sum_{i=1}^{n}|y_i - x_i|}{n} = \frac{\sum_{i=1}^{n}|e_i|}{n} \tag{3}$$

The formula of mean squared error:

$$MSE = \frac{1}{n}\sum_{i=1}^{n}(Y_i - \widehat{Y}_i)(Y_i - \widehat{Y}_i) \tag{4}$$

The formula of root mean squared error

$$RMSE = \sqrt{\frac{1}{N}\sum_{i=1}^{N}(\widehat{y_i} - y_i)(\widehat{y_i} - y_i)} \tag{5}$$

We create a ranking of algorithms for each indicator. We sum the ranking of each algorithm in each ranking. The algorithm that has the lowest score is the best algorithm in terms of predictive performance. R-squares is maximized while statistical errors are minimized. The machine learning algorithms have been trained with 80% of the data and the prediction was made with the remaining 20% of the data.

Based on the analysis, the following results were obtained:

- Polynomial Regression with an even payoff value 7;
- Gradient Boosted Trees with an even payoff value 9;
- Simple Regression Tree with an even payoff value 11;
- Linear Regression with an even payoff value 18;
- Tree Ensemble Regression e Random Forest Regression with an even payoff value 19;
- PNN-Probabilistic Neural Network with an even payoff value 25;
- ANN-Artificial Neural Network with an even payoff value 29.

Table 2. Statistical results of the Machine Learning algorithms

Statistical Results of the Machine Learning Algorithms				
Algorithms	**R^2**	**Mean Absolute Error**	**Mean Squared Error**	**Root Mean Squared Error**
ANN-Artificial Neural Network	0.981838	0.025922	0.001680	0.040993
PNN-Probabilistic Neural Network	0.984111	0.024687	0.001470	0.038343
Simple Regression Tree	0.995165	0.014137	0.000000	0.021151
Gradient Boosted Trees	0.996037	0.013366	0.000000	0.019148
Random Forest Regression	0.994291	0.016532	0.001000	0.022983
Tree Ensemble Regression	0.994347	0.016555	0.001000	0.022870
Linear Regression	0.997569	0.911196	1.796870	1.340474
Polynomial Regression	0.997568	0.010409	0.000000	0.015000

Overall, considering the average values, it appears that the value of renewable energy consumption is expected to grow from 32.99 up to 33.85 or a variation equal to an amount of 0.86 units equal to a 2.61%.

GOVERNMENT POLICIES BASED ON A PROCESS MINING APPROACH

The proposed example introduce a method to execute a possible process about sustainability process involving renewable energy management in a specific country. The use of machine learning algorithms in decision making processes can provide a support for governments planning their activities in policies, energy monitoring procedures and investments. An innovative approach to model decision processes is provided by Process Mining (PM) model (Massaro, Advanced Control Systems in Industry 5.0 Enabling Process Mining, 2022), (Massaro, Multi-Level Decision Support System in Production and Safety Management, 2022). The PM is an advanced approach integrating in processes the machine learning Decision Support Systems (DSSs) contributing to select specific sub-processes according to predicted results (Massaro, Advanced Control Systems in Industry 5.0 Enabling Process Mining, 2022), (Massaro, Multi-Level Decision Support System in Production and Safety Management, 2022). The Business Processing Modeling Notation (BPMN) is an engineering method suitable for the PM modeling (Massaro, Information Technology Infrastructures Supporting Industry 5.0 Facilities, 2021) representing by a standard graph symbols the processes of different application fields. In Figure 11 is illustrated a BPMN PM model concerning the process of policies to adopt for a specific country about decision and plans about renewable energy. The PM model is structured into two pools: the "Government Energy Management" main process, and the "Grid Network Energy Management" sub-process. The whole model is explained as follows:

- A parallel (simultaneous) evaluation of real data and predicted one (gateways "Parallel" of the main pool): the first check is about the observation of the trends of thresholds of the average values defining the gap between real renewable energy generated and renewable energy consumed (alignment/gap check);
- A decision making process ("Exclusive Event Based" gateway) following the yearly/seasonal check of energy production and energy consumption check, and selecting the sub-process to continue monitoring (when the gap decrease no further corrective actions are required) or the sub-process to intervene with an investment plan (or updating the previous plan) mainly in energetic infrastructure (when the gap decrease); in the case of aa no gap decrease is activated simultaneously the sub-process of the grid network check (second pool);
- A decision making process ("Exclusive Event Based" gateway) following the yearly check of energy production prediction and energy consumption prediction check selecting sub-process thus motivating the activation of the investment plan when the gap between these variables does not decrease; when the gap decreases will continue the production of the renewable energy;
- A decision making ("Parallel" gateway) concerning the check of the over production (when an over production is checked are defined new policies about the sale of the proper produced energy, in the case of a production under a specified threshold is checked the need of the internal energy request);
- A decision making ("Parallel" gateway) concerning of the check of the need of the internal energy request activating an increase of energy production (positive case), or a further estimation of energy needs taking into account the industrialization process (negative case) thus supporting to understand the quantity of renewable energy to increase (this estimation is further supported by the analysis of the yearly prediction of the energy consumption);
- A task about the support to define energy price policies by considering the prediction of yearly energy consumption of potential customers (countries linked with marketing agreement);
- a sub process of management of grid network (second pool) taking into account a preliminary simultaneous check of the energy balancing in the grid networks and the related storage systems enabling the check of the gap decrease ("Exclusive Event Based" gateway of the second pool); in the case of an energy gap decrease is continued the energy production, otherwise must be performed simultaneously a specific infrastructure investment and an importing of energy to avoid the risk to have not enough energy available for the standard national needs.

We observe that the main goal of the described process is to increase the increase of the renewable energy production (Laureti, Massaro, Costantiello, & Leogrande, 2023) also in secure conditions. The interventions can be performed in the grid connections (Massaro & Starace, Advanced and Complex Energy Systems Monitoring and Control: A Review on Available Technologies and Their Application Criteria, 2022), (Massaro, Galiano, Meuli, & Massari, 2018) or locally in each city by designing local renewable energy sources (Massaro, et al., 2021) and improving energy monitoring procedures (Massaro, Galiano, Meuli, & Massari, 2018), (Starace, Tiwari, Colangelo, & Massaro, 2022).

Figure 11. Process mining (PM) model applied to the definition of government policies about renewable energy decision

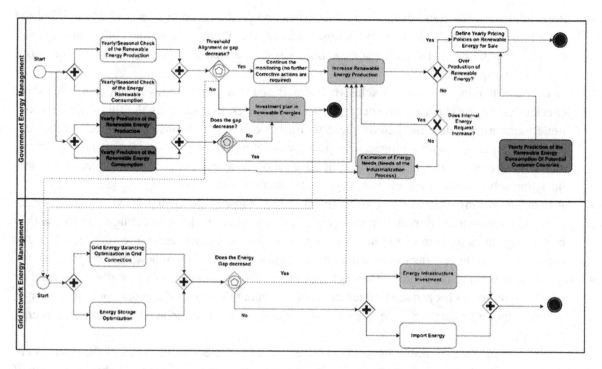

The green tasks indicates a possible correlation with industrialization advance, besides the red tasks are related to the application of machine learning algorithms as DSSs. The comparison function of the "Exclusive Event Based" gateway symbol highlighted in yellow (checkpoint symbol indicating the gap between renewable energy prediction and the renewable energy consumption) is modelled by ANN algorithms (see Figure 12).

As example we discuss the "checkpoint" of Figure 11 highlighted in yellow, which is executed by means of supervised machine learning algorithm as Artificial Neural Network (ANN). Specifically, the comparison between predicted energy consumption and predicted energy is performed by the Konstanz Information Miner (KNIME) (Massaro, Electronic in Advanced Research Industry: From Industry 4.0 to Industry 5.0 Advances, 2021) workflows of Figure 12 (a) providing the predicted results of Figure 12 (b): the predicted results allows to analyze the gap trend thus supporting the decision of the specific checkpoint (in the proposed example the gap decrease thus providing a secure condition).

Figure 12. (a) KNIME workflow related of the decision checkpoint highlighted in yellow in Figure 11. (b) Approach concerning gap trend estimation by means the plotting of renewable energy prediction and the renewable energy consumption (as example are estimated predicted data of the Afghanistan country).

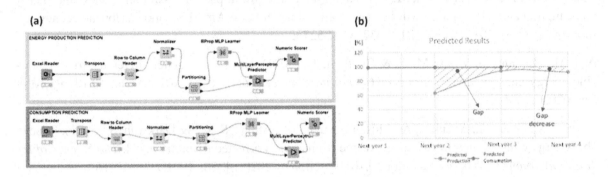

The hyper-parameters of the ANN network are: 70% as training dataset, 30% as testing dataset, 100 epochs, 1 hidden layer, 10 hidden neurons per layer.

CONCLUSION

The use of renewables on a global level is necessary to combat climate change, for environmental sustainability and to implement circular economy. However, at present, consistently with what is stated in the scientific literature cited, it is not possible to have a clear idea of the unique effects of the use of renewable energies either for economic growth either for the reduction of CO_2 emissions. In fact, not all the studies reported agree that the transition to the consumption of renewable energies can generate economic growth and greater environmental sustainability. From this point of view, it is necessary to consider that the countries that use the renewable energy are precisely the countries with low per capita incomes, with some rare exceptions such as in the case of Norway, Iceland and Austria. Probably, if we take technology constant, the application of international laws and agreements will reduce the probability of poor countries to afford economic growth due to energy constraints. In the future, the role of renewable energies will certainly increase. However, there are still some doubts as to whether renewables can support generalized economic growth or are instead a tool to create a further and more pernicious gap between high-growth countries that consume a mix of renewable and non-renewables energies and low-growth countries that consume predominantly renewables energies.

REFERENCES

Alola, A. A., Bekun, F. V., & Sarkodie, S. A. (2019). Dynamic impact of trade policy, economic growth, fertility rate, renewable and non-renewable energy consumption on ecological footprint in Europe. *The Science of the Total Environment*, *685*, 702–709. doi:10.1016/j.scitotenv.2019.05.139 PMID:31203164

Amri, F. (2017). The relationship amongst energy consumption (renewable and non-renewable), and GDP in Algeria. *Renewable & Sustainable Energy Reviews*, *76*, 62–71. doi:10.1016/j.rser.2017.03.029

Amuakwa-Mensah, F., & Nässtrom, E. (2022). Role of banking sector performance in renewable energy consumption. *Applied Energy*, *306*(118023), 118023. doi:10.1016/j.apenergy.2021.118023

Anser, M. K., Hanif, I., Alharthi, M., & Chaudhry, I. S. (2020). Impact of fossil fuels, renewable energy consumption and industrial growth on carbon emissions in Latin American and Caribbean economies. *Atmosfera*, *33*(3), 201–213. doi:10.20937/ATM.52732

Atif, M., Hossain, M., Alam, M. S., & Goergen, M. (2021). Does board gender diversity affect renewable energy consumption? *Journal of Corporate Finance*, *66*(101665), 101665. doi:10.1016/j.jcorp-fin.2020.101665

Baye, R. S., Olper, A., Ahenkan, A., Musah-Surugu, I. J., Anuga, S. W., & Darkwah, S. (2021). Renewable energy consumption in Africa: Evidence from a bias corrected dynamic panel. *The Science of the Total Environment*, *766*(142583). doi:10.1016/j.scitotenv.2020.142583 PMID:33143916

Brini, R., Amara, M., & Jemmali, H. (2017). Renewable energy consumption, International trade, oil price and economic growth inter-linkages: The case of Tunisia. *Renewable & Sustainable Energy Reviews*, *76*, 620–627. doi:10.1016/j.rser.2017.03.067

Can, M., & Ahmed, Z. (2022). Towards sustainable development in the European Union countries: Does economic complexity affect renewable and non-renewable energy consumption? *Sustainable Development*.

Deng, Q., Alvarado, R., Toledo, E., & Caraguay, L. (2020). Greenhouse gas emissions, non-renewable energy consumption, and output in South America: The role of the productive structure. *Environmental Science and Pollution Research International*, *27*(13), 14477–14491. doi:10.100711356-020-07693-9 PMID:31953767

Eren, B. M., Taspinar, N., & Gokmenoglu, K. K. (2019). The impact of financial development and economic growth on renewable energy consumption: Empirical analysis of India. *The Science of the Total Environment*, *663*, 189–197. doi:10.1016/j.scitotenv.2019.01.323 PMID:30711585

Hanlon, W. W. (2020). Coal smoke, city growth, and the costs of the industrial revolution. *Economic Journal (London)*, *130*(626), 462–488. doi:10.1093/ej/uez055

Hurrelmann, K., & Albrecht, E. (2021). *Gen Z: Between Climate Crisis and Coronavirus Pandemic*. Routledge. doi:10.4324/9781003128700

Ike, G. N., Usman, O., Alola, A. A., & Sarkodie, S. A. (2020). Environmental quality effects of income, energy prices and trade: The role of renewable energy consumption in G-7 countries. *The Science of the Total Environment*, *721*(137813), 137813. doi:10.1016/j.scitotenv.2020.137813 PMID:32197283

Ilechukwu, N., & Lahiri, S. (2022). Renewable-energy consumption and international trade. *Energy Reports*, *8*, 10624–10629. doi:10.1016/j.egyr.2022.08.209

Khan, H., Khan, I., & Binh, T. T. (2020). The heterogeneity of renewable energy consumption, carbon emission and financial development in the globe: A panel quantile regression approach. *Energy Reports*, *6*, 859–867. doi:10.1016/j.egyr.2020.04.002

Khan, M. I., Yasmeen, T., Shakoor, A., Khan, N. B., & Muhammad, R. (2017). 2014 oil plunge: Causes and impacts on renewable energy. *Renewable & Sustainable Energy Reviews, 68*, 609–622. doi:10.1016/j.rser.2016.10.026

Kwakwa, P. A. (2020). What determines renewable energy consumption? Startling evidence from Ghana. *International Journal of Energy Sector Management.*

Laureti, L., Massaro, A., Costantiello, A., & Leogrande, A. (2023). The Impact of Renewable Electricity Output on Sustainability in the Context of Circular Economy: A Global Perspective. *Sustainability (Basel), 3*(2160), 15. doi:10.3390u15032160

Li, R., & Leung, G. C. (2021). The relationship between energy prices, economic growth and renewable energy consumption: Evidence from Europe. *Energy Reports, 7*, 1712–1719. doi:10.1016/j.egyr.2021.03.030

Maji, I. K., Sulaiman, C., & Abdul-Rahim, A. S. (2019). Renewable energy consumption and economic growth nexus: A fresh evidence from West Africa. *Energy Reports, 5*, 384–392. doi:10.1016/j.egyr.2019.03.005

Massaro, A. (2021a). *Electronic in Advanced Research Industry: From Industry 4.0 to Industry 5.0 Advances.* Wiley IEEE. doi:10.1002/9781119716907

Massaro, A. (2021b). Information Technology Infrastructures Supporting Industry 5.0 Facilities. In Electronics in Advanced Research Industries (pp. 51–101). Wiley.

Massaro, A. (2022a). Advanced Control Systems in Industry 5.0 Enabling Process Mining. *Sensors (Basel), 8677*(22), 22. doi:10.339022228677 PMID:36433272

Massaro, A. (2022b). Multi-Level Decision Support System in Production and Safety Management. *Knowledge (Beverly Hills, Calif.), 2*(4), 682–701. doi:10.3390/knowledge2040039

Massaro, A., Birardi, G., Manca, F., Marin, C., Birardi, V., Giannone, D., & Galiano, A. M. (2021). Innovative DSS for Intelligent Monitoring and Urban Square Design Approaches: A Case of Study. *Sustainable Cities and Society, 102653*(102653), 65. doi:10.1016/j.scs.2020.102653

Massaro, A., Galiano, A., Meuli, G., & Massari, S. F. (2018). Overview and Application of Enabling Technologies Oriented on Energy Routing Monitoring, on Network Installation and on Predictive Maintenance. *Int. J. Artif. Intell. Appl., 9*(2), 1–20.

Massaro, A., & Starace, G. (2022). Advanced and Complex Energy Systems Monitoring and Control: A Review on Available Technologies and Their Application Criteria. *Sensors (Basel), 4929*(13), 22. doi:10.339022134929 PMID:35808429

Mazzucato, M., & Semieniuk, G. (2018). Financing renewable energy: Who is financing what and why it matters. *Technological Forecasting and Social Change, 127*, 8–22. doi:10.1016/j.techfore.2017.05.021

McGuire, S. A. (2020). Products of Industry: Pollution, Health, and England's Industrial Revolution. *The Bioarchaeology of Structural Violence: A Theoretical Framework for Industrial Era Inequality*, 203-231.

Meadows, D. H., Meadows, D. L., Randers, J., & Behrens, W. W. (2018). The Limits to Growth. In *Green planet blues* (pp. 25–29). Routledge. doi:10.4324/9780429493744-3

Mukhtarov, S., Mikayilov, J. I., Maharramov, S., Aliyev, J., & Suleymanov, E. (2022). Higher oil prices, are they good or bad for renewable energy consumption: The case of Iran? *Renewable Energy, 186*, 411–419. doi:10.1016/j.renene.2021.12.135

Narayan, S., & Doytch, N. (2017). An investigation of renewable and non-renewable energy consumption and economic growth nexus using industrial and residential energy consumption. *Energy Economics, 68*, 160–176. doi:10.1016/j.eneco.2017.09.005

Naz, S., Sultan, R., Zaman, K., Aldakhil, A. M., Nassani, A. A., & Abro, M. M. (2019). Moderating and mediating role of renewable energy consumption, FDI inflows, and economic growth on carbon dioxide emissions: Evidence from robust least square estimator. *Environmental Science and Pollution Research International, 26*(3), 2806–2819. doi:10.100711356-018-3837-6 PMID:30488245

Nordhaus, W. (2013). The climate casino: Risk, uncertainty, and economics for a warming world. Yale University Press.

Padhan, H., Padhang, P. C., Tiwari, A. K., Ahmed, R., & Hammoudeh, S. (2020). Renewable energy consumption and robust globalization (s) in OECD countries: do oil, carbon emissions and economic activity matter? *Energy Strategy Reviews, 32*(100535).

Pata, U. K. (2018). Renewable energy consumption, urbanization, financial development, income and CO2 emissions in Turkey: Testing EKC hypothesis with structural breaks. *Journal of Cleaner Production, 187*, 770–779. doi:10.1016/j.jclepro.2018.03.236

Pigou, A. C. (1920). *The Economics of Welfare*. Macmillan.

Qudrat-Ullah, H., & Nevo, C. M. (2021). The impact of renewable energy consumption and environmental sustainability on economic growth in Africa. *Energy Reports, 7*, 3877–3886. doi:10.1016/j.egyr.2021.05.083

Radmehr, R., Henneberry, S. R., & Shayanmehr, S. (2021). Renewable energy consumption, CO2 emissions, and economic growth nexus: A simultaneity spatial modeling analysis of EU countries. *Structural Change and Economic Dynamics, 57*, 13–27. doi:10.1016/j.strueco.2021.01.006

Shafiullah, M., Miah, M. D., Alam, M. S., & Atif, M. (2021). Does economic policy uncertainty affect renewable energy consumption? *Renewable Energy, 179*, 1500–1521. doi:10.1016/j.renene.2021.07.092

Shah, I. H., Hiles, C., & Morley, B. (2018). How do oil prices, macroeconomic factors and policies affect the market for renewable energy? *Applied Energy, 215*, 87–97. doi:10.1016/j.apenergy.2018.01.084

Smolović, J. C., Muhadinović, M., Radonjić, M., & Đurašković, J. (2020). How does renewable energy consumption affect economic growth in the traditional and new member states of the European Union? *Energy Reports, 6*, 505–513. doi:10.1016/j.egyr.2020.09.028

Starace, G., Tiwari, A., Colangelo, G., & Massaro, A. (2022). Advanced Data Systems for Energy Consumption Optimization and Air Quality Control in Smart Public Buildings Using a Versatile Open Source Approach. *Electronics (Basel), 11*(3904), 11. doi:10.3390/electronics11233904

Thorndike, R. (1953). Who belongs in the family? *Psychometrika, 18*(4), 267–276. doi:10.1007/BF02289263

Tugcu, C. T., & Topcu, M. (2018). Total, renewable and non-renewable energy consumption and economic growth: Revisiting the issue with an asymmetric point of view. *Energy, 152*, 64–74. doi:10.1016/j.energy.2018.03.128

Usman, O., Alola, A. A., & Sarkodie, S. A. (2020). Assessment of the role of renewable energy consumption and trade policy on environmental degradation using innovation accounting: Evidence from the US. *Renewable Energy, 150*, 266–277. doi:10.1016/j.renene.2019.12.151

WB. (n.d.-a). *Access to electricity (% of population)*. World Bank. Retrieved 01 30, 2023, from https://data.worldbank.org/indicator/EG.ELC.ACCS.ZS

WB. (n.d.-b). *Adjusted savings: natural resources depletion (% of GNI)*. World Bank. Retrieved 01 30, 2023, from https://data.worldbank.org/indicator/NY.ADJ.DRES.GN.ZS

WB. (n.d.-c). *Adjusted savings: net forest depletion (current US$)*. World Bank. Retrieved 01 30, 2023, from https://data.worldbank.org/indicator/NY.ADJ.DFOR.CD

WB. (n.d.-d). *Agricultural land (% of land area)*. World Bank. Retrieved 01 30, 2023, from https://data.worldbank.org/indicator/AG.LND.AGRI.ZS

WB. (n.d.-e). *Agriculture, forestry, and fishing, value added (% of GDP)*. World Bank. Retrieved 01 30, 2023, from https://data.worldbank.org/indicator/NV.AGR.TOTL.ZS

WB. (n.d.-f). *CO2 emissions (metric tons per capita)*. World Bank. Retrieved 01 30, 2023, from https://data.worldbank.org/indicator/EN.ATM.CO2E.PC

WB. (n.d.-g). *Cooling Degree Days*. World Bank. Retrieved 01 30, 2023, from https://databank.worldbank.org/metadataglossary/environment-social-and-governance-(esg)-data/series/EN.CLC.CDDY.XD

WB. (n.d.-h). *Energy imports, net (% of energy use)*. World Bank. Retrieved 01 30, 2023, from https://data.worldbank.org/indicator/EG.IMP.CONS.ZS

WB. (n.d.-i). *Forest area (% of land area)*. World Bank. Retrieved 01 30, 2023, from https://data.worldbank.org/indicator/AG.LND.FRST.ZS

WB. (n.d.-j). *Fossil fuel energy consumption (% of total)*. World Bank. Retrieved 01 30, 2023, from https://data.worldbank.org/indicator/EG.USE.COMM.FO.ZS

WB. (n.d.-k). *GHG net emissions/removals by LUCF (Mt of CO2 equivalent)*. World Bank. Retrieved 01 30, 2023, from https://data.worldbank.org/indicator/EN.CLC.GHGR.MT.CE

WB. (n.d.-l). *Maximum 5-day Rainfall, 25-year Return Level (projected change in mm)*. World Bank. Retrieved 01 30, 2023, from https://databank.worldbank.org/metadataglossary/environment-social-and-governance-(esg)-data/series/EN.CLC.PRCP.XD

WB. (n.d.-m). *Mean Drought Index (projected change, unitless)*. World Bank. Retrieved 01 30, 2023, from https://databank.worldbank.org/metadataglossary/environment-social-and-governance-(esg)-data/series/EN.CLC.SPEI.XD

WB. (n.d.-n). *PM2.5 air pollution, mean annual exposure (micrograms per cubic meter)*. World Bank. Retrieved 01 30, 2023, from https://data.worldbank.org/indicator/EN.ATM.PM25.MC.M3

WB. (n.d.-o). *Renewable electricity output (% of total electricity output)*. World Bank.

WB. (n.d.-p). *Energy use (kg of oil equivalent per capita)*. Retrieved 01 30, 2023, from https://data. worldbank.org/indicator/EG.USE.PCAP.KG.OE

Whelan, M. J., Linstead, C., Worrall, F., Ormerod, S. J., Durance, I., Johnson, A. C., & Tickner, D. (2022). Is water quality in British rivers "better than at any time since the end of the Industrial Revolution"? *The Science of the Total Environment*, *843*, 15. doi:10.1016/j.scitotenv.2022.157014 PMID:35772542

Yuping, L., Ramzan, M., Xincheng, L., Murshed, M., Awosusi, A. A., Bah, S. I., & Adebayo, T. S. (2021). Determinants of carbon emissions in Argentina: The roles of renewable energy consumption and globalization. *Energy Reports*, *7*, 4747–4760. doi:10.1016/j.egyr.2021.07.065

Zeren, F., & Akkuş, H. T. (2020). The relationship between renewable energy consumption and trade openness: New evidence from emerging economies. *Renewable Energy*, *147*, 322–329. doi:10.1016/j. renene.2019.09.006

Zhang, B., Wang, B., & Wang, Z. (2017). Role of renewable energy and non-renewable energy consumption on EKC: Evidence from Pakistan. *Journal of Cleaner Production*, *156*, 855–864. doi:10.1016/j. jclepro.2017.03.203

Zhang, M., Zhang, S., Lee, C. C., & Zhou, D. (2021). Effects of trade openness on renewable energy consumption in OECD countries: New insights from panel smooth transition regression modelling. *Energy Economics*, *104*(105649), 105649. doi:10.1016/j.eneco.2021.105649

Chapter 25
Meet Industry Needs in the Big Data Era:
Data Science Curricula Development

Liguo Yu
Indiana University, South Bend, USA

Yingmei Li
Harbin Normal University, China

ABSTRACT

The potential wide applications of big data analytics have created a high demand for data analysts in various industries, including business, healthcare, bioinformatics, politics, and management. As a result, higher education institutions are capitalizing on this opportunity by offering different data science programs to attract students and cater to industry needs. Over the past decade, there has been a rapid emergence of data science programs both nationally and globally. This chapter will begin by reviewing the impact of big data analytics on different industries. It will then proceed to describe various data science programs, including their curriculum design, course offerings, and target industry sectors for employment. Additionally, the chapter will address the weaknesses of some curricula and propose new teaching areas that are relevant to improve the learning outcomes of students. The aim of the suggestions is to better prepare data science students for the ever-evolving demands of big data analytics in the industry.

INTRODUCTION

Due to the evolution of information technology, including machine learning, statistical methods, and distributed computing, we are now able to analyze traditionally believed hard-to-dissect unstructured data, such as customer shopping history, business communication records, and personal activity records, which include financial activities, communication activities, and social media activities (Qiu et al., 2016; Wang et al., 2016; Liu et al., 2015). Big data analytics not only can help businesses, organizations,

DOI: 10.4018/979-8-3693-0049-7.ch025

institutions, and governments reduce operational costs, improve work efficiencies, and make strategic decisions, but it can also analyze data in real-time and respond to urgent and critical situations. This not only benefits institutions and corporations economically but can also save lives and prevent disasters (Berry & Linoff, 1999; Tansley & Tolle, 2009).

The potential wide applications of big data analytics have created a high demand for data analysts in many areas. Higher education institutions are taking this opportunity to grow their influence by offering different data science curricula to attract students of future data analysts or data scientists to meet the industry needs (De Veaux et al., 2017; Gil, 2014; Lyon et al., 2015). In the past ten years, we have witnessed the fast emergence of data science programs nationally and globally (Anderson et al., 2014; Clayton & Clopton, 2019; Demchenko, 2019). These programs range from bachelor's degree to PhD degree with various of business concentrations, such as finance, healthcare, bioinformatics, social informatics, politics, and management (Dogucu & Çetinkaya-Rundel, 2021).

However, because data science (big data analytics) is an interdisciplinary program, the current curriculum design might not fully satisfy the industry needs. In addition, big data analysis technologies and applications are both fast evolving, which require the data science curricula be reviewed and updated regularly to better fulfill the industries' dynamic needs (De Vaus, 2002; Provost & Fawcett, 2013; Tang & Sae-Lim, 2016). To our knowledge, academically there is a lack of summary of data science programs and their relations to industry needs.

This chapter describes different data science programs, their curriculum design, course offerings, and target industry sectors for employment. In addition, we discuss the weakness of some curriculum design and propose new teaching areas that are relevant to improve the learning outcomes of students. The aim of our suggestions is to better prepare future data science students for the ever-evolving demands of big data analytics in the industry. Our contributions to this field are twofold. First, we summarized current data science programs. Second, we provided guidance for future curriculum improvement to better meet the industry needs.

The remaining chapter is organized as follows. First, we review data science (big data analysis) and its impact on business and society. Next, we describe the common curriculum design of data science programs in the United States and across the world. Then, we analyze the strengths and weakness of some curriculum design and offer our suggestions for improvement. Finally, we conclude the chapter by summarizing the key points and illustrating the future work.

BIG DATA ANALYSIS AND ITS IMPACT

What is data? To answer this question, we need to define the concept of information. Let us say the world is made of entities. We human beings measure the properties of entities and observe the behaviors of entities. We understand the entities through observing and processing the information produced by the entity. The information could be in many different forms: electronic, acoustic, mechanic, chemical, biological, and sociological. It is worth noting that we might only be able to observe a fraction of the information produced by the entity. If we can collect more information, we can have a more accurate understanding of the entity (Seife, 2007; Gleick, 2012).

From information theory, we can define data as records of information, which is the fraction of information emitted from the entity that we observed and recorded. Because data is recorded information, we can analyze it later and reprocess it again and again in order to have a better understanding of the entity. That is the process of how human beings obtain knowledge, i.e., the cognitive process (McNurlin & Sprague, 2001; Wang & Chiew, 2010).

Data and knowledge are correlated. However, using data of an entity to obtain knowledge of an entity is not easy (Larose & Larose, 2014). This is mainly due to four factors. First, data is the expression of the property of the entity, not the property of the entity itself (Carey, 2015). We need to establish a correlation between them, which is part of the task of machine learning. Second, data is information transmitted through certain mediums and observed by human beings, which could result in missing data or distorted data. In addition, the observed data could also be affected by the observer and the observing process (Grice, 2011). Third, noise data is always present and more or less it can affect our understanding of the entity. Fourth, the entity that is under observation could be a complex system, which contains many interacting entities; the observed data is accordingly mixtures of properties and behaviors of different entities (Schmelzer et al., 1999). The difficulty of data analysis increases as the complexity of the observed entity increases (Tuomi, 1999). Data analysis of complex entities is part of the task of data mining.

Scientific research in general is about finding and refining ways to collect data, filter data, dissect data, and analyze data (Patten & Newhart, 2017). This applies to all disciplines, such as physics, chemistry, biology, engineering, sociology, history and more. Before the boom of information technology, data collection was limited in certain spectrum. Large amounts of data, especially personal, social, and business data were ignored or discarded. This is mainly because of the limitation of data storage and data processing power. However, as data storage is becoming cheaper, computing algorithms are becoming more efficient, and computer hardware is becoming more powerful, researchers, business, and government begin to realize the usefulness of traditionally ignored or discarded data. That is the beginning of the big data era (Cai & Zhu, 2015).

Big data in general refers to the large volume of data (usually unstructured) that are beyond the traditional processing techniques (Zikopoulos & Eaton, 2011). To process big data, we usually need to store data across different locations and storages, apply innovative algorithms, such as parallel programming, and utilize high performance computing devices, such as cloud-based services. Depending on different domains, big data have different properties. However, in general, big data can be described as five Vs — properties that are proposed by Oscar Herencia Rodrigo, Vice President of South of Europe & General Manager at MetLife Spain and Portugal.

- **Volume**. Some data are generated every day, such as social media data, personal communication data, stock transaction data, transportation and traffic data, and business transaction data. For example, in 2019, about 23 billion text messages are sent each day worldwide; in Nasdaq Stock Exchange Market, about 12 million trades are made per day; and about 294 billion emails are sent per day worldwide. These data are in large volume and beyond the storage and processing power of traditional technologies (Pedrycz & Chen, 2014). Another example is the surveillance camera data in metropolitan areas, which is continually generated all the time. The large volume of data generated every day poses challenges for data storage.
- **Variety**. Traditionally, useful data is most likely stored in text format. Nowadays, data is generated and stored in various formats. Text data could be in the files of csv, xml, and json format; image data could be in tiff, gif, and jpeg format. In addition, data could also be stored in different audio and video formats. Moreover, data could be structured, such as relational financial transac-

tion data, semi-structured, such as hash-tagged tweets data, and non-structured, such as Bigtable google map data (Chang et al., 2008).

- **Velocity**. Big data is often made available in real-time. For example, retail transaction data could be used instantly to recommend similar products to customers; traffic data could be used to provide real time alerts for drivers about road conditions in Google Maps or Apple Maps. IoT (Internet of Things) data could provide real time information about transportation, parking, and dining services (Gubbi et al., 2013).
- **Value**. Big data is valuable for sure. It has manty applications in many different domains, such as retail, finance, healthcare, marketing, transportation, government, cybersecurity, tourism, and entertainment. However, to mine useful information from big data is not easy. Storage and mining are two challenges in tapping the data value throughbig data analytics (Kaisler et al., 2013).
- **Veracity**. Data quality is another concern of big data analytics (Kwon et al., 2014). Wrong data, inaccurate data, and noise data are factors that affect big data quality. Low quality data present additional challenges for analytics and errors may result in management failures, business losses, or political damages.

Due to the potential benefits, big data analysis has been gaining attractions in many areas in the past decade. Here, we describe applications of big data analytics in business, healthcare, transportation, and politics.

In business, big data analytics is used in retail industry to help organize inventory, recommend products, and improve customers' shopping experiences (Sun et al., 2014). Big data analytics is also used in financial industry to help fraud identification and prevention, customer profiling, product cross-selling, and transaction optimization and automation (Fang & Zhang, 2016). For example, financial fraud is a serious side effect of digitalized financial transactions. Financial fraud has many different formats ranging from stolen credit numbers to fraudulent income tax returns. It is reported that people lost about $1.48 billion to financial fraud in 2018 – an increase of 38% over 2017. This number is expected to grow as more and more financial transactions are conducted online. Big data analytics provides tools that can help identify financial fraud and reduce the damage. For example, big data analysis systems coupled with machine learning can help identify credit card fraud: through profiling customers, an AI-based system could identify suspicious activities, such as transactions made from a new device, transactions made from an unusual location, or an uncommon large spending online. Once the operation is flagged as a suspicious activity, the customer will be contacted to verify the transaction to prevent possible fraud (Bolton & Hand, 2001).

In healthcare, big data analytics is used in preventive medicine design, diagnostic services, controlled and effective prescription, and chronic care (Raghupathi & Raghupathi, 2014). For example, research published in 2016 revealed that consuming white bread, bagels and rice increases the risk of lung cancer by 49 percent. This stunning finding is achieved based on big data analysis. Actually, new findings in healthcare and bioinformatics through big data analysis are published every day. Among many of the applications of big data in this area is the Human Genome Project, which intends to identify the human genome patterns and their correlations with certain diseases and therapeutic responses. Accordingly, big data analysis plays a key role in precision (personalized) medicine and gene engineering (Alyass et al., 2015).

In transportation, big data analytics is used in asset management, traffic management, logistics and supply-chain management (Rathore et al., 2015). Let us use Google Maps as an example to illustrate how big data has revolutionized our travel experience (Shekhar et al., 2012).

- **From paper maps to digital maps**. Digital maps, such as Google Maps, can be updated more easily than paper maps. Most importantly, together with their installed devices, digital maps can provide GPS services, which reduce customers' the driving anxiety. Through big data analysis, Google Maps could also recommend alternate routes to customers, which makes travel more flexible and enjoyable (Li & Lai, 2010).
- **Structured and informational surroundings**. Google Maps store business and natural environment data in order to better serve its users. Through big data analytics, Google Maps can recommend nearby gas stations, shopping centers, hospitals, and entertainment centers to map users.
- **Real-time traffic condition alert**. When we use Google Maps and travel on road, we are data producers as well as data consumers. Our travel data (location and speed) could be collected by Google Maps and used to analyze and monitor the traffic conditions. Traffic jam alerts could be sent to us from Google Maps when sustained slow group speed is identified.

In politics, big data is also widely used (Coté et al., 2016). An infamous case is the usage of Facebook data by Cambridge Analytica during the 2016 US presidential election, which might have affected the election result. In general, big data analytics can help campaign organizations identify potential swing states voters and target their campaign resources and effort on these voters. In fact, big data analysis also helped Obama win 2008 and 2012 elections. We have also seen many 2020 presidential candidates using big data to read public opinions and strategize their campaigns accordingly. In governance, big data could be used to better allocate various resources to fight poverty, prevent crimes, and improve education outcomes (Blumenstock et al., 2015).

STATUS OF DATA SCIENCE PROGRAMS

To meet the business needs of data analysts, many data science programs were created in the past ten years (Wilder & Ozgur, 2015). Basically, there are four types of data science programs in higher education industry. They are certificate, bachelor's degree, master's degree, and PhD degree. Based on the information provided on a GitHub website (Data Science Community, 2019), which collects data science programs nationally and worldwide, we extracted the following data: US-based data science programs and non US-based data science programs. It is worth noting here that (1) Data collected on this website is submitted voluntarily, which means it is possible that some data science programs are not reported; and (2) Data used in this study is downloaded on November 19, 2019, and we expect more data science programs will be developed and reported later.

Table 1 shows the number and percentage of different data science programs in the United States reported to the GitHub website. We can see majority of the programs are offering master's degrees. PhD programs are the smallest. In 475 listed programs, 305 are face-to-face programs and 170 are online programs. In these 170 online programs, majorities are certificate programs (46) and master programs (119).

Table 1. Number and percentage of different data science programs in the United States reported to GitHub website as of November 19, 2019

Program	Number	Percentage
Certificate	99	21%
Bachelor	49	10%
Master	308	65%
PhD	19	4%

Table 2 shows the number of data science programs by states in the United States. Forty-four states reported their data science programs. New York, California, Pennsylvania, Massachusetts, Illinois, Indiana, Colorado, Ohio, Florida, and Michigan are the top ten states by the number of data science programs reported. In contrast, the top ten states of the United States by population are California, Texas, Florida, New York, Pennsylvania, Illinois, Ohio, Georgia, North Carolina, and Michigan. We can see that in general, a larger state tend to have more data science programs. This is easy to understand: A state with more population tends to have a stronger economy and more advanced technology force and accordingly has a higher demand for data analysts.

Table 2. Number of data science programs by states in the United States (as of November 19, 2019)

State	Programs	State	Programs	State	Programs	State	Programs
NY	49	NJ	13	DC	7	ID	3
CA	42	VA	12	NE	7	SC	3
PA	36	NC	11	AL	6	KY	2
MA	32	TN	11	AR	6	KS	1
IL	27	WA	11	IA	6	LA	1
IN	21	GA	9	WI	6	MS	1
CO	20	MD	9	AZ	5	MT	1
OH	18	CT	8	OK	5	NV	1
FL	15	MN	8	SD	5	OR	1
MI	15	MO	8	UT	5	RI	1
TX	15	NH	8	HI	3	WV	1

Globally, data are collected from 136 programs of 27 countries. Details are shown in Table 3. It can be seen that European countries have more data science programs than other non-US countries. Table 4 shows the number and percentage of different data science programs of non-US countries reported to the GitHub website. Similar to the United States, majority of their data science programs are offering master's degrees. Internationally, out of the 136 reported programs, 3 are offered online.

Through analyzing data science programs in both the United States and non-US countries, we can see that master's degrees are the most popular programs. There are two major reasons. First, big data analytics is a new area. Many IT and business professionals with bachelor's degrees would like to switch to this field and accordingly they would pursue a master's degree. Second, big data analytics is interdisciplinary, which will be discussed in detail later. A four-year undergraduate education might not provide deep and advanced training in all disciplines. Therefore, graduates with a six-year master's degree are in high demand.

Table 3. Non-US countries and their number of data science programs (as of November 19, 2019)

Country	Programs	Country	Programs	Country	Programs
United Kingdom	46	Denmark	4	Israel	1
France	11	Italy	4	Korea	1
Ireland	11	Sweden	4	Lithuania	1
Spain	9	Austria	2	Philippines	1
Netherlands	7	Finland	2	Portugal	1
New Zealand	6	Hong Kong	2	Russia	1
Australia	5	Mexico	2	Singapore	1
Canada	5	Brazil	1	Turkey	1
Germany	5	Europe Union	1	Ukraine	1

Table 4. Number and percentage of different data science programs of non-US countries reported to GitHub website as of November 19, 2019

Program	Number	Percentage
Certificate	2	1%
Bachelor	12	9%
Master	118	87%
PhD	4	3%

DATA SCIENCE PROGRAM CURRICULUM STRUCTURE

We analyzed the data science programs listed in the GitHub website and summarized the program structures of certificate, bachelor, master, and PhD programs, which are detailed in Table 5 to Table 8, respectively.

Usually, data science graduate certificate programs are open to graduates of science majors, especially computer science and mathematics majors. Students need to take 4-6 courses to receive the certificate. More information can be found in Table 5.

Data science Bachelor of Science programs usually require 120 credit hours, where about 50-55 are general education credits and 10-15 are general elective credits. The remaining 50-55 credits are major required courses, which can be divided into three types: prerequisite computing and mathematics courses, data science core course, and data science elective courses. Details about these courses are shown in Table 6.

Table 5. Common data science graduate certificate program structure

Required Credits	12-16 Credit Hours
Core courses	Data Analysis Data Visualization Data Mining
Elective courses	Advanced Data Analysis Database Querying Machine Learning
Popular languages	Python, R

Table 6. Common data science bachelor's degree program structure

Prerequisite Courses (about 18 credits)	Calculus Discrete Math Linear Algebra Probability Statistics Programming in R Programming in Python
Core Courses (about 18 credits)	Data Ethics Data Analysis Data Visualization Database Querying Data Mining Advanced Data Analysis Machine Learning Big Data Analysis Capstone Project
Elective courses (about 18 credits)	Cloud Computing Data Security Database Design and Database Management Social Network Analysis Deep Learning Decision Optimization

Data Science Master of Science programs usually require 30-40 credit coursework plus a thesis or project option. It should be noted, most master's programs only require a capstone project, and the thesis is not needed. Table 7 lists the common program structure of data science mater programs.

Data Science PhD programs are not common yet. Usually, students need to take about 40-credit coursework plus a PhD dissertation. Table 8 shows its common structure. It is worth noting that usually, a PhD dissertation summarizes the research of applying big data analysis in a specific domain, such as business, social network, bioinformatics, and healthcare.

Table 7. Common data science master's degree program structure

Required Coursework	About 33 Credits
Core Courses (about 15 credits)	Programming in R Programming in Python Data Analysis Data Visualization Data Mining Advanced Data Analysis Database Querying Machine Learning Big Data Analytics
Elective Courses (about 15 credits)	Deep Learning Cloud Computing Social Network Analysis Natural Language Processing Decision Optimization Regression Analysis Decision Optimization Time Series Analysis
Capstone (3 credit)	Thesis or Project

Table 8. Common data science PhD program structure

Required Course Credits	About 40
Core Courses	Data Analysis Data Visualization Data Mining Advanced Data Analysis Machine Learning Big Data Analytics
Elective Courses	Database Design and Database Management Deep Learning Natural Language Processing Decision Optimization Time Series Analysis
Research	Dissertation

DISCUSSIONS AND SUGGESTIONS

In the previous session, we illustrated the common curriculum structures of data science programs, including certificate, bachelor, master, and PhD degrees. Data Science is an interdisciplinary program (Van Der Aalst, 2016). Mathematical analysis coupled with computing technologies are used to analyze data of a specific domain. Therefore, all programs should embrace these three branches, more or less.

- **Mathematical analysis**. Core courses in this branch include probability and statistics. Elective courses include differential equations, decision optimization, regression analysis, and time series analysis. Undergraduate (bachelor) programs should also include foundation courses, such as linear algebra, discrete math, and calculus. Through examining the data science programs listed in the GitHub website, we found that most of them (bachelor, certificate, master, and PhD) cover this branch well.

- **Computing technologies**. Core courses in this branch include data analysis, data visualization, data mining, machine learning, and big data analysis. Elective courses include database management, database design, deep learning, cloud computing, and social network analysis. Prerequisite programming techniques, such as R programming and Python programming are also needed. Through examining the data science programs listed on the GitHub website, we found that most of them cover this branch well. We also noticed that although Python and R are considered the most powerful programming languages for data analytics, a few programs chose to teach different programming languages, such as Java and MATLAB.
- **Application areas**. Data Science programs are created to meet industry needs. Currently, the three major applied areas are business, healthcare, and bioinformatics. Out of the 611 programs listed on the GitHub website, majority of them focus on general data science technologies. Table 9 shows the number of specialized data analytics programs.

Table 9. Number of reported specialized data science programs to the GitHub website as of November 19, 2019

Specialization	Number of Programs
Business Analytics	132
Healthcare Analytics	31
Management Analytics	12
Bioinformatics	9
Social Analysis	4
Earth and Environment Science Analytics	2
Industry Analytics	1

In general, we believe the design of these programs meets the industry needs of data analysts. However, through analyzing these programs and the status of industry demands, we believe certain components or courses are needed in some of these programs due to the unique work skill required for data analysts.

For graduate certificate programs, data privacy and data security courses are missing. Data analysts deal with data all the time. Some data could be sensitive requiring data analysts handle them carefully and follow data policies and business protocols. We believe this component should be added as a new course or embedded in some other courses in these programs.

For most bachelor's degree of data science programs, areas of focus are missing. Data science graduates not only should have general data analytics skills, but also need to know how to apply their knowledge and skills in a specific domain, such as financial industry, politics, and healthcare. Therefore, we recommend adding some elective domain specific data analysis courses. In addition, undergraduates should also be provided with opportunities to practice soft skills, such as teamwork skills, documentation skills, and communication skills. We believe these components should at least be embedded into the capstone project. Data analysts deal with data every day. However, they also interact with customers, coworkers, and other colleagues. These soft skills are necessary for them to complete their assigned work correctly, satisfying the customer's requirement, and fulfilling the business needs.

Many of the data science master programs focus on business analytics. These programs offer specific business data analysis courses. In contrast, few programs are offered in other specific domains. Therefore, we believe other specialized data science programs should be offered, such as healthcare analytics and bioinformatics. Due to the importance and wide application of healthcare data, experts in these areas will be in high demand.

For PhD programs, we recommend the dissertation research should not only focus on application of data analytic technologies, but also focus on uncovering new data mining techniques, data presentation methods, and data processing algorithms.

In addition, due to the growing application of data analytics in autonomous industry, such as self-driving vehicles, mobile technology, smart cities, and smart homes, we believe IoT (Internet of Things) should be included as an elective course for these data science programs, especially those bachelor's programs and master's programs. Because bachelor's graduates and master's graduates are major sources of IT industry workforce, who are contributing the most to technology application.

CONCLUSIONS AND FUTURE WORK

In this chapter, we reviewed the impact of big data analysis on different industries and described different data science programs, their curriculum design, course offerings, and target industry sectors for employment. In addition, we discussed the weakness of some curriculum design and proposed new teaching areas that are relevant to improve the learning outcomes of students. The aim of our suggestions is to better prepare students for the ever-evolving demands of big data analytics in the industry.

It is worth noting that our suggestions are based on the data science program data listed on the GitHub website. It is quite likely that not all data science programs are reported on the website. It is also possible that some well-designed data science programs are overlooked by this study. More importantly, big data analytics and its applications are fast growing and expanding, and our analysis of data science curricula will also need to be updated with technology evolution and business redefinition.

For future studies, we plan to apply quantitative analysis on current data science programs. The data items that could help us better understand the academia status include t=number of faculty of each program, number of enrolled students of each program, number of graduated students of each program, employment rate of each program, average starting salary, average salary of 5-year employment. We believe a comprehensive empirical study of data science programs can provide us detailed insights into their demands from industry and impact on industry.

REFERENCES

Alyass, A., Turcotte, M., & Meyre, D. (2015). From big data analysis to personalized medicine for all: Challenges and opportunities. *BMC Medical Genomics*, 8(1), 33. doi:10.118612920-015-0108-y PMID:26112054

Anderson, P., Bowring, J., McCauley, R., Pothering, G., & Starr, C. (2014). An undergraduate degree in data science: curriculum and a decade of implementation experience. In *Proceedings of the 45th ACM Technical Symposium on Computer Science Education* (pp. 145–150). ACM. 10.1145/2538862.2538936

Berry, M., & Linoff, G. (1999). *Mastering data mining: The art and science of customer relationship management*. John Wiley & Sons, Inc.

Blumenstock, J., Cadamuro, G., & On, R. (2015). Predicting poverty and wealth from mobile phone metadata. *Science, 350*(6264), 1073–1076. doi:10.1126cience.aac4420 PMID:26612950

Bolton, R. J., & Hand, D. J. (2001). Unsupervised profiling methods for fraud detection. *Credit Scoring and Credit Control, VII*, 235–255.

Cai, L., & Zhu, Y. (2015). The challenges of data quality and data quality assessment in the big data era. *Data Science Journal, 14*(0), 14. doi:10.5334/dsj-2015-002

Carey, B. (2015). *How we learn: The surprising truth about when, where, and why it happens*. Random House Trade Paperbacks.

Chang, F., Dean, J., Ghemawat, S., Hsieh, W. C., Wallach, D. A., Burrows, M., Chandra, T., Fikes, A., & Gruber, R. E. (2008). Bigtable: A distributed storage system for structured data. *ACM Transactions on Computer Systems, 26*(2), 4. doi:10.1145/1365815.1365816

Clayton, P. R., & Clopton, J. (2019). Business curriculum redesign: Integrating data analytics. *Journal of Education for Business, 94*(1), 57–63. doi:10.1080/08832323.2018.1502142

Coté, M., Gerbaudo, P., & Pybus, J. (2016). Politics of big data: Introduction. *Digital Culture & Society, 2*(2), 5–15. doi:10.14361/dcs-2016-0202

Data Science Community. (2019). *College & University Data Science Degrees*. Available at https://github.com/ryanswanstrom/awesome-datascience-colleges

De Vaus, D. (2002). Analyzing social science data: 50 key problems in data analysis. *Sage (Atlanta, Ga.)*.

De Veaux, R. D., Agarwal, M., Averett, M., Baumer, B. S., Bray, A., Bressoud, T. C., ... Kim, A. Y. (2017). Curriculum guidelines for undergraduate programs in data science. *Annual Review of Statistics and Its Application, 4*(1), 15–30. doi:10.1146/annurev-statistics-060116-053930

Demchenko, Y. (2019). Big data platforms and tools for data analytics in the data science engineering curriculum. In *Proceedings of the 3rd International Conference on Cloud and Big Data Computing* (pp. 60–64). ACM. 10.1145/3358505.3358512

Dogucu, M., & Çetinkaya-Rundel, M. (2021). Web scraping in the statistics and data science curriculum: Challenges and opportunities. *Journal of Statistics and Data Science Education, 29*(sup1), S112–S122.

Fang, B., & Zhang, P. (2016). Big data in finance. In *Big data concepts, theories, and applications* (pp. 391–412). Springer. doi:10.1007/978-3-319-27763-9_11

Gil, Y. (2014). Teaching parallelism without programming: A data science curriculum for non-CS students. In *Proceedings of 2014 Workshop on Education for High Performance Computing* (pp. 42–48). IEEE. 10.1109/EduHPC.2014.12

Gleick, J. (2012). *The information: A history, a theory, a flood*. Vintage.

Grice, J. W. (2011). *Observation oriented modeling: Analysis of cause in the behavioral sciences.* Academic Press.

Gubbi, J., Buyya, R., Marusic, S., & Palaniswami, M. (2013). Internet of Things (IoT): A vision, architectural elements, and future directions. *Future Generation Computer Systems, 29*(7), 1645–1660. doi:10.1016/j.future.2013.01.010

Kaisler, S., Armour, F., Espinosa, J. A., & Money, W. (2013). Big data: Issues and challenges moving forward. In *Proceedings of the 46th Hawaii International Conference on System Sciences* (pp. 995–1004). IEEE. 10.1109/HICSS.2013.645

Kwon, O., Lee, N., & Shin, B. (2014). Data quality management, data usage experience and acquisition intention of big data analytics. *International Journal of Information Management, 34*(3), 387–394. doi:10.1016/j.ijinfomgt.2014.02.002

Larose, D. T., & Larose, C. D. (2014). *Discovering knowledge in data: an introduction to data mining.* John Wiley & Sons. doi:10.1002/9781118874059

Li, H., & Lai, Z. (2010). The study and implementation of mobile GPS navigation system based on Google Maps. In *Proceedings of 2010 International Conference on Computer and Information Application* (pp. 87–90). IEEE. 10.1109/ICCIA.2010.6141544

Liu, S., McGree, J., Ge, Z., & Xie, Y. (2015). *Computational and statistical methods for analysing big data with applications.* Academic Press.

Lyon, L., Mattern, E., Acker, A., & Langmead, A. (2015). Applying translational principles to data science curriculum development. *Proceedings of the 12th International Conference on Digital Preservation.*

McNurlin, B. C., & Sprague, R. H. (2001). *Information systems management in practice.* Prentice Hall PTR.

Patten, M. L., & Newhart, M. (2017). *Understanding research methods: An overview of the essentials.* Routledge. doi:10.4324/9781315213033

Pedrycz, W., & Chen, S. M. (Eds.). (2014). *Information granularity, big data, and computational intelligence* (Vol. 8). Springer.

Provost, F., & Fawcett, T. (2013). *Data Science for Business: What you need to know about data mining and data-analytic thinking.* O'Reilly Media, Inc.

Qiu, J., Wu, Q., Ding, G., Xu, Y., & Feng, S. (2016). A survey of machine learning for big data processing. *EURASIP Journal on Advances in Signal Processing, 2016*, 1–16.

Raghupathi, W., & Raghupathi, V. (2014). Big data analytics in healthcare: Promise and potential. *Health Information Science and Systems, 2*(1), 3. doi:10.1186/2047-2501-2-3 PMID:25825667

Rathore, M. M., Ahmad, A., Paul, A., & Jeon, G. (2015). Efficient graph-oriented smart transportation using internet of things generated big data. In *Proceedings of the 11th International Conference on Signal-Image Technology & Internet-Based Systems* (SITIS) (pp. 512–519). IEEE. 10.1109/SITIS.2015.121

Schmelzer, J., Röpke, G., & Mahnke, R. (1999). *Aggregation phenomena in complex systems.* Wiley-Vch.

Seife, C. (2007). *Decoding the universe: How the new science of information is explaining everything in the cosmos, from our brains to black holes*. Penguin.

Shekhar, S., Gunturi, V., Evans, M. R., & Yang, K. (2012, May). Spatial big-data challenges intersecting mobility and cloud computing. In *Proceedings of the 11th ACM International Workshop on Data Engineering for Wireless and Mobile Access* (pp. 1–6). ACM. 10.1145/2258056.2258058

Sun, C., Gao, R., & Xi, H. (2014, July). Big data based retail recommender system of non e-commerce. In *Proceedings of the 5th International Conference on Computing, Communications and Networking Technologies* (pp. 1–7). IEEE. 10.1109/ICCCNT.2014.6963129

Tang, R., & Sae-Lim, W. (2016). Data science programs in US higher education: An exploratory content analysis of program description, curriculum structure, and course focus. *Education for Information*, *32*(3), 269–290. doi:10.3233/EFI-160977

Tansley, S., & Tolle, K. M. (2009). The fourth paradigm: Data-intensive scientific discovery (Vol. 1). Microsoft Research.

Tuomi, I. (1999). Data is more than knowledge: Implications of the reversed knowledge hierarchy for knowledge management and organizational memory. In *Proceedings of the 32nd Annual Hawaii International Conference on Systems Sciences* (pp. 103–117). IEEE. 10.1109/HICSS.1999.772795

Van Der Aalst, W. (2016). Data science in action. In *Process Mining* (pp. 3–23). Springer. doi:10.1007/978-3-662-49851-4_1

Wang, C., Chen, M. H., Schifano, E., Wu, J., & Yan, J. (2016). Statistical methods and computing for big data. *Statistics and Its Interface*, *9*(4), 399–414. doi:10.4310/SII.2016.v9.n4.a1 PMID:27695593

Wang, Y., & Chiew, V. (2010). On the cognitive process of human problem solving. *Cognitive Systems Research*, *11*(1), 81–92. doi:10.1016/j.cogsys.2008.08.003

Wilder, C. R., & Ozgur, C. O. (2015). Business analytics curriculum for undergraduate majors. *Transactions on Education*, *15*(2), 180–187. doi:10.1287/ited.2014.0134

Zikopoulos, P., & Eaton, C. (2011). *Understanding big data: Analytics for enterprise class hadoop and streaming data*. McGraw-Hill Osborne Media.

KEY TERMS AND DEFINITIONS

Big Data: Extremely large dataset that are generated in the digital age, which contains hidden useful information that can only be mined with modern computing technologies. Big data are usually unstructured have 5Vs property (volume, variety, velocity, value, and veracity).

Bioinformatics: The application of data science technologies in molecular biology, genetics, systems biology, and structural biology. The main objective of bioinformatics is to establish the correlation between genetic information and the behaviors and properties of organisms. The study in this field can facilitate the development of new drugs, gene alteration, organic farming, and synthetic meat.

Business Data Analytics: An interdisciplinary field that utilizes data science and data technologies in business practice to analyze customer data, product data, transaction data, in order to reduce cost, expend market, and improve customer experience.

Curriculum Design: The practice to systematically organize curriculum within a program. Important curriculum design activities include course selections, scheduling, and evaluation.

Data Analytics: The practice of using data science and data engineering technologies to analyze real-world big data in order to answer real-world questions or solve real-world problems.

Data Engineering: An interdisciplinary field that involves computer engineering, software engineering, artificial intelligence, and mathematics. The objectives of data engineering is to design, build, and integrate data processing programs and platforms that be used by data analysts.

Data Science: A branch of computer science that utilizes mathematical analytical methods to study big data in order to retrieve useful information.

Healthcare Data Analytics: The application of data science technologies in healthcare field. Through analyzing patient data and retrieving useful information, healthcare data analytics aims at improving patient service, reducing cost, promoting health, and preventing diseases.

Social Analytics: The application of data science technologies in social entities and social activities. Examples include web analysis, election analysis, and virtual network analysis.

APPENDIX: BRIEF DESCRIPTIONS OF MAJOR COURSES IN DATA SCIENCE CURRICULA

Part A. Prerequisite Courses

Calculus. This course should cover logarithm, trigonometric functions, real numbers and the completeness axiom, mathematical induction, single variable functions, set functions, limits, continuity, derivatives, mean value theorem, applications of the derivative, motion problems, optimization, antiderivatives, definite integral, indefinite integral, and other fundamental theorem of calculus.

Discrete Math. This course should cover formal logic, proof techniques, Boolean algebra, sets, number systems, functions, relations and counting.

Linear Algebra. This course should cover linear equations, matrix algebra, determinants, vector spaces, eigenvalues and eigenvectors, singular value decomposition, linear transformations, and linear dependence and independence.

Probability. This course should cover permutations, combinations, counting principles, binomial theorem, statistical experiments, conditional probability, independent events, random variables, probability density, cumulative distribution, expected values, standard deviations, Normal distribution, Binomial distribution, and Poisson distribution.

Statistics. This course should cover estimation and hypothesis testing, linear and nonlinear least square regression equation, t-distribution, chi-square distribution, and prediction and forecast.

Programming in Python. This course should cover fundamental Python programming concepts and technologies, including data types, control flow, functions, iteration, recursion, arrays, vectors, strings, algorithms, exceptions, and object-oriented programming.

Programming in R. This course should cover basic R programming techniques. Topics include variables, basic data types, and advanced data types, such as vectors, matrices, factors, data frames, and lists.

Part B. Core Courses

Data Analysis. This course should cover advanced statistical concepts, exponential distributions, monotone likelihood ratio, uniformly most powerful tests, minimum variance estimates, shortest confidence intervals, linear models, analysis of variance, and nonparametric tests. This course should include programming components so that students could utilize programming tools to practice these data analysis techniques.

Data Visualization. This course should cover visualization methods and tools for data exploration, data reporting, and data monitoring. Commonly used tools include R data visualization packages, such as ggplot2, Lattice, plotly, and dygraphs, and other tools, such as Power BI and Tableau.

Advanced Data Analysis. This course should cover advanced statistical techniques in data analytics. Topics include multiple regression, analysis of variance of one-way and two-way layouts under various models, multiple comparison, analysis of discrete data, comparison of variances, multivariate analysis, and discriminant analysis. This course should include programming components so that students could utilize programming tools to practice these data analysis techniques.

Data Mining. This course should cover data mining methods such as classification and clustering (linear classifiers, nearest neighbor, and support vector machines), decision trees, association rules, boosted trees, random forest, and neural networks rule-based learning.

Database Querying. This course should cover SQL language for rational database manipulation and Cypher language for graph database manipulation. Specific attention should be given to retrieval queries, such as SQL join and group operations.

Data Ethics. This course should cover the concepts of right and wrong conduct in relation to data, including practice and policies regarding data access and data management. Specifically, this course should cover conducts of both the traditional data and the modern day big data.

Big Data Analytics. This course should cover social media data (such as web posts, videos, audios, images, e-mails, and Tweets), personal financial data (such as shopping history and bank transaction record), healthcare data (such as patient illness history and doctor visit record), and more. Students should get familiar with important up-to-date technologies used in manipulating, storing, and analyzing big data. Such technologies include Hadoop, MongoDB, Spark, Kafka, and NoSQL (key-value store, document-based store, column-based store, and graph database).

Machine Learning. This course should cover supervised learning and unsupervised learning. Topics includes parametric learning, non-parametric learning, neural networks, support vector machines, clustering, dimension reduction, kernel methods, artificial neural networks, and reinforcement learning.

Capstone Project. Through taking this class, students will get an opportunity to apply the knowledge and skills they have gained throughout taking the series of data science courses to solve a real-world problem. This final project will test students' skills in combining data analysis, data visualization, and data reporting techniques.

Part C. Elective Courses

Data Security. This course should cover cybersecurity, cryptography, information security, data security, security management, and data privacy. The topics should include theories, practices, and policies.

Database Design and Database Management. This course should cover database modeling (ER Modeling and ERD Modeling), relational algebra, database design, database normalization, storage and indexing, query processing, query optimization, transaction processing, and database recovery.

Deep Learning. This course should cover invariance, stability, variability models, scattering networks, group formalism, convolutional neural network, covariance/invariance, dictionary learning, learned iterative shrinkage thresholding algorithm, deep unsupervised learning, autoencoders, and adversarial generative networks.

Social Network Analysis. This course should cover the concepts and methods of social network analysis. Specific topics include data extraction, data modeling, data management, and data visualization. Software tools are used to study social networks, such collaboration networks, communication networks, and social relations.

Cloud Computing. This course should cover cloud software architecture, storage, and services. Specifically, students will learn different communicating technologies such as JSON, REST API, RPC, and different clouds services such as IaaS (infrastructure as a service), PaaS (platform as a service), SaaS (software as a service), FaaS (function as a service; server-less architecture).

Natural Language Processing. This course should cover regular expressions, non-probabilistic parsing, language modeling, probabilistic context free grammar, information extraction, machine translation, automatic summarization, and interactive dialogue systems. The course should also cover knowledge-based and statistical approaches to language processing.

Decision Optimization. This course should cover theory and methods for the solution of optimization problems. Topics include Newton's method for minimization, iterative techniques for unconstrained optimization, which includes deterministic optimization, linear programming, nonlinear programming, network optimization, integer programming, constrained problems, simplex method, duality theory, and uncertainty.

Time Series Analysis. This course should cover time series relationships, univariate stationary and non-stationary models, regression with correlated errors, autoregressive models, autoregressive moving average models, frequency domain methods, spectral analysis, linear filtering, and prediction of time series.

Regression Analysis. This course should cover least square estimation of parameters, single linear regression, multiple linear regression, hypothesis testing and confidence intervals in linear regression models. This course should also cover data analysis using nonlinear regression models, such as logistic regression, Poisson regression, and generalized linear regression models.

Differential Equations. This course should cover mathematical models, first order differential equations, higher order linear differential equations, linear systems of arbitrary order and matrices, qualitative analysis of solutions, boundary value and initial value problems, nonlinear systems and phase plane analysis, numerical methods, and applications of differential equations.

Chapter 26
Empirical Study on the Impact of Select Green HRM Dimensions on Green Innovation Culture

Vasuki Boominathan
Theivanai Ammal College for Women, India

J. Tamil Selvi
Annamalai University, India

C. Dhilipan
ⓘD https://orcid.org/0000-0002-1580-922X
Jain University, India

M. Tamil Arasu
GRT Institute of Engineering and Technology, India

B. Elamurugan
Sri Manakula Vinayagar Engineering College (Autonomous), India

Palanivel Rathinasabapathi Velmurugan
ⓘD https://orcid.org/0000-0002-0395-9060
Berlin School of Business and Innovation, Germany

ABSTRACT

In a timeframe marked by intensifying ecological crises, the function of human resource management (HRM) in nurturing an environment-centric innovation ethos is significantly under-researched. This empirical inquiry aims to address this lacuna by investigating the nexus between chosen elements of green human resource management (GHRM) and the culture of green innovation in India's prominent cement manufacturing firms. Adopting a correlational research approach and making use of statistical methodologies like partial least squares (PLS), the study reveals a noteworthy positive linkage between green recruitment and selection (GRS), green training and development (GTD), and green performance appraisal (GPA) with green innovation culture (GIC). These insights add valuable dimensions to both the theoretical understanding and practical applications of HRM and sustainability, more so within the Indian cement industry.

DOI: 10.4018/979-8-3693-0049-7.ch026

INTRODUCTION

In recent times, there has been an escalating focus in both academic and industrial circles on the subject of environmental sustainability, colloquially termed "going green." The scholarly narrative has transitioned from an overarching emphasis on eco-conscious corporate activities to the specific "greening" of various organizational functions (Muisyo & Qin, 2021). In the prevailing cutthroat global business environment, enterprises are mandated to be not only operationally efficient and value-centric but also ecologically accountable. This heightened global sensitivity toward environmental aspects has fast-tracked the assimilation of green strategies in the business realm, enabling firms to achieve a dual character of being both "green and competitive" (Doghan et al., 2022).

Human Resource Management (HRM) is a crucial catalyst in propelling this green agenda, as corroborated by multiple studies including that of Muisyo et al., (2021). The infusion of green initiatives into HRM protocols can substantially elevate an organisation's likelihood of attaining enduring sustainability (Doghan et al., 2022).

In rapidly developing economies like India, cultivating a workforce that is attuned to environmental sustainability is critical. Recent alterations in the global economic dynamics have thrust emerging markets into prominence, chiefly due to their extensive resource utilization aimed at augmenting their Gross Domestic Product (GDP) (Al-Swidi et al., 2021). Owing to their abundant talent and resource pools, companies across various sectors worldwide find these markets increasingly appealing. Sharma et al., (2021) underscore that the preponderance of green HRM scholarship is predicated on Western frameworks, thereby accentuating the necessity for more geographically pertinent insights into green HRM practices within the Indian context.

The extant literature on green HRM has largely concentrated on its association with green innovation culture, according to current scholarly findings. While prior research has examined the nexus between Green HRM and eco-conscious creativity, the connection between green HRM and an organisation's green innovation culture remains inadequately probed. Supporting this viewpoint, Benevene and Buonomo (2020) argue that HRM can act as a facilitator in devising and executing green protocols across different organisational strata. Concurring with this, Muisyo et al. (2022) also underscore a notable research lacuna related to green HRM and green innovation culture. Reinforcing this notion, Yan and Hu (2021) found that enterprises with substantial investments in green HRM are not only compliant with rigorous global environmental norms but also gain a competitive upper hand owing to heightened consumer environmental consciousness. Hence, in rising economies, prioritizing green HRM becomes imperative for environmental stewardship, talent acquisition, and competitive positioning (Muisyo, Qin, Ho, et al., 2021). Therefore, delving deeper into this subject offers a fertile ground for prospective academic inquiries.

Research Objective

In consideration of these points, this study zeroes in on three key facets of Green HRM —specifically, Green Recruitment and Selection (GRS), Green Training and Development (GTD), and Green Performance Appraisal (GPA)—to scrutinize their Impact on the culture of green innovation. To achieve this objective, a survey involving 223 workers from significant cement production companies operating in India was carried out.

Research Question

This study seeks to unravel the intricate links between key elements of Green HRM and the organisational culture of green innovation. strategic HRM initiatives can markedly elevate an organisation's culture of innovation. Such initiatives equip senior executives with an exhaustive knowledge reservoir, thereby enabling them to make well-informed strategic HRM choices to navigate impending organizational obstacles (Muisyo, Qin, & Ho, 2021). One of the modern-day challenges confronting organisations in the 21st century pertains to the greening of HRM functions. In light of these findings and existing scholarly contributions, comprehending the association between green HRM and the culture of green innovation becomes crucial.

The research question to be investigated is as follows:

RQ1: Do green HRM practices, specifically GRS, GTD, and GPA, serve as predictors of an organizational culture of green innovation?

LITERATURE REVIEW

Green HRM

Today, GHRM is necessary for various reasons.

A historical record of adverse environmental incidents necessitates focus on sustainable practices (Krithika et al. 2019).

Organisations often engage in resource-intensive production processes, which not only consume natural resources, but also contribute to environmental pollution.

Excessive exploitation of natural resources for raw materials culminates in environmental degradation, ecosystem imbalance, and amplification of the greenhouse effect (Krithika et al., 2019).

In existing research, the "greening" of HRM is often explored within a spectrum that encompasses various HRM processes—ranging from job role analysis and recruitment to training & development (T&D), performance evaluation, and incentivization (Muisyo et al., 2022; Muisyo & Qin, 2021). Benevene and Buonomo (2020) have extended the scope of current research by examining multi-level mechanisms, innovative theoretical pathways, green HR systems, and individual employee behaviours. Their work has further enriched the Green HRM discourse by addressing its broader contextual factors and performance impact. According to Li et al. (2022), Green HRM practices initiate upon an employee's entry and continue through to their exit from the organization. Firms are advised to continually build a sustainable framework to fully leverage the philosophies of "mind-share" and "market-share". To mitigate confusion, the prefix "green" has been attached to each HRM activity, indicating the integration of environmental considerations into traditional HRM practices (Sharma et al., 2021).

GHRM holds a pivotal role in augmenting organizational competitiveness through various channels. For example, Muisyo et al. (2022) found that companies with inferior HR policies experience a more pronounced influence of environmental performance on their competitive edge. The study indicates that organizations with robust HR strategies secure a more comprehensive competitive advantage by synergizing improved environmental and organizational outcomes. The academic consensus posits that the adoption of Green HRM practices bolsters organizational sustainability. Benevene and Buonomo (2020) suggest that Green HR practices are geared toward aiding organizations in focusing on ecologically oriented components of their sustainability projects. Chen & Yan (2022) examined the paradoxes involved in HRM's role in fostering environmental sustainability. While existing literature posits a positive impact of GHRM on environmental sustainability, the relationship between Green HRM and green innovation remains under-investigated, leaving the evidential basis for such linkages relatively unclear.

Green Innovation Culture

In the organizational context, a "green" culture is defined as one where the workforce extends its objectives beyond mere profitability to include proactive environmental stewardship (Waqas et al., 2021). This culture is foundational to green innovation or eco-innovation, which focuses on elements like eco-design, waste reduction, and energy efficiency. Accelerated by heightened environmental awareness, regulatory pressures, and eco-conscious consumers, green innovation has become an indispensable strategic tool, especially for companies expanding into emerging markets (Sharma et al., 2021). Contemporary research underscores its role as a guidepost for balancing sustainability and competitiveness (Kodua et al., 2022). This balance is further substantiated by studies that elucidate the positive correlation between green innovation and organizational sustainability across various aspects, including product and process improvements aimed at ecological conservation (Muisyo, Qin, Ho, et al., 2021).

Innovation remains a cornerstone for bolstering an organization's competitive advantage, and green innovation adds layers of complexity to this equation by involving both product and process enhancements. These enhancements aim to optimize energy use, minimize pollution, and reduce the organization's environmental footprint. The imperatives of environmental conservation are also increasingly embedded within corporate governance frameworks, as compliance with ecological norms confers a competitive advantage (Doghan et al., 2022; Al-Swidi et al., 2021). Therefore, the adoption of green HRM practices and a green innovation culture is not just a matter of ethical or regulatory compliance but is integral to a firm's strategic positioning and long-term sustainability.

Hypotheses Development

The emergence of the "green movement," advocating foundational tenets like sustainability and environmental responsibility, has set the stage for the evolution of Green HRM. This shift in HRM is often commended for its potential to foster environmental guardianship. GHRM aims to create a collaborative environment between human resource professionals and senior leadership to harmonize employee-related processes with ecological initiatives. Hence, GHRM serves as a connective tissue between organizational goals and environmental preservation. Scholarly contributions highlight the broader implications of HRM and emphasize the positive outcomes of integrating GHRM into innovative production frameworks. Among various HRM practices, precedence is given to recruiting individuals whose values align with organizational eco-sustainability objectives and enhancing their green skills through focused training programs.

Additionally, documenting and evaluating employees' eco-friendly behaviors, thereby rewarding them based on their proficiency in specific green skills, is another crucial HRM initiative often termed as "green motivation." Existing HRM research has extensively probed the role of HR practices in shaping different dimensions of GHRM (Bhatti et al., 2021). Responding to the research gap outlined by Muisyo and Qin (2021), the present study aspires to offer intricate perspectives on the environmental ramifications of the robust relationship between Green Human Resource Management (GHRM) and Green Innovation Culture (GIC).

H1: A Green Innovation Culture (GIC) exhibits a Positive Correlation with Green Recruitment and Selection (GRS).

H2: A Green Innovation Culture (GIC) exhibits a Positive Correlation with Green Training and Development (GTD).

H3: A Green Innovation Culture (GIC) exhibits a Positive Correlation with Green Performance Appraisal (GPA).

Theoretical Background

The theoretical underpinnings of this study are rooted in the Ability-Motivation-Opportunity (AMO) theory, a framework suggesting that peak employee performance results from the enhancement of skill sets, promotion of employee engagement, and the generation of environments conducive to organizational innovation. Within this model, Green Human Resource Management (GHRM) emerges as a facilitator for both individual and organizational green innovation by recruiting eco-conscious staff, implementing green training initiatives, and incentivizing employee involvement in sustainable activities.

Hence, the AMO theory functions as the analytical lens through which this study examines the interconnected roles of Green Recruitment and Selection (GRS), Green Training and Development (GTD), and Green Performance Appraisal (GPA) in cultivating an organizational culture of green innovation. As articulated by Benevene and Buonomo (2020), a culture rooted in green innovation endows an organization with a competitive edge when it is intertwined with green human resource management practices.

Conceptual Model

This research study was conceptualized to analyze the relationship between GHRM, namely GRS, GTD, and GPA, and GIC. Figure 1 illustrates the conceptual model.

METHODOLOGY

Survey and Data Collection

This study utilized a correlational research methodology to investigate the impact of Green Human Resource Management (GHRM) practices—specifically Green Training and Development (GTD), Green Recruitment and Selection (GRS), and Green Performance Appraisal (GPA)—on Green Innovation Culture (GIC). To delve into these relationships and evaluate the conceptual model, a survey instrument with corresponding measurement scales was designed. Content validity of the pilot questionnaire was ascertained through consultation with three academic experts and three professionals from the industry, leading to subsequent refinements.

Figure 1. Proposed research model

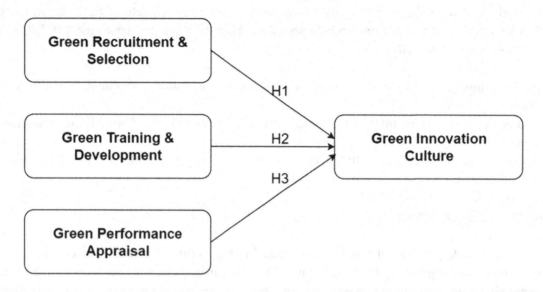

The study's unit of analysis encompasses individual firms, specifically targeting large cement manufacturing companies in India. These firms were chosen based on their structured HR processes, adherence to governmental regulations, and sensitivity to environmental concerns. The sampling frame was generated from the Confederation of Indian Industries (CII) Directory 2020 (CII, 2020). Ten major firms were selected, identified by their revenue listings in the directory. Given the comprehensive nature of the sampling frame and the potential for a high response rate via a postal survey, a judgmental sampling technique was employed. In line with the study's focus on both corporate and environmental aspects, questionnaires were distributed to HR managers or directors actively involved in HRM practices. Out of 1000 questionnaires disseminated, which were accompanied by a cover letter ensuring confidentiality and outlining the study's aims, 334 responses were obtained. Eleven of these were excluded for incompleteness or invalidity, resulting in 323 completed questionnaires and a response rate of 32.3%. Considering the historically low response rates for correlational research in the Indian context, this was deemed satisfactory.

Measurements

For the measurement of Green Human Resource Management (GHRM) variables, the study utilized the framework outlined by Renwick et al., (2013). Specifically, the study integrated the components of Green Performance Appraisal, Green Training and Development, and Green Recruitment and Selection (GRS). In terms of Green Innovation Culture (GIC), the research employed the four-item scale formulated by Y. S. Chen et al., (2006), which focuses on green production innovation. Participants were prompted to indicate their level of agreement or disagreement with the presented statements using a 5-point Likert scale, ranging from 'strongly disagree' (1) to 'strongly agree' (5). Importantly, each item included in the measurement scales was meticulously chosen for its theoretical relevance as substantiated by existing scholarly works.

DATA ANALYSIS

Data analysis in this study was conducted using SmartPLS 3.0 software, leveraging Partial Least Squares Structural Equation Modelling (PLS-SEM) to assess the formulated research model (Ringle et al., 2015). The advantage of employing PLS-SEM lies in its capability to accommodate smaller sample sizes, thus rendering it well-suited for this investigation (Hair et al., 2017). Upon confirmation of the measurement model's validity, the structural model was scrutinized following recognized guidelines set forth in existing literature (Silaparasetti et al., 2017)

Measurement Model

To evaluate convergent validity, metrics such as factor loadings, average variance extracted (AVE), and composite reliability (CR) were employed, adhering to the guidelines established by Hair et al., (2017). As delineated in Table 1, all components surpassed the stipulated benchmarks: factor loadings greater than 0.7, AVE exceeding 0.5, and CR above 0.7. These outcomes affirmed the measures' reliability and validity. Discriminant validity was subsequently scrutinized using criteria defined by Fornell and Larcker (1981), who posit that discriminant validity is attained when the square root of the AVE surpasses the inter-construct correlations. This condition was met, as illustrated in Table 2. Furthermore, the Heterotrait-Monotrait (HTMT) ratio aligned with the 0.85 threshold recommended by Zhang et al. (2021), offering additional validation of discriminant validity, as expounded in Table 3.

Structural Model

Hair et al. (2017) advocate for the utilization of a bootstrapping technique with 5,000 resamples to assess the R-squared value (R2), beta coefficients (β), and corresponding t-values for evaluating the structural model. Given that all Variance Inflation Factor (VIF) values were below five, multicollinearity was not a concern (Hair et al., 2017). Subsequently, the study examined the relationships between the independent and dependent variables, as outlined in Table 4. The R2 value of 0.425 indicated that the model accounted for 42.5% of the variance in Green Innovation Culture (GIC). According to Benevene and Buonomo (2020), an R2 value equal to or greater than 0.10 is deemed sufficient for evaluating the variance explained by an endogenous component. Hair Jr et al. (2017) noted that establishing universal benchmarks for acceptable R2 values is challenging, given the field-specific and model-specific contexts. In this study, with an R2 of 42.5% and three predictors, the variance explained was considered satisfactory.

Power analysis was conducted using Daniel Soper's website, resulting in a power value of 0.87, which is highly favorable. This calculation involved three predictors, a sample size of 0.425, and an R2 of 0.425. The findings corroborated that Green Training and Development (GTD) ($\beta = 0.268$, $p < 0.05$), Green Recruitment and Selection (GRS) ($\beta = 0.324$, $p < 0.05$), and Green Performance Appraisal (GPA) ($\beta = 0.279$, $p < 0.05$) were positively correlated with Green HRM, thereby affirming Hypotheses H1, H2, and H3. Among the predictors, GRS had the most significant Impact on Green HRM. The model's predictive relevance was further validated through a blindfolding procedure at a distance of seven. A Q2 value greater than zero, as stipulated by Fornell & Larcker (1981), indicates the model's predictive power for specific endogenous constructs. In this case, the Q2 value was 0.273, exceeding the zero threshold, thus confirming predictive relevance.

Table 1. Convergent validity

Variables and Indicators	Outer Loading	VIF	Composite Reliability	AVE	Cronbach's Alpha
Green innovation culture					
GIC1	0.778	1.58	0.871	0.63	0.803
GIC2	0.731	1.349			
GIC3	0.815	2.02			
GIC4	0.845	2.092			
Green Performance Appraisal					
GPA1	0.815	1.649	0.826	0.547	0.716
GPA2	0.767	1.464			
GPA3	0.774	1.541			
GPA4	0.78	1.135			
Green Recruitment & Selection					
GRS1	0.836	1.629	0.863	0.678	0.763
GRS2	0.787	1.46			
GRS3	0.845	1.584			
Green Training & Development					
GTD1	0.864	2.004	0.86	0.771	0.852
GTD2	0.875	2.148			
GTD3	0.895	2.136			

Table 2. Discriminant validity (Farnell Larcker criterion)

	GIC	GPA	GRS	GTD
GIC	0.793			
GPA	0.578	0.74		
GRS	0.631	0.547	0.823	
GTD	0.581	0.454	0.576	0.878

Table 3. Discriminant validity: Heterotrait-Monotrait ratio (HTMT)

	GIC	GPA	GRS	GTD
GIC				
GPA	0.76			
GRS	0.799	0.742		
GTD	0.697	0.59	0.709	

Table 4. Hypothesis testing

S.No	Hypothesis	Beta	T Statistics	p Value	Decision
H1	GPA -> Green Innovation Culture	0.279	5.16	0.001	Supported
H2	GRS -> Green Innovation Culture	0.324	6.725	0.001	Supported
H3	GTD -> Green Innovation Culture	0.268	3.465	0.001	Supported

DISCUSSION

This research serves as an inaugural endeavor to investigate the relationship between Green HRM and Green Innovation Culture (GIC). To the authors' best knowledge, this constitutes the first empirical study that utilizes this theoretical framework within the Indian milieu, with a particular emphasis on the cement manufacturing industry. By doing so, the study augments existing scholarship by enhancing our comprehension of green innovation practices within the scope of India's cement manufacturing sector.

Theoretical Contributions

The cement manufacturing sector serves as a crucial component of India's economic infrastructure, yet it is inextricably linked to significant environmental consequences. Accordingly, the integration of environmentally responsible strategies, such as cultivating a culture of green innovation, has garnered increased attention. While existing literature has highlighted the benefits of green innovation, such as cost-efficiency and talent management (Muisyo, Qin, Ho, et al., 2021), underscores a research gap in exploring the connection between Green HRM and a culture of green innovation. Addressing this gap, the current study investigates the Impact of three key GHRM elements—GRS, GTD, and GPA—on green innovation culture. Empirical data for this study were sourced from ten major cement manufacturing firms in India.

The study findings affirm a strong positive relationship between GRS and a culture of green innovation. This outcome is consistent with previous research, emphasizing that GRS activities are inherently aligned with eco-friendly objectives and knowledge dissemination (Gürlek & Koseoglu, 2021; Li et al., 2022). Sharma et al. (2021) also attests to the positive influence of GRS on fostering a culture of green innovation. Specifically, employees who bring environmental expertise from prior roles can act as catalysts for generating, applying, and disseminating environmental knowledge within their current organization. Such employees, equipped with specialized knowledge and skills, are well-positioned to contribute meaningfully to eco-friendly practices, thereby enriching the culture of green innovation.

The empirical data also validate the hypothesis that Green Performance Appraisal (GPA) positively impacts a culture of green innovation. GPA mechanisms measure employee contributions to sustainable work environments. Within the cement manufacturing sector, the adoption of green innovation strategies is crucial for enhancing employee engagement. Consequently, GPA can serve as an effective instrument for tapping into innovation cultures within organizations.

Furthermore, the study reveals a significant positive correlation between Green Training and Development (GTD) and a culture of green innovation. This aligns with the perspectives of Benevene and Buonomo (2020), who posit that GTD empowers employees with environmentally sustainable operational practices aimed at resource optimization, waste minimization, and energy conservation. Corroborate the positive role of GTD in nurturing a culture of green innovation. Green training promotes a work environment conducive to environmental stewardship, enhancing employees' capacity to undertake effective eco-friendly actions in their work settings. This study offers significant theoretical contributions by extending the Ability-Motivation-Opportunity (AMO) framework within the realm of Human Resource Management. AMO theory posits that employee performance is optimized when organizations focus on enhancing abilities, fostering motivation, and creating opportunities. Within this framework, green innovation emerges as a crucial intangible asset that can confer a competitive advantage to organizations. In doing so, this study emphasizes that a one-size-fits-all organizational model is not universally applicable, given that both internal and external environmental factors profoundly influence an organization's strategic direction.

Additionally, this research addresses a significant void in the literature by examining Human Resource Management through an environmental lens, particularly within the context of emerging economies like India. It provides novel insights into the interplay between GHRM practices and a culture of green innovation. By focusing on three core GHRM practices—GRS, GTD, and GPA - this study augments existing knowledge on GHRM and broadens the scope of HRM research. The findings suggest that cement manufacturing firms in India could cultivate a culture of green innovation by effectively implementing these GHRM practices. In this regard, the study resonates with the gaps identified by Kodua et al. (2022) regarding the Impact of HRM on innovation. It extends our understanding of how cement manufacturing firms can leverage green HRM practices to bolster their culture of green innovation, thereby providing both theoretical and practical validation for the integration of green HRM practices in the manufacturing sector.

Managerial Implications

This study carries significant practical implications for both industry stakeholders and policymakers. Its conceptual framework serves as a strategic guide for cement manufacturing organizations, particularly in developing economies, to understand the role of GHRM in cultivating a culture of green innovation. Given the burgeoning emphasis on sustainability, implementing this model can considerably augment organizational competencies in green manufacturing, thereby sustaining a competitive edge.

Empirically, the study illuminates the pivotal roles of GRS, GTD, and GPA in engendering a green innovation culture. For immediate organizational interventions, these facets of GHRM should be prioritized. Specifically, the study underscores the Impact of GRS as a cornerstone for shaping a green innovation culture. The adoption of innovative recruitment strategies, combined with cutting-edge technologies, can not only mitigate recruitment expenditures but also deliver compelling organizational outcomes. Likewise, the implementation of GPA systems can serve as a motivational lever, setting explicit performance standards and fostering an atmosphere conducive to green innovation. Furthermore, GTD emerged as instrumental in instilling a green innovation culture. Organizations can achieve enduring benefits by designing comprehensive green training programs that motivate employees to adopt sustainable practices in both professional and personal contexts.

On a policy level, the findings offer important considerations for enhancing the efficacy of green HRM practices among large-scale cement manufacturers. Policymakers might consider introducing specialized environmental training programs for staff, thereby amplifying the efficacy of Green Recruitment Systems (GRS). Additionally, investment in infrastructure focusing on environmental conservation, hosting environmental conferences, and fostering collaborative initiatives between organizations and stakeholders can contribute to the development of a more sustainable manufacturing landscape.

Limitations of the Study

While this study makes significant contributions to the existing literature, it is not without limitations that warrant careful consideration. First, the study's focus on large cement manufacturing firms in India raises questions about the generalizability of the findings. Although the research provides valuable insights into this specific industrial sector within the Indian context, its applicability to other industries or cultural settings remains untested. Future studies could extend this line of inquiry by replicating the research in diverse organizational and cultural contexts to enhance the generalizability of the conceptual model.

Second, the methodology of the study, particularly its reliance on self-reported, questionnaire-based data, introduces the potential issue of Common Method Variance (CMV). While statistical controls were implemented to mitigate the effects of CMV, it remains a recognized limitation associated with survey-based social science research. Future research should consider employing alternative data collection methods or statistical techniques to further address this concern.

Lastly, while the study establishes a robust link between green HRM and a culture of green innovation, its cross-sectional design limits its ability to examine the temporal effects of green HRM practices on the development of a green innovation culture. This limitation necessitates future research that employs a longitudinal approach to track the evolution of green HRM practices and their Impact on organizational culture over time.

Suggestions for Future Research

This study opens avenues for further scholarly exploration in the realm of GHRM and its Impact on green innovation culture. Future research could consider a more exhaustive set of GHRM dimensions and their individual and collective influences on green innovation. Comparative analyses across different industrial sectors and geographical contexts are recommended to enrich the discourse. Longitudinal studies can provide insights into the temporal effects of GHRM, and the framework can be extended to include metrics such as competitive advantage and long-term sustainability. These prospective studies would not only deepen the academic understanding but also offer practical implications for organizations aiming for environmental stewardship.

CONCLUSION

The imperative to adopt environmentally sustainable practices has gained traction among enterprises driven by escalating ecological concerns. In today's fiercely competitive business landscape, human resources often serve as a linchpin for organizational success, superseding financial prowess or innovative product offerings. Greening Human Resource Management (HRM) has become indispensable for enhancing HRM efficacy and organizational competitiveness. Despite its criticality, the domain of green HRM remains underexplored and its adoption among businesses is sporadic. This study endeavors to bridge this knowledge gap by scrutinizing the interplay between green HRM and the culture of green innovation, with a specific focus on India's leading cement manufacturing corporations.

The study employed a correlational research methodology and a survey instrument to measure the Impact of three green HRM practices—Green Training and Development, Green Recruitment and Selection, and Green Performance Appraisal—on Green Innovation Culture. The data was collected from 323 HR managers or directors from 10 major cement firms selected from the Confederation of Indian Industries (CII) Directory 2020. The data analysis was conducted using Partial Least Squares Structural Equation Modelling (PLS-SEM) with SmartPLS 3.0 software.

The results revealed that all three green HRM practices had a positive and significant effect on Green Innovation Culture, with Green Training and Development being the most influential factor. The study also found that Green Innovation Culture mediated the relationship between green HRM practices and organizational performance, indicating that fostering a culture of green innovation can enhance the competitiveness and sustainability of cement firms. The study contributed to the existing literature on green HRM by providing empirical evidence of its benefits and mechanisms in the context of the cement industry, which is one of the most polluting and energy-intensive sectors in the world.

REFERENCES

Al Doghan, M. A., Abdelwahed, N. A. A., Soomro, B. A., & Alayis, M. M. H. A. (2022). Organizational Environmental Culture, Environmental Sustainability and Performance: The Mediating Role of Green HRM and Green Innovation. *Sustainability (Basel)*, *14*(12), 1–20. doi:10.3390u14127510

Al-Swidi, A. K., Gelaidan, H. M., & Saleh, R. M. (2021). The joint Impact of green human resource management, leadership and organizational culture on employees' green behaviour and organisational environmental performance. *Journal of Cleaner Production*, *316*, 128112. doi:10.1016/j.jclepro.2021.128112

Benevene, P., & Buonomo, I. (2020). Green human resource management: An evidence-based systematic literature review. *Sustainability (Basel)*, *12*(15), 5974. doi:10.3390u12155974

Bhatti, S. H., Saleem, F., Murtaza, G., & Haq, T. U. (2021). Exploring the Impact of green human resource management on environmental performance: The roles of perceived organizational support and innovative environmental behavior. *International Journal of Manpower*.

Chen, Y., & Yan, X. (2022). The small and medium enterprises' green human resource management and green transformational leadership: A sustainable moderated-mediation practice. *Corporate Social Responsibility and Environmental Management*, *29*(5), 1341–1356. doi:10.1002/csr.2273

Chen, Y.-S., Lai, S.-B., & Wen, C.-T. (2006). The influence of green innovation performance on corporate advantage in Taiwan. *Journal of Business Ethics*, *67*(4), 331–339. doi:10.100710551-006-9025-5

Fornell, C., & Larcker, D. F. (1981). *Structural equation models with unobservable variables and measurement error: Algebra and statistics*. Sage Publications Sage CA.

Gürlek, M., & Koseoglu, M. A. (2021). Green innovation research in the field of hospitality and tourism: The construct, antecedents, consequences, and future outlook. *Service Industries Journal*, *41*(11–12), 734–766. doi:10.1080/02642069.2021.1929930

Hair, J., Hollingsworth, C. L., Randolph, A. B., & Chong, A. Y. L. (2017). An updated and expanded assessment of PLS-SEM in information systems research. *Industrial Management & Data Systems*, *117*(3), 442–458. doi:10.1108/IMDS-04-2016-0130

Hair, J. F. Jr, Matthews, L. M., Matthews, R. L., & Sarstedt, M. (2017). PLS-SEM or CB-SEM: Updated guidelines on which method to use. *International Journal of Multivariate Data Analysis*, *1*(2), 107–123. doi:10.1504/IJMDA.2017.087624

Krithika, J., DivyaPriyadharshini, N., & GokulaPriya, J. (2019). Green HRM-Practices In Organisations. *IOSR Journal of Business and Management (IOSR-JBM)*, *21*(3), 74.

Li, M., Tian, Z., Liu, Q., & Lu, Y. (2022). Literature Review and Research Prospect on the Drivers and Effects of Green Innovation. *Sustainability (Basel)*, *14*(16), 9858. doi:10.3390u14169858

Muisyo, P. K., & Qin, S. (2021). Enhancing the FIRM'S green performance through green HRM: The moderating role of green innovation culture. *Journal of Cleaner Production*, *289*, 125720. doi:10.1016/j.jclepro.2020.125720

Muisyo, P. K., Su, Q., Hashmi, H. B. A., Ho, T. H., & Julius, M. M. (2022). The role of green HRM in driving hotels' green creativity. *International Journal of Contemporary Hospitality Management*, *34*(4), 1331–1352. doi:10.1108/IJCHM-07-2021-0833

Renwick, D. W. S., Redman, T., & Maguire, S. (2013). Green HRM: Teaching and learning guide. *International Journal of Management Reviews*.

Ringle, C., Da Silva, D., & Bido, D. (2015). Structural equation modeling with the SmartPLS. *Brazilian Journal Of Marketing, 13*(2).

Sahoo, M. (2019). Structural equation modeling: Threshold criteria for assessing model fit. In *Methodological issues in management research: Advances, challenges, and the way ahead.* Emerald Publishing Limited. doi:10.1108/978-1-78973-973-220191016

Sharma, S., Prakash, G., Kumar, A., Mussada, E. K., Antony, J., & Luthra, S. (2021). Analysing the relationship of adaption of green culture, innovation, green performance for achieving sustainability: Mediating role of employee commitment. *Journal of Cleaner Production*, *303*, 127039. doi:10.1016/j.jclepro.2021.127039

Silaparasetti, V., Rao, G. V. R., & Khan, F. R. (2017). Structural equation modeling analysis using smart pls to assess the occupational health and safety (OHS) factors on workers' behavior. *Humanities & Social Science Reviews*.

Waqas, M., Honggang, X., Ahmad, N., Khan, S. A. R., & Iqbal, M. (2021). Big data analytics as a roadmap towards green innovation, competitive advantage and environmental performance. *Journal of Cleaner Production*, *323*, 128998. doi:10.1016/j.jclepro.2021.128998

Yan, J., & Hu, W. (2021). Environmentally specific transformational leadership and green product development performance: The role of a green HRM system. *International Journal of Manpower*.

Zhang, M. F., Dawson, J. F., & Kline, R. B. (2021). Evaluating the use of covariance-based structural equation modelling with reflective measurement in organizational and management research: A review and recommendations for best practice. *British Journal of Management*, *32*(2), 257–272. doi:10.1111/1467-8551.12415

Chapter 27
An Empirical Analysis on Issues Faced by the Users of Nykaa Product

K. Vidhya
Jain University, India

V. Selvam
Vellore Institute of Technology, India

Mani Kandan
Jain University, India

S. Ashwini
Jain University, India

M. Soumya
Jain University, India

Shimna Jayaraj
Jain University, India

ABSTRACT

These days people use computers more frequently. Because of rapid growth, many enterprises have started doing online business. The primary data for the study was collected through a questionnaire, which was distributed to the respondents via Google Forms. Secondary data is used to collect all published data through journals, magazines, and articles. The current study aims to identify the variables influencing ladies' beauty products. The study is also intended to identify the issues faced by the users of Nykaa products while purchasing them through online media and to find solutions to solve the issues and thus make online purchases easier and more convenient for the ladies.

DOI: 10.4018/979-8-3693-0049-7.ch027

1. INTRODUCTION

Tracing the history of cosmetics, one can find that it was prevalent in almost all global societies, even 7000 years from now. Even in a few of the primitive rituals in the history of human culture, the presence of cosmetics is observed (Charwak, 2016). The red mineral tints, otherwise called the red ochre, which includes crayons and a few of the same kind, are concurrent with the emergence of Homo Sapiens in Africa, and this turns out to be one of the solid proofs for the statement as mentioned earlier (Kumar & Ahuja, 2017). The Old Testament 2 also provides evidence regarding the use of cosmetics where Jezebel- believed to have lived during 840 BC, has daubed her eyelids (Ghazali et al., 2017). Another mention regarding cosmetics is connected with Esther, who explains various cosmetic therapies for human beings (Gopinath, 2019).

Ancient Roman literature also provides ample evidence regarding the usage of cosmetics by the people. But the cosmetic usages were looked upon with dismay during those times (Gopinath & Kalpana, 2019). The Roman women are believed to have invented cosmetics using lead and kohl to whiten their skin and line the eyes (Saravanakumar & Bojan, 2018). Consumer gratification is a crucial element in the creation of desired cosmetics, which are intended to be purchased again and again. Gratification is nothing but the difference between expected performance and the actual result. Most often, quality is sacrificed to achieve the desired outcome. There is no cross-opinion for the fact that cosmetics are one of the elementary prerequisites for human beings. The Mama Earth product is the most sought-after cosmetic product available (Alabdullah et al., 2021). It is made exclusively using natural components. It has mineral oil and is free of chemicals, making it skin-friendly. Organic cosmetics like these are in great demand as they do not harm the hair, complexion, and health.

Consumer buying behavior is the total consumer's attitudes, preferences, intentions, and decisions regarding consumer's behavior in the marketplace when purchasing a product or service. Anthropology, psychology, sociology, and other social science fields are all used to study consumer behavior. Identifying consumer purchasing patterns should be prioritized if a marketer wishes to target certain customers with certain items and services (Anjana, 2018). The requirements of the person, the group, and the organization drive consumer behaviour Therefore, it is necessary to have a thorough grasp of how those needs connect to customer purchasing behavior. Knowing how consumers interact with the marketing mix can help you better understand their purchasing habits. This is boatpeople's psychology toward goods and services varies depending on their culture, attitude, prior knowledge, and perception. Consumers base their subsequent decisions about whether or not to acquire the goods they prefer and where to do so on this information (Kanaan-Jebna et al., 2022).

Technology is the most important factor in Nykaa because it underpins nearly every aspect of business paratonia's technology development includes a variety of tasks, such as technology selection, process engineering, field testing, and component & feature desi Nykaa's human resource management helps the business with several crucial tasks, including recruiting and choosing employees, evaluating and develop employees' abilities, personnel planning, training, and remuneration. Nykaa targets clients while concentrating on a niche marketing strategy. company's primary clients are members of upper-middle-class society, primarily women (Gandotra Radhika, 2017). It also meets the needs of males in terms of fitness and appearance. The majority Nykaa's consumers are between the ages of 18 and 50. The organization that requires employees to appear presentable targets contemporary women. Customers between 19 and 25 who need all advice on cosmetics are active seekers. These consumers read blogs, shop online, and easily use technology. Due to its direct relationships with companies, Nykaa can provide brand-sponsored discounts on high-quality goods (Lakshmi & Babu, 2019).

The advertisements through social media and other channels have made Mama Earth products more popular. This popularity gained through the media- where they promote the brand by highlighting its quality; has made the cosmetics producers care about the needs of the audiences of the media. As a result, the brand is expected to produce a great financial turnover, which is again a subject of examination (Singh, 2003).

Marketing and advertising have a significant positive influence on consumer purchasing decisions and directly impact whether a consumer chooses to purchase a product from a well-known brand. Before purchasing a product, buyers did not give much thought to its characteristics in the past. Choosing what to buy has grown more complex in recent years and is influenced by consumer attitudes, beliefs, and behavior.

Meaning of customer: A customer is a person who purchases a product from a supplier against money or anything else of the same value. This customer is also called by other names such as client, buyer, or purchaser.

TYPES OF CUSTOMER

There are five main kinds of Consumers in the retail trade sector. They are:

Loyal consumers: These consumers make up only a minority of the consumer base but are good enough to make big sales.

Impulse customers: Consumers who do not have a particular item for consumption in mind and buy things when they seem good at a particular time.

Discount customers: Those consumers who wish to purchase on markdowns. They are usually frequent shoppers.

Need-based customers: Consumers who intend to buy any particular commodity.

Wandering customers: Consumers who are unaware of what they want to purchase.

Important 6 Techniques of Measuring Customer Satisfaction are as follows:

Important Six Rules for Customer Satisfaction

Feedback from the Consumers collected through Surveys: Of many methods to evaluate consumer gratification, surveys deserve special mention. Nothing is more trustworthy than listening right from the horse's mouth; hence, the surveys are considered the most authentic report on customer service. There are three ways through which the surveys can be conducted after providing the service. They are:

In-App Surveys: Unless caught in action, consumers will likely ignore such surveys. While the consumers avail facilities on the apps, honest feedback can be collected. A survey must be conducted immediately after the purchase. The response rate will be huge, and chances are there for the responses to become honest if taken immediately after the service. The survey should not hamper the consumer's experience while enjoying the service. For accurate and adequate responses, the survey questions must be kept short and smoothly integrated with the apps.

Post-Call Surveys: Once the interaction is over, the honest and finest feedback is received. Once the call is completed, the CSAT surveys can be conducted. The caller can give feedback by pressing a button automatically connected to the surveyor.

Email Survey: Consumers who go for repeated purchases can provide better feedback if email surveys are administered. Emails that include a form with relevant and significant questions that directly address the consumer needs should be sent to them. Since the responses tend to be descriptive, there are chances for the respondents to skip the survey. Even in that case, the surveyor must not give up the survey, for the data received through email surveys are of great value.

Voluntary Feedback: Even without any initiation from the service providers, the customers voluntarily provide feedback. The reasons for this can either be their extreme dissatisfaction with the product or service or out of extreme delight. However, the data received through voluntary feedback is highly reliable, and those respondents may not correspond to other automated surveys.

Customer Satisfaction Score: CSAT, or the customer satisfaction score, is a widely used metric to evaluate a consumer's latest interaction with the service providers. The metrics include 5 scale parameters ranging from highly satisfied to highly dissatisfied. The more positive the responses, the highest the score will be.

Being one of the elementary feedback collecting systems, the CSAT fails to provide any particular factor in the interaction, if any, that resulted in the high or low rating given by the consumers. One of the drawbacks of the CSAT system is that the consumers may carelessly select any of the scales in the parameters, which ultimately affects the reliability of the data. Nevertheless, CSAT cannot be avoided from the data collecting procedure as it is still significant due to its ease to the consumers to rate the service or product.

Net Promoter Score: NPS is a data-collecting system that, in a way, fills the gaps created in CSAT. A brand gets popularity and demand when consumers suggest it to their friends and relatives. A study conducted in 2020 reveals that 64% of consumers suggest the brand to their friends and relatives if it provides simple experiences and communications. NPS evaluates the chances for a brand or a particular product and its services to get suggested among consumer.

The scale ranges from 1-10, where '1' indicates 'not at all likely' and '10' suggests 'extremely likely'.

Since the NPS makes evaluations depending on an 'emotionally stirred question', the feedback rate is higher, and most often, the discontented consumers would never avoid a chance to respond to the survey questions. The contact centers should use this chance to maintain a few consumers and influence them with indubitable consumer service.

Customer Effort Score: Another consumer-oriented approach named the customer effort score, or CES, is used to evaluate the worth of consumer service. In this approach, the amount of effort that a consumer has put in to get a problem solved is observed. There will be questions regarding the organizational assistance in making the communication of the customers with the customer service team easy. The scale varies from 1 to 5, where 1'ignifies 'fewer 'hardships', and 'signifies 'extreme inconvenience'.

CES is a suitable parameter center's 'forts toward dissatisfied customers in the future. The consumers can point out the issue after the consumer survey, and for this purpose, most of the institutions put it in a text box. Approaches like this help an institution to make improvements in those areas.

It is understood that no single approach can bring in complete and reliable data. All the survey reports merge, and the data processed after the convergence provides a complete idea about consumer satisfaction more than any other stand-alone survey reports.

Web-Analytics: Analytics is a data-driven metric that works bereft of any direct consumer participation. Web analytics tracks the consumer's website searches effectively, evaluates the sales list and nature of sales, and predicts the possible future purchases of the consumer. Default attribution models provide clear information regarding the touch points, regularly checked FAQs, etc. Suppose the information thus gathered is assembled and operated cleverly. In that case, it can help the service providers to serve the customers better and thereby become the significant business differentiator in the market.

Social Media Metrics: In the current world, consumers are highly active on social media. They share reviews of their purchases through social media and bluntly criticize the brands they didn't like. Social media thus turns out to be a 'two-side blade'. Therefore, social media can be effectively used to realize what the customers say about the product, their expectations, and how to make improvements to meet their requirements. Social media platforms provide provisions to create a business account that offers an analytics console. Using this, the service providers can observe the comments of their customers and make modifications based on their suggestions. The consumer support teams can gather this data and formulate effective strategies to improve customer satisfaction and thereby make the best use of social media in advertising their brand.

REVIEW OF LITERATURE

Anjana, (2018) tries to find out the dissimilarities in the view of costumers regarding their attitude towards shopping-based on age, academic qualification, demographic features and gender in Nellore District of Andhra Pradesh. He describes the necessity of creating product awareness for the customers to stay in the mainstay of the market. The researcher concludes that when consumers are satisfied with company's sales will automatically grow.

Sharma et al., (2013) describe the significance of promotional offers for branded items in the market. He suggests that the service providers should consider the marketing strategies before implementation. As the FMCG sector is very active in India, one of the major aims should be the satisfaction of the customers in their purchases and thereby enhance the prominence of their brand in the market.

Jonathan, (2014) highlighted that in the age of globalization necessities and requirements of consumers also change. 'The Fast-Moving Consumer Goods (FMCG) sector contributes a lot to the development of the GDP of India. Hence, observing the changes in customer choices towards FMCG products is essential. The research evaluates the factors influencing the customer choices of FMCG products and their decision-making procedure. The research found that consumer behavior is immensely affected by location, product, value and advertisement, and physiological and psychological aspects. Nonetheless, the impact of these aspects also differs from product to product.

Prasad et al., (2019) define the term consumer gratification. According to them, it is the exaltation of the customers with firm product or its services. Customer satisfaction is considered one of the prime variables that provide positive inputs towards planning new marketing strategies. Their study aims to observe the issues encountered by the respondents while using Himalaya products. Ayurvedic products are opted by 45% of the respondents. As every Himalaya product is researched and trailed by the research and development wing of the Himalaya Company, the customers of Himalaya products do not have a second opinion regarding its quality and purity.

Lilly, (2010) conducted in Hisar City of Harya"a, observed the cosmetic preferences of the woman in the city. The researchers observed that the most number of females prefers cosmetics such as shampoo, powder, and cream. Among the brands, Lakme is the one they prefer the most.

Jadhav & Khanna, (2016) state that Ayurveda, which could be otherwise called 'the science of life', is a primal and all-inclusive method of diagnosis and treatment. It could be the oldest system of medical therapy ever known to mankind. They found that the research in Himalaya Company would commence with the raw herbs selected from the ancient textbooks. The conclusions are deduced from the observations of the behavior of the indigenous plants. The study also intends to evaluate the current status of herbal products in India. This information would help them to plan new marketing strategies.

Sharma et al., (2013) are purchasing personal products. Product quality, brand title, and price are the main factors affecting consumer choice. Apart from these factors, the trust the brands maintain among their customers also turns out to be a major factor influencing the customer's' choices. The major intention of the research is to evaluate the impact created by the influencers on the customers in their purchase of personal care products. The researcher conducted the study among 172 respondents, collected the samples, and conducted descriptive analysis, ANOVA, and Chi-Square tests using SPSS. The research reveals that customers get attracted to the advertisements first, and it gets enhanced if the product meets with quality.

Rastogi, (2010) observed that the purchase behavior of people has changed and has been positively affected by the growth of science and technology, improvement of the financial status and also by modern education. Media has a big role in creating awareness regarding hygiene, exquisiteness, and advanced lifestyle among the masses. The research also points out that 'women prioritize the 'brand names' of the products, followed by the product's contents and the magnitude of advertisements the product gets.

Nazir & Ul Haq, (2018) found that several factors such as interest, awareness, outlook, and knowledge with social and cultural elements and other factors such as value, advertising, and physical apparatus influence consumers behavior.

Madasu Bhaskara Rao & Lakshmi Hymavathi, (2018) suggest that healthy skin means being more than merely beautiful. Being one of the vital parts of the human body, healthy skin is one of the prime symbols of good health. The book describes the presence of anti-skin health factors, such as chemicals and bacteria, found everywhere on the globe. "Besides, overexposure to sunlight and bad food habits also affect skin health. Information regarding skin care is obtained mainly through advertisements and health magazines. The information received from these sources may not always be reliable as skin health improvement suggestions are practically wrong or contradictory. The book dwells deep into skin care and protection and throws no light on the impact of Ayurvedic cosmetics on skin health development.

Nizam & Mansor, (2019) identified the demographic influences on the customer choices towards Pathanjali products. They observed that certain factors such as hygiene, quality, and availability of the products at reasonable prices also affect consumer preferences.

Malarvizhi & Chitra, (2018) studied consumer perceptions of promotional strategies adopted by FMCG retailers in Kerala. Some of the concerns discussed included consumer understanding of various sales promotion techniques, their attraction to consumers, and their success in raising brand awareness, encouraging brand trial purchases, repeat purchases and brand loyalty. 300 customers from various regions of the state provided the data. The Chi-square test, t-test, ANOVA, and Duncan test were only among the mathematical and statistical techniques employed to analyze the data. study's findings indicate that customers from various categories are well aware of the various sales promotion techniques employed by marketers. In addition, buyers find discounts, gifts, and accessories to be the most alluring of the techniques used to increase sales. Also recommended are gifts and accessories, free samples, discounts, and premium offers for increasing brand recognition, trial purchases, repeat purchases, and brand loyalty.

RESEARCH METHODOLOGY

Objective of the Study

To explore the demographic profile of the respondents.
To evaluate the issues the NYKAA customers face on using the different products.

Research Question

What are the issues faced by NYKAA customers?
Are they satisfied with the product of NYKAA?

Sample Design

Sample Unit: This research is oriented on using Nykaa products only. The respondents are both men and women who have used cosmetics and personal care products that were purchased online at least once. Sample Size – 100 responses were collected for the current research.
Sampling Technique –Convenience Sampling through Google Forms.

Nature of the Study: This research is inclusive of both primary and secondary data. The primary data was collected through a questionnaire using an online Google format. The secondary data has been collected from previous research that has already been published in journals, magazines, newspapers and articles.

Statistical Tools used for the study: The study has adopted the ANOVA analysis to recognize the problems experienced by the customers of NYKAA users.

Limitations of the study

The study looks into the issues faced by the users of NYKAA products
It pertains to beauty and fashion accessories.

Statement of the Problem

Studies conducted on issues faced by the users of Nykaa are varied. It is as wide as the realities that we see in society, economics, and technology, which influence how customers behave. They address factors such as delay in delivery, damaged products, poor packaging, selling expired products, and a return policy unavailable for some products. In today's competitive world, for the success of any fresh product or service, it is necessary to know the customers' purchase behavior to adopt various approaches for bringing in and advertising fresh products or services. Therefore, the current research focuses on the issues faced by the users of Nykaa products.

DATA ANALYSIS AND INTERPRETATION

The following table 1 interprets about the analysis between independent and dependent variables.

Table 1. ANOVA analysis- Issues faced by the users of Nykaa products

		Sum of Squares	df	Mean Square	F	Sig.
Delay in delivery	Between Groups	.397	1	.397	.308	.580
	Within Groups	105.556	82	1.287		
	Total	105.952	83			
Damage Products	Between Groups	2.099	1	2.099	1.937	.168
	Within Groups	88.889	82	1.084		
	Total	90.988	83			
Poor package	Between Groups	4.166	1	4.166	3.891	.052
	Within Groups	87.787	82	1.071		
	Total	91.952	83			
Selling expired products	Between Groups	4.751	1	4.751	4.052	.047
	Within Groups	96.142	82	1.172		
	Total	100.893	83			
Return policy not available for some products	Between Groups	4.063	1	4.063	3.177	.078
	Within Groups	104.889	82	1.279		
	Total	108.952	83			
Lagging in tracking the products	Between Groups	3.291	1	3.291	2.813	.097
	Within Groups	95.947	82	1.170		
	Total	99.238	83			
Not as per the sample shown in the image	Between Groups	3.716	1	3.716	3.349	.071
	Within Groups	90.987	82	1.110		
	Total	94.702	83			
Lack of customer care contact	Between Groups	8.036	1	8.036	5.954	.017
	Within Groups	110.667	82	1.350		
	Total	118.702	83			
Incomplete order missing product	Between Groups	3.863	1	3.863	3.324	.017
	Within Groups	95.280	82	1.162		
	Total	99.143	83			
Mismatch or delivering the wrong products	Between Groups	3.111	1	3.111	2.786	.099
	Within Groups	91.556	82	1.117		
	Total	94.667	83			

Interpretation: From the Table 1, it is inferred that poor packaging, selling the expired products, lack of customer care contacts, and incomplete orders missing products are satisfied at a 5% level with F-Value of 3.891, 4.052, 5.954, and 3.324 with significant values of 0.052, 0.47, 0.017 and 0.017, states that there is a difference between gender and the issues faced by the users of mama earth products. The other variables like delay in delivery, damagee of products, return policy not available, lagging in tracking the products, not as per the sample shown in the image, and mismatch or delivering the wrong products are statistically insignificant at 5% level and fulfilling the null hypothesis that there is no difference between the gender and issues faced by the users of mama earth products.

Consumers nowadays hesitate to purchase product which is not up-to-date marketed. From the study, it is suggested that the manufactured product should be packed properly, more customer care attention must be provided on priority, and expired products should be checked. The delay in delivery, damaged products, and return policies must be provided to the customer on the prior hand. The discussion in this study is mainly focused on the issues faced by Mamaearth product users, and it is concluded that there is no difference in gender, and the product users are not that similar. So, the future study on this concept must target the services provided to the customers and the product developments and changes according to the upgradation in the market environment.

The cosmetics industry is moving toward the mountains and the clouds in the modern world. As customers become more aware of it, demand for it rises quickly. Therefore, professionals might use study's findings to evaluate their approaches to using cosmetic goods. The company Nykaa can pitch its beauty products for men, which do not have a great reach amongst the consumers. People switch to herbal products as they become more conscious of their skin. Nykaa can advertise its herbal items to raise interest in them, boosting sales. The business can offer coupons to its new and prospective consumers to encourage them to make huge purchases. From the study, it is clear that most people face issues with services provided with Nykaa, but still, people do have a fear of financial security. Most people still have a bad perception of using cosmetic products. An established brand like Nykaa should make efforts to change the mindset of people by making them aware of its use. It is important to make considerable effort to educate the public on the advantages of using cosmetics. They should be aware that using some of the cosmetic products daily act as a coverage to protect the skin from environmental pollution, etc.

CONCLUSION

A few years ago, industries like beauty and personal care thrived more on the store experience of touch, feel, and smell. We had no idea sectors like personal care and beauty would likely find their way onto digital platforms. We are all aware of how much easier, simpler, and more time-efficient life has become because of the development of e-commerce websites. This has demonstrated that the personal care and beauty sectors are not an exception to digital communication. Understanding consumer behavior is crucial for marketers because it enables them to communicate with customers effectively. They can narrow the market gap and highlight the required items and products no longer in use by studying how consumers choose a product. Nykaa is a direct-to-consumer e-commerce brand which has an inventory-based business model. Products bought directly from producers are kept in stock by the company Nykaa's strong marketing approach, built with digital marketing at its core, has helped it establish itself as one of the most capable companies in the beauty and fashion industries. Nykaa connects its audience and turns them into customers by offering a variety of consumables.

Current-day marketing is extremely challenging and interposed. An industry should decide on what could be sold and what methods could be adopted to satisfy the needs and preferences of the consumers. Nowadays, consumers hesitate to purchase the products which are on the mainstay of the market. Hence, undoubtedly, it is the consumer who decides the success or fiasco of a product. Thus, the current-day marketing strategies should be consumer-oriented. The research reveals that most respondents know about Mama Earth products. At present, people prefer personal care products for luxuries and for enhancing fitness. The Mama Earth Company should go for enormous advertising policies and select brand ambassadors to endorse the product. The company should bring new products and provide new services to the market. Nevertheless, consumers are contented with the brand and the obtainability of the products. The company will reach the highest goal soon, and whole customers will be satisfied globally if the suggestions mentioned above are considered are executed by the company.

REFERENCES

Alabdullah, T. T. Y., Al-Fakhri, I., Ahmed, E. R., & Kanaan-Jebna, A. (2021). Corporate Governance System and Firm Financial Performance. *Acta Scientific Computer Sciences*, *4*(6), 97–103.

Anjana, S. S. (2018). A study on factors influencing cosmetic buying behaviour of consumers. *International Journal of Pure and Applied Mathematics*, *118*(9), 453–459.

Charwak, B. (2016). The customer satisfaction towards Himalaya skin care products. *International Journal of Academic Research*, *3*(3).

Gandotra Radhika, A. V. (2017). *A Descriptive Study Of Brand Image And Consumer Perception On Consumer Loyalty And Preference Towards A Brand*. Patanjali Ayurveda Ltd.

Ghazali, E., Soon, P. C., Mutum, D. S., & Nguyen, B. (2017). Health and cosmetics: Investigating consumers' values for buying organic personal care products. *Journal of Retailing and Consumer Services*, *39*, 154–163. doi:10.1016/j.jretconser.2017.08.002

Gopinath, R. (2019). Factors Influencing Consumer Decision Behaviour in FMCG. *International Journal of Research in Social Sciences*, *9*(7), 249–255.

Gopinath, R., & Kalpana, R. (2019). A Study on Consumer Perception towards Fast Food Retail Outlet in Perambalur District. *International Journal for Research in Engineering Application & Management*, *5*(1), 483–485.

Jadhav, V., & Khanna, M. (2016). Factors influencing online buying behaviour of college students: A qualitative analysis. *The Qualitative Report*, *21*(1), 1.

Jonathan, B. (2014). Give Beauty an Online Makeover for Christmas. *Marketing Week*, p. 3.

Kanaan-Jebna, A., Baharudi, A. S., & Alabdullah, T. T. Y. (2022). Entrepreneurial Orientation, Market Orientation, Managerial Accounting and Manufacturing SMEs Satisfaction. *Journal of Accounting Science*, *6*(1), 1–14. doi:10.21070/jas.v6i1.1590

Kumar, A., & Ahuja, A. (2017). Consumer Behavior towards Patanjali Products: A Study on Consumers with Reference to Rohtak District of Haryana. *KIJECBM*, *4*(2), 404–410.

Lakshmi, Y. P. S. S., & Babu, M. (2019). Study of factors that influence the consumer behavior towards cosmetics -Conceptual framework. *Iconic Research and Engineering Journals*, 2(7), 21–28.

Lilly, J. (2010). Customer Perception and Preference towards Branded Products (With Special Reference to Television Sets). *Indian Journal of Marketing*, 40(2), 49–55.

Madasu Bhaskara Rao, C., & Lakshmi Hymavathi, M. M. (2018). Factors Affecting Female Consumer's Online Buying Behavior. *Academy of Marketing Studies Journal*, 22(2), 1–20.

Malarvizhi, J., & Chitra, D. (2018). A Study on Customer Satisfaction towards Patanjali Products in Theni Distr. International Research Journal of Management. *IT and Social Sciences*, 5(2), 75–79.

Nazir, S., & Ul Haq, Z. (2018). Exploring Women's attitude in Online Shopping-A review of Literature. *International Journal of Enhanced Research in Management & Computer Applications*, 7(3), 556–570.

Nizam, N. Z., & Mansor, N. (2019). Analyzing Customer Satisfaction: Consumer Behavior towards the Selection of Beauty Products in Klang Valley. *International Journal of Human and Technology Interaction*, 3(2), 55–60.

Prasad, A., Krithika, & Gudimetla, S. (2019). A study of digital shopping behaviour of women with respect to beauty and personal care products. SSRN *Electronic Journal*. doi:10.2139/ssrn.3307014

Rastogi, A. K. (2010). A study of Indian online consumers & their buying behaviour. *International Research Journal*, 1(10), 80–82.

Saravanakumar, A., & Bojan, S. K. (2018). A study on female customer satisfaction on hair oil and beauty cream with special reference to Himalaya products in Coimbatore district. *International Journal of Management Studies, 5*(Special4), 23.

Sharma, A., Bhola, S., Malyan, S., & Patni, N. (2013). Impact of brand loyalty on buying behaviour of women consumers for beauty care products-Delhi region. *Global Journal of Management and Business Studies*, 3(7), 817–824.

Singh, A. (2003). *Herbal drugs: US-EU move opens treasure trove*. Retrieved October 29, 2023, from Times of India website: https://timesofindia.indiatimes.com/city/lucknow/herbal-drugs-us-eu-move-opens-treasure-trove/articleshow/292287.cms

Compilation of References

Abbassy, M. M., & Ead, W. M. (2020). Intelligent Greenhouse Management System. In *2020 6th International Conference on Advanced Computing and Communication Systems (ICACCS)*. IEEE.

Abbassy, M. M. (2020). Opinion mining for Arabic customer feedback using machine learning. *Journal of Advanced Research in Dynamical and Control Systems*, *12*(SP3), 209–217. doi:10.5373/JARDCS/V12SP3/20201255

Abbassy, M. M., & Abo-Alnadr, A. (2019). Rule-based emotion AI in Arabic customer review. *International Journal of Advanced Computer Science and Applications*, *10*(9). Advance online publication. doi:10.14569/IJACSA.2019.0100932

Abdali, M. (2019). *The strategic use of digital learning solutions: An HRM perspective* (Doctoral dissertation).

Abdullahi, Y., Bhardwaj, A., Rahila, J., Anand, P., & Kandepu, K. (2023). Development of Automatic Change-Over with Auto-Start Timer and Artificial Intelligent Generator. *FMDB Transactions on Sustainable Energy Sequence*, *1*(1), 11–26.

Abid, A., Harrigan, P., & Roy, S. K. (2020). Online relationship marketing through content creation and curation. *Marketing Intelligence & Planning*, *38*(6), 699–712. doi:10.1108/MIP-04-2019-0219

Abu-Rumman, A. & Qawasmeh, R. (2021). Assessing international students' satisfaction of a Jordanian university using the service quality model. *Journal of Applied Research in Higher Education*. doi:10.1108/JARHE-05-2021-0166

Abu-Rumman, A. (2021). Effective Knowledge Sharing: A Guide to the Key Enablers and Inhibitors. In D. Tessier (Ed.), *Handbook of Research on Organizational Culture Strategies for Effective Knowledge Management and Performance* (pp. 133–156). IGI Global. doi:10.4018/978-1-7998-7422-5.ch008

Academy, M. (2022, December 6). *Exploring Blockchain-Based Messaging Apps*. Retrieved from Moralis Academy: https://academy.moralis.io/blog/exploring-blockchain-based-messaging-apps

Adams, R. L. (2017). 10 powerful examples of artificial Intelligence in use today. *Forbes*. https://www.forbes.com/sites/robertadams/2017/01/10/10-powerful-examples-of-artificial-intelligence-in-usetoday/#2fd895e9420d

Adisa, T. A., Aiyenitaju, O., & Adekoya, O. D. (2021). The work-family balance of British working women during the COVID-19 Pandemic. *Journal of Work-Applied Management*, *13*(2), 241–260. Advance online publication. doi:10.1108/JWAM-07-2020-0036

Adomavicius, G., & Tuzhilin, A. (2005). Personalization technologies: A process-oriented perspective. *Communications of the ACM*, *48*(10), 83–90. doi:10.1145/1089107.1089109

Aggarwal, C. C. (2011). *An introduction to social network data analytics*. Springer US. doi:10.1007/978-1-4419-8462-3

Aguiar, M., & Hurst, E. (2005). Consumption versus expenditure. *Journal of Political Economy*, *113*(5), 919–948. doi:10.1086/491590

Aguiar, M., & Hurst, E. (2007). Life-cycle prices and production. *The American Economic Review, 97*(5), 1533–1559. doi:10.1257/aer.97.5.1533

Ahmad, M. (2023). *Spatial Data as a Catalyst to Drive Entrepreneurial Growth and Sustainable Development.* doi:10.4018/978-1-6684-9843-9.ch004

Ahmad, M., & Ali, A. (2023). Mapping the Future of Sustainable Development Through Cloud-Based Solutions: A Case Study of OpenStreetMap. In Promoting Sustainable Management Through Technological Innovation (pp. 153–176). IGI Global. doi:10.4018/978-1-6684-9979-5.ch011

Ahmad, A., & Sharma, S. (2020). Sustainable digital preservation and access of heritage knowledge in India: A review. *DESIDOC Journal of Library and Information Technology, 40*(5), 321–325. doi:10.14429/djlit.40.05.15822

Ahmed, A., & Ramzan, M. (2013). Effects of job stress on employees' job performance a study on banking sector of Pakistan. *IOSR Journal of Business and Management, 11*(6), 61–68. doi:10.9790/487X-1166168

Ajanthan, D. (2017). The impact of a social media marketing on customer based brand equity- A special reference to travel and tourism industry in Sri Lanka. *Trans. Asian Journal of Marketing Management Research, 6*(11), 36–46.

Ajayakumar, K., Kumar, R., & Haridas, V. (2005). Influence of the subtending leaf on the growth of axillary bud and formation of banji bud in tea. *Indian Journal of Plant Physiology / Official Publication of the Indian Society for Plant Physiology, 10*(3), 267–272.

AjayiS. (2018). Effect of stress on employee performance and job satisfaction: A case study of Nigerian banking industry. Available at SSRN 3160620. doi:10.2139/ssrn.3160620

Akrich, M. (1992). *Shaping technology/building society: Studies in sociotechnical change.* MIT Press.

Akshaya, A., & Naachimuthu, K. P. (2022). Locavorism to Enhance Environmental, Social, & Economic Well-being. *Indian Journal of Agriculture Business, 8*(1), 25–33.

Al Doghan, M. A., Abdelwahed, N. A. A., Soomro, B. A., & Alayis, M. M. H. A. (2022). Organizational Environmental Culture, Environmental Sustainability and Performance: The Mediating Role of Green HRM and Green Innovation. *Sustainability (Basel), 14*(12), 1–20. doi:10.3390u14127510

Al Shraah, A., Abu-Rumman, A., Alqhaiwi, L. A., & AlSha'ar, H. (2022). The impact of sourcing strategies and logistics capabilities on organizational performance during the COVID-19 pandemic: Evidence from Jordanian pharmaceutical industries. *Uncertain Supply Chain Management, 10*(3), 1077–1090. doi:10.5267/j.uscm.2022.2.004

Al Shraah, A., Irtaimeh, H. J., & Rumman, M. A. (2013). The Strategic Human Resource Management Practices in Implying Total Quality Management (TQM): An Empirical Study on Jordanian Banking Sector. *International Journal of Management, 4*(5), 179–190.

Alabdullah, T.T.Y., & Ahmed, E.R. (2021). New Insights to Investigate the Impact of Internal Control Mechanisms on Firm Performance: A Study in Oman. *Riset Akuntansi dan Keuangan Indonesia, 6*(2).

Alabdullah, T.T.Y., Ahmed, E.R. (2021). New Insights to Investigate the Impact of Internal Control Mechanisms on Firm Performance: A Study in Oman. *Riset Akuntansi dan Keuangan Indonesia, 6*(2).

Alabdullah, T. T. Y., Al Fakhri, I., Ahmed, E. R., & Jebna, A. K. (2021b). Empirical Study of The Influence of Board of Directors' Feature on Firm Performance. *Russian Journal of Agricultural and Socio-Economic Sciences, 11*(119), 137–146. doi:10.18551/rjoas.2021-11.16

Alabdullah, T. T. Y., Al-Fakhri, I., Ahmed, E. R., & Kanaan-Jebna, A. (2021a). Corporate Governance System and Firm Financial Performance. *Acta Scientific Computer Sciences*, *4*(6), 97–103.

Alam, J. (2017). Human resource information system: A quality concept. *International Journal of Advanced Research*, *5*(9), 1423–1427. doi:10.21474/IJAR01/5462

Alara Efsun, Y. (2018). *Pink Tax, and the Law: Discriminating Against Women Consumers*. Academic Press.

Alayli, S. (2023). Unravelling the Drivers of Online Purchasing Intention: The E-Commerce Scenario in Lebanon. *F MDB Transactions on Sustainable Social Sciences Letters, 1*(1), 56–67.

Alayli, S. (2023). Unravelling the Drivers of Online Purchasing Intention: The E-Commerce Scenario in Lebanon. *FMDB Transactions on Sustainable Social Sciences Letters*, *1*(1), 56–67.

Ali, M. (2017). *Trust-to-Trust Design of a New Internet* [PhD dissertation]. Princeton University.

Allameh, E., Jozam, M. H., de Vries, B., Timmermans, H. J., & Beetz, J. (2011). Smart Home as a Smart Real Estate: a state of the art review. *18th International Conference of European Real Estate Society, Eindhoven, The Netherlands. ERES 2011.*

Al-maaitah, D. A., Tha'er Majali, M. A., & Almaaitah, T. A. (2021a). The role of leadership styles on staff job satisfaction in public organizations. *Journal of Contemporary Issues in Business and Government*, *27*(1), 772–783.

Al-Maaitah, D. A., Tha'er Majali, M. A., & Almaaitah, T. A. (2021a). The role of leadership styles on staffs job satisfaction in public organizations. *Journal of Contemporary Issues in Business and Government*, *27*(1), 772–783.

Al-maaitah, T. A., Tha'er Majali, M. A., & Almaaitah, D. A. (2021). The Impact of COVID-19 on the Electronic Commerce Users Behavior. *Journal of Contemporary Issues in Business and Government*, *27*(1), 772–783.

Almaamari, Q. A., Ali, B. M., & Almeer, S. (2022). Factors influencing organizational performance at petroleum products distribution company in Yemen. *Specialusis Ugdymas*, *1*(43), 2071–2083.

Almaamari, Q. A., & Salial, M. M. (2022). Influence of Job Satisfaction, Effective Teamwork and Social Media on Employee's Performance in Bahraini Telecommunication Sector. *Specialusis Ugdymas*, *1*(43), 2063–2070.

Almaamari, Q. A., & Salial, M. M. (2022). Influence of Job Satisfaction, Effective Teamwork, and Social Media on Employee's Performance in Bahraini Telecommunication Sector. *Specialusis Ugdymas*, *1*(43), 2063–2070.

Al-Naif, K. L., & Al Shraah, A. E. M. (2018). Working capital management and profitability: Evidence from Jordanian mining and extraction industry sector. *IUG Journal of Economics and Business.*, *2*(1), 42–60.

Alola, A. A., Bekun, F. V., & Sarkodie, S. A. (2019). Dynamic impact of trade policy, economic growth, fertility rate, renewable and non-renewable energy consumption on ecological footprint in Europe. *The Science of the Total Environment*, *685*, 702–709. doi:10.1016/j.scitotenv.2019.05.139 PMID:31203164

Al-Swidi, A. K., Gelaidan, H. M., & Saleh, R. M. (2021). The joint Impact of green human resource management, leadership and organizational culture on employees' green behaviour and organisational environmental performance. *Journal of Cleaner Production*, *316*, 128112. doi:10.1016/j.jclepro.2021.128112

Alt, E., Díez-de-Castro, E. P., & Lloréns-Montes, F. J. (2015). Linking employee stakeholders to environmental performance: The role of proactive environmental strategies and shared vision. *Journal of Business Ethics*, *128*(1), 167–181. doi:10.100710551-014-2095-x

Alyass, A., Turcotte, M., & Meyre, D. (2015). From big data analysis to personalized medicine for all: Challenges and opportunities. *BMC Medical Genomics*, *8*(1), 33. doi:10.118612920-015-0108-y PMID:26112054

Amado, A., Cortez, P., Rita, P., & Moro, S. (2018). Research trends on Big Data in Marketing: A text mining and topic modeling-based literature analysis. *European Research on Management and Business Economics, 24*(1), 1–7, 24. doi:10.1016/j.iedeen.2017.06.002

Amnesty International. (2018). Machine learning, and their application for growth, Adelyn Zhou. *SlideShare/LinkedIn.*

Amri, F. (2017). The relationship amongst energy consumption (renewable and non-renewable), and GDP in Algeria. *Renewable & Sustainable Energy Reviews, 76*, 62–71. doi:10.1016/j.rser.2017.03.029

Amuakwa-Mensah, F., & Näsström, E. (2022). Role of banking sector performance in renewable energy consumption. *Applied Energy, 306*(118023), 118023. doi:10.1016/j.apenergy.2021.118023

Anand, P. P., Kanike, U. K., Paramasivan, P., Rajest, S. S., Regin, R., & Priscila, S. S. (2023). Embracing Industry 5.0: Pioneering Next-Generation Technology for a Flourishing Human Experience and Societal Advancement. *FMDB Transactions on Sustainable Social Sciences Letters, 1*(1), 43–55.

Anand, P. P., Sulthan, N., Jayanth, P., & Deepika, A. A. (2023). A Creating Musical Compositions Through Recurrent Neural Networks: An Approach for Generating Melodic Creations. *FMDB Transactions on Sustainable Computing Systems, 1*(2), 54–64.

Anderson, A. J., Kaplan, S. A., & Vega, R. P. (2015). The impact of telework on emotional experience: When, and for whom, does telework improve daily affective well-being? *European Journal of Work and Organizational Psychology, 24*(6), 882–897. doi:10.1080/1359432X.2014.966086

Anderson, P., Bowring, J., McCauley, R., Pothering, G., & Starr, C. (2014). An undergraduate degree in data science: curriculum and a decade of implementation experience. In *Proceedings of the 45th ACM Technical Symposium on Computer Science Education* (pp. 145–150). ACM. 10.1145/2538862.2538936

Andrianto, N., Riyanto, D. Y., Riqqoh, A. K., & Fianto, A. Y. A. (2019). A conceptual framework for destination branding in jawa Timur, Indonesia. *Majalah Ekonomi, 24*(2), 149–157. doi:10.36456/majeko.vol24.no2.a2061

Ángeles, C. (2022). The legal-community obligations of the large digital service provider platforms in the metaverse era. *Cuad. Cuad. Transnational Law, 14*(2), 294–318.

Ángeles, C. (2023). The guardians of access to the metaverse. (Re)thinking the Competition Law of the European Union. *Cuad. Cuad. Transnational Law, 15*(1), 275–296.

Angeline, R., Aarthi, S., Regin, R., & Rajest, S. S. (2023). Dynamic intelligence-driven engineering flooding attack prediction using ensemble learning. In *Advances in Artificial and Human Intelligence in the Modern Era* (pp. 109–124). IGI Global. doi:10.4018/979-8-3693-1301-5.ch006

Anjana, S. S. (2018). A study on factors influencing cosmetic buying behaviour of consumers. *International Journal of Pure and Applied Mathematics, 118*(9), 453–459.

Annor Antwi, A., & Al-Dherasi, A. A. M. (2019) Application of Artificial Intelligence in Forecasting: A Systematic Review. SSRN *Electronic Journal.* doi:10.2139/ssrn.3483313

Anser, M. K., Hanif, I., Alharthi, M., & Chaudhry, I. S. (2020). Impact of fossil fuels, renewable energy consumption and industrial growth on carbon emissions in Latin American and Caribbean economies. *Atmosfera, 33*(3), 201–213. doi:10.20937/ATM.52732

Antenucci, J. C., Brown, K., Croswell, P. L., Kevany, M. J., & Archer, H. (1991). *Geographic Information Systems: a guide to the technology* (Vol. 115). Van Nostrand Reinhold.

Anuradha, T. A., Jan, N. A., & Subramani, A. K. (2019). Social Media Addiction, Culture Code and Mediation Effect of Mindfulness: A Structural Equation Modelling Access. *International Journal of Recent Technology and Engineering*, *8*, 1097–1102.

Anyim, F. C., Ikemefuna, C. O., & Mbah, S. E. (2011). Human resource management challenges in Nigeria under a globalized economy. *International Journal of Economics and Management Sciences*, *1*(4), 1–11.

Argiolas, M. (2014). Surveying housing market supply affordability using a spatial data mining approach. *WIT Transactions on Ecology and the Environment*, *191*, 125–137. Advance online publication. doi:10.2495/SC140111

Arif, S., Zainudin, H. K., & Hamid, A. (2019). Influence of Leadership, Organizational Culture, Work Motivation, and Job Satisfaction of Performance Principles of Senior High School in Medan City. *Budapest International Research and Critics Institute-Journal (BIRCI-Journal)*, *2*(4), 239-254.

Aristovnik, A., Keržič, D., Ravšelj, D., Tomaževič, N., & Umek, L. (2020). Impacts of the COVID-19 Pandemic on Life of Higher Education Students: A Global Perspective. *Sustainability (Basel)*, *12*(20), 8438. doi:10.3390u12208438

Armstrong, M. (2012). *A handbook of human resource management practice*. Kogan.

Arora, S., & Verma, A. (2019). M-commerce: Crusader for "Phygital" retail. In M-Commerce (pp. 163-182). Apple Academic Press.

Arslan, F., Singh, B., Sharma, D. K., Regin, R., Steffi, R., & Rajest, S. S. (2021). Optimization technique approach to resolve food sustainability problems. In *2021 International Conference on Computational Intelligence and Knowledge Economy (ICCIKE)*. IEEE. 10.1109/ICCIKE51210.2021.9410735

Arthanari, A., & Jambulingam, M. (2020). *Entertainmerce and phygital consumers–changing preferences for retail shopping destinations and retailtainment options*. Cengage learning Pvt Ltd.

Arthur, N., & Hack, J. (2022). A multiple scale, function, and type approach to determine and improve Green Infrastructure of urban watersheds. *Urban Forestry & Urban Greening*, *68*, 127459. Advance online publication. doi:10.1016/j.ufug.2022.127459

Arumugam, T., Jayakrishnan, B., Ranganathan, M., Kadiresan, V., & Mathai, R. (2020). A social network analysis on understanding pattern of shoppers' OmniChannel adoption and clustering based on channel switching and preference attributes. *SSRN Electronic Journal*.

Arumugam, T., Jayakrishnan, B., Ranganathan, M., Kadiresan, V., & Mathai, R. (2020, October). A Social Network Analysis on Understanding Pattern of Shoppers' OmniChannel Adoption and Clustering Based on Channel Switching and Preference Attributes. *International Conference on Business Management, Innovation & Sustainability (ICBMIS)*. 10.2139srn.3713754

Asemi, A., Safari, A., & Zavareh, A. A. (2011). The Role of Management Information System (MIS) and Decision Support System (DSS) for Manager's Decision Making Process. *International Journal of Business and Management*, *6*(7). Advance online publication. doi:10.5539/ijbm.v6n7p164

Ashfaque, Z. (2023). *Sentiment analysis with naive Bayes algorithm*. Retrieved October 25, 2023, from Medium website: https://medium.com/@zubairashfaque/sentiment-analysis-with-naive-bayes-algorithm-a31021764fb4

Asopa, V. N. (2007). *Tea industry of India the cup that cheers have tears*. IIMA-Research and Publications.

Aswathi, P., Sangavi, P., Naachimuthu, K. P., & Krishna, T. (2021). *Proceedings of the ICSSR Sponsored Webinar on Human Behavior and Environmental Sustainability*. Academic Press.

Atasever, M. (2023). Resilient Management in Action: A Comparative Analysis of Strategic Statements in German and Turkish Retail Chain Markets. *FMDB Transactions on Sustainable Management Letters*, *1*(2), 66–81.

Atif, M., Hossain, M., Alam, M. S., & Goergen, M. (2021). Does board gender diversity affect renewable energy consumption? *Journal of Corporate Finance*, *66*(101665), 101665. doi:10.1016/j.jcorpfin.2020.101665

Ayres, I., & Siegelman, P. (1995). Race and gender discrimination in bargaining for a new car. *The American Economic Review*, 304–321.

Babu, S. (2004). Tea Descriptors – Serie s-I. *Planters' Chronicle (Philadelphia, Pa.)*, *100*(5), 9–12.

Babu, S. (2005a). Tea descriptors: Series-2. *Planters' Chronicle (Philadelphia, Pa.)*, *101*(1), 12–15.

Babu, S. (2005b). Tea descriptors: Series- 3. *Planters' Chronicle (Philadelphia, Pa.)*, *101*(4), 27–30.

Babu, S., Saravanan, M., & Murugesan, S. (2007). Association of green leaf quality parameters in tea. *Newsletter - UPASI Tea Research Foundation*, *17*(1).

Baesens, B., Bapna, R., Marsden, J. R., Vanthienen, J., & Zhao, J. L. (2016). Transformational issues of big data and analytics in networked business. *Management Information Systems Quarterly*, *40*(4), 807–818. doi:10.25300/MISQ/2016/40:4.03

Baganz, G., Proksch, G., Kloas, W., Lorleberg, W., Baganz, D., Staaks, G., & Lohrberg, F. (2020). Site Resource Inventories-A Missing Link in the Circular City's Information Flow. *Advances in Geosciences*, *54*, 23–32. Advance online publication. doi:10.5194/adgeo-54-23-2020

Balas-Timar, D., & Lile, R. (2015). The story of Goldilocks told by organizational psychologists. *Procedia: Social and Behavioral Sciences*, *203*, 239–243. doi:10.1016/j.sbspro.2015.08.288

Balasudarsun, D., Sathish, D., Venkateswaran, D., Byloppilly, D. R., Devesh, S., & Naved, D. M. (2022). Predicting consumers' online grocery purchase intention within middle-class families. *Webology*, *19*(1), 3620–3642. doi:10.14704/WEB/V19I1/WEB19239

Bartzokas-Tsiompras, A. (2022). Utilizing OpenStreetMap data to measure and compare pedestrian street lengths in 992 cities around the world. *European Journal of Geography*, *13*(2), 127–141. Advance online publication. doi:10.48088/ejg.a.bar.13.2.127.138

Batool, K., Zhao, Z.-Y., Irfan, M., & Żywiołek, J. (2023). Assessing the role of sustainable strategies in alleviating energy poverty: An environmental sustainability paradigm. *Environmental Science and Pollution Research International*, *30*(25), 67109–67130. doi:10.100711356-023-27076-0 PMID:37103699

Baumbach, S., Rubel, C., Ahmed, S., & Dengel, A. (2019). Geospatial customer, competitor and supplier analysis for site selection of supermarkets. *ACM International Conference Proceeding Series, Part F148261*. 10.1145/3318236.3318264

Baye, R. S., Olper, A., Ahenkan, A., Musah-Surugu, I. J., Anuga, S. W., & Darkwah, S. (2021). Renewable energy consumption in Africa: Evidence from a bias corrected dynamic panel. *The Science of the Total Environment*, *766*(142583). doi:10.1016/j.scitotenv.2020.142583 PMID:33143916

Baytar, F., & Ashdown, S. (2015). An exploratory study of interaction patterns around the use of virtual apparel design and try-on technology. *Fashion Practice*, *7*(1), 31–52.

Beaver, D., Kumar, S., Li, H. C., Sobel, J., & Vajgel, P. (2010). Finding a needle in haystack: Facebook's photo storage. *9th USENIX Symposium on Operating Systems Design and Implementation (OSDI 10)*.

Becker, D., King, T. D., & McMullen, B. (2015, October). Big data, big data quality problem. In *2015 IEEE International Conference on Big Data (Big Data)* (pp. 2644-2653). IEEE. 10.1109/BigData.2015.7364064

Bell, B. S., Lee, S. W., & Yeung, S. K. (2006). The impact of e-HR on professional competence in HRM: Implications for the development of HR professionals. *Human Resource Management, 45*, 295–308.

Benevene, P., & Buonomo, I. (2020). Green human resource management: An evidence-based systematic literature review. *Sustainability (Basel), 12*(15), 5974. doi:10.3390u12155974

Benyamin, B., Uhl-Bien, M., Marion, R., Seers, A., Orton, J. D., & Schreiber, C. (2006). Complexity leadership theory: An interactive perspective on leading in complex adaptive systems. *Emergence, 8*, 2–12.

Berger, L., & Berger, D. (2010). *The Talent Management Handbook: Creating a sustainable competitive advantage by selecting, developing, and promoting the best people.* McGraw Hill Professional.

Berman, B., & Pollack, D. (2021). Strategies for the successful implementation of augmented reality. *Business Horizons, 64*(5), 621–630. doi:10.1016/j.bushor.2021.02.027

Berman, S. L., Wicks, A. C., Kotha, S., & Jones, T. M. (1999). Does stakeholder orientation matter? The relationship between stakeholder management models and firm financial performance. *Academy of Management Journal, 42*(5), 488–506. doi:10.2307/256972

Berry, M., & Linoff, G. (1999). *Mastering data mining: The art and science of customer relationship management.* John Wiley & Sons, Inc.

Beshr, B., Muhammad, S. K., Alaghbari, M. A., & Albo-Aainain, M. I. (2023). The mediating role of empowering workers in the relationship between the entrepreneurial orientation and operational performance of Bahraini family businesses. *Resmilitaris, 13*(1), 1331-1341.

Betz, A., Buchli, J., Göbel, C., & Müller, C. (2015). Food waste in the Swiss food service industry-Magnitude and potential for reduction. *Waste Management (New York, N.Y.), 35*, 218–226. doi:10.1016/j.wasman.2014.09.015 PMID:25305683

Bhanushali, M. M., Narang, P., Sabarirajan, A., & Turai, A. K., S. K., & U, K. S. (2022). Human Resource Management based Economic analysis using Data Mining. In *Proceedings of the 2022 3rd International Conference on Intelligent Engineering and Management (ICIEM)* (pp. 872-876). 10.1109/ICIEM54221.2022.9853202

Bhatnagar, J., & Sandhu, S. (2005). Psychological empowerment and organisational citizenship behaviour (OCB) in "IT" managers: A talent retention tool. Indian Journal of Industrial Relations, 449–469.

Bhatti, H. Y., Galan-Ladero, M. M., & Galera-Casquet, C. (2023). Socially responsible marketing: A systematic review of the literature. *International Review on Public and Nonprofit Marketing, 20*(1), 25–64. doi:10.100712208-021-00326-y

Bhatti, S. H., Saleem, F., Murtaza, G., & Haq, T. U. (2021). Exploring the Impact of green human resource management on environmental performance: The roles of perceived organizational support and innovative environmental behavior. *International Journal of Manpower.*

Blázquez, M. (2014). Fashion shopping in multichannel retail: The role of technology in enhancing the customer experience. *International Journal of Electronic Commerce, 18*(4), 97–116. doi:10.2753/JEC1086-4415180404

Bloch, T., & Sacks, R. (2018). Comparing machine learning and rule-based inferencing for semantic enrichment of BIM models. *Automation in Construction, 91*, 256–272. doi:10.1016/j.autcon.2018.03.018

Blumenstock, J., Cadamuro, G., & On, R. (2015). Predicting poverty and wealth from mobile phone metadata. *Science, 350*(6264), 1073–1076. doi:10.1126cience.aac4420 PMID:26612950

Boardman, R., Henninger, C. E., & Zhu, A. (2020). Augmented reality and virtual reality: new drivers for fashion retail? *Technology-Driven Sustainability: Innovation in the Fashion Supply Chain*, 155-172.

Bodhani, A. (2012). Shops offer the e-tail experience. *Engineering & Technology, 7*(5), 46–49. doi:10.1049/et.2012.0512

Bolton, R. J., & Hand, D. J. (2001). Unsupervised profiling methods for fraud detection. *Credit Scoring and Credit Control, VII*, 235–255.

Bondarouk, T., Schilling, D., & Ruël, H. (2016). eHRM adoption in emerging economies: The case of subsidiaries of multinational corporations in Indonesia: E-HRM Adoption in Emerging Economies. *Canadian Journal of Administrative Sciences / Revue Canadienne Des Sciences de l Administration, 33*(2), 124–137. doi:10.1002/cjas.1376

Bondarouk, T. V., & Ruël, H. J. M. (2009). Electronic Human Resource Management: Challenges in the digital era. *International Journal of Human Resource Management, 20*(3), 505–514. doi:10.1080/09585190802707235

Bondarouk, T., Ruël, H., & van der Heijden, B. (2009). e-HRM effectiveness in a public sector organization: A multi-stakeholder perspective. *International Journal of Human Resource Management, 20*(3), 578–590. doi:10.1080/09585190802707359

Bondi, E., Xu, L., Acosta-Navas, D., & Killian, J. A. (2021, July). Envisioning communities: A participatory approach towards AI for social good. In *Proceedings of the 2021 AAAI/ACM Conference on AI, Ethics, and Society* (pp. 425-436). 10.1145/3461702.3462612

Bonetti, F., Pantano, E., Warnaby, G., & Quinn, L. (2019). Augmenting reality: Fusing consumers' experiences and interactions with immersive technologies in physical retail settings. *International Journal of Technology Marketing, 13*(3-4), 260–284. doi:10.1504/IJTMKT.2019.104592

Bottrill, M. C., & Pressey, R. L. (2012). The effectiveness and evaluation of conservation planning. In Conservation Letters (Vol. 5, Issue 6). doi:10.1111/j.1755-263X.2012.00268.x

Bourini, F. (2011). Investigating the Relationship between Human Resource Information System and Strategic Capability among Employees). *Journal of Advanced Social Research, 6*(3).

Boyd, D., & Crawford, K. (2012). Critical questions for big data: Provocations for a cultural, technological, and scholarly phenomenon. *Information Communication and Society, 15*(5), 662–679. doi:10.1080/1369118X.2012.678878

Brand, A., & Gross, T. (2020). Paying the pink tax on a blue dress-exploring gender-based price-premiums in fashion recommendations. In *Human-Centered Software Engineering: 8th IFIP WG 13.2 International Working Conference* (Vol. 2020, pp. 190–198). Eindhoven, The Netherlands: Springer International Publishing. 10.1007/978-3-030-64266-2_12

Braun, V., & Clarke, V. (2006). Using thematic analysis in psychology. *Qualitative Research in Psychology, 3*(2), 77–101. doi:10.1191/1478088706qp063oa

Brini, R., Amara, M., & Jemmali, H. (2017). Renewable energy consumption, International trade, oil price and economic growth inter-linkages: The case of Tunisia. *Renewable & Sustainable Energy Reviews, 76*, 620–627. doi:10.1016/j.rser.2017.03.067

Bronfman, J. (2021, April 15). *How Do Messaging Apps Respond to Privacy?* Retrieved from Common Sense Media: https://www.commonsense.org/education/articles/tell-me-about-it-how-do-messaging-apps-respond-to-privacy

Brown, B., Bughin, J., Byers, A. H., Chui, M., Dobbs, R., Manyika, J., & Roxburgh, C. (2011). *Big data: The next frontier for innovation, competition, and productivity.* McKinsey Global Institute.

Buckley, R. (2012). Sustainable tourism: Research and reality. In Annals of Tourism Research (Vol. 39, Issue 2). doi:10.1016/j.annals.2012.02.003

Buhler, K. (2021, November 18). *The Rising Consumer Demand for Data Privacy and Autonomy.* Retrieved from Sequoia Capital: https://www.sequoiacap.com/article/the-rising-consumer-demand-for-data-privacy-and-autonomy/

Burawat, P. (2019). The relationships among transformational leadership, sustainable leadership, lean manufacturing, and sustainability performance in Thai SMEs manufacturing industry. *International Journal of Quality & Reliability Management, 36*(6), 1014–1036. doi:10.1108/IJQRM-09-2017-0178

Buzby, J. C., Wells, H. F., & Hyman, J. (2014). *The estimated amount, value and calories of postharvest food losses at the retail and consumer levels in the United States.* Economic Information Bulletin Number 121. Economic Research Service/USDA.

Cai, L., Qi, Y., Wei, W., Wu, J., & Li, J. (2019). mrMoulder: A recommendation-based adaptive parameter tuning approach for big data processing platform. *Future Generation Computer Systems, 93*, 570–582. doi:10.1016/j.future.2018.05.080

Cai, L., & Zhu, Y. (2015). The challenges of data quality and data quality assessment in the big data era. *Data Science Journal, 14*(0), 14. doi:10.5334/dsj-2015-002

Cajias, M., & Bienert, S. (2011). Does sustainability pay off for European listed real estate companies? The dynamics between risk and provision of responsible information. *Journal of Sustainable Real Estate, 3*(1), 211–231. doi:10.108 0/10835547.2011.12091823

Can, M., & Ahmed, Z. (2022). Towards sustainable development in the European Union countries: Does economic complexity affect renewable and non-renewable energy consumption? *Sustainable Development.*

Capon, N., & Mintzberg, H. (1996). The rise and fall of strategic planning. *Academy of Management Review, 21*(1), 298. doi:10.2307/258641

Capriotti, P. (2009). Economic and social roles of companies in the mass media. The impact media visibility has on businesses' being recognized as economic and social actors. *Business & Society, 48*(2), 225–242. doi:10.1177/0007650307305724

Carey, B. (2015). *How we learn: The surprising truth about when, where, and why it happens.* Random House Trade Paperbacks.

Castillo, M., Petrie, R., Torero, M. A., & Vesterlund, L. (2012). Gender differences in bargaining outcomes: A field experiment on discrimination. SSRN *Electronic Journal.* doi:10.2139/ssrn.2087134

Chan, J. P. (2013). *The promise of digital technology in brick and mortar retail* [Doctoral dissertation]. Massachusetts Institute of Technology.

Chang, F., Dean, J., Ghemawat, S., Hsieh, W. C., Wallach, D. A., Burrows, M., Chandra, T., Fikes, A., & Gruber, R. E. (2008). Bigtable: A distributed storage system for structured data. *ACM Transactions on Computer Systems, 26*(2), 4. doi:10.1145/1365815.1365816

Chang, T. Y., Zivin, J. G., Gross, T., & Neidell, M. (2019). The effect of pollution on worker productivity: Evidence from call center workers in China. *American Economic Journal. Applied Economics, 11*(1), 151–172. Advance online publication. doi:10.1257/app.20160436

Chapman, A. (2005). *Principles of data quality, version 1.0.* Global Biodiversity Information Facility.

Charwak, B. (2016). The customer satisfaction towards Himalaya skin care products. *International Journal of Academic Research, 3*(3).

Chaudhury, D. (2020). *Artificial Intelligence influencing and transforming the marketing function.* https://talkcmo.com/featured/artificial-intelligence-influencing-and-transforming-the-marketing-function/

Chen, H., Chiang, R. H., & Storey, V. C. (2012). Business intelligence and analytics: From big data to big impact. *Management Information Systems Quarterly, 36*(4), 1165–1188. doi:10.2307/41703503

Chen, K. Y., Chang, C. W., & Wang, C. H. (2019). Frontline employees' passion and emotional exhaustion: The mediating role of emotional labor strategies. *International Journal of Hospitality Management, 76,* 163–172. doi:10.1016/j.ijhm.2018.05.006

Chen, Y.-S., Lai, S.-B., & Wen, C.-T. (2006). The influence of green innovation performance on corporate advantage in Taiwan. *Journal of Business Ethics, 67*(4), 331–339. doi:10.100710551-006-9025-5

Chen, Y., & Yan, X. (2022). The small and medium enterprises' green human resource management and green transformational leadership: A sustainable moderated-mediation practice. *Corporate Social Responsibility and Environmental Management, 29*(5), 1341–1356. doi:10.1002/csr.2273

Chernikova, A. (2021, December 11). *Why More and More Companies Are Embracing Web 3.0.* Retrieved from Entrepreneur Media, LLC: https://www.entrepreneur.com/science-technology/why-more-and-more-companies-are-embracing-web-30/397262

Chéron, E., Kohlbacher, F., & Kusuma, K. (2012). The effects of brand-cause fit and campaign duration on consumer perception of Socially responsible marketing in Japan. *Journal of Consumer Marketing, 29*(5), 357–368. doi:10.1108/07363761211247479

Chhabra, B., & Mohanty, R. P. (2013). Effect of emotional Intelligence on work stress–a study of Indian managers. *International Journal of Indian Culture and Business Management, 6*(3), 300–313. doi:10.1504/IJICBM.2013.053104

Chiang, K. C., Wachtel, G. J., & Zhou, X. (2019). Corporate social responsibility and growth opportunity: The case of real estate investment trusts. *Journal of Business Ethics, 155*(2), 463–478. doi:10.100710551-017-3535-1

Chia, Y. M. (2005). Job offers of multi-national accounting firms: The effects of emotional intelligence, extra-curricular activities, and academic performance. *Accounting Education, 14*(1), 75–93. doi:10.1080/06939280042000229707

Chi, M., Plaza, A., Benediktsson, J. A., Sun, Z., Shen, J., & Zhu, Y. (2016). Big data for remote sensing: Challenges and opportunities. *Proceedings of the IEEE, 104*(11), 2207–2219. doi:10.1109/JPROC.2016.2598228

Chircu, A. M., & Kauffman, R. J. (2000). Limits to value in electronic commerce-related IT investments. *Journal of Management Information Systems, 17*(2), 59–80. doi:10.1080/07421222.2000.11045645

Chung, P. T., & Chung, S. H. (2013). On data integration and data mining for developing business intelligence. In *2013, IEEE Long Island Systems, Applications and Technology Conference (LISAT).* IEEE. 10.1109/LISAT.2013.6578235

Chung, H., & van der Lippe, T. (2020). Flexible working, work-life balance, and gender equality: Introduction. *Social Indicators Research, 151*(2), 365–381. doi:10.100711205-018-2025-x PMID:33029036

Chylinski, M., Heller, J., Hilken, T., Keeling, D. I., Mahr, D., & de Ruyter, K. (2020). Augmented reality marketing: A technology-enabled approach to situated customer experience. *Australasian Marketing Journal, 28*(4), 374–384. doi:10.1016/j.ausmj.2020.04.004

Clark, L. P., Millet, D. B., & Marshall, J. D. (2014). National patterns in environmental injustice and inequality: Outdoor NO2 air pollution in the United States. *PLoS One, 9*(4), e94431. Advance online publication. doi:10.1371/journal.pone.0094431 PMID:24736569

Claus, L. (2019). HR disruption Time already to reinvent talent management. *Business Research Quarterly, 22*(3), 207–215. doi:10.1016/j.brq.2019.04.002

Clayton, P. R., & Clopton, J. (2019). Business curriculum redesign: Integrating data analytics. *Journal of Education for Business, 94*(1), 57–63. doi:10.1080/08832323.2018.1502142

Cobero, C., Primi, R., & Muniz, M. (2006). Inteligencia emocional e desempenho no trabalho: Um estudo com MSCEIT, BPR-5 e 16PF. *Cadernos de Psicologia e Educação Paideia, 16*(35), 337–348. doi:10.1590/S0103-863X2006000300005

Cocchia, A. (2014). Smart and digital city: A systematic literature review. *Smart city: How to create public and economic value with high technology in urban space,* 13-43.

Coenen, M., & Kok, R. A. W. (2014). Workplace flexibility and new product development performance: The role of telework and flexible work schedules. *European Management Journal, 32*(4), 564–576. doi:10.1016/j.emj.2013.12.003

Cohen, A., & Liani, E. (2009). Work-family conflict among female employees in Israeli hospitals. *Personnel Review, 38*(2), 124–141. doi:10.1108/00483480910931307

Cohn-Gordon, K., Cremers, C., Dowling, B., Garratt, L., & Stebila, D. (2020). A Formal Security Analysis of the Signal Messaging Protocol. *Journal of Cryptology, 33*(4), 1914–1983. doi:10.100700145-020-09360-1

Columbus, L. (2018). *10 ways machine learning is revolutionizing marketing.* https://www.forbes.com/sites/louiscolumbus/2018/02/25/10-ways-machine-learning-is-revolutionizing-marketing/#701274705bb6

Colvin, G. (2008). *Talent is overrated: What really separated world-class performers from everybody else.* Penguin.

Conaty, B., & Charan, R. (2010). *The talent masters: Why smart leaders put people before numbers.* Random House Digital.

Conservancy, N. (2021). Wildlife Conservation Society. *WORLD (Oakland, Calif.).*

Contreras, F., Baykal, E., & Abid, G. (2020). E-leadership and teleworking in times of COVID-19 and beyond: What we know and where do we go. *Frontiers in Psychology, 11,* 590271. doi:10.3389/fpsyg.2020.590271 PMID:33362656

Conway, J. J. E. (2018). *Artificial intelligence and machine learning: current applications in real estate.* Academic Press.

Conway, D., Li, C. Q., Wolch, J., Kahle, C., & Jerrett, M. (2010). A spatial autocorrelation approach for examining the effects of urban greenspace on residential property values. *The Journal of Real Estate Finance and Economics, 41*(2), 150–169. Advance online publication. doi:10.100711146-008-9159-6

Corbett, C. J. (2018). How sustainable is big data? *Production and Operations Management, 27*(9), 1685–1695. doi:10.1111/poms.12837

Coté, M., Gerbaudo, P., & Pybus, J. (2016). Politics of big data: Introduction. *Digital Culture & Society, 2*(2), 5–15. doi:10.14361/dcs-2016-0202

Crawford, K., Gray, M. L., & Miltner, K. (2014). Big Data| Critiquing Big Data: Politics, ethics, epistemology| special section introduction. *International Journal of Communication, 8,* 10.

Daassi, M., & Debbabi, S. (2021). Intention to reuse AR-based apps: The combined role of the sense of immersion, product presence and perceived realism. *Information & Management, 58*(4), 103453. doi:10.1016/j.im.2021.103453

Dacko, S. G. (2017). Enabling smart retail settings via mobile augmented reality shopping apps. *Technological Forecasting and Social Change, 124,* 243–256. doi:10.1016/j.techfore.2016.09.032

Dalmia, V. P. (2021). *Cross border transactions: Cryptocurrency and foreign exchange management act (FEMA).* Retrieved November 2, 2023, from Vaish Associates Advocates website: https://www.mondaq.com/india/fin-tech/1023148/cross-border-transactions-cryptocurrency-and-foreign-exchange-management-act-fema

Dan Burden. (2006). *Urban Street Trees.* https://www.walkable.org/download/22_benefits.pdf

Das, S., & Sureshkrishna, G. (2019). Challenges of digitalization for HR Professionals: An Exploratory Study. *International Journal of Innovative Researchin Technology, 6*(1).

Data Science Community. (2019). *College & University Data Science Degrees*. Available at https://github.com/ryan-swanstrom/awesome-datascience-colleges

Davenport, T., Guha, A., Grewal, D., & Bressgott, T. (2020). How artificial Intelligence will change the future of marketing. *Journal of the Academy of Marketing Science, 48*(1), 24–42, 48. doi:10.100711747-019-00696-0

David, R., Steve, W., Melissa, W., & John, L. (2022). *Green Infrastructure Financing*. https://icma.org/sites/default/files/2022-05/Final%20Financing%20Green%20Infrastructure.pdf

Dawwas, M., & Zahari, I. (2014). Testing the Relationship between Human Resource Practices and Turnover Intention in a non-Western context of the Palestine. *Journal of Advanced Social Research, 4*(4), 10–22.

Dayal, U., Castellanos, M., Simitsis, A., & Wilkinson, K. (2009). Data integration flows for business intelligence. *Proceedings of the 12th International Conference on Extending Database Technology: Advances in Database Technology.* 10.1145/1516360.1516362

de Abreu e Silva, J., & Alho, A. R. (2017). Using Structural Equations Modeling to explore perceived urban freight deliveries parking issues. *Transportation Research Part A, Policy and Practice, 102,* 18–32. Advance online publication. doi:10.1016/j.tra.2016.08.022

De Regt, A., & Barnes, S. J. (2019). V-commerce in retail: nature and potential impact. *Augmented reality and virtual reality: The power of AR and VR for business,* 17-25.

De Vaus, D. (2002). Analyzing social science data: 50 key problems in data analysis. *Sage (Atlanta, Ga.).*

De Veaux, R. D., Agarwal, M., Averett, M., Baumer, B. S., Bray, A., Bressoud, T. C., ... Kim, A. Y. (2017). Curriculum guidelines for undergraduate programs in data science. *Annual Review of Statistics and Its Application, 4*(1), 15–30. doi:10.1146/annurev-statistics-060116-053930

DeLone, W., McLean, E., & Sedera, D. (2014). Future of information systems success: Opportunities and challenges. In Computing Handbook, Third Edition (pp. 70-1-70–19). Chapman and Hall/CRC.

Demchenko, Y. (2019). Big data platforms and tools for data analytics in the data science engineering curriculum. In *Proceedings of the 3rd International Conference on Cloud and Big Data Computing* (pp. 60–64). ACM. 10.1145/3358505.3358512

Demeter, E., Rad, D., & Balas, E. (2021). Schadenfreude and General Anti-Social Behaviours: The Role of Violent Content Preferences and Life Satisfaction. BRAIN. *Broad Research in Artificial Intelligence and Neuroscience, 12*(2), 98–111. doi:10.18662/brain/12.2/194

Deng, Q., Alvarado, R., Toledo, E., & Caraguay, L. (2020). Greenhouse gas emissions, non-renewable energy consumption, and output in South America: The role of the productive structure. *Environmental Science and Pollution Research International, 27*(13), 14477–14491. doi:10.100711356-020-07693-9 PMID:31953767

Desti, K., & Shanthi, R. (2015). A study on emotional intelligence at workplace. *European Journal of Business and Management, 7,* 147–154.

Devina, U., & Gupta, A. (2012). Morale, Welfare measure, job satisfaction: The key mantras for gaining competitive edge. *International Journal of Physical and Social Sciences, 2*(7), 80–94.

Dhani, P., & Sharma, T. (2016). Emotional intelligence; history, models and measures. *International Journal of Science Technology and Management, 5*(7), 189-201.

Dhani, P., & Sharma, T. (2017). Effect of Emotional Intelligence on Job Performance of IT employees: A gender study. *Procedia Computer Science, 122,* 180–185. doi:10.1016/j.procs.2017.11.358

Dickinson-Delaporte, S., Beverland, M., & Lindgreen, A. (2010). Building corporate reputation with stakeholders: Exploring the role of message ambiguity for social marketers. *European Journal of Marketing*, *44*(11/12), 1856–1874. doi:10.1108/03090561011079918

Dinerman, M. (1989). Book Reviews : Women's Quest for Economic Equality. By Victor R. Fuchs. Cambridge, MA: Harvard University Press, 1988, 171 pp., $18.95, paper. *Affilia*, *4*(3), 82–84. doi:10.1177/088610998900400310

Djanogly, H. (2018). Why Going Green Can Have a Positive Impact on Attracting Customers. *CustomerThink*. https://customerthink.com/why-going-green-can-have-a-positive-impact-on-attracting-customers/

Dogucu, M., & Çetinkaya-Rundel, M. (2021). Web scraping in the statistics and data science curriculum: Challenges and opportunities. *Journal of Statistics and Data Science Education*, *29*(sup1), S112–S122.

Dohlman, E., Hansen, J., & Boussios, D. (2022). *USDA Agricultural Projections to 2031 (No. 323859)*. United States Department of Agriculture.

Dohnalova, Z., & Zimola, B. (2014). Corporate Stakeholder Management", Procedia - Social and Behavioral Sciences 110. *Procedia: Social and Behavioral Sciences*, *110*, 879–886. doi:10.1016/j.sbspro.2013.12.933

Dou, Z., Ferguson, J. D., Galligan, D. T., Kelly, A. M., Finn, S. M., & Gie-gengack, R. (2016). Assessing U.S. food wastage and opportunities for reduction. *Global Food Security*, *8*, 19–26. doi:10.1016/j.gfs.2016.02.001

Dowling, P. J., Festing, M., & Engle, A. D. (2008). *International Human Resource Management - Managing people in a multinational context*. Cengage Learning.

Duarte, P., Silva, S. C., & Ferreira, M. B. (2018). How convenient is it? Delivering online shopping convenience to enhance customer satisfaction and encourage e-WOM. *Journal of Retailing and Consumer Services*, *44*, 161–169. doi:10.1016/j.jretconser.2018.06.007

Dubey, R., Gunasekaran, A., Childe, S. J., Papadopoulos, T., Luo, Z., Wamba, S. F., & Roubaud, D. (2019). Can big data and predictive analytics improve social and environmental sustainability? *Technological Forecasting and Social Change*, *144*, 534–545. doi:10.1016/j.techfore.2017.06.020

Duggan, J., Sherman, U., Carbery, R., & McDonnell, A. (2020). Algorithmic management and app-work in the gig economy: A research agenda for employment relations and HRM. *Human Resource Management Journal*, *30*(1), 114–132. doi:10.1111/1748-8583.12258

Dupre, D. (2020). Urban and socio-economic correlates of property prices in dublin's area. *Proceedings - 2020 IEEE 7th International Conference on Data Science and Advanced Analytics, DSAA 2020*. 10.1109/DSAA49011.2020.00070

Ead, W. M., & Abbassy, M. M. (2022). A general cyber hygiene approach for financial analytical environment. In *Financial Data Analytics* (pp. 369–384). Springer International Publishing. doi:10.1007/978-3-030-83799-0_13

Ead, W., & Abbassy, M. (2018). *Intelligent systems of machine learning approaches for developing E-services portals*. EAI Endorsed Transactions on Energy Web. doi:10.4108/eai.2-12-2020.167292

Economist. (2017). https://www.economist.com/business/2017/04/12/how-germanys-otto-uses-artificial-intelligence

Econsultancy. (2018). Vodafone's chatbot is delivering double the conversion rate of its website. *Ben Davis*. https://econsultancy.com/vodafones-chatbot-is-delivering-twice-the-conversion-rate-of-its-website/

Ekmeil, F. A. R., Abumandil, M. S. S., Alkhawaja, M. I., Siam, I. M., & Alaklouk, S. A. A. (2021, March). Augmented reality and virtual reality revolutionize rusiness transformation in digital marketing tech industry analysts and visionaries during Coronavirus (COVID 19). *Journal of Physics: Conference Series*, *1860*(1), 012012. doi:10.1088/1742-6596/1860/1/012012

El-Gayar, O., & Fritz, B. D. (2006). Environmental management information systems (EMIS) for sustainable development: A conceptual overview. *Communications of the Association for Information Systems*, *17*(1), 34. doi:10.17705/1CAIS.01734

Eller, R., Alford, P., Kallmünzer, A., & Peters, M. (2020). Antecedents, consequences, and challenges of small and medium-sized enterprise digitalization. *Journal of Business Research*, *112*, 119–127. doi:10.1016/j.jbusres.2020.03.004

Ellewala, U. P. (2020). Secure Messaging Platform Based on Blockchain. *2020 2nd International Conference on Advancements in Computing (ICAC)*. 10.1109/ICAC51239.2020.9357306

El-Manaseer, S. A., Al-Kayid, J. H., Al Khawatreh, A. M., & Shamim, M. (2023). The Impact of Digital Transformation on Combating Tax Evasion (Electronic Billing System as a Model). In *Artificial Intelligence (AI) and Finance* (pp. 679–690). Springer Nature Switzerland. doi:10.1007/978-3-031-39158-3_63

Elnahla, N., & Neilson, L. C. (2021). *The stressors faced by retail workers during the COVID-19 pandemic*. Academic Press.

Emerging Markets. (2021). Retrieved November 4, 2023, from Msci.com website: https://www.msci.com/our-solutions/index/emerging-markets

Eren, B. M., Taspinar, N., & Gokmenoglu, K. K. (2019). The impact of financial development and economic growth on renewable energy consumption: Empirical analysis of India. *The Science of the Total Environment*, *663*, 189–197. doi:10.1016/j.scitotenv.2019.01.323 PMID:30711585

Eriksson, M., Osowski, C. P., Malefors, C., Björkman, J., & Eriksson, E. (2017). Quantification of food waste in public catering services—A case study from a Swedish municipality. *Waste Management (New York, N.Y.)*, *61*, 415–422. doi:10.1016/j.wasman.2017.01.035 PMID:28161338

Etzion, D., & Aragon-Correa, J. A. (2016). Big data, management, and sustainability: Strategic opportunities ahead. *Organization & Environment*, *29*(2), 147–155. doi:10.1177/1086026616650437

Evseeva, O., Kalchenko, O., Evseeva, S., & Plis, K. (2019). Instruments of human resource management based on the digital technologies in Russia. In *Proceedings of the International Conference on Digital Technologies in Logistics and Infrastructure (ICDTLI 2019)*. Paris, France: Atlantis Press. 10.2991/icdtli-19.2019.29

Fang, B., & Zhang, P. (2016). Big data in finance. In *Big data concepts, theories, and applications* (pp. 391–412). Springer. doi:10.1007/978-3-319-27763-9_11

Fan, H., Yu, Z., Yang, G., Liu, T. Y., Liu, T. Y., Hung, C. H., & Vejre, H. (2019). How to cool hot-humid (Asian) cities with urban trees? An optimal landscape size perspective. *Agricultural and Forest Meteorology*, *265*, 338–348. Advance online publication. doi:10.1016/j.agrformet.2018.11.027

Fan, J., Han, F., & Liu, H. (2014). Challenges of big data analysis. *National Science Review*, *1*(2), 293–314. doi:10.1093/nsr/nwt032 PMID:25419469

Fedorova, A., Zarubina, A., Pikulina, Y., Moskovskikh, A., Balandina, T., & Gafurova, T. (2019). Digitalization of The Human Resource Management: Russian Companies Case. In *International Conference on Education, Social Sciences and Humanities* (pp. 1227–1230). Academic Press.

Feng, Y., & Xie, Q. (2019). Privacy concerns, perceived intrusiveness, and privacy controls: An analysis of virtual try-on apps. *Journal of Interactive Advertising*, *19*(1), 43–57. doi:10.1080/15252019.2018.1521317

Ferrell, O. C., Hartline, M., & Hochstein, B. W. (2021). *Marketing strategy*. Cengage Learning.

Fischer, J., & Lindenmayer, D. B. (2007). Landscape modification and habitat fragmentation: A synthesis. In Global Ecology and Biogeography (Vol. 16, Issue 3). doi:10.1111/j.1466-8238.2007.00287.x

Fitzpatrick, A. (2017). Shopping while female: Who pays higher prices and why? *The American Economic Review*, *107*(5), 146–149. doi:10.1257/aer.p20171127

Fletcher, P. (2005). *From Personnel Administration to Business Driven Human Capital Management: The Transformation of the role of HR in the digital age*. Jossey-Bass.

Florea, V. N., & Badea, M. (2013). Acceptance of new Technologies in HR: E-Recruitment in Organizations. In *Proceedings of the European Conference on Information Management & Evaluation* (pp. 344–352). Academic Press.

Folayan, M. O., Brown, B., Haire, B., Babalola, C. P., & Ndembi, N. (2021). Considerations for stakeholder engagement and COVID-19 related clinical trials' conduct in sub-Saharan Africa. *Developing World Bioethics*, *21*(1), 44–50. doi:10.1111/dewb.12283 PMID:32798320

Fonner, K. L., & Roloff, M. E. (2010). Why Teleworkers are More Satisfied with Their Jobs than are Office-Based Workers: When Less Contact is Beneficial. *Journal of Applied Communication Research*, *38*(4), 336–361. doi:10.108 0/00909882.2010.513998

Forest, M. (2008). *The Economic Value of Green Infrastructure*. http://www.greeninfrastructurenw.co.uk/resources/The_Economic_Value_of_Green_Infrastructure.pdf

Formánek, T., & Sokol, O. (2022). Location effects: Geo-spatial and socio-demographic determinants of sales dynamics in brick-and-mortar retail stores. *Journal of Retailing and Consumer Services*, *66*, 102902. Advance online publication. doi:10.1016/j.jretconser.2021.102902

Fornell, C., & Larcker, D. F. (1981). *Structural equation models with unobservable variables and measurement error: Algebra and statistics*. Sage Publications Sage CA.

Foundation, S. (2023). *Solana Foundation*. Retrieved from https://solana.com/news/announcing-the-formation-of-the-solana-foundation

Foundation, S. (n.d.). *Solana Foundation*. Retrieved from https://solana.com/

Frank, L. D., Sallis, J. F., Saelens, B. E., Leary, L., Cain, L., Conway, T. L., & Hess, P. M. (2010). The development of a walkability index: Application to the neighborhood quality of life study. In British Journal of Sports Medicine (Vol. 44, Issue 13). doi:10.1136/bjsm.2009.058701

Frank, M. J. (2021). *Approaches to resolving cross-border disputes between franchisee and franchisor*. Retrieved November 2, 2023, from Lexology website: https://www.lexology.com/library/detail.aspx?g=2d45293e-179e-4338-933a-72e5c13e283f

Gabriel, J. M. O. (2013). Management Information Systems and Corporate Decision-Making: A Literature Review. *International Journal of Management*, *2*(3).

Gabrys, J. (2014). *Programming environments: environmentality and citizen sensing in the smart city.*. doi:10.1068/d16812

Gajendran, R. S., & Harrison, D. A. (2007). The good, the bad, and the unknown about telecommuting: Meta-analysis of psychological mediators and individual consequences. *The Journal of Applied Psychology*, 92(6), 1524–1541. doi:10.1037/0021-9010.92.6.1524 PMID:18020794

Galan-Ladero, M. M., & Galera-Casquet, C. (2019). Corporate Social Responsibility and Digital Tools: The Socially responsible Marketing Case. In Handbook of research on entrepreneurship and marketing for global reach in the digital economy (pp. 1-16). IGI Global.

Gallardo-Gallardo, E., Thunnissen, M., & Scullion, H. (2020). Talent management: Context matters. *International Journal of Human Resource Management*, 31(4), 457–473. doi:10.1080/09585192.2019.1642645

Gallino, S., & Moreno, A. (2018). The value of fit information in online retail: Evidence from a randomized field experiment. *Manufacturing & Service Operations Management*, 20(4), 767–787. doi:10.1287/msom.2017.0686

Gandomi, A., & Haider, M. (2015). Beyond the hype: Big data concepts, methods, and analytics. *International Journal of Information Management*, 35(2), 137–144. doi:10.1016/j.ijinfomgt.2014.10.007

Gandotra Radhika, A. V. (2017). *A Descriptive Study Of Brand Image And Consumer Perception On Consumer Loyalty And Preference Towards A Brand*. Patanjali Ayurveda Ltd.

Gangwar, H., Mishra, R., & Kamble, S. (2023). Adoption of big data analytics practices for sustainable development in the e-commerce supply chain: A mixed-method study. *International Journal of Quality & Reliability Management*, 40(4), 965–989. doi:10.1108/IJQRM-07-2021-0224

Garg, A. (2015). Green Marketing for Sustainable Development: An Industry Perspective. *Sustainable Development (Bradford)*, 23(5), 301–316. Advance online publication. doi:10.1002d.1592

Gerard, L., McMillan, J., & D'Annunzio-Green, N. (2017). Conceptualising sustainable leadership. *Industrial and Commercial Training*, 49(3), 116–126. doi:10.1108/ICT-12-2016-0079

Ghazali, E., Soon, P. C., Mutum, D. S., & Nguyen, B. (2017). Health and cosmetics: Investigating consumers' values for buying organic personal care products. *Journal of Retailing and Consumer Services*, 39, 154–163. doi:10.1016/j.jretconser.2017.08.002

Gibb, R. G., Purss, M. B., Sabeur, Z., Strobl, P., & Qu, T. (2022). Global reference grids for big earth data. *Big Earth Data*, 6(3), 251–255. doi:10.1080/20964471.2022.2113037

Gill, C., & Meyer, D. (2013). Union presence, employee relations and high-performance work practices. *Personnel Review*, 42(5), 508–528. doi:10.1108/PR-07-2011-0117

Gillen, C. (2021, March 8). *Upselling vs. cross selling: What's the difference?* Retrieved October 25, 2023, from Zapier.com website: https://zapier.com/blog/cross-selling-vs-upselling/

Gillingham, P. (2019). Big data in social welfare. In *Big Data* (pp. 245–263). Edward Elgar Publishing. doi:10.4337/9781788112352.00016

Gillingham, P., & Graham, T. (2017). Big data in social welfare: The development of a critical perspective on social work's latest "electronic turn". *Australian Social Work*, 70(2), 135–147. doi:10.1080/0312407X.2015.1134606

Gill, J., & Johnson, P. (2010). *Research methods of managers*. Sage Publications Limited.

Gil, Y. (2014). Teaching parallelism without programming: A data science curriculum for non-CS students. In *Proceedings of 2014 Workshop on Education for High Performance Computing* (pp. 42–48). IEEE. 10.1109/EduHPC.2014.12

Girase, S., Powar, V., & Mukhopadhyay, D. (2017). A user-friendly college recommending system using user-profiling and matrix factorization technique. In *2017 International Conference on Computing, Communication and Automation (ICCCA)*. IEEE. 10.1109/CCAA.2017.8229779

Gleick, J. (2012). *The information: A history, a theory, a flood*. Vintage.

Gmb, H. S. R. (2021, March 22). *News & Announcements: V1.12 Release - Keycard on iOS, Crypto Onramps, and More*. Retrieved from Status Research & Development GmbH: https://our.status.im/v1-12-release-keycard-on-ios-crypto-onramps-and-more/

Goldberg, P. K. (1996). Dealer price discrimination in new car purchases: Evidence from the consumer expenditure survey. *Journal of Political Economy*, *104*(3), 622–654. doi:10.1086/262035

Goleman, D. (1995). *Emotional Intelligence*. Bantam Books.

Goleman, D. (1998, March). The emotionally competent leader. *The Healthcare Forum Journal*, *41*(2), 36–38. PMID:10177113

Gomez-Martinez, F., De Beurs, K. M., Koch, J., & Widener, J. (2021). Multi-temporal land surface temperature and vegetation greenness in urban green spaces of Puebla, Mexico. *Land (Basel)*, *10*(2), 155. Advance online publication. doi:10.3390/land10020155

Goodijk, R. (2002). Partnership at corporate level: The meaning of the stakeholder model. *Journal of Change Management*, *3*(3), 225–241. doi:10.1080/714042537

Gopinath, R. (2019). Factors Influencing Consumer Decision Behaviour in FMCG. *International Journal of Research in Social Sciences*, *9*(7), 249–255.

Gopinath, R., & Kalpana, R. (2019). A Study on Consumer Perception towards Fast Food Retail Outlet in Perambalur District. *International Journal for Research in Engineering Application & Management*, *5*(1), 483–485.

Graham, T. (2014). Technologies of choice: the structural shaping of choice on the World Wide Web. *Challenging Identities, Institutions and Communities: Refereed Proceedings of the TASA 2014*, 1-13.

Graham, B. (2002). Heritage as knowledge: Capital or culture? *Urban Studies (Edinburgh, Scotland)*, *39*(5-6), 1003–1017. doi:10.1080/00420980220128426

Grant, C. A., Wallace, L. M., Spurgeon, P. C., Tramontano, C., & Charalampous, M. (2019). Construction and initial validation of the E-Work Life Scale to measure remote e-working. *Employee Relations*, *41*(1), 16–33. doi:10.1108/ER-09-2017-0229

Grant, D., & Newell, S. (2013). Realizing the strategic potential of e-HRM. *The Journal of Strategic Information Systems*, *22*(3), 187–192. doi:10.1016/j.jsis.2013.07.001

Graves, S., Sandra, B., & Waddock, A. (2000). Beyond Build to Last... Stakeholder Relations in "Built to Last" Companies. *Business and Society Review*, *105*(4), 393–418. doi:10.1111/0045-3609.00090

Grice, J. W. (2011). *Observation oriented modeling: Analysis of cause in the behavioral sciences*. Academic Press.

Griffiths, P. (1967). *The History of the Indian Tea Industry*. Weidenfeld and Nicolson.

Gu, B., & Ye, Q. (2014). First step in social media: Measuring the influence of online management responses on customer satisfaction. *Production and Operations Management*, *23*(4), 570–582. doi:10.1111/poms.12043

Gubbi, J., Buyya, R., Marusic, S., & Palaniswami, M. (2013). Internet of Things (IoT): A vision, architectural elements, and future directions. *Future Generation Computer Systems, 29*(7), 1645–1660. doi:10.1016/j.future.2013.01.010

Guha, A. (1977). *Planteraj and swaraj: Freedom struggle and electoral politics in Assam 1820- 1947.* Delhi University Press.

Gunasundari, R., Kumar, R., & Ilango, R. V. J. (2002). Factors influencing leaf expansion time in tea. In K. Sreedharan & P. K. Kumar (Eds.), Codeword Process and Printers. Academic Press.

Guo, H. (2017). Big Earth data: A new frontier in Earth and information sciences. *Big Earth Data, 1*(1-2), 4–20. doi:1 0.1080/20964471.2017.1403062

Guo, H., Liu, Z., Jiang, H., Wang, C., Liu, J., & Liang, D. (2017). Big Earth Data: A new challenge and opportunity for Digital Earth's development. *International Journal of Digital Earth, 10*(1), 1–12. doi:10.1080/17538947.2016.1264490

Guo, H., Wang, L., Chen, F., & Liang, D. (2014). Scientific big data and digital Earth. *Chinese Science Bulletin, 59*(35), 5066–5073. doi:10.100711434-014-0645-3

Gupta, R. K. (2021b). Adoption of mobile wallet services: an empirical analysis. *International Journal of Intellectual Property Management, 12*(3), 341 – 353. doi:10.1504/IJIPM.2021.10035526

Gupta, R. K. (2021a). A study on occupational health hazards among construction workers in India. *International Journal of Enterprise Network Management, 12*(4), 325–339. doi:10.1504/IJENM.2021.119663

Gupta, R. K. (2022). Utilization of Digital Network Learning and Healthcare for Verbal Assessment and Counselling During Post COVID-19 Period. *Technologies Artificial Intelligence and the Future of Learning Post-COVID, 19*, 117–134.

Gupta, S. D., Raychaudhuri, A., & Haldar, S. K. (2015). Information technology sector in India and gender inclusivity. *Gender in Management.*

Gürlek, M., & Koseoglu, M. A. (2021). Green innovation research in the field of hospitality and tourism: The construct, antecedents, consequences, and future outlook. *Service Industries Journal, 41*(11–12), 734–766. doi:10.1080/026420 69.2021.1929930

Gustavsson, J., Cederberg, C., Sonesson, U., van Otterdijk, R., & Meybeck, A. (2011). *Global Food Losses and Food Waste: Extent, Causes and Prevention.* FAO.

Gutenschwager, K., McLeod, R. D., & Friesen, M. R. (2019). From Openstreetmap and Cell Phone Data to Road Network Simulation Models. *Proceedings - Winter Simulation Conference, 2019-December.* doi:10.1109/WSC40007.2019.9004833

Hair, J. F. Jr, Matthews, L. M., Matthews, R. L., & Sarstedt, M. (2017). PLS-SEM or CB-SEM: Updated guidelines on which method to use. *International Journal of Multivariate Data Analysis, 1*(2), 107–123. doi:10.1504/IJMDA.2017.087624

Hair, J., Hollingsworth, C. L., Randolph, A. B., & Chong, A. Y. L. (2017). An updated and expanded assessment of PLS-SEM in information systems research. *Industrial Management & Data Systems, 117*(3), 442–458. doi:10.1108/IMDS-04-2016-0130

Halevi, G., & Moed Dr, H. F. (2012). The evolution of big data as a research and scientific topic: Overview of the literature. *Research Trends, 1*(30), 2.

Hameed, S. S., Madhavan, S., & Arumugam, T. (2020). Is consumer behaviour varying towards low and high involvement products even sports celebrity endorsed. *International Journal of Scientific and Technology Research, 9*(3), 4848–4852.

Hamid, A., Ragab, M., Fatah, A., Mashat, S., & Khedra, A. M. (2012). Hybrid Recommender System for Predicting College Admission. In *12th International Conference on Intelligent Systems Design and Applications (ISDA)* (pp. 107–113). Academic Press.

Hamza, A. (2016). Impact of Management Information System (MIS) on Managers' Decision in Industrial Companies in India. *International Journal of Management, 7*(4), 172–178.

Hana, M., & Naachimuthu, K. P. (2023). A Comprehensive Model on Rejection Sensitivity. *South India Journal of Social Sciences, 21*(19), 19–31.

Hana, M., Vishnupriya, S., & Naachimuthu, K. P. (2022). Restorative Effect of Direct and Indirect Nature Exposure - A Systematic Review. *International Journal of Scientific Research, 11*(5), 10–15.

Hanlon, W. W. (2020). Coal smoke, city growth, and the costs of the industrial revolution. *Economic Journal (London), 130*(626), 462–488. doi:10.1093/ej/uez055

Hari Krishna, S., Madala, R., Ramya, P., Sabarirajan, A., Dobhal, D., & Sapate, S. (2023). Ethically Governed Artificial Intelligence Based Innovative Business Research in Finance and Marketing System. In *Proceedings of the 2023 Eighth International Conference on Science Technology Engineering and Mathematics (ICONSTEM)* (pp. 1-7). 10.1109/ICONSTEM56934.2023.10142352

Harris, R. (2018, April 3). *A Blockchain Messaging Platform That's Unstoppable.* Retrieved from App Developer Magazine: https://appdevelopermagazine.com/a-blockchain-messaging-platform-that%27s-unstoppable/

Hart, S. L., & Sharma, S. (2004). Engaging fringe stakeholders for competitive imagination. *IEEE Engineering Management Review, 32*(3), 28–28. doi:10.1109/EMR.2004.25105

Hassan, F. A. (2020). *Blockchain and the Future of the Internet: A Comprehensive Review.* https://arxiv.org/pdf/1904.00733.pdf

Hawking, P., Stein, A., & Foster, S. (2004). E-HR and employee self-service: A case study of a Victorian public sector organisation. *Issues in Informing Science and Information Technology, 1*, 1017–1026. doi:10.28945/795

Hawlitschek, F., Teubner, T., & Weinhardt, C. (2016). Trust in the sharing economy. *Die Unternehmung, 70*(1), 26–44. doi:10.5771/0042-059X-2016-1-26

Helm, S. (2007). One reputation or many? Comparing stakeholders' perceptions of corporate reputation. *International Journal (Toronto, Ont.), 12*(3), 238–254.

Henriques, I., & Sadorsky, P. (1999). The relationship between environmental commitment and managerial perceptions of stakeholder importance. *Academy of Management Journal, 42*(1), 87–99. doi:10.2307/256876

Henry, W. a. (2021, December 7). *Blockchain: Ready for Business.* Retrieved from Tech Trends 2022, Deloitte Insights: https://www2.deloitte.com/us/en/insights/focus/tech-trends/2022/blockchain-trends.html

Hiep, P. M., Tien, N. H., Dana, L. P., Kuc, B. R., Van Tien, N., & Ha, V. X. (2021). Enhancing social responsibility and sustainability in real estate industry. *Turkish Journal of Computer and Mathematics Education, 12*(14), 4999–5013.

Hilken, T., Heller, J., Chylinski, M., Keeling, D. I., Mahr, D., & de Ruyter, K. (2018). Making omnichannel an augmented reality: The current and future state of the art. *Journal of Research in Interactive Marketing, 12*(4), 509–523. doi:10.1108/JRIM-01-2018-0023

Hillenbrand, C., & Money, K. (2007). Corporate responsibility and corporate reputation: Two separate concepts or two sides of the same coin? *Corporate Reputation Review, 10*(4), 261–277. doi:10.1057/palgrave.crr.1550057

Hochbaum, D. S. (2018). Machine Learning and Data Mining with Combinatorial Optimization Algorithms. In Recent Advances in Optimization and Modeling of Contemporary Problems (pp. 109-129). INFORMS. doi:10.1287/educ.2018.0179

Hong, S., Kim, J., & Lee, H. (2008). „Antecedents of user-continuance in information systems: Towards and integrative view". *Journal of Computer Information Systems, 48*(3), 1–13.

Hooi, L. W. (2006). Implementing e-HRM: The readiness of small and medium sized manufacturing companies in Malaysia. *Asia Pacific Business Review, 12*(4), 465–485. doi:10.1080/13602380600570874

Hossain, A., Naser, K., Zaman, A., & Nuseibeh, R. (2009). Factors influencing women business development in the developing countries: Evidence from Bangladesh. *The International Journal of Organizational Analysis, 17*(3), 202–224. Advance online publication. doi:10.1108/19348830910974923

Hossain, M. S., Rahman, M. F., & Zhou, X. (2021). Impact of customers' interpersonal interactions in social commerce on customer relationship management performance. *Journal of Contemporary Marketing Science, 4*(1), 161–181. doi:10.1108/JCMARS-12-2020-0050

Huang, M. H., & Rust, R. T. (2018). Artificial intelligence in service. *Journal of Service Research, 21*(2), 155–172. doi:10.1177/1094670517752459

Huang, Y.-C., & Chen, Y.-J. (2019). Digital Image Design Research of Popular Culture Exhibition. *Proceedings of the International Conference on Signal and Image Processing.* 10.1109/SIPROCESS.2019.8868467

Hudson, J. B., & Durairaj, J. (2004). Cost control of tea cultivation. Planters'. *Chronicle (Philadelphia, Pa.), 100*(11), 8–21.

Hunt, C. (2014). *Transforming talent management: The impact of social and digital tech.* Academic Press.

Hurrelmann, K., & Albrecht, E. (2021). *Gen Z: Between Climate Crisis and Coronavirus Pandemic.* Routledge. doi:10.4324/9781003128700

Hussain, S., & Alam, F. (2023). Willingness to Pay for Tourism Services: A Case Study from Harappa, Sahiwal. *FMDB Transactions on Sustainable Management Letters, 1*(3), 105–113.

Husted, S. W., & Whitehouse, F. R. Jr. (2002). Socially responsible marketing via the world wide web: A relationship marketing strategy. *Journal of Nonprofit & Public Sector Marketing, 10*(1), 3–22. doi:10.1300/J054v10n01_02

Huurne, M., Ronteltap, A., Corten, R., & Buskens, V. (2017). Antecedents of trust in the sharing economy: A systematic review. *Journal of Consumer Behaviour, 16*(6), 485–498. doi:10.1002/cb.1667

Hwangbo, H., Kim, E. H., Lee, S. H., & Jang, Y. J. (2020). Effects of 3d virtual "try-on" on online sales and customers' purchasing experiences. *IEEE Access : Practical Innovations, Open Solutions, 8,* 189479–189489. doi:10.1109/ACCESS.2020.3023040

IBC Idea, Impressions and Implementation (2022). Retrieved November 2, 2023, from Gov.in website: https://ibbi.gov.in/uploads/whatsnew/b5fba368fbd5c5817333f95fbb0d48bb.pdf?cv=1

Ike, G. N., Usman, O., Alola, A. A., & Sarkodie, S. A. (2020). Environmental quality effects of income, energy prices and trade: The role of renewable energy consumption in G-7 countries. *The Science of the Total Environment, 721*(137813), 137813. doi:10.1016/j.scitotenv.2020.137813 PMID:32197283

Ilechukwu, N., & Lahiri, S. (2022). Renewable-energy consumption and international trade. *Energy Reports, 8,* 10624–10629. doi:10.1016/j.egyr.2022.08.209

Iles, P., Chuai, X., & Preece, D. (2010). Talent Management and HRM in Multinational companies in Beijing: Definitions, differences and drivers. *Journal of World Business, 45*(2), 179–189. doi:10.1016/j.jwb.2009.09.014

Indermun, V. (2014). Importance of human resource management practices and the impact companies face in relation to competitive challenges. *Singaporean Journal of Business Economics and Management Studies, 2*(11), 125–135. doi:10.12816/0006786

Iqbal, Q., & Piwowar-Sulej, K. (2022). Sustainable leadership in higher education institutions: Social innovation as a mechanism. *International Journal of Sustainability in Higher Education, 23*(8), 1–20. doi:10.1108/IJSHE-04-2021-0162

Islam, J., & Rahman, Z. (2017). The impact of online brand community characteristics on customer engagement: An application of Stimulus-Organism-Response paradigm. *Telematics and Informatics, 34*(4), 96–109. doi:10.1016/j.tele.2017.01.004

Jabbar, M., Yusoff, M. M., & Shafie, A. (2022). Assessing the role of urban green spaces for human well-being: a systematic review. In GeoJournal (Vol. 87, Issue 5). doi:10.100710708-021-10474-7

Jackson, L. T. B., & Fransman, E. I. (2018). Flexi work, financial well-being, work–life balance and their effects on subjective experiences of productivity and job satisfaction of females in an institution of higher learning. *Suid-Afrikaanse Tydskrif vir Ekonomiese en Bestuurswetenskappe, 21*(1). Advance online publication. doi:10.4102ajems.v21i1.1487

Jacobides, M. G., Brusoni, S., & Candelon, F. (2021). The evolutionary dynamics of the artificial intelligence ecosystem. *Strategy Science, 6*(4), 412–435. doi:10.1287tsc.2021.0148

Jadhav, V., & Khanna, M. (2016). Factors influencing online buying behaviour of college students: A qualitative analysis. *The Qualitative Report, 21*(1), 1.

Jagati, S. (2022, February 1). *Blockchain-based Decentralized Messengers: A Privacy Pipedream?* Retrieved from Cointelegraph: https://cointelegraph.com/news/blockchain-based-decentralized-messengers-a-privacy-pipedream

Jain, V., Gupta, M., Kevadia, J., & Shinde, P. K. (2018). College Recommendation System. *International Journal of Engineering Research & Technology (Ahmedabad), 5*(01).

Jara, A. J., Sun, T. Y., Song, H., Bie, T. R., Genooud, D., & Bocchi, Y. (2015). Internet of Things for Cultural Heritage of Smart Cities and Smart Regions. *Proceedings of the IEEE 29th—International Conference on Advanced Information Networking and Applications Workshops.* 10.1109/WAINA.2015.169

Javornik, A. (2016). Augmented reality: Research agenda for studying the impact of its media characteristics on consumer behaviour. *Journal of Retailing and Consumer Services, 30*, 252–261. doi:10.1016/j.jretconser.2016.02.004

Jee, K., & Kim, G. H. (2013). Potentiality of big data in the medical sector: Focus on how to reshape the healthcare system. *Healthcare Informatics Research, 19*(2), 79–85. doi:10.4258/hir.2013.19.2.79 PMID:23882412

Jennings, V., Baptiste, A. K., Osborne Jelks, N., & Skeete, R. (2017). Urban green space and the pursuit of health equity in parts of the United States. *International Journal of Environmental Research and Public Health, 14*(11), 1432. Advance online publication. doi:10.3390/ijerph14111432 PMID:29165367

Jiang, J. (2012). Information extraction from text. *Mining text data*, 11-41.

John, C. (2022, October 28). *Why Social Media and Messaging Apps on Blockchain May be a Better Option.* Retrieved from India Today: https://www.indiatoday.in/opinion-columns/story/why-social-media-messaging-apps-on-blockchain-may-be-a-better-option-opinion-2290395-2022-10-28

Jonathan, B. (2014). Give Beauty an Online Makeover for Christmas. *Marketing Week*, p. 3.

Jones, T. M. (1995). Instrumental stakeholder theory: A synthesis of ethics and economics. *Academy of Management Review, 20*(2), 404–437. doi:10.2307/258852

Jyoti, J. (2016). Impact of Demographic Variables on Emotional Intelligence: A Study among the Employees of Private Sector Banks in Madhya Pradesh, India. *Research Journal of Management Science.*, *5*(10), 20–24.

Kabaivanov, S., & Markovska, V. (2021, March). Artificial intelligence in real estate market analysis. In AIP Conference Proceedings (Vol. 2333, No. 1). AIP Publishing. doi:10.1063/5.0041806

Kadhim, R., & Sadikmohamadtaqi, B. (2012). Prototyping A Hospital Human Resource Information System). *International Journal of Independent Research and Studies*, *1*(1).

Kaisler, S., Armour, F., Espinosa, J. A., & Money, W. (2013). Big data: Issues and challenges moving forward. In *Proceedings of the 46th Hawaii International Conference on System Sciences* (pp. 995–1004). IEEE. 10.1109/HICSS.2013.645

Kanaan-Jebna, A., Baharudi, A. S., & Alabdullah, T. T. Y. (2022). Entrepreneurial Orientation, Market Orientation, Managerial Accounting and Manufacturing SMEs Satisfaction. *Journal of Accounting Science*, *6*(1), 1–14. doi:10.21070/jas.v6i1.1590

Kang, J., Lee, H. J., Jeong, S. H., Lee, H. S., & Oh, K. J. (2020). Developing a forecasting model for real estate auction prices using artificial intelligence. *Sustainability (Basel)*, *12*(7), 2899. doi:10.3390u12072899

Kardan, O., Gozdyra, P., Misic, B., Moola, F., Palmer, L. J., Paus, T., & Berman, M. G. (2015). Neighborhood greenspace and health in a large urban center. *Scientific Reports*, *5*(1), 11610. Advance online publication. doi:10.1038rep11610 PMID:26158911

Kavya, V., & Arumugam, S. (2016). A Review on Predictive Analytics in Data Mining. *International Journal of Chaos, Control, Modelling and Simulation*, *5*(1/2/3), 1-8.

Keels, G. N. (2021). *Brick-and-Mortar Retail Stores Disappearing in the Digital Age: Marketing Strategies for Sustainability* [Doctoral dissertation]. University of Maryland University College.

Keeso, A. (2014). *Big data and environmental sustainability: a conversation starter*. Smith School of Enterprise and the Environment. Working Paper Series, (14-04).

Keil, T., Maula, M., Schildt, H., & Zahra, S. A. (2008). The effect of governance modes and relatedness of external business development activities on innovative performance. In Strategic Management Journal (Vol. 29, Issue 8). doi:10.1002mj.672

Kerscher, A. (2015). *Corporate social responsibility and the market valuation of listed real estate investment companies* (Vol. 79). Universitätsbibliothek Regensburg.

Khan, H., Khan, I., & Binh, T. T. (2020). The heterogeneity of renewable energy consumption, carbon emission and financial development in the globe: A panel quantile regression approach. *Energy Reports*, *6*, 859–867. doi:10.1016/j.egyr.2020.04.002

Khan, M. A., Kumar, N., Mohsan, S. A. H., Khan, W. U., Nasralla, M. M., Alsharif, M. H., & Ullah, I. (2023). Swarm of UAVs for network management in 6G: A technical review. *IEEE Transactions on Network and Service Management*, *20*(1), 741–761. doi:10.1109/TNSM.2022.3213370

Khan, M. I., Yasmeen, T., Shakoor, A., Khan, N. B., & Muhammad, R. (2017). 2014 oil plunge: Causes and impacts on renewable energy. *Renewable & Sustainable Energy Reviews*, *68*, 609–622. doi:10.1016/j.rser.2016.10.026

Khawas, V. (2011). Status of Tea Garden Labourers in Eastern Himalaya: A Case of Darjeeling Tea Industry. In M. Desai & S. Mitra (Eds.), Cloud, Stone and the Mind: The People and Environment of Darjeeling Hill Area (pp. 1-19). ICIMOD Online Digital Library.

Khodabandehlou, S., & Zivari Rahman, M. (2017). Comparison of supervised machine learning techniques for customer churn prediction based on analysis of customer behavior. *Journal of Systems and Information Technology, 19*(1/2), 65–93. doi:10.1108/JSIT-10-2016-0061

Kidwell, J. (2011). Book Review: Ecological Hermeneutics: Norman C. Habel and Peter Trudinger, Exploring Ecological Hermeneutics, (Atlanta: Society of Biblical Literature, 2008. $24.95. pp. 183. ISBN: 978-1-58983-346-3). *The Expository Times, 122*(11), 563–563. doi:10.1177/00145246111220110107

Kim, D. E., & LaBat, K. (2013). Consumer experience in using 3D virtual garment simulation technology. *Journal of the Textile Institute, 104*(8), 819–829. doi:10.1080/00405000.2012.758353

Kim, H. Y., Lee, J. Y., Mun, J. M., & Johnson, K. K. (2017). Consumer adoption of smart in-store technology: Assessing the predictive value of attitude versus beliefs in the technology acceptance model. *International Journal of Fashion Design, Technology and Education, 10*(1), 26–36. doi:10.1080/17543266.2016.1177737

Kim, J., & Forsythe, S. (2008). Adoption of virtual try-on technology for online apparel shopping. *Journal of Interactive Marketing, 22*(2), 45–59. doi:10.1002/dir.20113

Kim, K. Y. (2014). Business intelligence and marketing insights in an era of big data: The q-sorting approach. *KSII Transactions on Internet and Information Systems, 8*(2), 567–582. doi:10.3837/tiis.2014.02.014

Kim, K., Kim, J. W., & Lee, H. (2018). Antecedents and consequences of customer loyalty in online shopping: A case of online travel agencies. *Journal of Travel Research, 57*(4), 481–495.

Kim, M. J., Lee, C.-K., & Jung, T. (2020). Exploring consumer behavior in virtual reality tourism using an extended stimulus-organism-response model. *Journal of Travel Research, 59*(1), 69–89. doi:10.1177/0047287518818915

Kiran, K. U., & Arumugam, T. (2020, December). Role of programmatic advertising on effective digital promotion strategy: A conceptual framework. *Journal of Physics: Conference Series, 1716*(1), 012032. doi:10.1088/1742-6596/1716/1/012032

Klimanova, O. A., & Illarionova, O. I. (2020). Green infrastructure indicators for urban planning: Applying the integrated approach for Russian largest cities. *Geography, Environment, Sustainability, 13*(1), 251–259.

Klimanova, O., Illarionova, O., Grunewald, K., & Bukvareva, E. (2021). Green infrastructure, urbanization, and ecosystem services: The main challenges for Russia's largest cities. *Land (Basel), 10*(12), 1292. Advance online publication. doi:10.3390/land10121292

Kohtamäki, M., Parida, V., Patel, P. C., & Gebauer, H. (2020). The relationship between digitalization and servitization: The role of servitization in capturing the financial potential of digitalization. *Technological Forecasting and Social Change, 151*, 119804. Advance online publication. doi:10.1016/j.techfore.2019.119804

Koivupuro, H.-K., Hartikainen, H., Silvennoinen, K., Katajajuuri, J.-M., Heikintalo, N., Reinikainen, A., & Jalkanen, L. (2012). Influence of socio-demographical, behavioral, and attitudinal factors on the amount of avoidable food waste generated in Finnish households. *International Journal of Consumer Studies, 36*(2), 183–194. doi:10.1111/j.1470-6431.2011.01080.x

Kong, L., Liu, Z., & Wu, J. (2020). A systematic review of big data-based urban sustainability research: State-of-the-science and future directions. *Journal of Cleaner Production, 273*, 123142. doi:10.1016/j.jclepro.2020.123142

Konrad, A. M., & Mangel, R. (2000). The impact of work-life programs on firm productivity. *Strategic Management Journal, 21*(12), 1225–1237. doi:10.1002/1097-0266(200012)21:12<1225::AID-SMJ135>3.0.CO;2-3

Köpsel, V., de Moura Kiipper, G., & Peck, M. A. (2021). Stakeholder engagement vs. social distancing-how does the Covid-19 pandemic affect participatory research in EU marine science projects? *Maritime Studies*, 20(2), 189–205. doi:10.100740152-021-00223-4 PMID:35300281

Koritnik, T., Bajd, T., & Munih, M. (2008). Virtual environment for lower-extremities training. *Gait & Posture*, 27(2), 323–330. doi:10.1016/j.gaitpost.2007.04.015 PMID:17596945

Köseoğlu, D., Ead, S., & Abbassy, W. M. (2022). Basics of Financial Data Analytics. In *Financial Data Analytics* (pp. 23–57). Springer International Publishing. doi:10.1007/978-3-030-83799-0_2

Kossek, E. E. (1987). Human resources management innovation. *Human Resource Management*, 26(1), 71–92. doi:10.1002/hrm.3930260105

Kossek, E. E., Lautsch, B. A., & Eaton, S. C. (2006). Telecommuting, control, and boundary management: Correlates of policy use and practice, job control, and work–family effectiveness. *Journal of Vocational Behavior*, 68(2), 347–367. doi:10.1016/j.jvb.2005.07.002

Kovach, K. A., & Cathcart, C. E. Jr. (1999). Human resource information systems (HRIS): Providing business with rapid data access, information exchange and strategic advantage. *Public Personnel Management*, 28(2), 275–282. doi:10.1177/009102609902800208

Kravariti, F., & Johnston, K. (2020). Talent management: A critical literature review and research agenda for public sector human resource management. *Public Management Review*, 22(1), 75–95. doi:10.1080/14719037.2019.1638439

Krishna, C. Y. S., & Bhaskar, S. V. (2011). Assessment of support and benefits of HRIS in medium-scale textile industries. *International Journal of Research in Economics & Social Sciences*, 1(2), 48–57.

Kristoff, H., Hoen, B. T., Adrian, L., & Stang, V. (2018). *Digitalization & HR*. Academic Press.

Krithika, J., DivyaPriyadharshini, N., & GokulaPriya, J. (2019). Green HRM-Practices In Organisations. *IOSR Journal of Business and Management (IOSR-JBM)*, 21(3), 74.

Krstic, N. (2014). Stakeholder management from the business perspective. *Megatrend Revija*, 11(2), 165–182. doi:10.5937/MegRev1402165K

Kshetri, N. (2014). Big data's impact on privacy, security, and consumer welfare. *Telecommunications Policy*, 38(11), 1134–1145. doi:10.1016/j.telpol.2014.10.002

Kumar, A., & Ahuja, A. (2017). Consumer Behavior towards Patanjali Products: A Study on Consumers with Reference to Rohtak District of Haryana. *KIJECBM*, 4(2), 404–410.

Kumar, A., & Naachimuthu, K. P. (2023). Market Potential for Shawarma Outlet in Coimbatore - An Analysis. *South India Journal of Social Sciences*, XXI(1), 130–140.

Kumari, K., Kataria, M., Limbani, V., & Soni, R. (2019). CAPSLG: College admission predictor and smart list generator. SSRN *Electronic Journal*. doi:10.2139/ssrn.3370798

Kumar, M., & Radhakrishnan, P. (2012). Tea in south India: present status and future prospects. *Souvenir. Plantation Crops Symposium*, 1–7.

Kumar, S. A., Rajest, S. S., Aravind, B. R., & Bhuvaneswari, G. (2023). Virtual learning styles based on learning style detection. *International Journal of Knowledge and Learning*, 1(1), 10057158. Advance online publication. doi:10.1504/IJKL.2023.10057158

Kumar, S., Tiwari, P., & Zymbler, M. (2019). Internet of Things is a revolutionary approach for future technology enhancement: A review. *Journal of Big Data*, 6(1), 1–21. doi:10.118640537-019-0268-2

Kumar, V. R., Selvaraj, M., Venkateswaran, P. S., Sabarirajan, A., Shatila, K., & Agarwal, V. (2022). The impact of training and development programs on employees performance: The case of Lebanese SMEs. *International Journal of Intellectual Property Management*, 12(3), 368. doi:10.1504/IJIPM.2022.124646

Kumar, V., & Vuilliomenet, A. (2021). Urban nature: Does green infrastructure relate to the cultural and creative vitality of European cities? *Sustainability (Basel)*, 13(14), 8052. Advance online publication. doi:10.3390u13148052

Kuragayala, P. S. (2023). A Systematic Review on Workforce Development in Healthcare Sector: Implications in the Post-COVID Scenario. *FMDB Transactions on Sustainable Technoprise Letters*, 1(1), 36–46.

Kwakwa, P. A. (2020). What determines renewable energy consumption? Startling evidence from Ghana. *International Journal of Energy Sector Management*.

Kwon, O., Lee, N., & Shin, B. (2014). Data quality management, data usage experience and acquisition intention of big data analytics. *International Journal of Information Management*, 34(3), 387–394. doi:10.1016/j.ijinfomgt.2014.02.002

Lakshmi, Y. P. S. S., & Babu, M. (2019). Study of factors that influence the consumer behavior towards cosmetics -Conceptual framework. *Iconic Research and Engineering Journals*, 2(7), 21–28.

Lama, S. (2022, April 4). *Secretum: The Messaging App of Web 3.0 Era*. Retrieved from BeInNews Academy: https://beincrypto.com/secretum-the-messaging-app-of-the-web-3-0-era/

Larose, D. T., & Larose, C. D. (2014). *Discovering knowledge in data: an introduction to data mining*. John Wiley & Sons. doi:10.1002/9781118874059

Laudon, K., & Laudon, J. (2010). *Managing the digital firm with management information systems* (11th ed.). Pearson Prentice Hall.

Lau, K. W., & Lee, P. Y. (2019). Shopping in virtual reality: A study on consumers' shopping experience in a stereoscopic virtual reality. *Virtual Reality (Waltham Cross)*, 23(3), 255–268. doi:10.100710055-018-0362-3

Laureti, L., Massaro, A., Costantiello, A., & Leogrande, A. (2023). The Impact of Renewable Electricity Output on Sustainability in the Context of Circular Economy: A Global Perspective. *Sustainability (Basel)*, 3(2160), 15. doi:10.3390u15032160

Le Texier, M., Schiel, K., & Caruso, G. (2018). The provision of urban green space and its accessibility: Spatial data effects in Brussels. *PLoS One*, 13(10), e0204684. Advance online publication. doi:10.1371/journal.pone.0204684 PMID:30332449

Leach, W. D. (2002). Surveying Diverse Stakeholder Groups. *Society & Natural Resources*, 15(7), 641–649. doi:10.1080/08941920290069245

Learn, O. S. M. (2016). *OpenStreetMap Data*. https://learnosm.org/en/osm-data/

Lee, C. S., & Cheang, P. Y. S. (2021). Predictive Analysis in Business Analytics: Application of Decision Tree in Business Decision Making. *Advances in Decision Sciences*, 26(1), 1–29. doi:10.47654/v26y2022i1p1-29

Lee, H., Xu, Y., & Porterfield, A. (2022). Antecedents and moderators of consumer adoption toward AR-enhanced virtual try-on technology: A stimulus-organism-response approach. *International Journal of Consumer Studies*, 46(4), 1319–1338. doi:10.1111/ijcs.12760

Lee, J., & Cheang, B. (2022). Predictive Analysis in Business Analytics: Application of Decision Tree in Business Decision Making. *Journal of Business Analytics*, 8(2), 123–136.

LeewayHertz. (2023). *How To Determine the Cost of Blockchain Implementation*. Retrieved from LeewayHertz: https://www.leewayhertz.com/cost-of-blockchain-implementation/

Lepak, D. P., Bartol, K. M., & Erhardt, N. L. (2005). A contingency framework for the delivery of HR practices. *Human Resource Management Review*, 15(2), 139–159. doi:10.1016/j.hrmr.2005.06.001

Lepak, D. P., & Snell, S. A. (1998). Virtual HR: Strategic human resource management in the 21st century. *Human Resource Management Review*, 8(3), 215–234. doi:10.1016/S1053-4822(98)90003-1

Lessmann, S., Haupt, J., Coussement, K., & De Bock, K. W. (2019). Targeting customers for profit: An ensemble learning framework to support marketing decision-making. *Information Sciences*, 15–22.

Liang, T.-P., & Liu, Y.-H. (2018). Bibliometrics study. *Expert Systems with Applications, 111*, 2–10. doi:10.1016/j.eswa.2018.05.018

Li, H., & Lai, Z. (2010). The study and implementation of mobile GPS navigation system based on Google Maps. In *Proceedings of 2010 International Conference on Computer and Information Application* (pp. 87–90). IEEE. 10.1109/ICCIA.2010.6141544

Liker, J. K. (2021). *Toyota way: 14 management principles from the world's greatest manufacturer*. McGraw-Hill Education.

Lilly, J. (2010). Customer Perception and Preference towards Branded Products (With Special Reference to Television Sets). *Indian Journal of Marketing*, 40(2), 49–55.

Li, M., Tian, Z., Liu, Q., & Lu, Y. (2022). Literature Review and Research Prospect on the Drivers and Effects of Green Innovation. *Sustainability (Basel)*, 14(16), 9858. doi:10.3390u14169858

Lindemann-Matthies, P., & Brieger, H. (2016). Does urban gardening increase aesthetic quality of urban areas? A case study from Germany. *Urban Forestry & Urban Greening*, 17, 33–41. Advance online publication. doi:10.1016/j.ufug.2016.03.010

Lin, Y., Wang, H., Li, J., & Gao, H. (2019). Data source selection for information integration in the big data era. *Information Sciences*, 479, 197–213. doi:10.1016/j.ins.2018.11.029

Li, R., & Leung, G. C. (2021). The relationship between energy prices, economic growth and renewable energy consumption: Evidence from Europe. *Energy Reports*, 7, 1712–1719. doi:10.1016/j.egyr.2021.03.030

Lishmah Dominic, M., Sowmiya, S., & Venkateswaran, P. S. (2023). Study on importance of entrepreneurship skill development programme (ESDP) for sustainable growth of MSMEs in India. *Proceedings on Engineering Sciences*, 5(3), 553–564. doi:10.24874/PES05.03.018

Liu, X., Sohn, Y. H., & Park, D. W. (2018). Application development with augmented reality technique using Unity 3D and Vuforia. *International Journal of Applied Engineering Research, 13*(21), 15068-15071.

Liu, Q., Browne, A. L., & Iossifova, D. (2022). A socio-material approach to resource consumption and environmental sustainability of tourist accommodations in a Chinese hot spring town. *Sustainable Production and Consumption*, 30, 424–437. Advance online publication. doi:10.1016/j.spc.2021.12.021

Liu, S., McGree, J., Ge, Z., & Xie, Y. (2015). *Computational and statistical methods for analysing big data with applications*. Academic Press.

Liu, W., Zhao, H., Sun, S., Xu, X., Huang, T., & Zhu, J. (2022). Green Space Cooling Effect and Contribution to Mitigate Heat Island Effect of Surrounding Communities in Beijing Metropolitan Area. *Frontiers in Public Health*, *10*, 870403. Advance online publication. doi:10.3389/fpubh.2022.870403 PMID:35586004

Liu, X. (2015). Research on the Service Platform to Realize Unified Retrieval and Revelation of Digital Cultural Resources. *Proceedings of the 8th International Symposium on Computational Intelligence and Design*. 10.1109/ISCID.2015.239

Liu, Y., Liu, Y., Xu, S., Cheng, K., Masuko, S., & Tanaka, J. (2020). Comparing VR-and AR-based try-on systems using personalized avatars. *Electronics (Basel)*, *9*(11), 1814. doi:10.3390/electronics9111814

Li, X., & Kao, C. (2022). Spatial Analysis and Modeling of the Housing Value Changes in the U.S. during the COVID-19 Pandemic. *Journal of Risk and Financial Management*, *15*(3), 139. Advance online publication. doi:10.3390/jrfm15030139

Loebbecke, C., & Picot, A. (2015). Reflections on societal and business model transformation arising from digitization and big data analytics: A research agenda. *The Journal of Strategic Information Systems*, *24*(3), 149–157. doi:10.1016/j.jsis.2015.08.002

López-Igual, P., & Rodríguez-Modroño, P. (2020). Who is teleworking and where from? Exploring the main determinants of telework in Europe. *Sustainability (Basel)*, *12*(21), 8797. doi:10.3390u12218797

Lorenzo, C. (2021). *Los Angeles Homeless Services Authority (LAHSA) Homelessness Prevention Program Evaluation* [Doctoral dissertation]. California State University, Northridge.

Lotz, S. L., Eastlick, M. A., Mishra, A., & Shim, S. (2010). Understanding patrons' participation in activities at entertainment malls. *International Journal of Retail & Distribution Management*, *38*(6), 402–422. doi:10.1108/09590551011045366

Lucivero, F. (2020). Big data, big waste? A reflection on the environmental sustainability of big data initiatives. *Science and Engineering Ethics*, *26*(2), 1009–1030. doi:10.100711948-019-00171-7 PMID:31893331

Ludwig, C., Hecht, R., Lautenbach, S., Schorcht, M., & Zipf, A. (2021). Mapping Public Urban Green Spaces Based on OpenStreetMap and Sentinel-2 Imagery Using Belief Functions. *ISPRS International Journal of Geo-Information*, *10*(4), 251. Advance online publication. doi:10.3390/ijgi10040251

Lu, L., Kao, S.-F., Chang, T.-T., Wu, H.-S., & Cooper, C. L. (2008). Work/Family Demands, Work Flexibility, Work/Family Conflict, and Their Consequences at Work: A National Probability Sample in Taiwan. *International Journal of Stress Management*, *15*(1), 1–21. doi:10.1037/1072-5245.15.1.1

Lyon, L., Mattern, E., Acker, A., & Langmead, A. (2015). Applying translational principles to data science curriculum development. *Proceedings of the 12th International Conference on Digital Preservation*.

Ma, Y., Brindley, P., & Lange, E. (2023). From Modelling and Analysis of Accessibility of Urban Green Space to Green Infrastructure Planning: Guangzhou as a Case Study. In Adaptive Urban Transformation: Urban Landscape Dynamics, Regional Design and Territorial Governance in the Pearl River Delta, China (pp. 249–266). Springer.

Macdonald, J. L., Dolega, L., & Singleton, A. (2022). An open source delineation and hierarchical classification of UK retail agglomerations. *Scientific Data*, *9*(1), 541. Advance online publication. doi:10.103841597-022-01556-3 PMID:36057644

MacKerron, G., & Mourato, S. (2013). Happiness is greater in natural environments. *Global Environmental Change*, *23*(5), 992–1000. Advance online publication. doi:10.1016/j.gloenvcha.2013.03.010

Madasu Bhaskara Rao, C., & Lakshmi Hymavathi, M. M. (2018). Factors Affecting Female Consumer's Online Buying Behavior. *Academy of Marketing Studies Journal*, *22*(2), 1–20.

Madhumitha, D., & Naachimuthu, K. P. (2023). Emotional Regulation among the Members of LGBTQ+ Community. *Education and Society*, *47*(2), 34–45.

Madyatmadja, E. D., Hiererra, S. E., Sembiring, D. J. M., Karya, S., & Pristinella, D. (2022, August). Social Media in Business Intelligence as a Solution Toward Social Problems: A Systematic Literature Review. In *2022 International Conference on Information Management and Technology (ICIMTech)* (pp. 505-510). IEEE. 10.1109/ICIMTech55957.2022.9915261

Mahdi, O. R., & Almsafir, M. K. (2014). The role of strategic leadership in building sustainable competitive advantage in the academic environment. *Procedia: Social and Behavioral Sciences*, *129*, 289–296. doi:10.1016/j.sbspro.2014.03.679

Mainali, B., Luukkanen, J., Silveira, S., & Kaivo-oja, J. (2018). Evaluating synergies and trade-offs among sustainable development goals (SDGs): Explorative analyses of development paths in south Asia and sub-Saharan Africa. *Sustainability (Basel)*, *10*(3), 815. doi:10.3390u10030815

Maji, I. K., Sulaiman, C., & Abdul-Rahim, A. S. (2019). Renewable energy consumption and economic growth nexus: A fresh evidence from West Africa. *Energy Reports*, *5*, 384–392. doi:10.1016/j.egyr.2019.03.005

Makower, J., & Pike, C. (2008). Strategies for the green economy : opportunities and challenges in the new world of business. In Strategies.

Malarvizhi, J., & Chitra, D. (2018). A Study on Customer Satisfaction towards Patanjali Products in Theni Distr. International Research Journal of Management. *IT and Social Sciences*, *5*(2), 75–79.

Malhotra, N. K., & Peterson, M. (2001). Marketing research in the new millennium: Emerging issues and trends. *Marketing Intelligence & Planning*, *19*(4), 216–232. doi:10.1108/EUM0000000005560

Manikandan, M., & Amsaveni, N. (2016). Management Information System Research Output: A Scientometric Study. *Global Journal of Library and Information Science*, *5*(1), 21–27.

Manzhong, L. (2017). The Application of Virtual Reality Technology in the Preservation of Mining and Metallurgy Culture in Huangshi Region. *Proceedings of the 2017 IEEE International Conference on Information, Communication and Engineering*. 10.1109/ICICE.2017.8479067

María, J. J. L., Polo, O. C. C., & Elhadary, T. (2023). An Analysis of the Morality and Social Responsibility of Non-Profit Organizations. *FMDB Transactions on Sustainable Technoprise Letters*, *1*(1), 28–35.

Marjamäki, P. (2023). *Evolution and trends of business intelligence systems: a systematic mapping study*. Academic Press.

Marlinspike, M. (2013, November 26). *Advanced Cryptographic Ratcheting*. Retrieved from Signal: https://signal.org/blog/advanced-ratcheting/

Massaro, A. (2021b). Information Technology Infrastructures Supporting Industry 5.0 Facilities. In Electronics in Advanced Research Industries (pp. 51–101). Wiley.

Massaro, A., Galiano, A., Meuli, G., & Massari, S. F. (2018). Overview and Application of Enabling Technologies Oriented on Energy Routing Monitoring, on Network Installation and on Predictive Maintenance. *Int. J. Artif. Intell. Appl.*, *9*(2), 1–20.

Massaro, A. (2021a). *Electronic in Advanced Research Industry: From Industry 4.0 to Industry 5.0 Advances*. Wiley IEEE. doi:10.1002/9781119716907

Massaro, A. (2022a). Advanced Control Systems in Industry 5.0 Enabling Process Mining. *Sensors (Basel)*, *8677*(22), 22. doi:10.339022228677 PMID:36433272

Massaro, A. (2022b). Multi-Level Decision Support System in Production and Safety Management. *Knowledge (Beverly Hills, Calif.)*, *2*(4), 682–701. doi:10.3390/knowledge2040039

Massaro, A., Birardi, G., Manca, F., Marin, C., Birardi, V., Giannone, D., & Galiano, A. M. (2021). Innovative DSS for Intelligent Monitoring and Urban Square Design Approaches: A Case of Study. *Sustainable Cities and Society*, *102653*(102653), 65. doi:10.1016/j.scs.2020.102653

Massaro, A., & Starace, G. (2022). Advanced and Complex Energy Systems Monitoring and Control: A Review on Available Technologies and Their Application Criteria. *Sensors (Basel)*, *4929*(13), 22. doi:10.339022134929 PMID:35808429

Massaro, A., Vitti, V., Galiano, A., & Morelli, A. (2019). Business Intelligence Improved by Data Mining Algorithms and Big Data Systems: An Overview of Different Tools Applied in Industrial Research. *Computer Science and Information Technology (Alhambra, Calif.)*, *7*(1), 1–21. doi:10.13189/csit.2019.070101

Mastracci, S., & Hsieh, C. W. (2016). Emotional Labor and Job Stress in Caring Professions: Exploring Universalism and Particularism in Construct and Culture. *International Journal of Public Administration*, *39*(14), 1–9. doi:10.1080/01900692.2015.1068327

Mattijssen, T. J., Dijkshoorn-Dekker, M. W., Kortstee, H. J., Polman, N. B., & Snep, R. (2023). Nature-inclusive urban development: Lessons learned in three real estate projects in Dutch cities. *International Journal of Urban Sustainable Development*, *15*(1), 152–171. doi:10.1080/19463138.2023.2216654

Mattis, J. (2018). *National Defense Strategy of the United States of America*. Department of Defense Washington United States.

Mazzucato, M., & Semieniuk, G. (2018). Financing renewable energy: Who is financing what and why it matters. *Technological Forecasting and Social Change*, *127*, 8–22. doi:10.1016/j.techfore.2017.05.021

McDonnell, A., & Heard, C. (2023). *Centralize your RFP Process With Olive*. Retrieved November 4, 2023, from Olive Technologies website: https://olive.app

McDonnell, A., & Wiblen, S. (2020). *Talent management: A research overview*. Routledge. doi:10.4324/9780429342301

Mcgee, S., & Moore, H. (2014). *Women's rights and their money: a timeline from Cleopatra to Lilly Ledbetter*. Lilly Ledbetter.

McGuire, S. A. (2020). Products of Industry: Pollution, Health, and England's Industrial Revolution . *The Bioarchaeology of Structural Violence: A Theoretical Framework for Industrial Era Inequality*, 203-231.

McKinsey & Company. (2013). *How retailers can keep up with consumers*. https://www.mckinsey.com/industries/retail/our-insights/how-retailers-can-keep-up-with-consumers

McNurlin, B. C., & Sprague, R. H. (2001). *Information systems management in practice*. Prentice Hall PTR.

Meadows, D. H., Meadows, D. L., Randers, J., & Behrens, W. W. (2018). The Limits to Growth. In *Green planet blues* (pp. 25–29). Routledge. doi:10.4324/9780429493744-3

Mears, A. (2010). Size zero high-end ethnic: Cultural production and the reproduction of culture in fashion modeling. *Poetics*, *38*(1), 21–46. doi:10.1016/j.poetic.2009.10.002

Merle, A., Senecal, S., & St-Onge, A. (2012). Whether and how virtual try-on influences consumer responses to an apparel web site. *International Journal of Electronic Commerce*, *16*(3), 41–64. doi:10.2753/JEC1086-4415160302

Mert, I. (2021a). Analyzing the Sustainability of the Accounting Valuation Practices in Romania during the Adaptation Period to the European Union. *Revista Argentina de Clínica Psicológica*, *30*(1), 787–798.

Mert, I. (2021b). The Effects of the Qualitative Parameters of Internal Auditing Works on the Preferences of Investment Funds' Analysts. *Economic Alternatives*, (1), 60–71.

Mert, I. (2022). *Assessment of Accounting Evaluation Practices, A Research-Based Review of Turkey and Romania.* Springer Cham. https://link.springer.com/book/10.1007/978-3-030-98486-1

Mert, I. (2022b). Investigation Techniques, Methods, Types, and Increasing Impact of Forensic Accounting in Digital Period. *Maliye ve Finans Yazıları*, (118), 13–32. doi:10.33203/mfy.1084274

Messenger, J. C., & Gschwind, L. (2016). Three generations of Telework: New ICTs and the (R)evolution from home office to virtual office. *New Technology, Work and Employment*, *31*(3), 195–208. doi:10.1111/ntwe.12073

Michaels, E., Handfield-Jones, H., & Axelrod, B. (2001). *The war for talent.* Harvard Business Press.

Mishra, L., Gupta, T., & Shree, A. (2020). Online teaching-learning in higher education during lockdown period of COVID-19 pandemic. *International Journal of Educational Research Open*, *1*(100012), 100012. doi:10.1016/j.ijedro.2020.100012 PMID:35059663

Mitchell, R. K., Agle, B. R., & Wood, D. J. (1997). Toward a theory of stakeholder identification and salience: Defining the principle of who and what really counts. *Academy of Management Review*, *22*(4), 853. doi:10.2307/259247

Mnyakin, M. (2020). Investigating the Impacts of AR, AI, and Website Optimization on Ecommerce Sales Growth. *ResearchBerg Review of Science and Technology*, *3*(1), 116–130.

Močarniková, K., & Greguš, M. (2019). Conceptualization of Predictive Analytics by Literature Review. In *Data-Centric Business and Applications* (pp. 205–234). Springer International Publishing.

Mohamad Rodzi, N. A. H., Othman, M. S., & Yusuf, L. M. (2015). Significance of data integration and ETL in the business intelligence framework for higher education. In *2015 International Conference on Science in Information Technology (ICSITech).* IEEE. 10.1109/ICSITech.2015.7407800

Möhring, K., Naumann, E., Reifenscheid, M., Wenz, A., Rettig, T., Krieger, U., … Blom, A. G. (2021). The COVID-19 pandemic and subjective well-being: longitudinal evidence on satisfaction with work and family. *European Societies*, *23*(sup1), S601–S617. doi:10.1080/14616696.2020.1833066

Mohsan, S. A. H., Othman, N. Q. H., Khan, M. A., Amjad, H., & Żywiołek, J. (2022). A comprehensive review of micro UAV charging techniques. *Micromachines*, *13*(6), 977. doi:10.3390/mi13060977 PMID:35744592

Moosmayer, D. C., & Fuljahn, A. (2010). Consumer perceptions of cause related marketing campaigns. *Journal of Consumer Marketing*, *27*(6), 543–549. doi:10.1108/07363761011078280

Moradi, S., Ansari, R., & Taherkhani, R. (2022). A systematic analysis of construction performance management: Key performance indicators from 2000 to 2020. *Civil Engineering (Shiraz)*, *46*(1), 15–31. doi:10.100740996-021-00626-7

Mora-Esperanza, J. G. (2004). Artificial intelligence applied to real estate valuation: An example for the appraisal of Madrid. *Catastro*, *1*, 255–265.

Moretti, E. (2013). Real Wage Inequality. American Economic Journal. *American Economic Journal. Applied Economics*, *5*(1), 65–103. doi:10.1257/app.5.1.65

Morgan, N. A., Whitler, K. A., Feng, H., & Chari, S. (2019). Research in marketing strategy. *Journal of the Academy of Marketing Science*, *47*(1), 4–29, 47. doi:10.100711747-018-0598-1

Mourad, M. (2016). Recycling, recovering, and preventing "food waste": Competing solutions for food systems sustainability in the United States and France. *Journal of Cleaner Production*, *126*, 461–477. doi:10.1016/j.jclepro.2016.03.084

Muisyo, P. K., & Qin, S. (2021). Enhancing the FIRM'S green performance through green HRM: The moderating role of green innovation culture. *Journal of Cleaner Production, 289*, 125720. doi:10.1016/j.jclepro.2020.125720

Muisyo, P. K., Su, Q., Hashmi, H. B. A., Ho, T. H., & Julius, M. M. (2022). The role of green HRM in driving hotels' green creativity. *International Journal of Contemporary Hospitality Management, 34*(4), 1331–1352. doi:10.1108/IJCHM-07-2021-0833

Mukhtarov, S., Mikayilov, J. I., Maharramov, S., Aliyev, J., & Suleymanov, E. (2022). Higher oil prices, are they good or bad for renewable energy consumption: The case of Iran? *Renewable Energy, 186*, 411–419. doi:10.1016/j.renene.2021.12.135

Muraleedharan, N., & Hudson, J. B. (2007). Tea cultivation in south India: Agricultural policies. *Planters' Chronicle (Philadelphia, Pa.), 103*(1), 6–41.

Naachimuthu, K. P., Ganga, S., & Mathiyoli, P. M. (2022). Psychosocial Impact of COVID-19 Lockdown. *IAHRW International Journal of Social Sciences Review, 10*(1), 52–59.

Nagarajan, G., & Naachimuthu, K. P. (2021). Positive Emotions and Experiences of Trans Men and Trans Women - A Grounded Theory Approach. *International Journal of Early Childhood Special Education, 14*(2), 6430–6447.

Narayan, S., & Doytch, N. (2017). An investigation of renewable and non-renewable energy consumption and economic growth nexus using industrial and residential energy consumption. *Energy Economics, 68*, 160–176. doi:10.1016/j.eneco.2017.09.005

Nations, U. (2018). *Renewable energy sources cut carbon emissions, efficiently increase electricity output worldwide, delegates say in second committee.* https://press.un.org/en/2018/gaef3501.doc.htm

Nazir, S., & Ul Haq, Z. (2018). Exploring Women's attitude in Online Shopping-A review of Literature. *International Journal of Enhanced Research in Management & Computer Applications, 7*(3), 556–570.

Naz, S., Sultan, R., Zaman, K., Aldakhil, A. M., Nassani, A. A., & Abro, M. M. (2019). Moderating and mediating role of renewable energy consumption, FDI inflows, and economic growth on carbon dioxide emissions: Evidence from robust least square estimator. *Environmental Science and Pollution Research International, 26*(3), 2806–2819. doi:10.100711356-018-3837-6 PMID:30488245

Nededog, J. (2015, May 27). *Mark Cuban's Cyber Dust is Producing its First Original Web Series.* Retrieved from Business Insider: https://www.businessinsider.in/mark-cubans-cyber-dust-is-producing-its-first-original-web-series/articleshow/47436464.cms

Neville, B. A., Bell, S. J., & Menguc, B. (2005). Corporate reputation, stakeholders and the social performance - financial performance relationship. *European Journal of Marketing, 39*(9), 1184–1198. doi:10.1108/03090560510610798

Ngoc, N. M. (2023). The relevance of factors affecting real estate investment decisions for post pandemic time. *International Journal of Business and Globalisation.*

Nguyen, T. S., Mohamed, S., & Panuwatwanich, K. (2018). Stakeholder management in complex project: Review of contemporary literature. *Journal of Engineering, Project, and Production Management, 8*(2), 75–89. doi:10.32738/JEPPM.201807.0003

Nilles, J. M. (1988). Traffic reduction by telecommuting: A status review and selected bibliography. *Transportation Research Part A, General, 22*(4), 301–317. doi:10.1016/0191-2607(88)90008-8

Nisar, Q. A., Nasir, N., Jamshed, S., Naz, S., Ali, M., & Ali, S. (2021). Big data management and environmental performance: Role of big data decision-making capabilities and decision-making quality. *Journal of Enterprise Information Management, 34*(4), 1061–1096. doi:10.1108/JEIM-04-2020-0137

Nizam, N. Z., & Mansor, N. (2019). Analyzing Customer Satisfaction: Consumer Behavior towards the Selection of Beauty Products in Klang Valley. *International Journal of Human and Technology Interaction, 3*(2), 55–60.

Nordhaus, W. (2013). The climate casino: Risk, uncertainty, and economics for a warming world. Yale University Press.

Obeidat, B. (2012). The Relationship between Human Resource Information System (HRIS) Functions and Human Resource Management (HRM) Functionalities). *Journal of Management Research, 4*(4). Advance online publication. doi:10.5296/jmr.v4i4.2262

Ocoró, M. P., Polo, O. C. C., & Khandare, S. (2023). Importance of Business Financial Risk Analysis in SMEs According to COVID-19. *FMDB Transactions on Sustainable Management Letters, 1*(1), 12–21.

Ogunjimi, A., Rahman, M., Islam, N., & Hasan, R. (2021). Smart mirror fashion technology for the retail chain transformation. *Technological Forecasting and Social Change, 173*, 121118. doi:10.1016/j.techfore.2021.121118

Ogunmola, G. A., Singh, B., Sharma, D. K., Regin, R., Rajest, S. S., & Singh, N. (2021). Involvement of distance measure in assessing and resolving efficiency environmental obstacles. In *2021 International Conference on Computational Intelligence and Knowledge Economy (ICCIKE)*. IEEE. 10.1109/ICCIKE51210.2021.9410765

Oh, H., Yoon, S. Y., & Hawley, J. (2004). What virtual reality can offer to the furniture industry. *Journal of Textile and Apparel. Technology and Management, 4*(1), 1–17.

Omar, M., Williams, R. L. Jr, & Lingelbach, D. (2009). Global brand market-entry strategy to manage corporate reputation. *Journal of Product and Brand Management, 18*(3), 177–187. doi:10.1108/10610420910957807

Osipova, O. (2019). Digital trasformation of personnel management services. In *International Conference on Digital Technologies in Logistics and Infrastructure (ICDTLI2019)*. Atlantis Press.

Osman, A. I., Chen, L., Yang, M., Msigwa, G., Farghali, M., Fawzy, S., Rooney, D. W., & Yap, P. S. (2023). Cost, environmental impact, and resilience of renewable energy under a changing climate: A review. *Environmental Chemistry Letters, 21*(2), 741–764. Advance online publication. doi:10.100710311-022-01532-8

Ostergren, K. A., Gustavsson, J., Hansen, O.-J., Møller, H., Anderson, G., Bellettato, C., Gaiani, S., & … . (2014). *FUSIONS Definitional Framework for Food Waste*. EU FUSIONS.

Overgoor, G., Chica, M., Rand, W., & Weishampel, A. (2019). Letting the computers take over: Using ai to solve marketing problems. *California Management Review, 61*(4), 156–185. doi:10.1177/0008125619859318

Ozcelik, A. B., & Varnali, K. (2019). Effectiveness of online behavioral targeting: A psychological perspective. *Electronic Commerce Research and Applications, 33*, 33. doi:10.1016/j.elerap.2018.11.006

Pachoulakis, I., & Kapetanakis, K. (2012). Augmented reality platforms for virtual fitting rooms. *The International Journal of Multimedia & Its Applications, 4*(4), 35–46. doi:10.5121/ijma.2012.4404

Padhan, H., Padhang, P. C., Tiwari, A. K., Ahmed, R., & Hammoudeh, S. (2020). Renewable energy consumption and robust globalization (s) in OECD countries: do oil, carbon emissions and economic activity matter? *Energy Strategy Reviews, 32*(100535).

Padmapriya, P., & Naachimuthu, K. P. (2023). Social and Philosophical Construction of Emotions in Bhagavad Gita & Plutchik Wheel of Emotions. *Journal of the Asiatic Society of Mumbai, XCVI*(27), 22–36.

Page, S. J., Forer, P., & Lawton, G. R. (1999). Small business development and tourism: Terra incognita? *Tourism Management, 20*(4), 435–459. Advance online publication. doi:10.1016/S0261-5177(99)00024-2

Pagourtzi, E., Metaxiotis, K., Nikolopoulos, K., Giannelos, K., & Assimakopoulos, V. (2007). Real estate valuation with artificial intelligence approaches. *International Journal of Intelligent Systems Technologies and Applications*, 2(1), 50–57. doi:10.1504/IJISTA.2007.011573

Pande, S. D., & Chetty, M. S. R. (2021). Fast medicinal leaf retrieval using CapsNet. In *Advances in Intelligent Systems and Computing* (pp. 149–155). Springer Singapore.

Pande, S., & Chetty, M. S. R. (2018). Analysis of Capsule Network (Capsnet) Architectures and Applications. *Journal of Advanced Research in Dynamical and Control Systems*, 10(10), 2765–2771.

Pande, S., & Chetty, M. S. R. (2019). Bezier Curve Based Medicinal Leaf Classification using Capsule Network. *International Journal of Advanced Trends in Computer Science and Engineering*, 8(6), 2735–2742. doi:10.30534/ijatcse/2019/09862019

Pandit, P. (2023). On the Context of the Principle of Beneficence: The Problem of Over Demandingness within Utilitarian Theory. *FMDB Transactions on Sustainable Social Sciences Letters*, 1(1), 26–42.

Pantano, E., Pedeliento, G., & Christodoulides, G. (2022). A strategic framework for technological innovations in support of the customer experience: A focus on luxury retailers. *Journal of Retailing and Consumer Services*, 66, 102959. doi:10.1016/j.jretconser.2022.102959

Pantano, E., & Willems, K. (2022). *Retail in a New World: Recovering from the Pandemic that Changed the World*. Emerald Group Publishing. doi:10.1108/9781801178464

Paoletti, J. B. (2012). Pink and Blue: Telling the Boys from the Girls in America. *America*.

Papahristou, E., & Bilalis, N. (2016). A new sustainable product development model in apparel based on 3D technologies for virtual proper fit. In *Sustainable Design and Manufacturing 2016* (pp. 85–95). Springer International Publishing. doi:10.1007/978-3-319-32098-4_8

Parent, M. M., & Deephouse, D. L. (2007). A case study of stakeholder identification and prioritization by managers. *Journal of Business Ethics*, 75(1), 1–23. doi:10.100710551-007-9533-y

Paroutis, S., Bennett, M., & Heracleous, L. (2014). A strategic view on smart city technology: The case of IBM Smarter Cities during a recession. *Technological Forecasting and Social Change*, 89, 262–272. doi:10.1016/j.techfore.2013.08.041

Pastorino, R., De Vito, C., Migliara, G., Glocker, K., Binenbaum, I., Ricciardi, W., & Boccia, S. (2019). Benefits and challenges of Big Data in healthcare: An overview of the European initiatives. *European Journal of Public Health*, 29(Supplement_3), 23–27. doi:10.1093/eurpub/ckz168 PMID:31738444

Pata, U. K. (2018). Renewable energy consumption, urbanization, financial development, income and CO2 emissions in Turkey: Testing EKC hypothesis with structural breaks. *Journal of Cleaner Production*, 187, 770–779. doi:10.1016/j.jclepro.2018.03.236

Pathak, S. K. (2022). *Role of sebi: Cross border merger, takeover code*. Retrieved November 2, 2023, from Ijirl.com website: https://ijirl.com/wp-content/uploads/2022/03/ROLE-OF-SEBI-CROSS-BORDER-MERGER-TAKEOVER-CODE.pdf

Patil, H. A. (2010). "Cry Baby": Using Spectrographic Analysis to Assess Neonatal Health Status from an Infant's Cry. *Advances in speech recognition: Mobile environments, call centers and clinics*, 323-348.

Patten, M. L., & Newhart, M. (2017). *Understanding research methods: An overview of the essentials*. Routledge. doi:10.4324/9781315213033

Paudel, P. K., Bastola, R., Eigenbrode, S. D., Borzée, A., Thapa, S., Rad, D., & Adhikari, S. (2022). Perspectives of scholars on the origin, spread and consequences of COVID-19 are diverse but not polarized. *Humanities & Social Sciences Communications, 9*(1), 1–11. doi:10.105741599-022-01216-2

Pedrini, M., & Ferri, L. M. (2019). Stakeholder management: A systematic literature review. *Corporate Governance (Bradford), 19*(1), 44–59. doi:10.1108/CG-08-2017-0172

Pedrycz, W., & Chen, S. M. (Eds.). (2014). *Information granularity, big data, and computational intelligence* (Vol. 8). Springer.

Peloza, J., Loock, M., Cerruti, J., & Muyot, M. (2012). Sustainability: How stakeholder perceptions differ from corporate reality. *California Management Review, 55*(1), 74–97. doi:10.1525/cmr.2012.55.1.74

Peng, J., Chen, X., Zou, Y., & Nie, Q. (2021). Environmentally specific transformational leadership and team pro-environmental behaviors: The roles of pro-environmental goal clarity, pro-environmental harmonious passion, and power distance. *Human Relations; Studies towards the Integration of the Social Sciences, 74*(11), 1864–1888. doi:10.1177/0018726720942306

Pereira, A. M., Moura, J. A. B., Costa, E. D. B., Vieira, T., Landim, A. R., Bazaki, E., & Wanick, V. (2022). Customer models for artificial intelligence-based decision support in fashion online retail supply chains. *Decision Support Systems, 158*, 113795. doi:10.1016/j.dss.2022.113795

Pham, H., & Kim, S.-Y. (2019). The effects of sustainable practices and managers' leadership competences on sustainability performance of construction firms. *Sustainable Production and Consumption, 20*, 1–14. doi:10.1016/j.spc.2019.05.003

Phan, D. D. (2003). E-business development for competitive advantages: A case study. *Information & Management, 40*(6), 581–590. Advance online publication. doi:10.1016/S0378-7206(02)00089-7

Philip, G., & Graham, T. (2017). *Big Data in Social Welfare: The Development of a Critical Perspective on Social Work's Latest*. Electronic Turn.

Phoek, S. E. M., Lauwinata, L., & Kowarin, L. R. N. (2023). Tourism Development in Merauke Regency, South Papua Province: Strengthening Physical Infrastructure for Local Economic Growth and Enchanting Tourist Attractions. *FMDB Transactions on Sustainable Management Letters, 1*(2), 82–94.

Pick, J. B., Turetken, O., Deokar, A. V., & Sarkar, A. (2017). Location analytics and decision support: Reflections on recent advancements, a research framework, and the path ahead. *Decision Support Systems, 99*, 1–8. doi:10.1016/j.dss.2017.05.016

Pigou, A. C. (1920). *The Economics of Welfare*. Macmillan.

Pinter, G., Mosavi, A., & Felde, I. (2020). Artificial intelligence for modeling real estate price using call detail records and hybrid machine learning approach. *Entropy (Basel, Switzerland), 22*(12), 1421. doi:10.3390/e22121421 PMID:33339406

Plotkina, D., & Saurel, H. (2019). Me or just like me? The role of virtual try-on and physical appearance in apparel M-retailing. *Journal of Retailing and Consumer Services, 51*, 362–377. doi:10.1016/j.jretconser.2019.07.002

Porter, M. E., & Kramer, M. R. (2011). Creating Shared Value. *Harvard Business Review*, 89.

Porter, M. E., & Kramer, M. R. (2019). Creating shared value: How to reinvent capitalism-and unleash a wave of innovation and growth. In *Managing Sustainable Business* (pp. 323–346). Springer Netherlands. doi:10.1007/978-94-024-1144-7_16

Pospiech, M., & Felden, C. (2015, October). Towards a big data theory model. In *2015 IEEE International Conference on Big Data (Big Data)* (pp. 2082-2090). IEEE. 10.1109/BigData.2015.7363990

Post, J. E., Preston, L. E., & Sachs, S. (2002). Managing the extended enterprise: The new stakeholder view. *California Management Review*, *45*(1), 6–28. doi:10.2307/41166151

Prasad, A., Krithika, & Gudimetla, S. (2019). A study of digital shopping behaviour of women with respect to beauty and personal care products. SSRN *Electronic Journal*. doi:10.2139/ssrn.3307014

Principato, L., Di Leo, A., Mattia, G., & Pratesi, C. A. (2021). The next step in sustainable dining: The restaurant food waste map for the management of food waste. *Ital. J. Mark.*, *2021*(3), 189–207. doi:10.100743039-021-00032-x

Principato, L., Mattia, G., Di Leo, A., & Pratesi, C. A. (2021). The household wasteful behavior framework: A systematic review of consumer food waste. *Industrial Marketing Management*, *93*, 641–649. doi:10.1016/j.indmarman.2020.07.010

Priscila, S. S., Rajest, S. S., Tadiboina, S. N., Regin, R., & András, S. (2023). Analysis of Machine Learning and Deep Learning Methods for Superstore Sales Prediction. *FMDB Transactions on Sustainable Computer Letters*, *1*(1), 1–11.

Priyadarshini, N. S., & Naachimuthu, K. P. (2020). Ancient and Modern Conception to Virtues: Comparing Naaladiyar and Positive Psychology. In *International Conference on Multi Facets of Sacred Literature* (pp. 1–12). Academic Press.

Provost, F., & Fawcett, T. (2013). *Data Science for Business: What you need to know about data mining and data-analytic thinking*. O'Reilly Media, Inc.

Pruitt, J., & Adlin, T. (2010). *The persona lifecycle: keeping people in mind throughout product design*. Elsevier.

PTI. (2022). Videocon Group insolvency: NCLAT junks Anil Agarwal-led firm's takeover, calls for fresh bids. *The New Indian Express*. Retrieved from https://www.newindianexpress.com/business/2022/jan/05/videocon-group-insolvency-nclat-junks-anil-agarwal-led-firms-takeover-calls-for-fresh-bids-2403388.html

Puncheva, P. (2008). The role of corporate reputation in the stakeholder decision-making process. *Business & Society*, *47*(3), 272–290. doi:10.1177/0007650306297946

Qasem, Z. (2021). The effect of positive TRI traits on centennials adoption of try-on technology in the context of E-fashion retailing. *International Journal of Information Management*, *56*, 102254. doi:10.1016/j.ijinfomgt.2020.102254 PMID:33106720

Qiu, J., Wu, Q., Ding, G., Xu, Y., & Feng, S. (2016). A survey of machine learning for big data processing. *EURASIP Journal on Advances in Signal Processing*, *2016*, 1–16.

Quasim, D. R. M. D. T. (2015). Artificial Intelligence as a business forecasting and error handling tool, COMPUSOFT an International Journal of Advanced Computer Technology. *Chattopadhyay R*, *4*(2), 1534–1537.

Qudrat-Ullah, H., & Nevo, C. M. (2021). The impact of renewable energy consumption and environmental sustainability on economic growth in Africa. *Energy Reports*, *7*, 3877–3886. doi:10.1016/j.egyr.2021.05.083

Rabby, F., Chimhundu, R., & Hassan, R. (2022). Digital Transformation in Real Estate Marketing: A Review. *Big Data: A Road Map for Successful Digital Marketing*, 39.

Rad, D., Balas, E., Ignat, S., Rad, G., & Dixon, D. (2020). A Predictive Model of Youth Bystanders' Helping Attitudes. *Revista romaneasca pentru educatie multidimensionala-Journal for Multidimensional Education*, *12*(1Sup2), 136-150.

Rad, D., Dughi, T., & Demeter, E. (2019). The Dynamics of the Relationship between Humor and Benevolence as Values. *Revista romaneasca pentru educatie multidimensionala-Journal for Multidimensional Education*, *11*(3), 201-212.

Rad, D., Rad, G., Maier, R., Demeter, E., Dicu, A., Popa, M., & Mărineanu, V. D. (2022). A Fuzzy logic modelling approach on psychological data. *Journal of Intelligent & Fuzzy Systems*, (Preprint), 1-11.

Rad, D., & Balas, V. E. (2020). A Novel Fuzzy Scoring Approach of Behavioural Interviews in Personnel Selection. BRAIN. *Broad Research in Artificial Intelligence and Neuroscience, 11*(2), 178–188. doi:10.18662/brain/11.2/81

Rad, D., Egerau, A., Roman, A., Dughi, T., Balas, E., Maier, R., & Rad, G. (2022). A Preliminary Investigation of the Technology Acceptance Model (TAM) in Early Childhood Education and Care. BRAIN. *Broad Research in Artificial Intelligence and Neuroscience, 13*(1), 518–533. doi:10.18662/brain/13.1/297

Rad, D., & Rad, G. (2021). Going Agile, a Post-Pandemic Universal Work Paradigm-A Theoretical Narrative Review. *Postmodern Openings, 12*(4), 337–388. doi:10.18662/po/12.4/380

Radhakrishnan, B., Durairaj, J., Mathew, M., Kumar, P., Udhayabahnu, K. G., Sankaranarayanan, P., & Liango, R. J. (2021). Performance of South Indian tea industry during last one decade and challenges ahead. *Bulletin of UPASI Tea Research Foundation, 56*, 3–15.

Radmehr, R., Henneberry, S. R., & Shayanmehr, S. (2021). Renewable energy consumption, CO_2 emissions, and economic growth nexus: A simultaneity spatial modeling analysis of EU countries. *Structural Change and Economic Dynamics, 57*, 13–27. doi:10.1016/j.strueco.2021.01.006

Raghupathi, W., & Raghupathi, V. (2014). Big data analytics in healthcare: Promise and potential. *Health Information Science and Systems, 2*(1), 3. doi:10.1186/2047-2501-2-3 PMID:25825667

Rainey, D. L. (2006). Sustainable business development: Inventing the future through strategy, innovation, and leadership. In *Sustainable Business Development*. Inventing the Future Through Strategy, Innovation, and Leadership. doi:10.1017/CBO9780511617607.015

Räisänen, J., Ojala, A., & Tuovinen, T. (2021). Building trust in the sharing economy: Current approaches and future considerations. *Journal of Cleaner Production, 279*(123724), 123724. doi:10.1016/j.jclepro.2020.123724

Rajabifard, A., & Williamson, I. P. (2001). Spatial data infrastructures: concept, SDI hierarchy and future directions. *Proceedings of GEOMATICS*, 10. https://doi.org/10.1.1.9.1919

Rajasekaran, N., Jagatheesan, S. M., Krithika, S., & Albanchez, J. S. (2023). Development and Testing of Incorporated ASM with MVP Architecture Model for Android Mobile App Development. *FMDB Transactions on Sustainable Computing Systems, 1*(2), 65–76.

Rajest, S. S., Singh, B. J., Obaid, A., Regin, R., & Chinnusamy, K. (2023a). Recent developments in machine and human intelligence. *Advances in Computational Intelligence and Robotics*. Advance online publication. doi:10.4018/978-1-6684-9189-8

Rajest, S. S., Singh, B., Obaid, A. J., Regin, R., & Chinnusamy, K. (2023b). Advances in artificial and human intelligence in the modern era. *Advances in Computational Intelligence and Robotics*. Advance online publication. doi:10.4018/979-8-3693-1301-5

Ramamoorthy, G., Suguna, M., Kumaravadivelu, P., & Sairam, C. (2012). Intercrop in tea with medicinal plants in the Nilgiris. In Abstracts of Papers. PLACROSYMXX.

Ramesh Kumar, V., Selvaraj, M., Venkateswaran, P. S., Sabarirajan, A., & Shatila, K., & Varsha Agarwal. (2022). The impact of training and development programs on employees' performance: The case of Lebanese SMEs. *International Journal of Intellectual Property Management, 12*(3).

Ramos, J. I., Lacerona, R., & Nunag, J. M. (2023). A Study on Operational Excellence, Work Environment Factors and the Impact to Employee Performance. *FMDB Transactions on Sustainable Social Sciences Letters, 1*(1), 12–25.

Ramu, V. B., & Yeruva, A. R. (2023). Optimising AIOps system performance for e-commerce and online retail businesses with the ACF model. *International Journal of Intellectual Property Management*, 13(3/4), 412–429. doi:10.1504/IJIPM.2023.134064

Ramya, N., & Dr Sa, A. M. (2019). Factors affecting consumer buying behaviour. *International Journal of Advanced Research*, 7(1), 563–568. doi:10.21474/IJAR01/8362

Ranasinghe, P., Wathurapatha, W. S., Mathangasinghe, Y., & Ponnamperuma, G. (2017). Emotional intelligence, perceived stress and academic performance of Sri Lankan medical undergraduates. *BMC Medical Education*, 17(1), 41. Advance online publication. doi:10.118612909-017-0884-5 PMID:28219419

Ranchordas, S. (2014). *Does sharing mean caring? Regulating innovation in the sharing economy.* Retrieved from https://papers.ssrn.com/abstract=2492798

Rastogi, A. K. (2010). A study of Indian online consumers & their buying behaviour. *International Research Journal*, 1(10), 80–82.

Rathore, M. M., Ahmad, A., Paul, A., & Jeon, G. (2015). Efficient graph-oriented smart transportation using internet of things generated big data. In *Proceedings of the 11th International Conference on Signal-Image Technology & Internet-Based Systems* (SITIS) (pp. 512–519). IEEE. 10.1109/SITIS.2015.121

Raunaque, N., Zeeshan, Md., & Imam, A. Md. (2016). Consumer perception towards online marketing in India, International Journal of Advanced Engineering. *Management Science*, 2(8), 1236–1240.

Reenu, M., & Panwar, J. S. (2013). Current trends in employee welfare schemes in Udaipur Retail Sector. *International Journal of Scientific Research Review*, 2(2), 44–54.

ReFed. (2018). *Restaurant Food Waste Action Guide.* Rethink Food Waste.

Regin, R., Khanna, A. A., Krishnan, V., Gupta, M., Bose, R. S., & Rajest, S. S. (2023). Information design and unifying approach for secured data sharing using attribute-based access control mechanisms. In Recent Developments in Machine and Human Intelligence (pp. 256–276). IGI Global.

Renwick, D. W. S., Redman, T., & Maguire, S. (2013). Green HRM: Teaching and learning guide. *International Journal of Management Reviews*.

Rest, K. D., & Hirsch, P. (2022). Insights and decision support for home health care services in times of disasters. *Central European Journal of Operations Research*, 30(1), 133–157. Advance online publication. doi:10.100710100-021-00770-5 PMID:34366709

Ricker, F., & Kalakota, R. (1999). Order fulfillment: the hidden key to e-commerce success. *Supply Chain Management Review*, 11(3), 60-70.

Rifat, M. R., Moutushy, S., & Ferdous, H. S. (2012). A Location Based Advertisement scheme using OpenStreetMap. *Proceeding of the 15th International Conference on Computer and Information Technology, ICCIT 2012*, 423–428. 10.1109/ICCITechn.2012.6509801

Rigby, D. (2011). The future of shopping. *Harvard Business Review*, 89(12), 65–76.

Ringle, C., Da Silva, D., & Bido, D. (2015). Structural equation modeling with the SmartPLS. *Brazilian Journal Of Marketing*, 13(2).

Roberts, M. L., Nguyen, L. D. B., Tra, M. C., & Nguyen, L. H. (2021). Artificial intelligence in personalized marketing: A systematic literature review. *International Journal of Electronic Commerce*, 25(3), 327–364. doi:10.1080/10864415.2021.1914232

Rodríguez-Rivero, R., Yáñez, S., Fernández-Aller, C., & Carrasco-Gallego, R. (2020). Is it time for a revolution in work–life balance? Reflections from Spain. *Sustainability (Basel)*, 12(22), 9563. doi:10.3390u12229563

Roman, A., Rad, D., Egerau, A., Dixon, D., Dughi, T., Kelemen, G., & Rad, G. (2020). Physical Self-Schema Acceptance and Perceived Severity of Online Aggressiveness in Cyberbullying Incidents. *Journal of Interdisciplinary Studies in Education*, 9(1), 100–116. doi:10.32674/jise.v9i1.1961

Rossini, P. (2000, January). Using expert systems and artificial intelligence for real estate forecasting. In *Sixth Annual Pacific-Rim Real Estate Society Conference, Sydney, Australia* (pp. 24-27). Academic Press.

Rousille, N. (2021). *The Central Role of the Ask Gap in Gender Pay Inequality*. Academic Press.

Runting, R. K., Phinn, S., Xie, Z., Venter, O., & Watson, J. E. (2020). Opportunities for big data in conservation and sustainability. *Nature Communications*, 11(1), 2003. doi:10.103841467-020-15870-0 PMID:32332744

Sabherwal, R., Jeyaraj, A., & Chowa, C. (2006). Information system success: Individual and organizational determinants. *Management Science*, 52(12), 1849–1864. doi:10.1287/mnsc.1060.0583

Sabti, Y. M., Alqatrani, R. I. N., Zaid, M. I., Taengkliang, B., & Kareem, J. M. (2023). Impact of Business Environment on the Performance of Employees in the Public-Listed Companies. *FMDB Transactions on Sustainable Management Letters*, 1(2), 56–65.

Sahoo, M. (2019). Structural equation modeling: Threshold criteria for assessing model fit. In *Methodological issues in management research: Advances, challenges, and the way ahead*. Emerald Publishing Limited. doi:10.1108/978-1-78973-973-220191016

Sahoo, N., Dellarocas, C., & Srinivasan, S. (2018). The impact of online product reviews on product returns. *Information Systems Research*, 29(3), 723–738. doi:10.1287/isre.2017.0736

Said, F. B., & Tripathi, S. (2023). Epistemology of Digital Journalism Shift in South Global Nations: A Bibliometric Analysis. *FMDB Transactions on Sustainable Technoprise Letters*, 1(1), 47–60.

Saleem, M., Qadeer, F., Mahmood, F., Ariza-Montes, A., & Han, H. (2020). Ethical leadership and employee green behavior: A multilevel moderated mediation analysis. *Sustainability (Basel)*, 12(8), 3314. doi:10.3390u12083314

Salovey, P., & Mayer, J. D. (1990). Emotional Intelligence. *Imagination, Cognition and Personality*, 9(3), 185–211. doi:10.2190/DUGG-P24E-52WK-6CDG

Sanjeev, M. A., Khademizadeh, S., Arumugam, T., & Tripathi, D. K. (2022). Generation Z and intention to use the digital library: Does personality matter? *The Electronic Library*, 40(1/2), 18–37. doi:10.1108/EL-04-2021-0082

Santos-Vijande, M. L., López-Sánchez, J. Á., & Trespalacios, J. A. (2012). How organizational learning affects a firm's flexibility, competitive strategy, and performance. *Journal of Business Research*, 65(8), 1079–1089. doi:10.1016/j.jbusres.2011.09.002

Sanyal, S., Kalimuthu, M., Arumugam, T., Aruna, R., Balaji, J., Savarimuthu, A., & Patil, S. (2023). Internet of Things and Its Relevance to Digital Marketing. In *Opportunities and Challenges of Industrial IoT in 5G and 6G Networks* (pp. 138–154). IGI Global. doi:10.4018/978-1-7998-9266-3.ch007

Saravanakumar, A., & Bojan, S. K. (2018). A study on female customer satisfaction on hair oil and beauty cream with special reference to Himalaya products in Coimbatore district. *International Journal of Management Studies, 5*(Special4), 23.

Sarkar, K. (2008). Globalization, restructuring and labor flexibility in tea plantations in West Bengal. *The Indian Journal of Labour Economics : the Quarterly Journal of the Indian Society of Labour Economics, 51*(4), 643–654.

Sattayaraksa, T., & Boon-itt, S. (2016). CEO transformational leadership and the new product development process: The mediating roles of organizational learning and innovation culture. *Leadership and Organization Development Journal, 37*(6), 730–749. doi:10.1108/LODJ-10-2014-0197

Savya, N., & Naachimuthu, K. P. (2022). Psychosocial Determinants of Name Dropping: A Conceptual Framework. *Madhya Bharti - Humanities and Social Sciences, 83*(14), 1–12.

Saxena, D., Khandare, S., & Chaudhary, S. (2023). An Overview of ChatGPT: Impact on Academic Learning. *FMDB Transactions on Sustainable Techno Learning, 1*(1), 11–20.

Sayers, R. C. (2012). The cost of being female: Critical comment on block. *Journal of Business Ethics, 106*(4), 519–524. doi:10.100710551-011-1017-4

SBNGP. (2019). *The Economic, Social, and Environmental Case for Green City, Clean Waters: An Update.* https://www.sbnphiladelphia.org/wp-content/uploads/2021/04/SBN-GCCW-Report-071219.pdf

Schanes, K., Dobernig, K., & Gözet, B. (2018). Food waste matters-A systematic review of household food waste practices and their policy implications. *Journal of Cleaner Production, 182*, 978–991. doi:10.1016/j.jclepro.2018.02.030

Schmelzer, J., Röpke, G., & Mahnke, R. (1999). *Aggregation phenomena in complex systems.* Wiley-Vch.

Schneider, D., & Seelmeyer, U. (2019). Challenges in using big data to develop decision support systems for social work in Germany. *Journal of Technology in Human Services, 37*(2-3), 113–128. doi:10.1080/15228835.2019.1614513

Schoech, D., Fitch, D., MacFadden, R., & Schkade, L. L. (2002). From data to intelligence: Introducing the intelligent organization. *Administration in Social Work, 26*(1), 1–21. doi:10.1300/J147v26n01_01

Seagraves, P. (2023). Real Estate Insights: Is the AI revolution a real estate boon or bane? *Journal of Property Investment & Finance.* Advance online publication. doi:10.1108/JPIF-05-2023-0045

Seddighi, H. R., & Mathew, S. (2020). Innovation and regional development via the firm's core competence: Some recent evidence from North East England. *Journal of Innovation & Knowledge, 5*(4), 219–227. doi:10.1016/j.jik.2019.12.005

Seife, C. (2007). *Decoding the universe: How the new science of information is explaining everything in the cosmos, from our brains to black holes.* Penguin.

Selvaraj, M. S., & Gopalakrishnan, S. (2016). Nightmares of an agricultural capitalist economy: Tea plantation workers in the nilgiris. *Economic and Political Weekly, 51*(18), 107–113. https://www.jstor.org/stable/44004242

Semenzato, P., & Bortolini, L. (2023). Urban Heat Island Mitigation and Urban Green Spaces: Testing a Model in the City of Padova (Italy). *Land (Basel), 12*(2), 476. Advance online publication. doi:10.3390/land12020476

Sentiment analysis. (2022). Retrieved October 25, 2023, from Thematic website: https://getthematic.com/sentiment-analysis/

Sethi, S., & Saini, N. K. (2020). COVID-19: Opinions and Challenges of School Teachers on WFH. *Asian Journal of Nursing Education and Research, 10*(4), 532–536. doi:10.5958/2349-2996.2020.00115.9

Shafiullah, M., Miah, M. D., Alam, M. S., & Atif, M. (2021). Does economic policy uncertainty affect renewable energy consumption? *Renewable Energy, 179*, 1500–1521. doi:10.1016/j.renene.2021.07.092

Shahhosseini, M., Silong, A. D., Ismaill, I. A., & Uli, J. N. (2012). The role of emotional intelligence on job performance. *International Journal of Business and Social Science*, *3*(21).

Shah, I. H., Hiles, C., & Morley, B. (2018). How do oil prices, macroeconomic factors and policies affect the market for renewable energy? *Applied Energy*, *215*, 87–97. doi:10.1016/j.apenergy.2018.01.084

Shahid, M. Z., & Li, G. (2019). Impact of artificial Intelligence in marketing: A perspective of marketing professionals of Pakistan, global. *Journal of Management and Business Research e Marketing*, *19*(2), 26–33.

Shang, S., Du, S., Du, S., & Zhu, S. (2021). Estimating building-scale population using multi-source spatial data. *Cities (London, England)*, *111*, 103002. Advance online publication. doi:10.1016/j.cities.2020.103002

Shankar, V., Kalyanam, K., Setia, P., Golmohammadi, A., Tirunillai, S., Douglass, T., Hennessey, J., Bull, J. S., & Waddoups, R. (2021). How technology is changing retail. *Journal of Retailing*, *97*(1), 13–27. doi:10.1016/j.jretai.2020.10.006

Sharma, D. K., Jalil, N. A., Regin, R., Rajest, S. S., Tummala, R. K., & Thangadurai. (2021). Predicting network congestion with machine learning. In *2021 2nd International Conference on Smart Electronics and Communication (ICOSEC)*. IEEE.

Sharma, D. K., Jalil, N. A., Regin, R., Rajest, S. S., Tummala, R. K., & Thangadurai. (2021a). Predicting network congestion with machine learning. In *2021 2nd International Conference on Smart Electronics and Communication (ICOSEC)*. IEEE.

Sharma, D. K., Singh, B., Raja, M., Regin, R., & Rajest, S. S. (2021a). An Efficient Python Approach for Simulation of Poisson Distribution. In *2021 7th International Conference on Advanced Computing and Communication Systems (ICACCS)*. IEEE.

Sharma, D. K., Singh, B., Raja, M., Regin, R., & Rajest, S. S. (2021b). An Efficient Python Approach for Simulation of Poisson Distribution. In *2021 7th International Conference on Advanced Computing and Communication Systems (ICACCS)*. IEEE.

Sharma, D. K., Singh, B., Regin, R., Steffi, R., & Chakravarthi, M. K. (2021b). Efficient Classification for Neural Machines Interpretations based on Mathematical models. In *2021 7th International Conference on Advanced Computing and Communication Systems (ICACCS)*. IEEE.

Sharma, D. K., Singh, B., Regin, R., Steffi, R., & Chakravarthi, M. K. (2021c). Efficient Classification for Neural Machines Interpretations based on Mathematical models. In *2021 7th International Conference on Advanced Computing and Communication Systems (ICACCS)*. IEEE.

Sharma, V., Trehan, T., Chanana, R., & Dawn, S. (2019). StudieMe: College Recommendation System. In *2019 3rd International Conference on Recent Developments in Control, Automation & Power Engineering (RDCAPE)*. IEEE.

Sharma, A., Bhola, S., Malyan, S., & Patni, N. (2013). Impact of brand loyalty on buying behaviour of women consumers for beauty care products-Delhi region. *Global Journal of Management and Business Studies*, *3*(7), 817–824.

Sharma, K., Singh, B., Herman, E., Regine, R., Rajest, S. S., & Mishra, V. P. (2021d). Maximum information measure policies in reinforcement learning with deep energy-based model. In *2021 International Conference on Computational Intelligence and Knowledge Economy (ICCIKE)*. IEEE. 10.1109/ICCIKE51210.2021.9410756

Sharma, S., Prakash, G., Kumar, A., Mussada, E. K., Antony, J., & Luthra, S. (2021). Analysing the relationship of adaption of green culture, innovation, green performance for achieving sustainability: Mediating role of employee commitment. *Journal of Cleaner Production*, *303*, 127039. doi:10.1016/j.jclepro.2021.127039

Shekhar, S., Gunturi, V., Evans, M. R., & Yang, K. (2012, May). Spatial big-data challenges intersecting mobility and cloud computing. In *Proceedings of the 11th ACM International Workshop on Data Engineering for Wireless and Mobile Access* (pp. 1–6). ACM. 10.1145/2258056.2258058

Shen, A. (2014). Recommendations as personalized marketing: Insights from customer experiences. *Journal of Services Marketing*, 28(5), 414–427. doi:10.1108/JSM-04-2013-0083

Shibly, A. (2011). Human Resources Information Systems Success Assessment). *Australian Journal of Basic and Applied Sciences*, 6(4).

Shifana, F., & Naachimuthu, K. P. (2022). Elements of Holistic Human Development in Naanmanikkadigai: A Hermeneutic Study. *Journal of Positive School Psychology*, 6(4), 2218–2231.

Shiksha.com. (2021). *Higher Education in India.* Retrieved November 14, 2023, from Shiksha.com website: https://www.shiksha.com

Shrinivas, K. T. (2013). A Study on employee welfare facilities adopted at Bosch Limited, Bangalore. Bangalore. *Research Journal of Management Sciences*, 2(12), 7–11.

Siddiquei, A., Asmi, F., Asadullah, M. A., & Mir, F. (2021). Environmental-specific servant leadership as a strategic tool to accomplish environmental performance: A case of China. *International Journal of Manpower*, 42(7), 1161–1182. doi:10.1108/IJM-07-2020-0350

Silaparasetti, V., Rao, G. V. R., & Khan, F. R. (2017). Structural equation modeling analysis using smart pls to assess the occupational health and safety (OHS) factors on workers' behavior. *Humanities & Social Science Reviews*.

Simon, J. P. (2019). Artificial Intelligence: Scope, players, markets and geography. *Digital Policy. Regulation & Governance*, 21(3), 208–237. doi:10.1108/DPRG-08-2018-0039

Singh, A. (2003). *Herbal drugs: US-EU move opens treasure trove.* Retrieved October 29, 2023, from Times of India website: https://timesofindia.indiatimes.com/city/lucknow/herbal-drugs-us-eu-move-opens-treasure-trove/articleshow/292287.cms

Singh, M., Sohani, P., Desai, J., Sharma, N. K., Chitte, P., & Gite, S. (2020). A Novel Approach for Colleges Recommendation for Admission Seekers Using Decision Tree. Ramrao Adik Institute of Technology.

Singh, R. C. (2021). Blockchain-Enabled End-to-End Encryption for Instant Messaging Applications. In *IEEE 23rd International Symposium on a World of Wireless, Mobile and Multimedia Networks (WoWMoM) 2022, Belfast* (pp. 501-506). IEEE.

Singh, M., Bhushan, M., Sharma, R., & Cavaliere, L. P. L. (2023). An Organized Assessment of the Literature of Entrepreneurial Skills and Emotional Intelligence. *FMDB Transactions on Sustainable Management Letters*, 1(3), 95–104.

Singh, N. (2022). Sustainable artificial intelligence tool strategy and customer experience in eye wear retail chain stores. *Journal of Contemporary Issues in Business and Government*, 28(4), 935–951.

Sivapriya, G. B. V., Ganesh, U. G., Pradeeshwar, V., Dharshini, M., & Al-Amin, M. (2023). Crime Prediction and Analysis Using Data Mining and Machine Learning: A Simple Approach that Helps Predictive Policing. *FMDB Transactions on Sustainable Computer Letters*, 1(2), 64–75.

Sjödin, D., Parida, V., Jovanovic, M., & Visnjic, I. (2020). Value Creation and Value Capture Alignment in Business Model Innovation: A Process View on Outcome-Based Business Models. *Journal of Product Innovation Management*, 37(2), 158–183. Advance online publication. doi:10.1111/jpim.12516

Skouras, T., Avlonitis, G. J., & Indounas, K. A. (2005). Economics and marketing on pricing: How and why do they differ? *Journal of Product and Brand Management, 14*(6), 362–374. doi:10.1108/10610420510624512

Slind, T. (2023). *How to Bring Location Services to Your Company and Customers.* https://www.locana.co/how-to-bring-location-services-to-your-company-and-customers/

Smith, P. A. C., & Sharicz, C. (2011). The shift needed for sustainability. *The Learning Organization, 18*(1), 73–86. doi:10.1108/09696471111096019

Smolović, J. C., Muhadinović, M., Radonjić, M., & Đurašković, J. (2020). How does renewable energy consumption affect economic growth in the traditional and new member states of the European Union? *Energy Reports, 6*, 505–513. doi:10.1016/j.egyr.2020.09.028

Soana, M.-G. (2011). The relationship between corporate social performance and corporate financial performance in the banking sector. *Journal of Business Ethics, 104*(1), 133–148. doi:10.100710551-011-0894-x

Sohlot, J., Teotia, P., Govinda, K., Rangineni, S., & Paramasivan, P. (2023). A Hybrid Approach on Fertilizer Resource Optimization in Agriculture Using Opposition-Based Harmony Search with Manta Ray Foraging Optimization. *FMDB Transactions on Sustainable Computing Systems, 1*(1), 44–53.

Song, H. K., Baek, E., & Choo, H. J. (2020). Try-on experience with augmented reality comforts your decision: Focusing on the roles of immersion and psychological ownership. *Information Technology & People, 33*(4), 1214–1234. doi:10.1108/ITP-02-2019-0092

Song, M. L., Fisher, R., Wang, J. L., & Cui, L. B. (2018). Environmental performance evaluation with big data: Theories and methods. *Annals of Operations Research, 270*(1-2), 459–472. doi:10.100710479-016-2158-8

Song, M., Cen, L., Zheng, Z., Fisher, R., Liang, X., Wang, Y., & Huisingh, D. (2017). How would big data support societal development and environmental sustainability? Insights and practices. *Journal of Cleaner Production, 142*, 489–500. doi:10.1016/j.jclepro.2016.10.091

Soni, N., Sharma, E. K., Singh, N., & Kapoor, A. (2019). Impact of artificial Intelligence on businesses: From research, innovation, market deployment to future shifts in business models. *Journal of Business Research.*

Springwater. (2021). *The economic value of parks and green spaces.* http://www.springwaterpcd.org/the-value-of-parks-and-recreation

Sri, G. P., Jayapriya, J., Poornima, T., & Naachimuthu, K. P. (2022). Hermeneutics of Iniyavai Naarpadhu and Inna Naarpadhu. *Journal of Positive School Psychology, 6*(8), 4358–4368.

Srinivasan, N. P., & Dhivya, S. (2020). An empirical study on stakeholder management in construction projects. *Materials Today: Proceedings, 21*, 60–62. doi:10.1016/j.matpr.2019.05.361

Srinivas, K., Velmurugan, P. R., & Andiyappillai, N. (2023). Digital Human Resources and Management Support Improve Human Resources Effectiveness. *FMDB Transactions on Sustainable Management Letters, 1*(1), 32–45.

Srivastava, D. K., & Roychoudhury, B. (2020). Words are important: A textual content based identity resolution scheme across multiple online social networks. *Knowledge-Based Systems, 195*, 105624. doi:10.1016/j.knosys.2020.105624

Srivastava, D. K., & Roychoudhury, B. (2021). Understanding the Factors that Influence Adoption of Privacy Protection Features in Online Social Networks. *Journal of Global Information Technology Management, 24*(3), 164–182. doi:10.1080/1097198X.2021.1954416

Stalin, K. G., Meharajan, T., & Venkateswaran, P. S. (2019). Impact of HRM practices on select IT companies' performance in Madurai. *International Journal of Scientific & Technology Research*, 8(12), 169–172.

Stamberg, S. (2014). Girls Are Taught To 'Think Pink. In ' But That Wasn't Always So. Academic Press.

Stang, M. (2023). *Real Estate Valuation in the Age of Artificial Intelligence–Modern Machine Learning Algorithms and their Application in Property Appraisal* (Doctoral dissertation).

Stankov, I. (2020, September). Environmental management information systems. In *2020 12th Electrical Engineering Faculty Conference (BulEF)* (pp. 1-7). IEEE. 10.1109/BulEF51036.2020.9326021

Stanton, J. M., & Coovert, M. D. (2004). Turbulent waters: The intersection of information technology and human resources. *Human Resource Management*, 43(2), 121–125. doi:10.1002/hrm.20010

Starace, G., Tiwari, A., Colangelo, G., & Massaro, A. (2022). Advanced Data Systems for Energy Consumption Optimization and Air Quality Control in Smart Public Buildings Using a Versatile Open Source Approach. *Electronics (Basel)*, 11(3904), 11. doi:10.3390/electronics11233904

Stevens, J. L., & Shanahan, K. J. (2017). Structured abstract: Anger, willingness, or clueless? Understanding why women pay a pink tax on the products they consume. In *Creating Marketing Magic and Innovative Future Marketing Trends* (pp. 571–575). Springer International Publishing. doi:10.1007/978-3-319-45596-9_108

Stolterman, E., & Fors, A. C. (2004). Information technology and the good life. In *Information Systems Research* (pp. 687–692). Springer US. doi:10.1007/1-4020-8095-6_45

Subramanyam, K. (1983). Bibliometric studies of research collaboration: A review. *Journal of Information Science*, 6(1), 33–38. doi:10.1177/016555158300600105

Sudheer, V., & Naachimuthu, K. P. (2022). Effect of JPMR on State-Trait Anxiety Among Young Female Adults During COVID-19 Pandemic Lockdown. *International Journal of Health Sciences*, 6(55), 1192–1202. doi:10.53730/ijhs.v6nS5.8848

Sugirtha, C. M. R., Hameed, S. S., & Arumugam, T. (2020). The impact of organizational identification and employee engagement on intellectual capital assets: An empirical study. *Test Eng. Manag*, 83, 6277–6285.

Sun, A. Y., & Scanlon, B. R. (2019). How can Big Data and machine learning benefit environment and water management: A survey of methods, applications, and future directions. *Environmental Research Letters*, 14(7), 073001. doi:10.1088/1748-9326/ab1b7d

Sun, C., Gao, R., & Xi, H. (2014, July). Big data based retail recommender system of non e-commerce. In *Proceedings of the 5th International Conference on Computing, Communications and Networking Technologies* (pp. 1–7). IEEE. 10.1109/ICCCNT.2014.6963129

Surbhi, S. (2020, February 3). *Difference between upselling and cross-selling*. Retrieved October 25, 2023, from Key Differences website: https://keydifferences.com/difference-between-upselling-and-cross-selling.html

Suriyankietkaew, S., & Avery, G. (2016). Sustainable leadership practices driving financial performance: Empirical evidence from Thai SMEs. *Sustainability (Basel)*, 8(4), 327. doi:10.3390/su8040327

Swartz, N. (2007). Data management problems widespread". *Information Management Journal*, 41(5), 28–30.

Taffese, W. Z. (2006). *A survey on application of artificial intelligence in real estate industry*. In 3rd International conference on artificial intelligence in engineering and technology, Kota Kinabalu, Malaysia.

Tambaip, B., Hadi, A. F. F., & Tjilen, A. P. (2023). Optimizing Public Service Performance: Unleashing the Potential of Compassion as an Indicator of Public Service Motivation. *FMDB Transactions on Sustainable Management Letters, 1*(2), 46–55.

Tambe, P., Cappelli, P., & Yakubovich, V. (2019). Artificial intelligence in human resources management: Challenges and a path forward. *California Management Review, 61*(4), 15–42. doi:10.1177/0008125619867910

Tănăsescu, R.-I., & Leon, R. (2013). Emotional intelligence, occupational stress and job performance in the Romanian banking system: A case study. *Management Dynamics in the Knowledge Economy, 7*(3), 322–335. doi:10.25019/MDKE/7.3.03

Tang, R., & Sae-Lim, W. (2016). Data science programs in US higher education: An exploratory content analysis of program description, curriculum structure, and course focus. *Education for Information, 32*(3), 269–290. doi:10.3233/EFI-160977

Tansley, S., & Tolle, K. M. (2009). The fourth paradigm: Data-intensive scientific discovery (Vol. 1). Microsoft Research.

Tan, X., & Wu, C. Y. X. (2016). Chinese Traditional Visual Cultural Symbols Recognition Based on Convolutional Neural Network. *Proceedings of the International Conference on Measuring Technology and Mechatronics Automation.*

Tan, Y. C., Chandukala, S. R., & Reddy, S. K. (2022). Augmented reality in retail and its impact on sales. *Journal of Marketing, 86*(1), 48–66. doi:10.1177/0022242921995449

Tawira, L., & Ivanov, A. (2023). Leveraging personalization and customization affordances of virtual try-on apps for a new model in apparel m-shopping. *Asia Pacific Journal of Marketing and Logistics, 35*(2), 451–471. doi:10.1108/APJML-09-2021-0652

tejaswipkle. (2023). *How Much Does It Cost to Develop Blockchain Apps?* Retrieved from geeksforgeeks: https://www.geeksforgeeks.org/how-much-does-it-cost-to-develop-blockchain-apps/

Templier, M., & Paré, G. (2015). A framework for guiding and evaluating literature reviews. *Communications of the Association for Information Systems, 37.* Advance online publication. doi:10.17705/1CAIS.03706

Thangam, D., Arumugam, T., Kommuri, U. K., Velusamy, K., Subramanian, M., Ganesan, S. K., & Suryakumar, M. (2022). COVID-19 pandemic and its brunt on digital transformation and cybersecurity. In Cybersecurity crisis management and lessons learned (pp. 15–42). IGI Global.

Thangam, D., Arumugam, T., Velusamy, K., Subramanian, M., Ganesan, S. K., & Suryakumar, M. (2022). COVID-19 Pandemic and Its Brunt on Digital Transformation and Cybersecurity. In Cybersecurity Crisis Management and Lessons Learned From the COVID-19 Pandemic (pp. 15-42). IGI Global.

Thangaraja, A. (2016a). An evolution of distributors' marketing intelligence system (DMIS) among FMCG distributors: A conceptual frame work. *International Journal of Multidisciplinary Education and Research, 1*(5), 11–13.

Thangaraja, A. (n.d.). *The role of culture code in acceptance of internet of things (IoT) among FMCG consumers: A positivist approach.* Academic Press.

Thangaraja, A. (2016b). Fast Moving Consumer Goods Distributors' source of Information and Marketing Intelligence System on Customer Feedback. *International Journal of Advance Research and Innovative Ideas in Education, 2*(1), 833–837.

Thangaraja, A. (2016c). The indispensability of information technology in marketing intelligence system: A conceptual approach. *International Journal for Scientific Research & Development, 4*(06), 118–121.

ThangarajaA. (2020). The veiling part of neuromarketing in developing brand preference in FMCG sector: A conceptual study. SSRN.

Thorndike, R. (1953). Who belongs in the family? *Psychometrika*, *18*(4), 267–276. doi:10.1007/BF02289263

Tian, Y., Zheng, B., Wang, Y., Zhang, Y., & Wu, Q. (2019). College library personalized recommendation system based on hybrid recommendation algorithm. *Procedia CIRP*, *83*, 490–494. doi:10.1016/j.procir.2019.04.126

Tony, M. (2011, August). *How do we put a value on green infrastructure?* Built Environment; The Guardian. https://www.theguardian.com/sustainable-business/value-green-infrastructure-spaces

Townsend, A. M., & Bennett, J. T. (2003). Human resources and information technology. *Journal of Labor Research*, *24*(3), 361–363. doi:10.100712122-003-1000-7

Tregouet, T. (2015). Gender-based price discrimination in matching markets. *International Journal of Industrial Organization*, *42*, 34–45. doi:10.1016/j.ijindorg.2015.05.007

Treleaven, P., Barnett, J., Knight, A., & Serrano, W. (2021). Real estate data marketplace. *AI and Ethics*, *1*(4), 445–462. doi:10.100743681-021-00053-4

Tripathi, D. S. (2021). *Guidelines for digitisation of archival material*. National Mission for Manuscripts. https://www.yumpu.com/en/document/view/33206162/standards-for-digitization-national-mission-for-manuscripts

Tripathi, K. P. (2011). Decision Making as a Component of Problem Solving. *International Journal of Information Technology and Management Information System*, *1*(1), 55–59.

Tripathi, S., & Al-Shahri, M. (2023). Problems and Prospects on the Evolution of Advertising and Public Relations Industries in Oman. *FMDB Transactions on Sustainable Management Letters*, *1*(1), 1–11.

Tucmeanu, E. R., Tucmeanu, A. I., Iliescu, M. G., Żywiołek, J., & Yousaf, Z. (2022). Successful management of IT projects in healthcare institutions after COVID-19: Role of digital orientation and innovation adaption. *Healthcare (Basel)*, *10*(10), 2005. doi:10.3390/healthcare10102005 PMID:36292452

Tugcu, C. T., & Topcu, M. (2018). Total, renewable and non-renewable energy consumption and economic growth: Revisiting the issue with an asymmetric point of view. *Energy*, *152*, 64–74. doi:10.1016/j.energy.2018.03.128

Tuomi, I. (1999). Data is more than knowledge: Implications of the reversed knowledge hierarchy for knowledge management and organizational memory. In *Proceedings of the 32nd Annual Hawaii International Conference on Systems Sciences* (pp. 103–117). IEEE. 10.1109/HICSS.1999.772795

Umbrello, S., & Van de Poel, I. (2021). Mapping value sensitive design onto AI for social good principles. *AI and Ethics*, *1*(3), 283–296. doi:10.100743681-021-00038-3 PMID:34790942

UNESCO. (1972). *Convención Sobre la Protección del Patrimonio Mundial, Cultural y Natural*. UNESCO.

UNESCO. (n.d.). *What is Intangible Cultural Heritage?* Retrieved from https://ich.unesco.org/en/what-is-intangible-heritage-00003

UPASI Tea Research Foundation. (2021). Retrieved November 12, 2023, from Upasitearesearch.org website: http://www.upasitearesearch.org

Ur Rehman, Z., Shafique, I., Khawaja, K. F., Saeed, M., & Kalyar, M. N. (2023). Linking responsible leadership with financial and environmental performance: Determining mediation and moderation. *International Journal of Productivity and Performance Management*, *72*(1), 24–46. doi:10.1108/IJPPM-12-2020-0626

Usman, O., Alola, A. A., & Sarkodie, S. A. (2020). Assessment of the role of renewable energy consumption and trade policy on environmental degradation using innovation accounting: Evidence from the US. *Renewable Energy*, *150*, 266–277. doi:10.1016/j.renene.2019.12.151

Van Der Aalst, W. (2016). Data science in action. In *Process Mining* (pp. 3–23). Springer. doi:10.1007/978-3-662-49851-4_1

Vandermeersch, T., Alvarenga, R. A. F., Ragaert, P., & Dewulf, J. (2014). Environmental sustainability assessment of food waste valorization options. *Resources, Conservation and Recycling*, *87*, 57–64. doi:10.1016/j.resconrec.2014.03.008

Varadarajan, P. R., & Menon, A. (1988). Socially responsible marketing: A coalignment of marketing strategy and corporate philanthropy. *Journal of Marketing*, *52*(3), 58–74. doi:10.1177/002224298805200306

Varadarajan, R., Srinivasan, R., Vadakkepatt, G. G., Yadav, M. S., Pavlou, P. A., Krishnamurthy, S., & Krause, T. (2010). Interactive technologies and retailing strategy: A review, conceptual framework and future research directions. *Journal of Interactive Marketing*, *24*(2), 96–110. doi:10.1016/j.intmar.2010.02.004

Vashishtha, E., & Dhawan, G. (2023). Comparison of Baldrige Criteria of Strategy Planning and Harrison Text. *FMDB Transactions on Sustainable Management Letters*, *1*(1), 22–31.

Vashishtha, E., & Kapoor, H. (2023). Implementation of Blockchain Technology Across International Healthcare Markets. *FMDB Transactions on Sustainable Technoprise Letters*, *1*(1), 1–12.

Vecco, M. (2010). A definition of cultural heritage: From the tangible to the intangible. *Journal of Cultural Heritage*, *11*(3), 321–324. doi:10.1016/j.culher.2010.01.006

Vega, R. P., Anderson, A. J., & Kaplan, S. A. (2015). A within-person examination of the effects of telework. *Journal of Business and Psychology*, *30*(2), 313–323. doi:10.100710869-014-9359-4

Venkateswaran, P. S. (2023). *Industry 5 - Challenges and Opportunities for business and industries*. Academic Press.

Venkateswaran, P.S., (2015), Influence of information systems in Engineering Institutions at Madurai District, Tamil Nadu, India. *International Journal of Applied Engineering Research*, *9*(21), 10513-10528.

Venkateswaran, P. S. (2015). influence of information systems in Engineering Institutions at Madurai District. *International Journal of Applied Engineering Research: IJAER*, *9*, 10513–10528.

Venkateswaran, P. S., Sabarirajan, A., Arun, B., Muthupandian, T., & Manimaran, D. S. (2018). Technology Acceptance Model for Making Decision to Purchase Automobile in Coimbatore District. *International Journal of Mechanical Engineering and Technology*, *9*(11), 1608–1613.

Venkateswaran, P. S., Sabarirajan, A., Rajest, S. S., & Regin, R. (2019). The theory of the Postmodernism in consumerism, mass culture and globalization. *Journal of Research on the Lepidoptera*, *50*(4), 97–113. doi:10.36872/LEPI/V50I4/201075

Venkateswaran, P. S., Singh, S., Paramasivan, P., Rajest, S. S., Lourens, M. E., & Regin, R. (2023). A Study on The Influence of Quality of Service on Customer Satisfaction Towards Hotel Industry. *FMDB Transactions on Sustainable Social Sciences Letters*, *1*(1), 1–11.

Venkateswaran, P. S., & Viktor, P. (2023). A Study on Brand Equity of Fast-Moving Consumer Goods with Reference to Madurai, Tamil Nadu. *FMDB Transactions on Sustainable Technoprise Letters*, *1*(1), 13–27.

Venter, Z. S., Shackleton, C. M., Van Staden, F., Selomane, O., & Masterson, V. A. (2020). Green Apartheid: Urban green infrastructure remains unequally distributed across income and race geographies in South Africa. *Landscape and Urban Planning*, *203*, 103889. doi:10.1016/j.landurbplan.2020.103889

Vesanen, J. (2007). What is personalization? A conceptual framework. *European Journal of Marketing*, *41*(5/6), 409–418. doi:10.1108/03090560710737534

Vesanen, J., & Raulas, M. (2006). Building bridges for personalization: A process model for marketing. *Journal of Interactive Marketing*, *20*(1), 5–20. doi:10.1002/dir.20052

Viana, C. M., Encalada, L., & Rocha, J. (2019). The value of OpenStreetMap historical contributions as a source of sampling data for multi-temporal land use/cover maps. *ISPRS International Journal of Geo-Information*, *8*(3), 116. Advance online publication. doi:10.3390/ijgi8030116

Violante, M. G., & Vezzetti, E. (2014). Implementing a new approach for the design of an e-learning platform in engineering education. *Computer Applications in Engineering Education*, *22*(4), 708–727. doi:10.1002/cae.21564

Violante, M. G., Vezzetti, E., & Piazzolla, P. (2019). How to design a virtual reality experience that impacts the consumer engagement: The case of the virtual supermarket. *International Journal on Interactive Design and Manufacturing*, *13*(1), 243–262. doi:10.100712008-018-00528-5

Viriato, J. C. (2019). AI and machine learning in real estate investment. *Journal of Portfolio Management*, *45*(7), 43–54. doi:10.3905/jpm.2019.45.7.043

Wang, Z., & Shi, Y. (2016). Prediction of the Admission Lines of College Entrance Examination based on Machine Learning. In *2nd IEEE International Conference on Computer and Communications* (pp. 332–335). IEEE.

Wang, C., Chen, M. H., Schifano, E., Wu, J., & Yan, J. (2016). Statistical methods and computing for big data. *Statistics and Its Interface*, *9*(4), 399–414. doi:10.4310/SII.2016.v9.n4.a1 PMID:27695593

Wang, C., Wang, Y., Wang, J., Xiao, J., & Liu, J. (2021). Factors influencing consumers' purchase decision-making in O2O business model: Evidence from consumers' overall evaluation. *Journal of Retailing and Consumer Services*, *61*(102565). doi:10.1016/j.jretconser.2021.102565

Wang, J., Rienow, A., David, M., & Albert, C. (2022). Green infrastructure connectivity analysis across spatiotemporal scales: A transferable approach in the Ruhr Metropolitan Area, Germany. *The Science of the Total Environment*, *813*, 152463. doi:10.1016/j.scitotenv.2021.152463 PMID:34952053

Wang, Y., & Chiew, V. (2010). On the cognitive process of human problem solving. *Cognitive Systems Research*, *11*(1), 81–92. doi:10.1016/j.cogsys.2008.08.003

Wang, Y., Ko, E., & Wang, H. (2022). Augmented reality (AR) app use in the beauty product industry and consumer purchase intention. *Asia Pacific Journal of Marketing and Logistics*, *34*(1), 110–131. doi:10.1108/APJML-11-2019-0684

Wanvestraut, R. (2020). *South Florida Water Management District Utility Rate Survey*. Academic Press.

Wan, Y., & Zhu, Q. (2020). The IT Challenges in Disaster Relief: What We Learned From Hurricane Harvey. *IT Professional*, *22*(6), 52–58. doi:10.1109/MITP.2020.3005675

Waqas, M., Honggang, X., Ahmad, N., Khan, S. A. R., & Iqbal, M. (2021). Big data analytics as a roadmap towards green innovation, competitive advantage and environmental performance. *Journal of Cleaner Production*, *323*, 128998. doi:10.1016/j.jclepro.2021.128998

Ward, J. S., & Barker, A. (2013). *Undefined by data: a survey of big data definitions*. arXiv preprint arXiv:1309.5821.

Ward, S., & Chapman, C. (2008). Stakeholders and uncertainty management in projects. *Construction Management and Economics*, *26*(6), 563–577. doi:10.1080/01446190801998708

WB. (n.d.-a). *Access to electricity (% of population).* World Bank. Retrieved 01 30, 2023, from https://data.worldbank.org/indicator/EG.ELC.ACCS.ZS

WB. (n.d.-b). *Adjusted savings: natural resources depletion (% of GNI).* World Bank. Retrieved 01 30, 2023, from https://data.worldbank.org/indicator/NY.ADJ.DRES.GN.ZS

WB. (n.d.-c). *Adjusted savings: net forest depletion (current US$).* World Bank. Retrieved 01 30, 2023, from https://data.worldbank.org/indicator/NY.ADJ.DFOR.CD

WB. (n.d.-d). *Agricultural land (% of land area).* World Bank. Retrieved 01 30, 2023, from https://data.worldbank.org/indicator/AG.LND.AGRI.ZS

WB. (n.d.-e). *Agriculture, forestry, and fishing, value added (% of GDP).* World Bank. Retrieved 01 30, 2023, from https://data.worldbank.org/indicator/NV.AGR.TOTL.ZS

WB. (n.d.-f). *CO2 emissions (metric tons per capita).* World Bank. Retrieved 01 30, 2023, from https://data.worldbank.org/indicator/EN.ATM.CO2E.PC

WB. (n.d.-g). *Cooling Degree Days.* World Bank. Retrieved 01 30, 2023, from https://databank.worldbank.org/metadataglossary/environment-social-and-governance-(esg)-data/series/EN.CLC.CDDY.XD

WB. (n.d.-h). *Energy imports, net (% of energy use).* World Bank. Retrieved 01 30, 2023, from https://data.worldbank.org/indicator/EG.IMP.CONS.ZS

WB. (n.d.-i). *Forest area (% of land area).* World Bank. Retrieved 01 30, 2023, from https://data.worldbank.org/indicator/AG.LND.FRST.ZS

WB. (n.d.-j). *Fossil fuel energy consumption (% of total).* World Bank. Retrieved 01 30, 2023, from https://data.worldbank.org/indicator/EG.USE.COMM.FO.ZS

WB. (n.d.-k). *GHG net emissions/removals by LUCF (Mt of CO2 equivalent).* World Bank. Retrieved 01 30, 2023, from https://data.worldbank.org/indicator/EN.CLC.GHGR.MT.CE

WB. (n.d.-l). *Maximum 5-day Rainfall, 25-year Return Level (projected change in mm).* World Bank. Retrieved 01 30, 2023, from https://databank.worldbank.org/metadataglossary/environment-social-and-governance-(esg)-data/series/EN.CLC.PRCP.XD

WB. (n.d.-m). *Mean Drought Index (projected change, unitless).* World Bank. Retrieved 01 30, 2023, from https://databank.worldbank.org/metadataglossary/environment-social-and-governance-(esg)-data/series/EN.CLC.SPEI.XD

WB. (n.d.-n). *PM2.5 air pollution, mean annual exposure (micrograms per cubic meter).* World Bank. Retrieved 01 30, 2023, from https://data.worldbank.org/indicator/EN.ATM.PM25.MC.M3

WB. (n.d.-o). *Renewable electricity output (% of total electricity output).* World Bank.

WB. (n.d.-p). *Energy use (kg of oil equivalent per capita).* Retrieved 01 30, 2023, from https://data.worldbank.org/indicator/EG.USE.PCAP.KG.OE

Weise, J., & Mostaghim, S. (2022). A Scalable Many-Objective Pathfinding Benchmark Suite. *IEEE Transactions on Evolutionary Computation, 26*(1), 188–194. Advance online publication. doi:10.1109/TEVC.2021.3089050

Weston, G. (2022, September 30). *Top 10 Web3 Applications You Must Know.* Retrieved from 101 Blockchains: https://101blockchains.com/top-web3-applications/

Whelan, M. J., Linstead, C., Worrall, F., Ormerod, S. J., Durance, I., Johnson, A. C., & Tickner, D. (2022). Is water quality in British rivers "better than at any time since the end of the Industrial Revolution"? *The Science of the Total Environment*, *843*, 15. doi:10.1016/j.scitotenv.2022.157014 PMID:35772542

WHO. (2016). *Urban green spaces and health*. WHO.

Widaningrum, D. L., Surjandari, I., & Sudiana, D. (2020). Discovering spatial patterns of fast-food restaurants in Jakarta, Indonesia. *Journal of Industrial and Production Engineering*, *37*(8), 403–421. Advance online publication. doi:10.108 0/21681015.2020.1823495

Wiki, O. (2023b). *About OpenStreetMap*. https://wiki.openstreetmap.org/wiki/About_OpenStreetMap

WikiO. (2023a). *Tags*. https://wiki.openstreetmap.org/wiki/Tags

Wilder, C. R., & Ozgur, C. O. (2015). Business analytics curriculum for undergraduate majors. *Transactions on Education*, *15*(2), 180–187. doi:10.1287/ited.2014.0134

Wong, C. S., & Law, K. S. (2002). The effects of leader and follower emotional intelligence on performance and attitude: An exploratory study. *The Leadership Quarterly*, *13*(3), 243–274. doi:10.1016/S1048-9843(02)00099-1

Wood, S. (2021, June 4). *The Security Implications for Private Messaging Apps*. Retrieved from TechRadar: https://www.techradar.com/news/the-security-implications-for-private-messaging-apps

Wu, J.-H., & Wang, Y.-M. (2006). Measuring ERP success: The ultimate users' view. *International Journal of Operations & Production Management*, *26*(8), 882–903. doi:10.1108/01443570610678657

Wu, Y.-C. (2011). Job stress and job performance among employees in the Taiwanese finance sector: The role of emotional intelligence. *Social Behavior and Personality*, *39*(1), 21–31. doi:10.2224bp.2011.39.1.21

Xiao, Y., & Watson, M. (2019). Guidance on conducting a systematic literature review. *Journal of Planning Education and Research*, *39*(1), 93–112. doi:10.1177/0739456X17723971

Xi, N., Chen, J., Gama, F., Riar, M., & Hamari, J. (2022). The challenges of entering the metaverse: An experiment on the effect of extended reality on workload. *Information Systems Frontiers*, 1–22. doi:10.100710796-022-10244-x PMID:35194390

Xue, L., Parker, C. J., & McCormick, H. (2019). A virtual reality and retailing literature review: Current focus, underlying themes and future directions. *Augmented Reality and Virtual Reality: The Power of AR and VR for Business*, 27-41.

Yamani, N., Shahabi, M., & Haghani, F. (2014). The relationship between emotional intelligence and job stress in the faculty of medicine in Isfahan University of Medical Sciences. *Journal of Advances in Medical Education & Professionalism*, *2*(1), 20. PMID:25512914

Yang, H. T., & Yen, G. F. (2018). Consumer responses to corporate Socially responsible marketing: A serial multiple mediator model of self-construal, empathy and moral identity. *European Journal of Marketing*, *52*(9/10), 2105–2127. doi:10.1108/EJM-07-2017-0468

Yang, J., Shen, G. Q., Ho, M., Drew, D. S., & Chan, A. P. C. (2009). Exploring critical success factors for stakeholder management in construction projects. *Journal of Civil Engineering and Management*, *15*(4), 337–348. doi:10.3846/1392-3730.2009.15.337-348

Yang, S. Y., Chen, S. C., Lee, L., & Liu, Y. S. (2021). Employee stress, job satisfaction, and job performance: A comparison between high-technology and traditional industry in Taiwan. The Journal of Asian Finance. *Economics and Business*, *8*(3), 605–618.

Yan, J., & Hu, W. (2021). Environmentally specific transformational leadership and green product development performance: The role of a green HRM system. *International Journal of Manpower*.

Yaoyuneyong, G., Foster, J. K., & Flynn, L. R. (2014). Factors impacting the efficacy of augmented reality virtual dressing room technology as a tool for online visual merchandising. *Journal of Global Fashion Marketing*, 5(4), 283–296. doi:10.1080/20932685.2014.926129

Ye, C., Zhao, Z., & Cai, J. (2021). The Impact of Smart City Construction on the Quality of Foreign Direct Investment in China. *Complexity*, 2021, 1–9. Advance online publication. doi:10.1155/2021/5619950

Yemenici, A. D. (2022). Entrepreneurship in the world of Metaverse: Virtual or real? *Journal of Metaverse*, 2(2), 71–82. doi:10.57019/jmv.1126135

Yeruva, A. R., & Ramu, V. B. (2023). AIOps research innovations, performance impact and challenges faced. *International Journal of System of Systems Engineering*, 13(3), 229–247. doi:10.1504/IJSSE.2023.133013

Ying, M., Faraz, N. A., Ahmed, F., & Raza, A. (2020). How does servant leadership foster employees' voluntary green behavior? A sequential mediation model. *International Journal of Environmental Research and Public Health*, 17(5), 1792. doi:10.3390/ijerph17051792 PMID:32164222

Younas, A., & Ali, P. (2021). Five tips for developing useful literature summary tables for writing review articles. *Evidence-Based Nursing*, 24(2), 32–34. doi:10.1136/ebnurs-2021-103417 PMID:33674415

Yuping, L., Ramzan, M., Xincheng, L., Murshed, M., Awosusi, A. A., Bah, S. I., & Adebayo, T. S. (2021). Determinants of carbon emissions in Argentina: The roles of renewable energy consumption and globalization. *Energy Reports*, 7, 4747–4760. doi:10.1016/j.egyr.2021.07.065

Zelniker, N. (2018). *Pink tax' means women still pay more for goods and services*. Academic Press.

Zeren, F., & Akkuş, H. T. (2020). The relationship between renewable energy consumption and trade openness: New evidence from emerging economies. *Renewable Energy*, 147, 322–329. doi:10.1016/j.renene.2019.09.006

Zhang, B., Wang, B., & Wang, Z. (2017). Role of renewable energy and non-renewable energy consumption on EKC: Evidence from Pakistan. *Journal of Cleaner Production*, 156, 855–864. doi:10.1016/j.jclepro.2017.03.203

Zhang, G., Wang, J., Huang, W., Yang, Y., Su, H., Yue, Y., Zhai, Y., Liu, M., & Chen, L. (2015). A Study of Chinese Character Culture Big Data Platform. *Proceedings of the International Conference on Cloud Computing and Big Data*. 10.1109/CCBD.2015.18

Zhang, M. F., Dawson, J. F., & Kline, R. B. (2021). Evaluating the use of covariance-based structural equation modelling with reflective measurement in organizational and management research: A review and recommendations for best practice. *British Journal of Management*, 32(2), 257–272. doi:10.1111/1467-8551.12415

Zhang, M., Zhang, S., Lee, C. C., & Zhou, D. (2021). Effects of trade openness on renewable energy consumption in OECD countries: New insights from panel smooth transition regression modelling. *Energy Economics*, 104(105649), 105649. doi:10.1016/j.eneco.2021.105649

Zhang, T., Wang, W. Y. C., Cao, L., & Wang, Y. (2019). The role of virtual try-on technology in online purchase decision from consumers' aspect. *Internet Research*, 29(3), 529–551. doi:10.1108/IntR-12-2017-0540

Zhang, Z. (2022). Globalized cross-border insolvency law: The roles played by China. *European Business Organization Law Review*, 23(3), 735–780. doi:10.100740804-021-00222-2

Zhao, H., & Zhou, Q. (2019). Exploring the impact of responsible leadership on organizational citizenship behavior for the environment: A leadership identity perspective. *Sustainability (Basel)*, *11*(4), 944. doi:10.3390u11040944

Zhu, C., Zhou, H., Leung, V. C., Wang, K., Zhang, Y., & Yang, L. T. (2017). Toward big data in green city. *IEEE Communications Magazine*, *55*(11), 14–18. doi:10.1109/MCOM.2017.1700142

Zhu, Z., Fan, M., Sun, C., & Long, R. (2017). Cultural symbiosis: Chu Culture and Course Teaching of Interface Design-A Case Study on a Chinese Bestiary. *Proceedings of the 2017 7th International Workshop on Computer Science and Engineering*.

Zikopoulos, P., & Eaton, C. (2011). *Understanding big data: Analytics for enterprise class hadoop and streaming data.* McGraw-Hill Osborne Media.

Zimmermann, R., Mora, D., Cirqueira, D., Helfert, M., Bezbradica, M., Werth, D., Weitzl, W. J., Riedl, R., & Auinger, A. (2023). Enhancing brick-and-mortar store shopping experience with an augmented reality shopping assistant application using personalized recommendations and explainable artificial intelligence. *Journal of Research in Interactive Marketing*, *17*(2), 273–298. doi:10.1108/JRIM-09-2021-0237

zur Heiden, P., & Winter, D. (2021). Discovering Geographical Patterns of Retailers' Locations for Successful Retail in City Centers. *Innovation Through Information Systems: Volume I: A Collection of Latest Research on Domain Issues*, 99–104.

Żywiołek, J., Tucmeanu, E. R., Tucmeanu, A. I., Isac, N., & Yousaf, Z. (2022). Nexus of transformational leadership, employee adaptiveness, knowledge sharing, and employee creativity. *Sustainability (Basel)*, *14*(18), 11607. doi:10.3390u141811607

About the Contributors

Sonia Singh, Director of Toss Global Management and Human Resource, Education and Management consultancy company with operations in India, UAE and UK, is a Researcher, Educator, Human Resource, Administrator and Corporate leader. She is also assessor for different quality awards of UAE. For over 22 years she served in India and abroad in different capacities and areas of expertise. Previously, Dr. Sonia Singh served as Group HR Director at LIN SCAN, one of the leading Oil and Gas companies with 8 offices around the world including UAE, Russia, India, Canada, Egypt, Minsk, Singapore and Malaysia, operations in 56 countries and more than 800 employees on board. She is a prominent speaker at different Universities and Government offices across UAE. She has been invited as Guest Speaker by SEWA (Sharjah Electricity and Water Authority). She was also a guest speaker for Emirates Canadian University College, (Umm Al Quwain), First Forum of "Year of Tolerance" under the patronage of Ruler of Umm Al Quwain. She is Recipient of the "Education Excellence Award" and honored by Hon. Penisimani Epenisa Fiftia, Minister of Education and Training, the Kingdom of Tonga for the support to African Community for Higher Education. She is the Editor, Guest editor of Scopus Indexed, ABDC and Web of science Journals. She is Board Member of GBRS (Research Forum of St. John University, USA, a collaboration between St. John's University's, Tobin College of Business and a diverse group of international scholars and Universities. She is an Advisory board member Gulf American University. Recognized for her excellent work in academics and corporate outside India and appeared in COFFEE BOOK TABLES launched in INDIA, UK, and UAE.

S. Suman Rajest is currently working as Dean of Research and Development (R&D) & International Student Affairs (ISA) at Dhaanish Ahmed College of Engineering, Chennai, Tamil Nadu, India. He is an Editor in Chief of the International Journal of Human Computing Studies and The International Journal of Social Sciences World, He is the Chief Executive Editor of the International Journal of Advanced Engineering Research and Science, International Journal of Advanced Engineering, Management and Science, The International Journal of Health and Medicines, The International Journal of Management Economy and Accounting Fields and The International Journal of Technology Information and Computer and also he is an Editorial Board Member in International Journal of Management in Education, Scopus, Inderscience, EAI Endorsed Transactions on e-Learning, and Bulletin of the Karaganda university Pedagogy series. He is also a Book Series Editor in IGI Global Publisher, Springer, etc. All of his writing, including his research, involves elements of creative nonfiction in the Human Computing learning system. He is also interested in creative writing and digital media, Learning, AI, student health learning, etc. He has published 200 papers in peer-reviewed international journals. He has authored and co-authored several scientific book publications in journals and conferences and is a frequent reviewer of international journals and international conferences and also, he is also a reviewer in Inderscience, EAI Journals, IGI Global, Science Publications, etc.

Slim Hadoussa is a Professor of Management Information System and Dean of the Faculty at Brest Business School France. He obtained his PhD in Management Information System from University of Toulouse I Capitole France in 2009 awarded by the Ministry of Foreign and European Affairs France. He has an international teaching experience as an Associate Professor at MENA and Gulf Region Universities especially at Saudi Electronic University, Saudi Arabia and University of Carthage Tunisia. He contributes to diverse research, cooperation and visiting programs at MENA Region (Saudi Arabia, Morocco, Egypt, Tunisia, etc.). His research and teaching interest focus on MIS and organizational change, performance in different sectors such health care, education, commerce, tourism, etc. His publications focus on digitalization process and organizational consequences. His research projects treat subjects dealing with social media, e-learning experiences at universities, e-commerce and e-marketing, e-health and decision-making process, etc. He has several publications at peer reviewed international journal indexed FNEGE France, ABS, Web of Science and Scopus.

Ahmed J. Obaid is a Asst. Professor at the Department of Computer Science, Faculty of Computer Science and Mathematics, University of Kufa, Iraq. Dr. Ahmed holds a Bachelor's in Computer Science, a degree in – Information Systems from the College of Computers, University of Anbar, Iraq (2001-2005), and a Master's Degree (M. TECH) in Computer Science Engineering (CSE) from School of Information Technology, Jawaharlal Nehru Technological University, Hyderabad, India (2010-2013), and a Doctor of Philosophy (Ph.D.) in Web Mining from College of Information Technology, University of Babylon, Iraq (2013-2017). He is a Certified Web Mining Consultant with over 14 years of experience working as a Faculty Member at the University of Kufa, Iraq. He has taught courses in Web Designing, Web Scripting, JavaScript, VB.Net, MATLAB Toolbox, and other courses on PHP, CMC, and DHTML from more than 10 international organizations and institutes in the USA, and India. Dr. Ahmed is a member of the Statistical and Information Consultation Center (SICC), University of Kufa, Iraq. His main line of research is Web mining Techniques and Applications, Image processing in Web Platforms, Image processing, Genetic Algorithm, information theory, and Medical Health Applications. Ahmed J. is an Associated Editor in the Brazilian Journal of Operations & Production Management (BJO&PM) and an Editorial Board member in the International Journal of Advance Study and Research Work (IJASRW), Journal of Research in Engineering and Applied Sciences(JREAS), GRD Journal for Engineering (GRDJE), International Research Journal of Multidisciplinary Science & Technology (IRJMST), The International Journal of Technology Information and Computer (IJTIC), Career Point International Journal Research (CPIJR). Ahmed J. was Editor in Many International Conferences such as: ISCPS_2020, MAICT_2020, IHICPS_2020, IICESAT_2021, IICPS_2020, ICPAS_2021, etc. (Scopus Indexed Conferences). He has edited Some books, such as Advance Material Science and Engineering (ISBN: 9783035736779, Scientific.net publisher), Computational Intelligence Techniques for Combating COVID-19 (ISBN: 978-3-030-68936-0 EAI/Springer), A Fusion of Artificial Intelligence and Internet of Things for Emerging Cyber Systems (ISBN: 978-3-030-76653-5 Springer). Ahmed J. has supervised several final projects for Bachelor's and Master's in his main line of work and authored and co-authored several scientific publications in journals, Books, and conferences with more than 75+ Journal Research Articles, 5+ book Chapters, 15+ Conference papers, 10+ Conference proceedings, 8+ Books Editing, 2+ Patent. Ahmed J. is also a Reviewer in many Scopus, SCI, and ESCI Journals e.g., CMC, IETE, IJAACS, IJIPM, IJKBD, IJBSR, IET, IJUFKS, and many others. Dr. Ahmed attended and participate as: Keynote Speakers (60+ Conferences), Webinars (10+), and Session Chairs (10+), in many international events in the following countries: India, Turkey, Nepal, Philippines, Vietnam, Thailand, Indonesia, and other countries.

R. Regin is currently working as an Assistant Professor in the Department of Computer Science and Engineering at the SRM Institute of Science and Technology, Chennai, Tamil Nadu, India. He has a specialization in the branch of information and communication. He holds experience of 10+ years in teaching faculty and research. He has also published papers in 55 reputed international journals, 40 international conferences, and 15 national conferences. He is a member of professional bodies like IE and IETE. He is also a Book Series Editor for IGI Global Publisher, Springer, etc. He is the Editor-in-Chief of the International Journal of Technology Information and Computers, Growing Scholar USA, and a member of the Journal Ilmiah Teunuleh's Editorial Advisory Board. He does research work in the fields of VANET, WSN, MANET, Cloud Computing, Network Security, and Information Security. He is a reviewer for many reputed journals like Springer, Inderscience, etc.

* * *

Shashank Agarwal is an analytics expert who has channeled his expertise within the healthcare space over the years. His experience cuts across various areas in market access, artificial intelligence, brand analytics, predictive modeling, launch strategy, and multi-channel marketing in several Fortune 500 companies such as CVS Health, AbbVie, and IQVIA

Munir Ahmad is a Ph.D. in Computer Science. over 23 years of extensive experience in spatial data development, management, processing, visualization, and quality control. He is dedicated expertise in open data, crowdsourced data, volunteered geographic information and spatial data infrastructure. A seasoned professional with extensive knowledge in the field, having served as a trainer for the latest spatial technologies. With a passion for research and over 25 publications in the same field. In 2022, he got PhD degree in Computer Science from Preston University Rawalpindi, Pakistan. He is dedicated to advancing the industry and spreading knowledge through my expertise and experience. #SpatialData #GIS #GeoTech.

R. Arun is an Assistant Professor in department of Management Studies, St,Josephs college of Engineering, Chennai. Dr. R.Arun has more than 15 years of teaching and research experience. He has presented more than 52 Papers in National and International Conferences and more than 26 publications in reputed National and International journals like SCOPUS, Web of Science and UGC Care Listed. He has been awarded various awards like Best Volunteer Award 2016, BEST Faculty Award 2017, Best Young Faculty Award 2018, Teaching And Research Excellence Award 2019, Global Achievement Award 2022 and recently he received BEST SOCIAL SCIENTIST AWARD 2023. He also received a Minor Research Project, Sanctioned an amount of RS.2, 55,000 by UGC-South Eastern Regional Office, New Delhi. He also published two Books and Filed 2 Patents. His research interests include Marketing, Human Resources Management, Hospitality Management, Digital Marketing, Financial Service and Security Markets, Entrepreneurial Development, Logistics and Supply Chain, Food Safety & Hygiene, Service Management, Culture and Tourism, Information Technology and Consumer Behavior. He holds a B.Sc., Catering Science & Hotel Management degree from Bharathiar University, Coimbatore, MBA from Annamalai University and Ph.D. in Management from the Bharathiar University, Coimbatore.

Vanitha B., M.Com, Assistant Professor, Department of Commerce, Government First Grade College, Channapatna. Her area of specialization is Accounting & Taxation. With more than 13 years of academic experience, she contributes extensively towards academic excellence and has published many research papers in national and international journals.

Seema Bhakuni is a Ph.D. in Management and have qualified UGC NET, CTET and UPTET exam. She has done her Masters in English, Sociology and Business Administration. She is an editorial board member in Journal of Human Resource Management and Global Scientific and academic research journal of economics, business and management. She is also an advisor to Global Leaders Foundation, New Delhi. She completed her education in Lucknow and moved to Rishikesh in 2015. She is presently working as an Assistant Professor at Doon Group of Institutions, Rishikesh and teaching her subject to students of Business Administration.

Manne Neelima Chaudhary is presently working as HOD, UG, Department of Commerce, SCS, JAIN (Deemed to be) University, Bangalore. Her area of specialization is Management and Finance. With more than 20 years of academic experience, she contributes extensively towards academic excellence and has published many research papers in national and international journals. She has been a part of organizing committee of national and international conferences. She has been presented with the Award of Excellence for achievement of excellence in enabling students to be Industry ready at the IMA-Wiley-Miles University Excellence Awards 2019.

Vidya Chandrasekar, MCom, MPhil, and PhD in Commerce, is currently working as Associate Professor, School of Commerce, JAIN (Deemed to be University), Bangalore. She has academic experience of 9 years at graduation level apart from 10 years of Industry experience.

Ruchi Doshi is having more than 16 years of academic, research and software development experience in Asia and Africa. Currently she is working as research supervisor at the Azteca University, Mexico and Adjunct Professor at the Jyoti Vidyapeeth Women's University, Jaipur, Rajasthan, India. She worked in the BlueCrest University College, Liberia, West Africa as Registrar and Head, Examination; BlueCrest University College, Ghana, Africa; Amity University, Rajasthan, India; Trimax IT Infrastructure & Services, Udaipur, India. She worked as a Founder Chair, Women in Engineering (WIE) and Secretary Position in the IEEE Liberia Subsection. She worked with Ministry of Higher Education (MoHE) in Liberia and Ghana for the Degree approvals and accreditations processes. She is interested in the field of Machine Learning and Cloud computing framework development. She has published numerous research papers in peer-reviewed international journals and conferences. She is a Reviewer, Advisor, Ambassador and Editorial board member of various reputed International Journals and Conferences.

Srinivas G., MCOM, Assistant Professor, is presently working as Co-coordinator, UG Department of Commerce, SCS, JAIN (Deemed to be University), Bangalore. His area of specialization is Accounting & Taxation. With more than 13 years of academic experience, he contributes extensively towards academic excellence and has published many research papers in national and international journals. He has been a part of organizing committee of national and international conferences; he has authored Income Tax, Advanced Corporate Accounting, Business Taxation, Indirect Taxes, for BCOM & BBA students from Kalyani Publishers.

Nidhi Raj Gupta, an accomplished academician with 16 years of experience, champions innovation's societal impact and sustainability. She began in Public Relations, excelling as a Technical Sales Specialist at Redington India Ltd. After a successful stint, she transitioned to academia, earning her doctorate. She led as brand director at Triangle A, a women-led startup, and trained in diverse domains including disaster management, emotional intelligence, and design thinking across Maharashtra, Goa, Patna, and Ahmedabad. Currently an Assistant Professor in Professional Accounting & Finance at Kristu Jayanti College, Bengaluru, Dr. Gupta's influence extends globally. She's authored books, presented papers at prestigious institutions, holds a UK design patent, and contributes to academic boards. Her notable accomplishments include being NET Qualified, a certified Life Skill trainer, NLP Trainer, NPTEL Mentor for Entrepreneurship, and Design Thinking practitioner. Committed to daily positive impact, she empowers through soft skill development, fostering holistic growth.

Sheetal V. Hukkeri is an experienced academician with a focus in the fields of Commerce and Management. Sheetal is currently working as a Program Coordinator and Assistant Professor at School of Commerce, JAIN (Deemed-to-be University). She has also published more than 30 articles in leading National and International Journals along with book chapters and books in Commerce and Management.

Yingmei Li is a full professor at Harbin Normal University, China. Her research interest is in software engineering and computer science education.

Nirmala M. is an academic professional with more than 15 years of experience in academics and industry. She has vast experience in curriculum development and designed a range of learning interventions, including behavioural and leadership programmes for various universities and institutions. She has published research papers in reputed journals and presented research papers in various national and international conferences.

Bhavesh Dilip Patil is a talented and passionate third-year Computer Engineering student at Vishwakarma Institute of Technology, Pune. With a strong inclination towards coding and software development, he has honed his skills as a Java developer and gained expertise in SQL, Salesforce, and React. In addition to their technical prowess, Bhavesh Patil has a keen interest in the field of Artificial Intelligence and Machine Learning. He is actively engaged in AI and ML projects, exploring the potential of these emerging technologies and their impact on various industries. Throughout their academic journey, Bhavesh Patil has demonstrated a commitment to continuous learning and staying updated with the latest advancements in the field. With a deep-rooted passion for technology and a drive to contribute to the ever-evolving IT landscape, Bhavesh Patil aspires to make a positive impact through their work. His dedication to innovation and his multidisciplinary approach make them a valuable asset in any project or team. He is doing his internship in Techrevive Technologies LLP as a full stack developer for now. As a published author of a book chapter in the prestigious IGI Global publication, Bhavesh Patil is excited to share his insights and contribute to the academic community. His chapter delves into the intersection of computer engineering, AI, and ML, offering valuable perspectives and practical knowledge for researchers and practitioners alike. Beyond his academic pursuits, Bhavesh enjoys staying abreast of industry trends, engaging in collaborative projects, and leveraging their skills to develop innovative solutions. He strives to make a meaningful contribution to the field of computer engineering and are committed to lifelong learning and professional growth. Follow Bhavesh Patil's journey on social media and stay connected to witness their continuous pursuit of excellence and dedication to the world of technology.

Usha Prabhu holds four Master degrees- MA, M. Phil, MBA, UGC- NET, Ph.D. She has more than 22 Years of teaching experience at the graduate and post-graduate levels. She was one of the member in the syllabus revision committee for the PG- MBA at Bangalore University. She is currently a Faculty at Jain (Deemed-to be University, Bangalore Karnataka, India. She co-authored the book- Organization Behaviour for PG Students.

Swetha Ramakrishnan is a final year student in the Department of Fashion Technology at the National Institute of Fashion Technology in Kannur, Kerala, India. She is passionate about the fashion industry and is committed to staying up-to-date with the latest trends and technologies. Throughout her academic career, Swetha has shown exceptional dedication and enthusiasm towards her studies, consistently demonstrating a strong work ethic and a desire to learn. Her coursework has focused on various aspects of the fashion industry, including design, merchandising, and production. In addition to her studies, Swetha has also participated in several extracurricular activities, including fashion shows and competitions.

Sandeep Rangineni is a Data Test Engineer at Pluto TV, with over 12 plus years of experience in the IT industry, primarily within the streaming media industry. He holds a Master's degree in Engineering Management and Master's degree in Information Technology. Sandeep has a diverse skill set, working with technologies such as PL/SQL, Azure Databricks, Salesforce, Informatica, and Snowflake. Currently, he is actively engaged in researching Data Engineering and Data Quality topics. Sandeep has professional certifications in Salesforce admin, AWS Data Analytics and Safe 5 practitioner. Sandeep is a senior member of IEEE, professional member of BCS and fellow of IETE, three esteemed technology organizations, and has served as a judge for reputable award organizations in Technology which including Globee Awards, Stevie Awards, NCWIT Aspirations, and Brandon Hall Group.

Patcha Bhujanga Rao is a highly qualified and accomplished individual with an exceptional academic background and a wealth of experience in the field of Human Resources, Legal and Soft Skills. Having completed his M.Com., DCFA., M.Phil., Ph.D, MBA (HR), M.Sc (Psychology), and LL.B, Dr Patcha Bhujanga Rao possesses a diverse range of educational qualifications. These qualifications have provided him with an extensive knowledge base and a broad understanding of various disciplines, allowing him to excel in his professional pursuits. With over 20 years of experience and presently working to the capacity of Professor at JAIN DEEMED-TO-BE-UNIVERSITY in Bengaluru, Dr Patcha Bhujanga Rao has made significant contributions to the academic community. His expertise lies in the field of Human Resources, where he has displayed a remarkable ability to understand and navigate the intricacies of this complex domain. He has been instrumental in training and guiding the next generation of HR professionals, equipping them with the necessary skills and knowledge to succeed in their careers. In addition to his expertise in HR, Dr Patcha Bhujanga Rao is also well-versed in Soft Skills. Recognizing the importance of effective communication, leadership, and interpersonal skills in today's professional landscape, he has dedicated himself to honing these skills in both students and professionals alike. His guidance and mentorship have proven invaluable to those seeking to enhance their personal and professional development. Dr Patcha Bhujanga Rao's drive for knowledge and excellence has been a driving force throughout his career. His multiple postgraduate degrees in diverse disciplines are a testament to his constant pursuit of higher education and his commitment to stay at the forefront of his field. His passion for imparting knowledge, coupled with his extensive experience, has enabled him to shape talent and facilitate positive changes in the professional lives of many. His dedication, expertise, and relentless pursuit of excellence make him a highly respected figure in the field of HR and Soft Skills.

Palanivel Rathinasabapathi Velmurugan is associated with BSBI, Berlin, as a professor in the Human Resource Management and Finance Stream. Prior to joining BSBI, he held the designation "Head" Faculty of Management at Sharda University, Uzbekistan, Central Asia, and "Dean of Arts" assignments at DMI St. John the Baptist University, Malawi, Central Africa. Also, he has been associated earlier with DMI St. Eugene University in Zambia, MAM Business School and various Engineering Colleges in India. He has a Ph.D. in Management from Mannonmanium Sundaranar University in India. Besides this, he holds an MBA Degree from SRM University in India and a BE Chemical Engineering degree from Annamalai University in India. Also, he completed six NPTEL Certificate Programs conducted by various IITs in India. He brings with him 15 years of rich working experience in teaching and research. Furthermore, he has a keen interest in the Case Method of teaching and research. He is an academic out of passion. Not only that, but he also takes a keen interest in guiding Ph.D. students. He has supervised three Ph.D. research scholars under his supervision at DMI St. Eugene University in Zambia.

Latha Thamma Reddi is a Principal Product Manager with two decades of IT industry experience in ERP, Digital Transformation, Software Engineering Development, Cloud Migration, Risk Management, Product, Portfolio & Program Management, Consulting & Presales. Latha is a seasoned leader with experience in managing larger teams, successfully led Global multi- disciplinary engineering teams for complex projects delivery in Hewlett Packard Inc, Hewlett Packard Enterprise and DXC Technology for HP, HPE, SABRE & Philips Clients. Latha is an IEEE Senior member and Fellow member. She is a Board Director for PMI Fort Worth Chapter as volunteer. Also, an "Advisory Committee" Member for Contact center world. Latha served as a judge for reputable award organizations in Technology and Business which include Globee Awards, Brandon Hall Group and Stevie Awards. Latha has published several research papers in major research publications and other major media Latha has strong track record of working with C-suite and senior executives on developing business strategy and execution. Latha also helps startups and corporations with insights on small-to-medium-large proposals that might not be visible through regular sources. Latha is a globally recognized, award-winning product coach, known for motivating and training young professionals across over 15 countries. Her expertise in product management transforms novices into competent professionals, elevating their careers. Latha can be reached @ .

Rupayan Roy is an Assistant Professor in the Department of Fashion Technology at the National Institute of Fashion Technology in Kannur, India. He received his Ph.D. in Textile Engineering from the Indian Institute of Technology Delhi in 2020, where he focused on the influence of fibre orientation on needle punched nonwoven properties. His research interests include textile structure, fibrous composites, protective textiles, and 2D and 3D woven textile structures. Dr. Roy has worked as a Teaching Assistant and Early Doc Research Scholar at IIT Delhi before joining as an Assistant Professor at the Technological Institute of Textile and Sciences Bhiwani. He has published numerous research papers and presented his work at various national and international conferences. Currently, he teaches and conducts research at NIFT Kannur, where he aims to contribute to the development of the Indian textile industry through his expertise in textile engineering.

N. Sathyanarayana has over 14 years of teaching experience at the UG and PG levels. He holds a Master's in Business Administration and Commerce and is pursuing a Ph.D. He currently holds the position of Assistant Professor in the School of Commerce at Jain (Deemed-to-be University), Bangalore. He has published 18 research papers in international journals, 3 research papers in national journals, and presented 12 research papers at international conferences and 8 research papers at national conferences.

Biswan Senapati is a Platinum-level ERP-SAP Consultant with more than 20 years of industry experience in domain consulting, business consulting, and solution architecture for large-scale ERP system design, development, implementation, rollout, support, and business process re-engineering capacity in supply chain, chemicals, hi-tech, CPG, pharmaceuticals, wholesale, fashion retail, health care, and manufacturing domains. Dr.Biswan has previously worked at Parker Hannifin, Home Depot, SONY, Gordon Foods, Constellations Brands, Olin Corporations, HPE, Ecolabs, TSC, Hanes Brands, PVH, Applexus, ECCO Denmark, Mindtree Germany, Ciber USA, Cognizant, Capgemini, and Deloitte Consulting, as well as the SAP Group of Consulting Companies. Here are some of the positions and duties I've had: -Led the SAP Competency (COE) and Delivery Centers in the USA, European Region, UK, EMEA, and ASEAN Geographies. -Solution architecture experience: I have designed solutions individually and have been part of the team for multiple opportunities or projects in SAP worth upward of $100 million. -ERP-SAP experience leading large business transformation projects for SCM, wholesale distribution, retail, fashion, manufacturing, utility, transportation management, and consumer goods industry verticals. -Managed more than 23 ERP-SAP projects in the US, Canada, EU, EMEA, and APAC geographies to support the global full life cycle implementation, upgrade support, and maintenance. Providing onsite delivery management oversight and direction to multiple IT application, implementation, and maintenance projects across multiple client engagements -Building IT architectures for industries 4.0 (chemicals, pharmaceuticals, CPG, hi-tech, apparel, manufacturing, retail domains, hi-tech, SCM, and e-commerce portfolios) in SAP HANA S/4 and C/4 HANA Box for the Large Enterprise -Expertise in AI, Deep Learning, ML, and IoT Skill for Digital Innovations (BPR), Applications Portfolio Rationalization, SAP Solution Designing, Testing, Data Migration, and Production Support -Rich expertise in HANA S/4 O2C manufacturing solutions, supply, and distribution business -Rich expertise on hybrids, cloud, and e-commerce implementation and support for global customers -Experiences in Quantum Computing (Quantum Machine Learning, QAI, and QIS) to solve real-world problems as per the industries 5.0) -Well versed in cloud infrastructure (AWS, Azure, and Google Cloud Platform). -Technologies: researcher, author, editor, invited speaker, and spiritual-technology consciousness leaders to solve real-world problems.

Anusha Thakur is an "Independent Researcher" with "25 Solo Research Papers" in World's reputed books and journals. She has been awarded the title of the "Best Woman Researcher of The Year" - (Category - Below 35 years) during the 4th International Inspirational Women Awards - (IIWA), 2023 in New Delhi, on 17th June 2023. Anusha has also been conferred the prestigious "Shiksha Bharati Award", in October 2023 by the "Indian Achievers Forum" in recognition of her extraordinary professional achievements and contribution towards nation-building. One of her published chapters, "Impact of Mood of the Millennial Customers on Purchase of Apparels Online," published by IGI Global, USA, was chosen to be included as a "Reprinted Chapter" in 2021 for the book "Research Anthology on E-Commerce Adoption, Models, and Applications for Modern Business (3 Volumes)" by the "Information Resources Management Association (USA). Anusha is also a reviewer for several publications with renowned publishers such as IGI Global, and Common Ground Research Networks journals & books. She has pursued B. Tech in "Electronics and Instrumentation Technology" from Tumkur, Karnataka, and Master's in Business Administration (MBA) in "Department of Economics and International Business" from the University of Petroleum & Energy Studies, (UPES) Dehradun. Anusha has also completed a post-Graduation certification course in "Market Research and Data Analytics" from MICA, Ahmedabad. She has a work experience of approximately 4+ years in the Market Research Industry as a Senior Research Analyst with extensive knowledge of market research in diversified industries.

P. S. Venkateswaran is currently working as a Professor in the Department of Management Studies, PSNA College of Engineering & Technology, Dindigul affiliated to Anna University, Chennai where he teaches courses in Advertising, marketing and Research Methods. He has served in various faculty positions from Assistant Professor to Professor in leading Arts & Colleges such as Cherran Arts and Science College, Kangeyam and Sree Saraswathi Thyagaraja College, Pollachi. He received MSc in Physics, an M.B.A., from Bharathiar University and MPhil from Alagappa University Karaikudi. He received his Ph.D in Business Administration from Madurai Kamaraj University, Madurai. He is having twenty two years of teaching and nine years of research & consultancy experience. His research activities include on Branding, Advertising and Digital marketing He conducted more than 90 Entrepreneurship Awareness Camps and trained around 8000 Engineering, Arts and Science College students and motivated them towards entrepreneurship. He also conducted 10 Faculty Development programmes, 10 EDP/WEDP programmes and 7 TEDP programmes. He trained more the 200 women entrepreneurs in Dindigul District.

Liguo Yu received his PhD degree in Computer Science from Vanderbilt University in 2004. He is an associate professor at Indiana University South Bend. He received his MS degree from Institute of Metal Research, Chinese Academy of Science in 1995. He received his BS degree in Physics from Jilin University in 1992. Before joining IUSB, he was a visiting assistant professor at Tennessee Tech University. During his sabbatical of Spring 2014, he was a visiting faculty at New York Institute of Technology-Nanjing. His research interests include software coupling, software maintenance and software evolution, empirical software engineering, and open-source development.

Index

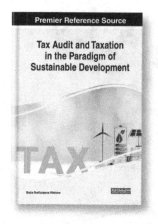
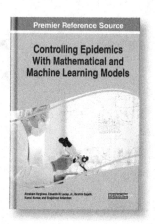

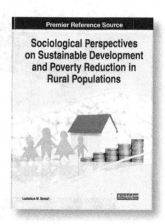

Printed in the United States
by Baker & Taylor Publisher Services